The Cassiopaea Experiment Transcripts 1994

The Cassiopaea Experiment is unique in the history of channeling, mediumship, and parapsychology. For years prior to the first Cassiopaean transmission, Laura Knight-Jadczyk went to great lengths to study the channeling phenomenon, including its history, its inherent strengths, weaknesses, dangers, and the various theories and methods developed in the past. After having exhausted the standard literature in search of answers to the fundamental problems of humanity, Laura and her colleagues (including her husband, mathematical physicist Arkadiusz Jadczyk) have held regular sittings for more than twenty years.

With the goal of applying true scientific standards and critical thinking, Laura began her experimentation with the spirit board, chosen for the optimum conditions of conscious feedback it offers. After two years of working through various levels of phenomena, including alleged discarnate entities and denizens of the 'astral realms', a new source came through in 1994. Unlike previous contacts, the Cassiopaeans came through strong and clear, often delivering full paragraphs' worth of complex material at one to two letters per second, with a high density of content and impeccable orthography. After telling Laura, "we are you in the future," the C's have been covering a wide range of topics by transmitting more than one million letters over the last twenty years, answering questions from practically all fields of knowledge, including physics, mathematics, psychology, philosophy, parapsychology, esotericism, history, politics, health, and astronomy. Where the material can be verified, the C's have proven to have an amazing track record, especially when compared to the variable quality of most examples of channeling from the past 150 years.

For the first time in print, this volume includes complete and extensively annotated transcripts of 36 experimental sessions conducted in 1994, beginning with the first contact with the Cassiopaeans on July 16. The sessions of this year introduced many of the themes that would recur in more detail over the next twenty years, including such topics as cyclical cometary bombardment of the Earth, the solar companion hypothesis, ancient history, metaphysics, the hyperdimensional nature of reality, and the possibility of evolution of humanity.

The Cassiopaea Experiment Transcripts 1994

Laura Knight-Jadczyk

Red Pill Press
2014

Copyright © 2014 Laura Knight-Jadczyk and Arkadiusz Jadczyk
First Edition, third printing
ISBN 978-1897244999
Red Pill Press (redpillpress.com)

No part of this publication may be reproduced, stored in a retrieval system, or transmitted in any form or by any means, electronic, mechanical, or otherwise, other than for "fair use", without the written consent of the author.

Contents

Editor's Note	i
Prophecies and Predictions	iii
Speculations on Time Travel and Superluminal Communication	xiii
"Feeling the Future": Elements of Practice and of a Theory	xxv
Introduction	1
July 16, 1994	15
July 22, 1994	23
July 27, 1994	29
July 30, 1994	31
September 30, 1994	39
October 5, 1994	61
October 7, 1994	73
October 9, 1994	83
October 16, 1994	93
October 18, 1994	109
October 19, 1994	115
October 20, 1994	119

October, 22 1994	**129**
October, 23 1994	**145**
October 25, 1994	**153**
October 28, 1994	**159**
November 2, 1994	**171**
November 4, 1994	**185**
November 6, 1994	**193**
November 7, 1994	**211**
November 9, 1994	**221**
November 12, 1994	**227**
November 16, 1994	**233**
November 19, 1994	**243**
November 24, 1994	**261**
November 26, 1994	**269**
November 27, 1994	**291**
December 1, 1994	**295**
December 3, 1994	**301**
December 5, 1994	**313**
December 9, 1994	**323**
December 10, 1994	**329**

December 17, 1994	343
December 23, 1994	351
December 28, 1994	361
December 31, 1994	371
Appendix: Images	383
Chapters of "The Wave"	391
Recommended Reading	395
Index	423

Editor's Note

In the last 20 years, session transcripts of the Cassiopaea Experiment were available only in an electronic format – first shared as text files in a private email group and later, in 2010, republished one by one in the public Cassiopaea Forum[1] for discussion.

Readers have been strongly discouraged from reading the Cassiopaean transcripts on their own, outside of the context provided by Laura's work, since it had been noted that readers often would understand them too literally, misinterpret them and would tend to project their own ideas, beliefs, and biases onto them. Therefore, readers were advised to read them *in context*, that is, by reading about the background of the Cassiopaea Experiment and the unfolding events 'behind the scenes'. Excerpts of the transcripts have been included, discussed and researched in Laura Knight-Jadczyk's books *Amazing Grace*, *The Wave* series Vols. 1–8, *The Secret History of the World* Vol. 1 and *High Strangeness*. In these and other books (see "Recommended Reading" section), Laura matches a small percentage of 'inspiration' from the C's with a lot of 'perspiration', i.e. hard work in researching the issues and conveying them to the readers.

For the upcoming 20th 'anniversary' of the first 'contact' with the Cassiopaeans on July 16, the same day that Comet Shoemaker-Levy 9 broke apart and collided with Jupiter, complete transcripts of 36 experimental sessions conducted in 1994 are for the first time prepared for publication in paper and electronic books. The advice about getting the necessary context to better understand the material still cannot be emphasized enough. For this reason, the editors have included more than 230 footnotes which point to the location where certain excerpts are discussed in detail in the above-mentioned books. The footnotes hopefully will encourage the reader to look up and study the context. A referencing footnote marks the first occurring line of a session excerpt

---

[1] http://cassiopaea.org/forum/

contained in the mentioned books. The footnotes give the book title and the chapter number where the excerpts can be found (e.g. *The Wave* 46). The section "Recommeded Reading" and the table "Chapters of 'The Wave'" at the end of this volume give additional details about the inserted references.

For the present volume, Laura has revisited the transcripts from 1994 and extensively annotated questions and answers in more than 450 footnotes, giving unprecedented insight into the background and interpersonal dynamics of the early Cassiopaea Experiment, and comparing certain statements and predictions of the C's with what she has learned since.

At the beginning of the present volume, three forewords are included, all giving essential information about the issues with and possibilities of communications with the future.

The sheer vastness of the transcript material became apparent only after a preliminary calculation of the required page count. It turned out that a minimum of eight books would be required to bring all the session transcripts from 1994 to 2014 to paper. Beginning with 1994, due to frequently held sessions, the first five volumes of this series are planned to include one year each, while later volumes are planned to include several years. To utilize paper space more efficiently, a two-column layout has been chosen.

In the early stages of the experiment, often several topics would be covered in a single session. For this reason, an exhaustive index at the end of this volume containing more than 560 keywords will hopefully enable the reader to quickly find topics of interest, even though the entire transcripts can and should be read as an amazing, unfolding story, containing numerous gems of wisdom, advice, and information.

Prophecies and Predictions

Foreword by Harrison Koehli

Whenever the topic of channeling or psychic abilities comes up, the issue of prophecy always comes to the fore. In fact, you could say that it was Laura's interest in prophetic possibilities and getting 'inside info' that partly drove her channeling experiment. Her extensive review of the enormous body of paranormal literature suggested to her that real prophecy is possible, but there are some very problematical issues that have to be considered, dealing with the nature of prophecy, and more fundamentally, the nature of reality itself.

At any given point in time there seems to be at least one charlatan running around predicting the imminent end of the world. In 2011, radio evangelist Harold Camping predicted the world's faithful would be 'Raptured' on May 21, 2011. Of course, the date turned out to be a total dud, prompting Camping to 'revise' his prediction to October 21. Needless to say, we didn't hold our breath back then, and with good reason. We might have passed out and missed another apocalyptic non-event! We got our wish during the last week of 2012, when once again the world didn't end, despite a library's worth of books, prophecies, and starry-eyed certainty (whether channeled or not).

But is there such a thing as valid prophecy or prediction of future events? The results of the Cassiopaean Experiment suggest that there is indeed such a thing, and more (e.g., remote access to unconventional knowledge, whether obscure or just previously unheard of). But the C's have presented a very unique take on the subject of prediction; it is intimately tied with their cosmology and their view on 'time.' According to the C's, our universe is a 'free will' universe and time is not a strictly linear 'one-off' phenomenon. That means the future is open. More on that below.

Most predictions are based on a pretty simplistic, and probably completely false, view of reality. According to this mechanistic idea, the universe was originally set in motion at some imaginary 'beginning' point in time by some equally imaginary 'first cause.' Religions have called this first cause 'God' while scientists have deemed it the 'Big Bang.' Once this machine has been set in motion, it obeys physical laws and plays itself out like clockwork. Theoretically, with enough data, every event in this mechanistic chain of cause and effect can be predicted. So when some prophet gives a prediction of a future event, he or she is basically operating on the assumption that because 'God' or some other divine being is omniscient and can see how everything will play itself out (and assuming this being actually exists, and that it is not simply pulling a cosmic practical joke on its subject), it's gotta be right. But things aren't that simple.

As we see in the cases of Harold Camping and countless others, their predictions are, more often than not, completely wrong. In such cases, the rationalization machine goes into overdrive and various explanations are given to account for the contradiction of a truth-telling God whose prophetic pronouncements have proven to be profoundly problematic. Usually, God simply changed his mind. Because even if the world follows mechanistic laws, God is the great supernatural exception. He's completely separate from our lowly physical world and can intervene at will and change the game whenever he chooses. Of course, most scientists reject God, or any other supernatural element, from their equations. According to them, Camping along with everyone else making such predictions are simply delusional crackpots or charlatans. (When was the last time you heard a prophet say, "Well, I may be completely off my rocker, but..."?)

But what about cases where predictions turn out to be true? What about the phenomena of prophetic dreams and premonitions? Even if we've experienced such a thing in our lives, or know someone who has, we lack a coherent explanation that accounts for all the data, and if we've resolved *not* to believe in such things, we simply write them off as coincidence and forget all about them. This is where the Cs' presentation is so interesting. According to them, we do not live in a strictly material, deterministic universe, nor is 'God' separate from Nature. As always, the devil is in the details. Unlike mechanistic scientists who reject the reality of free will, the Cs wholly endorse it. Indeed, it's an essential part of our reality. But what does this mean? Basically, *we all make choices*. And one choice, made during certain conditions, can change the course of the future.

This means that time is not some static line, like a film reel playing itself out to its predetermined end. Rather, at any given moment, based on the collective choices of the units of consciousness making up the whole, the future can go one way or another (or another, or another...). If people act in predictable, habitual ways and few 'new' choices enter the game, sure, the future can probably be predicted. But when an important choice affecting other future choices is made, it's as if we have entered a new timeline, one that previously existed only as a nebulous probability – one among billions of such probabilities.

In this sense, we *do* exist on one 'line of time.' It's the reality we experience as our lives: the events and interactions that make up the sum total of our experience. But it's merely one of many possible realities that we occupy based on our collective choices. A prediction that may have been true at one point in 'time,' following a choice that is significant to one degree or another on the part of one or more individuals, may not hold true beyond that point. What the C's are basically saying is that predictions that turn out to be wrong aren't necessarily wrong because the people were lying or delusional (although many undoubtedly are), or because the alleged sources of those predictions are stupid or playing cosmic pranks (although many may do so). Future events *can* be foreseen, but there are certain laws and conditions that need to be taken into account.

In volume five of her series, *The Wave, Petty Tyrants*,[1] Laura described it like this:

> My guess is that the real world of third density/dimensions, is a collapsed wave function reality. It is like the branch of a tree. At certain nodal points, there are other branches that have the possibility of "getting all the juice" and becoming the dominant branch, and what determines which it is depends on many factors.
>
> But, once one bud begins to dominate, the others become smaller and smaller and fall away eventually for lack of "juice." There is only one "real" reality. The others are only ghost or potential realities. Like a tree, with gazillions of branches, each individual's

---

[1] Originally published as the online series "Adventures with Cassiopaea" at cassiopaea.org

reality grows in this way. At certain points, there are alternate realities. But, depending upon choice, attention, and other factors, those realities that are undesirable can be "pruned" or deprived of sap so that they wither and fall away.

At the same time, each individual being their own "branch," has a slightly different reality from every other individual, and some responsibility for the way their branch grows. But it is all from the same tree, and thus has a more or less single reality. If their choices are "diseased," their branch will grow in a way that causes it to be pruned, or wither, or face some interference even from other branches, perhaps.

So, in a certain sense, at the nodal point, many possibilities may exist, just as several buds may put out on the end of a branch, but not all of them will continue the process of branching, and at such points, we have some freedom to choose, individually or collectively, depending on the nature of the branch.

The session transcripts that follow include many predictions. Some have come true; some haven't. Some seem symbolic after the fact, and some surprisingly literal. Some may even be both. So keep in mind the above ideas as you read the sessions themselves. But the Cassiopaean Experiment, while pretty 'out-there' to begin with (at least from the mainstream perspective), also deals with more 'down-to-earth' subject matter. Issues relating to more conventionally understood and practiced science of all types (albeit with often unconventional interpretations) make up a large portion of the received data.

Science: A Work in Progress

It's been my experience that people tend to forget that scientists are 'human' too, or more precisely, scientists can be just as willfully blind, self-serving, conformist, fearful and mendacious as anyone else. Some of them are even unabashed con men who falsify their data, or intellectual prostitutes who will produce the results they are paid to produce, whether they believe them or not. Just because it's been peer-reviewed, or written by a person with a string of letters after their name, doesn't mean it's true, or even remotely so. And if history tells us anything, it's that the history of science is a long history of wrong or incomplete ideas. So it's best to be skeptical whenever scientists speak in terms of absolutes with certainty, whenever they put the lid on testing alternate hypotheses. Chances are, they're simply deceiving themselves, and you.

Science is a work in progress. The theories that are taken for granted as being true may very well turn out to be completely bogus following the intervention of new discoveries and innovations. Sadly, space and weather science are two areas where innovation not only rarely occurs, but is also actively hindered by scientists and politicians with vested interests in keeping old, inadequate theories at the forefront of popular and academic belief systems.

Just as new discoveries in science can overturn a previously held 'consensus' in a heartbeat (often to the consternation or willful disbelief of those promoting the consensus), new historical data can turn our ideas of what we think happened in our history on their head. We often take for granted that event X occurred in year Y, forgetting that either or both of those variables may be completely false. The event may turn out to have been a fiction, created by scribes and leaders of the time (or years later) for purposes of political propaganda. Dating methods may be inaccurate or possess possible confounding factors, mucking up the accepted timeline. Or, when new documents or scientific data are discovered, the event may turn out to bear little resemblance to our previous ideas of how it happened. New actors emerge with new motivations, necessitating a revision of the history books and the way we see the events and personages of our near and distant past.

Then there are the problems inherent in the study of prehistory, before the advent of 'history' as we know it. There, we only have scarce clues to rely on, all built on sciences which are themselves built on certain assumptions about the way things work. Archeology, paleoanthropology, population and molecular genetics, climate science, geology ... all of these contribute to a story of the past that historians create for us. When we consider the relatively young age of many of these sciences, the amount of information that we have amassed in that short amount of time is pretty staggering. But it's important to keep in mind that history too is a work in progress; new theories and advancements in science can prompt a radical revision of old ideas.

Prehistory, for example, occupies a good portion of the C's transcripts. While archaeologists and anthropologists can piece together broad outlines of migrations, genetic mixing, human behaviors, population bottlenecks, etc., this was a period from which no written records appear to have survived. As such, it's hard to verify specific historical details and much of what the C's say about these times remains interesting conjecture. But while much of it is unverifiable, it also provides opportunities to test the material as new discoveries come to light: fossil finds, climate studies, evidence for catastrophes and extinctions, and more.

For those curious to know, the research inspired by the Cassiopaea Experiment has led Quantum Future Group to many of the topics that we focus on in our research, whether on our websites, which include the alternative news website SOTT.net and the main webpage for Laura's work and our international forum (cassiopaea.org), or in the books published by Red Pill Press. The diverse and long list of books in the "Recommended Reading" section of this volume is a case in point. Without those lines of research, and without the life experiences that we surely wouldn't have had if not engaged in this project, we probably never would have learned what we have about the history and danger of cometary catastrophe, the electrical nature of the universe, psychopathy, ponerology, polyvagal theory, and separating the wheat from the chaff when it comes to the vast number of 'conspiracy theories' on the market. Or at least, it would have taken us a lot longer.

After all, all of these fields have their respective authorities and advocates, those scientific mavericks who have come to the conclusion all was not right in their particular field of study, whether in history, politics, psychology, ufology, astrophysics, meteorology, or any other science. But this is usually done on their own, disconnected from the bigger picture and how to tie it all together. Often a lifetime of research will go into this process, with the downside that other possible areas of research are left untouched. (Witness researchers into the paranormal who deride 'conspiracy theories,' or '9/11 conspiracy theorists' who deride ufologists.) But we try to bring as many of them as possible together, to give as comprehensive and coherent as possible a view of reality as we can. This can bring us into areas often considered 'off limits' to scientists, including areas such as religious experience, spirituality, and the so-called paranormal.

Politics and Spirituality

Some readers may wonder what place so-called 'paranormal' research has in a project that endorses and strives towards real science and rationality. And others may, as I did just over a decade ago, wonder what on earth political conspiracies have to do with so-called 'spirituality.' In a world as controlled as our own, where lies can be glibly passed off as indisputable fact, with media, corporations, academia, and government acting as shapers of public opinion on every subject, an individual finds him or herself in a situation not dissimilar to that of Theseus in the Minotaur's labyrinth. At every turn we are confronted by lies, even (and perhaps especially) when it comes to our most basic views about the nature of reality. And we would be lost if not for the thread of Ariadne.

While I'm on a Greek bent, let me share something a member of our forum recently pointed out from Manly P. Hall's *The Secret Teachings of All Ages*:

> It is generally admitted that the effect of the Delphian oracle upon Greek culture was profoundly constructive. James Gardner sums up its influence in the following words: "Its responses revealed many a tyrant and foretold his fate. Through its means many an unhappy being was saved from destruction and many a perplexed mortal guided in the right way. It encouraged useful institutions, and promoted the progress of useful discoveries. Its moral influence was on the side of virtue, and its political influence in favor of the advancement of civil liberty."

In other words, there's our answer to the second question: a good oracle (or spiritual source) doesn't shy away from politics. Like a Greek Cynic, or the proverbial Cassandra, the prime role of an oracle is to present a vision of the world as it is, no matter how painful or unpopular the view, and provide the only alternative fit for a lie: the truth. So, yes, we track and study 'high strangeness,' and our worldview is quite at odds with the materialistic dictum peddled and enforced by PhD's and media pundits the world over. Everything you 'know' is a lie, and that includes all your metaphysical assumptions about the way the 'reality' really works. Luckily there's a way out of the labyrinth, and (please excuse me for going Biblical here!) the truth *will* set you free.

With politics, it's no different. Any 'spiritual' source that suggests otherwise – perhaps holding the view that such things are *un*spiritual – is no better than COINTELPRO, directing people to ignore the man behind the curtain, lie down and go back to sleep while unscrupulous individuals conspire to rob you of your money, your freedom, and the opportunity to live a fulfilling life where evil and abject mediocrity aren't the norm.

Think about it. Can you imagine a 'great spiritual leader' living under a corrupt government who is so stupid as to believe the lies 'the Party' tells him? Or one who would give her support to a leader who spouts high-sounding words while killing innocent people? Well, maybe those are dumb questions, because I can picture any number of such 'spiritual leaders.' But I hope the point is clear. A spiritual source that ignores politics is like a doctor who ignores disease.

Trying to make sense of chaos is human nature. Look at a blurry picture and your mind will try to 'piece it together' into something intelligible. And it's rewarding when it comes together. 'Aha!' However, say that picture is evidence of a crime. The criminal has a vested interest in *keeping* it obscure, whether that means burning the evidence or influencing your perception of the blur in question. When truth is an obstacle to one's ambition, lies are the only option, and that puts one at odds with anything truly human or spiritual in nature. It puts one in a position that goes *against* reality, forcing it into something it is not. Silencing those who question your manufactured reality – and thus risk waking others up to the truth and your own downfall – naturally follows.

This places those on the receiving end of the propaganda at a crossroads. It forces the questions: What do you truly value? Will you settle for being conned, if it means a relatively comfortable life? Or will you walk the 'thorny road of truth'? *That* is spirituality.

Critical Channeling: 10% inspiration, 90% perspiration

The subject matter covered in the Cassiopaean Experiment is extensive. I've been following it for over ten years and I still can't claim to have scratched the surface in terms of the research that has both gone into the experiment and which has been spurred on by it. A lot of it is obviously controversial. It's rooted in 'psychic phenomena,' after all! But without fail, no matter how far 'out there' the material may seem at first glance, it holds up if you dig deep enough. Not only has much of it been confirmed or supported by research; it's also coherent. It all tends to fit together. In other words, it is profoundly rational, despite whatever controversial directions it may take. And rationality is the basis of all science.

Broadly speaking, the topics involved can be placed into two fairly broad categories: science and spirituality. I hope this Foreword, culled from the pages of my upcoming book, *The Cassiopaeans' Greatest Hits*, will help shed some light on how these two subjects fit together, and place our approach to this experiment in a wider context. The approach the participants take to the Cassiopaean Experiment really is a case of 10% inspiration, 90% perspiration. One question asked, or one answer given, is often enough to inspire a whole line of research leading to data and conclusions that might only be tangentially related to the original question. That's the whole point: discovery, and in that sense, the data in the C's transmissions is more like the thread of Ariadne than a book of 'Divine Revelation.' The clues given lead those interested to take up the search through a vast labyrinth of information and 'disinformation' to what I like to think of as the heart of the matter: those areas of study that are not only highly relevant to coming to an understanding of the human condition and the nature of the cosmos, but which are also closely interrelated and always seemingly one step beyond what is currently accepted as 'common knowledge.'

In other words, one mystery reveals another, then another. It's a never-ending journey of discovery, which is what I think lies at the heart of science and mysticism. Anything else, like the belief that 'we finally know all there is to know on this subject,' only leads to intellectual stagnation and the death of curiosity. There's no such thing as an infallible text, and there's no such thing as free lunch.

Speculations on Time Travel and Superluminal Communication

Foreword by Arkadiusz Jadczyk, PhD

The term 'Cassiopaeans' appears in many places in this book. The name Cassiopaea was given by a source identifying itself by saying "we are you in the future" which Laura Knight-Jadczyk contacted via an experiment in superluminal communication in 1994.

"We are you in the future."

This is what 'they' declare: that 'they' – the Cassiopaeans – sixth density Unified Thought Form Beings – are us in the future. What a bizarre concept. Or is it?

Is that possible? Can such a statement find a place in accepted theories? Or is it an evident contradiction with everything that we – that is, physicists – know about Nature and its laws?

Putting aside for the moment the issue of whether existence in a pure state of consciousness is possible, is traveling in time possible, even if only in theory? Is sending and receiving information from the future or sending information into the past allowed by our present theories of relativity and quantum mechanics? If information can be sent, does this also imply that physical matter can be 'sent,' via some sort of TransDimensional Remolecularization? And if so what are the laws, what are the restrictions? What are the means?

Well, frankly speaking, we do not know, but we may have a clue. Kurt Gödel, after he became famous for his work on foundations of mathematics, went on to study the Einstein general theory of relativity and made an important contribution to physics: he discovered a class of otherwise reasonable cosmological solutions of Einstein equations – except for one point: they contained causal loops!

At first these causal loops were dismissed by relativists as being "too crazy." The arguments against these model universes even became rather personal, commenting upon the state of mind of the inventor! (A not terribly unusual phenomenon in the heated debates within the so-called 'ivory towers' of academia.)

A 'causal loop' means the same thing as 'time loop.' It can be described as going into the future and ending up where you started at the original time and place. It is called 'causal' because, in Einstein's Theory of Relativity, time is a relative concept and different observers can experience time differently, so the term 'causal' is used to avoid using the term 'time.'

But, little by little, it was realized that causal – or time – loops **can** appear in other solutions of Einstein equations as well – usually they correspond to some kind of 'rotation' of the universe.

Causal loops make time travel not only possible, but probable. But then, causal loops lead to unacceptable logical paradoxes, and physics does not like such paradoxes at all – they are a serious problem!

But, the subject of communicating with the past or receiving information from the future *is* being discussed in physics even in terms of the flat, not-curved-at-all space-time of Lorentz and Minkowski. Hypothetical faster-than-light particles – tachyons – can serve as the communication means. They make an 'anti-telephone' – a telephone into the past – possible.

But do tachyons exist? Or *can* they exist?

Well, that is still a question that has not been answered definitively for some.

And, the truth is that paradoxes must never be ignored. They always indicate that some important lesson is to be learned; that some essential improvement or change is necessary. The same holds true for the paradoxes involved in the idea of receiving information from the future. We cannot simply go back into Saturday and tell ourselves the winning lottery numbers of Sunday. If this were possible, then it should also be possible for some future, future self to tell a future self *not* to tell! Thus we have a paradox: we, in the future, have intervened into the past making our communication from the future impossible!

A paradox: if we communicated, we have not communicated, and if we do not communicate, then we have communicated! Impossible in a linear, non-branching universe!

Is there a possible escape from the paradox, an escape that leaves a door open, even if only a little – for our anti-telephone?

Indeed, there is, and not just one, but several ways out.

First of all – the evident paradox disappears if we admit the possibility that the communication channels are inherently noisy; that is a normal situation when we deal with quantum phenomena. So, if the communication into the past is a quantum effect – we are saved from evident paradoxes. Quantum Theory can be useful!

Sending a signal into the past, we are never 100% sure if the message will be delivered without distortion. And conversely, receiving info from the future we are never 100% sure if this comes from an authentic broadcast or is a spontaneous and random creation of the receiving end. If this is the case, and if certain quantitative information – that is, theoretic relations between receiving and transmitting ends – are secured to hold, then there are no more paradoxes even with reasonably efficient information channels.

In other words: there *can* be broadcasts from the future to the past, but *there will be few 'receivers'*, and of those few, *even fewer that are properly tuned*. And even those that are properly tuned may be subject to 'static.' Even if there is no static, those receivers that can receive pure information will experience the static of 'non-belief' and distortion after the fact from society.

There is also another aspect of such an information transfer which is that the probabilities involved are connected with a *choice event*; with the choosing of one among many possible futures.

It may happen that branching of the universe corresponds to each such event. Branching of the universe into an infinite tree of decisions has been discussed within quantum measurement theory – it even has the name of "Many Worlds Interpretation of Quantum Theory."

Two of the well-known physicists who consider the Many Worlds Interpretation more than just an exercise in theorizing are John Archibald Wheeler and David Deutsch.

The Many Worlds Interpretation has one serious weakness: it has no built in algorithm for providing the timing of the branchings. Thus it is a certain framework rather than a complete theory.

There is, however, a theory that fills in this gap in the Many Worlds Interpretation – and this theory I know quite well, and in fact I know it better than most others for the simple reason that I developed it in collaboration with Philippe Blanchard (University of Bielefeld) in 1988 as an integral part of the Quantum Future Project. It is called Event Enhanced Quantum Theory (EEQT for short notation). (A complete list of references and much more info on this subject can be found on my 'Quantum Future' project page[1] on the World Wide Web.)

The fact that our generally accepted theories of the present do not prevent us from thinking that time travel is, perhaps, possible, does not necessarily imply that we know how to build the time machine!

On the other hand, it is perhaps possible that the time machine already exists and is in use, even if we do not understand the principle of its work, because it goes much too far beyond our present theoretical and conceptual framework. It is also possible that some of the machines we think are serving a totally different purpose do, in fact, act as time machines. Many things are possible ...

Now, back to superluminal communication, or 'channeling' in general and the Cassiopaeans in particular: the fact that sending information into the past is possible does not necessarily imply that any information that pretends to be sent from the future is such indeed! But, if we generally accept that extraterrestrial life is possible, and we use all of our knowledge and resources to search for life beyond our Earth, then we also need to include the understanding that receiving information from the future is equally possible. With this perspective, science should search for any traces of such information.

What kind of information channels are to be monitored in search of such broadcasts? What kind of antenna arrays do we need? How must we direct them into a particular 'future time'? Say, into the year 3000? Or 30,000? Or 300,001?

My answer is: nothing like that is necessary. All that we need we already have, namely *our minds*.

And indeed, assuming that the knowledge and technology of the future is (or *can be*) much more advanced than ours, then it is only natural that any broadcast from the future *will be addressed directly into the mind*.

Even today there are techniques of acting directly on our minds. They are not always used for our benefit; nevertheless they do exist. But if

---

[1] http://quantumfuture.net/quantum_future

communications from the future are possible, why don't we receive these broadcasts on a daily basis? If our minds can serve as receivers, then why aren't we all aware of the transmissions?

I think that the answer has to do with multiple realities and branching universes, and perhaps any civilization which would receive messages from the future on a daily basis has ceased to exist because communication through time is a very dangerous game. You produce paradoxes, and these paradoxes remove the paradoxical universes from the repository of possible universes; if you create a universe with paradoxes, it destroys itself either completely or partially. Perhaps just intelligence is removed from this universe because it is intelligence that creates paradox. Perhaps we are very fortunate that even if we can receive *some* of these messages from the future, we still continue to exist.

Suppose our civilization were to advance to the point where everyone can communicate with themselves in the past; they have a computer with a special program and peripheral device that does this. It becomes the latest fad: everyone is communicating with themselves in the past to warn of dangers or upcoming calamities or bad choices, or to give lottery numbers or winning horses. But, what is seen as a 'good event' or 'benefit' for one, could be seen to be a 'bad choice' or 'calamity' to someone else!

So, the next step would be that 'hackers' would begin to break into the systems and send false communications into the past to deliberately create bad choices and calamities for some in order to produce benefits for themselves or others.

Then, the first individual would see that false information has been sent and would go into their system and go back even earlier to warn themselves that false information was going to be sent back by an 'imposter' and how to tell that it was false.

Then the hacker would see this, and go back in time to an even earlier moment and give false information that someone was going to send false information (that was really true) that false information (that was really false) was going to be sent, thereby confusing the issue.

This process could go on endlessly with constant and repeated communications into the past, one contradicting the other, one signal canceling out the other, with the result that it would be exactly the same as if there were *no* communication into the past!

There is also the very interesting possibility that the above scenario *is* exactly what is taking place in our world today.

It is also possible that, whenever a civilization comes to the point that it can manipulate the past and thereby change the present, it would most probably destroy itself, and probably its 'branch' of the universe, unless there comes a cataclysmic event before this happens which would act as a kind of 'control system' or way of reducing the technological possibilities to zero again, thus obviating the potentials of universal chaos. In this way, cataclysmic events could be a sort of preventive or pre-emptive strike against such manipulations, and may, in fact, be the result of engineered actions of benevolent selves in the future who see the dangers of communicating with ourselves in the past!

So, the probability is this: if there *is* communication from the future, it *may*, in fact, be constantly received by each and every one of us as an ongoing barrage of lies mixed with truth. Thus, the problem becomes more than just 'tuning' to a narrow band signal, because clearly the hackers can imitate the signal and have become *very* clever in delivering their lies disguised as 'warm and fuzzy' truths; the problem becomes an altogether different proposition of believing nothing and *acting* as though *everything* is misleading, gathering data from all quarters, and then making the most *informed* choice possible with full realization that it may be in error!

Using our computer analogy: we can't prevent hackers from hacking, but, what we can do is make every effort to prevent them from hacking into **our** systems by erecting barriers of knowledge and awareness. Hackers are always looking for an 'easy hack' (except for those few who really *like* a challenge), and will back away as you make your system more and more secure.

How do you make your computer (or yourself) immune to hackers?

It is never 100% secure, but if all preventative measures are taken, and we constantly observe for the signs of hackers – system disruption, loss of 'memory,' or energy, damaged files, things that don't 'fit,' that are 'out of context' – we can reduce the possibility of hacking. But, we can only do this if we are *aware* of hackers; if we *know* that they will attempt to break into our system in the guise of a 'normal' file, or even an operating system or program that promises to 'organize' our data for greater efficiency and ease of function or 'user friendliness,' while at the same time, acting as a massive drain on our energy and resources – RAM and hard drive.

As a humorous side note: we could think of Windows Operating System as the 'ultimate hacker from the future' who, disguised as a sheep, is a wolf devouring our hard disk and RAM, and sending our files to God only knows where every time we connect via the internet!

And of course, there are viruses. Whenever we insert a floppy disk or CD into our computer, we risk infection by viruses which can slowly or rapidly, distort or destroy *all* the information on our computer, prevent *any* peripheral functions, and even 'wipe' the hard disk of all files to replace them with endless replications of the viral nonsense. The human analogy to this is the many religions and 'belief' systems that have been 'programmed' into our cultures, and our very lives, via endless 'Prophet/God' programs, replacing, bit by bit, our own thinking with the 'dogma and doctrines of the faith.'

Enough of the computer analogies. I think that the reader can imagine any number of variations on the theme and come to an understanding of how vulnerable we are to 'disinformation' in the guise of truth from either the future, the past, or the present.

Among the many critics of 'channeling,' in general, and my wife's work in particular, which is quite different both in theoretical approach and content, there are those who say "Channeled Information is crap. It is 100% disinformation."

I can't take such claims seriously.

Why?

I am a scientist. I look at things in a somewhat different way than other people. I am more critical. I am even more critical than most of my colleagues. So, when I see a statements like these, or even "channeling is a satellite transmission," I get very suspicious.

Why so?

I immediately see that anyone who says things like this is speaking nonsense – in *these* sentences. And when I see someone speaking nonsense in couple of sentences, and when this somebody is so affirmative – *then* I can't take this person seriously in all the rest.

What are the facts? What are the possibilities?

Certainly there is a possibility that some (most?) of the channeling *today* comes via satellites or other means of programming. That *is* not only possible but probable.

The next question we should ask is: *Why?*

The evident answer is: to twist, to misinform, via New Age-type naive people. Based on an assessment of the facts of technology and the morality (or lack of) amongst the elite rulers of our world, it is highly probable that if there was information that would tend to free humanity from their controls, they would co-opt it immediately exactly as I have described above in my computer analogies.

Can the Cassiopaean channeling be disinformation or come as a result of such technology and/or programming?

This would not be so easy. We are not naïve, we are critical of our work. We think, we analyze, we test and do research.

Could *some* of our 'communications' have been influenced this way?

Yes. There is such a possibility.

Can *all*, or even 95% be received this way?

No. Because there are too many instances in which the Cassiopaeans were answering questions to which normal 'satellite type' of intelligence, without being able to instantly read the minds of everyone on this planet, could not have had access.

Therefore, I think the statement that *all* channeling is crap and disinformation, and that 95% is via satellites shows that the individuals who make such claims are:

- Unable to think logically,

- Not interested in discovering the truth.

This is the main difference between their approach and ours. While we are ready to question everything, and *always* look for new facts, other individuals declare, "*We know the Truth*. Here it is!" And then we find one or another easily detectable nonsense statement that is claimed to be absolute, and this discredits everything else they say.

The Devil is always in the details.

Whenever someone claims: "All white is black" – I get suspicious. And I am turned off to everything else they say. Not because "white being black" is impossible, we know there *are* paradoxes, but *because* the person uses this three letter word: "all."

As for parallel realities, yes, probably this is part of the clue. As for satellites trying, once in a while, their dirty tricks – yes, this is possible. And we *are* taking it into account. But *always* we are trying to apply our logical thinking, our 'judgment.' But we know that this third density reality check is *never sufficient* when dealing with possible hyperdimensional realities. But it is *always necessary*. Which means, in practical terms:

- Always use it to the max,

- Never think you can rely completely on it alone!

What I want to state clearly is this: this channeling, the Cassiopaean channeling, *is* different than other channeling. It was different from the very beginning, it continues to be so, and it will continue to be different. We may give it a name: Critical Channeling. It is such by intent, not by chance. It is channeling in which, by intent, the messenger is as important as the message itself. They are inseparably entangled in a quantum way; an interfering quantum amplitude. They form a oneness, a whole. To separate the message from the messenger would be, in this Cassiopaean quantum experiment, like closing one hole in a double-slit experiment. You close one hole, and the whole pattern is different, not just a part of it. As I have written above:

There *can* be broadcasts from the future to the past, but *there will be few 'receivers'*, and of those few, *even fewer that are properly tuned*. And even those that are properly tuned may be subject to 'static.' Even if there is no static, those receivers that can receive pure information will experience the static of 'non-belief' and distortion after the fact from society.

It is in this context – that my wife is one of those few receivers who has worked very hard to properly 'tune' to transmissions from the future – that I call the Cassiopaean Communication 'Critical Channeling.'

What is this 'Critical Channeling'? In what way is it different than other channeling?

It would take a lot of space and time to describe it in details. One day we will do it. But for now, let me just make this observation: the Cassiopaean channeling has characteristics of a scientific experiment.

Think of scientists in their lab, working on the great laws of the universe. They perform an important series of experiments. They are trained professionals, they know their stuff, they know their laboratory equipment and its quirks. But they are human beings. Once in a while someone will make some dirty joke, once in a while they will have to discard a series of data because mice have messed up their equipment during the night. Now, think, what advantage it would be if they would write in their paper the dirty joke, include the mice data, the ink blobs, etc., etc.

That is not the way of science. And the Cassiopaean experiment will proceed as a scientific one. With scientific standards in mind. The Cassiopaean channeling is Critical Channeling. It is in this respect that it is *different* from other channeling. And it will stay so.

The difference is in the approach. We are searching for the truth. Others who make unilateral statements that all channeling is crap are sure that they know it and would like to impose it on other people, or manipulate other people into believing what they say. And naturally, when such individuals state such things, they claim that it comes from God or some equally authoritarian source, but when someone else dares to have a different way of finding the truth, it is necessarily "100% disinformation" and "crap."

We try to share our thoughts, and when necessary, we are ready to learn and *change*. And that is what is most important. This attitude of being open.

What if such claims are right, that all channeling is crap and disinformation? Even if I consider it as highly improbable, can it be true?

Of course, being a scientist, and using my brain in order to judge, I had to consider also this possibility, however improbable it may look to me. And I concluded that such a claim cannot be true. Here is my reasoning: it goes via *reductio ad absurdum* – which is often used in logic and in mathematical proofs. You assume something to be true, and then by a chain of logical deductions you come to the conclusion that your assumption cannot be true. Somewhat tricky – but useful.

Applying this method to the claim that "all channeling is 100% disinformation because it is coming via satellite," let us suppose it is true. In order to be true it must include the capability of reading and controlling *everybody's* mind at *all* times.

But if that is the case, then why would the persons making such claims be exempt from this control?

Therefore, by logic, anyone who makes such a statement is also being influenced by programming and by satellites (if everybody is, then so is he). If so, then what such a person writes is skewed. And, because such debunkers are often so loud, and so sure, about this subject for no valid reason, it is a logical conclusion that what they are saying is *not* true, that the claim that all channeling is crap is, itself, disinformation.

So we see that starting from the assumption that such a claim is right (satellites affect everybody), we come to the conclusion that the claim is wrong (because it is simply repeating the satellite disinformation). So, here we have *reductio ad absurdum*.

But we can go even further. Can we find a reason why debunkers would state such evident nonsense with such certainty?

Well, here we can have a hypothesis too. If, as we know by the above analysis, *not all* channeling is from satellites, that *some* channeling can provide us with real information from 'benevolent higher beings,' from 'us in the future,' or from 'Mind-God and Oversoul,' call it as you will, then it is only natural that there will be forces trying to discredit *this* channeling. So, we have solved one problem here. If a critic calls all channelers disinformation agents, and if he is right, or even partly right, then we have reasons to suppose that such an individual is an agent of those forces.

There is one more exercise in logical reasoning and critical thinking that comes to mind. Most critics are not clear about what channeling is, so let me take the particular example of using the Ouija board, as my wife, Laura, does. Why does she use the Ouija board?

Laura went to great lengths to research the subject of channeling before she ever began her experiments. Based on facts and data, it was clear that using a 'peripheral device' in a full state of consciousness was the optimum method to screen out noise. In particular, such a method makes it far more difficult for satellites, or other programming signals coming from human and hybrid technology, when and if they come, to affect the message. At least two persons are needed, full consciousness, critical thinking, often coffee, fresh minds, loud discussion of the data as it comes, and the board. Thinking in terms of possible quantum physics involved in mind-matter interactions, it is clear to me that the methods she uses are more likely to be robust and shielded against deliberate bombarding from outside by mind-controlling signals, whether technological or 'psychic.' On the other hand, talking directly to 'Mind-God' as so many other channels do is far more susceptible to interference. For example, a weak outside EM signal can be talking directly to a tiny implant in our teeth, and we will take it for our Oversoul ...

So, by logical thinking and by critical analysis we come to a working hypothesis. But, please, do not jump to the conclusion that we have solved all the problems. Important problems are still out there and need to be addressed. The above analysis does not confirm anything 100%. It gives indications. To answer the question as to whether or not the Cassiopaean Communications is exactly what it says it is – transmissions from Us in the Future – a full analysis, which takes into account not one but many aspects, is necessary. Completely different methods must be used. If A is an opponent of B, and if we find that A is wrong, that does not mean that B is right! To see whether B is right or not – is a different problem.

Let me just note that we have discussed these issues on many occasions on our website[2] and forum,[3] with other groups or individuals and quite often, those who started as skeptics have later admitted openly that these Cassiopaeans have an amazing record.

---

[2] http://www.cassiopaea.org
[3] http://www.cassiopaea.org/forum

"Feeling the Future": Elements of Practice and of a Theory

Foreword by Arkadiusz Jadczyk, PhD

The subject of this article is precognition and premonitions, psychology, parapsychology, and quantum physics. It's a relatively long article. Glancing through it for sixteen seconds – the average time that the average reader spends on a web posting – is not enough to get a grasp of its content. Therefore, for those in a hurry, here's the comic-book version:

Dr. Daryl J. Bem – a not-so-serious-looking professor of psychology at Cornell University ...

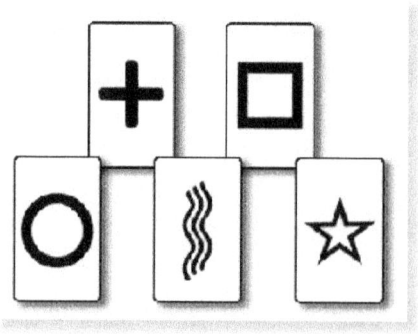

... recently wrote a serious-looking paper ...

... on the subject of parapsychology.

He argues that we can see our future, including the erotic one.

Others are attacking him ...

... but I have found a theoretical explanation of the phenomenon. The phenomenon is possible given an appropriate antenna and a kaironic mirror retransmitter.

Here is the essence of my invention:

> Knight went on again. "I'm a great hand at inventing things. Now, I daresay you noticed, that last time you picked me up, that I was looking rather thoughtful?"
> "You *were* a little grave," said Alice.
> "Well, just then I was inventing a new way of getting over a gate – would you like to hear it?"
> "Very much indeed," Alice said politely.
> "I'll tell you how I came to think of it," said the Knight. "You see, I said to myself, 'The only difficulty is with the feet: the *head* is high enough already.' Now, first I put my head on the top of the gate – then I stand on my head – then the feet are high enough, you see – then I'm over, you see."
> "Yes, I suppose you'd be over when that was done," Alice said thoughtfully: "but don't you think it would be rather hard?"
> "I haven't tried it yet," the Knight said, gravely: "so I can't tell for certain – but I'm afraid it *would* be a little hard."[1]

– *End of the comic part.* –

Now the long version. In everyday life we often meet cases to which we attribute the term miracle. Like it is discussed here: "Visions of the 9/11 Attack."[2]

'Miracles' are not recognized by official science. Nevertheless there exists a domain of research, closed to the boundary of official science, that deals with similar phenomena. Its name is parapsychology.

Let us therefore take, as a starting point, a paper recently accepted for publication in a peer-reviewed professional journal, the *Journal of Personality and Social Psychology*, "Feeling the Future: Experimental Evidence for Anomalous Retroactive Influences on Cognition and Affect."[3] The author of this paper, Daryl J. Bem,[4] is a professor emeritus at Cornell University. From his CV we learn that he first earned his MA in physics, then started graduate studies at MIT, but later followed his

---

[1] Lewis Carroll, *Through the Looking-Glass*
[2] http://paranormal.about.com/library/weekly/aa100101a.htm
[3] http://dbem.ws/FeelingFuture.pdf
[4] http://dbem.ws/

other calling and earned a PhD in social psychology. He retired from his position at Cornell in 2007.[5]

Dr. Bem's publication deals with parapsychology – a controversial domain whose very name is greeted with the condescending, knowing nod and smile from the majority of representatives of 'mainstream science'. The very fact that the paper has been accepted for publication does not necessarily mean that it will get published. Unsurprisingly, the attacks have already begun; there is probably also some pressure on the editorial board. Here is an example of a counter-offensive: "Why Psychologists Must Change the Way They Analyze Their Data: The Case of Psi."[6]

The authors of this paper state that they do not attack the very subject of Bem's paper, but merely question the statistical methods used in psychology.

Wagenmakers himself is a psychologist, Ruud Wetzels is his PhD student, Denny Borsboom has a PhD in psychology, and Han L. J. Van der Maas is a professor and the Head of Psychological Methods at the University of Amsterdam. **These scientists certainly represent what is called 'healthy science'.** But, since these people do not attack the phenomenon itself, we can tentatively assume that Daryl Bem is on to something, that his research indeed indicates the existence of the phenomenon, but that he has not been able to present his work in a form that would satisfy all. In fact, in his paper, he is explicit about why he has chosen this rather than another methodology. More sophisticated methods (Bayesian, etc.) do not always help, and sometimes they obfuscate the picture. Surely as an experienced psychologist he

---

[5]Note: The fact that the author of the paper is a professor emeritus provokes derisory smiles on the faces of those who have not yet retired. That tells us only about the owners of these faces and nothing about the value of the paper. Nevertheless a derisory smile excludes an objective judgment. I will add more: today, when a large part of research depends on the patronage of the employer, it is only in retirement that a scientist can busy him or herself with problems that he/she always, perhaps secretly, considered important. When we are on a payroll, then, for us and for our families, what is important for our employer is important for us. For the employer, on the other hand, 'important' is that what is important for politicians and funding institutions. We could follow this line farther, but there seems to be no end.

[6]Eric-Jan Wagenmakers, Ruud Wetzels, Denny Borsboom, & Han van der Maas, University of Amsterdam, http://dl.dropbox.com/u/1018886/Bem6.pdf

knows what he is talking about.

I am not going to enter into the technical details of the several experiments described in the paper; neither will I discuss the rather standard statistical evaluation methods used. That is not so important here. The paper has been accepted for publication in a peer-reviewed journal, it certainly passed through the hands of some referees, and there was a counter-attack that did not question the conclusions but only the methods used for drawing these conclusions. Moreover, since it is not the first paper reporting similar findings – there were many papers published on this subject in the past, with similar conclusions – I will therefore take it as a working hypothesis that the effect described by Bem is real. But what kind of an effect is it?

The effect consists simply of having a valid premonition about an event that is soon going to happen. And what is going to happen depends on random number generators. In the experiment, two kinds of random number generators were used: good software-based pseudo-random generators and hardware generators based on physical phenomena considered as random. On one of the blogs hosted on the *Psychology Today* web site, we can find an entry entitled: "Have Scientists Finally Discovered Evidence for Psychic Phenomena."[7]

The owner of this blog and the author of the charming entry is Melissa Burkley, PhD in psychology from Oklahoma State University. Dr. Burkley concludes that the effect, even though statistically small, is as large as or larger than the link, widely accepted by mainstream medicine, between aspirin and heart attack prevention, and the correlation, widely propagated in the media, between secondhand smoke and lung cancer. Dr. Burkley ends with an interesting remark. She writes:

> "**So although humans perceive time as linear, it doesn't necessarily mean it is so.** And as good scientists, we shouldn't let our preconceived beliefs and biases influence what we study, even if these preconceived beliefs reflect our basic assumptions about **how time and space work**."

I will not try to hide the fact that I like Dr. Burkley for these statements.

---

[7]http://www.psychologytoday.com/blog/the-social-thinker/201010/have-scientists-finally-discovered-evidence-psychic-phenomena

> **Do not keep saying ... 'But How Can It Be Like That?' ... Nobody knows how it can be like that.**
>
> *- Daryl Bem quoting physicist Richard Feynman*

So, what's the real deal with time and space? The author of the paper, Prof. Daryl Bem, devotes several pages to this problem. At the end he comes to the conclusion that physics has little to say about this matter. The fundamental laws of physics are time-symmetric and they do not give any reason why the future should be different from the past. "But wait!" I hear you say. "This is not the way *I* perceive time!" The problem of the arrow of time has been discussed by physicists and by philosophers throughout the ages without coming to any definite and generally satisfying conclusion. At the end the author quotes Richard Feynman with his famous line: **"Do not keep saying to yourself, if you can possibly avoid it, 'But how can it be like that?' Because you will go 'down the drain,' into a blind alley from which nobody has yet escaped. Nobody knows how it can be like that."**

But I do know how it can be like, and I want to share this knowledge. The whole thing is pretty simple. It is enough to look at modern physics and use its tools. In other words: **I have a theory**. Perhaps one day someone will be interested in this theory. Or maybe not. In any case I know it, but I am not going to pause at this place as there are problems more important than precognition that need to be solved. Technologically speaking, the way to some practical application is so long that it is more effective not to use any theory at all. Nevertheless I am going to explain the main idea, because **the theory allows us to answer the question "But can it be like that?"**

The whole secret is contained in my published paper "The Theory of Kairons."[8] Few people know that Kairos[9] is one of the gods of time. That is where the name comes from. Sometimes I like to play with things that are timeless.

In my theory of kairons I have introduced a new kind of physical object. **While particles propagate along time-like trajectories in space, my kairons propagate along space-like trajectories in time.**

So, they are propagating instantaneously, but **they are not tachions**. They are rather like shock waves with some quantum character – more like cracks in the fabric of time and space. Using them, as well as some kind of a quantum entanglement, **we can communicate with ourselves in the future**. There is, however, one condition: a 'friendly retransmitter' is needed, ideally somewhere far away, the distance is not an obstacle, it can be in some distant constellation. It can be somewhere near 3C 144 in the Crab nebula, or it can be 3C 461. What is important is that there should be a strong radio-source there that works in an appropriate nonequilibrium regime (right now received as a strong radio-source). 'We in the future' and 'we in the now' can become quantum-entangled with the retransmitter, the transmission is 'instantaneous,' and we receive the signal as 'us in the future'. That's all. The math is rather advanced, therefore no one, even a crippled dog, till now, has paid any attention to it. And if he has, perhaps he is not that crippled.

I am speculating that if the retransmitter is at the distance of x light years, reliable communication may take place with 'us in the future' at the time distance of $x/137$ years. The Sun is the strongest radio source, but the Sun does not have the supernova history, therefore its transmission regime is different, the noise is also probably rather high. The Sun is circa 8 light minutes from us. Therefore using the Sun would give us about 3 seconds of advance. That is enough for explaining Dr. Bem's data.

Figure 1 illustrates my hypothesis. And Figure 2 shows a map of

---

[8] Arkadiusz Jadczyk, "The Theory of Kairons", *Advances in Applied Clifford Algebras*, Volume 19, Number 1, 63–82, DOI: 10.1007/s00 006-008-0119-2

[9] http://en.wikipedia.org/wiki/Kairos

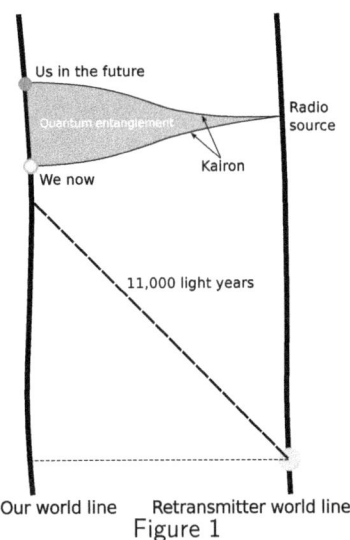

Figure 1

known radio-sources.[10]

About psychology

On the subject of psychology, psychologists, and the methods used by them, a PhD thesis can be written in the domain of satire. Tomasz Witkowski, also a psychologist, is the author of a version of the Sokal affair.[11] For fun he wrote, using a pseudo name, a 'scientific paper' on the subject of 'morphogenetic fields' and their possible use in psychology. Details can be found on Witkowski's site.[12] The result was that a respected journal readily accepted the paper, but when word got out that the paper was poking fun, a 'war' started that included attempts to remove all traces of the 'scandal,' including attempts to edit Wikipedia's entries. Not a pretty picture.

---

[10]Whitham D. Reeve, "Important Celestial Radio-sources", www.reeve.com/ Documents/ RadioScience/ CelestialRadioSources.pdf
[11]http://en.wikipedia.org/wiki/Sokal_affair
[12]http://www.tomaszwitkowski.pl/page16.php

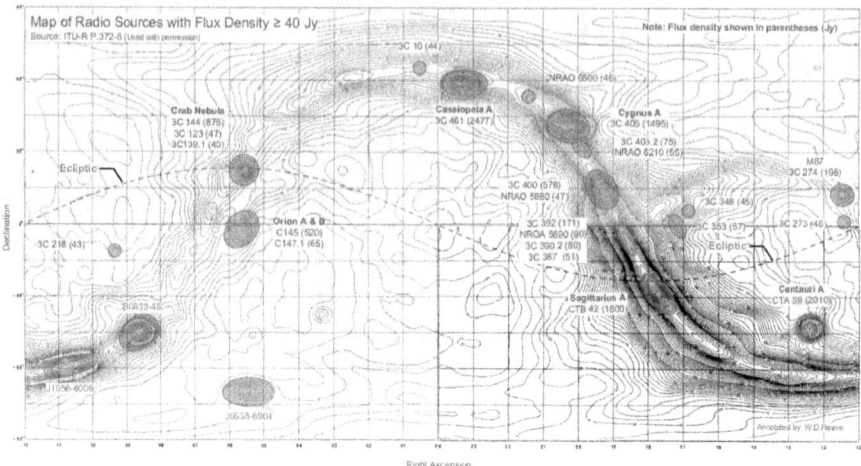

Figure 2: Annotations show the approximate locations of sources with flux density greater than or equal to 40 Jy. The contour lines represent lines of constant noise temperature as measured at 408 MHz.

Back to physics

Returning to physics I would like to give a hint about other physicists researching the subject of a 'super-luminal communication'. In a paper "Subquantum Information and Computation",[13] Dr. Antony Valentini (Theoretical Physics Group, Blackett Laboratory, Imperial College, London, England) writes in this abstract:

> It is argued that immense physical resources – for non-local communication, espionage, and exponentially-fast computation – are hidden from us by quantum noise, and that this noise is not fundamental but merely a property of an equilibrium state in which the universe happens to be at the present time. It is suggested that 'non-quantum' or non-equilibrium matter might exist today in the form of relic particles from the early universe. We describe how such matter could be detected and put to practical use. Non-equilibrium matter could be used to **send instantaneous signals**, to violate the uncertainty principle, to distinguish non-orthogonal quantum states without disturbing them, to eavesdrop on quantum key distribution, and to outpace quantum computation (solving NP-complete problems in polynomial time).

---

[13]http://arxiv.org/abs/quant-ph/0203 049

Figure 3

And figure 3 shows an interesting poster from Cambridge University (UK).

Postface

Like Dr. Daryl J. Bem, the author of the paper "Feeling the Future", I will also end with a quotation from Lewis Carroll's *Through the Looking Glass*:

> "I can't believe THAT!" said Alice.
> "Can't you?" the Queen said in a pitying tone. "Try again: draw a long breath, and shut your eyes."
> Alice laughed. "There's no use trying," she said: "one *can't* believe impossible things."
> "I daresay you haven't had much practice," said the Queen. "When I was your age, I always did it for half-an hour a day. Why, sometimes I've believed as many as six impossible things before breakfast."

Introduction

by Laura Knight-Jadczyk

Chances are that most readers of the transcripts published here in book format for the first time are already familiar with my work. But for those who aren't, a short intro may be helpful. I began what came to be known as the Cassiopaean Experiment in 1992. However, it was only after two years of applied efforts that we (myself and varied co-experimenters) made the contact that would help define the focus and direction of my work for the coming years. Thus, the contact with 'the C's' in mid-1994 was the result of a lifetime of questioning, seeking, research, planning, and experimentation. As these books go to press, it has been two decades, and what an adventure it has been!

The whole story – or a lot of it, at least – has already been told in my books *Amazing Grace* and *The Wave* (8 volumes). *Amazing Grace* tells the story of my life up to the time of the first contact with the C's, and *The Wave* focuses on the C's material itself, the research that both informed the sessions and in turn was inspired by the material we received. It also details the unique, informative, and often strange experiences I had as a result, the people with whom I interacted and the things I learned from those interactions. Much of this is only hinted at in the sessions that follow, so I've decided to add supplementary information in the form of introductions to many of the sessions, and footnotes throughout. Even so, it's highly recommended that new readers check out the mentioned volumes in order to get more details.

In early 1995, I gave a short talk about my work to the Clearwater MUFON group; in the audience was Tom French, a *St. Petersburg Times* (Florida) journalist, who approached me after the meeting and asked if he could meet with me privately. Though I was suspicious of his motives, I agreed. The upshot of the meeting was that he wanted to follow me in my daily life and work with a view to ultimately writing a special for his newspaper. Before agreeing, I asked for assurances that I would have at least some say-so in the final product and that it wasn't going to be a skeptical hit-piece. This turned out to be a rather long 'investigation' stretching over 5 years, during which a lot of changes manifested in my life as a result of the channeling experiment and Tom received a Pulitzer Prize for his book-length piece about a notorious murder that had interested both of us intensely long before we ever met.

The title of the piece about me, when it was finally published in February of 2000, ended up being "The Exorcist in Love,"[1] which I thought was horribly cheesy. But what can you do at the turn of the Millennium and you need a piece for Valentine's Day? The point it highlighted, however, wasn't cheesy at all: the channeling experiment led to extraordinary, dramatic changes in my life, including guiding me to a meeting with my husband, theoretical physicist Arkadiusz Jadczyk.

Getting back to the topic of channeling proper and the material contained in this set of books, of which this is the first volume, I want to point out that before even attempting to channel, I spent years reading and researching the topic. At an early age I had read the entire *Proceedings of the Society for Psychical Research*, founded in 1882 by some of the leading scientific figures of the time. Since then, the Society has published in-depth analyses of all sorts of psychic phenomena: hypnosis, mediumship, channeling, apparitions, poltergeists, psychokinesis, telepathy, and more. (For a highly readable account of this interesting period of history, and the personalities involved, see *New York Times* journalist Deborah Blum's *Ghost Hunters: William James and the search for scientific proof of life after death*). So I had a pretty good idea of what was out there and what I could expect before getting involved in my own experimentation.

As a result of this research, I trained as a hypnotherapist back in the mid-seventies. As mentioned above, I've chronicled this in my book *Amazing Grace*, so I won't go into details here. Let me just mention shortly that I began by doing past-life investigations, always looking for the 'perfect case', and gradually moved into more therapeutic modalities including what is generally known as Spirit Release, inspired by the work of psychologist Edith Fiore. The techniques were developed

---

[1] http://www.sptimes.com/News/webspecials/exorcist/index.html

and refined to some extent by William Baldwin, who called it Spirit Releasement Therapy. Spirit release operates on the premise that when people die, their spirits often stick around, 'attaching' to the living because of some sort of shared emotional resonance. The spirit attachment can then perpetuate or amplify emotional problems and behaviors, even introducing new proclivities and habits (for example, a desire for alcohol). Whether or not this is actually the case – whether these spirits actually exist or are simply creations of the subject's subconscious – is hard to say. All I *can* say is that in my practice, everyone had them, and I wasn't expecting them to be there and most assuredly wasn't asking leading questions. As I wrote in *Amazing Grace*, the only thing that concerned me was that it worked, and I was primarily concerned with results: relief for the client.

The main thing that can be said about my experience as a hypnotherapist, and specifically doing SRT, is that it was excellent training and preparation for engaging in a channeling experiment. Here, I won't kid you: indeed, 'messing around' with the supernatural or paranormal can be problematical and even dangerous. Channeling has a long history, from the trance-induced utterances of ancient shamans, seers, and prophets, to more modern phenomena and methods: Ouija boards, table-tipping, automatic writing, mediumship, and the 'trance channeling' typical of the older Spiritualism and the later New Age movements. As I explicate in some detail in *Amazing Grace*, using a prosthetic device, a 'talking board'-type instrument with several people involved, is probably the safest and least disruptive to the normal psychological functioning of the participants.

Psychologists refer to these various phenomena as 'automatisms', because the actions involved (e.g., the movement of the planchette on the board) occur without the conscious intent of the person or persons involved. Whether the alleged 'entities' who claim to make contact are real or not, the phenomenon itself is actually quite real and fascinating. For example, in a recent experiment with Ouija boards conducted by scientists at the University of British Columbia, participants are made to answer a series of questions on a computer, then asked to answer them using a Ouija board:

> During the Ouija board segment, participants are assigned a

partner and are blindfolded. Eventually, one of the pair is told to withdraw, leaving the other participant to play alone without knowing it.

The experiment has found participants who cannot answer some of the questions on the computer, can sometimes answer them correctly using the Ouija board, despite being blindfolded. Mr. Duncan said the remaining participant is told at the end that they were moving the board alone.

"Usually they don't believe us at first," he said. "When we tell them they were the only ones moving it ... usually they think that the deception was that we were just moving it around."

Ashwin Krishnamurthi, a second-year computer science student at UBC, was a participant in the Ouija experiment and was "amazed" when he found out he was the only one moving the board piece.

"I thought that the other participant was also playing along with me. I felt that the other person was trying to move the piece, but he wasn't. It was just me," Mr. Krishnamurthi said.[2]

Parapsychologists are divided as to whether the information coming through the Ouija board is simply coming from the subjects' own subconscious, clairvoyance of distant sources of information, telepathy from other living individuals, or other intelligences entirely. We tend to think that all are possibilities, but the devil is in the details, and discerning what may be the case in any specific situation requires much practice and research.

Many if not most 'channelers' approach the phenomenon as true believers. They may be aware of a wide array of previous channeled material, but very often they lack knowledge of the extensive history of scientific research into the 'paranormal', not to mention the wider range of relevant topics including science, history, psychology, psychopathology, religion, and philosophy. They approach the subject uncritically, assume that their 'contacts' are exactly who they say they are, and take their messages and prophecies as gospel truth.

My approach is much different. I call it 'critical channeling', and it was one of the reasons I decided on the board as opposed to something like trance channeling, where the channel or medium basically goes into

---

[2]Zoe Tenant, 'Researchers crowd-source funds to back Ouija board science project', *The Globe and Mail*, March 4, 2014

an altered state of consciousness and allows the communicating entity to control their body; in other words, no possibility for conscious feedback or participation on the part of the channel! Using the board, however, allows the participants to retain full control of their critical, conscious faculties while observing the 'automatic' movements on the board.[3]

Another important aspect often overlooked by New Age channelers is the importance of the channelers' own psychic hygiene, and how it may affect the 'level' of contact and the material coming through. At first, the only contacts we made were typical 'dead dudes' (similar to those encountered during spirit release), residents of the 'astral planes', and 'space brothers' with cheesy, New Age–sounding names and equally cheesy dialogs. After a couple years of working through all this, most of which was tedious and not informative (though we were learning a lot), the C's came through on July 16, 1994, pretty much in synch with the impacts of Comet Shoemaker-Levy on Jupiter. At the time, we didn't realize the significance of this, but it has proven to be an amazing key to many mysteries on our beleaguered planet.

Over the years, I've had a lot of people sit in on the sessions, either as guests or sitting directly at the board: close friends and family members, curious acquaintances, scientists, other professionals, and a few individuals we later found out did not have our best interests at heart. (See *The Wave* for details.)

One of the things early investigators of the paranormal discovered, and which became clear as I followed through with the experiment and learned from the experiences, is that psychic phenomena can be strongly influenced or 'colored' by a sitter's preconceived beliefs. In the case of the C's, it is not that they are 'controlled' by these prejudices; it rather seems that they do not contradict them out of scrupulous respect for free will. I was surprised to realize, after the fact, that on many occasions, the C's conveyed information in the presence of such individuals that was 'coded', so to say; in short, they managed to say what needed to be said without offending anyone. But, again, this sort of thing is covered in great detail in *The Wave*, where I cite specific instances and reveal

---

[3]There are several experimental trance channeling sessions included in this volume, but they were not satisfactory as there was a definite 'flavor' to them that was unpleasant, despite useful information coming through.

the machinations behind the scenes.

If you have read the history behind the sessions in *The Wave*, you will be aware that they were published online back in 2002 before they had been checked and verified against the original notes and tapes. There were many errors of various kinds that always creep into any lengthy discourse that is being transcribed from voice to text. In these volumes, you will find that I have more carefully checked the transcripts with the tapes and notes, made corrections where necessary, and redacted some private details. In some places, I've added explanatory footnotes above and beyond what is included in *The Wave*. There is also material here that has never been published before.

As alluded to above, the C's played 'match-maker' in my life with the result that my entire life changed suddenly and dramatically. You could even say that I entered a new reality, because that is certainly what it feels like. But the new reality has as much to do with knowledge and awareness as anything else and I am thankful that the C's did not just hand easy (and wrong) answers to me on a plate, but rather compelled me to go out and do research again and again and again; what is learned via labor becomes a part of your being and I have definitely grown and changed rapidly through the past 20 years in ways I never imagined possible. I think that this is true for everyone who was attracted to this experiment and became a permanent part of it as the years went by. Those who could not change, or who were not willing or able to do the work, fell away and now are a 'dream in the past.'

Of course, the world, too, has changed dramatically in ways none of us engaged in this experiment could imagine. The pre-9/11 world is as different from the post-9/11 world as though they were civilizations on different planets. The C's told us what was coming and explained many things about it, but our vision was so limited we could not conceive of how it could change from what was then to what is now. Whenever I wonder about things the C's have said about other matters that have not yet come to pass, when I struggle to imagine how such transitions could be made, I remember this.

Having said all of the above, let me make a few comments about the technical issues of channeling. People often ask me "how does it feel?" or "do you hear or otherwise perceive the answers before they are spelled out?" I guess the second question is related to "are you moving the pointer in response to what you know is the answer?"

For the first two or three years, yes, I felt a number of strange sensations at various places in my body both during the channeling sessions, and when not channeling. Most of these were rather like electrical buzzing or vibrations in the back of my neck and down my arm. On many occasions, the instant the contact began, I would get so hot I could barely tolerate it and you'll read a few remarks along this line in the sessions themselves. (We can't exclude early symptoms of menopause here, either!) A few times I had pinching feelings at the nape of my neck as though something was happening in the nerves there. And, as one would expect, there was a whole series of what can only be called paranormal occurrences running in the background, including multiple instances of what presented as psychokinesis, clairvoyance, clairaudience, etc. I took the approach that one should not be distracted or enamored of such things and should sort of 'will them to stop,' because they are actually of no spiritual value, they are just signposts along the way.

I generally sleep extremely deeply after a session, and sometimes it seems as though the communication continues at a subconscious level for several hours. I may wake up knowing further elaborations of answers to questions from the previous session. But that was just in the first few years. Now, the sessions seem to be so natural an activity that I only perceive some sort of a slight shift in nervous system orientation (for lack of a better way to describe it). I think it could be compared to learning to drive a car: in the beginning, you have to pay close attention to every little thing, but after awhile, it all becomes habitual and you can drive and carry on a conversation with a passenger at the same time. And certainly, I've got a well-developed left arm that easily suspends from the shoulder for long periods of time without getting tired!

As to what goes through my mind: in the beginning, there was absolutely, utterly, *no* pre-awareness of what was coming at all! The answers were as much a surprise to me as anyone else. That is still true to some extent, though now I sense (for lack of a better word) only the next letter, and the next and the next, just a fraction of a second before the pointer moves to it, and in a few instances, I have 'known' the answer just before it came. Usually, in the latter case, that is due to the obviousness of the response. For a very long time, I could not follow the string of letters with my conscious mind at all and *all* answers had to be read back to me. Nowadays, it seems that my conscious mind is able to follow better and I can connect the strings parallel to receiving them to some extent; it's like having two separate mental functions running at the same time. (Again, the learning-to-drive analogy.) When the answers are long and complex, though, I'm as lost as anyone else present. So, I would say that there have been some sort of changes to my brain/mind and the way I perceive and process things thanks to the years of engaging in this experiment; I can be totally aware of one aspect of reality in one way, while observing and appraising it from another angle at the same time. I've become a sort of parallel processor, I guess! (Or an experienced driver!)

From the C's point of view, there appear to be a number of issues that can affect the quality of the material that is transmitted as well as the mechanical aspects. In March of 1995, we had a communication session at a MUFON meeting with 25 or 30 people present. One of the members of MUFON wanted to place a Gauss meter on the table beside the board. A Gauss meter is a device that measures the intensity of magnetic fields. Well, interestingly, every time the C's began their response to a question, the needle on the meter buried itself to the right indicating a powerful magnetic field was manifesting from their side, though as soon as the transmission ended, the needle went back to the ambient measurement. Then, in January of 1996, we managed to obtain a Polaroid photo of the transmission as a light figure on the board. That was pretty exciting. (All of this will be presented with the related transcripts themselves.)

On a number of occasions, the individuals present in the room seemed to have a profound effect (positive or negative) on the strength, liveliness, and conciseness of the transmission. On a few occasions, energy bursts caused the pointer to literally fly off the board right out from under our fingers! That's always fun. One very peculiar thing I noted on several occasions was a sort of offsetting of the pointer: at these times, the motion would never hit the letters on the board directly on top of them, but would stop off to the side. It was as though the transmission was coming through at an angle of some sort. This factor was reflected in the responses, as well. So it seems that there are some energetic factors in such a process that could be investigated.

At a certain point, we finally caught on to the fact that receiving information from other realms was a process of breaking down – transducing – some sort of signal that arrives in what can only be called a universal language of metaphors which is focused and transferred as thought wave energy, which then gets further translated into what we know as phonetic (sound) language, which is then still further reduced to writing.[4] Obviously, there can be many a slip betwixt cup and lip in this process and I came to understand more deeply that there were problems of interpretation beyond simply transducing metaphoric signals into language. This was made very clear in a couple of exchanges, the first being on 26 November 1994 as follows:

Q: *(L)* In terms of these Earth changes, Edgar Cayce is one of the most famous prognosticators of recent note. A large number of the prophecies he made seemingly were erroneous in terms of their fulfillment. For example, he prophesied that Atlantis would rise in 1969, but it did not, though certain structures were discovered off the coast of Bimini which are thought by many to be remnants of Atlantis. These did, apparently, emerge from the sand at that time.

A: Example of one form of symbolism.

Q: *(L)* Well, in terms of this symbolism, could this be applied to the remarks you made about the two little boys who were missing in South Carolina?

A: Yes.

Q: *(L)* And the symbolism was that you were reading the event from 3rd density into 6th density terms and then transmitting it back into 3rd, and while the ideation was correct, the exact specifics, in 3rd density terms, were slightly askew. Is that what we are dealing with here?

A: 99.9 per cent would not understand that concept. Most are always looking for literal translations of data. Analogy is novice who attends art gallery, looks at abstract painting and says "I don't get it."

Q: *(L)* Well, let's not denigrate literal translations or at least attempts to get things into literal terms. I like realistic art work. I am a realist in my art preferences. I want trees to look like trees and people to have only two arms and legs. Therefore, I also like some literalness in my prognostications.

A: Some is okay, but, beware or else "California falls into the ocean" will always be interpreted as California falling into the ocean.

Q: [General uproar] *(F)* Wait a minute, what was the question? *(L)* I just said I liked literalness in my prophecies. *(F)* Oh, I know what they are saying. Peo-

---

[4]These ideas relate to our education and development in information theory, which is crucial for understanding any kind of channeling. Here the reader may wish to read Pierre Lescaudron's recent book *Earth Changes and the Human-Cosmic Connection* for an exposition of information theory.

ple believe that California is just going to go splat and that Phoenix is going to be on the seacoast, never mind that it's at 1800 feet elevation, it's just going to drop down to sea level, or the sea level is going to rise, but it's not going to affect Virginia Beach even though that's at sea level. I mean... somehow Phoenix is just going to drop down and none of the buildings are going to be damaged, even though its going to fall 1800 feet... *(T)* Slowly. It's going to settle. *(F)* Slowly? It would have to be so slowly it's unbelievable how slowly it would have to be. *(T)* It's been settling for the last five million years, we've got a ways to go in the next year and a half! *(F)* Right! That's my point. *(T)* In other words, when people like Scallion and Sun Bear and others say California is going to fall into the ocean, they are not saying that the whole state, right along the border, is going to fall into the ocean; they are using the term California to indicate that the ocean ledge along the fault line has a probability of breaking off and sinking on the water side, because it is a major fracture. We understand that that is not literal. Are you telling us that there is more involved here as far as the way we are hearing what these predictions say?

A: Yes.

Q: *(T)* Are we understanding what you are saying?

A: Some.

Q: *(T)* So, when we talk about California falling into the ocean, we are not talking about the whole state literally falling into the ocean?

A: In any case, even if it does, how long will it take to do this?

Q: *(LM)* It could take three minutes or three hundred years. *(T)* Yes. That is "open" as you would say.

A: Yes. But most of your prophets think it is not open.

Q: *(J)* Yeah, because they think they have the only line on it. *(T)* OK. So they are thinking in the terms that one minute California will be there and a minute and a half later it will be all gone. Is this what you are saying?

A: Or similar.

Q: *(T)* So, when we are talking: "California will fall into the ocean," which is just the analogy we are using, we are talking about, as far as Earth changes, is the possibility that several seismic events along the fault line, which no one really knows the extent of...

A: Or it all may be symbolic of something else.

Q: *(L)* Such as? *(J)* All the fruitcakes in California are all going to go off the deep end together. *(L)* Symbolic of what?

A: Up to you to examine and learn.

In addition to those issues, the 'time' conundrum became important, especially when one is dealing with an open universe, as the C's declare ours to be. Those concerns bring us face to face with the prophetic problem that exercised my mind a great deal back in those days, as I described in some detail in *Amazing Grace*. I would suggest that the 'time/open-universe' problem is parallel to the 'metaphor/information-realm-transduction-to-language' problem. If enough information is known to a source, more or less conditional predictions can be made. The longer the time in advance of an event a prediction is made, the more changes to the outcome might come into play by the shifts or changes in the reality, i.e. information field.

For example, I dreamed about the Challenger disaster a few hours before I witnessed it. I describe this in *Amazing Grace* in detail. How to explain this? Perhaps my subconscious mind accessed a sort of Universal Information Field and obtained the data that there were mechanical problems with the shuttle. Or perhaps I telepathically read the mind of one of the engineers who knew there were problems. (There are other possibilities as well.) The dream itself was a series of metaphoric images, but when the actual event happened, which I saw with my own eyes that sad January day, I realized the cleverness of this strange symbolic language of other realms.

So this metaphoric/symbolic element that requires transducing and translating is one main thing to keep in mind while reading the C's transcripts: much of what is in them is the consequence of arriving into language from a metaphoric and/or symbolic realm, though certainly there are things that are plain and simple. And keep in mind that time is always at least somewhat indefinite, because the Universe is open and things can change (thank goodness for that!). Finally, keep in mind that because the Universe *is* open, and inputs can change things, some events that are pretty certain to happen if things continue in a certain way with no major changes in trajectory, may change dramatically if there is a change in the dynamic. Sometimes things can be accelerated or delayed, too. If conspirators have a plan, and they are exposed and people are warned in advance, they are likely to change their plans. The end result may be the same, but it may take longer and go a different direction before getting there.

This brings up another aspect of predictions: most prophecies that we know of from ancient times were written after the fact, so we can't use them as models to study for extraction of principles. Most predictions of more recent times that I am aware of that have come to pass, so to say, have a peculiar characteristic. Let me give an example: the assassination of John F. Kennedy. This prediction was published in the Sunday supplement *Parade* on May 13, 1956: "As for the 1960 election

Mrs. Dixon thinks it will be dominated by labor and won by a Democrat. But he will be assassinated or die in office 'though not necessarily in his first term.'" But then, in 1960, when JFK was actually in the race, Ms. Dixon predicted that he would "fail to win the presidency." Was she then perceiving the machinations of a powerful group that stood against him?

So how did she get it so right in 1956 and so wrong in 1960? And keep in mind that, as far as we know, JFK was targeted by a conspiracy that only came into being because he actually did manage to obtain the presidency thanks to the countering machinations of his father (which Jeane Dixon apparently didn't perceive), and then he showed his true populist colors which either he had concealed up to then, or he had some sort of epiphany as is suggested by James W. Douglass in *JFK and the Unspeakable: Why He Died and Why It Matters*. If predictions are possible because a person can tap into an information field, or gather information from the minds of others telepathically as I suggest above, then this would mean that there was a conspiracy afoot already in 1956 to assassinate a president in 1960, whoever he was and no matter what he did. Or perhaps it wasn't a conspiracy at the human level; perhaps it was 'written in the stars' or due to some chaotic patch in the Cosmic Information Field? Or maybe it was something altogether different. I don't know.

In any event, going through these sessions to comment on them has been a remarkable experience for me; I came across things that I apparently remembered wrong, came across other things that I had forgotten entirely, and was able to better observe the flow of energy and how the communication actually was teaching me many things even when it was not being directly didactic. For example: the issue of lies vs. truth in various contexts. Our idea at the beginning was: can we get accurate predictions, can we prove it? Then it must be 'good.' It appears that it is not that simple.

The operative terms in the quantum-like hyperdimensional realities seem to be 'Service to Others' and 'Service to Self' rather than 'lies or truth.' It took me awhile to understand this but once I did, it really was a liberating, ecstatic feeling. And that doesn't mean that Truth isn't the highest value for those on the Service to Others pathway: it is. But we live in a Universe that exists by virtue of the myriad ways in which truth and lies, creation and entropy, spirit and matter combine. You could reduce the principle to positive and negative (charge) which emerges in our reality from a Cosmic Information Field. Or, think of the computer analogy of strings of 0s and 1s being the basic computing units. With the help of Michael Topper, who wrote a great deal of commentary on *The Ra Material*, from whence the terms STO and STS derive, I published an article[5] on this topic on my website. I also wrote about it in my book *The Secret History of the World* in some detail, so I won't repeat all of that here.

What I do want to point out is that during the course of annotating these sessions, I was able to see how this concept was conveyed through various interactions with the C's, myself, and the other participants or attendees at the sessions. I've made notes at various points where the C's were wrong – probably consciously – but I could see no fault or bad intent, because they were definitely working within the psychological parameters given them by those present. And this is a crucial thing to understand about this kind of work: it is definitely a reality where the observer/participant has a powerful influence and it is harder for a materially minded, black-and-white thinker to grasp the essence of this reality than that a camel should go through the eye of a needle!

In the C's sessions, you will encounter a whole lot of predictions about a coming reality that we could not even imagine at the time: the post-9/11 world. Much of this, in hindsight, fits the description of starting out as metaphoric and symbolic, transducing and translating into terms we were familiar with or which had certain symbolic meaning in our reality. Many of those 'off-side' predictions were obviously (now) about this and the means of change: the 9/11 attacks themselves. If my idea that prophecy is a product of tapping into this Information Field, or telepathically tuning into the minds of those who have information that the rest of us don't have, then that means the 9/11 attacks were already in the planning stage as early as 1994, just as the above remarks suggest that the plan to assassinate a president was already formulated four years before JFK was elected. Again, I don't know for sure; I just know that there are realms beyond our own that are surpassingly strange and deserve long and careful investigation and analysis that just

---

[5]http://cassiopaea.org/2010/09/14/michael-topper-on-stalking/

A session with the Cassiopaeans in 2014

isn't being done, because science has lost its way. But that's another topic for another day and another volume.

In closing, let me just say that the day the C's came an adventure began that has not ceased to amaze me for twenty years. There have been agonies and ecstasies and an unending parade of marvels that have enriched my life beyond anything I ever imagined possible, as well as the lives of the many others who have joined with me on this quest. I receive letters daily from people all over the world telling me how my work, inspired by the C's material, has changed their lives and how now, once again, their lives have become meaningful. And that's the bottom line: if it hadn't changed my life for the better, I wouldn't have begun to share it, and if it hadn't helped many others, this volume would not be seeing the light of day. But it did, I did, it has, and it continues... as the C's would say: "Stay tuned!"

July 16, 1994

Background: We had been sitting weekly for a bit over two years at this point and most of what had come through was a stream of alleged discarnates ('dead dudes') and 'space brothers.' One of the discarnates claimed to be an old friend of mine, science-fiction writer Keith Laumer, who had passed the previous year (January 23, 1993). A few weeks prior to this session presented here, we had asked a few general test questions about aliens and UFOs and the word 'Ra' had been spelled out several times. Except for the well-known Egyptian god, the only other references I had were from the Edgar Cayce channelings. However, just a few days after this, I came across an ad in a New Age–type magazine for a book entitled *The Ra Material* that was supposed to have been channeled from an 'ancient astronaut.' Intrigued, I ordered the book, and read it. I immediately knew that this was important material and even though we were becoming weary of our long vigil at the board, when I read about the many years this experimental channeling group put into a similar project, I took heart and, instead of giving up, as I was tempted to do, we persisted.

Participants: 'Frank',[1] Scarlett[2] and Laura

1 **Q**: Hello.

2 **A**: Hello.

3 **Q**: Do you have any messages for us?[3]

4 **A**: Keep doing what comes naturally.

5 **Q**: *(L)* In what respect?

6 **A**: Study.

---

[1] A pseudonym.
[2] Scarlett is identified as 'Candy' in *The Wave*. See introductory notes to session 1 December 1994.
[3] *Amazing Grace* 44; *High Strangeness* 5; *Riding The Wave* "Autobiographical Background"; *Facing the Unknown* "Appendix C"
[4] This was an unusual name. Up to this point in time, the names we had been given had all been, more or less, familiar. Names like 'Dave' or 'John' or 'Mary' were not uncommon with the 'dead dude'-type contacts. Some of them even used archaic, but still familiar names like 'Agamemnon' or 'Aquila.' So, a completely unfamiliar name with no known connection was a first.

7 **Q:** *(L)* What is your name?

8 **A:** Mucpeor.[4]

9 **Q:** *(L)* Are you an alien from another planet?

10 **A:** Alien from your perspective, yes.[5]

11 **Q:** *(L)* What is your group called?

12 **A:** Corsas.

13 **Q:** *(L)* Where are you from?

14 **A:** Cassiopaea.

15 **Q:** *(L)* Where is that?

16 **A:** Near Orion.

17 **Q:** *(L)* I heard that the Orions are the 'bad guys.' Are the Orion group bad?[6]

18 **A:** Some bad.

19 **Q:** *(L)* Do you serve self or others?[7]

20 **A:** I serve both.

21 **Q:** Are you bad or good?

22 **A:** Good.

23 **Q:** *(L)* What is your philosophy?

24 **A:** One.[8]

25 **Q:** *(L)* What are you here for tonight?

26 **A:** Prophecy.

27 **Q:** *(L)* What prophecies?

28 **A:** Tornadoes Florida – several.

29 **Q:** Where else?

30 **A:** Also Texas and Alabama.

31 **Q:** *(L)* When?

32 **A:** Sun is in Libra.[9]

33 **Q:** *(L)* What planet are you from?

34 **A:** Corsoca.[10]

---

[5] Please take careful note of this response. Contrary to the claims of many individuals who seek to dismiss this experiment by claiming that the C's are 'channeled aliens,' the C's have never, ever, at any point, stated that they are 'aliens.'

[6] In *The Ra Material*, the 'black hats' are called the "Orion Union" and the 'white hats' are the "Federation."

[7] The concept of "Service to Self" versus "Service to Others" as the modes of activity of the 'black hats' and the 'white hats' respectively, was something we had read in *The Ra Material*.

[8] "The Law of One," another concept from *The Ra Material* which may have been derived from the Cayce material.

[9] This remark about the "Sun in Libra" becomes extremely important later on, so it was interesting that this was brought up at the very first session.

[10] The term 'Corsoca' was one of the first 'clues' about hidden things in our reality the Cassiopaeans gave that related almost directly to a particular written work. In Jacques Vallee's book *Revelations*, at the beginning of each section, there are quotes from Cassilda's Song in *The King in Yellow*, Act 1, Scene 2, by Robert W. Chambers. The Song goes:

"*Strange is the night where black stars rise / And strange moons circle through the skies / But stranger still is ... Lost Carcosa – Songs that the Pleiades shall sing / Where flap the tatters of the King / Must die unheard in ... Dim Carcosa – Along the shore the cloud waves break / The twin suns sink behind the lake / The shadows lengthen ... In Carcosa.*"

So, of course, having just read this poem, I was immediately struck by the similarity of Corsoca to Carcosa. The reference to twin suns was also significant later on, but not of any significance to us at this point. Finally, considering the state of

Q: Where is that?

A: 2 DILOR.[11]

Q: What was that again?

A: You pay attention.

Q: *(L)* What else is going to happen?[12]

A: Seattle buried; Japan buckles; Missouri shakes; California crumbles; Arizona burns.

Q: [Unknown question.]

A: Go to Denver airports.

Q: *(L)* When is all this going to happen?

A: Scandal – Scandal – Denver Airport.

Q: *(L)* What about the Denver airport?

A: Scandal.

Q: I don't understand.

A: New Denver airport.

Q: I don't understand.

A: Pay attention.

Q: Okay, we are paying attention. What are you trying to tell us?

A: Denver new airport big, big, big, big scandal.

Q: *(L)* What kind of scandal?

A: Government.

Q: *(L)* Specifically what?

A: You will see. Dallas airport is secret base; Orlando too; Miami too.[13]

Q: *(L)* What about Denver airport and how does it relate to prophecies?

A: Denver reveals the government. Look for it. Pay attention.[14]

Q: *(L)* What else do you have to tell us?

A: Montana: Experiment with human reproduction. All people there – rays – radon gas.

---

the world at present, the description of "Lost, Dim Carcosa" become particularly poignant.

[11]Some confusion about this as the planchette had begun to move rather quickly and this is not complete.

[12]*High Strangeness* 9

[13]Retrospectively, with the connections in Texas and Florida to 9/11, and the Colorado NORAD involvement, again, it seems that this information is warning of 9/11 fully seven years in advance.

[14]Note that the answer is that "Denver reveals the government" and the emphasis on a "big, big, big scandal." We were very puzzled by this and our researches didn't produce much of interest. It was only in 1996 that I learned there was something 'scandalous' about the murals that had been commissioned to decorate the airport. (See session 29 March 1996.) The significant information needed didn't come until October of 1997 when a friend of mine undertook to get photographs of these murals for me [see Appendix for a selection of these photographs]. They are discussed in session 1 November 1997. It was then that the C's explicated that these murals were a pictorial representation of the elite controllers' plans for humanity. Thus, considering the connection between the Denver Airport murals and everything that has happened since 9/11/01, it seems to me that this warning about a "big, big, big scandal" was a very early intimation of 9/11 and the overt imposition of a police state, New World Order, or whatever you want to call it. Keep your eyes open, the C's dropped other clues in further sessions.

61 Q: *(L)* How are they doing this?

62 A: Compelled – Don't trust – Don't ignore – too strong urges – sinister plots.

63 Q: *(L)* What do you mean? I don't understand?

64 A: Strong urge is directed by sinister plot.[15]

65 Q: Plot by whom?

66 A: Consortium.

67 Q: *(L)* Who are the members of the consortium? Aliens? The government?

68 A: All.

69 Q: *(L)* All who?

70 A: Government and other.

71 Q: *(L)* Who is the other?

72 A: Unknown.

73 Q: *(L)* Why can't you tell us who is the other?

74 A: You know who.

75 Q: *(L)* Bob Lazar[16] referred to the fact that aliens supposedly refer to humans as containers. What does this mean?[17]

76 A: Later use.

77 Q: *(L)* Use by whom? How many?

78 A: 94 per cent.

79 Q: *(L)* 94 per cent of what?

80 A: Of all population.

81 Q: *(L)* What do you mean?

82 A: All are containers; 94 per cent use.

83 Q: I don't understand.

84 A: Will be used. 94 percent.

85 Q: *(L)* Used for what? You mean eaten?

86 A: Total consumption.[18]

87 Q: *(L)* What do you mean by consumption? Ingested?

88 A: Consumed for ingredients.

89 Q: *(L)* Why?

90 A: New race. Important. 13 years about when happens.[19]

---

[15] If, as it appears in hindsight, that this initial C's session contained warnings of a potential future event, it seems that it was in the planning stages already in 1994. The "strong urges" may refer here to the urges to acquire money and power that exist within the wealthy elite rulers of this planet.

[16] Bob Lazar is a fellow who claims to have worked at Area 51 on retro-engineering alien spacecraft that had been captured by the U.S. government. He talks about his experiences in a video presentation that is well worth watching. In this video, he mentions having read a Top Secret–Eyes Only file on the subject of aliens, in which it was said that they repeatedly refer to human beings as "containers." This struck me as extremely curious, and I didn't think that the standard explanation of a body as a "container" for the soul was exactly what was meant. We had been discussing this video while sitting at the board earlier in the evening, so that is why the question was asked.

[17] *High Strangeness* 9, 14; *The Wave* 68

[18] *The Wave* 68

[19] This response is not entirely clear and I regret that we were not saving the tapes of the sessions at the time. In any event, the topic was the "consumption of human beings" that was in some way related to the creation of a new race. On the surface, that doesn't make a lot of sense, but when one considers all the advances made

91 Q: *(L)* Why are humans consumed?[20]

92 A: They are used for parts.

93 Q: *(L)* We don't understand. How can humans be used for parts?

94 A: Reprototype. Vats exist. Missing persons often go there and especially missing children.[21]

95 Q: *(L)* Do we have any protection?

96 A: Some.

97 Q: *(L)* How can we protect ourselves and our children?

98 A: Inform them. Don't hide the truth from children.

99 Q: *(L)* How does truth protect us?[22]

100 A: Awareness protects. Ignorance endangers.

101 Q: *(L)* Why tell children such horrible things?

102 A: Need to know.

103 Q: I don't know how knowing this helps. This is awful. Why tell children such things?

104 A: Must know – ease pain with meditation.

105 Q: Why are you telling us this? It's awful!

106 A: We love you.

107 Q: Are we supposed to tell others?

108 A: Don't reveal to public. You would be abducted.

109 Q: *(L)* What is the purpose of this project?

110 A: New life here.

---

by science in understanding epigenetics and how our environment can shape gene expression, perhaps the concept is not so mysterious after all? One question that might have been asked at the time would have been "thirteen years from when?" Would that be 13 years from that moment in 1994 or 13 years after the "big, big, big scandal" that we had been discussing just previously? If it was after 1994, that would take us to 2007; that was certainly a bumper year for traumatizing events around the planet. See http://www.historyorb.com/ to get an idea. You may be shocked to see all those things lined up one after another. What I noted particularly were: Jan. 12th – Comet McNaught reaches perihelion becoming the brightest comet in more than 40 years; and, on Jan. 13th – Two thirds of Venus's southern hemisphere suddenly brightened as something triggered aerosols to form at a furious rate. Just as there were "storms/floods of the century" in tandem with the appearance of Comet Hale-Bopp in 1997, so 2007 had a series of extraordinary weather and geological events. Again, I refer you to the History Orb website for details. Having said all of that, if the reference of 13 years began counting down starting with 9/11/2001, then we will hit the 13 year mark in September of this year: 2014.

[20] *High Strangeness* 9

[21] I have discussed these comments about missing children in some detail in *Amazing Grace*. Suffice it to say here that, at the time, my knowledge of the problem was deficient to say the least. Over the years, the importance of this little exchange has become all-too-horribly real.

[22] That was a dumb question, for sure! The ancient saying "You shall know the truth and the truth shall set you free" takes on all new ramifications with the C's experiment and the material that has come out of it.

111 **Q:** *(L)* Are the aliens using our emotions and energies?

112 **A:** Correct; and bodies too. Each Earth year 10 percent more children are taken.

113 **Q:** *(L)* Do they suffer?

114 **A:** Some.

115 **Q:** *(L)* Do they all suffer?

116 **A:** Some.

117 **Q:** What happens to souls? Is this physical only?

118 **A:** Physical – souls recycled.

119 **Q:** Where do the souls go?[23]

120 **A:** Back here – most.

121 **Q:** Do some go elsewhere?

122 **A:** And go out of planet human.

123 **Q:** Who is responsible for this?

124 **A:** Consortium.

125 **Q:** *(S)* This is totally sick! I don't want to do this any more!

126 **A:** Sick is subjective.

127 **Q:** *(L)* But what you are telling us is so awful!

128 **A:** Understand, but all does not conform to your perspective.

129 **Q:** Why is this happening to us?[24]

130 **A:** Karma.

131 **Q:** *(L)* What kind of karma could bring this?

132 **A:** Atlantis.

133 **Q:** *(L)* What can protect us?

134 **A:** Knowledge.

135 **Q:** *(L)* How do we get this knowledge?[25]

136 **A:** You are being given it now.

137 **Q:** *(L)* What knowledge do you mean?

138 **A:** You have it.

139 **Q:** *(L)* How does the knowledge of what you have told us help us?

140 **A:** Gives great defense.

141 **Q:** *(L)* What knowledge gives defense?

142 **A:** Just gave it.

143 **Q:** *(L)* What specifically?[26]

144 **A:** Don't ask that not important.

145 **Q:** We don't understand.

146 **A:** Knowing about it gives psychic defense.[27]

147 **Q:** How do we tell other people? And who should we tell?

148 **A:** Inform indirectly only.

149 **Q:** *(L)* How?

150 **A:** Write.

151 **Q:** Should we use hypnosis to uncover such memories?

152 **A:** Open.

153 **Q:** *(L)* Have any of us been abducted?[28]

154 **A:** Yes.

155 **Q:** Who of us sitting here?

156 **A:** All.

---

[23] *High Strangeness* 9
[24] *The Wave* 62
[25] *The Wave* 10, 17
[26] *The Wave* 46
[27] The concept of how knowledge protects was expanded and developed over the years and it is very, very true that knowing about the darkest things in our reality affords great defense not only in terms of avoidance, but in terms of diminishment of same.
[28] *The Wave* 17

157 **Q:** *(L)* How many times?

158 **A:** Frank – 57; Scarlett – 56; Laura – 12.

159 **Q:** *(L)* Why has Laura not been abducted as much? [Laura laughs]

160 **A:** It is not over.[29]

161 **Q:** [Scarlett laughs]

162 **A:** Scarlett was abducted last month. Laura – 33.[30]

163 **Q:** *(L)* Who is abducting us?

164 **A:** Others.

165 **Q:** *(L)* What is the name of the group?

166 **A:** Different names.

167 **Q:** *(L)* Are we all abducted by the same group?

168 **A:** Mostly.

169 **Q:** *(L)* What did they do to us?

170 **A:** Gave false memories. Made you inhibited child – headaches – sick at school.

171 **Q:** *(S)* Where is my implant?

172 **A:** Head.

173 **Q:** Frank?

174 **A:** Same.

175 **Q:** Laura?

176 **A:** Same.

177 **Q:** *(L)* What are the implants for?

178 **A:** Study device.

179 **Q:** *(L)* To study what?

180 **A:** Soul composition.

181 **Q:** *(L)* Do any of the rituals we perform provide protection against further abduction?[31]

182 **A:** Don't need protection if you have knowledge.

183 **Q:** *(L)* How do we get this knowledge?[32]

184 **A:** Deep subconscious.

185 **Q:** *(L)* When did we get it?

186 **A:** Before birth.

187 **Q:** *(L)* Is there anything else we can do for protection?

188 **A:** Learn, meditate, read.[33]

189 **Q:** *(L)* Are we doing what we need to be doing at the present?

190 **A:** So far. Need awaken. Must go now. Out of Energy. I must go.

End of Session

---

[29] *The Wave* 43

[30] Years of age or years ago? See *Amazing Grace* for details and make your own call. There are strong indicators for both times.

[31] *High Strangeness* 9; *The Wave* 10

[32] *The Wave* 68

[33] This advice was most important and was repeated over and over again: knowledge protects. Here the C's were stating a fundamental principle that the communications were just inspirational; we had to do the the work of becoming fully educated.

July 22, 1994

Participants: 'Frank', Laura and Scarlett

about 10:30 p.m.

Q: Hello.

A: Hello.

Q: Is anyone with us?

A: Listen, Look. Learn. Stop eating.[1]

Q: What is the problem with eating?[2]

A: Not good connection.

Q: *(L)* What is your name?

A: Ellaga.[3]

Q: *(L)* Are you discarnate from Earth?

A: No.

Q: Are you an alien like we had the other night?[4]

A: Yes.

Q: *(L)* Are you from another galaxy?

A: No.

Q: *(L)* Where are you from?

A: Cassiopaea.

Q: *(L)* Is this the constellation we know as Cassiopeia?

A: Yes.

Q: *(L)* What can we do for a better connection?

A: Less noise.[5]

Q: *(L)* Do you have information for us this evening?

A: Space invasion soon. Four to six years. Battle between forces good and evil. Wait near. Look far. Listen. Mexico fall; Ethiopia quake; September – both – New Near – January – Paris bomb – London Blizzard – 109 die – Plane down – Tahiti – Cholera – Montana – January 1995 – government US – behind California quakes – Three soon –

---

[1] Scarlett was having a snack.
[2] *Amazing Grace* 44; *High Strangeness* 5; *Riding The Wave* "Autobiographical Background"
[3] Another unusual name; I was intrigued.
[4] Like so many others have done, I was making an assumption that we had been conversing with 'aliens' in the previous session. In fact, the Cassiopaeans have never described themselves as 'aliens.' What they had actually said was "alien from your perspective."
[5] There was activity in the next room. We shut the door.
[6] This odd collection of predictions that came out all in a rush is furiously interesting when one takes into account the urgent warning about the Denver Airport revealing the government involved in a "big, big, big scandal" in the previous session. If one takes the metaphor/symbolic interpretation into account, the warnings of a space

Oklahoma political abduction – February 95 – Big news.[6]

23 **Q**: *(L)* What is causing the Earth changes?[7]

24 **A**: Electromagnetic wave changes.

25 **Q**: *(L)* Can you be more specific?

26 **A**: Gap in surge heliographic field.[8]

27 **Q**: *(L)* I don't understand.

28 **A**: Put Frank on processor channel open.

29 **Q**: Do you mean that Frank can channel on the computer?

30 **A**: Yes. Do it now.[9]

31 **Q**: *(L)* Is a meteor or comet going to hit Earth?

32 **A**: Open.

33 **Q**: *(L)* What are the effects on us of the comet striking Jupiter?

34 **A**: Further field imbalance.

35 **Q**: *(L)* Was that comet meant for Earth as some psychics are saying?[10]

36 **A**: Open.

37 **Q**: [Unknown question.]

invasion and battle between good and evil could very well have been about the overt takeover of our world by psychopaths in power, effected so dramatically via the 'space attack' of 9/11. The events of this massive change in our reality, this 'invasion of the zombie psychopaths,' as we can see it now, actually took place seven years later, but one wonders if original plans, as they were formulated at the time of this session, did not include an earlier date?

The curious thing about the "Oklahoma political abduction" followed by "February 95" remark is that, in fact, on February 25 of 1995, in another session, we were given a warning of a terrorist bomb attack within a month. Connecting that back to this mention of Oklahoma "political abduction," and we find a curious relationship to the Oklahoma Bombing in March of 1995. Again, we see that something was possibly in the Information Field or, at least, in the minds of conspirators. In one of the earliest reports of the capture of Timothy McVeigh, he was quoted as saying that he was under the control of an implant that was in his hip, and that he believed he had been abducted and programmed by the government. In a later session, a connection is made between the Oklahoma bomb conspiracy and the 9/11 event even before 9/11/2001, so it appears that a proper reading of this would be that related groups were involved in both. Of course, all of this was still years in the future for us and we weren't taking anything as gospel, so this was just another data point in the experiment.

[7] *The Wave* 1, 34

[8] Keep this in mind also, along with the "Sun in Libra" remark from the first session, and the "twin sun" reference from the "Carcosa" clue.

[9] We tried it and it was nonsense. We concluded that this was an attempt at sidetracking the process.

[10] There were many rumors on the internet at the time of the Comet Shoemaker-Levy impacts on Jupiter that this comet had been meant to hit Earth, but a certain group of aliens, and I don't remember which one, had decided to 'save' the Earth by redirecting these comets to strike Jupiter instead. Naturally, all of mankind was supposed to be grateful to this particular group for saving our buns from the fire!

38 **A**: Bits childrens organs removed while wide awake – kidneys crushed – then next feet – next jaw examined on table – tongues cut off – bones stress tested – pressure placed on heart muscle until burst.

39 **Q**: Why are you saying these awful things?!

40 **A**: Must know what consortium is doing.

41 **Q**: What children are they doing this to?

42 **A**: Done mostly to Indian children.

43 **Q**: Why am I getting this horrible feeling while you are telling us this?

44 **A**: Because subject is distressing.

45 **Q**: Why do we need to know these things?

46 **A**: Very big effort on behalf of Orions and their human brethren to create new race and control.

47 **Q**: *(L)* Where are you from?

48 **A**: Cassiopaea.

49 **Q**: *(L)* Where do you live specifically?

50 **A**: Live in omnipresence.

51 **Q**: *(L)* What does that mean?

52 **A**: All realms.

53 **Q**: *(L)* Can you tell us what your environment is like?

54 **A**: Difficult.

55 **Q**: *(L)* Well take a stab at it.

56 **A**: What stab?

57 **Q**: *(L)* Do you serve self or others?

58 **A**: Both. Self through others.

59 **Q**: *(L)* Scarlett wants to know the details of her abductions.

60 **A**: Do you?

61 **Q**: *(S)* Yes.

62 **A**: Are you sure?

63 **Q**: *(S)* Yes.

64 **A**: Soon, vibrations not right at this time.

65 **Q**: *(L)* Does this mean Scarlett's vibrations are not right to receive this information?

66 **A**: Right.

67 **Q**: Why was information about our abductions given last time?

68 **A**: Was not I.

69 **Q**: And who are you?

70 **A**: Ellaga.

71 **Q**: *(L)* Is there a tenth planet as described by Zecharia Sitchin?[11]

---

[11] I had recently read Zecharia Sitchin's *The 12th Planet*, which posits that a superior race of alien beings once inhabited our world. Sitchin claims that they were travelers from the stars, that they arrived eons ago, and genetically engineered mankind to be slaves for them. He claims that the Sons of Anak mentioned in the Bible are the Annunaki, and also that they are the same as the Nefilim mentioned in the Bible. His claim is that they are a race of gold-seeking giants from a renegade planet in our own solar system that was known to the Sumerians as the 'Planet of the Crossing.' This planet 'crosses' the plane of the ecliptic every 3,600 years, and when it gets close enough, these beings make a 'hop' to Earth to check up on their creation. Supposedly, this will happen again soon. The title comes from the fact that Sitchin proposes that there are 12 houses of the zodiac because there were 12 'planets.' He includes the sun and moon in his count because they are zodiacally

72 **A:** No.

73 **Q:** *(L)* Was Venus ejected from Jupiter?[12]

74 **A:** No.

75 **Q:** *(L)* Did Venus follow a cometary orbit for a time?

76 **A:** Yes.

77 **Q:** *(L)* Did Venus appear in our solar system, from the area of Jupiter, coming from deep space as suggested by Velikovsky?

78 **A:** That is correct.

79 **Q:** *(L)* Was Venus the pillar of smoke by day and fire by night as seen by the Jews during the Exodus?

80 **A:** No.

81 **Q:** *(L)* What was seen by the Jews?

82 **A:** A Guideship.[13]

83 **Q:** *(L)* Were Sodom and Gomorrah destroyed by nuclear weapons?

84 **A:** Yes and no.

85 **Q:** *(L)* How were they destroyed?

86 **A:** EMP

87 **Q:** *(L)* What is "EMP"?

---

significant. But, in actuality, it is really a 10th planet, excluding the sun and moon. He also fails to note that the Earth is excluded from zodiacal considerations due to the fact that astrology is geocentric. But that is a minor point. More significantly, there does seem to be something to the idea of a 3,600-year 'event' of comet swarms due to the break-up of a giant comet as described by astronomers Victor Clube and Bill Napier in their books *The Cosmic Serpent* and *The Cosmic Winter*. This idea was given additional support by Firestone, West and Warwick-Smith in *The Cycle of Cosmic Catastrophes*. I am not aware of any other channeled source that has brought up and discussed these ideas and added information to the pool that later turned out to be correct based on scientific assessment.

[12]This was proposed by Immanuel Velikovsky as an explanation for why the ancient astronomers and myth makers claimed that Venus was born from Jupiter.

Velikovsky theorized by following the trail of Venus through world-wide myths and legends, that Venus intersected the Earth in its orbit sometime during the middle of the fifteenth century BC. This event was recorded in the Bible as the plagues of Egypt and the means by which the Jews escaped from bondage. Searching for verification of his theory, Velikovsky spent weeks trying to find an Egyptian account of the events of the Exodus. Finally he discovered a translation of an Egyptian papyrus which contained a description of a great catastrophe including the plagues of Egypt. It was called "Admonitions of a Sage," or the "Ipuwer Papyrus."

The reader will most certainly wish to read *Worlds in Collision* because it is one of the most rational books ever written. Even if Velikovsky was wrong about some of the conclusions he drew regarding myth and legend, his observations and proposals of a new way at looking at the cosmos have yet to be fully appreciated. And, according to the Cassiopaeans, he was, at least, partly correct.

[13]Understanding the problems of metaphoric transduction would suggest that a "guideship" could actually be a comet, though I think we can't discard alien/UFO explanations, even if I think they are largely paranormal phenomena.

[14]It's interesting that EMP was brought up at this point in the sessions. The problem of EMP as a weapon was generally popularized some years later (1998) in the book

88 **A**: Electromagnetic pulse.[14]

89 **Q**: *(L)* Was Jesus genetically engineered by aliens as some channeled sources suggest?

90 **A**: Close.

91 **Q**: *(L)* Can you explain?

92 **A**: Too complex.

93 **Q**: *(L)* Was Mary a true virgin when she gave birth?

94 **A**: No.

95 **Q**: *(L)* Did she conceive in the normal way?

96 **A**: Yes.

97 **Q**: *(L)* Who did she have sex with?

98 **A**: Her husband.

99 **Q**: *(L)* Was Jesus genetically altered?

100 **A**: After – in childhood. Use computer.[15]

101 **Q**: *(L)* We tried it. It wasn't satisfactory. Was Jesus special, Christed as it is called, in any way?

102 **A**: Quick exalted – Yontar[16] – ancient wars – civil entrancement – Zindar council.

103 **Q**: *(L)* What is the Zindar Council?[17]

[18]

104 **A**: Two cycle exchangers mission.

105 **Q**: *(L)* What does that mean?

106 **A**: References vast. Use Laura Channel computer.[19] Must go.

End of Session

The Day After Roswell by Colonel Philip J. Corso (Ret.), a member of President Eisenhower's National Security Council and former head of the Foreign Technology Desk in the U.S. Army. The blurb to the book says that he: "tells us how he spearheaded the Army's reverse-engineering project that led to today's integrated circuit chips, fiber optics, lasers, and super-tenacity fibers, and 'seeded' the Roswell alien technology to giants of American industry ... and how they used alien artifacts to change the course of twentieth-century history." He died just a year or two after publication. In regards to the experiences of Col. Corso, the following online article is fascinating: http://www.openminds.tv/corso-notes/3514

[15] Again, we are being urged to "use the computer" or a form of "automatic writing" for channeling purposes. Yes, it would certainly have been easier and faster, but I did not feel that the contact had been sufficiently checked out to warrant taking that step yet. One thing that occurs to me long after the fact is that this was a conflation of the idea of channeling with networking via computer.

[16] This reference to "Yontar" comes up again in another session as the name of a planet. The question that occurs here is: Are planets also beings as is suggested by this reference to "ancient wars"? Are comets and asteroids the munitions of 'the gods'?

[17] Zindar or Zendar also was given as a planetary name in a later session.

[18] *The Wave* 34

[19] Again the computer is being suggested, only this time it is specifically addressed to me. But, I wasn't buying it. Not yet, at least. Later, however, I felt that a lot of *The Wave* was written in a 'special state' and that is still true when I begin to 'ask myself questions and write down the answers.'

July 27, 1994

After a brief encounter with an easily identifiable 'dead dude,' whom we sent away, we used our Reiki symbols, asked specifically for our communicants from Cassiopaea and the following came through:

Participants: 'Frank', Scarlett, Laura

Q: We want to communicate with the Cassiopaeans.

A: I am Ra keeper of light.

Q: What are you here to tell us?

A: UFO not all bad.

Q: Why is the connection so bad tonight?

A: You see you are tired.

Q: [Unknown question.]

A: Level through 6.

Q: [Unknown question.]

A: Planet.

Q: [Unknown question.]

A: Always. Please let me go.

It was clear that the energy was very weak on this last contact. It was also curious that the character 'Ra' came through and identified himself as a "keeper of light." It was about the last of the 'intruders' before the C's became a fixture.

July 30, 1994

As the reader will see, we were asking a whole lot of random questions about aliens and abductions that were based on the many things we had read or heard about the topic. There are some interesting predictions made here in an extraordinary context.

Participants: 'Frank', Scarlett, Laura

1 **Q**: Hello.
2 **A**: Hello.
3 **Q**: And who do we have with us?
4 **A**: Name Panua Name Oz Name Pamala
5 **Q**: *(L)* Where are you from?
6 **A**: Corsoca.
7 **Q**: *(L)* Do you have messages for us?[1]
8 **A**: Be careful.
9 **Q**: *(L)* Of what?
10 **A**: Aliens.
11 **Q**: *(L)* Which Ones?
12 **A**: Orions.
13 **Q**: *(L)* What do they do?[2]
14 **A**: Follow you.
15 **Q**: *(L)* Did Ann, Scarlett and Laura see an alien craft last night?[3]
16 **A**: You better believe it.
17 **Q**: *(L)* Whose craft was it?
18 **A**: Orion.
19 **Q**: *(L)* Did it appear for us specifically?
20 **A**: No.
21 **Q**: *(L)* Do they know we saw them?
22 **A**: Yes.
23 **Q**: *(L)* Did they leave because we saw them?
24 **A**: Yes.
25 **Q**: *(L)* Were they planning to abduct somebody?
26 **A**: Maybe. You are next.
27 **Q**: *(L)* What?
28 **A**: To be abducted.
29 **Q**: *(L)* Who?
30 **A**: LK.
31 **Q**: *(L)* By whom?
32 **A**: Orion.
33 **Q**: *(L)* When?

---

[1] *The Wave* 17
[2] *Amazing Grace* 43
[3] The three of us had gone to visit a friend and had a very unusual sighting of a stationary, triangular craft with a bright light on each corner. When we pulled off the road under it and stopped, as soon as I got out of the car, it just zoomed away.

34 **A:** Open.

35 **Q:** *(L)* Why?

36 **A:** For Knowledge monitoring. Craft above now.

37 **Q:** *(L)* Above the house?

38 **A:** Absolutely.

39 **Q:** *(L)* Is it good for me to be abducted?[4]

40 **A:** Neutral.

41 **Q:** *(L)* Will I be abducted because I saw them last night?

42 **A:** Partly. Mike and John have reported you.[5]

43 **Q:** *(L)* Are they in cahoots with the aliens?

44 **A:** Not knowingly.

45 **Q:** *(L)* How, then?

46 **A:** Subconscious. Implants.

47 **Q:** *(L)* Do we have implants?

48 **A:** Two implants; one monitor.

49 **Q:** *(L)* What is the difference between a monitor and an implant?

50 **A:** All are monitors. Implant is permanent. Frank and Laura have permanent implants. Scarlett got monitor three months ago. Next is implant.

51 **Q:** *(L)* Why?

52 **A:** To watch and observe you.

53 **Q:** *(L)* Why?

54 **A:** You are all higher level beings. Frank implant: 4 years old. Laura implant: 5 years old.

55 **Q:** *(L)* Have Laura's children been abducted?

56 **A:** Not yet.

57 **Q:** *(L)* Have Scarlett's children been abducted?

58 **A:** One.

59 **Q:** *(L)* Which one?

60 **A:** Last.

61 **Q:** *(L)* Who is putting implants in us?

62 **A:** Orions.

63 **Q:** *(L)* And there is nothing we can do about it? That's sick!

64 **A:** A matter of perspective.

65 **Q:** *(L)* What do the Orions look like?

---

[4] I still had a lot of mixed feelings about the phenomenon of abduction. There were so many groups and sources propagating the idea that it was 'for the good of mankind,' even if such activity was based on violation of free will, pain, terror and suffering.

[5] The first individual mentioned here claimed to be a UFO investigator with a lot of supposed 'credentials' that later turned out to be fake. He was quite a character, going around in his white convertible, wearing a straw hat and safari-type clothing, with a 'UFO detector' in his pocket disguised as a cigarette pack that occasionally began to beep wildly, at which point he would dash off to a telephone to report the presence of a UFO to some secret organization to which he claimed to belong. He was obsessed with 'Bigfoot.' It was all pretty comical, and typical of the kinds of nuts that you find in the UFO milieu. The second individual was someone I would never have dreamed of being 'in cahoots' with aliens. He was most emphatically sure of one thing: if he ever met an alien, he would shoot first and ask questions later! Of course, he also believed firmly that the Annunaki were our gods and would return one day and he would be there to welcome them! He even thought that humanity should build giant houses for them in advance.

66 **A**: Grays.

67 **Q**: *(L)* Are they big-nosed Grays like I have read about in some sources?[6]

68 **A**: Both kinds of Grays.

69 **Q**: *(L)* Are they insectoid?

70 **A**: No.

71 **Q**: *(L)* Do they have hive souls?

72 **A**: No.

73 **Q**: *(L)* Do they have emotions?

74 **A**: No.

75 **Q**: *(L)* Do they want human bodies as hosts?

76 **A**: Some.

77 **Q**: *(L)* What is their planet like?

78 **A**: Similar to Earth.

79 **Q**: *(L)* What planet is it described in several books as a desert with huge spiders with legs like tree trunks?[7]

80 **A**: Uzuli.

81 **Q**: *(L)* Has any of us ever been abducted by the giant spiders?

82 **A**: No one has.

83 **Q**: *(L)* Well why have people seen this planet?

84 **A**: It is one of the planets of ZR 4.

85 **Q**: *(L)* What is ZR 4?

86 **A**: Zeta Reticuli 4. There are seven planets. The 4th one.

87 **Q**: *(L)* What other information can you give us?

88 **A**: Base of aliens near here small.

89 **Q**: *(L)* Are you the ones we refer to as the 'Boys in Brazil'?[8]

90 **A**: Yes. Anclote Gulf Park[9] used to be a military base. Underground.

91 **Q**: *(L)* Why underground?

92 **A**: To hide.

93 **Q**: *(L)* What group are you with?

94 **A**: Federation. Among many.

95 **Q**: *(L)* Is there any way we can prevent Orion abductions?[10]

96 **A**: No.

97 **Q**: *(L)* Why?

98 **A**: It would interfere with universal law of free will and service to self.

99 **Q**: *(L)* But we don't want to be abducted. Can't we stop it?

100 **A**: Not likely. They have more power than you.

101 **Q**: *(L)* Well then, why can't you help us?

102 **A**: Would interfere in natural progression of your race and theirs. Jews called upon us to save them – could not. And natives of your land from your race – could not stop that either. Natural progression, see?

103 **Q**: *(L)* Are we going to be wiped out by aliens as part of this natural progression?

104 **A**: Maybe. What makes you feel you are special?

---

[6]See Ray Fowler's *The Andreasson Affair*.

[7]See Whitley Strieber's *Majestic*.

[8]This is our joking reference to 'whoever is in charge of the universe.'

[9]This is a County Park next door to a power plant. The warm water outflow of the cooling towers makes a haven for manatees and many other fish. It is a little bit south of some ancient Indian mounds, also.

[10] *The Wave* 68

105 **Q:** *(L)* Jesus told us God loves us. Is this true?

106 **A:** But it is the soul that matters, not the body. The body dies not the soul.

107 **Q:** *(L)* Well, this whole thing just gives us the creeps.

108 **A:** No. You are energy. There is an energy that comes from soul and body connection; later the body is used for parts.[11]

109 **Q:** *(L)* What are they using our energy and bodies for?

110 **A:** Create a new race. Theirs fading out.

111 **Q:** *(L)* Well, do they just take people and kill them and do what with them?[12]

112 **A:** Slice them up.

113 **Q:** *(L)* Do they die?

114 **A:** Maximum matter and energy transfer during transition.

115 **Q:** *(L)* In other words, you are saying that a slow painful death gives them the most of what they want? This is totally sick.

116 **A:** You asked for truth. You say it is sick but it is merely the ultimate form of service to self.[13]

117 **A:** [14] What about your lab animals? Is that not service to self as well? What about unwanted insects et cetera?

118 **Q:** *(L)* We were here first!

119 **A:** So were insects. Grays now want your planet.

120 **Q:** *(L)* That is sick.

121 **A:** Is natural progression sick?

122 **Q:** *(L)* Is what is happening something like what Jesus described in the parable of the wheat where the workers come in to take out the weeds first?

123 **A:** Close.

124 **Q:** *(L)* What kind of people is this being done to?

---

[11] Refer back to the 16 July session where the exchange about the 94% use of human beings for creation of a new race occurred, predicted to begin 13 years from either 1994 or 2001 as I noted in a footnote to that session.

[12] *High Strangeness* 11

[13] This small exchange, disturbing though it may be, gives insight into why our world is subjected to so much propaganda and disinformation. It is the engineered suffering of humanity that feeds the entropic aspect of the universe. Also, consider the aspect of torture as was instituted by the Bush administration in the aftermath of 9/11: that may very well be the initiating of just the program described above. Considering how many dramatic changes have been made to our world since that day, under the guidance and direction of what can only be described as an invading force of psychopaths under the guidance of negative hyperdimensional forces, we can't even say that torture won't become as common as going to the supermarket. In fact, the practice, following the example of the Bush admin, does seem to be increasing everywhere, even in local police jurisdictions.

[14] At this point my daughter, who was standing by and watching, described reading a passage in a book which stated that Native Americans believed a slow torturous death of an enemy gave them more power. As she finished speaking, the Cassiopaeans continued.

125 **A**: Low level humans.[15]

126 **Q**: *(L)* What happens to the high-level humans?

127 **A**: Some will survive.

128 **Q**: *(L)* Will Jesus be reincarnated into a body?

129 **A**: No.

130 **Q**: *(L)* Is Jesus an alien?

131 **A**: One of us.[16]

132 **Q**: *(L)* Will there be atomic war?

133 **A**: No.

134 **Q**: *(L)* Will there be a war in the sky with the aliens?[17] [18]

135 **A**: Yes.

136 **Q**: *(L)* Will it be between Orions and the Federation?

137 **A**: Yes.

138 **Q**: *(L)* Will it be visible on Earth?

139 **A**: Oh, yes.

140 **Q**: *(L)* When will this be?

141 **A**: It has already started. Will intensify steadily.

142 **Q**: *(L)* Why are we not aware that it has already started?

143 **A**: Disguised at this point as weather. Fighting part still in other dimension. Will go to this one within 18 years. Anytime within this period. Not determinable exactly when. Could be tomorrow or 18 years.

144 **Q**: *(L)* Eighteen years from now is 2012. Is there some special significance to that time?

145 **A**: By then.[19]

146 **Q**: *(L)* Will the Earth be affected by a comet or planet?

147 **A**: Maybe. One at a time please. Stop thinking physical thoughts – they are low frequency.

148 **Q**: *(L)* What do you mean by physical thoughts? Who is thinking physical thoughts?

149 **A**: Anything to do with body or animal

---

[15]The question naturally arises as to what is meant by 'high-level humans' as opposed to 'low-level humans.' The reader should not get caught up in thinking that this is an 'elitist' or exclusionary definition in terms of the value of all human beings in their own context and reality. It has to do with, simply, the difference between those who are ready to graduate to a new level of being, and those who wish to continue in physical existence. In all cases, it is a choice that is demonstrated by one's frequency, rather than by whether or not one says that they are one or the other.

[16]"Us" meaning 6th density, not necessarily "Cassiopaeans." This will become clear as we go along.

[17]This was a recurring dream of mine, that there would be a 'space war.'

[18]*High Strangeness* 5; *Riding The Wave* "Autobiographical Background"

[19]Or anytime in between. I would suggest that it began on September 11, 2001, and that this war is being fought *through* human beings of various types: low level, high level, psychopathic, whatever. We may also notice that the level of the 'war' that is "disguised as weather" has really accelerated dramatically.

[20]This was a curious remark. I knew I wasn't thinking 'low-level' thoughts; I was pretty focused on my questions. I also knew Frank well enough to know that it wasn't him.

like – minimize as much as possible – that raises vibration level.[20]

150 Q: *(L)* Is vegetarianism then the way we should eat?

151 A: That is concentrating on the physical. The body is not important.

152 Q: *(L)* Does this mean that to worry about the body in any way is wrong?

153 A: Close. Don't concentrate on life in the body. Concentrate on the spirit.

154 Q: *(S)* Does this mean Laura should ignore her heart condition?

155 A: Don't worry about it. Treat the spirit.

156 Q: *(L)* Well, heart troubles mean that the heart is broken. Why is my heart broken?

157 A: Confused energy.

158 Q: *(L)* How can we improve the energy for reception?

159 A: Meditate in general.

160 Q: *(L)* But we like being in bodies and having opportunities to love and appreciate the natural world and all the beautiful things of creation. It is only natural to not want to terminate access to something that can be so pleasant.

161 A: Concentrating on trying to prolong life in the body. You will always have access.

162 Q: *(L)* Would we be happy moving to British Guyana?[21]

163 A: Not likely.

164 Q: *(L)* Will we be happy staying here and fixing this house?

165 A: More likely. No dish or clothes washers in Guyana. No electricity. No air conditioning. Are you ready for that?

166 Q: *(L)* But we don't want to stay here and be eaten by aliens!

167 A: Aliens eat Guyanans too.

168 Q: *(L)* But where should we go when Florida sinks?[22]

169 A: Who said Florida was going to sink?

170 Q: *(L)* Are we chosen?

171 A: What is chosen? Only you can choose. The choice comes by nature and free will and looking and listening. Where you are is not important. Who you are is and also what you see.[23]

172 Q: [Unknown question.]

173 A: Haven't you figured out by now?

174 Q: [Unknown question.]

So, the only logical candidate for a person thinking 'low-level thoughts having to do with 'animal-like' behavior was Scarlett.

[21] My ex-husband, to whom I was still married at the time, had been trying to convince me for a long time that we ought to sell everything we owned, pack up the children, and move to the rainforest in British Guyana. He was convinced that when the New World Order took over the country, this would be a safe place to be. I had my doubts, but with all the new information about aliens coming out, I was beginning to think that maybe it wasn't such a bad idea, even if we had two children with medical problems who needed to be close to proper facilities in case of the need for treatment.

[22] This was another of the endless rumors of prophecies being passed along via various channeled sources in books.

[23] *The Wave* 17

175 **A**: Up to you to discover. Use other medium for that.[24] Have given enough.

Must go.

End of Session

---

[24] Again, we are being urged to use another channeling medium. But, I still was not satisfied that this was proper advice based on all the analysis we had done.

September 30, 1994

It should be noted that, at this point, I was rather hung up on the idea that any communicant should be "Christian" and should support the Jesus story, so there is a lot of emotional investment going on here that could easily have skewed things significantly. In fact, based on ongoing research for the past 20 years, I would say that most of what is presented here as 'historical' are my own preferences for how the story should be told in the merging of my religious beliefs of the time and what I was learning in my explorations of the so-called 'alien reality.' What this means, I think, is that there were elements of it that were useful and semi-accurate, but it was still a bit of a mish-mash.

On the other hand it was otherwise a very good session, because when we moved to questions to which I had no particular attachment, the responses were remarkable. This was the session that introduced the idea of cyclical cometary bombardment as the reason for the cycle of catastrophes and extinctions on Earth. Well, in a sense, I was somewhat attached to my own theories about this and the C's were having none of it, so it is a definite example of when what I thought to be so conflicted with what the C's explicated. This is also the first session with a mention of the Wave. In general, you can see that I was all over the place and I was asking the questions rapidly and deliberately changing course to find out if I could catch the C's on their off foot, so to say. This was the first taped session, which was a decision we made because there was no one present to take notes.

Participants: 'Frank' and Laura

1 **Q**: Hello.

2 **A**: Hello.

3 **Q**: *(L)* Who are you?

4 **A**: Pamthora.

5 **Q**: *(L)* Are you the same individual who communicated with us last week?

6 **A**: No.

7 **Q**: *(L)* Are you from the same group?

8 **A**: Yes.

9 **Q**: *(L)* Why are you with us tonight instead of the one who was here last week?

10 **A:** Frequency waves.

11 **Q:** *(L)* The frequency waves are different?

12 **A:** Close.

13 **Q:** *(L)* Are you better able to communicate with us than the one who was here last week?

14 **A:** Same.

15 **Q:** *(L)* I don't understand what you mean about the frequency waves. Could you elaborate?

16 **A:** Too complex.

17 **Q:** *(L)* OK. Does this mean that you are not going to be able to communicate complex answers to us tonight?

18 **A:** No difference.[1]

19 **Q:** *(L)* Last week we were talking about Jesus of Nazareth who became the Christ. Can we continue that subject this week?

20 **A:** Yes.

21 **Q:** *(L)* Who was Jesus of Nazareth?[2]

22 **A:** Advanced spirit.

23 **Q:** *(L)* Was Jesus born from an immaculate conception; that is did his mother not have sex with a man in order to conceive him?

24 **A:** No.

25 **Q:** *(L)* She did have sex with a man in order to conceive him, is that correct?

26 **A:** Yes.

27 **Q:** *(L)* Who was the man with whom she had sex to conceive Jesus?

---

[1] *High Strangeness* 14
[2] *The Wave* 29
[3] From a book entitled *Lost Survivors of the Deluge*, by Gerd von Hassler, translated from the German by Martin Ebon, we find the following relating to this mysterious "Tonatha":

> This brings us to the crucial question. It is, indeed, so vital and controversial that St. Boniface, when he presented it to the Frisians during his missionary journey on June 5, 754, was put to death by the sword! Today, we may ask such a question without facing the sword; it is: Just what is the name of the God-Creator? What is the name of the god who governed the Earth even before the Deluge; this God of Gods, rightly called Father of the Gods, and thus Father of all Mankind? To put it even more simply: If a highly developed civilization existed more than 10,000 year ago, governing the world's then populated regions, and if the God-King was able to aid his contemporaries in surviving the Deluge catastrophe, surely the name of this ruler must have been handed down to later generations of survivors; who was he?
> We know from the Epic of Gilgamesh, of the horrible Enlil, who was responsible for the Deluge. The other gods did not think highly of him, but feared him a good deal. His influence never extended beyond Mesopotamia. His antagonist, Shamash, the Sun God, enjoyed greater prestige. He remains, notably in Asia even today, a figure of magical power, the epitome of the shaman. But even the early Egyptians called their Sun God by a different name, Ra. This need not mean much, because Plato tells us that the Egyptians had even then developed a unique and high level of civilization hostile toward the unknown earlier culture.
> The Egyptian term 'Ra' was integrated into the language of early Peru, where we encounter the annual sun festival Rami or Raymi. But this adaptation undoubtedly dates back only to the period following the Deluge, as does the word 'Wotan.' This enables us to draw a firm dividing line: we are able to eliminate all gods who

28 **A**: Tonatha.³   **Q**: *(L)* And who was this individual, To- 29

emerged from the post-Deluge civilizations as creators of cultures, builders of cities, magicians or agronomists. The ONE God for whom we search has to be the father – or even ancestor – of this post-Deluge generation of gods. Just as Tuisto, father of Mannus, was the ancestor of Germanic culture.

Tuisto? Can that be accurate? Or did Tacitus fail to understand the name correctly? The curious linking of the darkest and lightest vowel in our language brings back a curious association. Of course! It is Tiu, the god whom the early Germans recalled when they made up the calendar and named one day of the week after him: Tuesday. Otherwise he has been overshadowed by the ever-present Wotan-Odin, as the highest Ruler of the Heavens. This replacement took place, at the latest, during the Volkerwanderung, the Great Migration that caused a gigantic upheaval of populations on the Eurasian land mass. We may even assume that, just because Tiu (or Ziu) was removed heavenward, the very vigorous Wotan managed to take his place in human imagination and thought. It was a fate that Wotan experienced himself later on, when missionaries cut down the very oaks that had been dedicated to his divine presence.

Tiu-Ziu was just as much one of the Aesir as Wotan had been. And the Aesir had even managed to infiltrate the antagonist worlds of Egypt and Mesopotamia, representing the sun and divine wisdom. [..] I do think, however, that our search for the original name of the primal Creator-God should not get bogged down in such minute details. The survivors of the Deluge of whom we learn from the Bible and the earlier Gilgamesh Epic and other traditions, were themselves survivors of the earlier world of gods. [..] Over thousands of years, they passed on a handful of names. No doubt, precisely how much and what one name or another had originally meant may simply have been forgotten over the long, long years.

If we concentrate on the godlike of God Ziu, we discover the following points: Zius was the highest god of northern Europe; As Zeus, he was the highest god of ancient Greece; As Jupiter (Iu-Pitar = Tius-Pater) he was the Father God of ancient Rome; As Deus (from which we derive 'Deity') he was the basic concept of the heavenly, the only Deity in the Latin liturgy of the Church, and the God in all Romance languages, as well as in the word 'theology'; As Ometeotle (again, 'theology' is closely related) he was the highest god of the Mayan culture; As Cinteotl and God of Corn he is equivalent to Quetzalcoatl, the WHITE GOD; As TONATIUH, he was the Sun God, who provided the Aztecs with a sort of Valhalla for their war dead; As Xiuhtecutli, he was the Fire God of ancient Mexico; As Tirawa-Atius, the highest divinity of the Pawnee, he was credited with populating the world with 'giants'; As Tieholtsodi, the monster who caused the Deluge and ruled all waters, he exists in the traditions of the Navajos; As Szeu-kha, he is the son of the Creator-God whom the Pima Indians knew as floating above the Deluge; As the falcon Tiuh-Tiuh of the Guatemaltec Indians he mixed the blood of a snake with that of a tapir, kneaded it with corn-flour and 'thus created the flesh of man.' This tribe says that it came from Tulan, the Place of the Sun, across the sea.

We have previously mentioned the divine cities Tiahuanaco and Teotihuacan. To this should be added the holy plants, including the mushroom Teonacatl which caused divine visions.

All of this narrows down to one conclusion – which nevertheless is not definitive – and that is: our old Tuesday God, Tiu, was a divine Ruler-God in primeval times and his name imprinted itself so deeply into human memory that it has survived thousands upon thousands of years. [Von Hassler, 1976]

natha?

A: Acquaintance.

Q: *(L)* How old was Jesus' mother, Mary, when she conceived Jesus?

A: 19.

Q: *(L)* Was Joseph upset to discover that Mary was pregnant?

A: No.

Q: *(L)* How old was Joseph when he married Mary?

A: 39.

Q: *(L)* Was Joseph unable to father children?

A: Close.[4]

Q: *(L)* What date, counting backwards in our calendrical system, was Jesus born?

---

[4] As time went by, we learned that when the Cassiopaeans say "close," we needed to pay attention to the specific terms and assumptions we were making. Being "close" to "unable to father children" could as easily mean that he was unable because of choice or unable because of physical factors. It could even mean that the word "unable" was only close.

[5] January 6, 14 BC. This date is rather problematical as research over the past ten years or so has shown. Our calendrical system has been meddled with so much that it is taking a lot of time to sort through the texts, comparing one to another, comparing textual information to archaeology, etc., trying to find a fixed hook to hang historical events upon. An early tentative conclusion that I can mention here before publication of the initial volume of the *Chronicle of the Fall*, part of my Secret History project, is that there is a serious multi-year discrepancy on either side of the transition from BC to AD: the year -21 equates to what we would call year -1 and -20 equates to what we would call 1 AD. This date, 14 BC, taken at face value, without my adjustments, would equate to what we call 35 BC. With my adjustments, it would be 17 BC. In both years, 35 BC and 17 AD, there were several interesting events that might hint at what was really going on back then that led to the 'birth of the son of God,' i.e. Divus Filius, Octavian, who became Augustus.

First, in 35 BC, the last focus of opposition to the Second Triumvirate, Sextus Pompeius, son of Julius Caesar's opponent in the civil war, Pompeius Magnus, was executed without trial by order of Marcus Titius, Marc Antony's minion. His illegal death was later used by Octavian against Antony in his unilateral take-over. In the same year, Aristobulus III, the last scion of the Hasmonean royal house, brother of Herod the Great's wife Mariamne, was drowned by Herod's agents. It was the year of the Consulship of Cornificius and Sextus. Cornificius just happened to have served as the accuser of Marcus Junius Brutus in the court which tried the murderers of Julius Caesar, who was actually the real 'Jesus Christ.'

17 AD (14 BC with adjustments made) is interesting in its own right. This is the year that Octavian, now acclaimed as Augustus, celebrated the Ludi Saeculares for which Horace's hymn the Carmen Saeculare was commissioned. The Secular Games was a pagan celebration, involving sacrifices and theatrical performances, held in ancient Rome for three days and nights to mark the end of a saeculum and the beginning of the next. A saeculum is a length of time roughly equal to the potential

40 **A**: 01 06 minus 14.[5]

41 **Q**: *(L)* What time of day was he born?[6]

42 **A**: 6 am.

43 **Q**: *(L)* Was there any unusual celestial event in terms of star or planet alignments at that time?

44 **A**: No.

45 **Q**: *(L)* What was the star the Magi saw in the East that led them to the place where he was born? Was there an event where the Magi came to present gifts?

46 **A**: Close.

47 **Q**: *(L)* Who was it that came to present him gifts?

48 **A**: 3 prophets.

49 **Q**: *(L)* What country did these prophets come from?

50 **A**: Iran. Also known as Persia.

51 **Q**: *(L)* Was Jesus an individual who had psychic or unusual powers from birth?

52 **A**: Close.

53 **Q**: *(L)* Did he have an awareness from the earliest times of his life that he was in some way special or chosen?

54 **A**: Yes.

55 **Q**: *(L)* What was the 'star' that indicated to the prophets...

56 **A**: Spaceship.[7]

57 **Q**: *(L)* What kind of space ship?

58 **A**: Mother.

59 **Q**: *(L)* Where did this mothership come from?

60 **A**: Other realm.

lifetime of a person or the equivalent of the complete renewal of a human population. The term was first used by the Etruscans. Originally it meant the period of time from the moment that something happened (for example the founding of a city) until the point in time that all people who had lived at the first moment had died. At that point a new saeculum would start. According to legend, the gods had allotted a certain number of saecula to every people or civilization; the Etruscans themselves, for example, had been given ten saecula.

The hymn was sung by a chorus of twenty-seven maidens and twenty-seven young boys and was in the form of a prayer addressed to Phoebus (Apollo) and Diana. One of the lines says: *"When Sybilline verses have issued their warning/ To innocent boys, and the virgins we've chosen,/ To sing out their song to the gods..."* suggests that something had prompted Augustus to consult the Sybilline books, a generally rare occurrence that was only initiated in a serious situation, and the holding of the games was the appeasement of the gods. Additional verses suggest that the population of Rome was seriously decimated for some reason, possibly the many years of war since the assassination of Julius Caesar. *"... now protect gentle mothers/... nurture our offspring, bring to fruition/ The Senate's decrees concerning the wedlock/ Of women who'll bear us more of our children,/ ...So the fixed cycle of years, ten times eleven,/ Will bring back the singing again, bring back the games/... give/ Children and wealth to the people of Romulus..."* A marble inscription recording the ceremony and the part played by Horace still survives.

[6] *The Wave* 29

[7] I think we can discount this response as wishful thinking on my part.

61 **Q**: *(L)* Does that mean other realm as in dimension or density?[8]

62 **A**: Yes.

63 **Q**: *(L)* Do we know of these other realms or densities as other star systems or planets?

64 **A**: Partly.

65 **Q**: *(L)* Jesus grew up to the age of twelve, at which point he was Bar Mitzvahed, is that correct?

66 **A**: He was Bar Mitzvahed at the age of 10.

67 **Q**: *(L)* Did he at that time receive training elsewhere?

68 **A**: Aramaic rite.[9]

69 **Q**: *(L)* Did Jesus, during the course of his growing up years travel to other countries and study under other masters?[10]

70 **A**: No.

71 **Q**: *(L)* Where did he receive his teaching or training?

72 **A**: Channeled to him.

73 **Q**: *(L)* Did he at any point in his life travel to India?

74 **A**: No.

75 **Q**: *(L)* Did he travel to Egypt and undergo an initiation in the Great Pyramid?

76 **A**: No.

77 **Q**: *(L)* He lived his entire life in Palestine?

78 **A**: Near. In that general area. The Bible is not entirely accurate.

79 **Q**: *(L)* When Jesus attended the marriage at Cana, whose wedding was it?

80 **A**: Did not happen.

---

[8]We were still a bit confused as to the difference between 'dimension' and 'density.' We had all read *The Ra Material* by this time, and knew that there seemed to be some essential difference, but we had not yet formulated exactly how to use these terms.

[9]This refers to the previous remark about the Bar Mitzvah at the age of 10. I still haven't found an tradition that refers to this specifically. It may stand as a historical reality, but I think we can discard it as applying to any historical 'Jesus Christ' as a Jew.

[10]This is a fairly common explanation offered by many channeled sources over the past couple hundred years. It seems that none of these sources, even though they claimed to be using the technique themselves, could accept the idea of a truly 'miraculous' download of knowledge or grace. Thus, there were many attempts to explain the source of Jesus' teachings in the many schools and systems prevalent in the world at that time. I should also note that this was my first clue that we were definitely *not* dealing with the run-of-the-mill channeled source. It would have been so easy to just go with the flow of all other channeled sources and make up a long story about all the various initiations and teachings and so forth that would explain a historical Jesus' mission in 'realistic' or materialistic terms. But the Cassiopaeans were obviously not going to be seduced by taking the easy way. And, by so doing, even though they were operating within the parameters of my emotional beliefs at the time, they actually gave to the figure behind the Jesus story more honor and puissance than those channeled sources that had sought for so long to 'normalize' the existence of Jesus.

81 Q: *(L)* Did Jesus feed thousands of people with a few loaves and fishes?

82 A: No.

83 Q: *(L)* Are you saying that all the miracles of the Bible are myths?

84 A: Remember this is corrupted information altered after the fact for purposes of political and economic gain and control.

85 Q: *(L)* Tell us what Jesus really did.

86 A: He taught spiritual truths to those starving for them.

87 Q: *(L)* And what was the basis of these spiritual truths?

88 A: Channeled information from higher sources.

89 Q: *(L)* What is the truth that Jesus taught?

90 A: That all men are loved by the creator and are one with same.[11]

91 Q: *(L)* Did he perform miracles?

92 A: Some.

93 Q: *(L)* Can you tell us about one or two of them?

94 A: Healing.

95 Q: *(L)* Was he able to literally heal with the touch of his hand?

96 A: Yes.

97 Q: *(L)* Did he perform exorcisms?

98 A: Close.

99 Q: *(L)* Is Reiki the method he used to heal; or something similar?[12]

100 A: Yes.

101 Q: *(L)* Is there any way to enhance the Reiki energy to make it powerful enough that one could do in a very short time what now takes quite a while?

102 A: Yes.

103 Q: *(L)* What can one do to enhance the Reiki energy?

104 A: Attain lofty spiritual purity.

105 Q: *(L)* I have here two sets of Reiki symbols; which set is the correct or most powerful set: the first set or the second? [Holds up two sets of symbols][13]

106 A: The second set.

107 Q: *(L)* Are these the original Reiki symbols as given to Dr. Usui?

108 A: Close.

109 Q: *(L)* Are the Reiki symbols in the possession of Caroline the correct symbols?

110 A: No.

111 Q: *(L)* Are the symbols that Ann is using correct?

112 A: No.

113 Q: *(L)* Is Ann able to transmit the initiation in a full and powerful way?

114 A: No.

115 Q: *(L)* Is she just wasting her time thinking she is doing the transmitting, as I suspect?

116 A: Yours.

117 Q: *(L)* Is there someone I could go to for the correct initiation?[14]

---

[11] In this short series of questions and answers, the Cassiopaeans took with one hand and gave with the other. The result was, of course, that the figure of Jesus became more accessible and at the same time more remarkable.

[12] *The Wave* 17

[13] For illustrations see *The Wave* chapter 17.

[14] *The Wave* 17

118 **A:** Yes.

119 **Q:** *(L)* Do I know that person?

120 **A:** No.

121 **Q:** *(L)* Who do I know that may know that person?

122 **A:** Helen. VG has strongest ability.[15]

123 **Q:** *(L)* Does this mean that VG has the strongest Reiki ability of us all?

124 **A:** Yes.

125 **Q:** *(L)* Is her Reiki more powerful than my Reiki?

126 **A:** Yes. Scarlett has no ability. Crosses yours out.

127 **Q:** *(L)* Are you saying that Scarlett has given me Reiki that has cancelled my own Reiki out?

128 **A:** Precisely.

129 **Q:** *(L)* We did four hypnosis sessions with Scarlett where she discussed abduction experiences and so forth. Was any of that information that she gave embellished in any way?

130 **A:** Yes.

131 **Q:** *(L)* Was it embellished consciously or unconsciously?

132 **A:** Both.

133 **Q:** *(L)* Was she actually abducted by aliens?

134 **A:** Yes.

135 **Q:** *(L)* What was the purpose of her abduction? What were the aliens trying to do with or to her?

136 **A:** Vaginal probe.

137 **Q:** *(L)* For what purpose?

138 **A:** Reproductive efficacy.

139 **Q:** *(L)* But Scarlett has had a hysterectomy.

140 **A:** They found none.[16]

141 **Q:** *(L)* Was she abducted more than one time?

142 **A:** Yes.

143 **Q:** *(L)* How many times has she been abducted?[17]

144 **A:** 52.

145 **Q:** *(L)* How many times has Frank been abducted?[18]

146 **A:** 53.

147 **Q:** *(L)* Why have they been abducting Frank?

148 **A:** Mind.

149 **Q:** *(L)* What about his mind?

150 **A:** Programmed by advanced powers.

151 **Q:** *(L)* Did they abduct Scarlett 52 times just to do a vaginal probe?

152 **A:** No. That was the most recent.

153 **Q:** *(L)* What were all the previous ones for?

154 **A:** Study mind and tap emotions.

155 **Q:** *(L)* In other words, they have tapped her emotions?

156 **A:** Yes.

157 **Q:** *(L)* Do they feed off of her emotions?

158 **A:** Yes.

159 **Q:** *(L)* Do they feed off Frank's emotions?

160 **A:** Yes.

---

[15] VG was an occasional sitter with the experiment.
[16] That response strikes me as rather disingenuous.
[17] *High Strangeness* 8, "Appendix"; *The Wave* 21
[18] *The Wave* 34

161 **Q:** *(L)* Is there any way to break that tap?
162 **A:** It is not continuous.
163 **Q:** *(L)* Do they tap my emotions?
164 **A:** Yes.
165 **Q:** *(L)* Is this for our benefit?
166 **A:** No.
167 **Q:** *(L)* Is it the 'bad guys' who have been doing this?
168 **A:** Yes.
169 **Q:** *(L)* Is there any way we can disconnect these taps?
170 **A:** Keep channeling and meditating.
171 **Q:** *(L)* What does the channeling do to break the tap?
172 **A:** Informs.
173 **Q:** *(L)* Let's go back to Jesus. Are the only miracles he did healing?
174 **A:** No.
175 **Q:** *(L)* What other kinds of miracles did he do?[19]
176 **A:** Telekinesis.
177 **Q:** *(L)* Did he walk on water?
178 **A:** No.
179 **Q:** *(L)* Did he turn water into wine?
180 **A:** No.
181 **Q:** *(L)* Are these all just stories?
182 **A:** Yes.
183 **Q:** *(L)* What is the purpose of the stories?
184 **A:** Control.
185 **Q:** *(L)* Was Jesus crucified?
186 **A:** No.

187 **Q:** *(L)* Was somebody crucified?
188 **A:** Too vague.
189 **Q:** *(L)* Was somebody crucified on a cross and represented to be Jesus?
190 **A:** No.
191 **Q:** *(L)* There was no crucifixion, there was no resurrection after three days, is that correct?
192 **A:** Close.
193 **Q:** *(L)* OK, what is the truth on that matter?
194 **A:** Left Earth plane on ship after extended sleep state.
195 **Q:** *(L)* When did he go into this sleep state? Did he just go in one day and go to bed and go to sleep and then a ship came and picked him up?
196 **A:** Close.
197 **Q:** *(L)* So he appeared to his followers to have died?
198 **A:** They thought this.
199 **Q:** *(L)* Did he get up and say anything to anybody before he left on the ship?
200 **A:** Yes.
201 **Q:** *(L)* Did he come back to life...
202 **A:** Yes.
203 **Q:** *(L)* And then he told them things he had seen in his extended meditative sleep, is that what happened?
204 **A:** Close.
205 **Q:** *(L)* OK, what happened?
206 **A:** Told prophecies then proclaimed eventual return.
207 **Q:** *(L)* Was this information he got during this period of extended sleep?
208 **A:** Yes.

---
[19] *The Wave* 29

209 **Q:** *(L)* How long was he asleep, or in this state of semi-death?

210 **A:** 96 hours.

211 **Q:** *(L)* And then, a ship arrived and took him away, is that correct?

212 **A:** Yes. Upon pillar of light.

213 **Q:** *(L)* Are there any other miracles he did that are outstanding?

214 **A:** Miracles are subjective.

215 **Q:** *(L)* Did he raise Lazarus from the dead?

216 **A:** No.

217 **Q:** *(L)* Did he raise anybody from the dead?

218 **A:** No.

219 **Q:** *(L)* OK, when he got to this other plane, what did he do?

220 **A:** Vague question.[20]

221 **Q:** *(L)* Is there any special power or advantage in praying in the name of Jesus?

222 **A:** Yes.

223 **Q:** *(L)* Well, if he didn't die and release his spirit into the Earth plane, how is this power conferred?

224 **A:** Prayers go to him.

225 **Q:** *(L)* And what does he do when he hears the prayers?

226 **A:** Determines their necessity against background of individual soul development.

227 **Q:** *(L)* You said that when a person prays to Jesus that he makes some sort of a decision, is that correct?

228 **A:** Yes.

229 **Q:** *(L)* Well, how can he do that when millions of people are praying to him simultaneously?

230 **A:** Soul division.

231 **Q:** *(L)* What do you mean by soul division?

232 **A:** Self explanatory.

233 **Q:** *(L)* Do you mean soul division as in cellular mitosis where a cell splits and replicates itself?

234 **A:** No.

235 **Q:** *(L)* Does Jesus' soul divide?

236 **A:** Yes.

237 **Q:** *(L)* How many times does it divide?

238 **A:** Endlessly as a projection of consciousness.

239 **Q:** *(L)* And what happens to this piece of soul that is divided or projected?

240 **A:** Is not a piece of a soul.

241 **Q:** *(L)* What is it?

242 **A:** It is a replication.

243 **Q:** *(L)* Is each replication exactly identical to the original?

244 **A:** Yes. And no.

245 **Q:** *(L)* In what way is the replicated soul different from the original?

246 **A:** Not able to give individual attention.

247 **Q:** *(L)* Are any of us able to replicate in this manner if we so desire?

248 **A:** Could if in same circumstance. The way the process works is thus: When Jesus left the Earth plane, he went into another dimension or density of reality, whereupon all "rules" regarding the awareness of time and space are entirely

---

[20] *The Wave* 6

different from the way they are perceived in your realm. At this point in space time his soul which was/is still in the physical realm, was placed in a state of something akin to suspended animation and a sort of advanced form of unconsciousness. From that point to the present his soul has been replicated from a state of this unconsciousness in order that all who call upon him or need to be with him or need to speak to him can do so on an individual basis. His soul can be replicated ad infinitum – as many times as needed. The replication process produces a state of hyper-consciousness in each and every version of the soul consciousness.[21]

Q: *(L)* Who was Jack the Ripper?

A: Dr. Bates.

Q: *(L)* Did he commit suicide and is that why the Ripper killings stopped?

A: No.

Q: *(L)* Did he just stop doing it?

A: Yes.

Q: *(L)* Why did he do it?

---

[21] So, finally, the Cassiopaeans gave an explanation for the 'power of Jesus' that was, on the one hand, rational and, on the other hand, totally comprehensible from the human perspective no matter who Jesus was in the historical sense. Not only that, it could be inferred from what was said here that the mythicization of Jesus, the corrupting of the truth about his life (and I am convinced that Julius Caesar was Jesus, based on years of research), and the substituting of the myths of other 'dying savior' cults, amounts to the work of those who wish to confuse and corrupt mankind for purposes of control and domination. We can see that the idea was to present Jesus as a performer of miracles that are unavailable to humanity for the most part, so that this would distort human understanding of what the life experience of Julius Caesar, here on Earth, was all about; and further, how it applies to each and every one of us in a direct and meaningful way. That is to say, when words are put in Jesus' mouth, such as "these things I do, you can do too," it was far more attainable than standard religious teachings would have us believe. The idea that Jesus was actually Julius Caesar who was assassinated by Brutus/Judas and then was said to have ascended to heaven as a comet from where he would continue to aid and succor the common man also brings a whole new meaning to the saying: *"Greater love hath no man than that he should give up his life for his friends."* To submit oneself to crucifixion, knowing that one will "rise again to eternal life" in three days, is no real sacrifice. But to submit to a state of suspended animation in a "time warp cocoon" for thousands of years that may seem like eternity, is a very great sacrifice, indeed.

[22] I have a rather large collection of books on the subject of Jack the Ripper. Each and every one of them proposes a different solution to the identity of the killer. And each of these books is written logically, sincerely, and with a great deal of research to back up the conclusions. In the end, it is difficult to favor one solution over another. I wonder if the Cassiopaeans use of the term "Dr. Bates" was a sly allusion to the character of the movie *Psycho*, the unforgettable Norman Bates of the Bates Motel? And, if so, was it an indicator of a type of killer, rather than an actual name?

256 **A:** Experiment human organs; he was a mad surgeon.[22]

257 **Q:** *(L)* Was Adolf Hitler possessed by demons or evil spirits?[23]

258 **A:** Close.

259 **Q:** *(L)* Was Adolf Hitler under the control of the negatively oriented aliens?

260 **A:** Close.

261 **Q:** *(L)* Where is Adolf Hitler now?

262 **A:** Sleeping.

263 **Q:** *(L)* How long will he sleep?

264 **A:** Indefinite.

265 **Q:** *(L)* Will Adolf Hitler return to incarnation at some point in the future?

266 **A:** Yes.

267 **Q:** *(L)* Can you predict what kind of life he will lead in his future incarnation?

268 **A:** No.

269 **Q:** *(L)* The passages attributed to Jesus in Matthew 24 and Luke 21, where Jesus predicts the end of the age and his return, is that fairly accurately rendered?

270 **A:** Close.

271 **Q:** *(L)* Is Jesus, in fact, in a state of suspension, voluntarily, in another plane of existence, having chosen to give up his life on this plane in order to continuously generate replications of his soul pattern for other people to call upon for assistance?

272 **A:** Yes.

273 **Q:** *(L)* If one calls upon him more than once, does one get a double dose?[24]

274 **A:** Define.

275 **Q:** *(L)* If one repeatedly calls upon Jesus does one get repeated replications or additional strength, power or whatever?

276 **A:** No.

277 **Q:** *(L)* In other words, once one has truly made the connection, that's it?

278 **A:** That's all that's needed.

279 **Q:** *(L)* Has any other soul volunteered to perform this work?

280 **A:** Yes.

281 **Q:** *(L)* How many souls are doing this work at the present time?

282 **A:** 12.

283 **Q:** *(L)* Can you name any of the others?

---

[23] After reading several biographies of Adolf Hitler, there were several incidents in his life that stood out in my mind as having been potential points of possession by evil spirits in the terms described by Dr. William Baldwin in his book *Spirit Releasement Therapy*. One of these incidents was the fact that a brother of Hitler died when he was a child, and this was noted as a point in which his entire personality changed. His family home was next to a graveyard, and he was known to spend much time sitting on the wall, staring at the tombstones. Such morbidity in a young child is often precursor behavior for possession.

[24] *The Wave* 29

[25] I have never come across anything that seems remotely similar to this name, but it strikes me as having an Oriental flavor. Perhaps it is related to the Shinto religion of Japan?

[26] Again, the only relationship I can think of to make to this name is that it has the feel of India, with the term 'Naga' incorporated into it.

284 **A**: Buddha. Moses. Shintanhilmoon.[25] Nagaillikiga.[26] Varying degrees; Jesus is the strongest currently.

285 **Q**: *(L)* What year did the Exodus occur counting backward from now according to our calendrical system?

286 **A**: 4670.[27]

287 **Q**: *(L)* At that time did a cometary Venus pass close to the Earth and cause disruption?

288 **A**: Yes.

289 **Q**: *(L)* Was Venus born from the planet Jupiter?

290 **A**: No.

291 **Q**: *(L)* Did it appear in the sky from the area of Jupiter?

292 **A**: Yes.

293 **Q**: *(L)* Was the Earth knocked into a new orbital position because of this activity?

294 **A**: Yes.

295 **Q**: Is an event of this type going to take place in the not-too-distant future?

296 **A**: Maybe.

297 **Q**: *(L)* Did an event of this type take place at the time of the flood of Noah?

298 **A**: Yes.

299 **Q**: *(L)* How many years ago did the flood of Noah occur?

300 **A**: 12,656. (10,662 BC)

301 **Q**: *(L)* Was Noah an actual historical person?

302 **A**: Close.

303 **Q**: *(L)* Was Noah the same person described in the Babylonian or Sumerian texts as Utnapishtim?[28]

304 **A**: Close.

305 **Q**: *(L)* Which is the older civilization: Sumerian or Egyptian?

306 **A**: Sumerian.

---

[27]This would put the Exodus at 2676 BC. The fact is, there was some sort of discontinuity of many ancient cultures which occurred at both these periods: 3100–2500 BC and 1600 BC. I would also like to note that, considering the work of Iman Wilkens, *Where Troy Once Stood*, we can't rely on the Egypt we know today being the same Egypt of the Exodus, nor the Exodus being a Jewish phenomenon. See the work of Russell E. Gmirkin and Bruce Louden for insight. The Bible is not the history of the Jews and if there are historical elements there, they are most likely borrowed from other peoples and other times.

[28]In the Sumerian poems he is a wise king and priest of Shurrupak; in the Akkadian sources he is a wise citizen of Shurrupak. He is the son of Ubara-Tutu, and his name is usually translated as "He Who Saw Life." He is the protégé of the god Ea, by whose connivance he survives the flood, with his family and with "the seed of all living creatures." He is the main character of the Flood story in the eleventh tablet of the Gilgamesh epic. In a different version of this epic (such as the Atrachasis myth for instance) he is named Atrachasis, "the exceptional wise one." Old Babylonian Utanapishtim, Sumerian Ziusudra. He shows many similarities with the much more recent biblical Noah.

307 **Q:** *(L)* Who were Enlil[29] and Enki,[30] the Annunaki[31] of Sumerian stories?

308 **A:** Great teachers.

309 **Q:** *(L)* Were they human or extraterrestrial?

310 **A:** Extraterrestrial.

311 **Q:** *(L)* Where did they come from?

312 **A:** Cassiopaea.

313 **Q:** *(L)* Was the human race genetically

---

[29] In ancient Sumero-Babylonian myth, Enlil ("lord wind") is the god of air, wind and storms. Enlil is the foremost god of the Mesopotamian pantheon, and is sometimes referred to as Kur-Gal ("great mountain"). In the Sumerian cosmology he was born of the union of An heaven, and Ki earth. These he separated, and he carried off the earth as his portion. In later times he supplanted Anu as chief god. His consort is Ninlil with whom he has five children: Nanna, Nerigal, Ningirsu, Ninurta, and Nisaba. Enlil holds possession of the Tablets of Destiny which gives him power over the entire cosmos and the affairs of man. He is sometimes friendly towards mankind, but can also be a stern and even cruel god who punishes man and sends forth disasters, such as the great Flood which wiped out humanity with the exception of Atrahasis. Enlil is portrayed wearing a crown with horns, symbol of his power. In short, he is obviously a comet.

[30] The Sumerian high god of water and intellect, creation, wisdom, and medicine, who could restore the dead to life. He was the source of all secret and magical knowledge of life and immortality. Enki possessed the secret of *me*, "culture, civilization," which is the genius of progress in knowledge to lead humanity. He invented civilization for the people and assigned to each his destiny. He created order in the cosmos. He filled the rivers with fish. He invented the plough and the yoke so that farmers could till the earth with oxen. He made the grain grow. He is the father of all plants. In most myths his consort is Damkina, or Ninhursag, who gave him a daughter. Enki is depicted on a relief holding Zu, the storm-bird. He was called Ea in Babylonian, King of Apsu.

[31] The Annunaki are described by Z. Sitchin as the "sons of An," the Sumerian high God over all the other gods. He includes Enlil and Enki among them, though the facts may be somewhat confused. "Annunaku" was the Akkadian name for a group of gods of the underworld. They function as judges in the realm of the dead. Their counterparts are the Igigi (although in some texts the positions are reversed). The Annunaku show many similarities with the Sumerian Anunna. The Anunnaku are the offspring of Anu.

[32] Charles Fort, an obsessive collector of anomalous events, once remarked that the only conclusions he could draw from all his research, was that Earth was "owned" by some beings who we could neither see nor comprehend. All over the world, from time immemorial, gods have been represented with scales. Most analysts have interpreted this to be a symbolic representation of the 'powers' of the gods. Or the 'wisdom' of the serpent. But why a serpent would acquire any kind of cachet as wise simply does not compute in any way, shape or form. How do we explain the ubiquitous presence of a serpent race on Earth? Perhaps it is because at one time, or at various times, and even still, they are present in our realm, but as hyperdimensional beings; the secret Control System that owns Earth.

engineered to be slaves?

314 **A:** Yes.[32]

315 **Q:** *(L)* And who were the genetic engineers of this slavehood?

316 **A:** Lizard beings.[33]

317 **Q:** *(L)* Where do they come from: Earth or another planet?

318 **A:** Other.

319 **Q:** *(L)* What planet from?

320 **A:** Qaddeera.[34]

321 **Q:** *(L)* What star system is that in?

322 **A:** Zeta Reticuli.[35] [36]

323 **Q:** *(L)* Are the little gray beings from Zeta Reticuli also?

324 **A:** Yes.

325 **Q:** *(L)* Are the little gray beings...

326 **A:** Cybergenetic.[37]

327 **Q:** *(L)* Are they created by the lizards?

328 **A:** Yes.

329 **Q:** *(L)* Do they have souls?

330 **A:** They are Decoys.

331 **Q:** *(L)* Are the Lizzies currently with us?

332 **A:** Near.

333 **Q:** *(L)* Are the Lizzies planning to take over our planet?

334 **A:** Yes.

335 **Q:** *(L)* Are they planning on landing and doing this openly?

336 **A:** Close.[38]

337 **Q:** *(L)* Do they utilize such things as possession by dark energy forms to effect their control?

338 **A:** Yes.

339 **Q:** *(L)* What other groups are they in cahoots with?

340 **A:** Orions.

341 **Q:** *(L)* How many members are there in the Orion/Lizzie group?[39]

342 **A:** 16.

343 **Q:** *(L)* Who are the good guys? You say the Cassiopaeans are the good guys. Who else?

344 **A:** Pleiadeans and many others.

345 **Q:** *(L)* How many?

---

[33] *Secret History* 11; *The Wave* 29, 32

[34] I have never found anything that relates to this name.

[35] A binary star system that is roughly 37 light years away from Earth. The aliens that abducted Betty and Barney Hill (See: *The Interrupted Journey* by Raymond Fowler) were calculated to come from a planet in this system, and Bob Lazar claimed that the nine UFOs he saw in S-4 came from one of the planets in the Zeta Reticuli star system.

[36] *The Wave* 1

[37] Cyber – from a Greek word that means 'to steer, navigate, direct,' and 'genetic,' or creation. In other words, genetically engineered.

[38] Remember that "close" gets no cigar. It took us awhile to learn this and to go back to questions that had been answered this way to try and pin down exactly how close we were or were not!

[39] *The Wave* 65

346 **A:** 16.[40]

347 **Q:** *(L)* Are the sides equally balanced?

348 **A:** Yes.

349 **Q:** *(L)* Do the good guys abduct people?

350 **A:** No. They may contact and voluntarily transport.

351 **Q:** *(L)* Who really killed Abraham Lincoln?

352 **A:** Booth. Conspiracy.

353 **Q:** *(L)* Who was the head of the conspiracy?

354 **A:** Booth. But was not caught; was patsy stand in.

355 **Q:** *(L)* Was the story of Noah's flood the story of the breaking up of Atlantis?[41]

356 **A:** Yes. But symbolic.

357 **Q:** *(L)* How many people were on the planet at that time?

358 **A:** 6 billion.

359 **Q:** *(L)* Out of this six billion people, how many survived?

360 **A:** 119 million.[42]

361 **Q:** *(L)* Was Noah's flood caused by the close passage of another celestial body?

362 **A:** Yes.

363 **Q:** *(L)* Which body was that?

364 **A:** Martek.

365 **Q:** *(L)* Do we know this body in our solar system now?

366 **A:** Yes.

367 **Q:** *(L)* What name?

368 **A:** Mars.

369 **Q:** *(L)* Was Martek an inhabited planet at that time?

370 **A:** No.

371 **Q:** *(L)* Did it have water or other features?

372 **A:** Yes.

373 **Q:** *(L)* When it passed close to the Earth did it, in fact, overload our planet with water we did not have prior to that time?

374 **A:** Yes.

375 **Q:** *(L)* Did we, prior to that time, have a water-vapor canopy surrounding our planet?

376 **A:** Yes.

377 **Q:** *(L)* Was this the time of the major dying of the large dinosaurs?

378 **A:** Close.

379 **Q:** *(L)* What event transpired to kill off most of the dinosaurs?

380 **A:** Beasts.

381 **Q:** *(L)* What kind of beasts?

---

[40] This does not refer to individuals, but to distinct 'groups' or 'types' of 'aliens.' It seems to me that there may be some 'mystical' significance to this number 16. It is, in fact, the exact number of pieces on a chess board, and the chess board has been the symbol of mystical reality for millennia. And the game of chess is played on a board with 64 squares which is 4 times 16. Broken down in another way, on the chessboard there are 8 'dominant' pieces and 8 pawns to each side and the number 8 will be seen to figure significantly as we go along. Keep spiders and scorpions in mind, for example.

[41] *The Wave* 24

[42] Or 19 million? I am not sure of this figure. The early tapes were destroyed, and the notes have the number both ways with a couple of cross-outs.

382 **A**: Mastodon, sabertooth tiger, giant sloth, etc.[43]

383 **Q**: *(L)* Was it a cosmic event that brought about the death of some of the largest dinosaurs?

384 **A**: Yes.

385 **Q**: *(L)* It did not happen at the time of Noah, is that correct?

386 **A**: Yes.

387 **Q**: *(L)* Did it happen before the flood of Noah?

388 **A**: Yes.

389 **Q**: *(L)* How many thousands of years ago counting backward?

390 **A**: 27 million years ago.[44]

391 **Q**: *(L)* What event took place at that time that caused the death of the dinosaurs?

392 **A**: Comet impact.

393 **Q**: *(L)* Did a comet actually strike the Earth?

394 **A**: Yes.

---

[43] Despite the range of possible theories over the years, scientists are now virtually certain that the demise of the dinosaurs and thousands of other prehistoric plant and animal species was caused by the impact of a massive meteor on Earth some 65 million years ago.

Around this date, dinosaur evidence first began disappearing from the fossil record. But, far from popular belief, all the dinosaurs and other species were not wiped out with a bang, but instead gradually disappeared as a result of the consequences of the impact over a long period of time, perhaps millions of years.

When the 10-kilometre-wide meteor struck, the explosive equivalent was larger than the capabilities of the world's entire nuclear arsenal. Molten lava, created by the Earth being crushed beneath the meteor, spewed out over the area for hundreds of kilometers. Tidal waves made the effect of the impact travel even further afield, destroying coastal and marine life in the vicinity. While significant, these events alone would probably not have wiped out entire species.

But once the initial impact had died down, the major long term effects came into play. The atmosphere was filled with dust and microscopic debris which effectively blocked out the sunlight. The resulting death of plant life over time, and the plunging temperatures, radically altered the world's climate and hence the world's ecosystem. Based on the ocean floor samples, the researchers estimate that anything up to 70 percent of the planet's species were wiped out as a result of this prolonged and harsh winter.

The main survivors of this scenario were those species adapted to life underground or in the oceans, or those that ate meat.

[44] The accepted date of most scientists is 65 million years ago. However, after considerable study of the matter, we come to the idea that science may not be taking all things into consideration when setting up these dates. In particular, what is not being considered is the possibility that magnetic aberrations caused by ancient cataclysms might alter the isotopal imprints of matter. Electromagnetic surges could scramble the radiological dating, as well as other dating methods. These problems are discussed by some scientists, but they are generally not allowed to be heard in the mainstream journals.

395 **Q:** *(L)* Was it a large comet?

396 **A:** Yes.

397 **Q:** *(L)* How large?

398 **A:** 18 miles diameter.

399 **Q:** *(L)* Is there any regular periodicity or cycle to this comet business?

400 **A:** Yes.

401 **Q:** *(L)* What is the period?

402 **A:** 3600 years roughly.[45]

403 **Q:** *(L)* Was Velikovsky correct when he said Venus was on a 52 year orbit during a certain period in our history?

404 **A:** Close.

405 **Q:** *(L)* How many passes did Venus make through the solar system before it was precipitated into a regular planetary orbit?

406 **A:** 7.

407 **Q:** *(L)* Where did Venus originally come from?

408 **A:** 19 light years away.

409 **Q:** *(L)* So, it is actually an extra-solar system visitor?

410 **A:** Yes.

411 **Q:** *(L)* Is it true that at regular intervals the sun radiates massive amounts of electromagnetic energy which then causes the planets of the solar system to interact with one another to a greater or lesser extent?[46] [47]

412 **A:** Other irregular pulsations determined by external vibrational events.[48]

413 **Q:** *(L)* The sun is not the source of the periodicity of 'dyings,' is that correct?

414 **A:** Sometimes. Many causes.

415 **Q:** *(L)* Well what is the cause that recurs like clockwork? Is there some cause that is a regular pulsation?[49]

416 **A:** Cometary showers.

417 **Q:** *(L)* Where are these cometary showers from?

418 **A:** Clusters in own orbit.

---

[45] This is the same period suggested by Zecharia Sitchin for the 'return' of the 10th planet. And, the fact is, there is evidence that possible cataclysmic type activity does occur on Earth at exactly such an interval based on analysis of ice core samples.

[46] It was a theory of mine that the sun itself was responsible for the periodic cataclysms in the solar system; that it had major long-period oscillations that were capable of so charging the bodies of the solar system with electrical energy that their mutual attraction or repulsion would cause them to interact with one another without the need for an 'outside agent.' I was pretty fond of this theory, too!

[47] *The Wave* 1

[48] *The Wave* 24

[49] Sepkowski compiled a list of all the extinct species and supposed times of their extinction. He wanted to see if there was some biological pattern of dying out. The data revealed not only is there a pattern, there is a very definite cycle! Some of these 'Great Dyings' were more widespread and devastating than others, but it was unmistakably a regular pulsing of extinction! Formerly extinctions were thought to occur because a lot of things just coincidentally got bad all at once. The idea that the Dyings are a regular, cyclic thing implies "a single, powerful, and awesome cause, recurring like clockwork."

419 **Q:** *(L)* Where is the orbit of these clusters? Is it the Oort cloud?[50]

420 **A:** No.

421 **Q:** *(L)* Where is the orbit of clusters of comets located?

422 **A:** More specific.

423 **Q:** *(L)* A specific orbit containing clusters of comets?

424 **A:** Yes.

425 **Q:** *(L)* Does this cluster of comets orbit around the sun?

426 **A:** Yes.

427 **Q:** *(L)* Is the orbit perpendicular to the plane of the ecliptic?

428 **A:** Yes and no.

429 **Q:** *(L)* Does this cluster come into the plane of the ecliptic and cause havoc in the solar system?

430 **A:** Exactly.

431 **Q:** *(L)* How often does this cluster of comets come into the plane of the ecliptic?

432 **A:** 3600 years.

433 **Q:** *(L)* Is this cluster of comets the remains of a planet?

434 **A:** No.

435 **Q:** *(L)* Is the cluster of fragments in between the orbits of Mars and Jupiter the remains of a planet?

436 **A:** Yes.

437 **Q:** *(L)* What was that planet known as?

438 **A:** Kantek.

439 **Q:** *(L)* When did that planet break apart into the asteroid belt.

440 **A:** 79 thousand years ago approximately.

441 **Q:** *(L)* What body were the Sumerians talking about when they described the Planet of the Crossing or Nibiru?[51]

442 **A:** Comets.

443 **Q:** *(L)* This body of comets?

444 **A:** Yes.

---

[50] Once scientists had discovered that the Great Dyings occurred inexorably like clockwork, there was a lot of sweating going on to figure out when, where, how, and why. What they came up with was this: Way outside the edges of our solar system there is a ring of comets which circles around and around like good little comets should. Supposedly these are bits of matter which did not have sufficient impetus to amass into a planet, or are remnants of a planet or planets which were broken up billions of years ago. Also, spinning around out there in our galaxy somewhere is a dark star which swings close to this little band of comets (called the Oort Cloud), and the force of the Death Star's gravity sends billions of them spinning through our solar system and, of course, a few of them smack into the Earth. You will notice that this explanation does several important things. First, it maintains the steady state of our solar system – an outsider is the culprit. And, secondly, it makes the event chancy enough that we might escape if we are lucky. Based upon the dating of the extinct specimens, it is said that this event occurs once every 26 million years or so – give or take a day. And, curiously, this happens to be very close to the period of time in the past that the Cassiopaeans have assigned to the death of the dinosaurs though they say it is "years ago," not just that it is the cycle and we could be anywhere on that cycle.

[51] *The Wave* 24

445 **Q:** *(L)* Does this cluster of comets appear to be a single body?

446 **A:** Yes.

447 **Q:** *(L)* Is this the same object that is rumored to be on its way here at the present time?

448 **A:** Yes.

449 **Q:** *(L)* Who were the Annunaki?

450 **A:** Aliens.

451 **Q:** *(L)* Where were they from?

452 **A:** Zeta Reticuli.

453 **Q:** *(L)* Do they come here every time the comet cluster is approaching to sap the souls' energy created by the fear, chaos, and so forth?

454 **A:** Yes.

455 **Q:** *(L)* The two events are loosely interrelated?

456 **A:** Yes.

457 **Q:** *(L)* Is that why they are here now?

458 **A:** Close.

459 **Q:** *(L)* Is there a large fleet of spaceships riding a wave, so to speak, approaching our planet?[52]

460 **A:** Yes.

461 **Q:** *(L)* Where are these ships from?

462 **A:** Zeta Reticuli.

463 **Q:** *(L)* When will they arrive?

464 **A:** 1 month to 18 years.[53]

465 **Q:** *(L)* How can there be such a vast discrepancy in the time?

466 **A:** This is such a huge fleet that space/time warping is irregular and difficult to determine as you measure time.

467 **Q:** *(L)* Are these craft riding a 'wave' of some sort?

468 **A:** Yes.

469 **Q:** *(L)* How many planets are in our solar system?

470 **A:** 12.

471 **Q:** *(L)* Could you tell us the names of all the planets, their distances from the sun, the chemical composition, and the diameter.

472 **A:** Mercury=Opatanar, 36 million miles from Sun; 3000 mi. diameter. Venus=Pemuntar, 67 million miles from Sun; 7,500 mi. diameter. Earth=Saras, 93 million miles from Sun; 7,900 mi. diameter. Mars=Masar, 141,500,000 miles from Sun; 4,200 mi. diameter. Jupiter=Yontar, 483,400,000 miles from Sun; 88,700 diameter. Saturn=Zendar, 886,700,000 miles from Sun; 74,500 diameter. Uranus=Lonoponor, 1,782,700,000 miles from Sun; 31,566 diameter. Neptune=Jinoar, 2,794,300,000 miles from Sun; 30,199 diameter. Pluto=Opikimanaras, 3,666,100,000

---

[52] I asked this question because this was a phrase used by an abductee in a hypnosis session I conducted.

[53] Note that this is the same period given for the window of "space wars." On the other hand, the period given for the completion of a certain program having to do with readying a new prototype being in terms of the "creation of a new race," in the first session, was given as 13 years from either that time, or the time being discussed at that moment, a predicted event that was, itself, not locked-down in terms of time. Noting how some of the things the C's predicted have manifested, it appears that there will be a period of 'Rock 'n Roll' on the Big Blue Marble at some point, probably rather soon.

miles from Sun; 1,864 diameter. NI=Montonanas, 570,000,000,000 miles from Sun; solid matter; 7000 miles diameter. NII=Suvurutarcar, 830,000,000,000 miles from Sun; 18,000 miles diameter; hydrogen, ammonia. NIII=Bikalamanar, 1,600,000,000,000 miles from Sun; 46,000 miles diameter; hydrogen, ammonia.

End of Session

October 5, 1994

This was another session where I was asking rapid-fire questions, changing topics, reviewing things they had said already, and just generally trying to get the C's off-kilter as a way of testing them.

Participants: 'Frank' and Laura

1. **Q**: Hello.
2. **A**: You are good to do it this way without ritual.
3. **Q**: *(L)* What ritual do you want us to do?[1]
4. **A**: None.
5. **Q**: *(L)* Does ritual enhance or prevent communication?
6. **A**: Constricts.
7. **Q**: *(L)* What is your name?
8. **A**: Donarra.
9. **Q**: *(L)* Where are you from?
10. **A**: Cassiopaea.
11. **Q**: *(L)* Why is it every time we communicate with you Cassiopaeans we get a different person?
12. **A**: Energy disbursement.
13. **Q**: *(L)* Who is the energy disbursed to?
14. **A**: The next in order.
15. **Q**: *(L)* Does that mean that you utilize our energy to disburse?
16. **A**: No. We disburse.
17. **Q**: *(L)* We have a series of questions we want to ask.
18. **A**: Go ahead.
19. **Q**: *(L)* Assuming there is a fleet of spacecraft riding a wave, and approaching from the vicinity of Zeta Reticuli, what does it mean to say that the space-time warp is indefinite in terms of arrival? Why is this? Please specify.[2]
20. **A**: Mass affects electromagnetic transfer within gravity wave.
21. **Q**: *(L)* In other words, if there is a large mass you are trying to transfer, is the problem partly because the mass itself spreads out over such a large area of space-time and must be transferred in stages or something along that line?
22. **A**: Close.
23. **Q**: *(L)* Can you help us out anymore here?
24. **A**: Mass affects time cycle: small equal short cycle; large or dense equals long cycle.[3]

---

[1] *The Wave* 23
[2] *The Wave* 1
[3] The idea that mass affects time is extremely interesting but we didn't follow up on that at the time. Information Theory may also have some bearing on this if we can theorize that more information added to a system adds some sort of mass to it or

Q: *(L)* We would also like to have more information on Earth changes. Is the Japanese earthquake that just happened as you predicted last week, the last of the Japanese problem?[4]

A: No.

Q: *(L)* Can you give us more on that...

A: There will be activity about 8.9: 67 miles off Osaka coast; 9.7: central Tokyo.

Q: *(L)* Are all of these going to happen within this year?

A: No. Within 16 years.[5]

Q: *(L)* I would like more details about the man you say is the biological father of Jesus. Once again, what is his name?

A: Tonatha.

Q: *(L)* You said he was an acquaintance of Mary's?

A: Yes.

Q: *(L)* Was he selected for some reason to be the biological father of Jesus by other beings or powers?[6]

A: Close.

Q: *(L)* Can you give us any details about him? What was his lineage, where did he come from, etc?

A: He was a member of the White Sect.

Q: *(L)* What is the White Sect?

A: AKA Aryans. Andarans.[7]

---

that the information is reflected by the increase of mass. If there is anything to this idea, one might think that as a civilization loses its intelligence (as ours clearly has), becomes immersed in a sea of lies and disinformation, it would be losing mass, so to say, and this might accelerate time cycles, including cycles of catastrophe. One might even wonder if the diminishment of Earth's magnetic field is related to this in any way.

[4] An entire session had been lost due to tape malfunction. It consisted in part of a prediction of an almost immediate Japanese earthquake which did occur exactly as predicted.

[5] On Friday March 11, 2011 (17 years, not 16), a magnitude 9.0 (Mw) undersea megathrust earthquake occurred off the coast of Japan. The epicenter was approximately 70 kilometers (43 mi) east of the Oshika Peninsula of Tōhoku. It was the most powerful earthquake ever recorded to have hit Japan, and the fifth most powerful earthquake in the world since modern record-keeping began in 1900. I'd say that's close enough for horseshoes and considering the problems of transducing and translating. But, again, it raises the question of just what is in the Information Field that makes it possible to even make such a prediction that far in advance? Are some things more easily known because there is some sort of recompense that must be made to balance energy in an area? Or are the ponderous movements of the planet's tectonic plates more easily predicted (from another realm) than we think? Or was this earthquake deliberately triggered somehow and therefore, part of a conspiracy that could have been known at the time of this session? Just lots of questions here. One also thinks about the other earthquake mentioned here that has yet to occur, an even larger one inland that may or may not be centered on Tokyo.

[6] *The Wave* 29

[7] We didn't ask who were the Andarans, though it did come up again in a later session.

Q: *(L)* Was Mary a member of the Essene group?

A: Yes.

Q: *(L)* Was this man also a member of the Essenes?

A: No.

Q: *(L)* This person, Tonatha, was chosen to be the biological father of Jesus?

A: Yes.[8]

Q: *(L)* Why did Mary not marry him?

A: Feelings were extremely transient.

Q: *(L)* You are saying she was fickle?

A: No. Influenced by telepathic suggestion.

Q: *(L)* Was she already betrothed at this time?

A: No. Hypnotized level 1.[9]

Q: *(L)* Did Mary and Joseph, once together, subsequently have other children?[10]

A: No. But Jesus did.[11]

Q: *(L)* Jesus had children? Who was he married to?

A: Was not.

Q: *(L)* You mean he had illegitimate children?

A: Subjective institutionally.

Q: *(L)* Who was the mother of these children?

A: There were three women.

Q: *(L)* There were three women?

A: Yes.

Q: *(L)* Are they mentioned in the Bible?

A: One is but not by name.

Q: *(L)* Who was one of them?

A: Alicia.

Q: *(L)* What was the name of the second one?

A: Rafea.

---

[8] Note that the answer here is a "yes," while the previous similar question that was qualified by "other beings or powers" was "close."

[9] This term, 'Level 1,' comes up over and over again throughout the text when a 'predestined mission' is being discussed. So, we might assume that "hypnotized level 1" refers to behavior that is simply driven from the inner self with, perhaps, no conscious understanding of why one is being so driven.

[10] *The Wave* 30

[11] It's interesting that even though I was bound and determined to get answers that satisfied my belief system at the time, the C's kept managing to toss an interesting tidbit into the works. More recent sessions have returned to these issues without the deep assumptions and anticipation that colored religious questions in the early days of the experiment.

[12] In retrospect, this was a really big clue the C's were giving here: that the women who bore the children of 'Jesus' were Romans. That would put 'Jesus' in Rome, i.e. Julius Caesar. See the work of Francesco Carotta for how the gospels actually began as the stories of Caesar's exploits and after his assassination, after his deification and the beginning of his cult all over the Empire, the stories morphed in the telling over the years so that by the time of the Flavians, the story was ripe for being completely re-written, and was. This would explain the remark that one of the women involved with 'Jesus' AKA Julius Caesar, was "mentioned in the Bible."

69 **Q:** *(L)* The third one?

70 **A:** Vella. Romans.[12]

71 **Q:** *(L)* All three of them were Romans?

72 **A:** Yes.

73 **Q:** *(L)* And what happened to the children?[13]

74 **A:** Survived and multiplied fruitfully.

75 **Q:** *(L)* How many children were there from the three mothers?

76 **A:** Three.

77 **Q:** *(L)* Is that, as some people claim, the true meaning of the search for the Holy Grail, that it is not a cup but the 'Sang Real,' or holy blood line?[14]

78 **A:** Yes.

79 **Q:** *(L)* Are there any descendants of Jesus living today?[15]

80 **A:** 364,142.

81 **Q:** *(L)* Was Jesus Christed in the sense of having some special mantle of power falling over him at the time of his baptism?

82 **A:** Nearly correct.

83 **Q:** *(L)* Is Guyana a relatively safe place in terms of Earth crustal movements, Earth changes, etc?

84 **A:** What is? Earth includes all planet surface.

85 **Q:** *(L)* Are there any places that are going to be safer than others?

86 **A:** Changeable.

87 **Q:** *(L)* Is the North Caroline/Blue Ridge Mountain area relatively safe?

88 **A:** What did I just tell you? Depends on vibrational frequency changes. No specific Earth changes are accurately predictable until near event.[16]

89 **Q:** *(LM)* Ask what happened to those people that just died in Switzerland that were talked about on the news. Were they murdered?[17]

90 **A:** Pact. Agreement. Covenant.

91 **Q:** *(L)* They all made a pact to commit suicide together?

92 **A:** Yes.

93 **Q:** *(L)* Why? How many were there?

94 **A:** 48. Religious zealousy.

95 **Q:** *(L)* Did the United States government deliberately murder the Branch Davidians at Waco?[18]

96 **A:** Close. Led them to destroy themselves.

97 **Q:** *(L)* How?

98 **A:** Psychological warfare tactics.

99 **Q:** *(L)* Did the U.S. government set their compound on fire?

100 **A:** No.

---

[13] *The Wave* 30

[14] See *Holy Blood, Holy Grail* by Lincoln, Leigh and Baigent.

[15] *The Wave* 47

[16] This is an important clue that suggests that by changing the vibrational frequency of either ourselves or our planet, or both, that cataclysms can be mitigated.

[17] As we were conducting the session, my ex-husband was watching the 11 o'clock news and the story about the Solar Temple Cult suicide was aired. He came in to ask us to ask the Cassiopaeans what was really behind it since the story was just breaking and there were no details.

[18] *The Wave* 20, 59

101 Q: *(L)* Who set the compound on fire?

102 A: Branch Davidians. Drove them crazy.

103 Q: *(L)* Were ELF or subliminals used?

104 A: Yes. As well as other means.

105 Q: *(L)* Did O.J. Simpson kill his wife?

106 A: Yes.[19]

107 Q: *(L)* Did he take the murder clothes and weapon to Chicago and leave it there in a bag as some people are saying?

108 A: No.

109 Q: *(L)* Where is it?

110 A: LA dump. One of them.

111 Q: *(L)* What gifts did the magi/prophets bring to Jesus as a baby?

112 A: Gold; spices; clothing.

113 Q: *(L)* What other realm did the mother ship come from that was sighted by the magi?

114 A: 5th density.

115 Q: *(L)* And what was the purpose of the appearance of this mother ship at the time of the birth of Jesus?

116 A: Too vague.

117 Q: *(L)* Was it here for specific purposes relating to the birth of Jesus?

118 A: To lead the prophets.

119 Q: *(L)* Was that the main purpose?

120 A: No. Also observation of event and encoding.

121 Q: *(L)* Encoding of what?

122 A: Infant.

123 Q: *(L)* Was that encoding done physically or telepathically?

124 A: Both.

125 Q: *(L)* What realm or area did Jesus come from before he was born into the Earth in the body of Jesus of Nazareth?

126 A: 5th density.

127 Q: *(L)* He was a 5th density soul?

128 A: Yes.

129 Q: *(L)* Had he had any other incarnations in other human bodies on planet Earth?

130 A: Yes.

131 Q: *(L)* How many incarnations did he have before he achieved 5th density?

132 A: 1009.

133 Q: *(L)* Was Melchizedek an incarnation of Jesus?

134 A: No.

135 Q: *(L)* Was Joshua, the right hand man of Moses an incarnation of Jesus?

136 A: Yes.

137 Q: *(L)* Are there any other incarnations of Jesus with which we would be familiar if you were to name them?

138 A: Yes. Socrates.

139 Q: *(L)* What was the spiritual relationship of Jesus to John the Baptist?

140 A: Pact.

141 Q: *(L)* What was the spiritual relationship of Jesus to Mary, his mother?

142 A: Pact.

---

[19] Well, that was a hit, but a lot of people were already thinking that O.J. would beat the charges; he did, and later, a civil court found him guilty.

143 **Q:** *(L)* There was no other spiritual relationship in the sense of being combined souls?[20]

144 **A:** No.

145 **Q:** *(L)* Were either Mary or John the Baptist 5th density souls?

146 **A:** Both.

147 **Q:** *(L)* Are there any 5th density souls on the Earth today or any of recent times we would recognize?

148 **A:** Yes. Arafat. Sadat. Pope John V.

149 **Q:** *(L)* Do demons and evil spirits fear anything?

150 **A:** Yes.

151 **Q:** *(L)* Do they fear any power that we, as humans, possess?

152 **A:** Yes. Knowledge.

153 **Q:** *(L)* Do they fear religious symbols, signs or figures?

154 **A:** No.

155 **Q:** *(L)* Is there any name or sign or symbol that can halt their activity?

156 **A:** Sometimes.[21]

157 **Q:** *(L)* Were they afraid of Christ?

158 **A:** Yes. Because of his knowledge. The mass of his knowledge raised his vibrations. Knowledge is truly power.

159 **Q:** *(L)* Do pentagrams have any effect in slowing down or halting negative entities?

160 **A:** Only if you think they do.

161 **Q:** *(L)* Is the greatest power we have to resist demonic entities held in our free will: our power to say no?

162 **A:** No.

163 **Q:** *(L)* What is our greatest power?

164 **A:** Knowledge.

165 **Q:** *(L)* Does the accumulation of spiritual knowledge hold the key?

166 **A:** Yes.

167 **Q:** *(L)* Is there any other clue you can give us?

168 **A:** You do not need anything else than knowledge.

169 **Q:** *(L)* You said the Exodus occurred in 2676 BC, is that correct?

170 **A:** Close.

171 **Q:** *(L)* Was that the last passage of the cometary Venus?

172 **A:** Yes.

173 **Q:** *(L)* Was this activity of Venus interactive with the close passing of the cluster of comets you have mentioned?

174 **A:** Close. One of three cataclysms close together.

175 **Q:** *(L)* If Venus was one of the cataclysms and the cluster of comets was another, what was the third?

176 **A:** Mars.

177 **Q:** *(L)* Was Mars knocked out of its orbit by Venus?

178 **A:** Yes.

179 **Q:** *(L)* And the two appeared to do battle in the sky to the inhabitants of the

---

[20] I had read where another channeled source suggested that Jesus, John the Baptist and Jesus' mother, Mary, were all parts of a single soul that was too 'immense' to incarnate in a single individual.

[21] It is curious that the Cassiopaeans have said that "demons" do not "fear" religious symbols, signs, or figures, but that there may be some name, sign, or symbol that can halt their activity! A most interesting clue.

Earth as Velikovsky described, is that correct?

180 **A**: Close.

181 **Q**: *(L)* Now, this cluster of comets, when was the last time it came into the solar system?

182 **A**: 3582 yrs ago?

183 **Q**: *(L)* What is the cycle?

184 **A**: 3600 yrs.

185 **Q**: *(L)* So, when is this cluster expected to hit the plane of the ecliptic again?

186 **A**: 12 to 18 years.

187 **Q**: *(L)* Are the aliens traveling with this cluster of comets?

188 **A**: No.

189 **Q**: *(L)* What land did Noah/Utnapishtim live in, what continent?

190 **A**: Atlantis.

191 **Q**: *(L)* Where did the ark land after the receding of the waters?

192 **A**: Egypt.[22]

193 **Q**: *(L)* What caused Martek to pass close to the Earth at that time since that was many thousands of years before the Venus interaction?

194 **A**: Planetary alignment gravitational aberration related to Venus.

195 **Q**: *(L)* So, there was a planetary line-up that caused Mars to be pulled out of its orbit?

196 **A**: Yes.

197 **Q**: *(L)* What was the event a hundred or so years after the flood of Noah that was described as the confusing of languages, or the tower of Babel?[23]

198 **A**: Spiritual confluence.

199 **Q**: *(L)* What purpose did the individuals who came together to build the tower intend for said tower?

200 **A**: Electromagnetic concentration of all gravity waves.

201 **Q**: *(L)* And what did they intend to do with these concentrated waves?

202 **A**: Mind alteration of masses.

203 **Q**: *(L)* What intention did they have in altering the mind of the masses?

204 **A**: Spiritual unification of the masses.

205 **Q**: *(L)* Who were the 'gods' that looked down on the tower of Babel, at those who were building it with the intention of unification, and decided to destroy their works?

206 **A**: Lizards.

207 **Q**: *(L)* OK, so the Lizzies blew up the tower of Babel. What else did they do to the minds of mankind; did they do something causing literal disruption of their understanding of language?

208 **A**: Close.

209 **Q**: *(L)* What tool did they use to accomplish this divisiveness?

210 **A**: Brainwashing of masses.

211 **Q**: *(L)* Did they do this through implants and abduction?

212 **A**: Partly.

213 **Q**: *(L)* What is the true meaning, the original meaning, of the Hebrew word *shem*?

---

[22] Here the question needs to be asked: which Egypt? The ancient land or the land we know today as Egypt? I suspect it was the ancient one and that Iman Wilkens is correct locating it in Northwest France.

[23] *The Wave* 24, 25

214 **A**: Purity.

215 **Q**: *(L)* Why was this word related to the obelisks or standing stones later called *shems* by the Hebrews?

216 **A**: Symbolic of purity: unification. Uniformity.

217 **Q**: *(L)* Did these stones themselves actually possess any power?

218 **A**: Residual.

219 **Q**: *(L)* What object were the ancients going to place in the tower of Babel to...

220 **A**: Crystal.

221 **Q**: *(L)* Is *shem* also synonymous with 'crystal'?

222 **A**: Close.

223 **Q**: *(L)* Shem, the son of Noah, was the ancestor of the group that built the tower, is this correct?

224 **A**: Yes.[24]

225 **Q**: *(L)* How were Sodom and Gomorrah destroyed and the other cities of the plain? And by whom?

226 **A**: Nuclear; EM pulse. Who else?[25]

227 **Q**: *(L)* The Lizzies?

228 **A**: Yes.

---

[24] Z. Sitchen writes in *The 12th Planet*, Avon Books, New York, 1978:

> The Mesopotamian texts that refer to the inner enclosures of temples, or to the heavenly journeys of the gods, or even to instances where mortals ascended to the heavens, employ the Sumerian term *mu* or its Semitic derivatives *shu-mu* ("that which is a *mu*"), *sham*, or *shem*. Because the term also connoted "that by which one is remembered," the word has come to be taken as meaning "name." ... Thus G.A. Barton (*The Royal Inscriptions of Sumer and Akkad*) established the unchallenged translation of Gudea's temple inscription – that "Its MU shall hug the lands from horizon to horizon" – that "Its name shall fill the lands." A hymn to Ishkur, extolling his "ray-emitting MU" that could attain the heights of Heaven, was likewise rendered: "Thy name is radiant, it reaches Heaven's zenith." ... It is not too difficult to trace the etymology of the term, and the route by which the "sky chamber" assumed the meaning of "name." Sculptures have been found that show a god inside a rocket-shaped chamber, as in this object of extreme antiquity ... where the celestial nature of the chamber is attested by the twelve gloves decorating it. Many seals similarly depict a god (and sometimes two) within such oval "divine chambers"; in most instances these gods within their sacred ovals were depicted as objects of veneration. ... The ancient peoples developed the custom of setting up imitations of the god within his divine "sky chamber." Stone pillars shaped to simulate the oval vehicle were erected at selected sites ... That the purpose of the commemorative stone pillars was to simulate a fiery sky-ship can further be gleaned from the term by which such stone stelae were known in antiquity. The Sumerians called them NA.RU ("stones that rise"). The Akkadians, Babylonians, and Assyrians called them *naru* ("objects that give off light"). The Amurru called them *nuras* ("fiery objects" – in Hebrew, *ner* still means a pillar that emits light...).

So, we see where Sitchin is going: a *shem* is a rocket ship. Never mind the fact that the descriptions in the ancient writings fit much better with a comet and the stones that fall from the sky when comets and concomitant plasma activity are prevalent. Such stones are known to have been worshiped by the ancients as actual pieces of the god and therefore, objects of unification of a population.

[25] *The Wave* 24

Q: *(L)* Why?

A: To implant fear and obedience.

Q: *(L)* Weren't the Sodom and Gomorrans really evil and bad doing sodomy and Gomorrahy?[26]

A: That is a deception of history.

Q: *(L)* Did Lot's wife get turned into a pillar of salt?

A: No.

Q: *(L)* Is there any symbolism in that particular story for us today?

A: No.

Q: *(L)* Was the god who communicated with Abraham one of the Lizzies?

A: Yes.

Q: *(L)* Was the pact that Abraham made with the Lizzies?

A: Yes. Not directly.

Q: *(L)* Was Melchizedek a priest of the Lizzies?

A: No.

Q: *(L)* Did Melchizedek give Abraham the true information?

A: Close.

Q: *(L)* Is the Kaballah the true teachings of the good guys?

A: Close.

Q: *(L)* Is the Osirian cycle the exemplification of the action of the Lizzies upon mankind in terms of the cutting up of Osiris' body as the breaking apart of the strands of DNA?

A: Close.[27]

Q: *(L)* What was the fruit of the tree of knowledge of good and evil that was supposedly eaten by Eve and then offered to Adam?[28]

A: Knowledge restriction. Encoding.

Q: *(L)* What did it mean when it said Eve ate of the fruit of the tree of knowledge? What act did she perform to do that?

A: Consorted with wrong side.

Q: *(L)* What does consorted mean?

A: Eve is symbolic.

Q: *(L)* Symbolic of what?

A: Female energy.

Q: *(L)* The female energy did what when it consorted?

A: Lost some knowledge and power.

Q: *(L)* Why was the eating of the fruit of this tree called knowledge of good and evil feared by God or gods to enable Eve to be equated with gods?

A: What? Clarify please.

Q: *(L)* Who was the god that feared that the eating of this fruit would make Eve equal to him or them?

---

[26] Well, the word Sodom has been used to coin the word 'sodomy,' so why not Gomorrahy? I have *no* idea what it might be, so the reader can use their imagination.

[27] See my recent book *Comets and the Horns of Moses* for more up-to-date research on this. It seems obvious now that the myth of Osiris was just a take-off on the myth of the dismemberment of Dionysos by the Titans and was a 'comet story' at its root. However, as I discussed in *Comets and the Horns of Moses*, comet events may be the cause of mutations to DNA. So, yes, considering the imprecision of the question, the right answer was "close."

[28] *The Wave* 3, 23

262 **A:** No.[29]

263 **Q:** *(L)* The Bible says that these gods said that they were afraid that man would now take hold of the fruit of the tree of life and live forever. What does this mean? Why did the eating of this fruit make God afraid?

264 **A:** Did not.

265 **Q:** *(L)* What was the fruit of the tree of life?

266 **A:** Limitation.

267 **Q:** *(L)* How can the fruit of the tree of eternal life be limitation?

268 **A:** Conceptually limited.

269 **Q:** *(L)* I want you to know that this does not make a whole lot of sense.[30]

270 **A:** Yes it does. Think carefully.

271 **Q:** *(L)* Was the god who walked in the garden who warned Adam and Eve not to eat of the fruit of the tree of knowledge of good and evil, was that the original creator god, i.e. the good guy?

272 **A:** No.

273 **Q:** *(L)* Who was that god who ordered them not to eat of this tree?

274 **A:** Complicated. Laura you are missing the obvious.

275 **Q:** *(L)* In what sense would the fruit of the tree of life be limiting?

276 **A:** Believing that one source contains all knowledge is contradicting reality.

277 **Q:** *(L)* What was the flaming sword barring re-entry to Eden?

278 **A:** Do you not understand?

279 **Q:** *(L)* No I do not understand.

---
[29] They were right. I had the trees confused.
[30] *The Wave* 3, 23

280 **A:** Review. If the concept was the eating of the fruit of the tree of knowledge provides all knowledge, then one is being deceived, because no one particular source can provide all knowledge. Therefore, when one believes in the deception, one has now trapped oneself within parameters. And, forevermore, the human race, will be poisoned by the very same problem which is reflected in several different ways: one is always seeking the truth through one pathway instead of seeking it through a myriad of pathways; and also believing in simplistic answers to very complex issues and questions.

281 **Q:** *(L)* What was the flaming sword barring re-entry into the garden of Eden?

282 **A:** Symbolizes trap.

283 **Q:** *(L)* A self-imposed flaming sword?

284 **A:** Yes.

285 **Q:** *(L)* Where was Eden?

286 **A:** Earth.

287 **Q:** *(L)* The entire Earth was Eden?

288 **A:** Yes.

289 **Q:** *(L)* Was the 'Fall' in Eden, or the loss of the Edenic state, also accompanied by a cataclysm?

290 **A:** Yes.

291 **Q:** *(L)* What was the nature of that cataclysm?

292 **A:** Comets.

293 **Q:** *(L)* The cluster you have mentioned before?

294 **A:** Yes.

295 **Q:** *(L)* And, how long ago did this occur?

296 **A**: 309,882 years ago.

297 **Q**: *(L)* Was the loss of the Edenic state also accompanied by a takeover of mankind by the Lizzies?

298 **A**: Yes.

299 **Q**: *(L)* Who were the original creator gods?[31]

300 **A**: Us. Sixth density.

301 **Q**: *(L)* The Cassiopaeans? Were the Pleiadians also the original creator gods?

302 **A**: Same. Sixth density.[32]

303 **Q**: *(L)* What was the true identity of the serpent in Eden?

304 **A**: Lizards.

305 **Q**: *(L)* Who built the Great Pyramid?

306 **A**: Atlanteans.

307 **Q**: *(L)* What year was it built?

308 **A**: 10,643 years ago.

309 **Q**: *(L)* Why was it built? What purpose was it used for?

310 **A**: Capture cosmic energy.

311 **Q**: *(L)* And what was this cosmic energy used for once it was captured?

312 **A**: Many things. Power, transport, healing, mind control, climate, et cetera.

313 **Q**: *(L)* Who built the sphinx?

314 **A**: Same.

315 **Q**: *(L)* Was the sphinx built at the same time?

316 **A**: Yes.

317 **Q**: *(L)* Why was the sphinx built? What was its purpose?

318 **A**: Temple.

319 **Q**: *(L)* Are there records buried under the sphinx?

320 **A**: Yes.

321 **Q**: *(L)* What happened to Neanderthal man?[33]

322 **A**: Removed by Lizzies to other planets.

323 **Q**: *(L)* Is that removed as in taken off the planet physically?

324 **A**: Yes.

325 **Q**: *(L)* What planet were they taken to?

326 **A**: Others.

327 **Q**: *(L)* Of the several places around this country that we have thought about moving, which one would we be happiest in?

328 **A**: Indefinite.

329 **Q**: *(L)* Would we be happy in the Blue Mountains in Oregon.

330 **A**: Not determinable.

331 **Q**: *(L)* Shouldn't you be able to give prophetic insights?[34]

---

[31] *The Wave* 65

[32] Note that the Cassiopaeans do not claim to be *the* creator gods, but that it is a function of 6th density.

[33] *The Wave* 68

[34] I was still stuck on the idea that a truly 'valid' source would just give reams of prophecies that would come true. But, as we shall see, any source that does so as a 'habit' is doomed to failure because of the probabilistic nature of reality. The future is not absolutely fixed! And therefore, only probabilities can be given, and then, usually, only just before the event. However, the cyclical nature of 'time' does give us a field of probabilities, and we were learning gradually of what this field consisted.

332 **A**: Too many variables in this matter.[35]   End of session

---

[35] And that was, in the end, the crux of the matter of predictions: the many variables. But that then leaves us with those predictions that were made and were close enough that we can assume that in spite of variables, some things can be known in advance.

October 7, 1994

Participants: 'Frank' and Laura

1 **Q**: Hello.

2 **A**: Hello.

3 **Q**: *(L)* What's your name?

4 **A**: Bayreera.

5 **Q**: *(L)* Where are you from?

6 **A**: Cassiopaea.

7 **Q**: *(L)* Are you the next in line for the energy disbursement?

8 **A**: Precisely. You are learning well.

9 **Q**: *(L)* Are you disbursing the energy to us?

10 **A**: No.

11 **Q**: *(L)* Are we giving energy to you?

12 **A**: Near. Our disbursement is akin to taking turns.

13 **Q**: *(L)* Is there an advantage to taking turns as opposed to having one communicant?

14 **A**: Yes.

15 **Q**: *(L)* What is the advantage?

16 **A**: Energy equalization.

17 **Q**: *(L)* Is it difficult for you to make contact with us?

18 **A**: No.

19 **Q**: *(L)* Would it be difficult for you to make contact with others?

20 **A**: Becoming easier with you.

21 **Q**: *(L)* I would like to know the time of the Great Dying of the major dinosaurs, the big critters?

22 **A**: 27 million years as measured by your scale.

23 **Q**: *(L)* Regarding the 'Fall' in Eden and the loss of the Edenic state, how long ago did that happen?

24 **A**: 309,000 years ago approx. [1]

25 **Q**: *(L)* What was the situation... what happened... what was the state of mankind?

26 **A**: Loss of faith caused knowledge and physical restrictions by outside forces.

27 **Q**: *(L)* What did the snake or the 'tempter' represent?

28 **A**: Forces known to you as Lizzies; we have already taught you this.

29 **Q**: *(L)* I am just checking!

30 **A**: Faith dear.

31 **Q**: *(L)* I'm having faith, I'm just checking.

32 **A**: Suit yourself.

33 **Q**: *(L)* Who were the original creators of the human race?

34 **A**: Us.

35 **Q**: *(L)* The Cassiopaeans, correct?

36 **A**: Yes.

---
[1] *The Wave* 68

37 **Q:** *(L)* For what purpose did you create us? Was it a mandate from God?

38 **A:** Soul development or advancement.

39 **Q:** *(L)* The Sumerian story of the creation of human beings involves a story where they say they killed a god and mixed his blood and parts to mix with mud and then planted it in these female 'gestation' goddesses and that this is where the human race came from. Now, this sounds an awful lot like what the 'Grays' are doing at the present time. Did someone actually kill a 'god,' break his soul in pieces, and thereby make the human race? [2]

40 **A:** Symbolism and not correct event sequence. [3]

41 **Q:** *(L)* What was that story about? What was the real seed event?

42 **A:** Lizard beings genetically altering the human race after battle for their own feeding purposes. [4]

43 **Q:** *(L)* When did these events that these Sumerian stories are talking about take place?

44 **A:** 309,000 years ago, approx.

45 **Q:** *(L)* So, it happened so long ago that these stories have lost the truth?

46 **A:** Reflection passed down through psychic memory channel.

47 **Q:** *(L)* What killed off the major dinosaurs?

48 **A:** Comet impact.

49 **Q:** *(L)* What was the source of this comet?

50 **A:** Cluster.

51 **Q:** *(L)* How long has this comet cluster been with us in our solar system?

52 **A:** 890 million years.[5]

53 **Q:** *(L)* What was the origin of this comet cluster? Was it originally a large planet?

54 **A:** No.

55 **Q:** *(L)* You said the other night that there was a planet between Mars and Jupiter that was destroyed and became the asteroid belt. Was this planet ever inhabited by sentient beings?

56 **A:** Yes.

57 **Q:** *(L)* What caused this planet to be destroyed?

---

[2] *The Wave* 68

[3] *High Strangeness* 10

[4] After many more years of research this response makes more sense. The 'battle' is the bombardment of Earth by comets and/or fragments as has happened on repeated occasions. Keep in mind that a previous session described 4D battles manifesting as weather first and then moving into our realty as, I think, comets. Studying the ancient myths and legends in the light of the work of Victor Clube, Bill Napier, Mike Baillie, Firestone, West and Warwick-Smith, makes it clear that this 'breaking up of a god' was a violent cometary event. After the dust settled, the survivors possibly experienced genetic changes and went on to create myths about their gods and the origins of their own group. As to whether or not there was direct manipulation of genetics I can't say; research from the past 20 years suggests that such manipulation can easily be done by introducing a virus into a population. So, again, we see the metaphoric/symbolic nature of the communication.

[5] This differs from the ideas of Clube, Napier, et al., who suggest that a giant comet entered our solar system something like 40 thousand years.

58 **A**: Psychic energy.[6]

59 **Q**: *(L)* And where did the beings come from that lived on this planet? Did they evolve there?

60 **A**: No.

61 **Q**: *(L)* Were they also, like us, created beings?

62 **A**: Yes.

63 **Q**: *(L)* Who created them?

64 **A**: Same.

65 **Q**: *(L)* The Cassiopaeans?[7]

66 **A**: Yes.

67 **Q**: *(L)* OK, who created the Cassiopaeans?[8]

68 **A**: Your super ancient spiritual ancestors.

69 **Q**: *(L)* Do these beings have a name?

70 **A**: No.

71 **Q**: *(L)* What are they called?

72 **A**: Transient Passengers.[9]

73 **Q**: *(L)* Where are these "Transient Passengers" from?

74 **A**: Too difficult to explain on this medium; lengthy.

75 **Q**: *(L)* What is the closest you know to the original God/Creator force?

76 **A**: Seek other media. Computer.

77 **Q**: *(L)* This cluster of comets that you talk about that caused an impact, did one of the cluster impact the Earth at the time of the dinosaur dyings?

78 **A**: No one was large enough for event.

79 **Q**: *(L)* Was it some of these comets in the cluster that hit the Earth?

80 **A**: Yes. 14 hit at that occasion.

81 **Q**: *(L)* Does this cluster of comets orbit around the sun?[10]

82 **A**: Yes. Your government already knows they're coming close again.[11]

83 **Q**: *(L)* You said that the orbit is around the sun. Where does it enter the plane of the ecliptic?

84 **A**: Varies.

85 **Q**: *(L)* Does it enter between Mars and Jupiter, for example?

86 **A**: Sometimes.

87 **Q**: *(L)* Is the orbit perpendicular to the plane of the ecliptic? Or is it at an angle?

---

[6] See Pierre Lescaudron's book *Earth Changes and the Human-Cosmic Connection* to understand how human beings can be very much involved in the destruction of a planet and it's looking like ours is heading that direction.

[7] *The Wave* 9

[8] *Secret History* 12; *The Wave* 26

[9] This term is curious, for sure. It becomes even more interesting when taken in conjunction with another response that was to come in the session 3 December 1994, where the Wave is described as "feeling, hyperkinetic sensate." These terms considered in the light of Information Theory may actually make sense. But at the time, obviously, I was totally in the dark about many things.

[10] *The Wave* 1

[11] This is another very interesting remark in view of the conspiracies the C's expose throughout the transcripts. Apparently the Powers That Be *(PTB)* have some idea of what is coming but have no intention of informing the populace; for them, it's all about maintaining their control and dominance right to the bitter end.

88 **A**: In between.

89 **Q**: *(L)* What degrees of angle does it intersect the plane of the ecliptic?

90 **A**: Not correct idea structure. Picture a spirograph.

91 **Q**: *(L)* Do the comets orbit around themselves? Do they have a sort of axis?

92 **A**: No.

93 **Q**: *(L)* How many are in this cluster?

94 **A**: Varies.

95 **Q**: *(L)* Do they lose or pick any up from time to time?

96 **A**: Yes.

97 **Q**: *(L)* How big is the biggest one at this time?

98 **A**: 900 miles diameter. Spirograph.

99 **Q**: *(L)* The planet that was destroyed between Jupiter and Mars, you said was destroyed by psychic energy?[12]

100 **A**: Yes.

101 **Q**: *(L)* What was the source of this psychic energy?

102 **A**: Beings inhabiting the planet.

103 **Q**: *(L)* Do beings in this area of the galaxy just sort of destroy their planets from time to time? Is this getting to be a habit?

104 **A**: Close. Has been.

105 **Q**: *(L)* Did any of those beings leave that planet and come to Earth?

106 **A**: Yes.

107 **Q**: *(L)* Who were they? Were they humans like us?

108 **A**: Blond and blue eyed descendants.

109 **Q**: *(L)* Was that a colder planet?

110 **A**: No.

111 **Q**: *(L)* Was that planet much like Earth?

112 **A**: Yes.

113 **A**: Blue eyes. Eye pigment was because planet was farther from Sol.

114 **Q**: *(L)* How did the people of that planet come to Earth? Did they know it was going to be destroyed?

115 **A**: Some knew and were taken by Lizzies and they are the Annunaki.

116 **Q**: *(L)* Now, you say that the father of Jesus was an Aryan. Where did he come from?

117 **A**: Palestine.

118 **Q**: *(L)* What is the origin of the Aryan race?

---

[12] *The Wave* 24

[13]The asteroid belt is a doughnut-shaped concentration of asteroids orbiting the sun between the orbits of Mars and Jupiter, closer to the orbit of Mars. The asteroids have a slightly elliptical orbit. The time for one revolution around the sun varies from about three to six Earth years. The strong gravitational force of the planet Jupiter shepherds the asteroid belt, pulling the asteroids away from the sun, keeping them from careening into the inner planets. Whether or not the asteroid belt is the remains of a planet that was destroyed cannot be definitely affirmed or denied. After reading a number of books and papers on the subject, one finds that those who say 'impossible' don't have much to back them up, and those who think that it might be possible can't prove anything either. Those who think it was a planet suppose that it might have been fragmented by an impact by a large comet.

119 **A:** 5th planet now know as asteroid belt.[13]

120 **Q:** *(L)* When did they come to Earth?

121 **A:** 80 thousand years ago? Difficult for us to use your measuring system.

122 **Q:** *(L)* Were they similar in form and structure to what they are now?

123 **A:** Yes.

124 **Q:** *(L)* Why is it that our scientists have not been able to uncover evidence of such ancient existence?

125 **A:** They have. Do not want to acknowledge it.

126 **Q:** *(L)* Where do the Celts come from?

127 **A:** Same. Ferocious people. Came from fifth planet.

128 **Q:** *(L)* When was that planet destroyed?

129 **A:** 80 thousand years ago.

130 **Q:** *(L)* Were any of the descendants of Jesus famous individuals that we would know?

131 **A:** Yes. Yassar Arafat. Churchill.

132 **Q:** *(L)* You said that the Exodus occurred in 2676; is that BC or years ago?

133 **A:** B.C.

134 **Q:** *(L)* If the Exodus occurred in 2676 BC, that is 4,670 years ago more or less, this would mean that this was not related to the comet cluster which came in 1588 BC.

135 **A:** Correct.

136 **Q:** *(L)* Then, the comet cluster came by 8788 BC, is that correct?

137 **A:** Close enough.

138 **Q:** *(L)* Was there any historical cataclysm recorded in history that we could relate to that passing?

139 **A:** No.[14]

140 **Q:** *(L)* And Noah's flood occurred 12,388 BC, is that correct?

141 **A:** Close.

142 **Q:** *(L)* Now, the time of the passage of Venus was the time of the Exodus, is that correct? Was Venus a result of this cluster of comets?

143 **A:** Semi-stimulated by gravitational pull.

144 **Q:** *(L)* Venus was stimulated by the gravitational pull?

145 **A:** Attracted.

146 **Q:** *(L)* Venus was drawn into the solar system by the gravitational pull of the cluster of comets?

---

[14] In the years since this session, the research has turned up quite a few dates relating to wide-ranging environmental downturns, but you rarely find them all listed in a single source. From one ice-core study we have the following as years before 2000: 14,776, 14,692, 14,075, 12,896, 12,171, 11,703, 10,347, 8236, 7903. (S. O. Rasmussen et al. (2006) "A new Greenland ice core chronology for the last glacial Termination"; *Journal of Geophysical Research*, vol. 111, D06102) From Mike Baillie's tree rings we have 2354 BC, 1628 BC, 1159 BC, 208 BC, 540 AD. The 540 event is attested in tree-ring chronologies from Siberia through Europe and North and South America. This event coincides with the second largest ammonium signal in the Greenland ice in the last two millennia, the largest being in AD 1014, and both these epochs were accompanied by cometary apparitions. And so on. I won't list all the data and sources here but rather refer you to my recent book *Comets and the Horns of Moses*.

147 **A:** Yes.

148 **Q:** *(L)* Where did Venus get all its gases and clouds and so forth? What was its origin? Where did it get all this stuff?

149 **A:** Collected during fiery, friction filled journey and space matter in general.

150 **Q:** *(L)* Where was Venus originally from?

151 **A:** Ancient wanderer from near Arcturus.[15]

152 **Q:** *(L)* What are Mars's moons?

153 **A:** Disguised bases.

154 **Q:** *(L)* Who built them?

155 **A:** Who else? The Lizzies.

156 **Q:** *(L)* The film I saw at Andy's house, the Mars landing, was that an actual film of a Mars landing?

157 **A:** False.

158 **Q:** *(L)* Has there been a landing on Mars by the United States?

159 **A:** No.

---

[15] In 1967, a Russian space probe, Venera 4, and the American Mariner 5 arrived at Venus within a few hours of each other. Venera 4 was designed to allow an instrument package to land gently on the planet's surface via parachute. It ceased transmission of information in about 75 minutes when the temperature it read went above 500 degrees F. After considerable controversy, it was agreed that it still had 20 miles to go to reach the surface. The U.S. probe, Mariner 5, went around the dark side of Venus at a distance of about 6,000 miles. Again it detected no significant magnetic field but its radio signals passed to Earth through Venus's atmosphere twice – once on the night side and once on the day side. The results are startling. Venus's atmosphere is nearly all carbon dioxide and must exert a pressure at the planet's surface of up to 100 times the Earth's normal sea-level pressure of one atmosphere. Since the Earth and Venus are about the same size, and were presumably formed at the same time by the same general process from the same mixture of chemical elements, one is faced with the question: which is the planet with the unusual history – Earth or Venus? See also article "Rogue Planets Can Find Homes Around Other Stars" by Nancy Atkinson, *Universe Today*, http://www.sott.net/article/244 209

[16] Al Bielek is, apparently, a convincing speaker in the eyes of some people. He presents a wide range of popular references during his talks and weaves quite a tale in the telling. However, the information available prior to the 1983 movie, *The Philadelphia Experiment*, did not concern the prospect of time transport. The stated focus of the 'Philadelphia Experiment' project was to "achieve radar invisibility." Mr. Bielek states that his "memories began coming back *after* seeing the movie in 1988."

Many people get the impression that he incorporates new topics into his storyline as fast as he hears them, claiming that his "memory suddenly came back on that." One major flaw in his story is the statement that Nikola Tesla was in association with and in charge of the Philadelphia project. This is highly incredible since the experiment supposedly occurred in July 1943 and Tesla died on January 7, 1943, in New York City. Dr. Von Neumann (of computer fame) was supposedly involved in the 'Philadelphia Experiment' with Tesla, Einstein and LeBon. Bielek says he is recorded to have died in 1953 or 1957.

In Phoenix, 1986, Bielek's memories recalled a site in Montauk which, according to Bielek, "might be where Von Neumann currently resides in obscurity." Another

160 **Q:** *(L)* Is Al Bielek a phony?[16]
161 **A:** Semi.
162 **Q:** *(L)* Did he work on the Philadelphia project?
163 **A:** No.
164 **Q:** *(L)* Was he brainwashed to have fake outrageous memories?
165 **A:** No.
166 **Q:** *(L)* Is he lying deliberately?
167 **A:** Instructed by government for disinformation dissemination.
168 **Q:** *(L)* Did a spacecraft of the Lizzies piloted by the Grays crash in Roswell?
169 **A:** Yes.
170 **Q:** *(L)* What caused the crash?
171 **A:** Ionization.
172 **Q:** *(L)* Were the bodies and the craft recovered by the United States government?
173 **A:** Yes.
174 **Q:** *(L)* Are the Majestic 12 documents...
175 **A:** Semi-factual.
176 **Q:** *(L)* Were they dummied up?
177 **A:** Near.
178 **Q:** *(L)* Who did this and why?
179 **A:** To leak information and disinformation. Many were involved. ONI and CIA.
180 **Q:** *(L)* Is the information in the book *Majestic* by Whitley Strieber factual?
181 **A:** Semi-factual. There are many glaring falsehoods.
182 **Q:** *(L)* What is the source of the Native American Indians?
183 **A:** Asia.
184 **Q:** *(L)* Across the Bering Strait?
185 **A:** No. Rescued. Transferred.
186 **Q:** *(L)* By whom?
187 **A:** Grays.
188 **Q:** *(L)* What were they rescued out of?
189 **A:** Cataclysm.
190 **Q:** *(L)* When did that cataclysm occur?
191 **A:** 7200 years ago approx.
192 **Q:** *(L)* What was the nature of that cataclysm?[17]
193 **A:** Comets.
194 **Q:** *(L)* Where do the Basques come from?
195 **A:** Atlantis.
196 **Q:** *(L)* Is their language the Atlantean language?

---

major discrepancy, records indicate the original manned experiment occurred on October 28, 1943, *not* the 12th of August, 1943. Despite the irregularities, there were some interesting comments made in regard to time. The two most outstanding things about the public lecture was the showing of a slide purported to be a 'Zero Time Reference Generator' which looks strangely similar to an old Army field kitchen refrigeration unit, according to Chuck Henderson's military experience. No technical details were given or offered. This device was purported to be the oscillator which drove the coils of the experiment. Mr. Bielek claimed that the unit shown was used to synchronize two separate signals (one for each coil).

The literature of the 'Philadelphia Experiment' is replete with descriptions of the technology. If you get the chance to hear Mr. Bielek, it is highly recommended if only for entertainment. However, if you want usable data, good luck!

[17] *The Wave* 3

197 **A:** Derivative.

198 **Q:** *(L)* Which came first, the Sumerians or the Egyptians?

199 **A:** Sumerians.

200 **Q:** *(L)* Where did the Egyptians come from?

201 **A:** Atlantis.

202 **Q:** *(L)* Which came first, the Sumerians or Atlanteans?

203 **A:** Atlanteans.

204 **Q:** *(L)* Were the Sumerians a high civilization at the same time the Atlanteans were?

205 **A:** After.

206 **Q:** *(L)* Did the Atlanteans go to Sumeria and afterwards go to Egypt?

207 **A:** Traveled.

208 **Q:** *(L)* The Atlanteans traveled to Sumeria?

209 **A:** Yes.

210 **Q:** *(L)* Did they set up outposts in Sumeria?

211 **A:** Yes.

212 **Q:** *(L)* Then did the main Atlanteans move to Egypt when Atlantis was destroyed?

213 **A:** Yes. And elsewhere.

214 **Q:** *(L)* Where else did the Atlanteans go?

215 **A:** Americas. Inca. Aztec. Maya. Hopi Tribe. Pima tribe.

216 **Q:** *(L)* When the Jews were dispersed, did some of them come to America?

217 **A:** A few.

218 **Q:** *(L)* Who was the angel who communicated with the Prophet Daniel?

219 **A:** Us.[18]

220 **Q:** *(L)* Who gave John Revelation?

221 **A:** The Lizzies.[19]

222 **Q:** *(L)* Who did Paul encounter on the road to Damascus?

223 **A:** Spirit of the 6th density.

224 **Q:** *(L)* If the Revelations are from the 'bad' guys, are they an accurate portrayal of the end times?

225 **A:** Close.

226 **Q:** *(L)* What was the source of the prophecies of Isaiah?

227 **A:** Fiction.

228 **Q:** *(L)* What was the source of the so-called Cassiopaeans when Scarlett was present? Was that you guys?

229 **A:** Mixed.[20]

230 **Q:** *(L)* Does Jupiter have a solid core?

231 **A:** Yes.

232 **Q:** *(L)* Was Zecharia Sitchin correct in his naming of the planets?

233 **A:** No.

---

[18] That's even assuming that Daniel was a historical person, which I seriously doubt.

[19] Which does not, of course, mean that they can't tell the truth sometimes!

[20] Pay particular note to this remark above. It was my sensation that Scarlett was a corrupting influence in her participation and focus on personal issues, and here we have the C's confirming this. Keeping the connection clean has been an ongoing problem. Very often, the presence of a person with extremely negative, low or even aggressive attitude can 'skew' the reception. But even in such cases, we are often able to retrieve the Cassiopaean intent by careful study.

234 **Q:** *(L)* Was the interpretation I gave to it more correct.

235 **A:** Better but needs help.

236 **Q:** *(L)* True meaning of the word *shem*?[21]

237 **A:** Purity.

238 **Q:** *(L)* What language is the root of this word found in?

239 **A:** Atlantean. Hebrew.

240 **Q:** *(L)* Where did the Jews come from?

241 **A:** Atlantis.

242 **Q:** *(L)* Who was Yahweh?

243 **A:** Fictional being.

244 **Q:** *(L)* Who was the god that spoke to Moses on the mount?

245 **A:** Audible projection of Lizards.

246 **Q:** *(L)* Did Moses at any time realize that he had been duped by the Lizzies?

247 **A:** No.

248 **Q:** *(L)* Yet, the other night you said that Moses is also doing work with Christ on another plane, is that correct?

249 **A:** Yes.

250 **Q:** *(L)* Well, if he was misled by the Lizzies, how did he get to be a good guy?

251 **A:** Taught afterward.[22]

252 **Q:** *(L)* After what?

253 **A:** Plane transfer.

254 **Q:** *(L)* Did Moses die?

255 **A:** No.

256 **Q:** *(L)* Who took him?

257 **A:** Us.

End of Session.

---

[21] The reader will notice that I often ask the same questions over again, sometimes in a different way, and sometimes not. This was my way of 'testing' the source in terms of consistency over time.

[22] This is an important point because it signifies that even if a person is deceived while in the body, the true frequency of that individual, and their intent to be of Service to Others, means a lot.

October 9, 1994

Once again, this is a forensic session where I am asking many questions in order to gather analyzable data.

Participants: 'Frank' and Laura

1 **Q**: Hello.

2 **A**: Hello.

3 **Q**: Who do we have with us?

4 **A**: Baderea.

5 **Q**: *(L)* What do the Cassiopaeans look like?

6 **A**: Light form.

7 **Q**: *(L)* What do you mean by light form?

8 **A**: Humanoid light form.

9 **Q**: *(L)* Are you physical in atomic terms?

10 **A**: All according to the perceiver.

11 **Q**: *(L)* Do you mean you arrange yourselves according to what the perceiver wants?

12 **A**: No. It is according to perception capacity.

13 **Q**: *(L)* Can you appear to us?

14 **A**: No. Vibrational frequency envelope of your density prevents this.

15 **Q**: *(L)* Are you ever in any way physical?

16 **A**: Varying degrees according to realm.

17 **Q**: *(L)* Why are you communicating with us?

18 **A**: Because you called.

19 **Q**: *(L)* What are the differences between the Celts and the Aryans?

20 **A**: Geographic and cultural.

21 **Q**: *(L)* Are there any differences inherent from the former planetary home?

22 **A**: No. Post arrival difference development.

23 **Q**: *(L)* Were they the same prior to arrival?

24 **A**: Yes.

25 **Q**: *(L)* Was Mars ever inhabited?

26 **A**: Yes.

27 **Q**: *(L)* By whom?

28 **A**: By those you now know as Sasquatch or Bigfoot.

29 **Q**: *(L)* Do they now live on this planet as a result of being brought here by other beings?

30 **A**: They are transitory. Do not inhabit on a permanent basis.

31 **Q**: *(L)* Well, how do they come and go?

32 **A**: They are the slaves and "pets" of the Lizard beings.

33 **Q**: *(L)* How did the Sasquatch get here from Mars?

34 **A**: Brought by Lizard beings but they do not inhabit Earth.[1]

35 **Q**: *(L)* Why have Sasquatch been seen in remote places throughout history?

36 **A**: Put there for menial slave tasks.

37 **Q**: *(L)* Does that mean that whenever Sasquatch have been seen that there is a Lizard nearby?

38 **A**: No.

39 **Q**: *(L)* What menial tasks might they be doing?

40 **A**: Collecting samples.

41 **Q**: *(L)* Why has everyone who has ever come in contact with Sasquatch commented on the awful odor of them? Why do they stink?

42 **A**: Organic functions.

43 **Q**: *(L)* What is it about their organic functions that makes them stink?

44 **A**: Sweat.

45 **Q**: *(L)* Who killed Sir Harry Oakes?[2]

46 **A**: David Crofts.[3]

47 **Q**: *(L)* Who was St. Issa of India?[4]

---

[1] It's interesting that they repeat again, as if for emphasis, that Sasquatch/Yeti do not 'inhabit' Earth, but are more or less transitory.

[2] I was particularly interested in this case because my grandparents were acquainted with Harry Oakes through their mutual friend, Sir Roland Symonette, and after Oakes died, my grandmother purchased a number of pieces of porcelain ornaments from the estate sale which are now in my possession. The story of their acquisition was a thrilling tale of my childhood. Wikipedia:

> "Sir Harry Oakes, 1st Baronet (23 December 1874 – 7 July 1943) was an American-born British Canadian gold mine owner, entrepreneur, investor and philanthropist. He earned his fortune in Canada and in the 1930s moved to the Bahamas for tax purposes, where he was murdered in 1943 in notorious circumstances. The cause of death and the details surrounding it have never been entirely determined, and have been the subject of several books and four films." [http://en.wikipedia.org/wiki/Harry_Oakes]

[3] On the second day of the investigation, 36 hours after Oakes's body was discovered, they had arrested Oakes's son-in-law, Count Alfred de Marigny. He was committed for trial, and a rope was ordered for his hanging. However, he was acquitted in a trial that lasted several weeks, after the detectives were suspected of fabricating evidence against him. Oakes's murderer has never been found, and there were no court proceedings in the case after de Marigny's acquittal. The case received worldwide press coverage at the time.

[4] The use of the 'lost years' in the 'swoon hypothesis' suggests that Jesus survived his crucifixion and continued his life. This, and the related view that he avoided crucifixion altogether, has given rise to several speculations about what happened to him in the supposed remaining years of his life. In 1887 a Russian war correspondent, Nicolas Notovitch, claimed that while at the Hemis Monastery in Ladakh, he had learned of the document "Life of Saint Issa, Best of the Sons of Men" – Isa being the Arabic name of Jesus in Islam. Notovitch's story, with a translated text of the "Life of Saint Issa," was published in French in 1894 as *La vie inconnue de Jesus Christ (Unknown Life of Jesus Christ)*. But once his story had been re-examined by

48 **A**: Lama Kirtanah.[5]

49 **Q**: *(L)* Where was he from?

50 **A**: Palestine.

51 **Q**: *(L)* When was he in India?

52 **A**: 13 and 14 A.D.[6]

53 **Q**: *(L)* Is Frank's mind programmed?

54 **A**: Yes.

55 **Q**: *(L)* To do what?

56 **A**: To be an open channel.[7]

57 **Q**: *(L)* By whom?

58 **A**: Us.

59 **Q**: *(L)* You said one other time that he was also programed by the Grays.

60 **A**: Yes.

61 **Q**: *(L)* To do what?

62 **A**: To destroy himself.

63 **Q**: *(L)* Is this why it is important for him to channel?

64 **A**: Yes.

65 **Q**: *(L)* Why do they feed off emotions?

66 **A**: To fuel their energy.

67 **Q**: *(L)* Details about Jesus' extended 'sleep' state?

68 **A**: He spent 96 hours in a comatose state in a cave near Jerusalem. When he awoke, he prophesied to his disciples and then exited the cave. 27,000 people had assembled because of mother ship appearance and he was taken up in a beam of light.[8] [9]

---

historians, Notovitch confessed to having fabricated the evidence. Bart D. Ehrman states that "Today there is not a single recognized scholar on the planet who has any doubts about the matter. The entire story was invented by Notovitch, who earned a good deal of money and a substantial amount of notoriety for his hoax."

[5]Odd name. Encyclopedia Brittanica:

> "kirtana, form of musical worship or group devotion practiced by the Vaiṣṇava sects (followers of the god Vishnu) of Bengal. Kirtana usually consists of a verse sung by a soloist and then repeated by a chorus, to the accompaniment of percussion instruments. Sometimes the singing gives way to the recitation of a religious poem, the repetition of God's name (nama-kirtana), or dancing." [http://global.britannica.com/EBchecked/topic/319314/kirtana]

[6]Max Müller stated that either the monks at the monastery had deceived Notovitch (or played a joke on him), or he had fabricated the evidence. Müller then wrote to the monastery at Hemis and the head lama replied that there had been no Western visitor at the monastery in the past fifteen years and there were no documents related to Notovitch's story. J. Archibald Douglas then visited Hemis monastery and interviewed the head lama, who stated that Notovitch had never been there. (*Last Essays* by Friedrich M. Mueller, 1901 [republished in June 1973]) But notice that this does not exclude an Arabic-speaking visitor from Palestine two thousand years ago.

[7] *The Wave* 34

[8] *The Wave* 29

[9]I would say that this is a reflection of the workings of my own subconscious trying to find some way to explain the Jesus of myth and legend as a genuine historical figure. Much research has gone on since then and I am now convinced that the

69 **Q:** *(L)* Why did we have trouble with the tape recorder?

70 **A:** Influence of Lizard beings. In your head.[10]

71 **Q:** *(L)* Why didn't you guys tell me the tape was not recording?

72 **A:** Must experience to learn to practice precaution.

73 **Q:** *(L)* I am going to give a list of planets written about in the Sumerian texts which Dr. Sitchin has interpreted. I would like for you to give me the true translation of these names. What was meant by [the Sumerian word] Mummu?

74 **A:** Comet cluster.

75 **Q:** *(L)* Lahamu?

76 **A:** Venus.

77 **Q:** *(L)* Lahmu?

78 **A:** Earth.

79 **Q:** *(L)* The Hammered Bracelet?

80 **A:** Comet trail of Venus and cluster.

81 **Q:** *(L)* Anshar?

82 **A:** Jupiter.

83 **Q:** *(L)* Anu?

84 **A:** Moon.

85 **Q:** *(L)* Ea?

86 **A:** Sun.

87 **Q:** *(L)* Gaga?

88 **A:** Saturn.

89 **Q:** *(L)* Marduk?

90 **A:** Mars.

91 **Q:** *(L)* Tiamat?

92 **A:** Sirius.

93 **Q:** *(L)* You say that Christ gave into temptation. Could you please clarify what that means to us?

94 **A:** Three women represented sexual temptation. He felt bad after each. He washed himself and asked for strength and forgiveness.[11]

95 **Q:** *(L)* What did Christ write on the ground in the story about the adulteress who was about to be stoned?

96 **A:** Look into soul.

97 **Q:** *(L)* That is what he wrote?

98 **A:** Yes. Translation.

99 **Q:** *(L)* What, exactly, does the U.S. government know about aliens?

100 **A:** That they exist.

101 **Q:** *(L)* Does the government have or did they ever have a treaty with any aliens?

102 **A:** Yes.

103 **Q:** *(L)* Is the treaty still in effect?

104 **A:** Never was.

105 **Q:** *(L)* Did they try to get a treaty with them?

106 **A:** Yes.

107 **Q:** *(L)* Did the aliens refuse?

---

actual figure behind the Jesus Christ myth is Julius Caesar. But, it can take many years and a lot of work to rid oneself of wishful thinking and anticipation.

[10] Suggests some sort of PK action.

[11] Again, we are exposed to my own religious beliefs of the time. I'm not going to comment on these every time they come up as we go along; just take it for granted that I had a deep investment in finding a historical reality behind Jesus Christ as a Jew in Palestine, as close to the Gospel stories as possible. Thankfully, I am over that now!

108 **A:** No. Tricked.

109 **Q:** *(L)* How long before the U.S. government realized they had been tricked?

110 **A:** 19 years.[12]

111 **Q:** *(L)* What year was this?

112 **A:** 1972.

113 **Q:** *(L)* Does the government have any alien technology?

114 **A:** Yes.

115 **Q:** *(L)* Is this technology they were given?

116 **A:** Yes.

117 **Q:** *(L)* Is this mind control technology?

118 **A:** Close.

119 **Q:** *(L)* Does the government have the ability to say, walk through walls as the aliens do?

120 **A:** Incompetent.

121 **Q:** *(L)* Does the government listen to us on the telephone?

122 **A:** Can.

123 **Q:** *(L)* The individual in the Karla Turner book who had an experience similar to virtual reality, inside a blue bubble, who did this?[13]

124 **A:** Grays.

125 **Q:** *(L)* Who were the Grays working for when they did that?

126 **A:** Lizard beings.[14]

127 **Q:** *(L)* Is MF working for either the government or the aliens?

128 **A:** Aliens.

129 **Q:** *(L)* Which aliens is he working for?

130 **A:** Lizard beings. Unwittingly.[15]

131 **Q:** *(L)* What influence was Adolf Hitler under when he undertook to do the things he did? Who was guiding him?

132 **A:** Lizards. Indirectly.

133 **Q:** *(L)* What connection did they use to influence him?

134 **A:** Projected beings of human type, inspired forms of great Aryan spirits.[16]

135 **Q:** *(L)* Can you tell us more about the six billion people on the planet at the time of Noah's flood? Where were most of these beings living?

136 **A:** Atlantis.

137 **Q:** *(L)* In the upcoming cataclysms, which continent is going to suffer the most destruction?

---

[12] I was asking questions about many claims that were being circulated amongst the UFO/alien research crowd at the time. The reader might want to check out Colonel Corso's book *The Day After Roswell* as well as a critique of his claims here: http://www.bibliotecapleyades.net/exopolitica/esp_exopolitics_ZZO.htm

[13] Karla Turner, *Into the Fringe* (Berkley, 1992).

[14] *Secret History* 11; *The Wave* 29, 32

[15] See note to session 30 July.

[16] Quite a few years ago I acquired and read *The Mind of Adolf Hitler: The Secret Wartime Report* (1972, Basic Books), which was based on a World War II report by psychoanalyst Walter C. Langer. Apparently, based on testimony of various witnesses, Hitler was definitely seeing and hearing things when alone in his bedroom and was found cowering on the floor on a couple of occasions as a result of these episodes.

138 **A:** As yet undetermined.[17]

139 **Q:** *(L)* Why are there more abductions by the Grays in the United States than in other countries around the world?[18]

140 **A:** Government opened channel.

141 **Q:** *(L)* Are there alien bases in the United States?

142 **A:** Yes. New Mexico, Colorado, off Florida, Appalachia, California.

143 **Q:** *(L)* Are these underground bases?

144 **A:** Yes. Also under water.

145 **Q:** *(L)* What age was I the first time I was abducted?

146 **A:** Three.

147 **Q:** *(L)* Who abducted me?

148 **A:** Grays.

149 **Q:** *(L)* What was the purpose of that abduction?

150 **A:** Encoding.

151 **Q:** *(L)* To do what?

152 **A:** Kill yourself.

153 **Q:** *(L)* Why did they want me to kill myself?

154 **A:** Threat to reveal truth.

155 **Q:** *(L)* When did they abduct me next?

156 **A:** Age three.

157 **Q:** *(L)* Why?

158 **A:** Same.

159 **Q:** *(L)* Did they ever at any time do anything to my physical body to cause me problems?

160 **A:** Yes.

161 **Q:** *(L)* What did they do?[19]

162 **A:** Implant.

163 **Q:** *(L)* What kind of implant and where?

164 **A:** Brain silicon.

165 **Q:** *(L)* Did they ever put one in the lower part of my spine?

166 **A:** No.

167 **Q:** *(L)* Was I ever abducted by you guys?

168 **A:** No. Contacted at age three. We do not abduct.

169 **Q:** *(L)* How did the Grays know I would be a threat to them?

170 **A:** Image aural reading.

171 **Q:** *(L)* Is this the same reason they have abducted Frank so many times?

172 **A:** Yes.

---

[17] I think we can make a good guess at this point in time, especially when contemplating a recent mapping of the decline of the Earth's magnetic field, which shows the greatest loss over the Western hemisphere, concentrating on the United States and part of Canada. Nevertheless, we need to keep in mind that such events can be localized, though various effects can spread over wide territories. [https://www.youtube.com/watch?v=1OgRpLaeZBo]

[18] *High Strangeness* "Appendix"; *The Wave* 31

[19] *The Wave* 19

[20] *The Wave* 34

[21] Notice that this is different from the answers given to these questions in the first contact, 16 July. Frank: 57, Laura: 12. However, when I commented then on the few number of my alleged abductions, the C's said "It is not over." Then, on 30

173 **Q:** *(L)* How many times have I been abducted?[20] [21]

174 **A:** 17.

175 **Q:** *(L)* How many times have they abducted Frank?

176 **A:** 53.

177 **Q:** *(L)* Why have they abducted Frank more than me?[22]

178 **A:** You fight it.

179 **Q:** *(L)* When was the last time they abducted me?

180 **A:** Age 22.

181 **Q:** *(L)* When was the last time Frank?

182 **A:** Age 23.

183 **Q:** *(L)* So they haven't been abducting us for quite some time, is that it?

184 **A:** So far.

185 **Q:** *(L)* Do they have any plans to abduct either of us again?

186 **A:** Maybe.

187 **Q:** *(L)* Is there any way we can prevent it?

188 **A:** Knowledge channel.

189 **Q:** *(L)* Could you describe to me the true meaning of the Osirian cycle? What was the symbology of the killing of Osiris and the cutting up of the body?[23]

190 **A:** Removal of knowledge centers.

191 **Q:** *(L)* Knowledge centers in what?

192 **A:** Your DNA.

193 **Q:** *(L)* So, the breaking up of Osiris' body represents the breaking up of the DNA in our bodies?

194 **A:** Partly. Also means knowledge capacity reduction.[24]

195 **Q:** *(L)* What was the symbology of the throwing of the phallus into the river and its being eaten by three fishes?

196 **A:** Sexual violence energy introduction.[25]

197 **Q:** *(L)* What did Isis searching for her lord Osiris symbolize?

198 **A:** Separation of female energy from male energy union.

199 **Q:** *(L)* Does this have anything to do with brain activity?

200 **A:** Yes. The separating of the hemispheres of the brain.

201 **Q:** *(L)* Was this achieved through DNA modification?

202 **A:** Yes.

July, they told me "You are next." Nevertheless, 5 abductions in just a couple of months? Well, possible if it is the 'astral' type of abduction that is described in a session future to this one. And certainly, a lot of very weird stuff was going on in the background of our lives. What is new in this response is the "you fight it" angle being a factor in *not* being abducted so often. This also gets further development in a future session.

[22] *The Wave* 49

[23] *The Wave* 23

[24] See my footnote on this same question in the 5 October session.

[25] As mentioned in an earlier footnote, the Osiris story is a local version of the Ouranos/Kronos/Saturn/Zeus myth where the genitals of Ouranos were cut off by Kronos and tossed into the sea. The cometary imagery of this myth cycle and its various iterations is clear.

203 **Q:** *(L)* What did the son of Isis, Horus, represent?

204 **A:** New reality of limitation.[26]

205 **Q:** *(L)* What is the meaning of Horus avenging himself upon Set, the murderer of his father, Osiris?

206 **A:** Beginning of perpetual conflict energy to limit humanity.

207 **Q:** *(L)* Who did Set represent?

208 **A:** War.

209 **Q:** *(L)* What war?

210 **A:** All.

211 **Q:** *(L)* You say that part of what was done to the human race was that our capacity to retain or absorb knowledge was reduced genetically. Was there anything done to Frank or I either before or after birth in this regard?

212 **A:** In process of altering to make smarter. Ongoing since conception. Capacity for processing information will increase exponentially.

213 **Q:** *(L)* You mean we are going to get smarter than we already are?

214 **A:** Much. [Much laughter]

215 **Q:** *(L)* Who are the beings that have been abducting Karla Turner and her family?

216 **A:** Lizards.

217 **Q:** *(L)* Why have they been abducting that group of people?

218 **A:** Same reasons they have been abducting you and Frank.[27]

219 **Q:** *(L)* They have been abducting Karla Turner and her family because they perceive them as a threat?

220 **A:** Yes.

221 **Q:** *(L)* In one abduction where her son was involved, what was the black shadowy thing that seemed like a moving 'nothing' on the ground?

222 **A:** Blocked Grays. Son not as in tune as Karla. Careful driving alone to lectures and meetings.

223 **Q:** *(L)* Should she make sure there is always someone with her in the car?

224 **A:** At night and on lonely roads. Nephew must pay attention. Also son's friend.

225 **Q:** *(L)* Why did the Egyptians mummify their dead?

226 **A:** Superstition.

227 **Q:** *(L)* Was there really a curse on the tomb of King Tut that caused the deaths of many people?

228 **A:** Yes.

229 **Q:** *(L)* Who put the curse there?

---

[26] The research reveals that several of these esoteric ideas attached to the comet mythology may very well represent a change in the reality of significant proportions, including DNA changes due in part to cosmic interactions, and in other cases to population bottle-neck effects. So once again, we see 'through a glass darkly' via the symbolic/metaphoric language of the C's.

[27] *High Strangeness* 8

[28] Indeed; and I had learned this the hard way. See *The Wave* for details. Also, Alexandra David-Neel's book *Magic and Mystery in Tibet* is a fascinating tale that includes creative use of 'mental energy.' The C's further expand on this and how it can be utilized to block 'alien interference' in future sessions. Our own work has further proven the efficacy of strengthening the mind and enhancing its energy.

230 **A**: Egyptians. Anybody can create curse successfully with enough mental energy.[28]

231 **Q**: *(L)* What happened to Tiffany Sessions?

232 **A**: Murdered.

233 **Q**: *(L)* By whom?

234 **A**: Bob August.[29]

235 **Q**: *(L)* Where is the body?

236 **A**: Many sites. We are trying to contact Karla Turner's son's former roommate. But he is resisting. She does not realize the extreme importance. Communicate this to her now please Laura.

End of session.

---

[29]Interestingly, in February of this year, 2014, this case hit the news again. "Twenty-five years ago this month, Tiffany left her Gainesville apartment and went for a walk. She never came back. Her disappearance – along with the Danny Rolling serial murders in the months that followed – haunted the city for years." Apparently, the authorities decided that the killer was Paul Eugene Rowles, who died of cancer last year in the prison hospital at the South Florida Reception Center. Rowles killed Linda Fida and Elizabeth Foster. Fida was found in her bathtub. Foster's body was found in a shallow grave in the woods. Sessions has never been located. Though Rowles never confessed to this murder, the authorities think that a journal he left behind yields an important clue in Tiffany Sessions' case. Rowles wrote some of his victims' names in the book. Sessions isn't mentioned, but the date of her death is. On the bottom of a 2002 calendar, Rowles wrote: "#2 2/9/89 #2." So, they have concluded that Tiffany was his second victim, since her disappearance was on Feb. 9, 1989. Rowles didn't emerge as a serious suspect in Tiffany's case until his DNA was linked to another Gainesville cold case. By the time the connection was made in 2012, Rowles was suffering from cancer while in prison for kidnapping and raping a Clearwater girl. Another version says: "[Rowles] left behind an address book containing notes about the victims of the other three crimes – and what police and Tiffany's father believe is a coded reference to Tiffany's disappearance. Rowles lived in the Gainesville area at the time she vanished, and worked delivering scaffolding to a construction site along the route she regularly walked. ... Rowles had been a suspect in the murder of Foster for some time, but the presence of his DNA on her corpse convinced police that he was the killer, and they turned the case over to prosecutors. They decided to question him about Tiffany Sessions, who disappeared about a mile from where Foster's body was found. Rowles, already ravaged with cancer, angrily denied having anything to do with Tiffany. After the cops gathered more evidence, they wanted to question him again, but by then he had slipped into a coma from which he never awakened." [http://www.miamiherald.com/2014/02/05/3914313/25-years-later-cops-name-suspect.html] So, the authorities began to excavate a large area of ground near where Foster had been buried apparently with no results. [See: http://www.cbsnews.com/news/the-search-for-tiffany-sessions/] The name "Bob August" might be a symbol or metaphor: I've never found anything that pings my brain on that one.

October 16, 1994

This is one of the most interesting and informative sessions we ever had and it is in a unique format: reading prophecies from the Book of Revelations and asking the C's to elucidate the real meaning. In the course of this process, a fascinating description of a 'world to come' was given. What is crucially important about this is that almost every point of what the C's describe in this session has come to pass. What is more, they made certain identifications that have proven, as time has passed, to be absolutely correct. I won't put many notes in this one since it stands pretty well on its own, but there are a couple of acute points I will make.

Participants: 'Frank', Laura, V___

1 **Q**: Hello.
2 **A**: Hello. Music is Good.
3 **Q**: *(L)* Can you give us your name?
4 **A**: Cederra.
5 **Q**: *(L)* I would like to know what is the origin of the Freemasons?[1]
6 **A**: Osirians.
7 **Q**: *(L)* Can you tell us when the original Freemasons formed as a society?[2]
8 **A**: 5633 B.C.
9 **Q**: *(L)* Is Freemasonry as it is practiced today the same?
10 **A**: 33rd degree, yes.
11 **Q**: *(L)* So, there is a continuing tradition for over seven thousand years?
12 **A**: Yes.

[1] *Secret History* 11; *The Wave* 30
[2] *The Wave* 47

13 **Q**: *(L)* Is this organization with a plan to take over and rule the world?
14 **A**: Not exactly.
15 **Q**: *(L)* What is their focus?
16 **A**: Overseers.
17 **Q**: *(L)* Of what?
18 **A**: The status of Quorum.
19 **Q**: *(L)* What is the Quorum?
20 **A**: Deeper knowledge organization. Totally secret to your kind as of yet. Very important with regard to your future.
21 **Q**: *(L)* In what way?
22 **A**: Changes.
23 **Q**: *(L)* Can you get more specific? Is that changes to us personally?
24 **A**: Partly.
25 **Q**: *(L)* Earth changes?

26 **A:** Also.

27 **Q:** *(L)* What is the relationship between this Quorum and the Cassiopaeans?

28 **A:** They communicate with us regularly.

29 **Q:** *(L)* Do they do this knowing you are Cassiopaeans or do they do it thinking...

30 **A:** Yes.

31 **Q:** *(L)* Has there been an ongoing relationship between the Cassiopaeans and this Quorum for these thousands of years?

32 **A:** For some time as you measure it.

33 **Q:** *(L)* What is the origin of the Kabbalah?[3]

34 **A:** Channeled truths given to early pre-Mosaic Jews to use your terminology.

35 **Q:** *(L)* When the Jewish commentators began setting down the teachings, was this the first time this had been put into writing?

36 **A:** No. Not even close.

37 **Q:** *(L)* Is the form that it is in today very close to the original form and can it be relied upon?

38 **A:** No. Corrupted.

39 **Q:** *(L)* What is the origin of the books of Enoch?

---

[3] *The Wave* 32
[4] From Wikipedia:

> An ancient Jewish religious work, ascribed by tradition to Enoch, the great-grandfather of Noah, although modern scholars estimate the older sections (mainly in the Book of the Watchers) to date from about 300 BC, and the latest part (Book of Parables) probably to the end of the first century BC. It is not part of the biblical canon as used by Jews, apart from Beta Israel. Most Christian denominations and traditions may accept the Books of Enoch as having some historical or theological interest or significance, but they generally regard the Books of Enoch as non-canonical or non-inspired. It is regarded as canonical by the Ethiopian Orthodox Tewahedo Church and Eritrean Orthodox Tewahedo Church, but not by any other Christian group. It is wholly extant only in the Ge'ez language, with Aramaic fragments from the Dead Sea Scrolls and a few Greek and Latin fragments. For this and other reasons, the traditional Ethiopian belief is that the original language of the work was Ge'ez, whereas non-Ethiopian scholars tend to assert that it was first written in either Aramaic or Hebrew; E. Isaac suggests that the Book of Enoch, like the Book of Daniel, was composed partially in Aramaic and partially in Hebrew. No Hebrew version is known to have survived. The book itself claims to be written by Enoch himself before the Biblical Flood. The authors of the New Testament were familiar with the content of the story and influenced by it: a short section of 1 Enoch (1 En 1:9 or 1 En 2:1 depending on the translation) is quoted in the New Testament (Letter of Jude 1:14-15), and is attributed there to "Enoch the Seventh from Adam" (1 En 60:8). The text was also utilised by the community that originally collected the Dead Sea Scrolls. Some scholars speak even of an 'Enochic Judaism' from which the writers of Qumran scrolls were descended. The Book of Enoch was considered as scripture in the Epistle of Barnabas (16:4) and by many of the early Church Fathers, such as Athenagoras, Clement of Alexandria, Irenaeus and Tertullian, who wrote c. 200 that the Book of Enoch had been rejected by the Jews because it contained prophecies pertaining to Christ. However, later Fathers denied the canonicity of the book, and some even considered the letter of Jude uncanonical because it refers to an 'apocryphal' work. The oldest fragments of the Book of Watchers are dated 200-150

A: Sanskritian society in area now referred to as India.[4]

Q: *(L)* What evaluation can we give the books of Enoch as far as level of truth?

A: 50% of area was destroyed in nuclear conflagration in between.

Q: *(L)* In between what?

A: Then and now in the expanded present.

Q: *(L)* What is the "expanded" present?

A: The real measure of time.

Q: *(L)* Who was Hermes Trismegistus?[5]

A: Traitor to court of Pharaoh Rana.

Q: *(L)* Who is Pharaoh Rana?

A: Egyptian leader of spiritual covenant.

Q: *(L)* In what way was Hermes a traitor?

A: Broke covenant of spiritual unity of all peoples in area now known as Middle East.

Q: *(L)* Who did Hermes betray?

A: Himself; was power hungry.

Q: *(L)* What acts did he do?

A: Broke covenant; he inspired divisions within ranks of Egyptians, Essenes, Aryans, and Persians et cetera.

Q: *(L)* What was his purpose in doing this?

A: Divide and conquer as inspired by those referred to as Brotherhood in Bramley book you have read.

Q: *(L)* Is this the Brotherhood of the snake Hermes formed in rejection of unity?

A: Hermes did not form it; it was long since in existence.

Q: *(L)* Who was the originator of the Brotherhood of the Serpent as described in the Bramley book?

A: Lizard beings.[6]

Q: *(L)* Where did Moses get his knowledge?

BC. Since the Book of Watchers shows evidence of multiple stages of composition, it is probable that this work was extant already in the 3rd century BC. Returning to the idea of an Enochic Judaism, a form of Judaism older than that presented in the Septuagint, the main peculiar aspects are the following: the idea of the origin of the evil caused by the fallen angels, who came on the Earth to unite with human women. These fallen angels are considered ultimately responsible for the spread of evil and impurity on the Earth: 90; the absence in 1 Enoch of formal parallels to the specific laws and commandments found in the Mosaic Torah and of references to issues like Shabbat observance or the rite of circumcision. The Sinaitic covenant and Torah are not of central importance in the Book of Enoch:50–51; the concept of 'End of Days' as the time of final judgment that takes the place of promised earthly rewards: 92; the rejection of the Second Temple's sacrifices considered impure: according to Enoch 89:73, the Jews, when returned from the exile, "reared up that tower (the temple) and they began again to place a table before the tower, but all the bread on it was polluted and not pure"; a Solar calendar in opposition to the Lunar calendar used in the Second Temple (a very important aspect for the determination of the dates of religious feasts); an interest in the angelic world that involves life after death. [http://en.wikipedia.org/wiki/Book_of_Enoch, accessed on 2014-06-29]

So, it is not impossible that the C's answer may yet prove to be a serious clue.

[5] *Secret History* 11
[6] *The Wave* 29

64 **A**: Us.

65 **Q**: *(L)* OK, you told us before that he saw or interacted with a holographic projection created by the Lizard beings. Was that the experience on Mount Sinai?

66 **A**: Yes.

67 **Q**: *(L)* OK, well, if he got knowledge from you, did he get this prior to the interactions with the Lizard beings?

68 **A**: Yes. He was corrupted by imagery. He was deceived by the imagery a la Joseph Smith, for example.

69 **Q**: *(L)* Are you saying that Joseph Smith, the recipient of the Mormon texts, was deceived by the Lizards also?

70 **A**: Yes. They do that a lot.

71 **Q**: *(L)* Why did it take so long for us to get a 'good source' through this medium?[7]

72 **A**: Too many interactions with channel cancellers.

73 **Q**: *(L)* Who are the individuals who are channel cancellers?

74 **A**: It would not be our way to name names.

75 **Q**: *(L)* Do you mean people we have had involved in our lives?

76 **A**: Yes.

77 **Q**: *(L)* Does it have anything to do with our activities?

78 **A**: No.

79 **Q**: *(L)* Does it involve other entities that have tried to come through that have blocked the channel?

80 **A**: Yes.

81 **Q**: *(L)* Are they Lizards?

---
[7] *The Wave* 34

82 **A**: No.

83 **Q**: *(L)* Are there any exercises we can use to help our bodies transform into 4th density?

84 **A**: Not necessary. It is the soul that matters.

85 **Q**: *(L)* Does this mean that if we focus on soul development, that at the time of transformation that our bodies will automatically be transformed for us?

86 **A**: No. It is natural process. No preparation is needed.

87 **Q**: *(L)* So, if you are meant to transform, you will, if you are not you won't?

88 **A**: Yes.

89 **Q**: *(L)* Does this mean that when my body reacts to certain foods that I should stop eating them? Is my body trying to tell me something?

90 **A**: Up to you. Nothing needs to "tell" you anything.

91 **Q**: *(L)* Can you clarify that?

92 **A**: Why are you searching for guidance where it is not needed?

93 **Q**: *(L)* In other words, if we just do each day what naturally comes to us as the best choice in each moment, we are on the right track?

94 **A**: Precisely.

95 **Q**: *(V)* I find the information of transforming to the 4th dimension very exciting and natural which is why I ask if this is going to be something I will experience in the future excluding death?

96 **A**: Vague.

97 **Q:** *(L)* If, theoretically, an individual... I am getting a very unusual feeling right at this moment, why?[8]

98 **A:** Metabolic changes enhanced by accelerated learning.

99 **Q:** *(L)* Is this happening to all three of us?

100 **A:** Yes.

101 **Q:** *(L)* Now, as I was starting to say, if, theoretically an individual was to develop in a natural way by making all the proper choices, and was to arrive at the point in time when the major transition is to be made, would that individual's body pass through into that heightened dimension in a physical state? Remember, this is just a theoretical person...

102 **A:** Of course.

103 **Q:** *(L)* Now suppose this theoretical person were to pass through this transition to the other side, what state would they find their body in? Would it be exactly as it is now in terms of solidity? What would be the experience?[9]

104 **A:** The key concept here is variability of physicality.

105 **Q:** *(L)* Does this mean that everybody will be different or that an individual will have greater control over the substance and constitution of the body?

106 **A:** Not exactly either. Your physicality will be variable according to need and circumstance.

107 **Q:** *(L)* OK, does this mean that sometimes we will be more of a light body?

108 **A:** Close.

109 **Q:** *(L)* Does this mean that sometimes we will be more of a firm body as we have now?

110 **A:** Yes.

111 **Q:** *(L)* Will our bodies age differently?

112 **A:** Yes.

113 **Q:** *(L)* What will be the median lifespan?

114 **A:** 400 years

115 **Q:** *(L)* And will those who pass through this transition as, say, 50-year-olds, will they have an equal opportunity to live an additional 400 years?

116 **A:** Will regenerate in youthful appearance.

117 **Q:** *(L)* Now, when you say 400 years, will it be that the planet has a different orbit and that a year will be different?

118 **A:** No.

119 **Q:** *(L)* Will the days be different as to length of time light and dark as they are now?

120 **A:** Not the point. Planet will be 4th density as well.

121 **Q:** *(L)* But will the days and nights be different and will the orbit be different? Will the axial angle be changed?

122 **A:** You are thinking in terms of the 3rd level density. The rules will be so totally different that physical inspired comparisons are moot.

123 **Q:** *(L)* But I like the sunshine and birds singing and breezes. I just want to know if those things will be the same.

124 **A:** In some fashion.

---

[8]This was one of those moments I described in my introduction where I experienced sharp and definite electrical pinching feelings at the nape of my neck and going down my left arm, which is the hand I use for the pointer.

[9] *The Wave* 29

Q: *(L)* Can't you give a few clues?

A: We must let you see for yourself.

Q: *(V)* I had an experience with praying mantis beings. Who are they?

A: Minturians.

Q: *(L)* Where are they from?

A: Orion.

Q: *(L)* Are the Orions the bad guys?

A: Subjective.

Q: *(L)* Well, what group do they belong to?

A: Federation as do the Pleiadians.

Q: *(V)* Did they abduct me or what is the source of this memory?

A: It is a memory of a past life held in the deep subconscious level.

Q: *(V)* What did they do to me?

A: Retroprogramming for learning purposes.

Q: *(V)* For what?

A: Lessons are to be learned by you not told by us.

Q: *(L)* Why did the Grays abduct V_-_?

A: To try to encode her to destroy herself.

Q: *(L)* Has she overcome this programming?

A: Hopefully. There is always room for error. Remember, free will is the most important law of consciousness in creation.

Q: *(V)* I had a dream about being a teacher and showing small children how to use light and color. Was this precognition?

A: Probably.

Q: *(V)* Would this probability be within the next ten years?

A: Listen. Open.

Q: *(L)* What is the meaning of the number 666 in the book of Revelation?[10]

A: Visa.

Q: *(L)* You mean as in credit card?

A: Yes.

Q: *(L)* Are credit cards the work of what 666 represents?

A: Yes?

Q: *(L)* Should we get rid of all credit cards?

A: Up to you.

Q: *(L)* Would it be more to our advantage than not to disconnect ourselves from the credit system?

A: Isn't just credit also debit.

Q: *(L)* Is that an affirmative?

A: How are you going to do this?

Q: *(L)* Well, do you have any suggestions?

A: World will soon have nothing but credit and debit have you not heard of this new visa debit cards this is the future of money as controlled by the world banking system i.e. the Brotherhood i.e. Lizards i.e. antichrist.[11]

Q: *(L)* If I don't have a credit card then I don't have to belong to this system?

A: No. You will have no choices: belong or starve.

---

[10] *The Wave* 25

[11] This has certainly proven to be correct and we are well on our way to the final implementation. Many suggest that the door on this will slam shut in 2014.

165 **Q**: *(L)* What happened to free will?

166 **A**: Brotherhood aka Lizards aka antichrist has interfered with free will for 309,000 years. They are getting desperate as we near the change.

167 **Q**: *(V)* It has always been my nature to rebel against that which I did not feel was good for me. Is rebellion against this system possible?

168 **A**: If you are willing to leave the body.

169 **Q**: *(L)* Leave the body as in death, croak, kick the bucket?

170 **A**: Yes.

171 **Q**: *(L)* If we were to move...

172 **A**: Changes will follow turmoil be patient.

173 **Q**: *(L)* We would like to move into the country. Will it be possible to get along without this credit/debit card leading that kind of life?

174 **A**: No.

175 **Q**: *(L)* Are they going to have the kind of capability of controlling everything and everybody no matter where they are?

176 **A**: Yes.

177 **Q**: *(L)* Even if we moved to Guyana and built a log hut in the rainforest and didn't bother anybody, we'd still get sucked into this thing?

178 **A**: Laura you will feel the effect of the Lizard beings desperate push for total control no matter where you go.

179 **Q**: *(L)* That is inexpressibly depressing. Do you understand?

180 **A**: Why? Change will follow.

181 **Q**: *(L)* Will it follow soon?

182 **A**: You are slipping a bit. Refer to Literature "Bringers of the Dawn". Challenge will be ecstasy if viewed with proper perspective which is not, we repeat: not of third level reality, understand?

183 **Q**: *(L)* In the reference cited, Joan of Arc is described as feeling ecstatic while burning at the stake. Is that what you mean?

184 **A**: Sort of, but you need not burn at the stake.

185 **Q**: *(L)* That's small comfort. There's other ways to die.

186 **A**: We are not speaking of death, Laura. If you listen to those who are firmly rooted in 3rd level this is when you run the risk of slipping in your knowledge learned no matter how good the intentions i.e. LM.[12]

187 **Q**: *(L)* What do you mean about LM?

188 **A**: Guyana.

189 **Q**: *(L)* What do you mean "Challenge will be ecstasy"? What sort of challenge?

190 **A**: Living through the turmoil ahead.[13]

191 **Q**: *(L)* Several books I have read have advised moving to rural areas and forming groups and storing food, etc....

192 **A**: Disinformation. Get rid of this once and for all. That is 3rd level garbage.

193 **Q**: *(L)* We feel pretty helpless at the mercy of beings who can come in and feed off of us at will. Do we have someone on our side, pulling for our team, throwing us energy or something?

---

[12] My then husband, now ex-husband.

[13] We entered that period on September 11, 2001, and it has only been intensifying in the 13 years since.

194 **A:** Who do you think you have been communicating with?

195 **Q:** *(L)* Are you going to be able to assist us through this turmoil?

196 **A:** Yes.

197 **Q:** *(L)* Are you going to?

198 **A:** Up to you.

199 **Q:** *(L)* If we call, can we get your assistance?

200 **A:** All you have to do is ask.

201 **Q:** *(L)* Will we go through any periods when we may be cut off from help?

202 **A:** You are never ever cut off.

203 **Q:** *(L)* Oh, I don't want to suffer!

204 **A:** You need not suffer. Stop thinking 3rd level.

205 **Q:** *(L)* I don't want anybody I love to suffer either. I don't want any pain. I've suffered enough!

206 **A:** You are stuck at 3rd level tonight.

207 **Q:** *(L)* It's not just that. There is so much disinformation, you just don't know who to believe... I mean, how do we know we can believe you? There are so many sources out there deceiving and they do it so cleverly. Look at the Bible... for 2,000 years people have been believing that...

208 **A:** They deceive when you allow it.

209 **Q:** *(L)* I know you are supposed to take some things on faith... but, do you see my problem here?

210 **A:** Yes, but you don't.

211 **Q:** *(L)* What is my problem?

212 **A:** Mental block.

213 **Q:** *(L)* In the recent past you indicated that chapter 24 of Matthew and chapter 21 of Luke were given by Jesus after his extended sleep state. Now, both of those chapters refer to the present time as being like the days of Noah. Is that a correct assessment?

214 **A:** In a sense and individual events are as yet undetermined.

215 **Q:** *(L)* Well, the story of Noah tells us that Noah was told to build an ark.

216 **A:** Symbolic.

217 **Q:** *(L)* Yet Noah built an ark. Was it true that certain individuals, whoever they were, built boats or did things to survive that terrible cataclysm?

218 **A:** No. Look at it this way. Noah built a boat because it seemed like an enjoyable enterprise and when the flood came it came in handy, see?

219 **Q:** *(L)* So, you are saying that if we do what we do because we enjoy it that we will be in the right place at the right time, doing the right thing when whatever happens happens, right?

220 **A:** Close.

221 **Q:** *(L)* Are you saying that we will be led to do what we should be doing and be where we should be?

222 **A:** You will just fall into it but if you force things you run the risk of going astray.

223 **Q:** *(L)* Am I correct in thinking that many people who think they are channeling are just channeling earthbound spirits?

224 **A:** Sometimes.

225 **Q:** *(L)* Is it possible to channel dead people who have gone into the light?

226 **A:** Sometimes.

227 **Q:** *(L)* Would it be possible for us to do this with other people present so that they could ask questions also?

228 **A**: Yes.

229 **Q**: *(L)* Is Scarlett under the influence of other forces?

230 **A**: Yes.

231 **Q**: *(L)* Who?

232 **A**: Who else? The Lizzies.

233 **Q**: *(L)* Is it acceptable within universal law to do spirit release work on people without requesting their permission?

234 **A**: You already do this without inquiry.

235 **Q**: *(L)* Is it alright to do it without inquiry?

236 **A**: Open.

237 **Q**: *(L)* Is it possible that we could be loading ourselves with karmic debt by sticking our noses in where we may not be wanted?

238 **A**: Yes.

239 **Q**: *(L)* Would it be better to not do this without request?

240 **A**: You must answer within yourself.

241 **Q**: *(L)* Can one do a spirit release on another after asking the higher self permission?

242 **A**: Too many conflicting thought patterns.

243 **Q**: *(L)* Can one ask the higher self for permission to do a cleansing?

244 **A**: Be cautious not to interfere with karmic learning assignments.

245 **Q**: *(L)* Do some people have attachments that are part of karma?

246 **A**: Yes.

247 **Q**: *(L)* Let's go back to the subject of the Beast and the number 666. You say that following the enforcement of control by the Lizzies on the entire world that the change is going to take place, is that correct?

248 **A**: Yes.

249 **Q**: *(L)* How long following?

250 **A**: Open.

251 **Q**: *(L)* Several prophetic works have said that this period is going to last 6.3 or 7 years. Is that correct?

252 **A**: Open.[14]

253 **Q**: *(L)* On the subject of the 666, I was given an insight into this several years ago as to another meaning of it. Is that interpretation also correct?

254 **A**: Maybe. VI is 6 in Roman Numerals. S was 6 in ancient Egypt. A was 6 in Sanskrit. VISA, see, is 666. Interesting that to travel for extended periods one needs a "visa" also, yes?[15]

255 **Q**: *(L)* The other parts of chapter 13... Verse one says, "I stood on the sandy beach I saw a beast coming up out of the sea with ten horns and seven heads. On his horns he had ten royal crowns and blasphemous titles on his heads..." What does this verse mean?

---

[14] I suspect it will be a shorter time. If you refer back to my note to the C's remark "Mass affects electromagnetic transfer within gravity wave" in the 5 October session, I speculate that Earth's population is rapidly losing 'mass' due to the propaganda and disinformation campaign leading to all the many lies that are adhered to by the majority of humans at the present time.

[15] This actually turns out to be correct, though we had to do some digging to find it. S is 6 is Coptic and 6 is indeed A in Sanskrit. However, in a future session, there is more about the 'Mark of the Beast.'

256 **A:** Many meanings. Monetary control. 10 represents universal control of whole units of value.[16]

257 **Q:** *(L)* So, the ten horns represent units of value, so we are talking about money here. What are the blasphemous titles on his heads?

258 **A:** In God we trust.

259 **Q:** *(L)* "And the Beast that I saw resembled a leopard..."

260 **A:** New World Order.

261 **Q:** *(L)* "And to him the dragon gave his might and power and great dominion..." Who is the dragon?

262 **A:** Read again please.

263 **Q:** *(L)* "And the Beast I saw resembled a leopard..." What does the leopard signify?

264 **A:** Leopard is fast moving and distinctly patterned.

265 **Q:** *(L)* "His feet were like those of a bear..." What do the feet represent?

266 **A:** Russia.

267 **Q:** *(L)* Why are the feet like those of a bear?

268 **A:** Hidden power center in that geographic location.

269 **Q:** *(L)* What nature this power center?

270 **A:** Same as USA. Feet are not so easily seen.

271 **Q:** *(L)* Does this mean that Russia and the U.S. are secretly united?

272 **A:** Under same control.

273 **Q:** *(L)* Are these the Lizards?

274 **A:** At the root.

275 **Q:** *(L)* "His mouth was like that of a lion..." What does mouth represent and why is it like a lions?

276 **A:** Noisy and boastful.

277 **Q:** *(L)* Who is noisy and boastful and how is this going to manifest?

278 **A:** Economic power structure. Lion is powerful and commands attention by roaring. Who has been speaking loudly about a new world order?

279 **Q:** *(L)* The United States?

280 **A:** Close. Elements of same.

281 **Q:** *(L)* "One of his heads seemed to have a deadly wound, but his death stroke was healed and the whole earth went after the Beast in amazement and admiration..." What does it mean that one of his heads seemed to have a deadly wound?

282 **A:** Aliens.

283 **Q:** *(L)* The aliens will seem to be a deadly wound to the Beast?

284 **A:** Initially.

285 **Q:** *(L)* "But his death stroke was healed, and the whole earth went after the Beast with amazement and admiration..." What does this mean?

286 **A:** Initial fear gives way to worship and admiration.

287 **Q:** *(L)* "They fell down and gave homage to the dragon because he had bestowed on the Beast all of his dominion and authority..." Who is this dragon?

288 **A:** World Body Politic.

289 **Q:** *(L)* And who is this Beast?

290 **A:** New World Order aka Brotherhood aka Lizzies aka antichrist.

---

[16] What is known to us today as the IMF, which appears to be the instrument by which some group seeks to control the entire world.

291 **Q:** *(L)* "The Beast was given the power of speech uttering boastful and blasphemous words and was given freedom to exert his authority and exercise his will during 42 months..."

292 **A:** Timing is open. Power of speech is self explanatory in terms of audio and video media.

293 **Q:** *(L)* "And he opened his mouth to speak slanders against God blaspheming his name and his abode even vilifying those who live in heaven..." Does this mean that this group, this Beast are going to...

294 **A:** Disseminate disinformation with respect to encouraging worship, loyalty and obedience to antichrist.

295 **Q:** *(L)* "He was further permitted to wage war on God's holy people and to overcome them and power was given him to extend his authority over every tribe and people and every tongue and nation..." Does this mean trials and tribulations of those who refuse to submit?

296 **A:** No. See previous answer.

297 **Q:** *(L)* "And all the inhabitants of the earth will fall down in admiration... everyone whose name has not been recorded from the foundation of the world in the Book of Life of the Lamb that was slain in sacrifice from the foundation of the world..." What are "those whose names are recorded in the Book of Life..." What is the Book of Life?

298 **A:** Supercomputer.[17]

299 **Q:** *(L)* The Book of Life of the Lamb... everyone whose name has not been recorded... it is saying that the people who are going to worship the Beast are names that have not been recorded... does that mean that there is a supercomputer recording the names of those who do not worship the Beast?

300 **A:** Yes.

301 **Q:** *(L)* And who has this supercomputer?

302 **A:** Beast. All names will be recorded as being either obedient or disobedient.

303 **Q:** *(L)* Who is this 'Lamb'?

304 **A:** Beast.

305 **Q:** *(L)* "If anyone is able to hear let him listen: whoever leads into captivity will himself go into captivity; if anyone slays with the sword, with the sword will he be slain... herein is the call for the patience and fidelity of the saints (God's people)..." Who are God's people?

306 **A:** All.

307 **Q:** *(L)* What does it mean: "Whoever leads into captivity will go into captivity"?

308 **A:** Follow the leader.[18]

309 **Q:** *(L)* If they follow the leader they will become captive and if they fight with the leader they will be killed?

310 **A:** Yes.

311 **Q:** *(L)* "Then I saw another Beast rising up out of the land; he had two horns like a lamb and he spoke like a dragon..." What does this signify?

---

[17] Today, this makes a lot more sense with the revelations about the global spying of the NSA and the global manipulations of the CIA.

[18] Reminiscent of George W. Bush's announcement: "You are either with us, or you are with the terrorists." This actually echoes the position of Pompeius Magnus when he started the civil war against Julius Caesar, who made so many efforts to avoid war.

A: Other faces of the same entity.

Q: *(L)* What does it mean that he had two horns like a lamb? A lamb doesn't have horns. Why does it say he has horns?

A: Confusion by contradiction.

Q: *(L)* And what does the lamb represent?

A: Same face of the Beast.

Q: *(L)* What does it mean he "spoke like a dragon"?

A: Same.

Q: *(L)* "He exerts all the power and right of control as the former Beast in his presence and causes the earth and those who dwell upon it to exalt and deify the Beast whose deadly wound was healed and worship him..." Well, it seems to say that there is a second beast that is different from the first beast but you are saying that it is just another face of the Beast...

A: Yes. Look at it this way, aliens one face; God another; government another et cetera.

Q: *(L)* Did you mean to say that God was another face of the Beast?

A: As represented by religion.

Q: *(L)* "He performs great signs, startling miracles, even making fire fall from the sky to the earth in men's sight.." What does that mean?

A: Aliens perform "miracles".

Q: *(L)* And what is the 'image' of the Beast?

A: Aliens.

Q: *(L)* What does it mean to have been wounded by the sword and still live?

A: Perceived as scary then Godlike.

Q: *(L)* "And he was permitted to impart the breath of life into the Beast's image so that the statue of the Beast could actually talk and to cause all to be put to death that would not bow down and worship the image of the Beast." What does this mean?

A: Total control once deception is complete.

Q: *(L)* "Compels all alike, both small and great, rich and poor, free and slave, to be marked with an inscription on their right hand or on their foreheads...." What is this inscription?

A: Visa ID number.

Q: *(L)* Is this going to be actually physically put on our bodies?

A: Encoded.

Q: *(L)* How? Is that what the aliens do when they abduct people?

A: No.

Q: *(L)* How is it going to be done?

A: Stamped.

Q: *(L)* By what technical means?

A: Electronic encoding. A series of numbers.

Q: *(L)* Are they going to put these on our skins or imbed them in the skin on our heads or hand...?

A: Yes.

Q: *(L)* Does that mean that you will have to place your hand on an electronic scanner in order to conduct any type of monetary transaction?

A: Precisely.

Q: *(L)* OK, it says: "Here is room for discernment, a call for the wisdom of

346 interpretation, let him who has intelligence, penetration, insight enough calculate the number of the Beast, for it is a human number, the number of a certain man, his number is 666." What does this mean?

A: Visa as explained previously. Everyone will get their own number and it will be a Visa number, the number of the Beast.

347 Q: (L) "Then I looked and Lo! the Lamb stood on Mount Zion and with him 144,000 men who had his name and his father's name inscribed on their foreheads..." What does that mean?

348 A: ID. The Lamb is the Leadership council of the world bank. Many will think they are taking the "mark" of God when actually being marked by the Beast.[19]

349 Q: (L) "And I heard a voice from Heaven like the sound of great waters and like the rumbling of mighty thunder and the voice I heard seemed like the music of harpists accompanying themselves on their harps..." What is this voice from heaven and the sound like great waters and mighty thunder?

350 A: The return of Christ.

351 Q: (L) "And they sing a new song... No one could learn to sing that song except the 144,000 who had been ransomed from the earth..." You said the 144,000 are the leaders of the world bank and here it says they have been ransomed from the earth at the coming of Christ... it says "the 144,000 have not defiled themselves by relations with women for they are pure as virgins. These are they who follow the Lamb wherever he goes... they have been ransomed..."

352 A: Symbolism added later and this is not entirely accurate point. The symbols have been mixed. Tends to encourage elitism and divisiveness.

353 Q: (L) Are the 144,000 good guys or bad guys as we would term them?

354 A: Both. But they are ones who have supreme knowledge.

355 Q: (L) Are these human beings?

356 A: Yes.

357 Q: (L) There will be 144,000 people on the Earth who have supreme knowledge?

358 A: Approximately.[20]

359 Q: (L) Now, this 144,000, are we among that number? Just curious.

360 A: Maybe.

361 Q: (L) "No lie was found to be upon their lips for they are blameless, spotless, untainted without blemish. And I saw another angel flying in midair with an eternal gospel to tell to the inhabitants of the earth, every race and tribe and people, and he cried with a mighty voice: Revere God and give him glory, for the hour of his judgment has arrived, fall down before him, pay him homage and adoration and worship him who created heaven and earth and the sea and the springs of water..." What does this tell us?

362 A: Added later by questionable source.

363 Q: (L) "Then a second angel followed declaring: Fallen, fallen is Babylon the Great, she who made all nations drink of the wine of her passionate unchastity..." Who is Babylon and what does it mean she has fallen?

---

[19] Here the C's are quite explicit about the IMF as the Beast.
[20] *The Wave* 10

A: Same as previous answer.

Q: *(L)* "Another angel followed, a third, saying with a mighty voice saying whoever pays homage to the Beast and permits his stamp to be put on his forehead or on his hand he too shall have to drink of the wine of God's indignation and wrath poured undiluted into the cup of his anger, and he shall be tormented with fire and brimstone in the presence of the holy angels and in the presence of the Lamb..."

A: Disinformation. Intended to create fear and resistance so that the aliens can feed off of these emotions.

Q: *(L)* "Again I looked and lo! I saw a white cloud and sitting on the cloud one resembling a son of man with a crown of gold on his head and a sharp scythe in his hand..." Is that further additions?

A: Yes.

Q: *(L)* "Another angel came out of the temple saying with a mighty voice to the one sitting on the cloud: put in your scythe and reap for the hour has arrived to gather the harvest for the earth's crop is fully ripened..."

A: More fear based disinformation.

Q: *(L)* Now, I have compared certain passages of Revelations to the work of Immanuel Velikovsky. Were those sections accurate in what they describe?

A: Yes.[21]

Q: *(L)* And those are events that will transpire after the Lizzies have done their thing, after the Visa is in place, and before or after Christ returns?

A: Before.

Q: *(L)* So the cluster of comets is going to come before the return of Christ?

A: Yes. But return is just one event not the whole thing.

Q: *(L)* Is there going to be massive disruption on the planet and maybe a lot of people transitioning out of the body simultaneously because of the interaction of this cluster of comets and the Earth?

A: Close.

Q: *(L)* And, shortly following this event, Christ will return?

A: As part of the whole.

Q: *(L)* That is going to be part of the cluster of comets activity?

A: After.

Q: *(L)* What is Christ going to do after he returns?

A: Teach.

Q: *(L)* How many people are going to be on the planet to receive this teaching?

A: Open.

Q: *(L)* May we assume there will be six billion?

A: Assume as you please.

Q: *(L)* You keep saying that the return of Christ is a part of the whole as though there is some important thing that I am missing the question to discover. Consider that question asked... tell me what it is I am missing, please.

A: Obvious if you have been paying attention.

Q: *(L)* And that is...?

A: The transition to 4th density.

---

[21] The description of destruction at the 'End Times' in Revelation is almost identical to the description of the destruction of Egypt prior to and during the 'Exodus.' As I've written in a number of works, this is obvious comet catastrophe imagery.

393 **Q:** *(L)* Is the transition to 4th density going to happen before the comets or after?

394 **A:** After.

395 **Q:** *(L)* Is the interaction of the comets and the planet Earth going to...

396 **A:** Precede the transition.

397 **Q:** *(L)* Is it going to generate this change in some way?

398 **A:** No.

399 **Q:** *(L)* It's not going to have anything to do with electromagnetic interactions which would heighten the atomic vibrations of the planet?

400 **A:** No.

401 **Q:** *(L)* So, the comets are going to make a mess of things and then the transition is going to come as Christ comes?

402 **A:** Before.

403 **Q:** *(L)* The transition will happen and we will all be standing around glazed in the eyes or whatever, wondering what to do with ourselves, because we are finding ourselves in a new estate we have not been in before, and then Christ comes?

404 **A:** More or less.

405 **Q:** *(L)* Now, what is going to happen after Christ comes back and everything is sort of straightening out and he is teaching... is everybody on the planet going to be gathered together in one place to receive these teachings?

406 **A:** No.

407 **Q:** *(L)* Is he going to travel around and teach?

408 **A:** Technology.

409 **Q:** *(L)* He will teach via the media?

410 **A:** Yes.

411 **Q:** *(L)* And we are still going to have access to our media, television and radio and so forth?

412 **A:** Some.

413 **Q:** *(L)* Are some people at that point in time or just prior to this transition, going to leave in large groups with the Lizzies?

414 **A:** Yes.

415 **Q:** *(L)* Are there going to be large groups of people moving into domed cities on the planet living in 'cahoots' with the Lizzies?

416 **A:** Close.

417 **Q:** *(L)* In other words there may be areas of Lizzie control on the planet and areas under the control of Christ?

418 **A:** Christ does not control.

419 **Q:** *(L)* Will the Lizzie people come out of their cities from time to time and 'molest' the followers of Christ from time to time?

420 **A:** Maybe.

421 **Q:** *(L)* So, in other words, we will have a greatly reduced population, people here and people there, none of whom are totally united on the planet?

422 **A:** Goodnight.

End of Session.

October 18, 1994

Another data-gathering session. I wanted to know more about the C's themselves and their philosophy. What didn't occur to me was that philosophy is a human construct and is sort of oxymoronic in terms of Cosmic Light Beings. I also slipped in some 'checking questions.' I felt like a kid in a candy store, able to ask questions about all the mysteries of the world that had caught my attention over the years.

Participants: 'Frank' and Laura

1 **Q:** *(L)* Hello.

2 **A:** Hello.

3 **Q:** *(L)* Can you give us your name and opening statement?

4 **A:** Dedeba. Hello.

5 **Q:** *(L)* Are you a discarnate?

6 **A:** Cassiopaean.

7 **Q:** *(L)* Why do you not seem to have as much energy as the others?

8 **A:** Slow at first. Builds.

9 **Q:** *(L)* Has someone of you been looking over my shoulder during the day and reading the questions I have been preparing?[1]

10 **A:** Yes.

11 **Q:** *(L)* Are you prepared to answer my questions fully and completely tonight?

12 **A:** Yes.

13 **Q:** *(L)* Are you a male or female?[2]

14 **A:** Both.

15 **Q:** *(L)* Are all Cassiopaeans both male and female?

16 **A:** Yes.

17 **Q:** *(L)* Do you reproduce in anyway?

18 **A:** We are Light.

19 **Q:** *(L)* Have the Cassiopaeans ever been in physical bodies?

20 **A:** Ever is subjective.

21 **Q:** *(L)* OK, at any point in space-time have you occupied physical bodies?

22 **A:** Have, will and do.

23 **Q:** *(L)* Are you talking about the simultaneous past, present, and future?

24 **A:** Omnipresent.

25 **Q:** *(L)* Are you part of the collective subconscious, unconscious, or consciousness?

---

[1] As mentioned in the Introduction, I began to have sensations of connection sometimes hours in advance of a session. It was little more than just a feeling.

[2] I was still pretty stuck in trying to define and describe the C's in anthropogenic terms.

26 **A:** Too vague.

27 **Q:** *(L)* Are you part of our higher consciousness?

28 **A:** So is everything else.[3]

29 **Q:** *(L)* Are you prepared for my questions and to give practical answers because you know I am a practical person.

30 **A:** Yes.

31 **Q:** *(L)* Would anyone else be able to answer the sorts of questions we ask?

32 **A:** Anyone covers wide spectrum.

33 **Q:** *(L)* You understand our frustration with a lot of channeled sources?

34 **A:** Yes.

35 **Q:** *(L)* Our frustration lies in the fact that when a question is answered it is rarely, if ever, answered succinctly, directly, or anywhere near the point.

36 **A:** So your perspective, yes, to not do...

37 **Q:** *(L)* Is there any such thing as racial superiority regarding the races on the planet Earth?

38 **A:** Only karmically determined by physical confinement assignment.

39 **Q:** *(L)* It can be karmically determined to be born into one race or another?

40 **A:** Yes.[4]

41 **Q:** *(L)* Are the Aryan/Celts who came to this planet from the other one that was destroyed, were they, when they came, in any way superior to the humans already here?

42 **A:** Somewhat.

43 **Q:** *(L)* What was the nature of this superiority?

44 **A:** Durability.

45 **Q:** *(L)* Physical or mental?

46 **A:** Physical.

47 **Q:** *(L)* Well, blond-haired, blue-eyed people seem to be somewhat more delicate or thin-skinned compared to, say, the blacks.

48 **A:** In this environment on surface.[5]

49 **Q:** *(L)* Which race on Earth is the oldest?

50 **A:** All are same.

51 **Q:** *(L)* Even the Aryan/Celts from the other planet?

52 **A:** Yes.

53 **Q:** *(L)* Was there ever a time in history when Kantek, Martek, and Earth were all three occupied by sentient races which communicated with one another?

54 **A:** No.

55 **Q:** *(L)* Was there ever a time in history when all three planets were occupied simultaneously?

56 **A:** Yes.

57 **Q:** *(L)* Why are there different races?

58 **A:** Many reasons. Experimental creations. Partly.

59 **Q:** *(L)* Where did the Orientals come from?

---

[3] *The Wave* 10

[4] This won't make the white supremacists and neo-Nazis very happy, but as the saying goes: what goes around, comes around. Probably won't make the Jews happy either.

[5] I really dropped the ball here and didn't notice the implications of the response "on the surface." I just took it to mean 'surface appearances' when, in fact, as future sessions will show, it actually meant 'surface of the planet' vs. underground.

60 **A**: Same as all others. Result of experimentation.⁶

61 **Q**: *(L)* Did they originate on this planet? Are they native to this planet?

62 **A**: Both. Orientals reserved for souls most advanced; Aryans most aggressive; Negroes most naturally attuned to Earth vibrational frequency. So are "native Americans".

63 **Q**: *(L)* Can you determine my dominant genetic type?

64 **A**: Caucasian.

65 **Q**: *(L)* Is Caucasian different from Aryan or Celtic?

66 **A**: Aryan subgroup Caucasian.⁷

67 **Q**: *(L)* In terms of being Caucasian, do I have any negro blood in me?

68 **A**: Faint trace.

69 **Q**: *(L)* Who were the blue-skinned people written about in the Vedas?

70 **A**: Aryans.

71 **Q**: *(L)* Were the Aryans originally blue skinned?

72 **A**: No.

73 **Q**: *(L)* Why did the Vedas talk about blue-skinned people and why are there

---

[6] Keep in mind the metaphoric/symbolic nature of the communication. These 'experiments' could manifest in our world from an Information Field as virii that change DNA.

[7] I think this means that Aryan is a subgroup of Caucasian, not the reverse.

[8] An entire family from isolated Appalachia was tinged blue. Their ancestral line began six generations earlier with a French orphan, Martin Fugate, who settled in Eastern Kentucky. He married a red-haired American named Elizabeth Smith – who had a very pale complexion – and their union formed a genetic mutation that resulted in their descendants being born with blue skin. The most detailed account, "Blue People of Troublesome Creek," was published in 1982 by the University of Indiana's Cathy Trost. Methemoglobinemia is a blood disorder in which an abnormal amount of methemoglobin – a form of hemoglobin – is produced, according to the National Institutes for Health. In methemoglobinemia, the hemoglobin is unable to carry oxygen and it also makes it difficult for unaffected hemoglobin to release oxygen effectively to body tissues. Patients' lips are purple, the skin looks blue and the blood is 'chocolate colored' because it is not oxygenated, according to Tefferi. The disorder can be inherited, as was the case with the Fugate family, or caused by exposure to certain drugs and chemicals such as anesthetic drugs like benzocaine and xylocaine. The carcinogen benzene and nitrites used as meat additives can also be culprits, as well as certain antibiotics, including dapsone and chloroquine. The genetic form of methemoglobinemia is caused by one of several genetic defects. The Fugates probably had a deficiency in the enzyme called cytochrome-b5 methemoglobin reductase, which is responsible for recessive congenital methemoglobinemia. Because the rural Kentucky area in which the Fugates lived offered few opportunities to expand the gene pool, intermarriage allowed the rare met-H gene to come into contact with other carriers much more frequently. Today eastern Kentucky has a vastly larger population, and the condition has for all intents and purposes disappeared. (http://www.dailymail.co.uk/news/article-2101911/Talk-blue-face-The-extraordinary-tale-Blue-Family-Appalacia.html)

blue skinned people in remote areas of the Appalachians?[8]

74 **A:** Are whites real "white"?

75 **Q:** *(L)* Were there ever any really blue people?

76 **A:** No. They were perceived as blue due to thinness of skin and contrast with native population.

77 **Q:** *(L)* What is the origin of the swastika.

78 **A:** Oriental. Signified supremity.

79 **Q:** *(L)* Were Adam and Eve attempting to obtain knowledge to free themselves from bondage when they ate of the fruit of the tree of knowledge?

80 **A:** Adam and Eve are symbolic.

81 **Q:** *(L)* But were they in bondage and trying to help free themselves with the help of a benevolent 'serpent'?

82 **A:** Not benevolent.

83 **Q:** *(L)* Were they already in bondage to someone else when the Lizzies came?

84 **A:** No. They were free. The symbolic story of Adam and Eve was a story of enticement to false knowledge. The tree of knowledge of good and evil was focused, imprisoned knowledge.

85 **Q:** *(L)* Is the solar system sort of a giant atom?

86 **A:** No. But similar; remember your atomic knowledge is still mostly theoretical.

87 **Q:** *(L)* Could the orbits of the planets be described as energy 'shells' such as the shells occupied by the various electrons around an atom?

88 **A:** Close.

89 **Q:** *(L)* Does the solar system, at different points in time absorb or emit energy and do planets move from one shell to another? And, does the nature of the solar system change what it 'is' by adding or taking away bodies?

90 **A:** First, if a solar system adds or subtracts bodies then of course it changes. Next, the fundamental changes occur as a result of interaction with outside forces.

91 **Q:** *(L)* What outside forces?

92 **A:** Plane convergence.

93 **Q:** *(L)* What is plane convergence?

94 **A:** What will happen to Earth.

95 **Q:** *(L)* Is this going to happen soon?[9]

96 **A:** Yes.

97 **Q:** *(L)* Is this plane convergence a phenomenon that occurs frequently in the universe, galaxy, or solar system?

98 **A:** Yes.

99 **Q:** *(L)* What is it caused by or manifested by?

100 **A:** Passing through realm border.

101 **Q:** *(L)* What is a realm border?

102 **A:** Too complex.

103 **Q:** *(L)* What is the source of the legend of the phoenix?

104 **A:** Ancient Indian destruction and rebuilding.

105 **Q:** *(L)* Who created the Lizzies?[10]

106 **A:** Ormethion.

107 **Q:** *(L)* And who is this individual?

108 **A:** Thought center.

109 **Q:** *(L)* Located where?

---

[9] *The Wave* 39
[10] *Secret History* 12; *The Wave* 26

110 **A**: Everywhere.

111 **Q**: *(L)* Can you give us a little more of a clue?

112 **A**: Another sector of reality.[11]

113 **Q**: *(L)* Is this a sentient, self-aware being that created the Lizzies?

114 **A**: Yes and no.

115 **Q**: *(L)* Is this individual one of what you called the Transient Passengers?

116 **A**: No.

117 **Q**: *(L)* Is it similar?

118 **A**: No.

119 **Q**: *(L)* And who created this Ormethion?

120 **A**: Not being; thought center.

121 **Q**: *(L)* Thought center of what?

122 **A**: Too complex.

123 **Q**: *(L)* Who was it who appeared to Ezekiel?

124 **A**: Lizard beings.[12]

125 **Q**: *(L)* What do you intend for us to do with all this information?

126 **A**: Put in book.

127 **Q**: *(L)* Any suggestion for title?

128 **A**: Up to you.

129 **Q**: *(L)* Should we let it out gradually? Some of the information is pretty heavy.

130 **A**: All at once.

131 **Q**: *(L)* Is there only one ultimate creator of the universe?[13]

132 **A**: All is one. And one is all.

133 **Q**: *(L)* From the one what was the first division?

134 **A**: Mass division and disbursement.

135 **Q**: *(L)* Was this simultaneous?

136 **A**: Yes.

137 **Q**: *(L)* Was this what we refer to as the 'Big Bang'?

138 **A**: Yes.

139 **Q**: *(L)* Is there any reference to this event in terms of time?

140 **A**: Always.

141 **Q**: *(L)* Can we say that all that exists in the material universe is, say, 'x' number of years old?

142 **A**: No. It is the eternal now. Not only did happen, is happening and going to happen. The expanded presence.

143 **Q**: *(L)* What is the true source of the Brotherhood of the Snake in terms of human members?

144 **A**: Adam and Eve.

145 **Q**: *(L)* Were Adam and Eve real people?

146 **A**: No.

147 **Q**: *(L)* A group of people?

148 **A**: Thought pattern change not a giving into temptation.

149 **Q**: *(L)* What or who were these people? What country did they live in?

150 **A**: All people. Realm border crossing.

151 **Q**: *(L)* You mean this occurred at a time when realms crashed or crossed each other?

152 **A**: Yes.

---

[11] Here the C's were probably referring to Information Theory, but my knowledge of that was years in the future.
[12] *Secret History* 11; *The Wave* 29, 32
[13] *Secret History* 12; *The Wave* 26, 68

Q: *(L)* Did this involve a war of some sort between one group of beings and another group?

A: Realm crossing has many manifestations.

Q: *(L)* So, in other words, if it hadn't been the Lizzies it would have been someone else?

A: Yes.

Q: *(L)* Was this just sort of destined to happen?

A: Yes.

Q: *(L)* Is it just part of a great cosmic drama?

A: Yes.

Q: *(L)* Is the ultimate creator self-conscious and self-aware?

A: Yes and no.

Q: *(L)* These events that occur in our universe just sort of happen?

A: Close.

Q: *(L)* Are there other universes besides ours?

A: Yes.

Q: *(L)* Are these other universes also spun off from 'our' ultimate creator?

A: Yes.

Q: *(L)* Are these universes countable?

A: Counting is artificially limiting concept.

Q: *(L)* Are the numbers of universes limitless?

A: In a sense.

Q: *(L)* Do universes ever crash into each other?

A: Too complex.

End of Session

October 19, 1994

This session was rather personal because we were basically discovering that everyone we met who was involved in the UFO/alien research and New Age communities were a bunch of loopers; two-faced, backstabbing, egocentric nutcases! There were self-proclaimed magicians, witches, contactees, almost-ascended masters, and more. It was an absolute zoo and we were trying to navigate it because it seemed that this would be the community that might be most interested in the C's experiment results. However, that turned out not to be the case. As soon as we revealed that we were getting interesting results a whole series of personal (and psychic) attacks commenced. I've written about this period at some length in *The Wave*.

Participants: 'Frank' and Laura

1 **Q**: *(L)* Hello.

2 **A**: Hello.

3 **Q**: *(L)* Do we have anybody with us tonight?

4 **A**: We are always with you.

5 **Q**: *(L)* Who are we talking with tonight?

6 **A**: Nonigera.

7 **Q**: *(L)* Is it true that when we ask an individual under hypnosis about an alien abduction scenario to try to tune in to aliens... can we do that?

8 **A**: Yes. The individual is aware on every level and the information you seek was known at the time. The questions you ask are merely an accessing of information that is already in awareness at some level. Budd Hopkins and David Jacobs are too regimented.[1]

9 **Q**: *(L)* Why does Mike F think that people are trying to come between him and Scarlett?[2]

---

[1] *High Strangeness* 8

[2] Mike F was a self-proclaimed UFO/abduction expert who "took over" the alien abduction case of Scarlett as written about in *Soul Hackers*.

[3] I had begun to suspect that Mike F's intentions toward Scarlett were not just academic, to put it one way. She came to me for a hypnosis session after claiming she had been abducted by aliens yet again. She displayed bruises on the backs of her legs and upper arms which could have been evidence of being carried by the arms and legs, *or* could have been evidence of rough sex. I tell ya, that whole crowd was just a Peyton Place, for sure!

10 **A**: Paranoia.

11 **Q**: *(L)* Is Mike F engaged in physical relationship with Scarlett?[3]

12 **A**: Trying.

13 **Q**: *(L)* Why did Scarlett just suddenly turn cold to everything and everybody?

14 **A**: Embarrassment.

15 **Q**: *(L)* About what?

16 **A**: Cream.

17 **Q**: *(L)* Because she backed out on the cream deal?[4]

18 **A**: Close.

19 **Q**: *(L)* Well, embarrassed in what way?

20 **A**: Realized how stupid she looked and two faced also. Usually when someone stops contact with you it is because of embarrassment.

21 **Q**: *(L)* Why did she stop contacting V__-__ [Mutual friend and occasional participant in the sessions]?

22 **A**: V___ is connected to you.

23 **Q**: *(L)* Is Scarlett still having serious problems at this time [i.e. more abductions and related emotional fallout]?

24 **A**: Scarlett is having problems she perceives as serious.

25 **Q**: *(L)* But they are not, is that correct?

26 **A**: Subjective.

27 **Q**: *(L)* How does John W really feel about me and Frank?[5]

28 **A**: Questions your intent.

29 **Q**: *(L)* In what respect? Does he think I am up to something?

30 **A**: Thinks you are volatile.

31 **Q**: *(L)* Am I?

32 **A**: Subjective.

33 **Q**: *(L)* How does he feel about Frank?

34 **A**: Resents him.

35 **Q**: *(L)* Why?

36 **A**: Intelligence.

37 **Q**: *(L)* What are John W's intentions toward me?

38 **A**: Make you a follower.[6]

39 **Q**: *(L)* Is he jealous?

40 **A**: Yes.

41 **Q**: *(L)* Is it because Frank has a strong mind?

42 **A**: Yes. He only wants followers.

43 **Q**: *(L)* I am asking you to help me out here.[7]

44 **A**: Can't help with karmic level 1 processes.

45 **Q**: *(L)* What is a karmic level 1 process?

46 **A**: Major predestined lesson or mission.

47 **Q**: *(L)* Are Frank and I going through all of these things right now to create

---

[4]Scarlett had the idea to make and sell a face cream and had gotten a number of people involved and investing and it flopped.

[5]JW is cousin written about in *Amazing Grace*.

[6]JW was an almost religiously devoted follower of the ideas of Zecharia Sitchin.

[7]A recent event had occurred when JW was present with Frank and myself, and he was 'preaching' the Sitchin line. Frank and I both perceived a flash of light (as I write this, there was a flash of lightning), following which, JW became very angry and aggressive and I had to step in and say that I felt extremely ill and he should leave. It was bizarre.

some change in our state of being or our living...

48 **A**: To open memories, psychic record.

49 **Q**: *(L)* Have we been through these experiences in other lifetimes?

50 **A**: Yes.

51 **Q**: *(L)* When we do this channeling does it magnetize our bodies to bring benefits into our lives?

52 **A**: Yes.

53 **Q**: *(L)* Is this work a destined mission?

54 **A**: Yes.

55 **Q**: *(L)* If one is in process of fulfilling one's destiny in terms of performing a mission, is not the universe capable of meeting one's needs?

56 **A**: Yes.

57 **Q**: *(L)* Is this, in fact, going to happen for both of us as we focus on this work?

58 **A**: If you keep pushing forth.

59 **Q**: *(L)* So all the things we are doing now...

60 **A**: And coordinate each others input equally.

61 **Q**: *(L)* Did Scarlett make any money selling her jewelry?

62 **A**: No.

63 **Q**: *(L)* What does Scarlett think about Frank?

64 **A**: Resents his superior intelligence.

65 **Q**: *(L)* Me?

66 **A**: Resents same. Thinks you're weird.

67 **Q**: *(L)* What does AB really think about me?[8]

68 **A**: Resents your power.

69 **Q**: *(L)* CH?[9]

70 **A**: Fears your power. She is misguided.

71 **Q**: OK, thank you for the help.

72 **A**: Good Night.

End of Session

---

[8] This was a guy in St. Pete who claimed to be the highest-level Golden Dawn initiate in the State of Florida. My impression of him was that he was not the brightest crayon in the box.

[9] A local psychic reader whom I generally liked very much. She was a former nun and had a wicked sense of humor, but after the C's experiment began, she started to distance herself because some of the material contradicted her beliefs.

October 20, 1994

After dealing with some personal issues, this is another 'kid-in-the-candy-store' data-collecting session. I figured if I just asked about everything that was an item of curiosity to me, I would have enough material to begin researching the responses to try to come up with some sort of percentage of 'correct' answers. I really didn't realize how much my world view was going to change as a consequence!

Participants: 'Frank', Laura, V___

1 **Q:** *(L)* Hello.
2 **A:** Hello.
3 **Q:** *(L)* Who do we have with us tonight?
4 **A:** Elminoia.
5 **Q:** *(L)* And where are you from?
6 **A:** Cassiopaea.
7 **Q:** *(L)* Last year both V___ and I went to visit a psychic surgeon named C___. Is this individual legitimate?
8 **A:** Not in the way presented.
9 **Q:** *(L)* Does she actually insert her hand into your body and do what she claims to do?
10 **A:** No.
11 **Q:** *(L)* Is it all faked?
12 **A:** Delusional.
13 **Q:** *(L)* Where does the bloody water come from?
14 **A:** Trickery.
15 **Q:** *(L)* Does Reverend Rita know that she [the psychic surgeon] is a fraud?[1]
16 **A:** No. She believes her.
17 **Q:** *(L)* Is there any psychic activity that occurs when this woman works on one?
18 **A:** Yes.
19 **Q:** *(L)* What is the nature of it?
20 **A:** Transference of energy.
21 **Q:** *(L)* What is the source or root of this energy?
22 **A:** Intense concentration of psychic thought power.
23 **Q:** *(L)* She is not influenced by any negatives such as the Lizzies or anything like that?
24 **A:** Some, for confusion purposes.
25 **Q:** *(L)* So C___ works with the Lizzie energy?
26 **A:** Somewhat.

---

[1] Rev. Rita was the head honcho of the local spiritualist/metaphysical church as written about in *Amazing Grace* and *Soul Hackers*. Some of it was pretty funny, other parts, not so much.

[2] Members of the spiritualist church and a local Reiki group.

27 **Q:** *(L)* What is the force or background of R___, G___, J___, et al?²

28 **A:** Bogus but some sincere healing does occur as a result of faith.

29 **Q:** *(L)* In the incident that occurred in the spring at Ann B's house when 'Rev. B___' came up and sort of zapped me, who or what was behind that activity and what did he do?³

30 **A:** Dark energies of terrestrial nature were temporarily concentrated upon you.

31 **Q:** *(L)* What was the intent?

32 **A:** Harm out of jealousy.

33 **Q:** *(L)* Did they intend to kill me?

34 **A:** Hurt.

35 **Q:** *(L)* Who put this Reverend B___ up to this activity?

36 **A:** Rita.

37 **Q:** *(L)* Anybody else involved with her in that decision?

38 **A:** Scarlett.

39 **Q:** *(L)* Why?⁴

40 **A:** Fear reaction to overtaking of influence she wanted.

41 **Q:** *(L)* Is Ann B once again involved with the characters at that metaphysical church?

42 **A:** Yes.

43 **Q:** *(L)* What are they up to?

44 **A:** Strange thinking patterns.

45 **Q:** *(L)* Why did B___ call V___ the other day?

46 **A:** Try to steer her away from you and Frank.

47 **Q:** *(L)* Why does B___ think she has to steer V___ away from me and Frank?

48 **A:** You are powerful influence and so is Frank.

49 **Q:** *(L)* What do these people think we are that makes them behave so cruelly and fearfully toward us?

50 **A:** Don't agree with your knowledge.

51 **Q:** *(L)* Well, what's the story here? Am I completely in left field? Or, is Laura right and them wrong?

52 **A:** Close. You are far closer to the supreme truth than they.

53 **Q:** *(L)* Is Jeannie a good psychic?

54 **A:** Like Aunt Clara on Bewitched.

55 **Q:** *(L)* How do aliens control people?

56 **A:** Which ones?

57 **Q:** *(L)* How many choices do I have?⁵

58 **A:** Open.

59 **Q:** *(L)* Well, how do the Grays and Lizzies do it?

60 **A:** Mind and body interference with electrical response patterns.

61 **Q:** *(L)* Can they do this remotely?

62 **A:** Less effectively.

63 **Q:** *(L)* So they need to work directly on you or be in contact with you by some means that is somewhat material?

---

³Written about in *Amazing Grace* and *Soul Hackers*.

⁴That answer actually shocked and hurt me. I had no idea that Scarlett felt that way about me, since she was so nice and complimentary to my face. I was definitely learning a few hard lessons about people.

⁵This is an indication that I was beginning to learn that a dialog with the C's was best conducted without expectations!

64 **A**: Yes.

65 **Q**: *(L)* Are there other aliens on the planet abducting people?

66 **A**: Much less often.

67 **Q**: *(L)* What was the flying boomerang the kids and I saw last year?[6]

68 **A**: Lizard projection multiple reality station.

69 **Q**: *(L)* Did they fly over my house deliberately for me to see them?

70 **A**: Yes.

71 **Q**: *(L)* What was the purpose of them showing themselves to me?

72 **A**: Make you aware of existence.

73 **Q**: *(L)* Why did they want to make me aware of their existence?

74 **A**: That is an extremely complicated situation.

75 **Q**: *(L)* Did that little flap that occurred in Pasco county in spring of 1993 happen as a result of Frank's and my activities?[7]

76 **A**: Yes.

77 **Q**: *(L)* Was there a craft over my house the night I hypnotized Pat Z?

78 **A**: Tuned into visual stimuli from implants. And Z implants alerted scout craft of Grays and Lizzies.

79 **Q**: *(L)* Is Pat Z___ under the control of the Lizzies?

80 **A**: Yes.[8]

81 **Q**: *(L)* How many people are not under the control of the Lizzies nowadays?!

82 **A**: Open.

83 **Q**: *(L)* We would like to know what is the origin of the Gypsies?

84 **A**: Genes spliced. Slaves of dark forces.

85 **Q**: *(L)* Who are these dark forces?

86 **A**: Same.

87 **Q**: *(L)* As what?

88 **A**: Brotherhood.

89 **Q**: *(L)* Does this Brotherhood consist of Lizzies and various humans?

90 **A**: Yes.

91 **Q**: *(L)* If the Gypsies were gene spliced, who were they gene spliced with?

92 **A**: Alien race, humanoid, and Atlantean drone workers.

93 **Q**: *(L)* What were Atlantean drone workers?

94 **A**: Slave people controlled by crystal.

95 **Q**: *(L)* Why do the Gypsies remain so cohesive? Is that genetically programed?

96 **A**: Yes. And mind control.

97 **Q**: *(L)* There are legends of half-human creatures, minotaurs, centaurs, etc. Were any of these creatures real?

---

[6]Written about in "Autobiographical Background" of *Riding the Wave*, *High Strangeness* 2, *Amazing Grace* 39.

[7]See *Amazing Grace* as well as Tom French's article in the *St. Pete Times*: http://www.sptimes.com/News/webspecials/exorcist/index.html

[8]I could hardly believe this at the time. Also, Pat Z reentered our lives further down the road with fairly dramatic side-effects. Again, some of this is written about in *Amazing Grace*, some written about in Tom French's article, and some in *The Wave*. It was quite an adventure when we learned who Pat Z really was, and who her dying husband was and what his occupation had been.

98 **A:** Experiments known as beasts in Atlantis. VG is part Gypsy. Hiding this.[9]

99 **Q:** *(L)* Does she know it?

100 **A:** Some.

101 **Q:** *(L)* Who built the city of Baalbek?[10]

102 **A:** Antereans and early Sumerians. We meant Atlanteans.[11]

103 **Q:** *(L)* What is the reason for the enormous proportions of this building?

104 **A:** Giants.

105 **Q:** *(L)* Who were the giants?

106 **A:** Genetic effort to recreate Nephalim.

107 **Q:** *(L)* Did the Atlanteans and Sumerians succeed in recreating the Nephilim?

108 **A:** No.

109 **Q:** *(L)* Why did they build this enormous city?

110 **A:** Retarded subjects.

111 **Q:** *(L)* The results of their efforts were retarded?

112 **A:** Yes.

113 **Q:** *(L)* Why did they build the enormous city?

114 **A:** In anticipation of success.

115 **Q:** *(L)* Why would someone come along and build a city of the proportions of Baalbek in anticipation of a genetic project that could take many years to accomplish?

116 **A:** Project took only three years. Speeded up growth cycle using nuclear hormonal replication procedure. Why failed.

117 **Q:** *(L)* That's why it failed, because of the speeded up growth?

118 **A:** Did not take properly.

119 **Q:** *(L)* What technical means did they use to cut the stones and transport them?[12]

120 **A:** Sound wave focusing.[13]

121 **Q:** *(L)* What happened to interrupt or halt the building of this city?

122 **A:** Venus first appearance and pass.

123 **Q:** *(L)* What year was this project brought to a halt?

---

[9]The C's here were obviously trying to give me a clue. Our relationship with VG was problematical at times but we kept trying to operate based on normal human dynamics and surface appearances. This was rapidly fading as an option in our lives, as we were learning. Seeing and identifying essential energies was becoming a theme of the experiment as well as our 'real lives.'

[10]*High Strangeness* 14; *The Wave* 44. I should also like to mention here that in more recent years, while researching material from the sessions, I came across the fact that the people of the ancient Roman Empire, as late as the 6th Century, knew the great temple at Baalbek as 'The Temple of Solomon.' So obviously, the idea that there was a 'Temple of Solomon' in Jerusalem was a development after this time.

[11]Who are the Antereans?

[12]*The Wave* 44

[13]*The Wave* 24

[14]Here we have the first 'appearance' and close pass of Venus in 3218 BC. The prior sessions include info about Venus as follows: 30 September: appeared in the sky from the area of Jupiter; Earth moved into new orbital position as a result of this interaction (one assumes that this is the Baalbek time); an event of this type (but

124 **A:** 3218 B.C.[14]

125 **Q:** *(L)* Who built the city of Mohenjo Daro?

126 **A:** Lizards directly. Coatzlmundi legend ties in to this directly look at illustrations on stones now.[15]

127 **Q:** *(L)* Who is Coatzlmundi?

128 **A:** Other deity of the Lizards worshipped by the Atlanteans and their descendants because of the direct contact with humans for 1000 years.

129 **Q:** *(L)* Now, you said Mohenjo Daro was built by the Lizzies directly. Did they occupy this city themselves?

130 **A:** No.

131 **Q:** *(L)* When was this city last inhabited continually?

132 **A:** 3065 years ago.

133 **Q:** *(L)* When was it built?

134 **A:** 6092 years ago.

135 **Q:** *(L)* I would like to go back to the subject of the Nephilim. Now you said the Nephilim were a group of humanoid types brought here to Earth to be enforcers, is that correct?[16]

---

not necessarily Venus) took place at the time of the flood of Noah, i.e. 10,662 BC; Noah's flood caused by close passage of Martek; Venus on close to a 52-yr orbit after entering the solar system; makes 7 passes before being precipitated into a stable orbit; originally came from 19 light years away. 5 October: Exodus was the last passage of Venus before settling into orbit, i.e. 2676 BC (542 years after the Baalbek event); at the time of the Flood of Noah (10,662 BC) Martek was sent running amok due to "Planetary alignment gravitational aberration related to Venus," which suggests that the approach of Venus to the solar system was felt long before it was seen. 7 October: Venus pass at the time of the Exodus, 2676 BC; Venus from near Arcturus (Arcturus is 36.66 light years from Earth); Venus was drawn into the solar system by the gravitational pull of the cluster of comets. In the 19 November session, we find the following: Atlantis suffered damage by a close passage of Martek and a mass of comets (one assumes this was the Flood of Noah event and includes Victor Clube's giant comet that breaks up into many pieces). "Part of landmass, but not all, was destroyed." But then, there was partial recovery (building of pyramids and other such mega-monuments?). Then, a second destruction of Atlantean civilization was caused by Venus, which we may assume to have been the Baalbek event of 3218 BC. Much later, 23 August 2001, in what is obviously a corrupt session due to the presence of guest, it is said that Venus cause the eruption of Thera in 1627 BC.

[15] The idea of a connection between a civilization on the Indian sub-continent, and what was obviously a Central or South American reference, did not make much sense until some years later when the book *Gods of the Cataclysm: A revolutionary investigation of man and his gods before and after the Great Cataclysm* by Hugh Fox fell into my hands. Fox presents some fascinating theories and evidence about how early civilizations before the flood/cataclysm could have interacted with one another despite being separated by vast oceans and great distances. As it happens, the book is full of illustrations that demonstrate conclusively that there was a connection.

[16] *High Strangeness* 14

136 **A:** Yes.

137 **Q:** *(L)* When were they brought here?

138 **A:** 9046 B.C. one reference.

139 **Q:** *(L)* They were giants, is that correct?

140 **A:** Yes.

141 **Q:** *(L)* They were presented to the people as the representatives, or 'sons' of God, is that correct?

142 **A:** Yes.

143 **Q:** *(L)* You say these dudes were 11 to 14 feet tall...

144 **A:** Yes.

145 **Q:** *(L)* You and the ancient literature say that these sons of god intermarried with human women, is that correct?

146 **A:** Yes.

147 **Q:** *(L)* Did they do that the same way it is done today, that is, sexual interaction?

148 **A:** No.

149 **Q:** *(L)* How was it done?

150 **A:** Forced insemination.

151 **Q:** *(L)* So, it was artificial insemination?

152 **A:** Close.

153 **Q:** *(L)* Were these beings like us, including their sexual apparati?

154 **A:** Close.

155 **Q:** *(L)* Any significant differences?

156 **A:** Three gonads.

157 **Q:** *(L)* Was their sexual apparatus otherwise similar?

158 **A:** Yes.

159 **Q:** *(L)* Did they mate with human females in a normal way at any time?

160 **A:** No.

161 **Q:** *(L)* Why not?

162 **A:** Size difference.

163 **Q:** *(L)* Just for the sake of curiosity, just how different in terms of size?

164 **A:** 23 inches long.

165 **Q:** *(L)* Were they circumcised?[17]

166 **A:** No.

167 **Q:** *(L)* Just what was the origin of the practice of circumcision?

168 **A:** Same as all Judaic traditions hygiene.

169 **Q:** *(L)* Where do the Tibetans come from?

170 **A:** Asia.

171 **Q:** *(L)* Were they special in any way? Hybrids or anything?

172 **A:** No. All are hybrids. At some juncture.

173 **Q:** *(L)* What is the origin of the Nubians?

174 **A:** Caucus range.

175 **Q:** *(L)* How come they are so terribly black?

176 **A:** Genetic mixing.

177 **Q:** *(L)* With what? Anything particularly special about them?

178 **A:** East Indian aborigines.

179 **Q:** *(L)* Who was the Queen of Sheba?

180 **A:** Fictional.

---

[17] Yes, I know that was a dumb question but I had a theory that circumcision had been invented to 'imitate' some 'godly type' individual, so I was just throwing it out there in case.

Q: *(L)* Did a great queen come to visit King Solomon?

A: Alien influence.

Q: *(L)* Who was Arjuna?

A: Same as Sheba.

Q: *(L)* Who is Shiva?

A: Same.

Q: *(L)* Rama?

A: Indian. High priest influenced by Confederation.

Q: *(L)* Is Ormethion who the Lizzies worship?

A: Close.

Q: *(L)* Who do they worship? What do they call their god?

A: Physical universe.

Q: *(L)* The physical universe is their god?

A: Yes.

Q: *(L)* What happened to KW?[18]

A: Killed.

Q: *(L)* By whom?

A: Demented human named Carl.

Q: *(L)* What happened to Dale W and Clarke S?[19]

A: Abducted by aliens for experimentation.

Q: *(L)* Were they killed through these experiments?

A: Yes.

Q: *(L)* How were the walls of Jericho brought down?

A: Earthquake.

Q: *(L)* What happened to the army of Sennacherib?

A: Destroyed by cosmic rays energy concentration by Lizards.[20]

---

[18] Little girl missing in another state.

[19] Two local men who had disappeared without a trace in October 1979. One of them, Dale W, was the elder brother of one of my school classmates. An article from the Mid-Pinellas *Evening Independent* of Jan 1, 1980, referred to the area where Clarke and Dale were lost as the "Hudson Triangle" because there were three boats and six men lost in about three months. The Coast Guard source is the one who gave this name to the area. He reported that "These were really all-out searches..." As it happens, Clarke was a retired Air Force major and B-52 pilot. Absolutely nothing has ever been found. The disappearances have been blamed on drug-running on the FL coast.

[20] By now we should know that "cosmic ray concentration by Lizards" can very well mean something that we might label otherwise, though I admit that here I don't know what. In 701 BC, a rebellion backed by Egypt and Babylonia broke out in Judah, led by King Hezekiah. In response Sennacherib sacked a number of cities in Judah. He laid siege to Jerusalem, but soon returned to Nineveh, with Jerusalem not having been sacked, in order to put down an attempted coup. This event was recorded by Sennacherib himself, by Herodotus, Josephus, and by several Biblical writers. According to the Bible, Sennacherib also withdrew because the "angel of Yahweh went out and put to death 185,000 in the Assyrian camp" (2 Kings 19:35). Assyrian records date it to 689 BC and do not treat it as a disaster, but a great victory – they maintain that the siege was so successful that Hezekiah was forced to give a monetary tribute, and the Assyrians left victoriously, without losses of thou-

207 Q: *(L)* Is there such a thing as sound that can kill?

208 A: Yes. Anything properly concentrated can kill.

209 Q: *(L)* Are there words that can kill by their simple pronunciation?

210 A: No.

211 Q: *(L)* Are there words of power that invoke energies by their pronunciation?

212 A: Maybe.

213 Q: *(L)* Could you tell us any of them?

214 A: No. You might use unwisely.

215 Q: *(L)* Sitchin says that the pyramid was built as a permanent marking system to navigate the planets of our solar system. Could you give comments on this please?

216 A: It was not built for that.

217 Q: *(L)* Who was Jehovah?

218 A: Lizard projection.

219 Q: *(L)* What is the Melchizedek priesthood?

220 A: False rite.

221 Q: *(L)* Is there an order of priests to which the original Melchizedek belonged that was true?

222 A: Yes.

223 Q: *(L)* I had an experience under hypnosis several years ago while in the mountains of North Carolina. What was that?[21]

224 A: Soul memory awakening.

225 Q: *(L)* What was the significance of the necklace?

226 A: Symbolic of ability to communicate supreme knowledge.

227 Q: *(L)* Another experience on the boat one night, I am remembering now. What was that event?[22]

228 A: Similar.

229 Q: *(L)* What was the source of these two events?

230 A: Us.

231 Q: *(L)* Alright, another event during meditation followed by period of intense crying. What was this event?

232 A: Soul cleansing.

233 Q: *(L)* The source?

---

sands of men, and without sacking Jerusalem. The Greek historian Herodotus, who wrote his *Histories* ca. 450 BC, speaks of a divinely-appointed disaster destroying an army of Sennacherib (2:141): "As the two armies lay here opposite one another, there came in the night, a multitude of field-mice, which devoured all the quivers and bowstrings of the enemy, and ate the thongs by which they managed their shields. Next morning they commenced their fight, and great multitudes fell, as they had no arms with which to defend themselves. There stands to this day in the temple of Vulcan, a stone statue of Sethos, with a mouse in his hand, and an inscription to this effect – 'Look on me, and learn to reverence the gods.'" Josephus' *Jewish Antiquities*, book ten, verses 21–23, relate an account by the Babylonian historian Berossus, in which Berossus claims a disease befell an Assyrian army led by Rabshakeh, and one hundred eighty-five thousand men were lost. Earlier in the book, the account of Herodotus is also mentioned. So, maybe "cosmic ray concentration" is a metaphor for a plague virus?

[21] Written about in *Amazing Grace*.
[22] The "Boatride to Damascus," written about in *Amazing Grace*.

234 **A**: Us ridding you of dark influences.²³

235 **Q**: *(L)* When did the Aryans invade India?²⁴

236 **A**: 8243 years ago.

237 **Q**: *(L)* Who was there before that?

238 **A**: Asian tribes and number 3 prototype.

239 **Q**: *(L)* What is a number 3 prototype?

240 **A**: Known as Neanderthal man.

241 **Q**: *(L)* And what are we?

242 **A**: Number 4 types C and D. Translation into English comprehension.

243 **Q**: *(L)* Were the Aryan/Celts the original giants?

244 **A**: No.

245 **Q**: *(L)* What white men were seen in South America and talked to the tribes there and promised to return one day and were worshipped as gods?²⁵

246 **A**: Egyptians and Atlantean descendants.

247 **Q**: *(L)* What did the Atlanteans do to bring this karma on us such that the Grays and Lizzies...

248 **A**: Worshipped and served self to extreme.²⁶

249 **Q**: *(L)* Does the act of channeling actually change our genetics or DNA or some element around our being in some way that we are not even conscious of?

250 **A**: Steadily yes.

251 **Q**: *(L)* Will this channeling have effects on us that will cause changes our lives and lifestyle?²⁷

252 **A**: Yes.

253 **Q**: *(L)* Will there be benefits brought into our lives because of dedication to this work?

254 **A**: Yes.

255 **Q**: *(L)* If we dedicate ourselves does this mean that we will be protected or cared for in any way?

256 **A**: Close.

257 **Q**: *(L)* We got some information from the first session when we were working with S___ which said some awful things about bits of children's organs were removed, etc. What was the source of that information? Did that come from you guys?

258 **A**: Yes. Sorry for shock but necessary for broadening channel.²⁸

259 **Q**: *(L)* You say that there is an effort on the part of the Orions or Lizards... Are the Orions and Lizards synonymous?

260 **A**: Close.

261 **Q**: *(L)* OK. You say that there is an effort on the part of these beings to create a new race. Why do they want or need a new race?

262 **A**: Theirs no longer satisfies them.

---

²³I can only say that it was definitely a profound event of cleansing of some sort. I've written about it in *Amazing Grace*.
²⁴*The Wave* 68
²⁵As written about by Graham Hancock.
²⁶*High Strangeness* 9
²⁷It was already happening. It was as though the C's and their communications had become a powerful polarizing influence: people loved or hated it.
²⁸*The Wave* 10

263 **Q:** *(L)* When we asked you in the session on July 30th where you were from you said Corsoca, is that correct?

264 **A:** Yes.

265 **Q:** *(L)* Is that a planet?

266 **A:** No.

267 **Q:** *(L)* What is Corsoca?

268 **A:** Point of energy confluence between realms that reflects locator when we were 3rd level.[29]

269 **Q:** *(L)* When we do this channeling, Frank and I together, is it different than if Frank were to do it alone?

270 **A:** Yes.

271 **Q:** *(L)* OK, when we are doing it together with the board, where are you in space-time relative to us as we sit here?

272 **A:** Above at 6000 miles at border between 3 realms.

273 **Q:** *(L)* Once again, you said that if we called on you for help, you would come if we ask. Is there any special way to call and how can we know if you answer?

274 **A:** Will feel it.

End of Session

---

[29] Since the C's further explicate "we are you in the future," and here they mention having been at this "point of energy confluence between realms that reflects locator when we were 3rd level," what is the implication? I can't help but recall that strange poem from "The King in Yellow" quoted by Jacques Vallee in his book *Revelations* that I mentioned in the notes to the first session: *"Strange is the night where black stars rise,/ And strange moons circle through the skies, / But stranger still is... Lost Carcosa. / Songs that the Pleiades shall sing,/ Where flap the tatters of the King,/ Must die unheard in ... Dim Carcosa./ Along the shore the cloud waves break,/ The twin suns sink behind the lake,/ The shadows lengthen... In Carcosa."* If that is applicable, it is a sad prospect for my world.

October, 22 1994

This was an experimental session undertaken because Frank kept insisting on taking over the whole channeling experiment and turning it into trance channeling with him as the sole channel. As those who have read *Amazing Grace* and *The Wave* know, I don't trust that kind of channeling any further than I can throw an elephant. However, in this case, the information seems to be very good, and I've noted elsewhere that Frank was an extremely talented psychic who could look at your palm, tune into you in some way, and pull out all kinds of astonishingly accurate things – not because they came to him from some outside source, but because he extracted it in some way from the individual he was 'channeling for.' Thus it seems that this session was just an enhanced version of that type of thing – that I was there with the questions and he was somehow extracting this information *through* me. (I also suspect that this was the same mechanics of the Ra channeling with Don Elkins as the 'antenna' and receiver and Carla Rueckert as the 'speakers'.) So, as I said, the info is good, some of it beautiful even, when reading the words – though most of it is unverifiable. The only thing I can say is that you had to be there to understand why, despite the apparent excellence of the material, nobody else present wanted to continue in this way. There was a certain very subtle 'taste' to the tone and attitude of Frank that was unpleasant. Also, notice the verbosity. We all had the feeling that if this practice was continued, Frank would be co-opted in some way.

Direct channeling with 'Frank' under hypnosis. Participants: Laura, Terry, Jan

Q: *(L)* Who is with us?

A: Enduanda and Alorra.[1]

---
[1]That two 'energy sources' are named is interesting.

Q: *(L)* What is the significance of the earthquake that occurred a few months ago that was called the superdeep earthquake that was 400 miles deep?

A: A magma shift caused by gradual heating from within. Just part of a periodic cycle.

Q: *(L)* Any other comments on that?

A: No.

Q: *(L)* We would like to have comments on the thumping noises reportedly heard off the coast of California.

A: Expansion of a base.

Q: *(L)* What kind of base?

A: It's a transfer center for those beings known as the Grays.

Q: *(L)* And what was the thumping?

A: They are expanding it.

Q: *(L)* Is it construction work?

A: Yes except that they are using sound waves to disintegrate rock in the crust under the ocean. This disintegration causes the atomic structure of the particles being disintegrated to completely disappear, which has something to do with why those sounds are heard in that particular rhythm.

Q: *(L)* Any other comments?

A: There is some awareness on the part of the U.S. government as to what is going on there. They are suspicious.

Q: *(L)* What was the source of knowledge accessed by Edgar Cayce?

A: Well, he had a unique biochemical composition which allowed for easy opening and closing of his consciousness from outside sources without interference with his electromagnetic flow stream. It is a very unique and unusual situation. The first manifestation of this was when he asked for help. If he had not asked for help from a higher source, possibly his awareness of his abilities would never have come forth.

Q: *(L)* What is the source of Lama Singh's knowledge?

A: Lama Singh has studied long and hard in metaphysical fields through meditation and other areas and therefore a doorway or channel can be opened voluntarily. This requires the cooperation of the host and is not as easily opened or closed as it was in the case of Cayce.

Q: *(L)* In terms of access levels, which one of the two had access to the greatest field of subjects or information?

A: Actually Cayce was accessing a somewhat different source, but the overall accuracy level and the overall intensity level were greater with Cayce.

Q: *(L)* In terms of relationships relative to the Cassiopaean level of knowledge, how would Cayce and Lama Singh relate?

A: The access level is much greater and broader.

Q: *(L)* When and how did planet Earth acquire its moon?

A: Was caused by the regular passage of a large comet cluster which caused a gravitational disruption allowing a large chunk of the original Earth's surface, which was somewhat less solid at that point in space-time, to break away from the main body and assume a locked-in orbit around the main body.

Q: *(L)* When did this happen?

A: This occurred approximately 3 billion years ago.

Q: *(L)* Can a spiritual being become entrapped in physical matter?[2]

A: It's possible but very unlikely.

---

[2] *The Wave* 68

Q: *(L)* Are human beings entrapped in physical matter?[3]

A: By choice.

Q: *(L)* Why did they make this choice?

A: To experience physical sensations. It was a group mind decision.

Q: *(L)* Who was in charge of the group?

A: The group.

Q: *(L)* Does the interaction between the spirit/soul and the body/physical produce some by-product that is desirable to other beings?

A: Well, all things have desirable consequences as well as undesirable consequences, but it must also be mentioned here that everything that exists in all realms of the universe can experience existence in one of only two ways. That would be defined as a long wave cycle and a short wave cycle. Going back to your previous question about why humans are "entrapped" in physical existence, which, of course, is voluntary and chosen, this was due to the desire to change from the long wave cycle experience of completely what you would call ethereal or spiritual existence, to the short wave cycle of what you call physical existence. The difference is that a long wave cycle involves only very gradual change in evolution in a cyclical manner. Whereas a short wave cycle involves a duality. And this is the case with souls in physical bodies as is experienced on this Earth plane because the soul experiences an ethereal state for half the cycle and a physical state for the other half of the cycle. While these halves are not measured in time the way you measure time, the totality of experience is equal in each half. The necessity to form the short wave cycle was brought about through nature through the natural bounds of the universe when the group mind of souls chose to experience physicality as opposed to a completely ethereal existence.

Q: *(L)* Does this interaction produce a by-product?

A: It produces equal by-products of a positive and negative nature.

Q: *(L)* And what are these by-products?

A: Which one first?

Q: *(L)* Positive.

A: Positive by-product is an increase in relative energy which speeds up the learning process of the soul and all of its one dimensional and two dimensional interactive partners. In other words, flora and fauna, minerals, etc. All experience growth and movement towards reunion at a faster rate on the cycle through this short wave cycle physical/ethereal transfer. Of a negative nature, it also produces many negative experiences for these very same entities which otherwise would not exist because being of a first level and second level nature, flora and fauna would ordinarily experience a long term or long wave cycle on the physical plane as opposed to a short wave cycle physical and ethereal, as they do now because of their interaction with the human species in its short wave ethereal/physical cycle.

Q: *(L)* The comment was made at one point that certain alien beings abduct humans and subject them to cruel and torturous deaths in order to create "maximum energy transfer." In this respect, what is this maximum energy

---

[3] *The Wave* 8, 23

transfer that occurs during a long, slow, torturous dying process?[4]

46 **A:** Extreme fear and anxiety builds up fear/anxiety energy which is of a negative nature, which fuels the beings that you speak of in that they draw from that and produce a sort of a fueling energy which keeps them going as one of their forms of nourishment based on their metabolic structure.

47 **Q:** *(L)* What is their metabolic structure?

48 **A:** That is very complex and very difficult to describe because it is on the fourth level of density which you do not understand. But, part of their reason for existence on the fourth level is their ability to nourish themselves both through ethereal methods and through physical methods. Therefore, this energy transfer would represent the ethereal method of nourishment and other means are achieved physically.

49 **Q:** *(L)* What other means?

50 **A:** Well, the drinking of blood and blood by-products would be an example of that.

51 **Q:** *(L)* Do they do that?

52 **A:** Yes, but the manner of intake is different than what you may be thinking. It is done through pores.

53 **Q:** *(L)* In what manner?

54 **A:** Bathing and then absorbing the necessary products and then disposing of the remaining product.

55 **Q:** *(L)* Did Arthur Clarke channel *Childhood's End*?

56 **A:** No. Used imagination.

[4] *High Strangeness* 7
[5] *The Wave* 5

57 **Q:** *(L)* Is the amnesia related to UFO abductions deliberately induced or is it a product of the mind's inability to deal with the event?

58 **A:** It is an equal commingling of both.

59 **Q:** *(L)* The part that is deliberately induced, how is that accomplished?

60 **A:** By using a cosmic energy flow to influence memory function through a combination of spiritual and chemical interaction.

61 **Q:** *(L)* Can you be more specific?

62 **A:** Being more specific would be in another way less specific, but a good way to put it is altering the flow of electromagnetic energy in the brain. Electromagnetic energy, electromagnetism, is the life force that exists within all that evolves through long wave or short wave cycles.

63 **Q:** *(L)* Going back to the beings that absorb nutrients through their pores, what kind of beings are they?

64 **A:** Both those that you describe as the Lizard beings and those you describe as the Grays. This is necessary for their survival in each case. Even though the Grays are not natural parts of the short wave cycle, but rather an artificial creation by the Lizard beings, but nevertheless they mimic the nourishment functions.

65 **Q:** *(L)* Since they are artificially created by the Lizard beings, does this mean they have no souls?

66 **A:** That's correct.[5]

67 **Q:** *(L)* How do they function? Are they like robots?

68 **A**: They function by interaction with the souls of the Lizard beings. This technology is extremely far in advance of that with which you are familiar, but the Gray beings are not only built and designed artificially, but also function as a projection mentally and psychically of the Lizard beings. They are like four dimensional probes.

69 **Q**: *(L)* As four dimensional probes, what are their capabilities?

70 **A**: They have all the same capabilities of the Lizard beings except for the fact that their physical appearance is entirely different and they do not have souls of their own and also their biological structure is internally different. But, their functioning is the same and in order to remain as projection beings they also must absorb nutrients in the same fashion both spiritually and physically as the Lizard beings do. The reason the negative energy is necessary fuel is that the Lizard beings and the Grays are both living in the fourth level of density, which is the highest level of density one can exist in serving only self as these entities do. So, therefore, they must absorb negative energy because the fourth level of density is the highest example of self service which is a negative thought pattern. The fourth level of density is a progression from the third level of density. With each progression upward in density level, the existence for the individual conscious entity becomes less difficult. So, therefore, the fourth level of density is less difficult to exist in that the third, the third is less difficult than the second and so on. It puts less strain on the soul energy. Therefore, beings existing on the fourth level of density can draw from beings existing on the third level of density in terms of absorption of negative soul energy. Likewise, beings on the third level of density can draw from beings on the second level of density, though this type of drawing is not as necessary but is done. This is why human beings existing on the third level frequently cause pain and suffering to those of the animal kingdom who exist on the second level of density because you are drawing negative soul energy as beings who primarily serve self, as you do, from those on the second level, and on the first, and so on. Now, as you advance to the fourth level of density which is coming up for you, you must now make a choice as to whether to progress to service to others or to remain at the level of service to self. This will be the decision which will take quite some time for you to adjust to. This is what is referred to as the "thousand year period." This is the period as measured in your calendar terms that will determine whether or not you will advance to service to others or remain at the level of service to self. And those who are described as the Lizards have chosen to firmly lock themselves into service to self. And, since they are at the highest level of density where this is possible, they must continually draw large amounts of negative energy from those at the third level, second level, and so on, which is why they do what they do. This also explains why their race is dying, because they have not been able to learn for themselves how to remove themselves from this particular form of expression to that of service to others. And, since they have such, as you would measure it, a long period of time, remained at this level and, in fact, become firmly entrenched in it, and, in fact, have increased themselves in it, this is why they are dying

and desperately trying to take as much energy from you as possible and also to recreate their race metabolically.

71 **Q:** *(L)* Well, if we are sources of food and labor for them, why don't they just breed us in pens on their own planet?[6]

72 **A:** They do.

73 **Q:** *(L)* Well, since there are so many of us here, why don't they just move in and take over?[7]

74 **A:** That is their intention. That has been their intention for quite some time. They have been traveling back and forth through time as you know it, to set things up so that they can absorb a maximum amount of negative energy with the transference from third level to fourth level that this planet is going to experience, in the hopes that they can overtake you on the fourth level and thereby accomplish several things. 1: retaining their race as a viable species; 2: increasing their numbers; 3: increasing their power; 4: expanding their race throughout the realm of fourth density. To do all of this they have been interfering with events for what you would measure on your calendar as approximately 74 thousand years. And they have been doing so in a completely still state of space-time traveling backward and forward at will during this work. Interestingly enough, though, all of this will fail.

75 **Q:** *(L)* How can you be so sure it will fail?[8]

76 **A:** Because we see it. We are able to see all, not just what we want to see. Their failing is that they see only what they want to see. In other words,

[6] *The Wave* 22
[7] *The Wave* 31
[8] *High Strangeness* 17

it's the highest manifestation possible of that which you would refer to as wishful thinking. And, wishful thinking represented on the fourth level of density becomes reality for that level. You know how you wishfully think? Well, it isn't quite reality for you because you are on the third level, but if you are on the fourth level and you were to perform the same function, it would indeed be your awareness of reality. Therefore they cannot see what we can see since we serve others as opposed to self, and since we are on sixth level, we can see all that is at all points as is, not as we would want it to be.

77 **Q:** *(L)* Zecharia Sitchin proposes that the pyramid was built as a permanent marking system to navigate the solar system. Could you comment on that idea?

78 **A:** That is incorrect. The pyramids were built as energy storage and transference facilities. They were built by the descendants of those known to you as the Atlanteans who are, of course, your ancestors in soul matters. They were not built to be markers for anything.

79 **Q:** *(L)* Did any aliens at all, and specifically the Lizzies, ever live among mankind and receive worship?

80 **A:** They did not live among mankind, but they did interact directly with human beings, at various points in the past. It was at those points when human beings were ready, willing and able to accept deities appearing directly from outside sources and then worship them. Such things would not have occurred in the recent past. But, beware,

81 **Q:** *(L)* Who made the Nazca lines in South America and what was their purpose?

82 **A:** Those were natives living in the area at the particular time who were highly advanced spiritually and they put those lines there to call to others that were coming from what they perceived to be an outer space location.

83 **Q:** *(L)* Were they symbols of power in any way?

84 **A:** Well, some may have perceived them as such but they were mainly an effort to call forth those who had been worshipped and had appeared to them previously from the outside including not only the Lizard beings, but other travelers.

85 **Q:** *(L)* Who built the city of Angkor Wat?

86 **A:** That was built by the Lizard beings themselves. Built approximately 3108 years ago.

87 **Q:** *(L)* Who built the city of Mohenjo Daro?

88 **A:** That also was built by the Lizard beings directly.

89 **Q:** *(L)* Did they live in these cities?

90 **A:** No, as stated before, they did not live there, they visited or occupied on a temporary basis, but did not live there.

91 **Q:** *(L)* Who did they build the cities for?

92 **A:** They built the cities for themselves and their worshippers amongst humans.

93 **Q:** *(L)* In an earlier reading, the question was asked as to what planet you are from, and the response was Corsoca. The question was then asked: "Can you be more specific?" and the answer was 2 DILOR. Is this an incorrect spelling or what does this mean?

94 **A:** That which you refer to as Corsoca is actually not what you would refer to as a planet in your understanding, because you must understand it is at the sixth level of density which is completely out of reach of any of your senses except for the sixth one, therefore you do not have any concept of the level of being at that density. So, the term "planet" simply cannot apply here. But, that is, indeed, our residence. But it is best left at that because to try to explain to you what exactly it is like there would not be possible for you to imagine.[9]

95 **Q:** *(L)* Alright. You mentioned in this earlier reading something about a "Denver Airport Scandal." Recently it has come to my attention that this is a possible development. Is this scandal going to develop into a far worse situation and, if so, what are the ramifications?

96 **A:** Yes, that will be an ongoing problem, to say the least.[10]

97 **Q:** *(L)* Are there any rituals that can be performed to provide protection for one against intrusion by the Lizzies?[11]

---

[9] This appears to contradict the information given towards the end of the 20 October session.

[10] No cigar for trance channeling there! As noted earlier, everything taken in context suggests that 9/11 was the event being predicted in the early sessions though the specifics were off since, probably, the planning of the conspirators was not yet congealed.

[11] *High Strangeness* 9; *The Wave* 10, 23

98 **A**: Rituals are self-defeating.

99 **Q**: *(L)* Are there any technological means we can use?

100 **A**: The only defense needed is knowledge. Knowledge defends you against every possible form of harm in existence. The more knowledge you have, the less fear you have, the less pain you have, the less stress you feel, the less anguish you feel, and the less danger you experience of any form or sort. Think of this very carefully now for this is very important: Where is there any limitation in the concept behind the word "knowledge"? Being that there is no limitation, what is the value of that word? Infinite. Can you conceive of how that one concept, that one meaning frees you from all limitation? Use your sixth sense to conceive of how the word, the term, the meaning of knowledge can provide with all that you could possibly ever need. If you think carefully you will begin to see glimpses of how this is true in its greatest possible form.

101 **Q**: *(L)* Does this include knowledge learned from books?

102 **A**: This includes all possible meanings of the concept of the word. Can you think of how it would be that simply with one term, this one word can carry so much meaning? We sense that you are not completely aware. You can have glimpses of illumination and illumination comes from knowledge. If you strive perpetually to gain and gather knowledge, you provide yourself with protection from every possible negative occurrence that could ever happen. Do you know why this is? The more knowledge you have, the more awareness you have as to how to protect yourself. Eventually this awareness becomes so powerful and so all encompassing that you do not even have to perform tasks or rituals, if you prefer, to protect yourself. The protection simply comes naturally with the awareness.

103 **Q**: *(L)* Does knowledge have a substance or an existence apart from its possession or its acceptance?

104 **A**: Knowledge has all substance. It goes to the core of all existence.

105 **Q**: *(L)* So acquiring knowledge includes adding substance to one's being?

106 **A**: Indeed. It includes adding everything to one's being that is desirable. And also, when you keep invoking the light, as you do, truly understand that the light is knowledge. That is the knowledge which is at the core of all existence. And being at the core of all existence it provides protection from every form of negativity in existence. Light is everything and everything is knowledge and knowledge is everything. You are doing extremely well in acquiring of knowledge. Now all you need is the faith and realization that acquiring of knowledge is all you need.

107 **Q**: *(L)* I just want to be sure that the source that I am acquiring the knowledge from is not a deceptive source.

108 **A**: If you simply have faith, no knowledge that you could possibly acquire could possibly be false because there is no such thing. Anyone or anything that tries to give you false knowledge, false information, will fail. The very material substance that the knowledge takes on, since it is at the root of all existence, will protect you from absorption of false information which is not knowledge. There is no need to fear the absorption of false information when you are simply openly seeking to acquire knowledge. And knowledge forms the

protection – all the protection you could ever need.

109 **Q**: *(L)* There are an awful lot of people who are being open and trusting and having faith who are getting zapped and knocked on their rears.

110 **A**: No. That is simply your perception. What you are failing to perceive is that these people are not really gathering knowledge. These people are stuck at some point in their pathway to progress and they are undergoing a hidden manifestation of what is referred to in your terms as obsession. Obsession is not knowledge, obsession is stagnation. So, when one becomes obsessed, one actually closes off the absorption and the growth and the progress of soul development which comes with the gaining of true knowledge. For when one becomes obsessed one deteriorates the protection therefore one is open to problems, to tragedies, to all sorts of difficulties. Therefore one experiences same.

111 **Q**: *(L)* While we are on the subject of knowledge and experiencing things that may or may not be pleasant, I would like to ask for Frank what it is he needs to learn.

112 **A**: He is moving in the right direction at the present time even though he is not completely aware of that fact. He can appear to be under more stress than he actually is and also he has an extreme store of innate information which is one reason why we are able to work through him because we opened those channels a long time ago. Interestingly enough, though you are not aware of it, your own existence has been influenced by this very same factor.

---

[12]'Dane' in *Amazing Grace*.
[13]July 22, 1994.

113 **Q**: *(L)* Which factor?

114 **A**: The natural progression being experienced by the one you know as Frank.

115 **Q**: *(L)* In what respect?

116 **A**: You are being driven and you are driving yourself in the right direction because of your interaction with this individual even though you are not completely aware of that fact, that is, in fact, what is happening.

117 **Q**: *(L)* What caused Frank to spend so many years interacting with a person such as Norman E?[12]

118 **A**: That was part of the learning process and was also karmic in nature.

119 **Q**: *(L)* And what brought that whole situation to a halt?

120 **A**: It was time to end.

121 **Q**: *(L)* During a previous reading[13] we asked several questions about Jesus of Nazareth known as the Christ. The question was asked: "Was Jesus special, that is, Christed, in some way?" The answer came back was: "Quick exalted; wars; civil entrancement. Zindar council." I would like to know the meaning of these references.

122 **A**: Quick exalted refers to a sudden boost of awareness level as related to your previous questions about knowledge. Sometimes that acquisition can occur in a surge and sometimes this is referred to as illumination. Jesus acquired his knowledge by having complete faith in his ability to acquire the knowledge from a higher source. This faith caused an equal balancing interaction with higher sources, which allowed him to gain supreme knowledge

simply by having that faith. Remember that the resources for the acquisition of knowledge in the space-time ere of Christ were much more limited than they are now. There were few options open for acquiring true knowledge except total and complete faith. And this one was instilled with the awareness that total and complete faith would cause dramatic and spectacular acquisition of knowledge; also would cause dramatic and spectacular progression of the soul being. Therefore, the faith was felt, the knowledge was received.[14]

123 **Q:** *(L)* What was the source of the knowledge?

124 **A:** The source was the sixth level of density which is where we reside and we also were involved in that as well.

125 **Q:** *(L)* What does the term "Civil entrancement" mean?

126 **A:** Civil entrancement is a complete balancing of one's useful energies to a level where there is no experiencing of over balancing on the positive or negative side which is preferable for meditation in a mass form.

127 **Q:** *(L)* What is the Zendar Council?

128 **A:** Zendar Council is a sixth level density council which spans both physical and ethereal realms and which oversees dramatic development points at various civilizational sectors in lower density levels.

129 **Q:** *(L)* I would like you to expound a bit on the life of Christ in terms of chronology of events. Could you tell us about his understanding about himself, his interaction with higher sources, his state of being Christed, and what was the true work he came here to do and how did he accomplish it?

130 **A:** His awareness of who and what he was gradually came as he grew. He was taught by us through his faith as described previously. And you should have faith as well because you would find things would come to you as "knowings" more often than even now. Jesus' awareness of his mission and his actions pertaining to it were part of the natural progression of his growth and development. The information about his "miracles" has been largely corrupted by writings which have been passed down after the actual event period. Most of these writings are by entities who wish to confuse and corrupt all humanity for previously stated purposes. The idea was that if one perceived Jesus as performing physical miracles, then your entire understanding of what the life experience here on Earth and on this plane is, and the meaning for it all, is also corrupted and the knowledge is blocked which is the goal of those who have done this. Jesus' purpose and plan was to teach knowledge to all who sought but did not have the strength to express as great a level of faith as he had to acquire the knowledge as he did from higher sources. If they were open and willing to learn they could be taught by hearing. He had only very limited success in imparting faith to others because faith comes solely from within and that is one of the most difficult things for beings on

---

[14]Knowing what I know now, having done the hard research, I'd say this answer – and the rest of what is said in this session about Jesus – was a load of bologna! But then, if Frank was pulling it through me, as seemed to be the case, then the problem was with me and my repeated insistence on revisiting this topic.

your plane to acquire.

131 **Q:** *(L)* Now, it has been discussed before that Jesus was probably the product of a genetically selected impregnation. Could you comment on this and why this would be?

132 **A:** There was no genetic selection of the impregnation. That is incorrect.

133 **Q:** *(L)* OK, then what was it?

134 **A:** It was a natural conception.

135 **Q:** *(L)* Well what I meant was that the person was selected to be the biological father.

136 **A:** Well, that is always the case in every single birth that occurs in your level of density.

137 **Q:** *(L)* Could you comment on the idea that is implicit in this that Jesus was illegitimate?

138 **A:** Obviously if one feels that this would put a shadow or stain on him in some way, or the knowledge that he imparted, then you have not been paying attention. Did you not hear what was said about obsession as opposed to knowledge? Those who are truly, within themselves, at all points of development, trying to seek greater knowledge, will not be blocked by any ideas relating to illegitimacy as you refer to it. Those who are obsessed, by choice, rather than trying to seek true knowledge, will indeed be blocked at that point. It is all up to the choice of the individual. If you choose to develop and gain knowledge then you are never blocked or obsessed at any point about anything ever. However if you choose to limit your knowledge or become obsessed then you are constantly finding yourself blocked and this will manifest in all your life experiences. That is part of the individual soul development pattern. It is all based on choice. Therefore it is not possible for you to interfere with another's choice to acquire knowledge or not and how it is or is not done. There is no need to try to alter another's perceptions because that would be to interfere with free will. If one chooses to be obsessed rather than to be illumined, that is their choice!

139 **Q:** *(L)* We talked about the planet Martek. Is this an ancient human name for Mars or is it an alien designation?

140 **A:** Combination of both as were many things at various levels of the development of your history.

141 **Q:** *(L)* The remark was made that the planet Earth, prior to its interaction with Martek, had a water vapor canopy. How was this water vapor canopy suspended?

142 **A:** The water vapor canopy was a natural element of the particular composition of your atmosphere at that particular measure point in space-time.[15]

143 **Q:** *(L)* Was the gravity level the same as what it is now?

144 **A:** It was somewhat different. But not perceptible to you. That difference is part of the explanation of why that vapor canopy remained suspended.

145 **Q:** *(L)* Did that condition prior to the flood of Noah, the altered gravitational state as well as the water vapor canopy, was that condition more conducive to extended life spans than the conditions that exist on the planet now?

146 **A:** Not only those things but all the other conditions that existed on the

---

[15] *The Wave* 24

planet at that particular point in space-time were more conducive to longer life spans. And, by the way, Noah is a symbolic message rather than an historical event.

Q: *(L)* Do you mean a historical event in the terms of Noah being in an ark or historical event in terms of the flood?

A: First of all, there was no Noah. Secondly there was no actual real flood as depicted in that story. Thirdly, the whole story was a symbolic message as opposed to an actual event.

Q: *(L)* What did actually occur and what does the symbolism have to tell us?

A: It is a very broad representation. It simply means that there was a cataclysmic event that did envelop the whole planet at that time and that those that were ready to experience that as part of their soul development without exiting the body, were warned ahead of time. But not by trying to manipulate events, but by simply allowing faith to let them acquire knowledge and being naturally drawn into position to experience what they needed to experience to survive the event.

Q: *(L)* At that time was Martek drawn close to the Earth and did it have water on its surface which the Earth then robbed or borrowed?

A: That is very close to being the case. It is far more complicated than that so we will leave that at this time.

Q: *(L)* Tell me about the Nephilim.[16]

A: That was a race of beings in the third level of density which came from an actual planet at another point in this

---

[16] *High Strangeness* 14

particular galaxy also in the third level of density, who were taken, or shall we say kidnapped, reprogrammed and retrained by the Lizard beings to act as enforcers during a particular era of what you would measure as your past.

Q: *(L)* What era was that?

A: That was an era... it would have been approximately 8 to 5 thousand years ago but there are also dates relating to 12 to 14 thousand years ago and others. Dating system is not ours and does not exist for us.

Q: *(L)* For how many years did these beings exist on our Earth?

A: Approximately 15 to 18 hundred years. They died off because they were not able to reproduce naturally in the atmosphere of the Earth and experimentation to try to cause them to intermix with the human population did not succeed.

Q: *(L)* When did the last of them die off?

A: Probably near 6 to 7 thousand years ago. But there is also a reference point of 12 to 14 thousand years as well.

Q: *(L)* What was the name of the planet they came from?

A: Dorlaqua.

Q: *(L)* Where was this planet located?

A: This planet was located in the Orion complex.

Q: *(L)* After the 'flood of Noah' approximately how many people survived that cataclysm on the whole Earth?

A: Approximately 19 million.

167 **Q:** *(L)* Why did the population of the Earth continue to decline from that point?

168 **A:** Because of disease and inability to adjust due to artificial manipulations of the genetic pool.

169 **Q:** *(L)* What did the tower of Babel look like?

170 **A:** Looked very similar to your Washington monument. Which re-creation is an ongoing replication of a soul memory.

171 **Q:** *(L)* Would the great pyramid in Egypt still work if someone knew how to use it?

172 **A:** It still works today even though it isn't being artificially used. It was also a preservative chamber. If you were to walk inside the confines of the great pyramid and then leave the body, your body would retain its structure for quite some time. This ability has contributed to the preservation of the actual structure.

173 **Q:** *(L)* What did the original face on the sphinx look like?

174 **A:** Looked like a representation of a feline and a human.

175 **Q:** *(L)* At one point in a previous transmission it was stated that the Lizard beings altered the human race after a battle for their own 'feeding' purposes. Could you clarify this?[17]

176 **A:** It would not be possible for these beings to completely control your existence. If it were you would not be able to do the things your race has done. There has been interference by the Lizard beings in the physical structure of the human beings for their own benefit. Remember what we told you before. They have been interfering with the time cycle experienced on this plane, for quite some time as you measure it. For 74 thousand years they have been interfering in a backwards and forwards time reference manner in order to set up circumstances that they perceive to be beneficial for them in the measure of time that you would consider to be forward, that is, in the future. They have been going backwards and forwards in time to do this. They are suspended in the time cycle as they do this. So what they perceive as being your equivalent of one hour could be as long as 74 thousand years.

177 **Q:** *(L)* So they haven't been here for 300 thousand years?

178 **A:** They originally set up circumstances for their benefit 309 thousand years ago, however, they have been using the particular bracketed period of the 74 thousand year period to alter things in all the various ways mentioned earlier.

179 **Q:** *(L)* Now you mentioned the creators of your group as the super ancient ancestors called the Transient Passengers. What is the meaning of this term and who are these beings?

180 **A:** Transient Passengers are not beings. Transient Passengers are unified thought form.[18]

181 **Q:** *(L)* Why are they called Transient Passengers?

182 **A:** Because they transit all forms of reality. And they spring forth from the Unified form of existence.

---

[17] *The Wave* 68
[18] *Secret History* 12; *The Wave* 26

183 **Q:** *(L)* The planet that was destroyed between Jupiter and Mars that we now know as the asteroid belt, you said was destroyed by psychic energy. Could you clarify that?

184 **A:** The occupants of that planet, many of whom are your soul ancestors, simply decided to develop a service to self atmosphere that was so super charged in the negative that it actually caused their home planet to be destroyed because the energy levels became so intense crashing back upon themselves that they actually destroyed the atomic structure of the planet, causing it to physically explode.

185 **Q:** *(L)* Was this done technologically or was it strictly done by mind power?

186 **A:** They are one and the same.[19]

187 **Q:** *(L)* Did they do something like drop bombs?

188 **A:** No, no. This was done by psychic energy. There has been in a transient fashion of reality the danger of the same thing happening on your planet. Although we are quite confident it won't because we see all reality, past, present, and future. But, you must understand also that even in our particular perspective point, all reality is nonetheless fluid. There are still many choices of realities and possible futures and possible pasts and possible presents. But we feel fairly confident that that particular fate will not befall your planet, although it did the one then known as Kantek.

189 **Q:** *(L)* On a couple of occasions it has been mentioned that Yasser Arafat was a 5th density soul and that he was a descendant of Jesus of Nazareth. What is there about him that demonstrates these qualities or these genetics?

190 **A:** Have you not seen? Imagine what it would be like to be Yasser Arafat. Look at your perception. What is he doing now?

191 **Q:** *(L)* Well the pro-Jewish point of view is not favorable to him.

192 **A:** Well, what you describe as pro anything is an obsession. And, as we know, obsession blocks knowledge which in turn blocks the ability to protect oneself against negative occurrences. Not a good idea. If you were following circumstances, Yasser Arafat is now trying to take the world upon his shoulders by making peace with the Israelis who have been enemies for a very long time. And, therefore, he is now a peace maker and knowledge dispenser.

193 **Q:** *(L)* In that particular conflict between the Jews and the Arabs, which side has the greater validity?

194 **A:** All sides have equal validity. It is only with individuals we find negativity or positivity.

195 **Q:** *(L)* In discussion of a purported crash of a spacecraft in Roswell, it was remarked that this crash was caused by ionization. Could you be more specific?

196 **A:** That reference simply means the bouncing of what you call radar beams off of the ions existing in the atmosphere at the time, caused electromagnetic disturbance which interfered the gravitational balancing system of that particular craft.

197 **Q:** *(L)* Why were the ions present at that time and not at other times?

198 **A:** The ions were charged at that time because of storm activity.

---

[19] *High Strangeness* 8, 11; *The Wave* 41

Q: *(L)* You said that there were bodies recovered by the government. How many bodies were recovered?

A: Three dead and one still in operation.

Q: *(L)* How long did the one live?

A: Remained in operation for approximately 3 and a half years. It was a robotic biogenetic being rather than a soul encompassing physical existence.

Q: *(L)* Did the government know that it was a robotic being?

A: No.

Q: *(L)* Do they still think it was a living being?

A: The government is not one individual. Some are now aware that these are biogenetic engineered beings.

Q: *(L)* In another transmission we were told that we would receive information from a different being each time of contact in order to get good information. Why is this?

A: That is to make sure that balance and equilibrium is maintained and also informational sources are fresh in the interaction between the giver and the receiver.

Q: Well, that is it for tonight. Thank you.

A: Good Night.

End of Session

October, 23 1994

See the 22 October session – direct channeling with Frank – for context respecting the first part of this sesson. As for the rest, other than a personal question asked on behalf of a friend, my 'kid-in-the-candy-store' type of questions resumed. If I was curious about anything, I asked. There was, of course, some method to what I was doing: collecting data, checking answers to the same questions against each other, getting answers that I could research as well as answers that nobody would ever know the answer to just to see what the C's would say. And, of course, I was still interested in philosophical and religious things, though the intensity of this was beginning to lessen every so slightly.

Participants: 'Frank', Laura, VG

Q: *(L)* Hello.

A: Hello. Join mirth Laura.

Q: *(L)* I am not unmirthful. Who is with us tonight?

A: Onokoia.

Q: *(L)* Where are you from?

A: Same.

Q: *(L)* Are you a Cassiopaean?

A: Yes.

Q: *(L)* Last night we tried direct channeling through Frank, I was not entirely satisfied with the results. Can you tell me what the status was and should we pursue that avenue?

A: Yes.

Q: *(L)* Was Frank operating as a clear channel last night?[1]

A: Partly.

Q: *(L)* What was the nature of the interference?

A: Static electromagnetic.

Q: *(L)* What was the origin of this static?

A: Various. Channels must be grooved as this one has been.

Q: *(L)* Is it correct that we should persist with practice for him to become a clear channel?

A: Yes.

Q: *(L)* How often should we do this?

A: Open, but one time per week would be work.

Q: *(L)* How long will it take to 'groove' or clear the channel?

A: Open.

---
[1] *The Wave* 34

Q: *(L)* Was the trance technique acceptable?

A: Choose another.

Q: *(L)* Could you give a suggestion?

A: Opening.

Q: *(L)* So I should suggest another thing for the opening of the channel?

A: Good idea: subject, you are drifting, falls, etc.

Q: *(L)* What visual image should I give him in suggestion to open the channel?

A: Up to you. You are now probing in lieu of learning.

Q: *(L)* Evelyn L: Can you tell me about her physical condition?

A: Thyroid and estrogen count. Psychological problems caused by thyroid.

Q: *(L)* Is there anything wrong with her heart or her aorta?

A: Thyroid.

Q: *(L)* How long after mankind was engineered by the Cassiopaeans did they live on the Earth in a harmonious, Edenic, condition before the zapping by the Lizards?

A: Mankind was not engineered by us.

Q: *(L)* Well, were we created by you?

A: No.

Q: *(L)* Well, then how did mankind come to be here?[2]

A: Combination of factors. Numerous souls desired physical existence then was altered by three forces including principally Lizards through Grays, Nephalim and Orion union.[3]

Q: *(L)* Tell us again who are the Nephilim?[4]

A: Enforcers. Slaves of Orion. From Planet 3C, or 3rd star, 3rd planet.

Q: *(L)* You said the other night that the Nephalim came from some area around the constellation Scorpio, is that correct?

A: Originally seeded there but you were too.

Q: *(L)* We were originally seeded somewhere else? Where? Orion? What is the name of that planet?

A: D'Ankhiar. Ankh is ancient symbolism of this planet. Is female symbol. Stands for mother planet.

Q: *(L)* Is this other planet our original home?

A: Yes.

Q: *(L)* What is it like back Home?

A: Spent. Cindered. Burned up.

Q: *(L)* So it's true, you can't go home?

A: Yes.

Q: *(L)* These Nephilim, how tall were they again?

A: Up to 15 feet maximum.

Q: *(L)* Was Goliath, who was killed by David, one of the Nephilim?

A: Yes. In legend. Actual event depicted in story was earlier.

---

[2] *The Wave* 3, 66, 68
[3] *High Strangeness* 11
[4] *High Strangeness* 14
[5] The story also probably has nothing at all to do with Jewish 'history' as suggested by the response that the "actual event was earlier."

57 **Q**: *(L)* Was it actually David and Goliath?

58 **A**: Yes.[5]

59 **Q**: *(L)* Did he actually slay him with a stone from a slingshot?

60 **A**: Close.

61 **Q**: *(L)* Were these Nephilim genetically intermixed with human beings?

62 **A**: Temporarily.

63 **Q**: *(L)* Why only temporarily?

64 **A**: DNA conflict.

65 **Q**: *(L)* Were they smarter than us?

66 **A**: No.

67 **Q**: *(L)* Were they bigger and dumber?

68 **A**: No.

69 **Q**: *(L)* About the same?

70 **A**: Yes.

71 **Q**: *(L)* Was it difficult for them to live on our planet because of their size and gravity and so forth?

72 **A**: Yes.

73 **Q**: *(L)* Did they have physical problems here?

74 **A**: Yes.

75 **Q**: *(L)* And when did the last of them die off?

76 **A**: 6000 B.C. Approximately. One reference.

77 **Q**: *(L)* When were they originally brought here?

78 **A**: 12 000 B.C. approx. one reference. Please understand your measurements don't make sense.

---

[6] *The Wave* 3, 68
[7] *High Strangeness* 11

79 **Q**: *(L)* Let's go back to the three forces. You said numerous souls desired physical existence. When the numerous souls did this, how did physical existence come to be?

80 **A**: First was apelike.[6]

81 **Q**: *(L)* And then what happened? Did these apelike being just pop into the air? What did the souls do with these apelike beings?

82 **A**: Souls altered them by transfer.

83 **Q**: *(L)* Transfer of what?

84 **A**: Souls into seeded bodies. Orion Union was first into Neanderthal.

85 **Q**: *(L)* The Orion souls came into Neanderthal bodies?[7]

86 **A**: No. Put humans there for incubation process.

87 **Q**: *(L)* Were altered ape embryos put back into ape females for gestation?

88 **A**: No. Souls only.

89 **Q**: *(L)* They put the souls into the ape bodies?

90 **A**: Close.

91 **Q**: *(L)* Did the soul's presence in the ape body cause its genetics and DNA to change?

92 **A**: Yes.

93 **Q**: *(L)* They entered into living creatures on this planet to experience 3D reality and by entering in caused mutation?

94 **A**: Yes. Then were altered by Orion Union first. They resemble you.

95 **Q**: *(L)* Who resembles us?

96 **A**: The Orions.

97 **Q:** *(L)* We haven't talked too much about the Orions...

98 **A:** Orion Union. There are others in Orion Community.

99 **Q:** *(L)* Are some of the Orions not good guys as we would term it?

100 **A:** Yes.

101 **Q:** *(L)* Are some of them good guys?

102 **A:** Yes.

103 **Q:** *(L)* So, you are saying that the original creators or genetic engineers were Orions?

104 **A:** Close. The original engineers but not inhabitants.

105 **Q:** *(L)* Where did the souls come from that entered into the bodies on the planet Earth? Were they in bodies on other planets before they came here?[8]

106 **A:** Not this group.

107 **Q:** *(L)* Were they just floating around in the universe somewhere?

108 **A:** In union with the One. Have you heard the super ancient legend of Lucifer, the Fallen Angel?

109 **Q:** *(L)* Who is Lucifer?

110 **A:** You. The human race.

111 **Q:** *(L)* Are the souls of individual humans the parts of a larger soul?

112 **A:** Yes. Close. The One. All who have fallen must learn "the hard way."

113 **Q:** *(L)* Are you saying that the act of wanting to experience physical reality is the act of falling?

114 **A:** You are members of a fragmented soul unit.

115 **Q:** *(L)* What is it about wanting to be physical is a 'fall'?

116 **A:** Pleasure for the self.

117 **Q:** *(L)* How many people on the planet know what you are teaching us?

118 **A:** A few.

119 **Q:** *(L)* Are we 'special' in some way to receive this?

120 **A:** All are special.

121 **Q:** *(L)* How many know?

122 **A:** 8 so far.

123 **Q:** *(L)* Will we be able to teach others?

124 **A:** Up to you.

125 **Q:** *(L)* Who are the others?

126 **A:** No contact right now.

127 **Q:** *(L)* Did, at any time, the human race live for a long time in an Edenic state, where they were able to use bodies and still have a spiritual connection?[9]

128 **A:** Yes. But not long. No addiction takes long to close the circle.[10]

129 **Q:** *(L)* So, mankind was addicted to pleasuring the self?

130 **A:** Became quickly.

131 **Q:** *(L)* How long from the time of the moving of souls into bodies did the 'Fall' in Eden occur?

132 **A:** Not measurable. Remember Laura, there is no time when this event occurred. Time passage illusion did not exist at that point as well as many other falsehoods.

133 **Q:** *(L)* So you are saying that the Fall in Eden was also the beginning of time?

134 **A:** Yes.

---

[8] *High Strangeness* 11; *The Wave* 23, 68
[9] *The Wave* 68
[10] *The Wave* 3, 23

135 **Q:** *(L)* These many other falsehoods that you mention, could you tell us about a couple? We know that the first one is time...

136 **A:** You must learn on your own.

137 **Q:** *(L)* [One of my kids] wants to know what the Loch Ness Monster is?

138 **A:** Serpent. 40 feet long average. There are 51 in the lake. They live in underwater cavern system and are leftovers from pre-cataclysmic times.

139 **Q:** *(L)* Are there any huge monsters at the bottom of the ocean?

140 **A:** Giant squid about 1000 feet long. There are about 20,000 of them more or less.

141 **Q:** *(L)* Are there any leftover dinosaurs in the jungles of Africa or South America?

142 **A:** No.

143 **Q:** *(L)* Is a vegetarian style of eating good for one?

144 **A:** Not usually.

145 **Q:** *(L)* What did human beings eat before the Fall?

146 **A:** Vegetarian.

147 **Q:** *(L)* So, until we go through the transition we are not really designed to be vegetarian?

148 **A:** Correct.

149 **Q:** *(L)* Would we be able to use this source to do readings for other people to give them information that they need?

150 **A:** Open.

151 **Q:** *(L)* Would you be willing to help us to give readings for other people?

152 **A:** OK.

153 **Q:** *(L)* I would like to know if the teachings of Gurdjieff were in any way accurate or near the truth.

154 **A:** Open.

155 **Q:** *(L)* We would like to know the source of information coming through Billy Meier.

156 **A:** Grays.

157 **Q:** *(L)* He is not channeling Pleiadians?

158 **A:** Was but not now.

159 **Q:** *(L)* Are the Minturians associated with the Lizzies?[11]

160 **A:** Yes.

161 **Q:** *(L)* Are the Minturians assisting in abductions?

162 **A:** No.

163 **Q:** *(L)* Are the Minturians on the planet at this time?

164 **A:** No.

165 **Q:** *(L)* Are they nearby our planet?

166 **A:** No.

167 **Q:** *(L)* Are they in any way involved with the activities going on on the planet at this time?

168 **A:** No.

169 **Q:** *(L)* Are they slaves of the Lizzies?

170 **A:** No.

171 **Q:** *(L)* Are they living on a free will planet?

172 **A:** Yes. All are.

173 **Q:** *(L)* How tall are they?[12]

174 **A:** 11 feet tall average but in 4th density realm.

175 **Q:** *(L)* Do they eat?

---

[11] Name of alien group given in a text we had read in Val Valerian's *Matrix*, I believe.
[12] *High Strangeness* 7

176 **A**: No.

177 **Q**: *(L)* Do they reproduce?

178 **A**: Mechanically.

179 **Q**: *(L)* When the Earth becomes 4th density will we still eat?

180 **A**: Differently.

181 **Q**: *(L)* Will we still reproduce?

182 **A**: Differently.

183 **Q**: *(L)* Will people still have sexual relations?

184 **A**: Wait and see for yourself. Absorb nutrients through the skin.

185 **Q**: *(L)* In the same way as the Lizzies and Grays do?

186 **A**: They are 4 level.

187 **Q**: *(L)* And they also absorb nutrients through their skin?

188 **A**: Yes.

189 **Q**: *(L)* What nutrients do they use?

190 **A**: Many.

191 **Q**: *(L)* What source do they use for these nutrients?

192 **A**: Answered by Frank previous session.

193 **Q**: *(L)* Are you saying that we will be feeding ourselves the same way?

194 **A**: No.

195 **Q**: *(L)* Is it true they throw people in the blender and then absorb their bodies?

196 **A**: Close.

197 **Q**: *(L)* Was Jeffrey Dahmer abducted by the Lizzies at an early age?

198 **A**: Yes.

199 **Q**: *(L)* Did he get his perversions from the Lizzies?

200 **A**: Yes.

201 **Q**: *(L)* Is he genetically connected to the Lizzies?

202 **A**: No.

203 **Q**: *(L)* I have a book in the bedroom called *The P'taah Tapes* channeled by a gal named Jani King. Who is Jani King channeling?

204 **A**: Herself.

205 **Q**: *(L)* We want to know about the *Ra Material* by Elkins, Rueckert and McCarty. Where is the *Ra Material* coming from?

206 **A**: Us.

207 **Q**: *(L)* Would you say that the *Ra Material* comes through a clear channel?

208 **A**: Yes.

209 **Q**: *(L)* If we had a book with the inscriptions from the city of Mohenjo Daro, would you be able to translate them for us?

210 **A**: Maybe.

211 **Q**: *(L)* Who built Stonehenge?[13]

212 **A**: Druids.

213 **Q**: *(L)* Who were the Druids?

214 **A**: Early Aryan group.

215 **Q**: *(L)* How did they move the stones and set them up?

216 **A**: Sound wave focusing; try it yourself; coral castle.

217 **Q**: *(L)* Who taught the Druids to use the sound waves?

218 **A**: They knew; handed down.

219 **Q**: *(L)* When was Stonehenge built?

220 **A**: 6000 approx. B.C.

---

[13] *The Wave* 24, 44

221 **Q:** *(L)* What was Stonehenge built to do or be used for?

222 **A:** Energy director.

223 **Q:** *(L)* What was this energy to be directed to do?

224 **A:** All things.

225 **Q:** *(L)* Was the energy to be directed outward or inward to the center?

226 **A:** Both.

227 **Q:** *(L)* Are you suggesting we should get together and try to move something with sound?

228 **A:** Yes.

229 **Q:** *(L)* Does this sound come from our bodies?

230 **A:** Learn. Laura will find answer through discovery.

231 **Q:** *(L)* It says in the Kaballah that when a group meets regularly with intent and purpose to acquire spiritual awareness, that they create what is called a vessel. Is this what we have done these past three years?

232 **A:** Yes.

233 **Q:** *(L)* Now, since we have created this vessel, into which this information can flow, can we add other people to the use and benefits of this vessel?

234 **A:** Maybe.

235 **Q:** *(L)* We have heard about a movie called *The Puppet Master*. Is this movie a depiction of truth?

236 **A:** Close.

237 **Q:** *(L)* Were the events surrounding the death of JFK depicted correctly in the Oliver Stone movie, *JFK*?

238 **A:** Close.

239 **Q:** *(L)* Is it true that he was shot by one of his own bodyguards?

240 **A:** No.

241 **Q:** *(L)* Why was he killed?

242 **A:** Corruption.

243 **Q:** *(L)* Was he the one who was corrupt?

244 **A:** Too many facts to discuss in this medium.

245 **Q:** *(L)* Did Marilyn Monroe commit suicide?

246 **A:** No.

247 **Q:** *(L)* Was she murdered?

248 **A:** Yes.

249 **Q:** *(L)* Was she murdered because of her connection with JFK?

250 **A:** Yes.

251 **Q:** *(L)* What did she know that made them want to murder her?

252 **A:** A lot.

253 **Q:** *(L)* Who was the man in the velvet or iron mask who was imprisoned by Louis XIV?

254 **A:** An heir to the throne.

255 **Q:** *(L)* If that was an heir, what relation was he to the king?

256 **A:** Bastard son. Using your terminology.

257 **Q:** *(L)* Did Elvis Presley really die?

258 **A:** Yes.

259 **Q:** *(L)* Is he really in his grave?

260 **A:** Yes.

261 **Q:** *(L)* Did he die of an overdose?

262 **A:** Close. Heart attack.

263 **Q:** *(L)* Do the tabloids print truth about UFOs?

264 **A:** Very often.

Q: *(L)* Was the woman who reappeared in Berlin who said she was the Princess Anastasia really who she said she was?[14]

A: Yes.

End of Session

---

[14]There have been books claiming she was not, that a DNA test on a tissue sample proved she was not. However, this was done after she had died and there were powerful financial reasons to dismiss her claims, so there was motivation to either fake this test or replace the tissue sample with another. The most compelling book about her claims used sophisticated analysis – including intel agency – developed ear-matching techniques – to prove that she was the Grand Duchess, Anastasia. I'll believe the ear matching since I am can't be confident of the chain of provenance of a tissue sample.

October 25, 1994

You will see from the notes that I have a number of criticisms of this session. In retrospect, I wonder if the presence of VG was suppressive in some way?

Participants: 'Frank', Laura, VG

Q: *(L)* Who do we have with us tonight?

A: Batuva.

Q: *(L)* Are you a discarnate Earth spirit?

A: No.

Q: *(L)* Where are you from?

A: Cassiopaea.

Q: *(L)* Are you prepared to answer our questions this evening?

A: Yes.

Q: *(L)* The first question is what is the meaning of the winged circle that is so common throughout ancient religions?

A: Life energy.

Q: *(L)* Why was life energy represented this way?

A: Closed circle. Free spirit in closed circle.[1]

Q: *(L)* What is the meaning of the eye of Horus?

A: Psychic energy.[2]

Q: *(L)* What was the origin of the serpent god?

A: Lizard rule.[3]

Q: *(L)* Who appeared to Joan of Arc?

---

[1] That's a facile esoteric explanation. However, I tend to think that it represented comets as gods. Of course, that was the origin of the ideas of the gods 'in the sky' and as time passed, the gods were reduced to abstract concepts by the Greeks. See my book *Comets and the Horns of Moses* for details. So this answer is true enough, it just doesn't go deep enough.

[2] Again, another esoteric explanation of something I think was a representation of a comet.

[3] As is explained in both *Comets and the Horns of Moses* and *Earth Changes and the Human-Cosmic Connection* (Lescaudron), the origin of the idea of the serpent god is most likely due to witnessing dramatic cometary-caused plasma discharge events in the Earth's atmosphere. But then, considering the metaphoric nature of the communication, and previous remarks about weather being how humans witness/experience global 4th density battles, and the likelihood that comets are just the next stage in this 'space war' that enters our reality from what is best described as a semi-paranormal realm, this answer is entirely understandable; it is both literal and metaphoric.

A: Lizard projection.

Q: *(L)* What is the true origin of Halloween?

A: All Hallows Eve.

Q: *(L)* Is there something older than that?

A: No.[4]

Q: *(L)* Are there alien bases on the moon?

A: Yes.

Q: *(L)* Who do the bases belong to?

A: Grays.

Q: *(L)* Was there ever at any time such a thing as mermaids?

A: No.

Q: *(L)* What is the origin of this legend?

A: Sailors delirium.[5]

---

[4]This answer is wrong. The last day of October is a holiday that is said to be the ancient Celtic celebration of the 'End of Summer,' Samhain, Halloween, or All Hallows Eve. I think, when we look at Halloween, we are seeing something very ancient that is filtered through many layers of interpretation. What is consistent throughout, however, is the theme of easy traversal of the border between life and death, leading mainly to death, which suggests that death on a massive scale came on Halloween a very long time ago. Whatever it was, it was so terrifying, so widespread, that cultures the world over have commemorated it, and the days following it, in ways that appear to be designed to ward it off, to prevent it from ever happening again. In the book *The Worship of the Dead, or the Origin and Nature of Pagan Idolatry and Its Bearing Upon the Early History of Egypt and Babylonia* by John Garnier (1904, London: Chapman & Hall; Chapter One, pages 3–11), the author writes that the modern-day celebrations for the dead focused around All Hallows Eve, including the following few days, originated to memorialize the people who died in the Deluge brought by God on a wicked world. The research of Victor Clube and Bill Napier and others suggests that the cometary bombardment (Taurids) that brought the last ice-age to an end probably occurred around Halloween, which is why it is called 'All Hallows Eve' and the next day, November 1st, is the Day of the Dead. According to Clube and Napier, et al., in the same way that Jupiter was struck repeatedly in 1994 by the million-megaton impacts of the comet Shoemaker-Levy, so Earth was bombarded 13,000 years ago by the fragments of a giant comet that broke up in the sky before the terrified eyes of humanity. The multiple impacts on the rotating planet caused tidal waves, raging fires, atomic bomb–like blasts, the mass extinction of many prehistoric species such as the mammoth and sabre-toothed tiger, most of humanity, and left the world in darkness for months. (See: *The Cosmic Serpent* and *The Cosmic Winter* by Clube and Napier. See also: *The Origin of the Universe and the Origin of Religion*, Anshen Transdisciplinary Lectureships in Art, Science, and the Philosophy of Culture, by Fred Hoyle.) Bottom line: no cigar for the C's on this one!

[5]I don't think I agree with this one either. There is very good evidence that human beings spent a considerable period of their evolutionary time adapting to a semi-aquatic existence. The hypothesis was first proposed by German pathologist Max Westenhöfer in 1942, and then independently by English marine biologist Alister Hardy in 1960. After Hardy, the most prominent proponent was Welsh writer Elaine

Q: *(L)* Are there alien bases on Mars?

A: Yes.

Q: *(L)* Whose?

A: Grays and Lizards.

Q: *(L)* The kids want to know what the giant squids eat?

A: Various things.

Q: *(L)* Do they have a purpose for being on the planet?

A: Does anything?

Q: *(L)* Does it?

A: We asked you. Rhetorical question.

Q: *(L)* The kids also want to know how long it takes a squid to grow that big and how long they live?

A: 200 to grow and live up to 700 years.

Q: *(L)* What procedure or technology do the Grays use to pass through solid matter?[6]

A: Transdimensional atomic rearrangement.

Q: *(L)* How do aliens transport themselves or others on beams of light?

A: By electron focusing and previous answer.

Q: *(L)* How do aliens create the virtual reality scenarios as described in Karla Turner's second book?

A: Mental image restructuring.[7]

Q: *(L)* Why does this phenomenon involve the use of the 'blue bubble' or light?

A: Hypnotic suggestion trigger.

Q: *(L)* What is the basis of the Gnostic texts such as the Apocryphon of John?

A: Ancient atheists.[8]

Q: *(L)* What was the energy fueling the crazy sick life of Aleister Crowley?

A: Lizards.

Q: *(L)* Are Lizards responsible for paranoid schizophrenia?[9]

A: Some.

Q: *(L)* In a general sense, in the majority of cases, what is the cause of paranoia or schizophrenia?

A: Lizard manipulation of energies.

Q: *(L)* Why?

A: To feed off the negative results.

Q: *(L)* So it isn't necessarily attachments?

A: No.

Morgan, who wrote a series of books on the topic. My thought is that it is quite possible that just as there was a branch that finally made a choice for life on dry land, there may as well have been a branch that chose the other way. After all, it is said that whales evolved from land mammals. So, in my view, no cigar for the C's on this one.

[6] *High Strangeness* 6
[7] *High Strangeness* 8
[8] I would say that this answer is also wrong. A very good case can be made that the Gnostics, far from being atheists, developed out of the intensely fundamentalist Orphic ideas of extreme purity. The same can be said for Judaism: it's just another take on Orphism.
[9] *The Wave* 63

Q: *(L)* Do Lizards use attachments of dark energies to effect their purposes?

A: Yes.

Q: *(L)* In a lot of cases of paranoid schizophrenia are attachments used?

A: Yes.

Q: *(L)* Are they perpetuating schizophrenia through genetics?

A: Can. Or mental and emotional. Environmental life experiences.

Q: *(L)* Why does it not usually show up until adolescence? Is this because adolescents are being abducted and having implants put in?

A: Not necessarily.

Q: *(V)* Do I have an implant in my right ear?

A: Yes.

Q: *(V)* It has been going off a lot lately.

A: Caused by your interactions with these powerful channels.

Q: *(V)* What do you mean by powerful channels?

A: Laura and Frank.

Q: *(V)* Are they Lizard implants?

A: Yes. Monitoring heavily lately.

Q: *(V)* When did I get the implants?

A: Age 3.

Q: *(L)* How come Frank and I cause her implant to buzz? *(V)* It buzzes when I'm not with you guys, too.

A: Set off.

Q: *(L)* Does that mean that we are controlled by Lizards?

A: They are concerned by VG's communication with us through you.

Q: *(L)* What is their concern?

A: Losing mole.

Q: *(L)* As in espionage terminology. Is VG a mole?

A: Were subconsciously.

Q: *(L)* VG wants to know if she is detrimental to the project by being here?

A: No. Beneficial but the Lizards may resist.

Q: *(L)* How would they do this resistance?

A: Make her life more difficult just like they have with you two.

Q: *(V)* But it seems that my life is more on track that it has ever been before.

A: Watch out. Too late to leave project.

Q: *(V)* I just heard something in my left ear. Is that also an implant?

A: Yes.

Q: *(V)* Do they know what we are doing right at this moment?

A: Yes.

Q: *(V)* Should I stop and go home?

A: Up to you.

Q: *(L)* Why do the implants go off when they do?

A: Monitoring. They have reasons to monitor when they do. They can turn on the monitor and read everything that has gone on since the last monitoring. It is done at their convenience.

Q: *(V)* Do I have an implant in my left sinus which causes thick discharge?

A: Yes.

Q: *(V)* Am I going to be able to blow it out?

A: No.

107 **Q:** *(L)* I want you to translate for me this phrase: Enuma elish lanabu shamamu.

108 **A:** All are seen together.

109 **Q:** *(L)* Translate: Apsu.

110 **A:** Life.

111 **Q:** *(L)* Nudimmud.

112 **A:** World.

113 **Q:** *(L)* Marduk.

114 **A:** Mars.

115 **Q:** *(L)* Kingu.

116 **A:** Light.

117 **Q:** *(L)* Duggae.

118 **A:** Ground.

119 **Q:** *(L)* What is the Enuma Elish really about?

120 **A:** Ascent.

121 **Q:** *(L)* Ascent of what?

122 **A:** Gods.

123 **Q:** *(L)* What gods were these?

124 **A:** Lizards.[10]

125 **Q:** *(L)* How many planets did the Sumerians know about?

126 **A:** They thought 12.

127 **Q:** *(L)* What is a "tablet of destinies"?

128 **A:** Map.

129 **Q:** *(L)* How did Marduk slay Tiamat?

130 **A:** Wrong.

131 **Q:** *(L)* Marduk did not slay Tiamat?

132 **A:** No.

133 **Q:** *(L)* What did it mean when it said "putting Tiamat's head into position"?

134 **A:** Mars conjunct Moon.

135 **Q:** *(L)* How did Tiamat's head form the "hammered bracelet"?

136 **A:** Comet trail.

137 **Q:** *(L)* Is the Quorum composed of members who are humans on this planet?[11]

138 **A:** Partly.

139 **Q:** *(L)* Would we know any of them as well known figures?

140 **A:** Hidden. None you would know.

141 **Q:** *(L)* How is the Quorum important in regard to the Earth changes?

142 **A:** Watchers.

143 **Q:** *(L)* Why is it important to have watchers?

144 **A:** Keep track of prophecies.

145 **Q:** *(L)* How do the Masons relate to the Illuminati?

146 **A:** Masons are low level branch.

147 **Q:** *(L)* I would like to know the approximate years of the life of Hermes Trismegustus.

---

[10] Wrong again, in my view. Again, I refer the reader to my book *Comets and the Horns of Moses*. Nearly all ancient legends and myths can be traced back to very dramatic electro-plasmoid interactions between the Earth and comets. It's odd to me that the C's keep pushing this 'Lizard business' when they have been so open about the comet bombardment issue. But then, again, as I said, if we take the metaphoric nature of the communication into account, then it can be correct if one understands 4th density manipulations as including comets and weather 'wars' so to say.

[11] *The Wave* 30

148 **A:** 5211 approx.[12]

149 **Q:** *(V)* What were the red and green balls of light Eric[13] saw several months ago?

150 **A:** Grays probing.

151 **Q:** *(V)* Was he abducted at that time?

152 **A:** No.

153 **Q:** *(V)* Were the probes there because of him or because of me?

154 **A:** Him.

155 **Q:** *(V)* Has he ever been abducted?

156 **A:** Yes.

157 **Q:** *(V)* How old when first abducted?

158 **A:** Two.

159 **Q:** *(VG)* [My son's] dream of being choked?

160 **A:** Past life memory disconnection.

End of Session

---

[12]Years ago or BC? Recall that a previous question was asked about Hermes in the 16 October session and he was described as a "traitor to court of Pharoah Rana ... Egyptian leader of spiritual covenant" and that he broke the covenant of spiritual unity in the Middle East. I think it was 'years ago' because that puts it at 3211 BC right about the time of the takeover of Egypt by Narmer. "Narmer was an ancient Egyptian pharaoh of the Early Dynastic Period (c. 31st century BC). Probably the successor to the Protodynastic pharaohs Scorpion and/or Ka, some consider him the unifier of Egypt and founder of the First Dynasty, therefore the first pharaoh of unified Egypt. (Also identified as Menes.)" Obviously, something significant happened around this time that we can barely see through the mists of the years.

[13]Her son.

October 28, 1994

This is what I would consider a 'so-so' session for the most part. What is most remarkable about it are the 'coded messages' to me that it contains. On questions where there was no emotional investment, the responses are good.

Participants: 'Frank', Laura, VG

1   **Q**: *(L)* Hello.
2   **A**: Hello.
3   **Q**: *(L)* Is someone with us?
4   **A**: As always.
5   **Q**: *(L)* Can we have your name please?
6   **A**: Gursaea.
7   **Q**: *(L)* Are you a discarnate human?
8   **A**: No.
9   **Q**: *(L)* What are you?
10 **A**: Cassiopaean.
11 **Q**: *(L)* There were two little boys stolen from their mother in South Carolina. We would like to know if we can obtain any information regarding this matter?
12 **A**: House in Union South Carolina in closet.[1]
13 **Q**: *(L)* Can you give us any details about the house and how it could be found?
14 **A**: On street with lots of other houses white clapboard.
15 **Q**: *(L)* Any other details? Name of street?
16 **A**: Oak in name.[2]
17 **Q**: *(L)* How close is this to where their parents are?
18 **A**: Close.

---

[1] No cigar, though I suppose you could say that metaphorically, the little boys were in a sort of closet, i.e. a closed vehicle. Generally, I don't think that the the C's are very good at this type of 'cold-reading' question, especially when the room is full of emotional investment in the responses.

[2] There is an Oak St. in Union, SC, but no cigar for that! I have no idea if there is any relationship between anything in this case and an "Oak St."

[3] Well, they were partly right about this. The lake where the boys were found is in the woods west of Union, SC, but no mention of water in the response, so I don't give the C's a cigar! Curiously, in September of 1996, the same lake was the scene of another tragedy. From the *NY Times*:

> "Seven people, including four children, died in John D. Long Lake on Saturday night after they came to see the spot where Susan Smith drowned her two young sons in late 1994 in a murder that drew worldwide attention to this usually quiet town and

19 **Q:** *(L)* Where is the vehicle?

20 **A:** In woods West.[3]

21 **Q:** *(L)* Are the little boys alright?

22 **A:** Will be found soon for comparison to ultimate results.[4]

23 **Q:** *(L)* Why am I having these current headaches?

24 **A:** Changes DNA.

25 **Q:** *(L)* AB suggested an ozone generator to enhance the contact. Is this a good idea?

26 **A:** He means well. Have him supply it.

27 **Q:** *(L)* Is it alright for me to send the edited version of our transcripts to AB?

28 **A:** B___ may share with questionable individuals.

29 **Q:** *(L)* Will that be detrimental to us?

30 **A:** What do you think?

31 **Q:** What was AB's purpose in calling me today?

32 **A:** Curiosity generated by UFO grapevine gossip.

33 **Q:** *(L)* What was the gossip?

34 **A:** John W and Mike F inspired intrigue.

35 **Q:** *(L)* Do these two have more contact than we would think?

36 **A:** Yes.

37 **Q:** *(L)* John W and F___!?

38 **A:** Yes.

39 **Q:** *(L)* John W hates Mike F, isn't that correct?

40 **A:** Variable.

41 **Q:** *(L)* Should I not share information with John W?

42 **A:** All is learning process.

43 **Q:** *(L)* Are they all in a tizzy about what we are doing here?

44 **A:** Generally yes. Terry and Jan are OK.

45 **Q:** *(L)* So Terry and Jan are not saying anything to John W or Mike F about this?

46 **A:** Yes. But that's not the point.

47 **Q:** *(L)* What is the point?

48 **A:** Motives are good omnipresently.

49 **Q:** *(L)* What do you mean by that? Are we talking just about Jan and Terry?

50 **A:** Yes.

51 **Q:** *(L)* Are AB's motives good?

52 **A:** Variable.

53 **Q:** *(L)* Are John W's motives good?

54 **A:** Same.

55 **Q:** *(L)* Would John W ever do anything that would damage me or this work?

56 **A:** Search within self for answer.

57 **Q:** *(L)* Why should we take the melatonin?

58 **A:** Is mild hallucinogen.

59 **Q:** *(L)* Why do we need this?

---

lured thousands to the lip of the lake."

[4]This was a rather bizarre answer: "found soon" and "ultimate result" seem to say, metaphorically, that the children were dead. Obviously, this was not what any of us wanted to hear emotionally, though you can give the C's half a cigar for this. As mentioned, I suspect that the emotions in the room had a lot to do with mixing this one up!

60 **A**: Keeps exercising psychic abilities and opens paths. Don't be alarmed by vividly erotic dreams.

61 **Q**: *(L)* Should we expect to have vividly erotic dreams?

62 **A**: Possible as psyche passes through levels on ascension.

63 **Q**: *(L)* Is there a problem with the energy level tonight?

64 **A**: With board.

65 **Q**: *(L)* What is wrong with board?

66 **A**: Getting crumpled.

67 **Q**: *(L)* We need to get a new board?

68 **A**: Good idea.

69 **Q**: *(L)* If I get a piece of glass to put on the board and felt for the planchette will that do it?

70 **A**: Maybe.

71 **Q**: *(L)* Better to get a new board?

72 **A**: Open.

73 **Q**: *(L)* I wonder if there is a chance of getting the old Lizzies involved if we are not careful about who we tell?

74 **A**: Always chance of that.

75 **Q**: *(L)* We would like to have a rundown of certain UFO-related individuals:

76 **Q**: *(L)* William Cooper?

77 **A**: Independent; good intentions; slightly overactive imagination; a little misled.

78 **Q**: *(L)* Bob Lazar supposedly worked on alien craft retro-engineering?

79 **A**: Did but sinister. Involved with questionable types.

80 **Q**: *(L)* His video about working at Area 51 and descriptions of propulsion systems and alien craft was or was not truth?

81 **A**: Close to the truth. Craft tech: minor points were off.

82 **Q**: *(L)* What about Stanton Friedman?

83 **A**: Pure, good man.

84 **Q**: *(L)* William Moore who co-wrote *The Roswell Incident* with Charles Berlitz?

85 **A**: Same as Friedman.

86 **Q**: *(L)* What about the incident where he admitted to disinformation?

87 **A**: Was coerced to say that by complex sources. That situation is very complex.

88 **Q**: *(L)* What about Jaime Shandera?

89 **A**: Misled by same as Moore. Has mixed intentions.

90 **Q**: *(L)* What about Don Ware?

91 **A**: Disinformation artist.

92 **Q**: *(L)* What about John Lear?

93 **A**: Good but overcareful.

94 **Q**: *(L)* What about Dr. Richard Boylan whose book I just read? This guy says he had an experience where he was abducted and overnight his attitude about aliens changed. Who was responsible for that abduction that changed his attitude?

95 **A**: The Grays changed Boylan's attitude.

96 **Q**: *(L)* What was the motivation in doing so?

97 **A**: Get him to dispense selective info.

98 **Q**: *(L)* What is the intent of this selective information?

99 **A**: Confuse investigators.

100 **Q**: *(L)* Was his mind taken over when the Grays abducted him?

101 **A**: In a sense.

102 **Q:** *(VG)* A Navy plane crashed on Tuesday, why did the plane crash?

103 **A:** Guidance system malfunction.

104 **Q:** *(VG)* Why wasn't the pilot able to eject?

105 **A:** It was her time to go.

106 **Q:** *(VG)* So none of this had anything to do with aliens?

107 **A:** No.

108 **Q:** *(VG)* I listened to a woman named Janet Dailey who says that women who have abortions have a higher incidence of breast cancer but that spontaneous abortion or miscarriage do not cause the same reaction. Is this true?

109 **A:** Yes. But women who have their first pregnancy later in life also have higher instances of breast cancer and same for those who never get pregnant.

110 **Q:** *(VG)* Does abortion create karma resulting in breast cancer?

111 **A:** Hormonal anomalies cause breast cancer. Karma is interconnected with physical experiences.

112 **Q:** *(L)* Are you saying that having an abortion can create karma?

113 **A:** Of course.

114 **Q:** *(VG)* Is this research funded by pro-life activists?

115 **A:** Some.

116 **Q:** *(L)* I think that V___ wants to ask if she has karma in this regard?

117 **A:** Yes.

118 **Q:** *(L)* She has not worked it out?

119 **A:** No.

120 **Q:** *(L)* Bill Baldwin says abortions lead to serious spiritual attachment situations. Is this true?

121 **A:** Semi-accurate.[5]

122 **Q:** *(L)* Is there some way to release this kind of karma for V___ or others who have it?

123 **A:** Yes.

124 **Q:** *(L)* Could you tell us?

125 **A:** If we tell you, you won't learn.

126 **Q:** *(L)* Now, several people have told me that there is a small child who is with me constantly. Who is she and why is she here?[6]

127 **A:** Next in line.

128 **Q:** *(L)* Next in line for what?

129 **A:** Birth.

130 **Q:** *(L)* Am I going to have another child?

131 **A:** Maybe.

132 **Q:** *(L)* How many are there in line?

133 **A:** One.

134 **Q:** *(L)* Male or female?

135 **A:** Female.

136 **Q:** *(L)* Is this to happen within the next year?

137 **A:** Open.

138 **Q:** *(L)* I am 42 years old. If I were to get pregnant would I be able to have a normal pregnancy and produce a healthy infant?

---

[5] *High Strangeness* 7; *The Wave* 10
[6] *The Wave* 34

139 **A**: Yes. Your consciousness will soon give you spectacularly sharp, exact and correct information.[7]

140 **Q**: *(L)* Will this be due to ingesting the melatonin?

141 **A**: Partly.

142 **Q**: *(L)* Is soon within a month?

143 **A**: You will know.

144 **Q**: *(L)* I get the feeling that this has a lot to do with trusting my own intuition.

145 **A**: Yes.

146 **Q**: *(L)* I had a very serious physical attack yesterday. What was the nature of that attack?

147 **A**: Gallbladder.

148 **Q**: *(L)* What should I do about it?

149 **A**: See ultrasound specialist.

150 **Q**: *(L)* Will Reiki heal it?

151 **A**: Open.

152 **Q**: *(L)* When V___ had her hands on my heart area and they were visually vibrating, is that a sign of transmission of a great deal of energy?

153 **A**: Yes.

154 **Q**: *(L)* And what part of the body was that energy going to?

155 **A**: Chest area.

156 **Q**: *(L)* V___'s hands are tingling right now. Is that Reiki energy happening right now?

157 **A**: Yes.

158 **Q**: *(VG)* Is my Reiki energy going to Frank and Laura as we are doing this?

159 **A**: All ways. You have strong natural healing power.

160 **Q**: *(VG)* So, it isn't necessarily the Reiki initiation?

161 **A**: No. Ann B is misguided.

162 **Q**: *(L)* If VG had the correct initiation would this power her up so that she could do near miracles?

163 **A**: Precisely.

164 **Q**: *(VG)* Does Eric also have this ability?

165 **A**: Some ability.

166 **Q**: *(L)* This evening Eric was acting up, what was going on with him?

167 **A**: Hormonal upsurge.

168 **Q**: *(VG)* Is this due to interacting with females?

169 **A**: Close.

170 **Q**: *(VG)* Female energy?

171 **A**: More physical.

172 **Q**: *(VG)* Are they having a good time?

173 **A**: Fluctuating.

174 **Q**: *(VG)* Is L___ [VG's friend] OK?

175 **A**: Yes.

176 **Q**: *(VG)* How much longer do I have to deal with this hormone thing with Eric?

177 **A**: 6 years.

178 **Q**: *(L)* Is patience the key?

179 **A**: Yes.

180 **Q**: *(VG)* Can Reiki clear marijuana residue from the lungs?

---

[7]This was one of those instances where I was certain the C's were trying to convey something to me indirectly that might have otherwise been blocked by the emotions of other present and participating. Of course, I didn't understand that at the time or even dream of how things would turn out. Best to read *The Wave* for the details!

A: Partly but what if there are continuous infusions?

Q: *(L)* Is there ever a case when ingestion of pot or alcohol are beneficial in a spiritual way?

A: Yes.

Q: *(L)* V___ used pot within past two weeks. Why?

A: Search within.

Q: *(L)* Was it an outside influence?

A: All uncomfortable events are influenced either directly or indirectly.

Q: *(L)* Was this the passing of her uncle?

A: Search within.

Q: *(L)* Many years ago I was with a friend and we pulled off the road to let me drive. We both walked around the car and got in and I believe we sat there for a very long time. Was that because of the potency of what she had smoked or what?

A: You were abducted due to the open state produced by the drug.

Q: *(L)* What was in that stuff?

A: Strychnine.

Q: *(L)* Have I done great physical damage to my body through drugs?[8]

A: Some.

Q: *(L)* Is it irreversible?

A: Not likely.

Q: *(L)* If I went on a fast would I be able to reverse the damage to my body?

A: Good chance.

Q: *(L)* Is that the same for Frank and V___?

A: Yes.

Q: *(L)* Is it advisable to take colonics with the fasting?

A: Good idea.

Q: *(L)* Also to take vitamin supplements?

A: No.

Q: *(VG)* Is the Godspark the portion of the Creator that lives within us, the soul, so to speak?[9]

A: Sounds good.

Q: *(L)* If the Godspark is the soul within us, does anybody have Godsparks times 2 or 3 or so on? That is more than others?

A: Yes.

Q: *(L)* What type of person would have more Godspark than anybody else?

A: Jesus has Godsparks ad infinitum.[10]

Q: *(L)* How does Jesus have Godsparks ad infinitum?

---

[8] I'm not talking about illegal drugs here but the myriad of drugs prescribed for me for various conditions since I was quite young. I had taken Tylenol for arthritis pain 3 or 4 times a day for years until I began having liver/gall bladder problems. See *Amazing Grace* for details.

[9] VG had been reading a book that described the soul as a "godspark" more or less.

[10] Here begins another segment on Jesus that I think is strongly colored by my own beliefs, though, of course, read as metaphor, or extracting the 'tenor' of the responses, a different interpretation could be drawn that better matches the research findings. I do think that Julius Caesar was such an extraordinary human being that the remarks the C's have made about the abilities of Jesus could very well apply.

213 **A**: Soul replication for communication purposes.

214 **Q**: *(L)* So, every time we call upon Jesus, we are replenishing our Godspark?

215 **A**: Yes.

216 **Q**: *(L)* Would you describe these soul replications as being more like a template or hologram?

217 **A**: Hologram.

218 **Q**: *(L)* And what is his connection to the Creator that enables him to do this soul replication?

219 **A**: Volunteered.

220 **Q**: *(L)* Rudolf Steiner called Christ "The most sublime human principle ever to unfold on Earth." Is this an accurate statement?

221 **A**: One interpretation.

222 **Q**: *(L)* He also said: "The Christ, who in the course of this evolution lived 3 years in the body of Jesus of Nazareth..." Is this a correct statement? Did the Christ statement enter Jesus at age 30?

223 **A**: Formed then.

224 **Q**: *(L)* How did this sublime being, the Christ, dwell in a human body?

225 **A**: Natural process caused by supremely pure faith and thought.

226 **Q**: *(L)* Yet previously you said that Jesus had sexual relations with women after he was Christed, is that correct?

227 **A**: No. Before.

228 **Q**: *(L)* So, after he was Christed he had no sexual relations?

229 **A**: Correct.

230 **Q**: *(L)* Did the Christ spirit descend into the body of Jesus in his 30th year?

231 **A**: No.

232 **Q**: *(L)* What happened?

233 **A**: Formed within him. And it could do thusly in anyone who reaches such levels of service to others plus faith and supreme levels of pure thought.

234 **Q**: *(L)* What was the source of the belief that Christ descended into hell during the course of his so-called death?

235 **A**: Superstitions created hundreds of years after his work.

236 **Q**: *(L)* When is the credit/debit card system going to be put into effect?

237 **A**: 4 to 11 years.

238 **Q**: *(L)* According to shamanistic teachings, one can have animal spirits or guides. Is this correct?[11]

239 **A**: Partly. You have them if you believe you have them.

240 **Q**: *(L)* If believing in them makes it so, is this belief beneficial?

241 **A**: All belief is beneficial at some level.

242 **Q**: *(L)* Did Jesus of Nazareth believe in animal spirits or totems?

243 **A**: No.

244 **Q**: *(L)* Is it just New Age revival of superstition?

---

[11] *High Strangeness* 9

[12] Perhaps shamanism as it is understood and practiced today is "Lizard inspired," but my research suggests that it was quite different thousands of years ago. From another angle, if shamanism developed in response to cometary cataclysms, which could be "lizard inspired" as I've mentioned previously, then this could be considered "close enough."

245 **A**: Shamanism is subjective and limits. Lizard inspired.[12]

246 **Q**: *(L)* This book that is being promoted, *M.A.P.*, what is the inspiration behind that book?

247 **A**: Not good.

248 **Q**: *(L)* Just for fun, if I had an animal spirit what would it be?

249 **A**: Peacock.

250 **Q**: *(L)* Frank?

251 **A**: Deer.

252 **Q**: *(L)* V___?

253 **A**: Cat.

254 **Q**: *(L)* Do the Cassiopaeans have pets?

255 **A**: Not exactly.

256 **Q**: *(L)* What do you guys do for fun?

257 **A**: All is fun when perceived correctly.

258 **Q**: *(L)* Should I hook up to the computer internet to use as a source to propagate channeled messages?

259 **A**: Yes. Go for it.

260 **Q**: *(L)* Does Frank need caffeine as he takes it.

261 **A**: Up to him.

262 **Q**: *(L)* Is this beneficial to him?

263 **A**: Believe it or not, yes.

264 **Q**: *(L)* Is it good for VG?

265 **A**: Yes. Adjusts your thinking and vice versa.

266 **Q**: *(L)* Is smoking detrimental to any of our bodies?

267 **A**: Not if mild. Not if mind is in right mode.

268 **Q**: *(L)* Does smoking enhance psychic abilities?

269 **A**: Yes.

270 **Q**: *(L)* Is it true that the government program to stamp out smoking is inspired by the Lizzies?

271 **A**: Yes because they know it may heighten psychic abilities.

272 **Q**: *(L)* What is causing the lung cancer they are attributing to smoking?

273 **A**: Mental conditioning and subliminal programming to expect it.

274 **Q**: *(L)* So, it only happens if you are convinced that it can and must happen?

275 **A**: Correct.

276 **Q**: *(L)* Is there any particular brand of cigarettes to smoke?

277 **A**: No.

278 **Q**: *(L)* Should I accept a job offer?

279 **A**: Will take you away from this work somewhat.

280 **Q**: *(L)* Would it be better if I turn it down?

281 **A**: Your inner self communicates this to you.

282 **Q**: *(L)* Is my idea to form a hypnosis association and teach and get clients thereby a good concept?

283 **A**: Up to you.

284 **Q**: *(L)* I get the idea sometimes that when you say "Up to You" that it may not be the best idea, is this correct?

285 **A**: Sometimes but not the only motivation.

286 **Q**: *(L)* VG is jittery.

287 **A**: Mind control, V___. Try exercise.

288 **Q**: *(L)* Breathing or physical?

289 **A**: Physical.

290 **Q**: *(L)* *Bringers of the Dawn* advised spinning, is this advisable for all of us?

291 **A**: Major yes.

292 **Q:** *(L)* How many times a day?

293 **A:** 3.

294 **Q:** *(L)* How many times [to spin]?

295 **A:** 33.

296 **Q:** *(L)* Is it OK to do it in the pool?

297 **A:** Okay.

298 **Q:** *(L)* Is the altar beneficial to have in one's house?[13]

299 **A:** Okay.

300 **Q:** *(L)* Is that OK beneficial?

301 **A:** Be careful not to jump to conclusions.

302 **Q:** *(L)* What conclusions? That the altar is OK beneficial. Is it highly OK for us?

303 **A:** No.

304 **Q:** *(L)* Mediocre OK?

305 **A:** No. No. No.

306 **Q:** *(L)* What?

307 **A:** Laura has been hurt by jumping to Lizard inspired conclusions.

308 **Q:** *(L)* So the altar is useless?

309 **A:** No. Just be careful remember metaphysical church group.

310 **Q:** *(L)* Is it a matter of misguided alliances?

311 **A:** Has been frequent problem.

312 **Q:** *(L)* Should I dismantle the altar?

313 **A:** Altar is okay but other things are not okay like silly rituals.

314 **Q:** *(L)* Is V___'s altar OK?

315 **A:** Yes.

316 **Q:** *(L)* OK, during the period of time I was getting the hassle from the metaphysical church group, my pool was green. Was this symbolic of the attack I was under?[14]

317 **A:** Yes but you left yourself open by association and buying too many concepts without careful examination.

318 **Q:** *(L)* Do you mean that, if, at that time, I had refused to acknowledge that any harm could come to me, that that would have made it impossible for any harm?

319 **A:** Close. But investigate before buying and practicing in future okay?

320 **Q:** *(L)* Investigate what? Ideas?

321 **A:** Yes. And concepts and especially practices.

322 **Q:** *(L)* The ideas of candle burning, salt, sage, shamanistic rituals and so forth? Is all this useless?[15]

323 **A:** Maybe.

324 **Q:** *(L)* Is sage not useful?

325 **A:** You are learning; remember when we say "good no ritual"?

326 **Q:** *(L)* In other words, your knowledge and your strength which comes from your knowledge and knowing is the point and the protection?

327 **A:** Precisely. This is extremely important.

---

[13] We were typical New Agey types with little tables or shelves in our houses converted to 'altars' with stones and candles and incense that were supposed to create 'good energy' or 'attract benefits' or whatever. As the C's pointed out, it wasn't the altars that were the problem, but mindless rituals for which the real meaning had been forgotten.

[14] *The Wave* 19

[15] *The Wave* 10

328 **Q:** *(L)* Alexandra David-Neel quoted a lama who said we must beware of the children of our own minds as well as the children of the minds of others, such as thought forms perhaps created by higher negative beings. If we do not acknowledge that such things exist, are we then subject to being devoured by them?

329 **A:** Ritual drains directly to Lizard beings.

330 **Q:** *(L)* Even our saying of the Lord's prayer?

331 **A:** It is okay to pray. Why do you think organized religion is obsessed with rituals?

332 **Q:** *(L)* Is the same thing true of shamanistic practices and so forth?

333 **A:** Exactly.

334 **Q:** *(L)* What occurred to make my pool clear up?[16]

335 **A:** You restored your own energy.

336 **Q:** *(L)* And it had nothing to do with rituals?

337 **A:** Correct. In spite of rituals but you were lucky could have gone the other way.

338 **Q:** *(L)* What prevented this from happening?

339 **A:** Divine intervention. [Energy surge and pointer nearly flies off the board]

340 **Q:** *(L)* Well, my life seems to have been full of incidents of Divine intervention. Is this true?

341 **A:** Yes.

342 **Q:** *(L)* What is the purpose of this intervention?

343 **A:** To preserve and prepare you for work.[17]

344 **Q:** *(L)* What is this work?

345 **A:** You are extremely valuable to all on your planet.

346 **Q:** *(L)* What particular value? Is this common to all people?

347 **A:** No.

348 **Q:** *(L)* Is this something meaningful? What is the mission?

349 **A:** Faith in your opening channel; you will learn as you go. We cannot tell you all at once.

350 **Q:** *(L)* Since the energy is high at this time, we would like to know if you have anything to give in the form of a teaching.

351 **A:** Not ready for that yet; establish clear channel and forum first; one step at a time.[18]

352 **Q:** *(L)* What is the forum?

353 **A:** What do you think?

354 **Q:** *(L)* Do you mean that we need to bring more people into this work?

355 **A:** Close.

356 **Q:** *(L)* We need to create a forum.[19]

357 **A:** Yes. A direction will open if you persevere.

---

[16] *The Wave* 34

[17] This next series of questions and answers are actually quite remarkable and another instance of the C's sending coded messages through to me. The terms that are used describe exactly the conditions surrounding my meeting of my husband, Ark.

[18] *The Wave* 64. In January 2006, we created a public forum for research and discussion: http://cassiopaea.org/forum/

[19] *The Wave* 44

Q: *(L)* So things will be brought to us and happen for us if we just persevere?

A: Soon expect big opportunity.

Q: *(L)* I assume that we are not to ask what it is, we are to have faith, is that correct?

A: Yes. Danger you may misinterpret opportunity.

Q: *(L)* Should we all three be able to realize in congruence whether the opportunity is good?

A: Varying degrees.

Q: *(L)* If there is a danger we may misinterpret the opportunity, could you give us a couple of clues so that when it occurs we won't miss it?

A: At least one of you will have instant recognition but others may not. Wait and see.[20]

Q: *(L)* This misinterpretation, does this mean we can count on this misinterpretation?

A: Open.

Q: *(L)* Are we an experiment?

A: Maybe.

Q: *(L)* How many others are receiving this level of information?

A: Less than 100 on entire planet. Less in this mode.

Q: *(L)* Are some of the others using other modes? What?

A: Many different ones.

Q: *(L)* Is channeling with three-way energy as we are doing in a purer source of information than direct channeling through a single individual?

A: Equal.

Q: *(L)* Can any one of us do direct channeling?

A: All have equal potential.

Q: *(L)* Is AB attached in a major way?

A: Yes.

Q: *(L)* Is he going to order the Bill Baldwin book [as was suggested to him]?

A: Yes.

End of Session

---

[20] I certainly had instant recognition of Ark, but all the other members of the channeling experiment were against him at first.

November 2, 1994

This is one of the more interesting sessions, since the main topic was 'the Nephilim.' The secondary topic was crop circles. As usually happened, the discussion of one topic brought in answers that begged for following, which we often did. That's why it seems we had a hard time staying on topic!

The session began with a question about Frank's 'state' the night before. I was regularly subjected to his hours-long rants about how hard his life was and how no one appreciated him or treated him with respect. I've written about this at some length in *The Wave* series of books. What is interesting in this session is that the C's mentioned that there was a sort of conflict between good and evil within Frank himself and it was uncertain which side would win. Later developments (chronicled in the books mentioned) answered this question.

VG, as was usual, mainly asked questions about things that concerned her personally.

Participants: 'Frank', Laura and VG

1 **Q:** *(L)* Hello.

2 **A:** Hello.

3 **Q:** *(L)* What is your name please?

4 **A:** Fori.

5 **Q:** *(L)* Why was Frank in such a state last night?[1]

6 **A:** Because his life is difficult.

7 **Q:** *(L)* What is making his life difficult?

8 **A:** Destiny.

9 **Q:** *(L)* Is it his destiny for his entire life to be difficult?

10 **A:** Open.

11 **Q:** *(L)* Is that choice up to him?

12 **A:** No.

13 **Q:** *(L)* Well then, why is it open?

14 **A:** Will dark or light forces win?

15 **Q:** *(L)* Win what?

16 **A:** Battle.

17 **Q:** *(L)* Battle where?

18 **A:** All.

19 **Q:** *(L)* Well, I thought you said that the forces of light were definitely going to win. Is that not correct?

20 **A:** Too simplified.

---

[1] *The Wave* 35

21 **Q:** *(L)* Is there anything Frank can do in this battle to assist getting over this problem?

22 **A:** Fight.

23 **Q:** *(L)* Why does V___'s friend T___ snipe at her the way she does?[2]

24 **A:** Jealousy.

25 **Q:** *(L)* So should she just keep all this information to herself?

26 **A:** Up to her. All will be okay. We feel important matters need discussion from here forward please.[3]

27 **Q:** *(L)* Could you define important matters for us?

28 **A:** Of importance to all.

29 **Q:** *(L)* Who or what group is responsible for crop circles?

30 **A:** Us. You bet.

31 **Q:** *(L)* What is the purpose of the crop circles?

32 **A:** Messages to world. All.

33 **Q:** *(L)* Do these crop circles mean an idea, an energy, a concept; how do they transmit messages?

34 **A:** Translate; it can be done.

35 **Q:** *(L)* This one here,[4] what does it mean?

36 **A:** You.

37 **Q:** *(L)* Do you mean the human race?

38 **A:** Yes. Symbol for human race.

39 **Q:** *(L)* What does this one mean?[5]

40 **A:** Planet.

41 **Q:** *(L)* What was the meaning of the circle my husband found in his driveway?[6]

42 **A:** Mars.

43 **Q:** *(L)* What message did that convey?

44 **A:** Astrological.

45 **Q:** *(L)* Did it convey any message other than astrological?

46 **A:** What does Mars represent?

47 **Q:** *(L)* War... anger, energy, struggle, assertiveness, sex, life...

---

[2]This had been a large part of the pre-session discussion, triggered by a recap of Frank's rant episode the previous night.

[3]This is the first occasion out of many where the C's explicitly urged to not focus too much on personal questions, but to address questions of a universal nature. The reader will discover more of such requests in later sessions.

[4]See Appendix, Figure 1

[5]See Appendix, Figure 2

[6]A year or so before I married my now ex-husband, he had called me (as the local knowledgable person about strange phenomena) to come and look at a strange figure marked out in the sand and grass at the front of his house. It was quite large (maybe 35 or 40 feet across) and precisely marked. I tried various ways to imitate the way it had been drawn with no success, so I finally concluded that it had been 'stamped.' But that would have been very difficult because there were undisturbed over-hanging trees. It was quite a puzzle. After this session, I later found an image in a book [see Figure 3 in the Appendix] that was very similar to the symbol marked in the ground; it was indeed an ancient symbol for the planet Mars. It originally appeared in Barrett's *Magus* (1801).

[7]See Appendix, Figure 4

48 **A**: First four.

49 **Q**: *(L)* [Holding up images of crop circle] Now, what does this circle represent?[7]

50 **A**: Interdimensionality.

51 **Q**: *(L)* This one here, what does it represent?[8]

52 **A**: Atomic structure.

53 **Q**: *(L)* This squiggly one, what does it mean?[9]

54 **A**: Struggle.

55 **Q**: *(L)* In what way?

56 **A**: Learning from change and adversity.

57 **Q**: *(L)* Well, that is all the pictures I have...

58 **A**: Need more soon.

59 **Q**: *(L)* In the library?

60 **A**: Maybe. This is of the utmost importance.

61 **Q**: *(L)* Is this going to help with the 'forum'?

62 **A**: Yes.

63 **Q**: *(L)* Who carved the stone heads on Easter Island?[10]

64 **A**: Lemurian descendants.

65 **Q**: *(L)* The natives say the stones walked into position. Is this true?

66 **A**: No.

67 **Q**: *(L)* Well, how?

68 **A**: Tonal vibration.

69 **Q**: *(L)* And what did these stones represent?

70 **A**: Nephalim.[11]

71 **Q**: *(L)* Is this what the Nephilim looked like?

72 **A**: Close.

73 **Q**: *(L)* Does that mean that the Nephilim were present in Lemuria?

74 **A**: Close.

75 **Q**: *(L)* Where was Lemuria located?

76 **A**: Pacific off South America.

77 **Q**: *(L)* So when the Easter Island natives talk about their ancestors they are talking about people who came from the direction of South America?

78 **A**: No. Right near all around. Easter Island is remnant of Lemuria.

79 **Q**: *(L)* What happened to Lemuria?

80 **A**: Submerged close to time you refer to as Fall of Eden, approximately.[12]

81 **Q**: *(L)* Well if the Nephilim were brought here 9 to 12 thousand years ago...

82 **A**: Last visit. Have been here 5 times. Will return.[13]

---

[8] See Appendix, Figure 5
[9] See Appendix, Figure 6
[10] *High Strangeness* 14; *The Wave* 1
[11] This is one of those instances where a question brings back a surprising answer and the questions go off on another topic.
[12] The 'Fall' had already been dated to 309,882 years ago. See session 5 October.
[13] This obviously didn't answer my implied question about how the Nephilim could have been known from Lemuria when it had 'sunk' so very, very long ago. Well, obviously, I was asking the initial question with the assumption that the Easter Island people were survivals of Lemuria. And when I asked if the Nephilim had been present in Lemuria, the C's only said "close." The C's then pointed out that

83 **Q:** *(L)* The Nephilim are going to return? Where do the Nephilim currently live?

84 **A:** Orion.

85 **Q:** *(L)* They live in the constellation Orion? Where is their planet?

86 **A:** Don't have one. In transit.

87 **Q:** *(L)* The whole dadgum bunch is in transit?

A: Three vehicles.

88 **Q:** *(L)* How many Nephilim does each vehicle hold?

89 **A:** About 12 million.

90 **Q:** *(L)* Are they coming to help us?

91 **A:** No. Wave comet cluster all using same energy.[14]

the areas around Easter Island were areas of survival of the Lemurians and that Easter Island itself was a remnant of the land area. So, I guess it is like the story about Atlantis where survivors were scattered and tried to reconstitute their civilization for some time following a major destruction and there could be survivals of tales or other elements handed down for thousands of years. But still, it seems like 310 thousand years is a very, very long time! At a later session, the C's say that Atlantis and Lemuria are not the oldest civilizations on Earth, that others, far older, have come and gone. In still another session, they say that the Oriental peoples are the survivors of the Lemurian genetic stock. Of course, that is interesting when one reads a book I've mentioned previously in my notes, *Gods of the Cataclysm*, which is loaded with images showing the connections between South America and the Orient. Wikipedia says about the island:

> "Estimated dates of initial settlement of Easter Island have ranged from 300 to 1200 CE, approximately coinciding with the arrival of the first settlers in Hawaii. Rectifications in radiocarbon dating have changed almost all of the previously posited early settlement dates in Polynesia. Rapa Nui has more recently been considered to have been settled in the narrower range of 700 to 1100 CE. An ongoing study by archaeologists Terry Hunt and Carl Lipo suggests a still-later date: 'Radiocarbon dates for the earliest stratigraphic layers at Anakena, Easter Island, and analysis of previous radiocarbon dates imply that the island was colonized late, about 1200 CE.'" [http://en.wikipedia.org/wiki/Easter_Island, accessed on 5 July 2014]

So it is assumed that the statues were erected by these settlers. I suspect that this is not proven at all, that when the settlers arrived, they found the statues already there. According to *National Geographic*: "Most scholars suspect that the moai were created to honor ancestors, chiefs, or other important personages, However, no written and little oral history exists on the island, so it's impossible to be certain." [http://travel.nationalgeographic.com/travel/world-heritage/easter-island/]

[14] Now, notice that the C's say that the Nephilim have no planet of their own and they talk about them arriving in "three vehicles" and that the "Wave," the "comet cluster," and these "vehicles" are "all using the same energy." In the session of 23 October, the C's said that the Nephilim were "Enforcers. Slaves of Orion." And then, you will see in the very next session, 4 November 1994, that the C's say that the Nephilim use "stun guns" to do their enforcing. Considering the police state that has been imposed on our planet since 9/11, and that the "enforcers" of this state are the police who are notoriously using stun guns, one gets the feeling that

93 **Q:** *(L)* Using same energy to what?

94 **A:** Pass through space/time.

95 **Q:** *(L)* Does this mean that without this comet cluster they cannot pass through space-time?

96 **A:** No. Slower. Message follows here. Quiet for one moment please: From now on when word to follow is in quotes we will designate as follows: mark then word then mark. Now, "slower."[15]

97 **Q:** *(L)* So, it is slower for them to come here without this wave. Where is the wave coming from?

98 **A:** Follows cluster.

99 **Q:** *(L)* It follows the cluster. What does this wave consist of?

100 **A:** Realm border.[16]

101 **Q:** *(L)* Does the realm border wave follow the comet cluster in a permanent way?

102 **A:** No.

103 **Q:** *(L)* Is the realm border loosely associated with the comet cluster each time it comes?

104 **A:** No. Realm border follows all encompassing energy reality change; realm border will follow this cluster passage and has others but not most.

105 **Q:** *(L)* Is this realm border a dimensional boundary?

this, again, was symbolism and/or metaphor for events that would transpire on our planet.

What if the 'coming Nephilim' are actually genetically modified humans? What if the 'vehicles' that were traveling on some kind of energy wave were 'soul transporters' rather than transporting actual physical, 14-foot-tall dudes? In other words, what if, in essence, the Nephilim are already here? Now, I won't discount the possibility that actual craft could bring them, but I'm just opening the door to a different way of understanding how things transpire between density levels. As I discussed in *Comets and the Horns of Moses*, nearly all the ancient stories of comet cataclysms include tales of giants, dwarfs, cannibals, etc. I also noted in that volume how comets may be able to modify DNA either by some direct EM effect, or by bringing virii that alter DNA. What if that is what is meant here?

What if the transporters are bringing (or have already brought) virii that will infect the population with DNA-altering pathogens resulting in more violent and aggressive individuals? Look at the increase in mass shootings; look at the increase in 'zombie'-type attacks; look at the increase in mob-type violence; look at the increase in psychopathy and overt psychopathic behavior in the top levels of government! Even individuals who previously managed to come across as relatively normal humans seem to have gone over the edge or come out of the closet somehow in the manifestation and demonstration of their Evilness! Dick Cheney, Tony Blair, George Bush, Condoleeza Rice, Hillary Clinton, Barack Obama, and on and on the list goes. At the present moment, the only group that seem to be behaving in a human sort of way – and it could be a mask – are the Russians under the leadership of Vladimir Putin.

[15] We installed quote marks on the board after this. From this point on, when words in the Cassiopaean responses are in quotes, it is because they have spelled it so.

[16] *The Wave* 9

106 **A**: Yes.

107 **Q**: *(L)* OK, this realm border, do dimensions...

108 **A**: Pulsating realms. Fluctuating realms.

109 **Q**: *(L)* Is our realm fluctuating or pulsating?

110 **A**: No.

111 **Q**: *(L)* But this other realm does?

112 **A**: No.

113 **Q**: *(L)* What fluctuates?

114 **A**: Residence.

115 **Q**: *(L)* Whatever is in that realm fluctuates?

116 **A**: No. Your planet fluctuates between realms.

117 **Q**: *(L)* How often does this fluctuation occur?

118 **A**: About every 309,000 years.

119 **Q**: *(L)* In other words we can expect to be in 4th density for about 300,000 years?

120 **A**: Yes.

121 **Q**: *(L)* Does this mean that the Edenic state existed for about 300.000 years before the 'Fall'?

122 **A**: Yes.

123 **Q**: *(L)* Now, you say these Nephilim are coming and there is about 36 million of them, correct?

124 **A**: Yes.

125 **Q**: *(L)* And they are the enforcers of the Grays and Lizzies, is that correct?

126 **A**: Yes.

127 **Q**: *(L)* Well, let's sit back and watch the show! You are saying that the planet fluctuates...

128 **A**: No, realms do planet merely occupies realm.

129 **Q**: *(L)* What is the source in space-time of this other realm?

130 **A**: Too complex.

131 **Q**: *(L)* What is the generative source?

132 **A**: Part of grand cycle.

133 **Q**: *(L)* Is this the cycle understood by the Mayans?

134 **A**: They understood partially.

135 **Q**: *(L)* Their calendar extends to 2012... is that accurate as to the time of the realm border change?

136 **A**: Close. Still indefinite as you measure time. Lizzies hoping to rule you in 4th density. Closer to 18 years.[17]

137 **Q**: *(V)* Is Eric[18] home in bed?

138 **A**: Yes. And No.

139 **Q**: *(V)* He is at home but not in bed?

140 **A**: Yes.

141 **Q**: *(V)* Was he out earlier?

142 **A**: Yes.

143 **Q**: *(V)* Is this the same individual as before?

144 **A**: Yes. Eric going through many changes.

145 **Q**: *(V)* Is he asleep?

146 **A**: No.

147 **Q**: *(V)* Should I call him?

---

[17]I guess if my metaphoric interpretation of the Nephilim matter is correct, we are already moving into 4th density and the control system of "Enforcers with stun guns" is already in place.

[18]Teenage son.

148 **A**: No.

149 **Q**: *(L)* Is the present arrangement better?[19]

150 **A**: No.

151 **Q**: *(L)* Better before?

152 **A**: Yes.

153 **Q**: *(L)* What was better?

154 **A**: You and Frank switch places.

155 **Q**: *(L)* Why?

156 **A**: Energy vortex.[20]

157 **Q**: *(L)* If the Nephilim are coming 36-million strong as enforcers for the Lizzies, does the Confederation have a like amount for defense?

158 **A**: We don't operate that way.[21]

159 **Q**: *(L)* Are we just going to have to fight them off ourselves?

160 **A**: Think of The Wizard of Oz. It was inspired by us.

161 **Q**: *(L)* Does the witch represent the Lizzies?

162 **A**: Yes.

163 **Q**: *(L)* So, is there something we have or can do...

164 **A**: Glenda like us.

165 **Q**: *(L)* And who is the Wizard? Is that the Beast or the U.S. government?

166 **A**: Close. Illuminati.

167 **Q**: *(L)* Are the monkeys the Nephilim?

168 **A**: Close enough.[22]

169 **Q**: *(L)* If water destroyed the witch, and the witch represents the Lizzies, can we destroy the Lizzies?

170 **A**: Knowledge.

171 **Q**: *(L)* But there are only a few on the planet who have the knowledge, am I correct?

172 **A**: What do you mean? Against all when time comes.

173 **Q**: *(L)* So the 36 million will be against all on the planet when the time comes?

174 **A**: Of course.[23]

---

[19] We had switched seats.

[20] The C's apparently wanted me to sit with my back to the East, facing West, and Frank with his back to the North, facing South. I have continued to do this ever since, even using a compass to align the table properly.

[21] *The Wave* 3

[22] I had forgotten the soldiers in *The Wizard of Oz*. "The Winkie Guards are the Wicked Witch of the West's foot soldiers from The Wizard of Oz. ... After the Witch died, the Winkies redeem themselves and thank Dorothy for killing her. This strongly implies that they were merely slaves to the Witch and did her evil bidding because they had no choice and feared her wrath." I think that a study of the Right Wing Authoritarian personality as identified by psychologist Bob Altemeyer goes a long way toward explaining the behavior of the police and other enforcement organizations nowadays.

[23] This little exchange implies an interesting proposition: that the global population will, at some point, turn against the 'enforcers' en masse and that this is related in some way to the arrival of the comets following which the Wave and realm change will manifest. We return to these topics numerous times in further sessions so keep these ideas in mind. I've only come to them after observing the changes that have manifested in our world over the past 20 years and noting how correct the C's were

175 **Q:** *(L)* And those who have the knowledge and can dispense it to others ...

176 **A:** Yes.

177 **Q:** *(V)* Have you inspired other movies we could watch?

178 **A:** We have but different meanings and subjects.

179 **Q:** *(V)* Is *Cocoon* one of yours?

180 **A:** No. Hollywood.

181 **Q:** *(L)* Who were the original inhabitants of the city of Jericho?

182 **A:** Aramaic.[24]

183 **Q:** *(L)* There was a stone tower at one of the lower levels. What was it built for?

184 **A:** Energy disbursement. Attempt to duplicate tower of Babel and Atlantean crystal towers.[25]

185 **Q:** *(L)* Who carved the crystal skull found in Central America?

186 **A:** Mayans.

187 **Q:** *(L)* What was the purpose of that skull?

188 **A:** Study brain. Long message follows pause: Now: Skull was to learn about soul; reflective remolecularization imaging. Grays do this with abductees.

189 **Q:** *(L)* Through what kind of instrument?

190 **A:** Energy focusing.

---

in so many respects, though much of it seems to have been metaphoric. As I like to say nowadays: "Who needs aliens when we have psychopaths?"

[24] More accurate than trying to identify a specific people. The Aramaic language is of the Semitic family of languages which includes variations spoken by the Assyrians, Babylonians, Chaldeans, Arameans, Hebrews, and Arabs.

[25] I'm not too sure about that; for all we know, it was just a look-out tower! But, it *is* very old. It is an 8.5-metre-tall (28 ft) stone structure, built in the Pre-Pottery Neolithic A period around 8000 BC. The tower was constructed with an internal staircase of twenty-two steps and is almost 9 meters (30 ft) in diameter at the base, decreasing to 7 meters (23 ft) at the top with walls approximately 1.5 meters (4.9 ft) thick.

Recent studies by Ran Barkai from Tel Aviv University and Roy Liran have suggested astronomical and social purposes in the construction of the tower. Showing an early example of archaeoastronomy, they used computer modelling to determine that the shadow of nearby mountains first hit the tower on the sunset of the summer solstice and then spread across the entire town. Noting that there were no known invasions of the area at the time of construction, the defensive purpose of the tower, wall and ditch at Jericho has been brought into question. No burials were found and suggestions of it being a tomb have been dismissed. Discussing in the *Jerusalem Post*, Barkai argued that the structure was used to create awe and inspiration to convince people into a harder way of life with the development of agriculture and social hierarchies. He concluded with, "We believe this tower was one of the mechanisms to motivate people to take part in a communal lifestyle." (Parry, Wynne., "Tower of Power: Mystery of Ancient Jericho Monument Revealed," *LiveScience*, 18 February 2011, and O'Sullivan, Arieh, "World's first skyscraper sought to intimidate masses," *Jerusalem Post*, 14 February 2011) So maybe the C's were quite right about this one?

191 **Q:** *(L)* What is behind their eyes?[26]

192 **A:** Camera like system.

193 **Q:** *(L)* Is that system also able to send signals?

194 **A:** Yes.

195 **Q:** *(L)* At what spectrum level?

196 **A:** Thought paralysis.

197 **Q:** *(L)* Do they implant thoughts with their eyes also?

198 **A:** Can.

199 **Q:** *(L)* What do they do with implants?

200 **A:** Monitor.

201 **Q:** *(L)* Do they monitor our thoughts?

202 **A:** Yes.

203 **Q:** *(L)* Do they monitor what we see?

204 **A:** Yes.

205 **Q:** *(L)* Hear and feel?

206 **A:** Yes.

207 **Q:** *(L)* Do the implants just monitor?

208 **A:** And control.

209 **Q:** *(L)* Do all of us have implants?

210 **A:** Yes.

211 **Q:** *(L)* Are we under the control of the Grays?

212 **A:** Attempt.

213 **Q:** *(V)* How many times have I been abducted?

214 **A:** 55.

215 **Q:** *(L)* Laura

216 **A:** 12.[27]

217 **Q:** *(L)* A___? [Daughter]

218 **A:** None.

219 **Q:** *(L)* J___? [Son]

220 **A:** Yes.

221 **Q:** *(L)* Can I protect them from abduction?

222 **A:** Maybe. Tried A___.

223 **Q:** *(L)* What stopped it?

224 **A:** You.

225 **Q:** *(V)* When was I last abducted?

226 **A:** June.

227 **Q:** *(V)* Was that when I was perceiving being attacked...

228 **A:** Yes.

229 **Q:** *(V)* When I called on the hand of God did that help?

230 **A:** No.

231 **Q:** *(L)* Who carved friezes in French caves as well as executing the cave paintings?

232 **A:** People. Aryans. In caves because struggling to survive conflicts between many forces including Lizard being domination.[28]

233 **Q:** *(L)* Why did the Egyptians draw sideways?

---

[26] *High Strangeness* 7

[27] Notice that this is the same number given the first time this question was asked, but then a second asking gave 17 as the answer, an increase of five. Now, we are back to 12. Does this reflect the quality of the transmission? Is 12 the correct number (assuming there is any factuality to the concept at all)?

[28] If "Lizard Being domination" includes cometary bombardment or climate stress on the planet as the C's have indicated, then this answer is easy to understand. It's pretty certain by now that it was not 'hunting magic' as the earliest theories proposed.

234 **A**: Atlantean method handed down. Simply artistic stylization.

235 **Q**: *(L)* What about the passages in the pyramid? Why so odd?

236 **A**: Used energy vortex for movement. Floated, levitated. Can still do this if you know how. In the pyramid the passages created the energy by their placement and relationship to other space/solid configurations. And passages sometimes changed their structure atomically and still do.[29]

237 **Q**: *(L)* What is the purpose of the sarcophagus in the 'King's' chamber?

238 **A**: Energy storage.

239 **Q**: *(L)* Was there ever anything in this object?

240 **A**: Yes.

241 **Q**: *(L)* What?

242 **A**: Many things.

243 **Q**: *(L)* So, there was nothing permanent in it, you could put various things in it for various reasons?

244 **A**: Yes.

245 **Q**: *(L)* In our machinery we generally have dials and tuners which can adjust the machine to do a specific job or deliver a particular amount or flow of energy. What was the equivalent of dials and tuning devices in the pyramid?

246 **A**: Thoughts.

247 **Q**: *(L)* Was it the thoughts of a person in there or of a specific individual whose job it was to do this 'thinking'?

248 **A**: Both on occasion.

249 **Q**: *(L)* Could just anybody go into the pyramid, get into this sarcophagus, and have something done to them as they specified? Or, was it the culmination of some other long process?

250 **A**: All.

251 **Q**: *(L)* When you say that the passages changed atomically, did you mean that they might actually become larger or smaller?

252 **A**: Yes. And change position as well.

253 **Q**: *(L)* Is the theory of Petrie anywhere near correct?

254 **A**: In 1967 the U.S. Army Corps of Engineers did study. Look it up.[30]

255 **Q**: *(L)* Was there ever at any point in

---

[29] Interestingly, this answer turns out to be amazingly correct. A number of different teams have done georadar and microgravimetry work in the great pyramid and a number of additional chambers have been 'discovered' this way. Permission to go any further in this investigation has been thus far denied by Egyptian authorities. See: http://www.touregypt.net/featurestories/pyramidchambers.htm

[30] I've never found an "Army Corps of Engineers" study on the Great Pyramid. I have noticed that they do a lot of studies about areas that are prone to flood and also some georadar studies as mentioned in the previous note that were carried out by a French team, I believe. However, I did find a book by an engineer, Christopher Dunn, that gives an interesting take on the use of the monument. (*The Giza Power Plant: Technologies of Ancient Egypt*) He has a website also: http://www.gizapower.com/ Another interesting book on the topic is *Ancient Egypt 39,000 BCE: The History, Technology, and Philosophy of Civilization* by Edward F. Malkowski. I also found *Before the Pharaohs: Egypt's Mysterious Prehistory*, also by Malkowski, to be interesting.

time such a thing as a unicorn as is described in legends?

256 **A**: No.

257 **Q**: *(L)* What is source of this legend?

258 **A**: Atlantis beast was similar to unicorn. All died in cataclysm. Looked similar to horse and some had horn but not all.

259 **Q**: *(L)* What is the origin of the Sanskrit language?

260 **A**: Atlantis.

261 **Q**: *(L)* When the Aryans were brought here, were they brought to Atlantis?

262 **A**: No. The Aryans were different from the Atlanteans.

263 **Q**: *(L)* Is there any language in existence today that is descended from the Aryan language? Or, that has remained more similar in development from Indo-European?

264 **A**: Yes. All Germanic.

265 **Q**: *(L)* Is Celtic considered to be one of these?

266 **A**: Yes.

267 **Q**: *(L)* What was the origin of the Minoan civilization?

268 **A**: Atlantean descendants.[31]

269 **Q**: *(L)* What was 'bull leaping'?

270 **A**: A test, a sport, a religious rite.

271 **Q**: *(L)* When Thera blew, it seems to have destroyed all the Minoan cities except for Knossos.

272 **A**: Thera was result of close passage by Maldek. Knossos was not destroyed because structures were fundamentally stronger and blast wave was perpendicular.[32] Underground shelters saved a few of the people.

273 **Q**: *(L)* Knossos lasted for about another 75 years after the events which destroyed most of the Minoan civilization. What were the events which brought about the final downfall of the Minoans?

274 **A**: Meteor borne parasites. Meteor destroyed city.[33]

275 **Q**: *(L)* The Mycenaeans built a city with a 50-foot-thick wall. Why was this wall built so if the only dangers were warriors armed with spears and arrows?

276 **A**: Protected against frequent cataclysmic events during that period. It worked. Much of wall is still standing.

---

[31] *The Wave* 24

[32] We missed this "blast wave" reference at the time. It was later, as I began digging deeply into the problem of cometary bombardment, that I learned that much of the destruction is not due to body impacts, but due to explosions of the body in the atmosphere as happened in Tunguska and elsewhere, then, in February 2013, in Chelyabinsk. I have written numerous articles reporting on this research over the years and believe me, "blast wave" is a terrifying prospect. Oddly enough, looking back, the 'primary weapon' of the alien craft depicted in the movie *Independence Day* comes pretty darn close to giving us an idea of what a large comet fragment exploding in our atmosphere would be like.

[33] We also missed this one: "meteor borne parasites." It wasn't until I later read Mike Baillie's book *New Light on the Black Death* that the research in this area expanded with help from Gabriela Segura, MD. She wrote an article on our findings, "New Light on the Black Death: The Viral-Cosmic Connection", http://www.sott.net/article/228189

277 **Q:** *(L)* Now, when you talk about the comet cluster, as you have on many occasions, the technical definition of a comet is that it is a chunk of ice. Is this the case with the comets in this cluster?

278 **A:** And other substances, primarily iridium cores.

279 **Q:** *(L)* Now you say there are 36 million Nephilim heading this way. Are they 4th density beings?

280 **A:** No. They live in 4D but are 3D. They are as physical as you. Behave like gestapo. Gestapo was inspired by Nephilim through Lizard beings' influence over Hitler. It was a practice run.[34]

281 **Q:** *(L)* Are any of the Nephilim going to be friendly toward us?

282 **A:** No.

283 **Q:** *(L)* Now, you said that the Nephilim were seeded on a planet called D'Ankhiar as were human beings. When you said we were seeded there, what did you mean?[35]

284 **A:** Was proper environment for molecularization.

285 **Q:** *(L)* Are you saying that the physical bodies on planet Earth, the various types of mankind such as Neanderthal, Cro-Magnon, Australopithicus, etc., were generated on that other planet and then brought here?

286 **A:** Yes.

287 **Q:** *(L)* I am assuming that if the Nephilim are 3D that they die like we do. Is this correct?

288 **A:** Yes.

289 **Q:** *(L)* So, we can shoot them and they will die?

290 **A:** Correct. But wrong approach.

291 **Q:** *(L)* What is the right approach?

292 **A:** Knowledge protects.

293 **Q:** *(L)* Well, if a 15-foot-tall guy comes at me and wants to knock me around, what is knowledge going to do to protect me?

294 **A:** You will be in 4th density.

295 **Q:** *(L)* So, before they get here we will be 4th density?

296 **A:** Crossing.[36]

297 **Q:** *(L)* All three of us?

298 **A:** Yes, and many others.

299 **Q:** *(L)* So, we are not going to have to deal with the Nephilim?

300 **A:** Not correct.

---

[34] Another clue given in 1994 about what is now our reality. And all thanks to the events of 9/11, the "big, big, big scandal."

[35] *The Wave* 68

[36] Since we have something in the way of 'Nephilim' in the various "enforcers using stun guns" on our planet at the present time, I think we can take this to mean we are currently in the early stages of transition. Further sessions will talk about this somewhat more, and among the symptoms are things like the crazy weather we have been experiencing since 9/11, increasing and accelerating it seems, and disappearances such as the recent vanishing of Malaysian Flight 370. The radar glitches in Europe (e.g. http://www.sott.net/article/280 431) are also a symptom, and the current events in Ukraine are mentioned as a marker. But all that will be coming up in the sessions; I just want to mention them here so you will have your eyes and mind open as you read.

Q: *(L)* Does this mean that there will be 3 and 4D beings on the planet at the same time and that some will have to deal with these guys and some won't?

A: But you will have to too.

Q: *(L)* I don't understand. Are these Nephilim coming here to transition to 4D also?

A: They already live there as 3 density beings. Demonstration: When you are abducted you are 3rd density but you are taken into 4th density.

Q: *(V)* In June I had a dream where I was taken up and there were light beings and I was also a light being; I was trying on different clothes. I was led into a room where I was told I could write there and when I was told it was time to leave, I had shoes on that had written on them 'Earth Star.' Was this an abduction?

A: Yes.

Q: *(V)* Talk about illusions, I thought that was a good thing! Was this a bad thing?

A: Subjective.

Q: *(V)* Who were the abductors?

A: Grays.

Q: *(V)* When I woke up I felt so tall and so electric. I thought it had been the best thing... that was my abduction in June?

A: Yes.

Q: *(L)* We would like to know about this plane crash. Early report from a witness said that there were no bodies. Is that the case?

A: No.

Q: *(L)* Where are the bodies?

A: Scattered.

Q: *(L)* What caused the crash?

A: Just like USAir. Was Lizard attack. Will be covered up.

Q: *(V)* The night before the USAir crash several of us had headaches and woke up drained.

A: Precognition and soul transfer of energy.

End of Session

November 4, 1994

Before commencing this session, we had been sitting around the table drinking coffee and talking about a couple of large crystals I had acquired at the local rock shop, which were on a nearby table.

Participants: 'Frank' and Laura

1 **Q:** *(L)* Hello.
2 **A:** Hello. Rocks.
3 **Q:** *(L)* What about the rocks?
4 **A:** Put in sunlight for two days.
5 **Q:** *(L)* And what will that do?
6 **A:** Energize.
7 **Q:** *(L)* Energized to do what?
8 **A:** Provide power to you.[1]
9 **Q:** *(L)* And who do we have with us tonight?
10 **A:** Rolla.
11 **Q:** *(L)* Are you a discarnate?
12 **A:** No.
13 **Q:** *(L)* Where are you from?
14 **A:** Cassiopaea. Did you see the article

---

[1] I've continued to do this with my various stones and crystals over the years. I sometimes even put them outside in the sun in containers of water. It is usually done intentionally, with some particular problem needing a solution in mind.

[2] From Wikipedia:

> The Sagittarius Dwarf Spheroidal Galaxy (Sgr dSph), also known as the Sagittarius Dwarf Elliptical Galaxy (Sgr dE or Sag DEG), is an elliptical loop-shaped satellite galaxy of the Milky Way. It consists of four globular clusters, the main cluster having been discovered in 1994. Sag DEG is roughly 10,000 light-years in diameter, and is currently about 70,000 light-years from Earth, travelling in a polar orbit (i.e. an orbit passing through the galactic poles) at a distance of about 50,000 light-years from the core of the Milky Way (about 1/3 the distance of the Large Magellanic Cloud). In its looping, spiraling path, it has passed through the plane of the Milky Way several times in the past. [..]
>
> Sag DEG was immediately recognized as being the nearest known neighbor to our Milky Way at the time. (Since 2003, the newly discovered Canis Major Dwarf Galaxy is considered the actual nearest neighbor.) Although it is one of the closest companion galaxies to the Milky Way, the main parent cluster is on the opposite side of the galactic core from Earth, and consequently is very faint, although it covers a large area of the sky. [..] Sag DEG has four known globular clusters with one, M54, apparently residing at its core. [..] Sag DEG has multiple stellar populations, ranging in age from the oldest globular clusters (almost as old as the universe itself) to trace populations as young as several hundred million years (mya). [..] Based on its current trajectory, the Sag DEG main cluster is about to pass through the galactic disc of the Milky Way within the next hundred million years, while the extended

Q: *(L)* Yes I did and I was curious about that. Is there something about that that you would like to tell us?

A: Our energy transference line to you.

Q: *(L)* What is the energy transference line, this newly discovered galaxy?

A: In a sense.

Q: *(L)* Why was the information received about the little boys so unclear?

A: Need to interpret for practice.

Q: *(L)* Does this mean that all information we get has to be interpreted also?

A: Not as much. That was a particularly sensitive subject with many focusing at once.

Q: *(L)* Was there interference from the people focusing on it?

A: Close. Remember Allison is good but not when too many are focusing.

Q: *(L)* Who is Allison? *(F)* Dorothy?

A: Yes. Dorothy.

Q: *(F)* Yeah, the psychic who finds dead people. *(L)* Well, I don't even know who she is. *(F)* She's very famous. *(L)* Well, I must be living in a cave. I was reading today in *Bringers of the Dawn* about people who are keepers of frequency. Is this an accurate concept?

A: Yes.

Q: *(L)* Are Frank and I keepers of frequency?

A: Yes.

Q: *(L)* Are we nearly at the frequency we need to keep?

A: Yes.

Q: *(L)* Helen D gave me a reading a few month's ago when she told me about two people in a partnership and she said no others should be brought in. Was this about S___ or Frank and me?

A: Interference caused reading to be askew.

Q: *(L)* Well, was she referring to this work with Frank and I or was she talking about S___?

A: Maybe.

Q: *(L)* In that reading she also said that I was going to meet somebody in the month of November who was going to become a very important part of my life in some way. Could you tell me a little bit about that?

A: Wait and see. Time to rattle the bushes again.[3]

---

loop-shaped ellipse is already extended around and through our local space and on through the Milky Way galactic disc, and in the process of slowly being absorbed into the larger galaxy, calculated at 10,000 times the mass of Sag DEG. [...] A simulation published in 2011 suggested that the Milky Way may have obtained its spiral structure as a result of repeated collisions with Sag DEG.

[http://en.wikipedia.org/wiki/Sagittarius_Dwarf_Spheroidal_Galaxy]

[3]This is an interesting remark considering a few things that the local psychic, Helen, had said to me. As the C's said, it was kind of skewed, but darned if it doesn't look pretty good in retrospect. Though, of course, the issue of interpretation is always problematic. But mainly, it seems that Helen was picking up on my meeting Ark and the many coming changes in my life. Among the things she said were:

"There is a spiritual gift coming to you and it is coming soon. And it is going to help

39 Q: *(L)* Which bushes?

40 A: Manner of speech.

41 Q: *(L)* Of all the different bushes I have rattled and people I have contacted, which ones in particular?

42 A: UFO people.

43 Q: *(L)* How can I do that?

44 A: Re-contact. Some doubt. Re-contact.

45 Q: *(L)* Re-contact some who doubt?

46 A: No. Re-contact some do doubt.

47 Q: *(L)* Which ones in particular?

48 A: Must just rattle without prejudice.[4]

49 Q: *(L)* Does this mean sending out scripts from our sessions?

50 A: Good idea. Spark interest.

51 Q: *(L)* Well, that is what I have been planning to do.

> you move on. Your potential is extremely high. There is a lot you are going to be able to do and it is a little unusual. ... There is going to be a proposal made to you that will involve a new interest, an adding onto what you are already considering, what you have already started to do, which I feel is going to be successful, but slow. And I feel you may have to add something more to it, you may have to involve a new educational tool in some way. [Going online?] There is some sort of an education involved with it. Something either to do with classes or teaching or something. ...I think that what you are doing is going to build up and I think that next year is going to do real well. ... The person who is going to come to you with an idea is a male and it probably won't be until into October [October is Ark's birth month], and I feel that he is mature, perhaps even retired. He has some good ideas. He is going to just stumble on you and really be interested. There is a lot of personal happiness coming for you. There is future happiness for you. Future from right now, that is. There is fulfillment coming. ... you are going to help a lot of people... You two will learn from each other and from the people. There is a possibility that this will lead to a church or meeting place. This looks good. Spirit are showing a lot of possibilities. There is a lot of harmony and balance coming into your life which I saw before. Whatever is not right just now is going to be resolved. The interesting thing are the four twos. There are a lot of decisions you are going to make. ... Independence is coming for you. A second chance. Payback time. A lot of challenges coming having to do with communication. You are too honest and not tactful enough. Be careful of this. Definitely on a spiritual path. A new friend coming into your circle, if you are already married then it is a spiritual friend. Because of what you are doing you are going to draw a lot of people to you and there is going to be one who is going to stand out and turn out to be important to you. Won't be until the end of the year. At least November."

Of course, it was not until July of 1996 that Ark came along, so that was still 20 months in the future. But, you will notice, again and again, the intimations of the future. The C's kept hammering on the "go on the Net" idea and I kept resisting. It might be said that, had I actually hooked up to the internet sooner than I did, I may have met Ark sooner, but no way to tell for sure.

[4]This turned out to be the case. In the spring of 1996, I finally shared some transcripts with a UFO mailing/discussion list run by a retired AF colonel. One of the recipients on this list, unbeknownst to me, sent my session transcripts to Ark, who was immediately intrigued and then contacted me. A lot of this is described in *The Wave* books. So keep in mind what happened as you continue to read.

52 **A**: It takes more than one spark of the flint to ignite the fire.

53 **Q**: *(L)* Should Frank get the Reiki initiation?

54 **A**: Okay.

55 **Q**: *(L)* Would it be good for him to get the Reiki initiation?

56 **A**: It is always.

57 **Q**: *(L)* Who are the Nordic type aliens?

58 **A**: Your ancestors.

59 **Q**: *(L)* What planet did they come from?

60 **A**: Several and transitory.

61 **Q**: *(L)* What is their type called? Just the Nordic types?

62 **A**: That is as good as any description.

63 **Q**: *(L)* What is their purpose here on the planet at this time?

64 **A**: Observation.

65 **Q**: *(L)* Haven't they been seen with the Lizzies on occasion?

66 **A**: Yes.

67 **Q**: *(L)* Are they involved with the Lizzies?

68 **A**: Some are.

69 **Q**: *(L)* Are some of them not nice?

70 **A**: Fifty-fifty.

71 **Q**: *(L)* Do they ever abduct people?

72 **A**: Have but not too often. When they do, they do not give back.[5]

73 **Q**: *(L)* What do they do with the ones they abduct?

74 **A**: Take away to too many other places to mention. Purpose is multiple. Too complex.

75 **Q**: *(L)* I get the feeling that maybe it is not too complex, but that you just don't want to answer, is this correct?

76 **A**: Open. Not at this moment.

77 **Q**: *(L)* What about the Vilas-Boas case; who were these beings and what was the purpose for this interaction?

78 **A**: Aryan's breeding experiment.[6]

79 **Q**: *(L)* Where do these Aryans live?

80 **A**: In transit.

81 **Q**: *(L)* When they get to where they are going, where do they live?

---

[5]Well, that's a pretty creepy answer!

[6]Antônio Vilas-Boas was a Brazilian farmer who claimed to have been abducted by extraterrestrials in 1957. Though similar stories had circulated for years beforehand, Vilas Boas' claims were among the first alien abduction stories to receive wide attention. At the time of his alleged abduction, Antônio Vilas-Boas was a 23-year-old who was working at night to avoid the hot temperatures of the day. On October 16, 1957, a red star-like craft landed and though Antonio tried to get away on his tractor and then on foot, the aliens out-maneuvered him with their technology and he ended up inside their ship being subjected to what seem to be decontamination procedures. Following this, he was induced to have sexual intercourse with an odd-looking, but attractive, female. After this, he was taken on a tour of the ship and then released. Following this event, Antonio apparently suffered from radiation sickness. Vilas-Boas later became a lawyer, married and had four children. He stuck to the story of his alleged abduction for his entire life. He died in 1991 at the age of 57.

82 **A:** They don't. There are many who do not live specifically anywhere. They are perpetually in transit.

83 **Q:** *(L)* Why is this?

84 **A:** There is no need to be grounded; it is only your perception because that is your familiarity. A planet is a vehicle too.[7]

85 **Q:** *(L)* Why were there 3 pyramids? Did they each have separate purposes?

A: Variance in energy levels and age. 86 Did you research about the 1967 engineer's study yet?[8]

87 **Q:** *(L)* What book would that be in?

A: Look at Mystery volume. Now, 88 please.[9]

89 **Q:** *(L)* Why was Moses not allowed into the promised land?

---

[7] This exchange was extremely unsettling to me because I get claustrophobic just thinking about living on a spaceship ever-traveling through endless space. It was very *Star Wars*-like and I found that creepy.

[8] No, I hadn't! For crying out loud, it had only been a couple of days since they mentioned it and the internet was just getting going at the time. How the heck was I supposed to research it?

[9] I looked and there was nothing there that seemed to fit the bill.

[10] And that's assuming that any part of that story is true. If it is, the most likely candidate for Moses is the student (or son) of Orpheus, Mousaios AKA Musaeus, a legendary polymath, philosopher, historian, prophet, seer, priest, poet, and musician, said to have been the founder of priestly poetry in Attica. He composed dedicatory and purificatory hymns and prose treatises, and oracular responses.

Herodotus reports that, during the reign of Peisistratus at Athens, the scholar Onomacritus collected and arranged the oracles of Musaeus but inserted forgeries of his own devising. Artapanus of Alexandria, Alexander Polyhistor, Numenius of Apamea, and Eusebius identify Musaeus with Moses the Jewish lawbringer and it is likely that the Exodus story was a rip-off of the Homeric epics with Musaeus added in as the Egyptian/Jewish hero, and this was done sometime in the early 3rd century BC.

If he was an actual person in relationship to Orpheus, he would have lived before or around the time of the Trojan War. The ancient Greeks thought that the Trojan War was a historical event that had taken place in the 13th or 12th century BC, but it is nowadays considered to be non-historical. I would suggest that it was not a war, per se, but rather an event of cometary bombardment, the one that brought on the collapse of the Bronze Age. The BBC published a report on research about this saying:

> "Evidence is growing that a huge comet smashed into the Earth about 4,000 years ago. Scientists are pointing to studies of tree-rings in Ireland which have revealed that about 2,354–2,345 BC there was an abrupt change to a colder climate. They have also highlighted discoveries by archaeologists in northern Syria of a catastrophic environmental event at about the same time. This is also about the time that Bronze Age civilisations collapsed. Dr Bill Napier, an astronomer at Armagh Observatory, and Dr Victor Clube, from Oxford and Armagh universities, say the evidence points to a comet hitting the Earth, and have called for more research." [http://news.bbc.co.uk/2/hi/science/nature/100101.stm]

90 **A:** Because he became tyrannical.[10]

91 **Q:** *(L)* Were the Lizards the ones who led the Jews to the 'Promised Land'?

92 **A:** No. Were not led; followed their own paths in effort to escape the effects of cataclysms.[11]

93 **Q:** *(L)* Why have they got this big legend about being chosen and led to the Promised Land?

94 **A:** More Brotherhood influence and nonsense.

95 **Q:** *(L)* What kind of weapons do the Nephilim use to do their 'enforcing'?[12]

96 **A:** Stun guns.[13]

97 **Q:** *(L)* Do they actually use some kind of material weapon?

98 **A:** Yes.

99 **Q:** *(L)* And could you tell us what the Lizzies look like?

100 **A:** Upright alligators with some humanoid features in face.[14]

101 **Q:** *(L)* I heard one theory that the Lizzies originally evolved on planet Earth. Is this true?

102 **A:** No. Neither did you.

103 **Q:** *(L)* Do you mean us in the sense of the early human prototypes?

104 **A:** All prototypes.

105 **Q:** *(L)* When these prototypes were evolved on another planet, did they have souls at that time?

106 **A:** Were added.

107 **Q:** *(L)* What souls occupied those prototypes on that other planet?

108 **A:** Same.

109 **Q:** *(L)* So, the legend of the fall of Lucifer as the origin of the souls incarnating into physical life was an event that actually took place on this other planet?

110 **A:** Yes.

111 **Q:** *(L)* Do the Lizzies have more than one heart?

112 **A:** No.

113 **Q:** *(L)* Do they have more than one brain?

114 **A:** No.

115 **Q:** *(L)* This fellow, Eddie Page, who claims that he was abducted, and taken by the aliens and altered in physical ways, was any of this true?

116 **A:** No.

117 **Q:** *(L)* Was he abducted, in fact?

118 **A:** Yes.

119 **Q:** *(L)* What was done to him?

120 **A:** Same routine as other abductees.

121 **Q:** *(L)* Does Eddie Page know that he is deceiving other people?

122 **A:** Yes. He is a fraud. Misguided by delusions.[15]

End of Session

---

[11] Which fits with my idea that the Trojan War was really about cometary cataclysms.

[12] *High Strangeness* 14

[13] See my notes about this in the previous sessions and how factual this has turned out to be for our current time.

[14] *High Strangeness* 7

[15] This turned out to be absolutely correct, though for a couple of years I had to deal with people who believed the nonsense this guy was spouting! It's just amazing how gullible people are.

November 6, 1994

As part of my ongoing efforts to help Frank, who spent a lot of time complaining about how he suffered in life, I discussed with him a book I had recently read about how to change your mental state by changing your posture. That was the topic of discussion before this session began. Right at the end of this session, a question was asked about the 'Gulf Breeze Six' that is interesting and I've had a number of thoughts about that since then that I will share.

Participants: 'Frank' and Laura

1 **Q**: *(L)* Are you there?

2 **A**: Wait.

3 **Q**: *(L)* Are you there?

4 **A**: Yes.

5 **Q**: *(L)* Who do we have with us tonight?

6 **A**: Vedeeba.

7 **Q**: *(L)* Are you a discarnate from Earth?

8 **A**: No.

9 **Q**: *(L)* Who are you?

10 **A**: Cassiopaean.

11 **Q**: *(L)* Have you been listening in on our discussion?[1]

12 **A**: As always.

13 **Q**: *(L)* In this particular discussion we have been talking about freeing up life energy which can be blocked by emotional traumas and so forth, and that, according to this book I read, you can tell the life energy is blocked by the way a person holds or moves their body. From this information I think that Frank's life energy is blocked. Am I correct?

14 **A**: No.

15 **Q**: *(L)* Then why is Frank so ill at ease in his body?

16 **A**: Book not entirely incorrect but remember not to take anything entirely on face value.

17 **Q**: *(L)* Is there some part of that idea that would benefit Frank and help him to feel more at ease?

---

[1] *The Wave* 35

[2] This and the rest of this exchange was certainly a coded message to me, but I was unable to really understand it at the time. After the events of later years transpired, I revisited some of the many subtle hints and warnings the C's were giving me about Frank (and others) in my book *Petty Tyrants* (part of *The Wave* series of books). With the insights of our long research into psychopathology culminating in finding the book *Political Ponerology*, little clues like the fact that people reacted negatively

18 **A**: Frank is ill at ease because most others are ill at ease with him.[2]

19 **Q**: *(L)* Well, who started out being ill at ease, him or others?

20 **A**: Others.

21 **Q**: *(L)* And why were they ill at ease with him?

22 **A**: Sensed differences.

23 **Q**: *(L)* If Frank were to do some bodywork and bring his energies into focus where his physical sensations are concerned, would this, in some way, help to overcome this particular difficulty or situation?

24 **A**: Won't work.

25 **Q**: *(L)* Is there anything Frank can do to free up his energies and to become more at ease with himself?

26 **A**: He is more at ease now than before because he no longer listens to others' criticisms.

27 **Q**: *(L)* Is Frank correct in saying that his body and mode is that of the future?

28 **A**: Closer. But not there yet.

29 **Q**: *(L)* There was a comment made in an earlier reading when we were told we needed to equalize our input in this project. I am curious as to the exact meaning of equalize the input? Does that refer to use of the board or what?[3]

30 **A**: Many meanings. One must not dominate decision making. Be open all ideas and input. Once we have made financial arrangements that will be your cue to dedicate full time efforts to this endeavor.[4]

31 **Q**: *(L)* Are you making financial arrangements for us to be taken care of?

32 **A**: Will.

33 **Q**: *(L)* When will this be?

34 **A**: Open.

35 **Q**: *(L)* Does it depend on our dedication and increasing of this channel strength, etc?

36 **A**: Just wait. Continue as you are.

37 **Q**: *(L)* Now, I was just reading in *Bringers of the Dawn* about male energy and female energy and it says: "We have said that the male vibration will transform in a very short period of time. We will not tell you why or how because some of you will consider it to be entirely too ominous, however, we will

---

to Frank because they "sensed differences" and that he "no longer listens to others' criticisms," as well as the info from a previous session about a battle between good and evil going on within him, began to add up and make sense. But these are the kinds of things that we are conditioned to shove under the rug, to ignore, to make nice about.

[3]I had a hidden motive in this question. I had noticed that I was the one doing all the work in the experiment and Frank was the one taking all the credit and making sure that everyone knew – because he told them – that he, and he alone, was 'the channel.' This was despite the fact that the C's had given very broad hints otherwise. So, I was quite interested in how the C's would handle answering this question.

[4]This was an odd answer since, as far as I could tell, no one was "dominating decision making." However, as time went by, I began to realize that this was exactly what Frank was doing. And, indeed, much, much later, I was able to devote myself wholly to this work – and much, much more – though Frank was left behind.

say that as the waves continue to come there will be a unilateral rising of consciousness within the population. At a certain point, when men are in the deepest point of mastering feeling, the feeling center will be activated. This will either occur gently or it will be blown wide open." What will be "entirely too ominous"?[5]

38 **A**: Energy redirection.

39 **Q**: *(L)* Energy direction is going to happen and that is what you are saying is the ominous thing here?

40 **A**: Overview.

41 **Q**: *(L)* Well, what does energy direction specifically mean? What kind of energy?

42 **A**: Sexual.

43 **Q**: *(L)* And this is going to be the ominous event that would frighten people?

44 **A**: Repercussions.

45 **Q**: *(L)* What are the repercussions?

46 **A**: Many.

47 **Q**: *(L)* Could you tell us some of them?

48 **A**: First you must figure out answer to number one.

49 **Q**: *(L)* Well, sexual energy 'redirected'; does this mean women will stop having sex with men?

50 **A**: Not exactly.

51 **Q**: *(L)* Am I close?

52 **A**: Yes. Men will lose most of their drive in favor of more spiritual pursuits. It is the sex drive that is at the root of most

---

[5] I can't say that this exchange is much clearer now than it was then. I can say that there has *not* been a "unilateral rising of consciousness" and as far as I can tell, the only way that the "male vibration" of our Earth has transformed has been to go deeper into entropy and war. Perhaps that is what the Pleiadians actually meant?

[6] We certainly haven't seen men on Earth losing their drive in favor of more spiritual pursuits! In fact, the opposite seems to have occurred: aggression and lack of feeling on the part of large segments of populations all over the planet. Maybe the problem was that I introduced Marciniak's material and Frank was very taken with it and had some emotional investment in rejecting sex, as described in *Petty Tyrants*? Or the C's hint about "redirected sexual energy" being the "root of most of the historical aggression" has to do with what Gurdjieff said about the wrong usage of sexual energy in *In Search of the Miraculous*:

> "Speaking in general, there are only two correct ways of expending sexual energy – normal sexual life and transmutation. All inventions in this sphere are very dangerous. [..] You must understand where lies the chief evil and what makes for slavery. It is not in sex itself but in the abuse of sex. But what the abuse of sex means is again misunderstood. It means [..] the functioning of the sex center with energy borrowed from other centers and the functioning of other centers with energy borrowed from the sex center. [..] The energy of the sex center in the work of the thinking, emotional, and moving centers can be recognized by a particular 'taste,' by a particular fervor, by a vehemence which the nature of the affair concerned does not call for. The thinking center writes books, but in making use of the energy of the sex center it [..] is always fighting something [..] The emotional center preaches Christianity, abstinence, asceticism, or the fear and horror of sin, hell, the torment of sinners, eternal fire, all this with the energy of the sex center. [..] Or on the other hand it works up revolutions, robs, burns, kills, again with the same energy."

of the historical aggression and lack of feeling on the part of the male.[6]

53 Q: *(L)* Can we tell others?

54 A: Might cause turmoil but up to you.

55 Q: *(L)* I noticed that at about the same time I began meditating heavily that my drive plummeted. Is this because of the meditation?

56 A: Yes. Females will lose some drive too. But how will humans react to this, that is the question. Will they be prepared?[7]

57 Q: *(L)* Does this mean that everybody is going to lose interest in sex?

58 A: Will have much less and must learn to relate to each other more spiritually.

59 Q: *(L)* Is this because one of the major drives of the human being is for contact and, up to now, this has been manifested through sexual union and without the sexual urge they will be forced to find other ways to relate?

60 A: One would hope so. You are all moving toward 4th level which is less physical thus you must learn this existence in order to pass through into the 4th level.

61 Q: *(L)* And those who do not learn will not pass, is that correct?

62 A: Yes. Some will be relieved. It depends upon how advanced one is.[8]

63 Q: *(L)* I have drawn a sort of conclusion about some of the activities of the Lizzies and their abductions through the Grays and so forth, and it seems to me that these excessive numbers of exams, gynecological, reproductive or whatever exams might possibly be a screen for a process that is used to extract life force or energy from the human being, through the basal chakra, the sexual chakra, as I understand where the life force enters in. Is this idea correct or on track?

64 A: Close.

65 Q: *(L)* It does seem that the Grays and Lizzies are abnormally interested in sexual activities of human beings, is that correct?[9]

66 A: Yes.

67 Q: *(L)* Why are they so inordinately interested in this and why do they practice sex, sexual aberrations, or do they have a tremendous sex drive even though they are 4th density beings?

68 A: Too many questions; one at a time.

69 Q: *(L)* Do they have tremendous sex drives even though they are in 4th density?

70 A: No.

71 Q: *(L)* Are they interested in sexual energy simply because it is life force?[10]

---

[7] Well, if humans have actually lost any sex drive, I would say it is due simply to overall loss of vigor of the species. We also now know the reaction: Viagra and other sex-stimulating drugs.

[8] That was how Frank felt; as I have written about in *Petty Tyrants*, he was certain that he was an advanced type of human because he had no interest in sex. Well, more than that, he had an aversion to it. So, these responses about sex could have been skewed by his emotional investment. But I doubt that it was evidence of his superior state of being, which proved to be not-so-superior in later years.

[9] *High Strangeness* 7

[10] *High Strangeness* 17

72 **A:** Partly and also desperate to stave off change in order to retain control.

73 **Q:** *(L)* What changes are they desperate to stave off?

74 **A:** To 4th level.[11]

75 **Q:** *(L)* They are trying to stave off the 4th level change. Can they do that?

76 **A:** No. Also hoping to retain control even if change occurs.

77 **Q:** *(L)* By what means do they do this through these gynecological exams? Is there some technical activity they undertake?

78 **A:** Yes. Too complex.

79 **Q:** *(L)* Are these supposed memories people have from their abductions of these exams just screens of procedures used to take life force from them?

80 **A:** Yes.[12]

81 **Q:** *(L)* When they sample an abductee's tissue and take the little scoops or chunks out of them, what do they take these chunks of flesh for?

82 **A:** Cloning.

83 **Q:** *(L)* If they clone, why do they need such a large chunks?

84 **A:** You don't know all details of cloning process yet.[13]

85 **Q:** *(L)* Do they take twins, or one of

---

[11] Which makes one wonder how harvesting sexual energy from human beings could aid in staving off the changes to 4th density? Maybe that relates back to the previous topic, the loss of sex drive in the human species; the loss of vigor? Perhaps that loss of vigor is what makes human beings so easily controlled and manipulated? Maybe that loss of vigor is due to this constant harvesting? Maybe normal, healthy sex drives in human beings, that are balanced with spiritual inclinations and strivings, are what humanity needs to progress, as alluded to by Gurdjieff? It certainly isn't happening with Viagra putting the focus on the animalistic aspects of the thing.

[12] Notice that the answer was "close" earlier when I posed the question with qualifiers about the basal chakra or sex chakra. Apparently, the chakras have nothing to do with it.

[13] The only reason I can think of as to why so much tissue is needed is because a lot of cloning is going on! If you have a nice chunk, you can make many copies and discard the ones that are faulty.

[14] I had recently become aware of the research of a member of the Clearwater MUFON group, Caryl Dennis, who focused on what she called 'The Vanishing Twin' phenomenon:

> "While engaged in research involving extraterrestrial contactees who became geniuses, she came upon the Vanishing Twin Phenomenon (1 in 8 people actually begin life as twins – seventy-five percent of the women diagnosed with twins only deliver one baby). Her research revealed that many of the contactees were twins, were supposed to be twins, or had twins in their family. Through this research, Caryl discovered that she herself had a twin sister in utero who did not survive. That discovery enabled Caryl to establish extra-dimensional telepathic contact with her "missing" twin, whose name is Karyl (pronounce Kuh-rill). Karyl informed Caryl that her ever-expanding psychic ability is one result of the stimulation of the pineal gland that occurs in the process of that contact."

> In January of 1997, Caryl, with her partner Parker Whitman, published *The Mil-*

a pair of twins, and raise one artificially?[14]

86 **A:** Have done so.

87 **Q:** *(L)* Have they done this to a great extent?

88 **A:** Define.

89 **Q:** *(L)* Is this done frequently?

90 **A:** No.

91 **Q:** *(L)* What is the purpose of taking one of a pair of twins?

92 **A:** Study to determine which is best soul receptacle: one of twins or clone.[15]

93 **Q:** *(L)* Do these twins they raise, do they raise them on their ships or in their enclave wherever they are?

94 **A:** Yes.

95 **Q:** *(L)* And do they treat them well?

96 **A:** Open.

97 **Q:** *(L)* Do they teach them a great deal?

98 **A:** Yes.

99 **Q:** *(L)* Do they do this to test the brain capacity of the human being?

100 **A:** And other reasons.

101 **Q:** *(L)* Was I one of a pair of twins?

102 **A:** No.

103 **Q:** *(L)* For what purpose are they trying to decide which is the best receptacle, the clone or the twin? Receptacle for what?[16]

104 **A:** Future project.

105 **Q:** *(L)* To do what?

106 **A:** Switch physical realities.

107 **Q:** *(L)* And who is going to switch physical realities? Are they going to enter into bodies they have prepared for themselves and force human souls to enter into their bodies?

108 **A:** No.

109 **Q:** *(L)* They are going to enter into the bodies themselves so that they can switch their reality?

110 **A:** Yes.

111 **Q:** *(L)* So, they are preparing a bunch of soulless bodies into which they can enter in themselves?

112 **A:** Will try.[17]

---

lennium Children: Tales of the Shift, which tells of her research into the growing number of children who are born retaining pre-birth memories and/or displaying marked psychic abilities, as well as the ability to see beyond the visible light spectrum (frequently, their other senses are highly developed, as well), and who often report contact with extra-terrestrial or extra-dimensional entities. Their IQs are usually in the genius range, and they display a variety of inventive and creative talents. *The Millennium Children* (subsequently referred to as Indigo Children) offers possible reasons for this consciousness "shift", as well as the most extensive exploration of the Vanishing Twin Phenomenon in print at the time it was written."
[http://caryl.ipower.com/wordpress/about-us/]

[15]This raises the question as to why the choice has to be either. Is there some connection between clones and the original body and one twin and another that is vital to the purpose of the Lizzies?

[16]*High Strangeness* 7

[17]Right about now, with the apparent tremendous increase in psychopaths on our planet, I'd say that this experiment was working, at least partly. This also gives another angle to any so-called 'alien invasion.' Heck, if they've been abducting

113 **Q**: *(L)* You said the other night that the Lizzies were like upright alligators only with somewhat humanoid features to their faces, is that correct?

114 **A**: Yes.

115 **Q**: *(L)* Do they have tails?

116 **A**: Yes.

117 **Q**: *(L)* How tall are they?

118 **A**: Six to eight feet tall.

119 **Q**: *(L)* Do they wear clothing?

120 **A**: Yes.

121 **Q**: *(L)* I know this is a silly question, but does their clothing have an opening for the tail?

122 **A**: Yes.

123 **Q**: *(L)* Do they defecate?

124 **A**: No. They are 4th level.

125 **Q**: *(L)* So, when you are 4th level you neither eat nor defecate in the regular way?

126 **A**: Correct.

127 **Q**: *(L)* Do the Lizzies have the ability to change their shape or appearance?

128 **A**: Temporarily.

129 **Q**: *(L)* In the Karla Turner book, the son's roommate encountered a female alien type. Who was that?[18]

130 **A**: One of us. But several individuals sharing form.

131 **Q**: *(L)* Karla Turner had a visit with several entities in her kitchen while she was cooking. Who were they?

132 **A**: Others.

133 **Q**: *(L)* Others who?

134 **A**: Different group.

135 **Q**: *(L)* What different group?

136 **A**: Not necessary to know.

137 **Q**: *(L)* Were they 'good' guys or 'bad' guys?

138 **A**: Open. We only rarely appear as human.

139 **Q**: *(L)* The other night my daughter A___ thought she saw a spirit figure standing near as we were channeling. Did she, in fact, see an old woman figure?

140 **A**: Yes.

141 **Q**: *(L)* And who was that individual?

142 **A**: Us.

143 **Q**: *(L)* Why did that individual say "remember me"? Was that the entire message or was there more message?

144 **A**: Message is for A___ to interpret.

145 **Q**: *(L)* Why did A___ say that she had some questions as to whether that was a positive or negative source? She first felt that it was positive but then she had doubts. She wondered about being deceived. Can you help her with that?

146 **A**: All must search to learn.

---

people, cloning, stealing babies, whatever, for years now, they have enough bodies to 'invade' without ever appearing in the skies as an 'alien armada' that has to be fought and resisted as depicted in the movie *Independence Day*. I keep saying: "Who needs aliens when we've got psychopaths!" Well, maybe the psychopaths *are* 'aliens'!

[18]The book is *Into the Fringe* as has already been mentioned. Well worth reading, as are all Karla's books.

147 **Q:** *(L)* The kids want me to ask about fairies. Are there such things?

148 **A:** There is such thing as all things in one reality or another.

149 **Q:** *(L)* A___ wants to know about dwarfs or midgets.

150 **A:** Karma.

151 **Q:** *(L)* They are not Lizzie experiments?

152 **A:** No. Predictions will arrive spontaneously when needed.[19]

153 **Q:** *(L)* Do you have any predictions for us at this time?

154 **A:** Not at this juncture.

155 **Q:** *(L)* Is there anyone I should add to the list of people to send the transcript to?

156 **A:** Marciniak.

157 **Q:** *(L)* What is wrong with the A drive on my computer?

158 **A:** Hardware glitch.

159 **Q:** *(L)* Is it repairable?

160 **A:** Yes.

161 **Q:** *(L)* How much is it going to cost?

162 **A:** Open.[20]

163 **Q:** *(L)* All the UFO sightings in Gulf Breeze, are these aliens or government experiments?[21]

164 **A:** Some are and some are projections.

165 **Q:** *(L)* And who is responsible?

166 **A:** Multiple sources.

167 **Q:** *(L)* Positive or negative?

168 **A:** Both.

169 **Q:** *(L)* And the Gulf Breeze Six, as they call them, the AWOL military personnel who were taken into custody and who were receiving messages on a Ouija board, what information were they receiving and who was it from?

170 **A:** Some from us and some from others.

171 **Q:** *(L)* Was there something terribly frightening about this information that caused the government to confiscate these people and their transcripts?

[The last part of this session was lost due to tape malfunction. This is unfortunate because it is a fascinating case. And since the only persons present were Frank and myself, there are no handwritten notes to this session.]

Phil Coppens has written a concise article about the Gulf Breeze Six from which I will quote several chunks below. You can visit his site[22] to read the whole story. My comments to the quotation will be in footnotes.

> On July 9, 1990, six US military intelligence analysts from the 701st Military Intelligence Brigade at Augsburg, West Germany,

---

[19] I have no recall as to why this announcement was made. Perhaps it was another subtle clue for me to collect and ponder?

[20] I thought I would check their 'predictive abilities'!

[21] *The Wave* 52

[22] http://www.philipcoppens.com/gulfbreeze6.html

at that time the biggest NSA (National Security Agency) listening post²³ in the world outside the United States, deserted their posts, somehow convinced that the end of the world was nigh. It is one of the most extra-ordinary stories...

Spc. Kenneth Beason, Spc. Vance Davis, Sgt. Annette Eccleston, Pfc. Michael Hueckstaedt, Pfc. Kris Perlock and Pfc. William Setterberg went AWOL²⁴ ... The group left their station in Germany, travelled to Chattanooga, Tennessee, where they bought a van, and drove to Gulf Breeze, Florida, at the time a noted UFO hotspot. ... most of these men had done their basic training at Curtiss Station in nearby NAS (Naval Air Station) Pensacola, which meant that they were familiar with the area.²⁵

Five days after their flight, on Saturday July 14, a broken taillight on the van resulted in a routine traffic stop, and Hueckstaedt, the driver of the van, was detained by police when a computer check indicated that he was wanted for desertion. The remaining five were later rounded up and taken to Fort Benning, Georgia, where they were kept in solitary confinement, incommunicado. Their fate – a possible execution – hung in the balance, until their families leaked their predicament to the press, resulting in reactions from Senators Casman and Dole.

Surprisingly enough, three weeks after their arrest, instead of being severely punished by a military tribunal, they were [slated to be?] discharged from Fort Knox – with full honours! Following Colin Powell's dissent to this incredible verdict – after all, they were deserters – this was withdrawn.²⁶ Instead, they were reduced to the lowest rank and forfeited half a month's pay. Since, military officials have refused to discuss the investigation. ... When the case

---

²³Considering all the recent scandal about the NSA eavesdropping on the whole planet, and the discussion of the 'Beast of Revelation' and the "supercomputer" recording everything about everyone in a previous session, I find it utterly fascinating that these guys were working for the NSA and went off the deep end like this. Just what does this reveal about the inner workings of that agency?

²⁴Military abbreviation for 'Absence Without Leave.'

²⁵Coppens wonders if the spate of UFO sightings there was related to the activities of these individuals, or if they were drawn there because of the UFO sightings. My own experience was that it seems that my activities attracted UFOs and this is reported in the *St. Petersburg Times* article: http://www.sptimes.com/News/webspecials/exorcist/index.html

²⁶Curious that Colin Powell, minion of the Bush Administration that brought us 9/11, was involved here. Surely he was privy to what was going on. Gives an all new perspective on what the Bush gang might have been aware of.

was declassified, 1400 out of 1600 pages were withheld. ...

[Vance] Davis states that as a teenager, he had enrolled in Silva Mind Control courses ... and mastered techniques of self-hypnosis through active imagination. During one of his trances, he met a green-skinned, yellow-clad alien female named Kia, who, over one night, corrected his flat-footedness. Davis said that Kia "told me that she came from a planet forty-five light years away from Earth, that had been destroyed by another race. Her race, the Kiasseions,[27] were telepaths that were enroute to Earth to assist the Alliance[28] in protecting the human race. They were scheduled to arrive by late 1992.[29] The Kiasseion civilization had been reduced to five spacecraft carrying about three thousand people per ship [...] Her husband had been killed, and she had taken his place as Commander of this small armada, with her two grown sons in charge of two of the remaining ships." Kia became Vance's guardian.

Nothing unusual so far, if at least you are familiar with what many other channelers have stated about their contacts. But Davis held the "toppest" security clearances in the country.[30]

But what caused them to go AWOL? "Ouija board sessions." According to Davis, the Ouija board put the six soldiers in touch with an entity that named herself Safire, and others, including those presenting themselves as the Old Testament prophet Zechariah, Mark and Timothy of New Testament, and the Blessed Virgin Mary herself.[31]

Between December 1989 and July 1990, the Ouija-summoned spirits gave the group a series of predictions of coming world events which, Davis claims, were passed along to military authorities upon their arrest, together with the copious notes that were taken

---

[27] Odd homophony to 'Cassiopaea.'

[28] Similar word to 'Federation' used first by the Ra group and then picked up by the C's.

[29] As you will see, the biggest problems with this whole story are the attached dates. If such ships did actually arrive at any point, they certainly didn't make themselves widely known!

[30] Indeed the story is pretty much the New Age/UFO contactee schtick even to the acquisition of a 'space brother-type' guardian. As I mentioned in my introduction, we waded through a lot of that sort in the two years leading up to the contact with the C's and sent them all on their way.

[31] These types of entities are a dime a dozen when channeling. But obviously, this group didn't know that nor did they know how to deal with it.

by the group during the eight Ouija sessions. ...[32]

When some of Safire's prophecies, both minor and significant, started to come true, one stating the exact dynamics and the number of casualties of a major earthquake in Iran (292,236 deaths),[33] it convinced the six that they were dealing with genuine transhuman encounters. ... They asked Safire how to carry out their divine mission. Safire instructed them to flee the military, regardless of consequences, because they were needed to help lead the world through an impending cataclysm. So they did.[34]

Davis states that in 1989, he "began to sense that the lines of demarcation between the physical world and the spiritual one were beginning to blur." It is here that we need to introduce Beason, who was even more instrumental in the group's flight. He believed in reincarnation and believed that he had been sacrificed to the gods in a previous life. He also believed that the US government was in cahoots with aliens and that evidence for this could actually be found in Augsburg, the NSA site where they worked.[35] It was

---

[32] I don't know what they mean by "copious notes" taken during their sessions. As long as there is a third person present at my sessions, notes are taken to record the movements of the pointer and, if possible, a quick note about the question. But usually things move so fast, it is hard to keep up with the strings of letters being recognized and called out, so I'm not sure what else these folks could have been writing.

[33] I have no idea what Coppens is talking about here since the only earthquake in Iran I could find that had a significant mortality was on June 20, 1990, and the death toll is listed as "at least 35,000." http://en.wikipedia.org/wiki/List_of_earthquakes_-in_Iran

[34] Oh boy! Big mistake. These guys should have been doing research instead of believing everything they were told by a 'channeled' source. At the very least, they should have read John Keel's books where he exposes the Cosmic Trickster nature of most of these types of communications.

[35] Well, as far as I can see, he could have been quite correct on all these points. The important thing is what one does with this kind of information. Research would be the first step. I don't know that we can ever prove that "aliens are in cahoots with the US government," even though the C's have said the same thing, and though it does appear plausible based on circumstantial evidence; but I think I'd have some qualms about taking advice *from* aliens if you suspect aliens to be 'in cahoots.' I'd be doing the research first. Also, if the evidence was supposed to found at Augsburg, why weren't these guys working on digging that up and exposing it like Edward Snowden did? Funny that Snowden was able to get away with it, and some of the info he has released is a little questionable in my opinion, and if the Gulf Breeze Six actually did do any digging and copying of documents, we have heard nothing about it. Maybe that is part of the "copious notes" they were taking that have been

also Beason who knew Anna Foster, at whose house in Gulf Breeze most of the group would later be hiding – and arrested. He was in love with her. ...

Davis states that Safire warned them of a coming war. Mankind was about to make an evolutionary step, which is why many alien entities were in orbit, on or under the Earth – and/or in telepathic contact with the likes of him. There were two alien groups: the Alliance, the good guys, who believed in free will, and "the Others", who were abducting people and performing medical experiments on them. Safire "confirmed" to the group that the US government was in cahoots with the aliens, as they had suspected all along.[36]
...

What is at the bottom of this story? At its most basic level, it shows that certain NSA operatives were dabbling with alien-Christian eschatology – and went AWOL as a consequence.[37] But is that all there is to it? We only have Davis' word and his interpretation for it, but he does suggest that they may have been part of an experiment – as some observers noted at the time when their story hit the press. ...

Davis also had an intriguing career. He noted that he had his initial posting in Ft. Meade, which was rare. "I had done work in psychic research back at Fort Meade, and was surprised at the seriousness with which our military approached this subject. I realized then that my fast-track to NSA was probably due to my Silva Mind Control background." It suggests that Davis was followed – if not singled out – by the NSA early on.[38]

---

so heavily redacted?

[36] Not that much different from things the C's have said.

[37] This is not the first time I've heard this kind of story from the UFO/alien research/dabbling community. I read a long document some years ago where it was claimed that the ONI (Navy) was still involved in time-travel research and were busy going back into the past to plant religious ideas for mind-control purposes to be activated in the present, including the whole Christianity schtick. Fact is, the Christianity myth could grow and develop out of real historical events, such as the life and doings of Julius Caesar, by perfectly normal means; well-known principles of social memory, text transmission, language shifts, and all that sort of thing apply. So we don't need time-traveling sailors to get us there. Just like we don't need aliens when we have psychopaths. I'm not closing the door on that, but I keep pointing out that the alien/UFO phenomenon is a paranormal thing, para-physical, and unlikely to manifest in our world as those folks who would like to see a UFO land on the White House lawn wish.

[38] Or that these guys were an experiment and this story and or memory was 'implanted'

You can get Vance Davis's book, *Unbroken Promises: A True Story of Courage and Belief* for more details, and you can read further about it on Phil Coppens's website linked in the footnote. At this point, I think we can take a look at some of the Gulf Breeze Six's more interesting predictions[39] that they received via the Ouija board. I'm not sure how subsequent predictions were made; perhaps they went to direct channeling, which I wouldn't trust any further than I can fly. However, these predictions that came via the board are very interesting if we completely discard the dates attached to them. Text in curly brackets seem to come from one of the original editors of the material.

Gulf Breeze Six Prophecies

- War between the U.S. and Iraq – 1990. This will last 100 days if the state of Israel does not get involved. (Occurred.)

- Los Angeles earthquake in late 1993 – 8.3 or higher.

- Riots in Los Angeles in 1992. (Occurred)

- An earthquake in Seattle, Washington, in the magnitude of 5.4 or higher will lead to the eruption of Mount Rainier.

- Mount Rainier will blow and destroy a large portion of Seattle in late 1993 or the spring of 1994.

- The U.S. stock market will crash in 1994.

- A huge explosion in New York 1993. (Occurred) {The World Trade Center bomb could be the first huge explosion this year.

---

by the now proven-as-real mind-control experiments. However, having said that, Ft. Meade *is* an interesting place, as is Ft. Detrick. Further on in the sessions, we will encounter the same woman who 'brought the UFOs' to my small town the night I did hypnotherapy with her about what appeared to have been an alien abduction. Again, see the *St. Petersburg Times* special linked above for details, and more details in *The Wave*. This woman's husband was doing secret research at Ft. Detrick and she, herself, had a security clearance. So, no wonder there was a little UFO flap the night I put her under hypnosis to find out some details!

[39]Quoted in *Heave-Up: Phase One* (books.google.at/books?id=3nQHkFA1VKQC), allegedly coming from *The Gulf Breeze Prophecies* (www.amazon.com/ dp/ B004WT3ZYI)

Another explosion caused by a gas-line rupture will take out a large portion of Manhattan. This will be caused by a 6.0 quake outside of New York City that will rupture the aging gas mains. This will actually be caused by a continental flux after the 8.3 quake in Los Angeles.}

- Destruction of New York City and Manhattan by many disasters, natural and manmade between 1996 to 1998.

- Race riots in all major cities – 1993 to 1994.

- Martial law enacted in major cities – 1994/1995.

- Russian earthquake which will kill 1,000. (Occurred.)

- Government will lose AWOL military intelligence soldiers in Atlanta, Georgia – 1990. (Occurred.)

- European economic community will be in power by 1992. (Occurred.)

- Borders dropped in all of Europe – 1992. (Occurred.)

- Military troops will be controlling Chicago – 1996.

- Terrorist activity in the United States increases – 1993 to 1995.

- All U.S. air space will be restricted by martial law – 1995.

- The constitution will be suspended for 90 days – 1994/1995.

- A house will be destroyed in Massachusetts with 140 people killed.

- Major universities will be shut down.

- 50 of the worlds top scientists will disappear.

- An explosion at a supermarket in 1994 will injure 50 persons with no deaths.

- Gun laws passed in 1994.

- Explosion in space in 1993. (Occurred–satellite explodes.)

- Shuttle not launched due to fuel leak–1990. (Occurred) {This prediction actually stated that another American Space Shuttle would explode just like the Challenger disaster, if the fuel leak was not caught in time. The fuel leak was found seconds before lift-off, a classic example of cause and effect probabilities and dual timelines.}

- Terrorism increases in Israel – 1993. (Occurring.)

- Homeless and social undesirables rounded-up – 1994.[40]

- Systematic marking of government employees and all general military personnel takes place – 1994/1995.

- The Rapture occurs – 1995/1996. {This is one point Vance and I are in vehement disagreement over. This may have to do with the 'taking up' of all of those who have been abducted and 'marked' in the form of nasal or body probes. Is this benevolent, or is it just the negative aliens' way of protecting their precious breeding program?}

- True spiritual leaders arise – 1996.

- The hidden keepsake comes forth with the true teachers. {This will be a book about the lost true religion of Man. The new teachers of truth will talk about our co-creatorship with God and our own divine intervention. This will be the beginning of the new "True" religion.}

- The Seven Thunders will be revealed. {In the Book of Revelation, John The Beloved was shown, on the Isle of Patmos, seven books which were called "The Great Books of Thunder". They were so awesome that John was not allowed to speak of them. They were to be revealed in the last days, by God's "Witnesses and Prophets". The Vatican now possesses two of these books, according to Vance, and the other five will be revealed here in America and around the world.}

---

[40] This is increasingly common in recent years. See for example: "Florida City About To Make It Illegal For Homeless People To Have Possessions In Public" http://www.sott.net/article/277883

- Biblical treasures are found – 1994. {Many great truths about the true nature of the Bible will be revealed that will turn Christianity upside-down. [...]}

- Earth magnetic tilt – 2011

- Increase in volcanic eruptions – 1993 to 1995.

- Increase in severe weather causes mass destruction – 1992 to 1996. (Occurring.)

- Insurance companies collapse – 1993 to 1994.

- Quantum leaps in the evolution of Mankind after 2032.

- Fear of the new religion, the New World Order. (Here now!)

Now, what to make of all of this, especially considering the fact that the C's said that their sources of information were "some from us and some from others"? That appears to be possible, since we are theorizing that the C's information comes from a connection to the Cosmic Information field, a realm of metaphors that get 'shaped' into symbols and then transduced into language both oral and written. I notice that some of these predictions are very close to some the C's have made (or will make in sessions further on, and we didn't have this text at the time). Some others are things that we can see have actually happened or begun to happen in our world in the years since 9/11. Some haven't happened yet, assuming they will. What is glaringly obvious is the fact that the dates are way, way off! Why?

Well, I suppose that if I was a power-mad Denizen of Darkness and I wanted to guard my realm, I would want to turn people off to any idea that I even existed. As the old saying goes, the Devil's greatest defense is that no one believes in him anymore. Well, I don't believe in the Devil, per se, but I've had enough experiences and seen enough evidence to be 99% confident that our reality is embedded in another, 'higher,' hyperdimensional realm where all the rules are different. And I've studied this long and deeply and know the Cosmic Trickster does what s/he/it does mainly to discourage, dishearten, discombobulate and deter further explorations and incursions into that reality. That critter just *loves* to get people all worked up and then make fools of them. Read John Keel's research; read Jacques Vallee's books. Just as importantly, do as much reading of actual paranormal research as you can because you will find the same patterns in both fields. So the business of assigning specific dates to specific predictions is part of the pattern.

As I noted in the introduction, we live in an open universe and variables can change at any instant, and changed variables often mean changed outcome. This strange realm in which our 'hard 3D reality' is embedded is very definitely a macro-quantum world where things are only statistically probable. You can't investigate it with the rules of material science. Heck, in some cases, you can't even investigate the material world with the rules of science: the observer/experimenter effect has messed up enough of that sort of thing to put good scientists on guard about making unilateral declarations of how things are. That doesn't mean that a lot of scientists and material-minded people don't still demand hard and fast rules, specific predictions with specific dates, in order to 'believe,' but that's a dangerous path to walk because inevitably, the probabilistic nature of reality will bite you. And that seems to be what happened here with the Gulf Breeze Six. But still, it was a fascinating little excursus, and I think that we can see that these guys were picking up some real signals, but there was so much interference from their 'spirits and space brothers' that it was like running the vacuum cleaner in front of the TV. (At least older TVs, where the cleaner would produce so much snow and static you couldn't see the picture.) This is exactly the sort of thing that I knew must be avoided in any channeling experiment. Yes, I know that a lot of excellent information comes through – even fantastic information – but you have to take care sorting through it. You have to take care cleaning your conduit/transmission line; you have to learn how to research, to translate, to interpret, and that takes time and attention and practice.

November 7, 1994

In this session, I resumed my combination of 'kid-in-the-candy-store' and 'researcher-collecting-data' approach to questioning the C's. I wanted lots of checkable data, but I also was thinking: "What if this is a super source? I'd be crazy not to ask about as many mysterious things as possible so as to get some ideas or answers!"

Participants: 'Frank' and Laura

1 **Q:** *(L)* Hello. Who do we have with us tonight?

2 **A:** Goonian.

3 **Q:** *(L)* Are you a discarnate?

4 **A:** No.

5 **Q:** *(L)* Where are you from?

6 **A:** Cassiopaea.

7 **Q:** *(L)* Are you ready for our questions?

8 **A:** Yes.

9 **Q:** *(L)* I would like to know what is the origin and meaning of the Biblical story of the 'mark of Cain'? Was it a physical mark?

10 **A:** Knot at top of spine.

11 **Q:** *(L)* Do you mean like a humpback?

12 **A:** No. Signified.

13 **Q:** *(L)* Was it a physical knot on top of the spine?

14 **A:** Is yours and all others. Feel your head.

15 **Q:** *(L)* The occipital ridge?

16 **A:** Close.

17 **Q:** *(L)* Well if I have it does it mean that I am a murderer?

18 **A:** No. More superstitions spread by Brotherhood.

19 **Q:** *(L)* Well, what did the mark of Cain signify?

20 **A:** Jealousy.

21 **Q:** *(L)* Jealousy of whom?

22 **A:** All humans.

23 **Q:** *(L)* Was there a group of people who were set apart by this mark?

---

[1]I didn't know anything about Neanderthal anatomy at the time, but there is actually a good correlation here. It seems that the Neanderthals had something called an occipital bun, which is a prominent bulge, or projection, of the occipital bone at the back of the skull. Some scientists think that occipital buns might correlate with the biomechanics of running, while others attribute them to enlargement of the cerebellum, a region of the brain which mediates the timing of motor actions and spatial reasoning. It was common among many of humankind's ancestors, primarily

24 **A:** No. All it is is one of your shortcomings genetically engineered by the Lizards.[1]

25 **Q:** *(L)* What was the 'Ark of the Covenant'?[2]

26 **A:** Power cell.

27 **Q:** *(L)* What was the origin of this power cell?

28 **A:** Lizards given to the Jews to use for manipulation of others.[3]

29 **Q:** *(L)* Why was it that if you came close to this object or touched it you would die?

30 **A:** Energy overload; scrambling by reverse electromagnetism.

31 **Q:** *(L)* What is reverse electromagnetism?

32 **A:** Turned inward.

33 **Q:** *(L)* What effect does it produce?

34 **A:** Liquification of matter.

35 **Q:** *(L)* Well, that is pleasant. This 'cell' was kept in an ornate box of some sort, is that correct?

36 **A:** Yes.

37 **Q:** *(L)* Why was it only the priests who could handle it?

38 **A:** Only those who would not try to use for selfish reasons.

39 **Q:** *(L)* But then did just coming near it injure a person?

40 **A:** Yes.

41 **Q:** *(L)* Well why were these individuals able to come near it?

42 **A:** Nonselfish energy field.

43 **Q:** *(L)* So it could tune into thought fields?

44 **A:** Yes.

45 **Q:** *(L)* Why are UFOs frequently sighted over geological fault lines?

46 **A:** Electromagnetism. Use electrical free waves as fuel for power restoration.

---

the robust relatives such as Neanderthal, but it is relatively rare in modern Homo sapiens – though some populations have them. One study provides evidence that individuals with narrow heads (dolicocephalic) or narrow cranial bases and relatively large brains are more likely to have occipital buns as a means of resolving a spatial packing problem. [Lieberman DE, Pearson OM, Mowbray KM (2000). "Basicranial influence on overall cranial shape." *J. Hum. Evol.* 38 (2): 291–315] A couple of studies in recent years have demonstrated that there have been several instances of archaic human admixture with modern humans through interbreeding of modern humans with Neanderthals, Denisovans, and/or possibly other archaic humans over the course of human history. Neanderthal-derived DNA accounts for an estimated 1–4% of the Eurasian genome, but it is absent within the Sub-Saharan African genome. A later study revised the proportion to an estimated 1.5–2.1%. The best model was a recent admixture event that was preceded by a bottleneck event among modern humans, i.e. a possible major catastrophe and severe reduction in population; exactly what we would expect to see with the C's metaphors about genetic manipulation occurring across density/realm barriers by pragmatic means such as virii.

[2] *The Wave* 22

[3] The unasked question at this moment is: who are 'the Jews' really? Stay tuned!

Q: *(L)* Could it be that the UFOs are a manifestation of the geomagnetic energies emitted at fault lines?

A: No. Not all theories are correct and some are not even sincere.

Q: *(L)* What is the connection between UFOs and earthquakes?

A: Is none. Coincidence. If they are there, some fault breaks produce EM fields which are visible briefly as red or yellow light flashes.

Q: *(L)* How do UFOs affect the electrical systems of automobiles and so forth and why is this phenomenon also associated with hauntings?

A: Electromagnetic pulse. Can be manifestations of hauntings also.

Q: *(L)* Would this indicate that both phenomena are originating from the same source or utilizing the same power?

A: Laura, do you not know by now that all these phenomena are interdimensional?

Q: *(L)* Is there something about moving from one dimension to another that creates this electromagnetic pulse?

A: Yes. Kind of like breaking the sound barrier.

Q: *(L)* OK, we talked about the fact that the brown-eyed people are Earth-seeded for much longer than blue-eyed people, who were seeded on another planet. Where did green-eyed people come from?

A: Green and blue are the same in terms of origin.

Q: *(L)* Who was Seth, channeled by Jane Roberts?

A: Higher plane Earth spirit.

Q: *(L)* Were the teachings in the Seth material accurate and was that a good source?

A: Yes but rapidly becoming obsolete as you move toward new reality.

Q: *(L)* What happens to people who commit suicide?

A: Varies according to circumstance.

Q: *(L)* In a general sense, is there some negative karma involved in committing suicide?

A: There can be negative karma involved with many things.

Q: *(L)* What about the death penalty?

A: Specify.

Q: *(L)* Is putting a criminal to death the equivalent of reducing society to the level of the criminal?

A: You are all put to death.

Q: *(L)* What do you mean?

A: In one way or another.

Q: *(L)* Well, is there any negative karma on society, the judge, the jury, the executioner, if a criminal is brought to trial, found guilty of a heinous crime and then put to death?

A: What about war? What is better? This is open because all are murderers and suicides. It is the supreme lesson you all must learn before you can graduate to ethereal existence. Your thinking is too simplified.

Q: *(L)* Is there ever a situation where execution helps relieve the criminal of some of his karma that may be caused by the commission of the crime for which he is being executed?

A: No.

77 **Q**: *(L)* Is it better to take a criminal, such as Dahmer, and have all of society support and take care of him?

78 **A**: These are all past issues. Will be resolved soon.[4]

79 **Q**: *(L)* Are there any other physical creatures on planet Earth which have souls?

80 **A**: All do.

81 **Q**: *(L)* Is the human soul different from, say, animal souls?

82 **A**: Of course.

83 **Q**: *(L)* Are there any other physical creatures on the Earth which have souls like human souls? On the same level, so to speak?

84 **A**: No.

85 **Q**: *(L)* Well, I have heard that dolphins, porpoises, and whales have very advanced souls. Is that true?

86 **A**: All souls are advanced.

87 **Q**: *(L)* But are whales sentient, thinking, self-aware as humans are?

88 **A**: Apples and oranges.

89 **Q**: *(L)* Well, since whales are so big, do they have bigger souls?

90 **A**: Irrelevant.

91 **Q**: *(L)* Is there some way to communicate with whales or dolphins and can one find a way to translate the differences and have a reasonable, intelligent exchange with a whale or a dolphin or even an elephant?

92 **A**: You don't need conversation "with" when a higher telepathic level.[5]

93 **Q**: *(L)* Dolphins and whales communicate telepathically?

94 **A**: Yes. So do dogs and cats and snakes etc. etc. only humans have learned the "superior" art of verbal communication.

95 **Q**: *(L)* But, at the same time, verbal communication can be quite limiting, is that correct?

96 **A**: That is the point.

97 **Q**: *(L)* So, you were being sarcastic with me, weren't you?

98 **A**: Humorous.

99 **Q**: *(L)* Do whales form long-lasting bonds and feel love?

100 **A**: Yes.

101 **Q**: *(L)* Do dogs feel love?

102 **A**: Dogs feel need as love.

103 **Q**: *(L)* Who would make a better governor, Bush or Chiles?

104 **A**: Either.

105 **Q**: *(L)* Which one is going to win?

106 **A**: Open.

107 **Q**: *(L)* Carlos Casteneda writes about the peyote beings called 'Mescalitos.' This being supposedly is part of the peyote plant, a sort of being from the plant. Is this true?

108 **A**: No.

109 **Q**: *(L)* What beings does one encounter when one eats a bunch of peyote?

110 **A**: Hallucination.

---

[4]There might have been a double meaning here: 1) within a couple of weeks of the date of this session, Jeffrey Dahmer would be bludgeoned to death in prison on November 28, 1994, or 2) with the coming of the Wave, we will 'graduate' to where we don't have to argue about death penalties. I'd give the C's a small cigar for this one.

[5]"when a higher": that is how the C's spelled it.

111 **Q:** *(L)* Why are these hallucinations so consistent?

112 **A:** Because those that do have that expectation. If you ate enough peyote you would encounter Santa Claus if that was your expectation. [Much laughter]

113 **Q:** *(L)* What happens if you give someone LSD while they are dying? Does it help them die easier?

114 **A:** No.

115 **Q:** *(L)* Does it make dying more difficult?

116 **A:** No.

117 **Q:** *(L)* Is there any essential difference or effect of note?

118 **A:** No.

119 **Q:** *(L)* What is the 'philosopher's stone'?[6]

120 **A:** Idea center.

121 **Q:** *(L)* How can this idea center be accessed?

122 **A:** Many ways: meditation is the best.

123 **Q:** *(L)* Is there any visual image of the philosopher's stone that one could use to access it in meditation?

124 **A:** Yes. Diamond or prism.

125 **Q:** *(L)* Was there or is there such a thing as a literal, physical philosopher's stone that can transmute lead into gold?

126 **A:** No.

127 **Q:** *(L)* Was anybody ever able to transmute lead into gold by any means?

128 **A:** Everybody is able.

129 **Q:** *(L)* How?

130 **A:** You must discover this yourself.

131 **Q:** *(L)* Is this knowledge written down somewhere on the planet?

132 **A:** Yes, but it will be easier in 4th level.[7]

133 **Q:** *(L)* Comte St. Germaine claimed to be able to transmute lead into gold. Was this true?

134 **A:** Yes.

135 **Q:** *(L)* He also claimed to have discovered the secret of eternal youth. Was this true?

136 **A:** No.

137 **Q:** *(L)* Did he die like everybody else at the regular age?

138 **A:** Yes.

139 **Q:** *(L)* Is Elizabeth Clare Prophet channeling St. Germaine?

140 **A:** No.

141 **Q:** *(L)* Who does she channel?

142 **A:** Imposter.

143 **Q:** *(L)* Who was Merlin?

144 **A:** English jolly fellow.

145 **Q:** *(L)* He wasn't a great magician?

146 **A:** He was the Houdini of his time.

147 **Q:** *(L)* There was a very famous case of haunting called the Bell Witch case. Can you tell us about it?

148 **A:** Inform, ask and we will access.

149 **Q:** *(L)* Is that why we have to ask every question in such detail?

150 **A:** Yes.

151 **Q:** *(L)* When we ask a question how does it enable you to access the information?

---

[6] *The Wave* 29

[7] Which suggests that transiting densities is part of the alchemical process; if the being isn't able, the substances won't transmute.

152 **A**: Puts in visual image.

153 **Q**: *(L)* Who or what was the Bell Witch?

154 **A**: Connected spirit. Karmic.

155 **Q**: *(L)* Was this spirit connected to Betsy Bell or her father?

156 **A**: Both.

157 **Q**: *(L)* Why did this spirit so brutalize her father until he died?

158 **A**: Revenge for previous life wrongs.

159 **Q**: *(L)* Is it true, as Dr. Nandor Fodor suggested, that this was an aspect of Betsy Bell's own personality which attacked her father because he had been sexually molesting her?

160 **A**: No.

161 **Q**: *(L)* What is the cause of Alzheimer's disease?

162 **A**: Genetic.

163 **Q**: *(L)* Is there anything that can be done to prevent it or lessen its effects?

164 **A**: Biogenetic engineering but will resolve anyway in the near future. And much other as well.

165 **Q**: *(L)* Do Anne Boleyn and Catherine Howard haunt the Tower of London and Hampton Court?

166 **A**: Spirit reflection.

167 **Q**: *(L)* Is a ghost or haunting just an image imprinted in space-time?

168 **A**: Sometimes.

169 **Q**: *(L)* Are there some cases where the actual spirit of the person hangs around causing phenomena?

170 **A**: Yes.

171 **Q**: *(L)* Can they do this for untold centuries?

172 **A**: Yes because there is no time.

173 **Q**: *(L)* Is T. C. Lethbridge's theory about dowsing correct?

174 **A**: Yes.

175 **Q**: *(L)* Is it possible to dowse things in other dimensions by lengthening the string?

176 **A**: Yes.

177 **Q**: *(L)* Is it possible by using this technique to dowse winning lottery numbers?

178 **A**: Difficult; intentions must be pure.

179 **Q**: *(L)* It is very difficult to have pure intentions about money, isn't it?

180 **A**: Yes.

181 **Q**: *(L)* But if, theoretically, one did have pure intentions, would they be able to dowse numbers...

182 **A**: Tall order. Yes.

183 **Q**: *(L)* Are lottery numbers... fixed?

184 **A**: Everything is at some level. But choice is at what level will be experienced.

185 **Q**: *(L)* Recently I read an article about bursts of gamma rays in the upper atmosphere. What are these bursts of gamma rays?[8]

186 **A**: Increasing energy with approach of wave.

187 **Q**: *(L)* So, these bursts of gamma rays are not effects of battling UFOs in other dimensions?

188 **A**: No.

189 **Q**: *(L)* Why are there so many crop circles in Britain?

---

[8] *The Wave* 1

190 **A**: Window. Why Stonehenge was built there.

191 **Q**: *(L)* What is the relationship between UFOs and clouds?

192 **A**: Can create clouds or appear as clouds but no other relationship.

193 **Q**: *(L)* What is ball lightning?

194 **A**: Electromagnetic spark. Pass from 4th to 3rd density.

195 **Q**: *(L)* Is the Ayurvedic system a superior system to others?

196 **A**: Free will.

197 **Q**: *(L)* What are the implications of the fact that the Lizzies worship the physical universe?

198 **A**: Self service.

199 **Q**: *(L)* What do they see in the physical universe that they feel is superior to the spiritual universe?

200 **A**: All who serve self yearn for physicality.

201 **Q**: *(L)* These bodies they are creating for themselves, are they creating some kind of super physical beings they can then move into and occupy which will have very advanced abilities that would enable them to serve self better, longer, or more completely?

202 **A**: Yes.

203 **Q**: *(L)* There has been a lot of scuttlebutt about Walt Andrus, the head of MUFON. I would like to know what energies are behind him and what his motivations are.

204 **A**: He is okay. Paranoia is his chief problem.

205 **Q**: *(L)* What about LS?

206 **A**: Muddled thoughts.

207 **Q**: *(L)* Jenny Randles?

208 **A**: Okay. She means well.

209 **Q**: *(L)* What are the copper scrolls discovered in Israel?

210 **A**: Essenes. The treasure described was real but no longer intact as described.

211 **Q**: *(L)* Who was or is Baal?

212 **A**: Lizard.

213 **Q**: *(L)* Beelzebub?

214 **A**: Same.

215 **Q**: *(L)* Were these actual names of individual Lizards?

216 **A**: No. Personifications.

217 **Q**: *(L)* What was the beast known as Leviathan?

218 **A**: Sea god. Same as Neptune.

219 **Q**: *(L)* I discovered the name Nibiru in a list of demonic names. What is the origin of this name?

220 **A**: Dark teacher.

221 **Q**: *(L)* What is the origin of the name Appolyon?

222 **A**: Light being?

223 **Q**: *(L)* Why is Appolyon called the "destroyer" in Revelation?

224 **A**: Backward for sake of deception. Bible corrupted.

225 **Q**: *(L)* You have often stated that the Bible is corrupted. I would like to know who, exactly, corrupted the Bible and when and how they did this?

226 **A**: Illuminati brotherhood for a thousand Earth years.

227 **Q**: *(L)* Does this mean that up until a thousand years ago the Bible was fairly accurate?

228 **A**: No.

229 **Q:** *(L)* Is there any possibility that the Catholic church had anything to do with this corrupting influence?

230 **A:** Yes.

231 **Q:** *(L)* Does the Catholic church have in its possession actual original texts of the Bible that have not been corrupted?[9]

232 **A:** No.

233 **Q:** *(L)* Were there ever such texts in existence?

234 **A:** No.

235 **Q:** *(L)* Who wrote the book of Matthew?

236 **A:** Greek enforcers.

237 **Q:** *(L)* What are Greek enforcers?

238 **A:** Like your FBI.

239 **Q:** *(L)* Who wrote the book of Mark?

240 **A:** Same.

241 **Q:** *(L)* Luke and John?

242 **A:** Same.

243 **Q:** *(L)* Acts?

244 **A:** Same.

245 **Q:** *(L)* Are any books of the New Testament written by who they claim to be written by?

246 **A:** No. Remember this is 70% propaganda.

247 **Q:** *(L)* Is 30% then the truth or the actual teachings?

248 **A:** Close. Enough you must decipher from instinct through meditation.

249 **Q:** *(L)* Why did my son's leg suddenly start giving him problems at about the age of three?

250 **A:** Reflection of past life. Leg was torn off at death. SAM missile shot by North Vietnamese Army. He was flying a jet. This was 1969. Name was George Raymond. Shot down over Phan Bien.[10]

251 **Q:** *(L)* Is there anything that can be done to help him release this problem?

252 **A:** Will be difficult.

253 **Q:** *(L)* Is his past life very strong for him?

254 **A:** Yes.

255 **Q:** *(L)* Is it stronger than in the other children?

256 **A:** Yes.

257 **Q:** *(L)* Will hypnosis help him to release this?

258 **A:** Yes.

259 **Q:** *(L)* How old was he when he was shot down?

260 **A:** 25.

261 **Q:** *(L)* Was he married?

262 **A:** No.

263 **Q:** *(L)* Why did he pick me to be his mother?

264 **A:** Previous life connection.

---

[9] *The Wave* 66

[10] This was an interesting response to a question that I expected some kind of medical answer to. This bit of information was a significant hit. See Tom French's article for details: http://www.sptimes.com/News/webspecials/exorcist/index.html However, note that it doesn't confirm the identity of the C's! As I've mentioned, Frank was a very good psychic. Well, of course that gives some weight to reincarnation and psi abilities, which is interesting in and of itself.

265 **Q:** *(L)* In his previous life was he abducted by aliens?

266 **A:** Yes.

267 **Q:** *(L)* What country did he live in?

268 **A:** Which lifetime?

269 **Q:** *(L)* When he was shot down?

270 **A:** USA.

271 **Q:** *(L)* What about the lifetime when he was connected to me? When was that and what was the relationship?

272 **A:** 1600s brother.

273 **Q:** *(L)* Does his leg cause him pain?

274 **A:** All violent deaths reflect difficulties in next incarnation.

275 **Q:** *(L)* Is that why I have so many difficulties, because of a violent death?

276 **A:** Yes.

277 **Q:** *(L)* How did I die in my last life?

278 **A:** Head hit pavement.

279 **Q:** *(L)* How is that reflected in this life?

280 **A:** Non-specific pains in body. You have a lot of those because of the violent trauma.

281 **Q:** *(L)* Scars of the soul, so to speak?[11]

282 **A:** Yes, exactly.

283 **Q:** *(L)* Does Frank have physical aches and pains because of violent trauma?

284 **A:** Mental in his case.

285 **Q:** *(L)* What brings it on?

286 **A:** Continuation of past life. Victimization by many. Left unresolved.

287 **Q:** *(L)* What could he have done to resolve that in that lifetime?

288 **A:** Fought back.

289 **Q:** *(L)* Is Frank telling the truth when he says he has no repressed anger?

290 **A:** Yes.

291 **Q:** *(L)* But how can he fight back if he has no anger to fuel the fighting?

292 **A:** Does not need to. Not the problem exactly. Different circumstances now. Needs to be patient and ride out the storm.

293 **Q:** *(L)* This situation will pass?

294 **A:** Open. Will pass if can withstand; didn't last time.

295 **Q:** *(L)* If he doesn't ride it out this time does this mean he has to come back into 3rd density and do it over?

296 **A:** Yes.

End of Session

---

[11]In fact, based on dreams, meditation visions, and many psychic flashes throughout my life, I was aware that I had committed suicide in a past life in Nazi Germany by jumping out of a window.

November 9, 1994

Participants: 'Frank' and Laura

Q: *(L)* Hello.

A: Hello. Promia.

Q: *(L)* Is that your name?

A: Yes.

Q: *(L)* And where are you from?

A: Cassiopaea.

Q: *(L)* Having you as communicants, does this protect us from the intrusion of earthbound spirits?[1]

A: Earthbound spirits yes but others no.

Q: *(L)* What others do you mean?

A: Aliens.

Q: *(L)* So your presence protects us from earthbound spirits but other aliens can come through if they choose?

A: Not through while with this connection but around.

Q: *(L)* They are around?

A: Not now.

Q: *(L)* Have they been around on other occasions when we were communicating?

A: Yes.

Q: *(L)* Have they ever, on any occasion, contaminated or corrupted our channel?

A: Tried but failed because you recognized it the one time.

Q: *(L)* When was the one time?

A: Several sessions ago.

Q: *(L)* Is that one of the sessions on tape? What was the name of the individual that came through that time?

A: Not named.[2]

Q: *(L)* I was reading today about the theory that if you get the name of an entity you then have power over it. Is this true?

A: No. There is much foolishness to muddle through.

Q: *(L)* We want to thank you for your help, by the way, and the good and precise answers we get through this source.[3]

A: You are welcome. More to come.

Q: *(L)* Well, I want people to be just awestruck with the accuracy of this information.

A: They will be.

---

[1] *The Wave* 35

[2] They were probably referring to the trance channeling with Frank. I think we all recognized that there was an influence around.

[3] I had just received an answer from a professor of languages at the University in Tampa that the C's explication of 666 as VISA was correct. I was pretty impressed!

29 **Q:** *(L)* I was reading an article about Cayce's teachings on the root races. Is this idea as presented by him basically correct?

30 **A:** Close.

31 **Q:** *(L)* What is that phenomenon we commonly call a poltergeist?

32 **A:** Many causes.

33 **Q:** *(L)* Each situation is different?

34 **A:** No. The causes are multiple.

35 **Q:** *(L)* Could you list these?

36 **A:** No. There are many causes but some are the same as others. One cause is female pubescent children giving off life force aura burst.[4]

37 **Q:** *(L)* What is this thing we call hypnosis?

38 **A:** The 2nd step to open consciousness union with level 5.

39 **Q:** *(L)* What's the first step?

40 **A:** Dream state.

41 **Q:** *(L)* What's the third step?

42 **A:** Trance.

43 **Q:** *(L)* What's the fourth step?

44 **A:** Expiration of body functions.

45 **Q:** *(L)* You mean as in death, kicked the bucket?

46 **A:** Of body.

47 **Q:** *(L)* In many ancient ruins there are found certain symbols which interest me, specifically the coil or spiral which seems to be ubiquitous throughout the world. This is also very similar to one of the Reiki symbols. What is the origin and meaning of this symbol?

48 **A:** Energy collector translevel; Stonehenge was one. Stonehenge is a coil. The missing stones form a coil arrangement. People have been "zapped" at Stonehenge.[5]

49 **Q:** *(L)* If I had a large place in my yard and I arranged plants and a walkway in a coil and then I walked that spiral, would it give me power?

50 **A:** Yes. Do it. If you do it you will actually see us when 3 levels are right. Move the pool.

51 **Q:** *(L)* Move my pool!

52 **A:** Which is more important? We did not say get rid of it.

53 **Q:** *(L)* What about the area next to the pool?

54 **A:** Up to you.

55 **Q:** *(L)* Do you know how hard it was to put that pool in?

56 **A:** Yes.

57 **Q:** *(L)* Now, JW and AB think the Ouija board should work without us putting our hands on it. Is that true. Would or could it work that way?

58 **A:** If it did it would not be us. Self serving forces do that only. Remember there is much foolishness. W___ and B___ are suspicious.

---

[4] This is pretty much in line with psychical research conclusions. There is obviously more to it than that, as the C's indicate.

[5] *The Wave* 24

[6] These fellows have appeared before in the transcripts: John W, the cousin who was a Sitchin devotee; AB, the MUFON member and friend of Terry and Jan who claimed to be the baddest magician of the Golden Dawn variety in the whole Southeast; and

59 **Q:** *(L)* AB told me that Mike F said he caused John W's wreck. Did he?[6]

60 **A:** No.

61 **Q:** *(L)* Why would he say he did?

62 **A:** Tales are easy to sew when the past is yours only to know.

63 **Q:** *(L)* AB also said he disintegrated a man with his mental powers. Is this true?

64 **A:** Rubbish.

65 **Q:** *(L)* Was he able to cause SS's TV to act up with his powers of mind?

66 **A:** Nonsense.

67 **Q:** *(L)* Does AB have any powers?

68 **A:** The same as yours.

69 **Q:** *(L)* Do I have any powers?

70 **A:** Yes, but when was the last time you zapped someone's TV?[7]

71 **Q:** *(L)* Archaeologists repeatedly find grotesque little carvings of fat bellied, big-breasted women and they call them mother goddesses. What were they?

72 **A:** They were children's toys. More foolishness.

73 **Q:** *(L)* Who built the temple complex on the island of Malta?

74 **A:** Moors.[8]

75 **Q:** *(L)* When?

76 **A:** 800 A.D.

77 **Q:** *(L)* Is the Sufi path a good one to study?[9]

78 **A:** Up to you.

79 **Q:** *(L)* I know that but I want to know if it is valid or better than another?

80 **A:** We don't want to judge that for you.

81 **Q:** *(L)* What percentage of truth is in that path?

82 **A:** In one sense all teachings are truths.

83 **Q:** *(L)* Can't you just tell me?

84 **A:** Subjective. Would you like us judge Reiki?

Mike F, the self-proclaimed UFO investigator who carried around a UFO detector disguised as a cigarette pack in his shirt pocket and was known to leap to his feet in the middle of MUFON meetings, run to a pay-phone, and talk into the handset without ever dialing a number. (Yeah, somebody watched him doing that!) I tell ya, it was a circus! JW hated MF and declared he was a fraud (probably true) and AB was sort of friends with the two of them. JW had been in a minor accident and apparently, MF (who equally hated JW because JW hated him I guess) claimed responsibility when he was having a conversation with AB with Terry and Jan present, which is how I heard about it. It seems that the two of them were telling tall tales of one-upmanship at a social gathering in an effort to impress everyone. Zoo, huh?

[7] Bottom line. Is it any wonder that I soon began to distance myself from these people?

[8] Wrong, in my opinion. Well, maybe I should have been more specific about the question. Perhaps there were Moorish buildings there, but that wasn't what I was talking about. The experts say they were built during three distinct time periods between 3000 BC and 700 BC approximately. That sort of leaves out the Moors on the temples I had in mind. However, it turns out that the Arabs occupied and ruled the islands from 869 to 1090. See http://ambassadors.net/archives/issue29/features.htm for a discussion of the Arabic influence on the area, architecture, language, etc.

[9] *The Wave* 67

85 **Q:** *(L)* Well, yes before I spend any money on it. Will I waste my money?

86 **A:** Not if you go to right source. Now we have led you to answer we want you to continue to exercise your mind. That is how you progress.

87 **Q:** *(L)* So you want me to study Sufi for the exercise?

88 **A:** Yes. If we answered all your questions you would not learn.[10]

89 **Q:** *(L)* In this book I am reading it talks about knowledge that is only given to the elect and that certain things are passed down through secret organizations. Most people think this organization is the Illuminati and that they hold many deep, dark secrets. Is that true?[11]

90 **A:** Close. But now there is a knowledge explosion. The Illuminati is no longer exclusive; but they still think they are.

91 **Q:** *(L)* Compared to the big high mucky mucks in the Illuminati, what percentage of their knowledge do Frank and I possess?

92 **A:** 2 per cent.

93 **Q:** *(L)* You mean they know 98 per cent more than we do? That's depressing! How much knowledge, relative to the Illuminati, does the average college graduate have?

94 **A:** 0.02 per cent.[12]

95 **Q:** *(L)* Is there any one person who holds a major chunk of knowledge on this planet?

96 **A:** By this time next year you will have 35 per cent as much.

97 **Q:** *(L)* That means I have to work hard!

98 **A:** No. It will flow into you. Stop listening to those that block.

99 **Q:** *(L)* Who in my life is blocking me now?

100 **A:** Can't say. You must find this out.

101 **Q:** *(L)* Is it myself?

102 **A:** Only through others.[13]

103 **Q:** *(L)* DM called today about an antique bracelet she put in the keeping of a jewelry dealer who was supposed to have it repaired for her...

104 **A:** Woman sold it to a dealer in Atlanta. D___ must confront her and she will break. Sold for 11,000 dollars.[14]

---

[10] This pretty much encapsulates the major Cassiopaean attitude towards us: they are here to help, to give clues, to give advice or information when really needed, but we are supposed to be doing the work to learn things through our own efforts.

[11] *The Wave* 35

[12] I wasn't surprised to learn that the C's assessed us as having more knowledge than the average college graduate; I had worked with many of them over the years and they were an abysmally ignorant bunch overall. Many of them never again crack a book after graduation.

[13] In retrospect, it is interesting that I can see how Frank, himself, was one of the blocks, as well as my ex-husband.

[14] The last I heard about it the jeweler claimed it had been stolen and DM was unable to get anything done about it.

[15] True enough. However, he died within three months of the UFO sighting that the kids and I had in our backyard where Dannyboy was also present. Following this event, I also suffered what could be described as radiation sickness for months.

105 **Q:** *(L)* What did my dog Dannyboy die from?

106 **A:** Heart condition.[15]

107 **Q:** *(L)* Is there another Dannyboy puppy out there for me?

108 **A:** Maybe.[16]

109 **Q:** *(L)* Why have I been so depressed today?

110 **A:** Too much interaction with negative energy coming from others.

111 **Q:** *(L)* Is Babaji living in Tibet?

112 **A:** Yes.

113 **Q:** *(L)* How old is Babaji?

114 **A:** 190.[17]

115 **Q:** *(L)* In the book of Revelation it describes a being with copper skin and white hair. Is this a real Nephilim from the planet Nibiru? Who is that being?

116 **A:** Nephalim descendant but not from Neburru.

117 **Q:** *(L)* This was a giant?

118 **A:** Yes.

119 **Q:** *(L)* Is there a planet Nibiru?

120 **A:** No.

121 **Q:** *(L)* What does Nibiru mean in the Sumerian language?[18]

122 **A:** Slave owner.

123 **Q:** *(L)* Back about a year or so ago we got an individual [communicating via the board] who claimed to be Keith. Was this, in fact, Keith Laumer?

124 **A:** Yes.

125 **Q:** *(L)* How does he feel about being dead?

126 **A:** Okay.

127 **Q:** *(L)* Was it like he expected?

128 **A:** Better.

129 **Q:** *(L)* Was it his influence that caused me to continuously play opera?

130 **A:** Yes.[19]

131 **Q:** *(L)* Was he around me for a period of time after he died?

132 **A:** Yes.

133 **Q:** *(L)* Has he gone into the light now?

134 **A:** Yes.

End of Session

---

[16] I do, currently, have a Dannyboy replica named Elvis along with 7 other wonderful doggums.

[17] You can check Babaji out on Wikipedia. It's an interesting story and we probably can't get any confirmation about it. But I do think that 190 years old is a lot more reasonable than almost 2000 years old.

[18] *The Wave* 24

[19] Keith was an opera devotee; he listened to opera as loud as could be borne almost every waking moment. At the time, I detested opera but oddly, after Keith passed, I felt his presence and decided to play some opera for him and I found that I liked it better when I was the one who chose to play it! I've been an aficionado ever since and I always think about Keith when I listen to opera.

November 12, 1994

There were many things the C's said that we did not, and have not, followed up on, but there was one thing that bugged me – the information about 'The Quorum' – so this session is devoted to discussing that. It is a remarkable example of the C's teaching style and demonstrates the didactic nature of the interaction.

Just to refresh your memory, the first reference to the term 'Quorum' was from the 16 October 1994 session:

Q: *(L)* Is Freemasonry as it is practiced today the same?

A: 33rd degree, yes.

Q: *(L)* So, there is a continuing tradition for over 7 thousand years?

A: Yes.

Q: *(L)* Is this organization with a plan to take over and rule the world?

A: Not exactly.

Q: *(L)* What is their focus?

A: Overseers.

Q: *(L)* Of what?

A: The status of Quorum.

Q: *(L)* What is the Quorum?

A: Deeper knowledge organization. Totally secret to your kind as of yet. Very important with regard to your future.

Q: *(L)* In what way?

A: Changes.

Q: *(L)* Can you get more specific? Is that changes to us personally?

A: Partly.

Q: *(L)* Earth changes?

A: Also.

Q: *(L)* What is the relationship between this Quorum and the Cassiopaeans?

A: They communicate with us regularly.

Q: *(L)* Do they do this knowing you are Cassiopaeans or do they do it thinking...

A: Yes.

Q: *(L)* Has there been an ongoing relationship between the Cassiopaeans and this Quorum for these thousands of years?

A: For some time as you measure it.

The next reference was on 25 October 1994:

Q: *(L)* Is the Quorum composed of members who are humans on this planet?

A: Partly.

Q: *(L)* Would we know any of them as well known figures?

A: Hidden. None you would know.

Q: *(L)* How is the Quorum important in regard to the Earth changes?

A: Watchers.

Q: *(L)* Why is it important to have watchers?

A: Keep track of prophecies.

Q: *(L)* How do the Masons relate to the Illuminati?

A: Masons are low level branch.

I wanted to get to the bottom of this but, as you will see, my problem was black-and-white thinking. The C's undertook here to teach me a more nuanced mode of viewing metaphysical concepts. There are a few notes I'll add to this as we go along.

Participants: 'Frank' and Laura

1 **Q:** *(L)* Hello.

2 **A:** Cassiopaea calling.

3 **Q:** *(L)* What does that mean?

4 **A:** We are beginning to tune into your humor.

5 **Q:** *(L)* What do you mean.

6 **A:** "Cassiopaea calling."

7 **Q:** *(L)* I get it![1] What are the dogs barking at?

8 **A:** Someone in alley.

9 **Q:** *(L)* What are they doing in the alley?

10 **A:** Passing.[2]

11 **Q:** *(L)* Do you have any specific messages for us?

12 **A:** No.

13 **Q:** *(L)* On a number of occasions we talked about the Quorum and the Illuminati. They both seem to be the highest levels of secret organizations. What is their relationship to each other?

14 **A:** Please put new music on; this a little disruptive.[3]

15 **Q:** *(L)* How is this?[4]

16 **A:** Better.

17 **Q:** *(L)* You don't like the Native American stuff?

18 **A:** It is okay but disruptive to vibrations.[5]

---

[1] It was interesting that the C's were in a "good humor" and felt like joking when I was feeling deadly serious!

[2] With all the weird behavior of the local metaphysical/paranormal UFO community that we had been witnessing, and all our reading on the UFO phenomenon, plus the communications with the C's, I was feeling just a tad paranoid!

[3] "Creation Chant" was playing.

[4] I changed to "Celtic harp."

[5] That was an interesting remark to me. I had been playing the tape because it was given to me and guaranteed to create the 'right' ambiance!

19 **Q:** *(L)* Back to the Quorum and Illuminati.

20 **A:** Quorum mostly alien; Illuminati mostly human.⁶

21 **Q:** *(L)* Well, the Quorum has been described...

22 **A:** Meet; two halves of whole.

23 **Q:** *(L)* Well the Quorum seems to be described as being in touch with the Cassiopaeans, that is, yourselves, which you have described as beneficial beings, is this correct?

24 **A:** Close.⁷

25 **Q:** *(L)* The Illuminati has been described as being behind or with the Brotherhood, which has been described as being in connection with the Lizard beings...

26 **A:** Close. But not that simple.

27 **Q:** *(L)* Well, if the Quorum is the good guys and the Illuminati is the bad guys, and they both are at the high levels of Freemasonry, what is the story here?

28 **A:** Picture a circle or cycle first now then contemplate for a moment before follow up.

29 **Q:** *(L)* OK, I am contemplating a cycling circle.

30 **A:** Now, two halves representing positive and negative. Two halves.

31 **Q:** *(L)* Well, what I am getting out of that is the two halves and both sides are playing with the human race. Is that it?⁸

32 **A:** No. This is complicated but if you can learn and understand, it will be a super revelation.

33 **Q:** *(L)* Well, go ahead and explain.

34 **A:** Ask step by step.

35 **Q:** *(L)* Why do we so often have to ask things step by step?

36 **A:** In order to absorb the information.

37 **Q:** *(L)* The Quorum is described as the good guys. The Illuminati is described as bad guys. And yet, they are both Masonic. When a person in the Masonic organization reaches the higher levels, are there individuals at the higher levels recruiting Masons to one side or the other?

38 **A:** First, not exactly one side or another.

39 **Q:** *(L)* I am beginning to not understand something here because if the Lizzies...

40 **A:** Unblock.

41 **Q:** *(L)* I don't have a block here. If the Brotherhood AKA Illuminati AKA Lizzies AKA Beast are the ones who are going to do detrimental things to this planet, how are they related or connected to the Quorum which is in touch with...⁹

42 **A:** This will take time to explain be patient it will be worth it.

---

⁶It's interesting that up until just now, as I am reading through all the sessions to comment on them, I didn't recall that the C's had said that the Quorum that they introduced to us was "mostly alien."

⁷I think that the "close" refers to the idea that the C's may not be 'beings' as we understand it, but rather contact points with the Universal Information Field.

⁸I was being really dense here; the easiest way to picture what the C's were describing is the ancient Yin-Yan symbol.

⁹Actually, I was blocked; black-and-white thinking was dominating my mind.

43 **Q:** *(L)* Well, are you going to explain it right now?

44 **A:** Ask step by step.

45 **Q:** *(L)* OK. What is the nature of evil?

46 **A:** Blend.[10]

47 **Q:** *(L)* Are the Lizzies what we would consider to be evil?

48 **A:** Yes.

49 **Q:** *(L)* Are the Cassiopaeans what we would consider to be good?

50 **A:** Yes.

51 **Q:** *(L)* Yet, do the Cassiopaeans use and manipulate the Lizzies to accomplish certain things?

52 **A:** No.[11]

53 **Q:** *(L)* The Lizzies work independently and in opposition to the Cassiopaeans?

54 **A:** Independently, not in opposition.

55 **Q:** *(L)* Well then, is there somebody over and above this whole project...

56 **A:** We serve others therefore there is no opposition. Careful now. Step by step. If you do not fully understand answer ask another.

57 **Q:** *(L)* Part of a whole. Part of a circle.

58 **A:** Blend.

59 **Q:** *(L)* Does this mean...

---

[10] What did "blend" mean? I think this is something that is well described by Gurdjieff in his discussion of good and evil reported by Ouspensky in Chapter VIII of *In Search of the Miraculous*:

> "The idea of morality is connected with the idea of good and evil conduct. But the idea of good and evil is always different for different people, always subjective in man number one, number two, and number three, and is connected only with a given moment or a given situation. A subjective man can have no general concept of good and evil. For a subjective man evil is everything that is opposed to his desires or interests or to his conception of good.
>
> "One may say that evil does not exist for subjective man at all, that there exist only different conceptions of good. Nobody ever does anything deliberately in the interests of evil, for the sake of evil. Everybody acts in the interests of good, as he understands it. But everybody understands it in a different way. Consequently men drown, slay, and kill one another in the interests of good. The reason is again just the same, men's ignorance and the deep sleep in which they live.
>
> "This is so obvious that it even seems strange that people have never thought of it before. However, the fact remains that they fail to understand this and everyone considers his good as the only good and all the rest as evil. ...
>
> "The idea of good and evil is sometimes connected with the idea of truth and falsehood. But just as good and evil do not exist for ordinary man, neither do truth and falsehood exist.
>
> "Permanent truth and permanent falsehood can exist only for a permanent man. If a man himself continually changes, then for him truth and falsehood will also continually change. And if people are all in different states at every given moment, their conceptions of truth must be as varied as their conceptions of good. A man never notices how he begins to regard as true what yesterday he considered as false and vice versa."

[11] Again I was making assumptions based on my own narrow thinking. I assumed that communication with the C's involved being used and manipulated.

60 **A:** Picture a blending colored circle image.

61 **Q:** *(L)* Are you saying that at some levels the two halves overlap?

62 **A:** Close.

63 **Q:** *(L)* Are you saying that some of the Quorum are good guys and bad guys and the same for the Illuminati because the two are on opposing sides of the circle but at the point of blending one is weighted more to one side and the other to the other side? And these organizations are where the interactions come together?

64 **A:** Closer.

65 **Q:** *(L)* Let's leave it for the time being.

66 **A:** No. Now please.

67 **Q:** *(L)* OK. So it is a blending. Does it have something to do with ... in your case service to others means that you even serve those who serve self, is that correct?

68 **A:** Yes; we serve you and the Lizards have programed your race to self service remember.

69 **Q:** *(L)* Well, I am down a notch or two. So, I am still a service to self individual to some extent, is that correct?

70 **A:** But moving slowly toward service to others. Not all humans are.

71 **Q:** *(L)* Does this mean that when people who are members of the Quorum or Illuminati call for information or help, that you, because of your service to others orientation, are obliged to answer whoever calls?

72 **A:** Yes and no.

73 **Q:** *(L)* What is the no part?

74 **A:** If vibrational frequencies are out of pattern we do not connect.

75 **Q:** *(L)* Is the work of the Lizzies part of an overall grand plan or design?

76 **A:** All is.[12]

77 **Q:** *(L)* Let's go on. I am depressed because you guys told me I was a bad person.

78 **A:** You are not a bad person.

79 **Q:** *(L)* Well, I am feeling pretty crummy right now.

80 **A:** Lizzies induced.

81 **Q:** *(L)* You mean my crummy feelings are Lizzie induced?

82 **A:** As always.

83 **Q:** *(L)* Well I am feeling crummy because you guys let me know that I am in the same sinking boat as the rest of the poor slobs on this miserable planet. I was working pretty hard to get out of the boat.

84 **A:** Silliness; you're in your own boat.

85 **Q:** *(L)* I would like to know where Dr. Usui got the Reiki symbols.

86 **A:** Must answer question.

87 **Q:** *(L)* What question? The Quorum and Illuminati question?

88 **A:** You will feel ecstasy once answered.[13]

---

[12] This answer is the closest: that the All blinks neither at the light nor the darkness and even the Devil says in Faust: "I am part of that power which eternally wills evil and eternally works good." Roses grow best in manure and it is only by suffering that we acquire wisdom.

[13] It is true. It is a very liberating thing to finally let go of anger against God and the Universe for not being the perfect fairy-land that we childishly want it to be.

89 **Q:** *(L)* OK. A blending. Yet two halves.

90 **A:** Of a circle.

91 **Q:** *(L)* Who designed this circle?[14]

92 **A:** Natural frequency wave. Some near conjunction blend both service patterns and each "camp" to create perfect balance.

93 **Q:** *(L)* OK, so the Illuminati are the higher level on the pathway of service to self and somehow, by reaching these higher levels may have come to realizations, or [achieved] frequencies, which have caused their position to be modified or blended to where service to self becomes, or incorporates, or moves them, to service to others realizations, is this correct?

94 **A:** Continue.

95 **Q:** *(L)* OK, the ones in the Quorum are those who are focused on service to others and they, in their pathway of service to others begin to understand that some service to self is service to others.

96 **A:** Close.

97 **Q:** *(L)* And the whole idea is to blend both pathways no matter which direction you come to it from?

98 **A:** Service to others provides the perfect balance of those two realities; service to self is the diametrical opposite closing the grand cycle in perfect balance.[15]

99 **Q:** *(L)* So it is necessary to have a pathway of service to self in order for the pathway of service to others to exist?

100 **A:** Yes.

101 **Q:** *(L)* And those who are in the Quorum and the Illuminati ...

102 **A:** Blends in middle.

103 **Q:** *(L)* So it is necessary to have the darkness in order to have the light...

104 **A:** Yes.[16]

105 **Q:** *(L)* And it is necessary to have the Lizzies in order to have the Cassiopaeans...

106 **A:** Close.

107 **Q:** *(L)* And both groups evolved through the Masonic organizations..

108 **A:** Freemasonry is human reflection in physical of these processes.

109 **Q:** *(L)* OK, thank you very much. I think that is all for tonight.

110 **A:** Good Night.

End of Session

---

[14] *The Wave* 30

[15] Somehow, reading this now, it seems to be part of the predictions of the C's, that the world is moving into an intensified Service to Self mode that will act to close a Grand Cycle so that Service to Others can be restored in our reality. But obviously, if that is the case, then from the purely human perspective, things will get a lot worse before they get better.

[16] The error that so many make is the assumption that the 'darkness' is an error, a rebellion, a flaw in Creation. It isn't; it is an essential element. If there was no darkness, the light would not stand out. Everywhere you look, there is the Face of God.

November 16, 1994

The reader may have noticed from the dates that we were sitting to communicate with the C's every couple of days at this period. At this point, the contact had been going on for four months and was probably still not fully developed, so I wasn't expecting perfection. Still, I continued to ask testing questions as well as getting in as many questions as possible on mysteries that puzzled me. Obviously, many of the questions I asked were about things that there probably could never be any proof found to confirm or deny the C's answers. As you will see, I quickly got in deep water in this session.

Participants: 'Frank' and Laura

1 **Q:** *(L)* Hello.

2 **A:** Hello. How are you?

3 **Q:** *(L)* Well I guess we are fine this evening. Who do we have with us?

4 **A:** Roligea.

5 **Q:** *(L)* And where are you from?

6 **A:** Cassiopaea.

7 **Q:** *(L)* I have been reading recently about the shrine at Lourdes where the Virgin Mary supposedly appeared to Bernadette Soubirous...

8 **A:** Energy focusing center.

9 **Q:** *(L)* What kind of energy is focused there?

10 **A:** Positive due to consistent prayer patternings.

11 **Q:** *(L)* OK, what appeared to Bernadette?

12 **A:** Imaging energy consciousness wave.

13 **Q:** *(L)* Was this image out of her own mind?

14 **A:** Close.

15 **Q:** *(L)* The healings that take place...

16 **A:** Because of the concentration of positive energy.

---

[1] From October 13, 1990, through October 13, 1998, Conyers housewife Nancy Fowler claimed that the Virgin Mary appeared to her and relayed messages to all citizens of the United States. The messages ranged from admonitions to prayers to warnings of war. The Virgin's supposed visits to Conyers, a suburban community about thirty miles east of Atlanta, make Conyers one of the longest-lived Marian apparition sites in the nation. In the early 1990s the roads to Conyers were clogged with pilgrims. Fowler was a homemaker and the divorced wife of a retired air force officer. Her mystical experiences began in the 1980s, but it was not until October 13, 1990, that

17 **Q:** *(L)* What or who has been causing the apparitions of the Virgin Mary at Conyers, Georgia?[1]

18 **A:** Deceptive field.

19 **Q:** *(L)* What energy is behind this?

20 **A:** Lizards.

21 **Q:** *(L)* Why?

22 **A:** Confusion campaign part of bigger picture and plan.

23 **Q:** *(L)* What is the bigger picture and plan?

24 **A:** Conquest.

25 **Q:** *(L)* How will that aid their conquest?

26 **A:** By dispersing knowledge.

27 **Q:** *(L)* Dispersing as in breaking apart or scattering?

28 **A:** Spreading thin. Confusion does this. You are being bombarded with confusion in this era.[2]

29 **Q:** *(L)* [My daughter] A___ had a dream where she saw some symbols[3] and would like to know what the symbols represented in her dream.

30 **A:** One by one.

31 **Q:** *(L)* The first one? [Displays drawing for each symbol in series]

32 **A:** Battle.

33 **Q:** *(L)* The second one?

34 **A:** Life force.

35 **Q:** *(L)* The third?

36 **A:** Spiritual union with higher planes.

37 **Q:** *(L)* The fourth?

38 **A:** Destruction.

39 **Q:** *(L)* The fifth one?

40 **A:** Fear.

41 **Q:** *(L)* What is the entire message?

42 **A:** Up to her to learn; remember if we tell you certain things you will not gain adequate protection for the time ahead.

43 **Q:** *(L)* I dreamed last night about a puppy belonging to my sister in law. As I was walking away in the dream, I turned back and saw a car run over the dog. It was quite graphic and I awoke very upset. What was the cause or purpose of this dream?

44 **A:** This one was not particularly pertinent.

45 **Q:** *(L)* Was it just a dream?

46 **A:** Yes.

47 **Q:** *(L)* Now, relating to what we have been discussing lately, did any groups of the black race, on their own, ever create a high civilization as has been reported by several archaeologists or other individuals?

48 **A:** Yes.

49 **Q:** *(L)* On their own without assistance?

50 **A:** No.

51 **Q:** *(L)* Who did they have assistance from?

---

[1] Fowler said the Virgin Mary instructed her to take her message to the public. Until May 13, 1994, the messages continued monthly. After that date they came only on October 13 of each year and after October 13, 1998, ceased completely.

[2] To understand how confusion and believing lies can aid in the conquest/destruction of Earth, read Pierre Lescaudron's book *Earth Changes and the Human-Cosmic Connection*.

[3] See scan of original drawing in Appendix, Figure 14.

A: Lizards.[4]

Q: *(L)* Why have black people, in general, for most of recorded history, been living in such primitive conditions with such primitive mind set?

A: Isolation from modern interaction.

Q: *(L)* Why is this?

A: Karma. Punishment for past society which was cruel master hierarchical.

Q: *(L)* Are black people being abducted by the Lizzies as frequently as white people?

A: Yes.

Q: *(L)* Why do we hear so little, if any, about this?

A: You hear little of black culture in general.

Q: *(L)* Are black people, within their cultural confines, aware of aliens and alien abductions?

A: Less aware and discuss it less.

Q: *(L)* We are aware that we are being manipulated by the media. We would like to know what types of methods do they use and what is their objective?

A: More precise.

Q: *(L)* What kind of technical means do they use to project mental manipulation by way of TV or movies?

A: Simple bombardment visual and verbal.

Q: *(L)* Do they use subliminal implantation of ideas?

A: Not needed most often.

Q: *(L)* The music that kids listen to, is there any effort to program them in this media?[5]

A: Yes.

Q: *(L)* Do they use subliminals?

A: Yes.

Q: *(L)* Do they use electronic signals?

A: Yes.

Q: *(L)* Do they use electronic signals on television programming?

A: Have but not that often.

Q: *(L)* Is there any signal being sent over the test of the emergency broadcast signal?

A: No.

Q: *(L)* If the Lizzies have been feeding off of us frequently and are planning to come and take over our planet, why, when they achieved their domination 300,000 years ago, did they not just move here and take up residence and be in charge?[6]

A: No desire to inhabit same realm.

Q: *(L)* Why was this?

A: You are 3rd level they are 4th level.

Q: *(L)* Why are they planning to now?

A: They want to rule you in 4th density.

Q: *(L)* If the mother planet that the human race was seeded on originally is burned up, or turned into a cinder, I would like to know how it burned up.

A: Star expanded.

Q: *(L)* Well, if the star expanded, it must have expanded recently, is that correct?

---

[4] Which seems to be true of all civilizational developments.
[5] *The Wave* 20
[6] *The Wave* 22, 71

88 **A:** Time does not measure that way in that realm.

89 **Q:** *(L)* What realm is that?

90 **A:** Time/space warp.

91 **Q:** *(L)* What do you mean by a time/space warp?

92 **A:** Too complicated but you already have some understanding of concept.

93 **Q:** *(L)* So, the star expanded and the mother planet was turned into a cinder. If this was the case, it means that it must have turned into a cinder very close to the point, using time loosely, when human beings were created?

94 **A:** You can't even use it loosely.

95 **Q:** *(L)* Would you help me out here? I'm trying to figure out why, if that planet was turned into a cinder, why were human beings seeded there... what was the point in being brought into being on a planet that was very shortly to become a cinder... a crispy critter...

96 **A:** Okay. Now: "Shocker" for you. It hasn't become a cinder yet.

97 **Q:** *(L)* OK. What is it? You told us it was a cinder... burned up... what is the real story here?

98 **A:** It will be at the same "time" that you go to 4th density. The human race is currently being formed on D'Ahnkiar.

99 **Q:** *(L)* What do you mean that the human race is currently being formed on that planet? Is that because that planet is this planet?

100 **A:** No. That closes realm grand cycle.

101 **Q:** *(L)* Are you saying that there are human beings being created on that planet at this current time...

102 **A:** Yes, you are. Your race is forming there.

103 **Q:** *(L)* How?

104 **A:** Realm crossing understand?

105 **Q:** *(L)* Are you saying that there are 4th density bodies being formed there...

106 **A:** No. 3rd.

107 **Q:** *(L)* There are 3rd density bodies... are we going to leave the bodies we are in and go into other bodies?

108 **A:** You are drifting... Think carefully. Realm is derivative of reality. Cycle.

109 **Q:** *(L)* So the human race is being formed on this other planet at the present time...

110 **A:** Yes.

111 **Q:** *(L)* And at the time of the realm border crossing, this other planet will then become cindered... burned up...

112 **A:** Yes.

113 **Q:** *(L)* Where will the human beings go that are being formed on that planet at the time of the realm border crossing?

114 **A:** Ancient Earth.

115 **Q:** *(L)* They will go to ancient Earth?

116 **A:** There is no time as you know it; it's all just lessons for the collective consciousness.[7]

117 **Q:** *(L)* So at the closing of this grand cycle everything will just start all over again?

118 **A:** Not exactly; you see, there is no start.

119 **Q:** *(L)* Are a lot of souls on the Earth going to recycle into these new bodies coming onto the Earth?

120 **A:** Yes.

---

[7] *The Wave* 10

121 **Q**: *(L)* As ancient mankind?

122 **A**: Yes.

123 **Q**: *(L)* And do the whole thing all over again?

124 **A**: Yes.

125 **Q**: *(L)* So, in other words, a lot of people are going back to square one?

126 **A**: Close.

127 **Q**: *(L)* Is this punishment?

128 **A**: No. Nature.

129 **Q**: *(L)* Are some of the souls, at that point, going to move into a higher density level?

130 **A**: Yes.

131 **Q**: *(L)* Could you give us a percentage on this?

132 **A**: No. Open at this point.

133 **Q**: *(L)* Now, getting back to the planet, if at some point in the cycle, bodies were generated on this planet and brought to Earth, who brought them?

134 **A**: Realm crossing.

135 **Q**: *(L)* It was not a who, it was a what, is that correct?

136 **A**: All is who and what.

137 **Q**: *(L)* Well, the other night you mentioned something about the Transient Passengers hauling these bodies off that planet and bringing them to Earth, is that correct?

138 **A**: Yes.

139 **Q**: *(L)* Well, are these Transient Passengers 'realms'?[8]

140 **A**: Yes. So are you.

[8] *Secret History* 12; *The Wave* 26
[9] *High Strangeness* 6

141 **Q**: *(L)* Do you guys know what you are doing to the linear mind here?

142 **A**: Can of worms.

143 **Q**: *(L)* You said something the other night when we lost the tape about the expansion of the star being conducive to creation. Could you give us a little bit on that aspect?

144 **A**: Transdimensional Atomic Remolecularization.[9]

145 **Q**: *(L)* What is remolecularization?

146 **A**: Being reassembled.

147 **Q**: *(L)* Reassembled from what to what?

148 **A**: Complex. Density collision.

149 **Q**: *(L)* Collision of one density with another. Which?

150 **A**: Learn 4 level assembly.

151 **Q**: *(L)* How?

152 **A**: Study.

153 **Q**: *(L)* Does this mean that this was a point in space-time when pure energy could form around a framework of a thought pattern and thus become solid matter?

154 **A**: Close.

155 **Q**: *(L)* Is this transitioning of energy from higher densities into 3rd density or solid matter kind of a traumatic event for universal energy?

156 **A**: Subjective.

157 **Q**: *(L)* Is it a form of death?

158 **A**: Death and birth are the same.

159 **Q**: *(L)* Was it a requirement to be on a planet with a dying star for this remolecularization to take place?

160 **A**: If 3rd density remolecularization.

161 **Q**: *(L)* So, for energy to go into 3rd density physical level... is energy moving down when it comes into 3rd level?

162 **A**: No. Upward.

163 **Q**: *(L)* What moves upward?

164 **A**: Molecules, atomic matter. Light is first density and unifies all densities.

165 **Q**: *(L)* Does that mean that by us moving from 3rd density into 4th density that we are getting further away from unification with the source?

166 **A**: No. Light and darkness unify all densities.

167 **Q**: *(L)* How many levels of density are there?

168 **A**: 7.

169 **Q**: *(L)* When you reach the 7th level, how would you describe that if 1st level is light?

170 **A**: 7th is core of existence.

171 **Q**: *(L)* Well, if 7th density is the core of existence, would that mean that 1st density is the outer edge of existence?

172 **A**: Base.

173 **Q**: *(L)* When one has reached 7th density, then what does one do?

174 **A**: When one reaches 7th all do.

175 **Q**: *(L)* Are there any beings on 7th level?

176 **A**: Time does not exist.

177 **Q**: *(L)* When light is transferred to electrical energy, does it actually change density?

178 **A**: Yes.

179 **Q**: *(L)* Is it from 1st to 3rd when it becomes electricity?

180 **A**: Yes.

181 **Q**: *(L)* Once again, are there any beings on 7th level?

182 **A**: Big bang.

183 **Q**: *(L)* Big bang is at 7th level?

184 **A**: Close enough.

185 **Q**: *(L)* So, when we all reach 7th level we will all blow up? We will all become one and it will all start all over again?

186 **A**: Close.

187 **Q**: *(L)* Well, that's not a pleasant thought!

188 **A**: Why? There is no time, you dwell there eternally. 7th is the light you see at death of the body.

189 **Q**: *(L)* So, when you die and leave the body, do you go to 7th level?

190 **A**: See it.

191 **Q**: *(L)* Well, I have a book over on the shelf called *Messages from Michael*... this entity says that souls are being continually flung off from some sort of soul generator somewhere in the universe... what was this source?

192 **A**: Entity at 3rd incarnate.

193 **Q**: *(L)* Was this information valid in absolute terms?

194 **A**: No. Souls are already created.

195 **Q**: *(L)* You mean from the first instant of time (excuse the term)?

196 **A**: Yes.

197 **Q**: *(L)* Well, it all seems pretty amorphous.

198 **A**: Amorphous is perceptive.

199 **Q**: *(L)* I want to ask what is the source of the pain L___, J___ and I have been

experiencing identically for the past week or so?[10]

200 **A:** DNA changes.

201 **Q:** *(L)* And what is the source of these DNA changes?

202 **A:** Moving to 4th density.

203 **Q:** *(L)* How soon are we going to make it?

204 **A:** Open.

205 **Q:** *(L)* In referring to the Nephilim you used the term "forced insemination." How does this differ from artificial insemination?[11]

206 **A:** No difference.

207 **Q:** *(L)* At the time of the tower of Babel it says that the Nephilim looked on the daughters of men and took wives as if there were some friendly interaction of some sort... does this mean they broke ranks and had feelings for their human 'wives'?

208 **A:** No. Another deception of history. Picturesque way of describing genetic experiments.

209 **Q:** *(L)* Why did the sphinx look like a feline human?

210 **A:** Symbolism of feline energy.

211 **Q:** *(L)* Was this why the Egyptians worshipped cats or held cats in such high regard?

212 **A:** At root of this.

213 **Q:** *(L)* What was the origin of this feline god?

214 **A:** Atlantean tradition.

215 **Q:** *(L)* Where did the Atlantean tradition of the feline god originate?

216 **A:** Superstition.

217 **Q:** *(L)* What was the superstition about?

218 **A:** Not important.

219 **Q:** *(L)* Well, it is possibly important because such an enormous monument was built to honor this god and I am sure the world would like to know what is at the root of this!

220 **A:** What is at root of Statue of Liberty?

221 **Q:** *(L)* A principle. So, a feline principle is at the root of the sphinx?

222 **A:** Close.

223 **Q:** *(L)* It does not represent any alien beings, gods or goddesses?

224 **A:** No.

225 **Q:** *(L)* And what was this god's name?

226 **A:** Endurra.

227 **Q:** *(L)* Why did the worship of this god or goddess stop?

228 **A:** Fizzled out.

229 **Q:** *(L)* You said that the Lizzies lived among humans for a thousand years. When, in our illusion of time, did this occur?

230 **A:** During peak of Atlantis.

231 **Q:** *(L)* And how long was the Atlantean civilization in existence?

232 **A:** 70,000 years

233 **Q:** *(L)* Was mankind living on the Earth as a sentient being during the time of the large dinosaurs?

234 **A:** Yes and no.

235 **Q:** *(L)* What does that mean?

---

[10] I can only describe it as feeling like a hot steel ball about the size of a marble, under the shoulder blade.

[11] *High Strangeness* 14

236 **A**: Transitory time warp.

237 **Q**: *(L)* Was there ever a time when there was a physical human race that contained within a single body both sexes?

238 **A**: No.

239 **Q**: *(L)* Was the physical human race always two sexes, that is, male and female?

240 **A**: Yes.[12]

241 **Q**: *(L)* Did Atlantis go down as a series of destructions?

242 **A**: Yes.

243 **Q**: *(L)* How many cataclysms?

244 **A**: Three.

245 **Q**: *(L)* Were these cataclysms all caused by the same source?

246 **A**: No.

247 **Q**: *(L)* And you said that the 'flood of Noah' was the story of the final deluge and destruction of Atlantis?[13]

248 **A**: Yes.

249 **Q**: *(L)* And that was caused by what?

250 **A**: Venus.

251 **Q**: *(L)* I thought you said it was caused by Martek?

252 **A**: Yes.

253 **Q**: *(L)* Well, how can it be caused by Venus if it was caused by Martek?

254 **A**: Venus also "caused" Martek.[14]

255 **Q**: *(L)* You said that the Earth, up to that time, was surrounded by a water vapor canopy, correct?[15]

256 **A**: Yes.

257 **Q**: *(L)* And when Mars came by it overloaded the Earth's atmosphere and it fell as a deluge, correct?

258 **A**: Close.

259 **Q**: *(L)* When did Venus enter the solar system?

260 **A**: 80,000 years approximately.

261 **Q**: *(L)* How many close passes to the Earth did Venus make?

262 **A**: Seven.

263 **Q**: *(L)* Was Venus involved with the planet Kantek which you said exploded due to psychic energies generated by its inhabitants?

264 **A**: No.[16]

265 **Q**: *(L)* When L___ took the melatonin the other night, how come he was unable to sleep?

266 **A**: Adjusting to the melatonin.

267 **Q**: *(L)* Is everything going to work out for Frank in a positive way?

268 **A**: Eventually if he can withstand the rough period.

---

[12]So much for esoteric myths about hermaphrodites.

[13]The date of the 'Flood' was given on 30 September 1994 as 10,662 BC. In the 7 October 1994 session, I repeated the date incorrectly as 12,388 BC and the C's response was "close," so they weren't being fooled.

[14]For a recap on the previous questions about Venus see sessions: 22 July, 30 September, 5 October, and 7 October. Consistent responses, even if I was making a lot of assumptions in my questions that made it difficult.

[15]I asked this question on 30 September 1994.

[16]Consistent.

269 **Q:** *(L)* Is it true that once we have gotten through rough periods and established faith and patience, we don't have to do it anymore?

270 **A:** Open.

271 **Q:** *(L)* How long is it seen that mother will be staying with this lady in Largo?[17]

272 **A:** 4 to 6 months longer.

273 **Q:** *(L)* Why has AB not called me back about crop circles?[18]

274 **A:** UFO grapevine gossip.

275 **Q:** *(L)* Saying what?

276 **A:** Your source is not valid.

277 **Q:** *(L)* Who started that grapevine rumor?

278 **A:** Two people.

279 **Q:** *(L)* Who are they?

280 **A:** MF and JW. Ego again.[19]

281 **Q:** *(L)* Well guys, let me ask you: did you start this communication because you wanted this information given out to the world in a general way? Or just simply because we were driven to have answers?

A: Yes. Both.

282

283 **Q:** *(L)* If we are going to get this information out, it should just happen...

284 **A:** Yes, but resistance and interference too. Persevere.[20]

285 **Q:** *(L)* Well, with all this resistance and this grapevine it is real discouraging.

A: Not right people.

286

287 **Q:** *(L)* Well, can you tell me about a few of the right people?

288 **A:** Not problem. Just press those you have.

289 **Q:** *(L)* OK, thank you and good night.

A: Good Night.

290

End of session

---

[17] My mother was working as a home-care nurse and this was kind of a sideways question about when the woman might pass on.

[18] Again, our notorious local Golden Dawn guy who would call now and then and inquire how the channeling experiment was going, I would send him some info, and then he would go around trashing it and me.

[19] Remember good ole MF and JW? The UFO investigator and the Sitchin devotee? See previous notes.

[20] There was resistance, interference, defamation, attacks, right from the very beginning. It was bizarre. I wonder, if I had known how bad it would ultimately get, if I would have persisted. Probably, but it sure has been a rough road. And we were so blissfully naive at the time!

November 19, 1994

This is the first C's session in which Terry and Jan participated. They had come up on a couple of occasions in the earlier days of the experiment when nothing much was happening except endless wading through dead dudes and occasional space brothers. In the months since the C's had appeared, I had talked to both of them frequently, telling about the contact. However, at the same time, AB, MF, and JW, mentioned several times in previous sessions, had been lobbying against what we were doing as being worth anyone's time, though they all wanted to know what was coming through. So, finally, Terry and Jan made the effort to come up again and check things out. VG also attended, so it was a funny mix of energies and emotional agendas. It's a great session that covers a lot of territory with fascinating tidbits about time travel, the Philadelphia Experiment, Men in Black, famous UFO cases, demonic possession, poltergeists, the Bermuda Triangle, Earth changes, government disinformation about UFOs and aliens, time warps, Atlantean crystals, and much more!

Participants: 'Frank', Laura, VG, Terry and Jan

1 **Q**: *(L)* Hello.

2 **A**: Hello. Please no rituals. They constrict energy flow.[1]

3 **Q**: *(L)* Who do we have with us this evening?

4 **A**: Xora.

5 **Q**: *(L)* Are you a discarnate?

6 **A**: No.

7 **Q**: *(L)* Where are you from?

8 **A**: Cassiopaea.

9 **Q**: *(V)* I met a young man named J___- this evening who claims to be a psychic vampire. Do you know of the person I am speaking of? The conversation I am speaking of?

10 **A**: No.

11 **Q**: *(V)* What I want to know is has he mislabeled himself?

12 **A**: Yes.

13 **Q**: *(V)* Is he under demonic possession?

14 **A**: No.

15 **Q**: *(V)* Is he playing games with me?

16 **A**: No.

---

[1] VG was doing some kind of New Agey ritual thing.

17 **Q:** *(V)* What's his problem?

18 **A:** Delusional.

19 **Q:** *(V)* He wants to, more to the point of questioning, he wants to speak with me more. I figure it's for one of two reasons, one is he wants to take my energy, or two because he is calling out for help. Is he wanting to take my energy?

20 **A:** In a sense.

21 **Q:** *(V)* Does he want my help as in counseling?

22 **A:** No.

23 **Q:** *(L)* Does he want to waste her time?

24 **A:** Open.

25 **Q:** *(V)* So he's not attached? I find that hard to believe. Is he attached?

26 **A:** Most likely.

27 **Q:** *(L)* Terry wants to ask why he has such deep-rooted anger?

28 **A:** Victim of much circumstances related to this life.

29 **Q:** *(L)* Is it karmic?

30 **A:** It always is.

31 **Q:** *(L)* Can you give us a clue about how to deal with this and relieve it?

32 **A:** It's already in progress.

33 **Q:** *(L)* Is there anything to speed the process?

34 **A:** Not necessary.[2]

35 **Q:** *(T)* Is there something I can do about it or will it relieve itself in its own course?

36 **A:** You are already on right path.

37 **Q:** *(T)* Have I been abducted?

38 **A:** Childhood.

39 **Q:** *(L)* Has he been abducted since he was grown?[3]

40 **A:** Maybe in level 3.

41 **Q:** *(L)* What is level 3?

42 **A:** Type of abduction.

43 **Q:** *(L)* How many levels and types of abductions are there?

44 **A:** Six.

45 **Q:** *(L)* What is level 3?

46 **A:** Consciousness altered to "alpha" state.

47 **Q:** *(T)* Does this mean screen memories?

48 **A:** Close.

49 **Q:** *(T)* In other words I will be seeing something other than what is actually happening? Or remembering something other than what actually happened?

50 **A:** Yes but not physical as in childhood.

51 **Q:** *(V)* Has he been to the caves? Have the Grays taken him to the caves?

52 **A:** This is strange question.

53 **Q:** *(L)* How many times has he been physically abducted?

54 **A:** 27.

55 **Q:** *(L)* How many times have they interfered with his consciousness by inducing an alpha state?

56 **A:** 196.

57 **Q:** *(T)* Is this when I am asleep that they induce this alpha state?

58 **A:** Sometimes.

59 **Q:** *(V)* Has it ever happened when he's in front of his computer?

---

[2] *The Wave* 24
[3] *High Strangeness* 8

60 **A**: At work.

61 **Q**: *(T)* At work for Honeywell?

62 **A**: Inside large white building.

63 **Q**: *(L)* Where is the large white building? *(T)* That's the Honeywell complex. *(F)* Are they all white? *(T)* They're all white. *(V)* Is the Honeywell corporation agents of the Lizzies?

64 **A**: No. US government.

65 **Q**: *(T)* Yes they are. They are a government contractor. Has it happened since I worked at my new job?

66 **A**: No.

67 **Q**: *(T)* Is it because I am no longer working for a government facility?

68 **A**: Partly.

69 **Q**: *(T)* What would the other part be?

70 **A**: You have recently had consciousness raising experience.

71 **Q**: *(L)* And this consciousness raising experience has made it more difficult for them to play with his head?

72 **A**: Yes.

73 **Q**: *(T)* What was the consciousness-raising experience?

74 **A**: Soul searching period.

75 **Q**: *(V)* Have you been doing a lot of soul searching? *(T)* I've been saying that I have been at 100% depression for six or seven weeks now. *(L)* What is causing Terry's depression?

76 **A**: Change of DNA.

77 **Q**: *(T)* What brought about the change in DNA?

78 **A**: Moving toward 4th level of density reality.

79 **Q**: *(L)* Why does this always seem to cause pain, suffering, or depression?

80 **A**: All level 1 changes do.

81 **Q**: *(L)* What are level 1 changes?

82 **A**: We use "level" designation to denote significance.

83 **Q**: *(L)* Is level 1 most significant?

84 **A**: Yes.

85 **Q**: *(L)* As the numbers go higher does the significance get lessened?

86 **A**: Close.

87 **Q**: *(L)* What is causing the pain in Jan's right shoulder, since several of us have been having this exact same symptom?

88 **A**: DNA changes.

89 **Q**: *(L)* Can Reiki be used to help alleviate the discomfort?

90 **A**: Not necessary or recommended.

91 **Q**: *(L)* Do we just have to suffer through this one?

92 **A**: Each "suffering" will be closely followed by dramatic life changes.

93 **Q**: *(V)* Is there any reason why I have not experienced this discomfort?

94 **A**: You will.

95 **Q**: *(T)* Will I continue to be abducted now that I have had this change of consciousness?

96 **A**: Open.

97 **Q**: *(T)* Are the same beings doing all the abductions or are there different groups?

98 **A**: Two groups.

99 **Q**: *(T)* What is one group?

100 **A**: Grays.

101 **Q**: *(T)* What is the other group?

102 **A**: Lizards.

103 **Q**: *(T)* Is the woman Marissa T channeling the Lizzies?

104 **A:** Yes.

105 **Q:** *(T)* Are these Lizzies she is channeling intentions beneficial toward human beings?

106 **A:** No.

107 **Q:** *(T)* Was I in some kind of danger by ticking her off?[4]

108 **A:** Not at this point.

109 **Q:** *(T)* Is there anything further you would like to say about this woman channeling the Lizzies?

110 **A:** Further interactions with Lizards are not encouraged. Be careful of some in "MUFON".

111 **Q:** *(T)* Is it true that the government is using MUFON as their grassroots information-gathering organization?[5]

112 **A:** Yes.

113 **Q:** *(T)* I received information during a dream. Was the information real or was it just a dream?

114 **A:** Corrupted.

115 **Q:** *(T)* By whom or what?

116 **A:** Conflicting energies.

117 **Q:** *(L)* What are the sources of these energies? Are these within Terry himself or outside him?

118 **A:** Both.

119 **Q:** *(T)* Can the information that was sent through be retrieved?

120 **A:** Will be repeated. Have you noticed your repeating dream patterns?

121 **Q:** *(T)* I have not been remembering most of my dreams.

122 **A:** Try melatonin; avoid any antidepressants. Some have suggested.

123 **Q:** *(L)* Is pot considered an antidepressant?

124 **A:** No.

125 **Q:** *(T)* Is the information of the dream important not only to me but to everybody?

126 **A:** All is.

127 **Q:** *(T)* Are different people receiving different pieces of information or are some people receiving as much as they can handle and then it moves to another person to receive more of the information in varying amounts?

128 **A:** Too many questions.

129 **Q:** *(T)* Is this information being given out in pieces to different people to be put together?

130 **A:** Close.

131 **Q:** *(T)* The information I have would not then be whole unto itself?[6]

132 **A:** Network. Use computer net. There are others communicating and piecing together in this way.

133 **Q:** *(T)* How do I retrieve the information?

134 **A:** Ask.

135 **Q:** *(L)* Start taking the melatonin?

136 **A:** No. On computer network.

---

[4] As best as I can recall, Terry and Jan had attended some channeling sessions of this woman and Terry had asked some challenging questions which upset the woman and others attending the session.

[5] And no doubt they will pick the best and brightest and feed them disinfo to send them offtrack!

[6] *The Wave* 18

137 **Q:** *(T)* Ask on the computer network how to retrieve the information?

138 **A:** No. Others ask.

139 **Q:** *(L)* Ask if others are having dreams of a similar nature?

140 **A:** Open dialogue.

141 **Q:** *(T)* I received a dream one night, I saw what was presented to me, I would describe it as a holographic or virtual-reality computer screen. It was a glowing outline of a screen and information scrolled past. The information was in different colors. There were a lot of different documents. The long documents I believe were some kind of technical references. It was just a black void; I wasn't even there; it was just there in front of me like I was watching a screen. There were red documents, very short, that I took to be some kind of statement; they scared me. I don't remember what they were. There were green documents, there were yellow documents. The outline of the screen changed the color of the documents as they scrolled through. There was a lot of them. I know I read all of them but I don't know what any of them said.

142 **A:** Hypnotize Terry.

143 **Q:** *(L)* In that hypnosis with my son, was that an abduction in a previous lifetime?

144 **A:** End of life information session. Read "Majestic".

145 **Q:** *(L)* When a person dies and leaves the body, are the beings who take charge of the soul and direct the end-of-life review and the next life plan, are these beings similar to what we call aliens?

146 **A:** Sometimes. But on individual basis and level 5 density.

147 **Q:** *(L)* So, are you saying that any 'aliens' that would be assisting with this type of thing would be of the level 5 density? Or, that the individual would be of the 5th level?

148 **A:** Alien is based on one's perspective.

149 **Q:** *(L)* But, does this mean that the 'being' is the level 5 density person?

150 **A:** Yes. Reflective of experience vibration.

151 **Q:** *(L)* Why is the planchette moving so slowly tonight?

152 **A:** V___'s attention is diverted.

153 **Q:** *(L)* Diverted to what?

154 **A:** Writing.

155 **Q:** *(T)* One last question and I will be gone for now. Who sent me the information in the dream?

156 **A:** You don't have to "go". Complex.

157 **Q:** *(T)* Was the information sent by the good guys or the bad guys?

158 **A:** Different concept.

159 **Q:** *(T)* What race of beings? Did it come from a specific race?

160 **A:** Not exactly.

161 **Q:** *(L)* Can you give us just a few words on this?

162 **A:** Okay, Laura. Cosmic retrieval system.

163 **Q:** *(L)* What does the cosmic retrieval system retrieve?

164 **A:** Remember computer was inspired by cosmic forces and reflects universal intelligence system of retrieval of reality.[7]

---

[7] Interesting concept in view of Information Theory!

Q: *(T)* This is a computer network, yes or no?

A: Strange thought pattern.

Q: *(T)* What you have described, on a very large scale, sophisticated...

A: Grand scale, close.

Q: *(T)* Can I access it through our earthly computer system?

A: In a sense, but not directly as of yet. But just wait.

[Break]

Q: *(L)* OK, we are back guys. Have you been listening to us?

A: We are always with you now.

Q: *(L)* With all of us?

A: We have added Jan and Terry. Will add more as needed.

Q: *(J)* Is there a specific pattern to the phone calls that I have been getting in the mornings?

A: No.

Q: *(J)* Is there any outside agent causing my phone to ring to help me to wake up when I need to?

A: No. Just coincidence.

Q: *(J)* Is there any significance to the high number of hang-ups I have been getting on both our phone lines?

A: Three calls were monitors because of MUFON involvement.

Q: *(L)* Are Terry and Jan's phones tapped?

A: Phone "taps" are no longer necessary.

Q: *(L)* Why?

A: Technology advancements.[8]

Q: *(L)* You mean they can listen to us without tapping our phones?

A: Yes.

Q: *(L)* Can they listen to us over the phones even when the phones are hung up?

A: Can.

Q: *(T)* Can they listen to us through the TV through the infra-red frequency?

A: Again, technology has advanced beyond that. Walls have "ears." Satellites can monitor any conversation or meeting.

Q: *(J)* Is this conversation being monitored at this point in time?

A: No.

Q: *(T)* Can our movements be tracked through the electronic ignition systems in our cars?[9]

A: Not necessary. You are not yet aware of the extent to which humans have been "aided" in technological advancement.

Q: *(T)* By whom?

A: This requires long and complicated response.

Q: *(T)* The object behind using the electronic ignitions, from what I have heard, whether the source is true or not I can't say, but I had a strange confirmation of part of it.

A: Beware of disinformation. It diverts your attention away from reality thus leaving you open to capture and conquest and even possible destruction.

---

[8]This suggests that the recently revealed NSA phone information gathering has been going on a lot longer than anyone has supposed.

[9]*The Wave* 51

199 **Q:** *(L)* Is the information about the electronic ignition systems correct?

200 **A:** Disinformation comes from seemingly reliable sources. It is extremely important for you to not gather false knowledge as it is more damaging than no knowledge at all. Remember knowledge protects, ignorance endangers. The information you speak of, Terry, was given to you deliberately because you and Jan and others have been targeted due to your intense interest in level of density 4 through 7 subject matter. You have already been documented as a "threat."

201 **Q:** *(L)* Can you tell Terry what event occurred (referring to 'confirmation' of electronic ignition subject)...

202 **A:** Remember, disinformation is very effective when delivered by highly trained sources because hypnotic and transdimensional techniques are used thereby causing electronic anomalies to follow suggestion causing perceived confirmation to occur.

203 **Q:** *(T)* Who was the guy in the Camaro?

204 **A:** Diversion.

205 **Q:** *(T)* About two weeks after I saw the video tape where I heard this information, a guy pulled up out of nowhere driving a souped up Camaro... (Jan: No! It was the night we were watching it!) We had watched it before and we were talking about it and decided to watch it again. So, Gary and I had decided to go outside to take the dog around the block and we had just gotten back and put the dog on the porch and we were standing outside smoking a cigarette when the guy in the Camaro pulls into the driveway with steam coming out from under the hood. He asked to use the hose. I told him yes. He gets out wearing jeans, tee shirt and scraggly blond hair. He says: "I overheated. I'm coming back from Gulfport and was going back to Ocala and was on the interstate," when his car overheated. Now, 275 is a little ways from my house and he came all the way, passed a gas station and convenience store, turned off the main drag and then onto my street to get water... then he started talking about how the new electronic ignitions are designed to shut down when the car exceeds a certain speed so he had installed a special racing ignition but ever since his car had been overheating... we had just finished watching this movie about electronic ignitions and we were flabbergasted... What I want to know is who has the power and ability to set up these kinds of 'confirmations' or synchronicities?

206 **A:** Same forces spreading disinformation: Brotherhood / consortium / Illuminati / New World Order / "Antichrist" / Lizards.[10]

207 **Q:** *(T)* But I'm just a nobody. Why would they go to all trouble to send somebody in a Camaro to drive up on my lawn...

208 **A:** Several answers follow: Number One, nobody is a "nobody." Number two, it is no trouble at all for aforementioned forces to give seemingly individualized attention to anybody. Number three, Terry has been targeted and so has Jan and others because you are on the right track. Number four, this area is currently a "hot bed" of activity and extremely rapidly expanding awareness.

---

[10] *The Wave* 20

[Talk about the Philadelphia Experiment during break]

209 **Q:** *(L)* I suppose you have been listening to us talk. What do you have to comment about the Philadelphia Experiment?

210 **A:** We are always listening. [Laura makes error in calling out letters.] More coffee, Laura. [Terry takes V___'s place at the board for a time.]

211 **Q:** *(L)* Are you, in a sense, part of the cosmic computer network retrieval system?

212 **A:** All are in one way or another.[11]

213 **Q:** *(L)* Did the Philadelphia Experiment, as described by Terry's scoutmaster, occur in the way it was described?

214 **A:** That description was not of Philadelphia Experiment.

215 **Q:** *(L)* Was that the ship that was part of the Philadelphia Experiment?

216 **A:** One of three.

217 **Q:** *(L)* Were the effects that ship experienced a result of the Philadelphia Experiment as we understand it?

218 **A:** Reality molecular residual.

219 **Q:** *(L)* Did the Philadelphia Experiment, as we have read about it, occur in the way it was described?

220 **A:** Close.

221 **Q:** *(L)* Was Al Bielek part of the experiment?[12]

222 **A:** Yes.

223 **Q:** *(L)* Was the information he has given out about this factual?

224 **A:** Close.

225 **Q:** *(L)* Is the information he gives about being aged regressed in the body and his brother coming into a new body accurate?

226 **A:** No.

227 **Q:** *(T)* Is his brother, Duncan, really who he claims to be?

228 **A:** No.

229 **Q:** *(L)* Is Al Bielek really who he claims to be?

230 **A:** No. Was technician but not aboard vessel.

231 **Q:** *(L)* So he did not go back and forth in time?

232 **A:** Correct.

233 **Q:** *(T)* So he's trying to make himself out to be more than he actually is?

234 **A:** Yes.

235 **Q:** *(J)* He is a wannabe?

236 **A:** No. He is an agent of the government.

237 **Q:** *(T)* Is Preston also a government agent?

238 **A:** Yes.

---

[11] Another hint in the direction of a Universal Information Field.

[12] Al Bielek gained a degree of public recognition within the UFO/alien research community with his testimony at the MUFON conference in 1990. At that time he stated that he was a true eyewitness and participant to the Philadelphia Experiment. What remains amazing is that Bielek's story was widely accepted by the media and his 'fan community' without criticism. People of all backgrounds were quick to repeat his quotes, often just borrowing them from someone else's web page, without checking the claims or presenting any critical analysis of whether they 'could' be true. See: http://www.bielek-debunked.com/

239 **Q:** *(T)* Why are they coming out with this story? Besides disinformation...

240 **A:** Slow revelation to effect gauge of public response.

241 **Q:** *(L)* Should V___ stand behind Terry and put her hands on his shoulders for energy?

242 **A:** Not necessary because Terry has adequate energy of his own. George Bush was involved with Philadelphia Experiment.[13]

243 **Q:** *(T)* He was Navy, World War II. *(L)* I would like to know what happened to Ambrose Bierce?[14]

244 **A:** Dead. Spontaneous combustion.

245 **Q:** *(L)* What happened to Marcia Moore, who was working on drug-enhanced outer-space contact via altered consciousness?[15]

246 **A:** Permanent abduction victim by Lizards.

247 **Q:** *(L)* Why?

248 **A:** Too close to truth.

249 **Q:** *(L)* Well, are we close to the truth too?

250 **A:** Yes.

251 **Q:** *(L)* Will we be permanently abducted by the Lizards?

252 **A:** Knowledge protects.

---

[13] Now this statement was furiously interesting. Recall my comments about Jeane Dixon's prediction about the death of John Kennedy in the Introduction along with the well-known (to alternative research community) apparent fact that George H.W. Bush was involved in the Kennedy assassination. Then consider that the C's have previously stated that the government (at least those with 'need to know') are aware of coming Earth changes. Now, we have something a bit further back that might provide a context for some of these things: time-travel experiments conducted by ONI. Funny that the new offices of the ONI were destroyed in the Pentagon Strike on 9/11, and that one doesn't, in general, hear much about the ONI – it's all CIA and NSA these days. In a previous note I mentioned that I had read a document that claimed that the ONI was engaged in time traveling to create religious memes at various points in the past, including Christianity, so as to be able to utilize these in the present. Inquiring minds wonder...

[14] Ambrose Bierce was an American editorialist, journalist, short-story writer, fabulist, and satirist. He wrote the short story "An Occurrence at Owl Creek Bridge" and compiled a satirical lexicon, *The Devil's Dictionary*, which consists of satirical definitions of English words that lampoon cant and political double-talk. His vehemence as a critic, his motto "Nothing matters," and the sardonic view of human nature that informed his work, all earned him the nickname 'Bitter Bierce.' His style often embraces an abrupt beginning, dark imagery, vague references to time, limited descriptions, impossible events, and the theme of war. Bierce was considered a master of pure English by his contemporaries, and virtually everything that came from his pen was notable for its judicious wording and economy of style. He wrote in a variety of literary genres. In 1913, Bierce traveled to Mexico to gain first-hand experience of the Mexican Revolution. While traveling with rebel troops, he disappeared without a trace.

[15] *High Strangeness* 8

Q: *(L)* But didn't she have a lot of knowledge too?

A: Scrambled with drugs.

Q: *(L)* I would like to know what is the specific mode of time travel?

A: Complex.

Q: *(L)* Well, just give us a clue here?

A: Transdimensional transfer utilizing electromagnetic adjustment of atomic structure to alter speed of time cycle convergence.

Q: *(L)* Who or what are the individuals called 'Men in Black'?[16]

A: Lizard projections.[17]

Q: *(T)* Does that mean that they are just projecting an image of a being?

A: Yes.

Q: *(T)* The MIBs are not real, then, in our physical terms?

A: Partly correct. You do not understand technology but we will describe it if you like.

Q: *(L)* We like. Please describe this.

A: Okay. Get ready. First we must explain further time "travel" because the two concepts are closely related. The first step is to artificially induce an electromagnetic field. This opens the door between dimensions of reality. Next, thoughts must be channeled by participant in order to access reality bonding channel. They must then focus the energy to the proper dimensional bridge. The electrons must be arranged in correct frequency wave. Then the triage must be sent through realm "curtain" in order to balance perceptions at all density levels.

Q: *(L)* Information in the event that has to be balanced or taken into consideration as to importance so that the program runs correctly. Is this the correct interpretation of triage as you have used it?

A: Sort of. Triage is as follows: 1. Matter, 2. Energy, 3. Perception of reality. That is it folks.

---

[16] *High Strangeness* 6; *The Wave* 52

[17] *The Wave* 64

[18] A famous abduction case written about by Ray Fowler. Fowler received a B.A. degree in liberal arts from Gordon College (Massachusetts). He graduated with honors when he received the degree magna cum laude. He then joined the U.S. Air Force in 1952, attended a special school for electronic espionage, after which he was assigned to the USAF Security Service under the auspices of the NSA. His civilian career included work on U.S. government projects including the Minuteman Project weapons system. Fowler served as Director of Scientific Investigations for MUFON and authored an older edition of the MUFON Field Investigators Manual. He also served as the Scientific Associate for the Center for UFO Studies. Fowler had also served as an associate member and eventually chairman of NICAP (National Investigations Committee on Aerial Phenomena). J. Allen Hynek, who developed the Hynek UFO classification system, recognized Fowler as one of the outstanding investigators in the UFO field. "An outstanding UFO investigator ... I know of no one who is more dedicated, trustworthy or persevering," Hynek said about Fowler's investigative work. He wrote *The Andreasson Affair* in 1979. See: http://www.ufocasebook.com/Andreasson.html

269 **Q:** *(L)* Who abducted Betty Andreasson.[18]

270 **A:** Grays.

271 **Q:** *(L)* Was the information that Betty Andreasson was given by these beings who abducted her screen information or false information of information for disinformation?

272 **A:** All of the above and some factual.

273 **Q:** *(L)* In the Ann Haywood case which is supposed to be a case of demonic possession or obsession, who or what are the beings that are afflicting this woman and her family?[19]

274 **A:** 3rd density section "B" energy anomalies same as "poltergeist."

275 **Q:** *(L)* The case that is described in the book *The Haunted*, about the Smurl family, with quite a bit of phenomena occurring in their house including the sighting of a Bigfoot-type creature, what is the source of the phenomena in that case?

276 **A:** Same.

277 **Q:** *(L)* So, neither of those cases are 'alien' related?

278 **A:** Correct.

279 **Q:** *(L)* Why are there such marked similarities between those two cases and the case described by Karla Turner and other alien abductions?

280 **A:** Similarities are open to interpretation. Turner household was opened to multiple types of phenomena due to interaction with Grays and others.

281 **Q:** *(L)* Does that occur frequently in interactions with Grays?

282 **A:** When there is excessive activity of this sort it leaves open channels or "windows" which allows all sorts of things to come through.

283 **Q:** *(L)* Well, who are these old hags who have sex with people...?

284 **A:** Poltergeistal entities.

285 **Q:** *(L)* What is a poltergeist entity?

286 **A:** Self explanatory.

287 **Q:** *(L)* Is the poltergeist entity generated by the subconscious energy of the individual to which the poltergeist effect occurs or takes place?

288 **A:** Interaction just like everything else between perceived and perceiver.

289 **Q:** *(L)* And what is, in this case, being perceived? Is it an energy construct or is it an actual being?

290 **A:** Both. Remember, Laura, you too are an energy construct.

291 **Q:** *(L)* OK, in S___'s regression to the time she experienced a meeting on a ship, there was a woman very similar to the woman described in these other cases. Who or what was that woman and why was she there?

292 **A:** This "woman" is becoming quite popular isn't she?

293 **Q:** *(L)* Who, the woman in the hypnosis or S___?

294 **A:** The "Hag."

295 **Q:** *(L)* Why is she becoming so popular? *(J)* She must be good!

296 **A:** We don't know.

297 **Q:** *(L)* When my daughter A___ did a spirit viewing of me she saw a cord attached to me and at the end of this cord

---

[19]See: *The Demon Syndrome* by Nancy Osborn. This is really a terrifying case and I had some private correspondence with the author that makes me tend to think that everything she wrote about really happened as she described it. Truly creepy!

there was a blue astronaut. What was the blue astronaut she saw?

A: Guide.

Q: *(L)* Well, we disconnected him. Should we have left him alone?

A: Up to you.

Q: *(L)* Who were the beautiful Nordic beings seen by George Adamski?

A: Figment of George Adamski's highly evolved imagination.

Q: *(L)* Several times I have heard reference to big flying rectangular boxes. I would like to know who these belong to?[20]

A: Lizard projections.[21]

Q: *(L)* Why do they have so many different types of craft?

A: Not all are theirs.

Q: *(L)* Now, we went to the recommended person to take the Reiki initiation. Do we now, at this point in time, have the true Reiki initiation?[22]

A: Getting there. Must allow energy to solidify. Do you understand the concept of imprinting?

Q: *(L)* Yes.

A: Then you know.

Q: *(L)* Practicing Reiki is the thing that will solidify the force?

A: Partly.

Q: *(L)* Are there symbols for Reiki that are even older and stronger than the ones we have been given?

A: Yes.

Q: *(L)* Are the original symbols in Sanskrit?

A: Yes.

Q: *(L)* Where are we going to find them?

A: You are not.

Q: *(L)* And the Reiki symbols we learned from Sally are the closest we can get?

A: Yes. Good enough.

Q: *(L)* When one receives the Reiki initiation does it reverse the flow of intake and output, positive or negative polarity of the energy flow in the hands?

A: Yes.

Q: *(L)* Does the left hand then become the output hand?

A: Yes.

Q: *(L)* Is the right hand then the intaking hand?

A: Yes.

Q: *(L)* Is the Sui Ching attunement Sally gives more powerful than anything we could have received from any other person?

A: Yes. Have faith.

Q: *(L)* The spiritual exercises she teaches, are those beneficial for us both to practice?

A: They are okay.

Q: *(L)* Is that so-so or really good?

A: Remember some things must be learned by your own path.

Q: *(L)* What or who are the South American aliens I have read about who are described as being gray with thick

---
[20] *The Wave* 52
[21] *High Strangeness* 6, 8; *The Wave* 64
[22] *The Wave* 17

lips, rudimentary features, gray uniforms, and are called by the South Americans 'Malos'?[23]

334 **A**: Lizard projections.[24]

335 **Q**: *(L)* Were these also the clay-like beings seen by Betty Andreasson, only she saw them wearing blue suits?

336 **A**: Yes.

337 **Q**: *(L)* Where was Betty Andreasson taken to when she saw the Phoenix in her abduction?

338 **A**: Another dimension of reality.

339 **Q**: *(L)* Is Betty Andreasson correct in believing that her experiences are positive and are bringing her closer to God?

340 **A**: No.

341 **Q**: *(L)* Is Betty Andreasson deluded?

342 **A**: No. She is a victim.

343 **Q**: *(L)* What happened to the Australian pilot Frederick Valentich?[25]

344 **A**: He was taken by the Lizards and dissected.

345 **Q**: *(V)* It just gets uglier and uglier! *(L)* OK, I want to ask about this purple energy plate. Is this something that would be worth spending money on?

346 **A**: No. Is bogus. Pretty color though.

347 **Q**: *(L)* How long should I wait to get the master initiation?

348 **A**: Up to you.

349 **Q**: *(L)* Sally likes for her students to wait six months. Is it necessary or beneficial for me to wait that long since I have been doing Reiki for so long?

350 **A**: Up to you.

351 **Q**: *(V)* We would like to know why we have all been under such attack lately?

352 **A**: Because you are now connected to a valid source.

353 **Q**: *(L)* Is Bob Oeschler a government plant?

354 **A**: Semi.[26]

355 **Q**: *(L)* Was the Carp, Ontario, UFO landing a real UFO landing?

---

[23] *High Strangeness* 8; *The Wave* 52
[24] *High Strangeness* 6; *The Wave* 64
[25] Frederick Valentich disappeared while on a 125-mile (235 km) training flight in a Cessna 182L light aircraft over Bass Strait in Australia on October 21, 1978. Valentich radioed Melbourne Flight Service at 7:06 PM to report an unidentified aircraft was following him at 4,500 feet and was told there was no known traffic at that level. Valentich said he could see a large unknown aircraft which appeared to be illuminated by four bright landing lights. He was unable to confirm its type, but said it had passed about 1,000 feet (300 m) overhead and was moving at high speed. Valentich then reported that the aircraft was approaching him from the east and said the other pilot might be purposely toying with him. Valentich said the aircraft was "orbiting" above him and that it had a shiny metal surface and a green light on it. Valentich reported that he was experiencing engine problems. Asked to identify the aircraft, Valentich radioed, "It isn't an aircraft," when his transmission was interrupted by unidentified noise described as being "metallic, scraping sounds" before all contact was lost. No trace of Frederick or his aircraft was ever found.
[26] You can search the internet and read about the Oeschler situation. The C's were correct: "Semi" because it does seem that some real phenomena was going on in that case.

356 **A:** Yes.

357 **Q:** *(L)* Who was involved in that?

358 **A:** Grays.

359 **Q:** *(L)* Anyone else?

360 **A:** No, but government wants to use it as in "opportunity knocks." UFO per se was not staged. Guardian story was.

361 **Q:** *(L)* Was the UFO actually flown by aliens?

362 **A:** Yes. Government has miles of UFO footage in its possession. May use at its discretion.

363 **Q:** *(T)* What does it mean that the Guardian story was staged? How? Is the videotape real?

364 **A:** Used tape to concoct story around.

365 **Q:** *(T)* Did the individual calling himself Guardian actually film that?

366 **A:** No.

367 **Q:** *(T)* Who filmed it?

368 **A:** Military.

369 **Q:** *(T)* How did they know to be there in the middle of Ontario, Canada, to film that landing?

370 **A:** Landing took place near where regiment of NATO reservists were training.

371 **Q:** *(T)* Did it take place where they said it did?

372 **A:** Near.

373 **Q:** *(T)* Was the woman in the farmhouse part of the plot?

374 **A:** Saw UFO. Was part of "flap".

375 **Q:** *(T)* Was the UFO experience that the woman in the farmhouse had, was that the same event on the Guardian tape?

376 **A:** No. But similar.

377 **Q:** *(T)* So we have a woman who saw a UFO landing, had one that they had on tape, and when she came forward to talk about her sighting, they decided to use the footage to corroborate her story, is that correct?

378 **A:** Yes.

379 **Q:** *(T)* Did the woman know about the NATO maneuvers?

380 **A:** No.

381 **Q:** *(T)* Were the NATO maneuvers near where she was?

382 **A:** Yes. All major military exercises are plagued by UFOs.

383 **Q:** *(T)* Is the government planning to stage an invasion by aliens to cause the populace of the world to go into such a fear state that they will accept total control and domination?[27]

384 **A:** Open. But if so, will "flop".

385 **Q:** *(T)* Why?

386 **A:** Many reasons: 1. Visual effects will be inadequate and will have "glitches". 2. Real invasion may take place first. 3. Other events may intercede.

387 **Q:** *(T)* Such as what?

388 **A:** Earth changes.

389 **Q:** *(T)* Am I correct in assuming that some of these hot-shot, big-wig guys in the government who have plans for taking over the whole world and making everything all happy and hunky-dory with them in charge, are just simply not in synch with the fact that there are some definite Earth changes on the agenda? Are they missing something here?

390 **A:** Close. They are aware but in denial.

---

[27] *The Wave* 22

391 **Q:** *(T)* Are these Earth changes going to occur prior to the arrival of the cometary cluster?

392 **A:** No. But "time" frame is, as of yet, undetermined.

393 **Q:** *(T)* Am I correct in saying that if they knew what was really going to happen that they would still continue with their stupid little plans to make money and try to control the world?

394 **A:** Yes. Greed is a sickness.

395 **Q:** *(T)* Is there such a thing as 'Alternative 3,' the plan to take all the brains off the planet?

396 **A:** No.

397 **Q:** *(T)* Is that more disinformation?

398 **A:** Yes. So is Mars landing but not Mars monuments.

399 **Q:** *(TL)* Who made the monuments on Mars?

400 **A:** Atlanteans.

401 **Q:** *(T)* So, the Atlanteans had interplanetary ability?

402 **A:** Yes. With ease. Atlantean technology makes yours look like the Neanderthal era.

403 **Q:** *(T)* Who created the structures on the moon that Richard Hoagland has discovered?

404 **A:** Atlanteans.

405 **Q:** *(T)* What did they use these structures for?

406 **A:** Energy transfer points for crystalline power/symbolism as in monuments or statuary.

407 **Q:** *(T)* What statuary are you referring to?

408 **A:** Example is face.

409 **Q:** *(T)* What power did these crystals gather?

410 **A:** Sun.

411 **Q:** *(T)* Was it necessary for them to have power gathering stations on Mars and the moon. Did this increase their power?

412 **A:** Not necessary but it is not necessary for you to have a million dollars either. Get the correlation? Atlanteans were power hungry the way your society is money hungry.

413 **Q:** *(T)* Was the accumulation of this power what brought about their downfall?

414 **A:** Yes.

415 **Q:** *(T)* Did they lose control of this power?

416 **A:** It overpowered them the same way your computers will overpower you.

417 **Q:** *(V)* Is it similar to them gaining a life and intelligence of their own?

418 **A:** Yes.

419 **Q:** *(L)* You mean these crystalline structures came to life, so to speak?

420 **A:** Yes.

421 **Q:** *(L)* And then what did they do?

422 **A:** Destroyed Atlantis.

423 **Q:** *(L)* But I thought that Atlantis was destroyed because of the close passage of another body of the solar system?

424 **A:** Was damaged but recovered.

425 **Q:** *(L)* So Atlantis was damaged by a close passage of Mars or whatever and then recovered from that damage, is that correct?

426 **A:** Part of landmass, but not all, was destroyed.

427 **Q**: *(L)* So, how many separate destructions did Atlantis experience?

428 **A**: Three.

429 **Q**: *(L)* One was caused by the close passage of Mars?

430 **A**: Yes. And comets.

431 **Q**: *(L)* Were Mars and the comets loosely interactive?

432 **A**: Yes.

433 **Q**: *(L)* And the second was caused by what?

434 **A**: Venus.

435 **Q**: *(L)* And the third and final destruction was caused by what?

436 **A**: Crystals.

437 **Q**: *(T)* Are the crystals still active?

438 **A**: Bermuda triangle.

439 **Q**: *(L)* I thought that was a myth.

440 **A**: No.

441 **Q**: *(L)* And what does that crystal do? Is it continuously active?

442 **A**: No. Erratic.

443 **Q**: *(L)* Is it still active in the sense of being a conscious or sentient entity?

444 **A**: No.

445 **Q**: *(L)* What activates it?

446 **A**: Many factors.

447 **Q**: *(L)* And when it is activated, what does it do?

448 **A**: Transdimensional window is blasted open.

449 **Q**: *(L)* Say a person was sailing along in the Bermuda Triangle and the window was blasted open and these people passed through or were engulfed in it or whatever, in what condition would they find themselves?

450 **A**: Something akin to suspended animation.

451 **Q**: *(L)* Would they be conscious of their state of suspended animation or would their consciousness also be suspended?

452 **A**: Either or.

453 **Q**: *(L)* Do they stay in this state forever, or do they come back out, or do they come out somewhere else?

454 **A**: Open. All are possible. Same thing happened to Philadelphia Experiment participants.

455 **Q**: *(L)* If an individual were in this interdimensional state of suspended animation, does this mean they are stuck there forever?

456 **A**: Maybe.

457 **Q**: *(L)* Can they not die, is that what you are saying?

458 **A**: To them they may perceive something like waiting for millions of years.

459 **Q**: *(L)* Is there no one or no way to rescue them from this state?

460 **A**: Why do you think those sailors were hopelessly insane?[28]

461 **Q**: *(L)* Besides the crystal in the Bermuda Triangle, are any of the others still active?

462 **A**: Yes.

463 **Q**: *(T)* Does the government know about them?

464 **A**: Semi.

465 **Q**: *(L)* Where are the others located?

466 **A**: Off Japan; in Brazil; in Ural mountains of Russia; North and South Poles.

---

[28]The Philadelphia Experiment.

467 Q: *(T)* Are the ones on the moon and Mars active also?

468 A: Yes.

469 Q: *(V)* Are they responsible for any of the earthquakes like the one in Japan?

470 A: Yes.

471 Q: *(L)* If one crystal is found and the technology is deciphered, and another is found, does it increase the power...

472 A: Let us answer this way: If Neanderthals found a 747 would they know how to use it?

473 Q: *(L)* What were the physical dimensions of these crystals and were they cut or naturally grown?

474 A: Varied. Were synthetic.

475 Q: *(L)* Were they faceted?

476 A: Yes.

477 Q: *(L)* In their faceting, what was the general configuration?

478 A: Pyramid.

479 Q: *(L)* Was that an absolute pyramid with the same proportions as say, the Great Pyramid at Gizeh?

480 A: Close.

481 Q: *(L)* How large was the largest from base to apex?

482 A: 5000 feet.

483 Q: *(L)* What was the average size?

484 A: 500 feet.

485 Q: *(L)* And was the one that was 5,000 feet tall, is that one still in existence?

486 A: Yes.

487 Q: *(L)* Where is that one located?

488 A: 380 miles due East of you?

489 Q: *(L)* Some years ago a pilot reported seeing a pyramid near there in the water...

490 A: That is just the top sticking out of the ocean floor. It is 90 per cent buried.

491 Q: *(V)* In meditation, I saw crystals coming up during Earth changes. Is this what is going to happen?

492 A: Yes.

493 Q: *(L)* How come this crystal didn't shatter or break up during the subsidence of Atlantis?

494 A: Extraordinarily strong. An atomic bomb would not shatter it. The chain reaction of a thermonuclear explosion would be absorbed into the crystal and transferred into pure energy. That relates to the design function.

495 Q: *(L)* And then what would happen?

496 A: Energy dispersal unless focused as engineered by the Atlanteans.

497 Q: *(L)* Where did they get this technology?

498 A: They evolved it.

499 Q: *(L)* They invented it themselves?

500 A: Yes.

501 Q: *(L)* Did they interact with any aliens?

502 A: Yes.

503 Q: *(L)* Did they get any help at all from these extraterrestrials?

504 A: Yes.

505 Q: *(L)* And who were these aliens?

506 A: Lizards.

507 Q: *(L)* What kind of power frequency did these crystals use?

508 A: Full range.

509 **Q:** *(T)* How many of the crystals have been discovered by the governments of the world?

510 **A:** All.

511 **Q:** *(T)* Are they trying to use them?

512 **A:** Pointlessly.

513 **Q:** *(T)* Are they trying?

514 **A:** Maybe.

515 **Q:** *(T)* Is that why they backed off from the moon and stopped the space program?

516 **A:** No. Government doesn't understand technology.

517 **Q:** *(T)* Have they backed off from their activities on the moon?

518 **A:** Open.

519 **Q:** *(T)* Are the crystals on Mars why they want to get there so badly?

520 **A:** Yes.

521 **Q:** *(T)* Because of the crystals or because of what is stored in the monuments?

522 **A:** Neither.

523 **Q:** *(T)* Why do they want to get to Mars?

524 **A:** Explore.

525 **Q:** *(T)* Are the top echelons of the human race all the fools that they seem?

526 **A:** Subjective.

527 **Q:** *(L)* Can we utilize that crystalline shape to generate electricity?

528 **A:** Possible and has been done.

529 **Q:** *(L)* Is it complicated?

530 **A:** Yes.

531 **Q:** *(L)* What effect does wearing hematite have on the physical body?

532 **A:** Open.

533 **Q:** *(V)* What about this fellow Stephenson?

534 **A:** If all parties have faith in it.

535 **Q:** *(V)* Did Laura receive healing on her heart today?

536 **A:** Yes.

537 **Q:** *(V)* Where did Stephenson get his information?

538 **A:** Read it.

539 **Q:** *(L)* Jan has asked about doing a spirit release.

540 **A:** Okay.

541 **Q:** *(L)* She wants to know how many attachments she has.

542 **A:** Three. Two positive. One negative.

543 **Q:** *(L)* Terry?

544 **A:** Four 3/1.

545 **Q:** *(L)* How did they get them?

546 **A:** Find out.

547 **Q:** *(L)* Earlier the suggestion was made to hypnotize Terry. Is that what they are saying we should do?

548 **A:** Yes.

549 **Q:** *(T)* Can I trust Jerry?

550 **A:** Maybe.

551 **Q:** *(T)* Does Commodore Kirk die at the end of the movie? *(V)* Does *X-Files* have the Lizzie influence?

552 **A:** No.

553 **Q:** *(T)* Does *X-Files* tell the people what they need to hear?

554 **A:** Yes.

End of session.

November 24, 1994

The reader may wish to refer back to the 9 October 1994 session where we had asked some questions about the Karla Turner case written about in the book *Into the Fringe*. During the course of the discussion, the C's had warned that Karla should be "Careful driving alone to lectures and meetings." At the end of this session, the C's had spontaneously said: "We are trying to contact Karla Turner's son's former roommate. But he is resisting. She does not realize the extreme importance. Communicate this to her now please Laura." I had printed out all the sessions up to, and including, that session and sent it to her by snail mail. (Not everybody was on the Net then!) When there were additional questions in session 25 October 1994, I forwarded that to her as well. Karla wrote back:

> "Thank you again for sharing your work and information with me. The entire situation is very intriguing to me as a researcher, and I wish I were able to personally investigate it. But of course, from this distance, that isn't possible. I would like to see the dynamics of your involvement in this, along with the others, and understand the development of the scenario: the changes in individual alien activity, the internal changes in values, perspective, motivation, etc., the evolution of each of your ideas about the entire alien scenario. And I'm very interested in the channeling, especially since doing the research that has resulted in my latest book, *Masquerade of Angels*. I've enclosed a flier...
>
> "In the channeling sessions, I saw that you sometimes tried to elicit information which could actually be checked out, in addition to all the unverifiable 'data' the channel delivered. And as you also saw, with the information about the two missing boys in South Carolina, the channel proved to be either wrong or a liar. If the channel gave you false information once, on something you could verify, then I hope you are no longer willing to believe anything else it delivers at face value. Instead, I'm hoping you are concentrating on understanding the mechanism and motivation of whatever is giving you the info. Some of the things I've heard elsewhere (although I haven't personally verified the reports) point to the possibility that our human military/intelligence folks have technology that allows the broadcast of 'channeled' info to a person in

some manner — perhaps through a human-installed implant or the use of mind-altering or mind-activating electronics. So that has to be one possibility.

"And even if the info is coming from an 'alien,' there should still be plenty of skepticism on your part, I would think. We know very well that the aliens have no problem appearing in 3-D reality to us, so why the need for remote channeling at all? Or if the channels are indeed discarnate spirits, presumably with access to a wider time-space continuum, why would they deliver false information? All it takes is one confirmed lie to make the rest of the data unreliable, and you now have that. [..]

"As far as your situation and the info you've shared, please let me know what, if anything, you would like for me to do, and I'll see if it's possible to be of help. ... I would very much like to meet with you in person, and I'll let you know if [I will be in your area].

"I care very much about your situation, about all our situations, and I realize that we are all seeking truths that are constantly eluding us. But we'd better get educated as quickly as possible, and I'll assist you in any way I can and in turn will be grateful for help from you, too." (Signature, etc.)

This began a correspondence between us that went on for a little while, and then... silence. I had no way of knowing that Karla had been diagnosed with cancer in early 1995. It was only in late 1995 (November 23) that we were back in touch again. She was dead in less than two months after that (January 10, 1996). I can't help but think that the C's warnings to her in the Fall of 1994 were some sort of reflection of the danger she was in. In her last email to me she wrote:

> "The medical treatment I'm pursuing occurs daily, in this phase of the therapy, and we have to travel several hours a day to take care of it, so I really don't have a free moment other than maybe 15 minutes a day to check my email. ... I'll look forward to your updates. This adventure keeps on rolling, doesn't it? Hold tight to your loved ones, and make sure the seat belts are on! With my love and good wishes for your journey."

In any event, the following session begins with a discussion of the letter I had just received where Karla insisted that what the C's had said about the two little boys in South Caroline was an outright *lie*, which was not, in fact, the case, though as long as we are stuck in black-and-white thinking and not really considering elements of higher-density contact and the difficulties of transducing and translating such material, it might appear that way.

Participants: 'Frank' and Laura

Q: *(L)* Hello.

A: Greetings.

Q: *(L)* Who do we have with us tonight?

A: Peehmi.

Q: *(L)* Have you ever lived on Earth?

A: No. There is little need to ask question each time as this is now grooved channel.

Q: *(L)* Does that mean that the vibrations have been adjusted for you specifically and that others cannot utilize it?

A: Cannot unless you request.

Q: *(L)* Are you aware of the letter I got today from Karla Turner?

A: We are Cassiopaean.

Q: *(L)* Does that mean that you are aware?

A: We are aware of your entire life aura.

Q: *(L)* What caused her to react to the channeled information the way she did? Obviously something upset her. What was it?

A: Miffed by personal references; suspicious of motives; send her this session verbatim.[1]

Q: *(L)* Well, OK, what would you say to her... obviously she thinks you, as a source, were caught in a lie and that put her off. What can you say in response to that accusation, I guess you would call it?

A: There are no lies.

Q: *(L)* Well, obviously that is something that can be said, but she thinks that since you did not come right out and describe everything in precise detail about those two little boys in South Carolina, that what little you did say, she interpreted as a lie. What else is going on here that...

A: There are no lies only interpretations.

Q: *(L)* Is it important for her to receive information from this source?

A: It is important for all on planet to learn at their own pace.

Q: *(L)* Is Karla's pace slower?

A: Apples and Oranges.

Q: *(L)* I would like to address the issue of accuracy. How can we increase or determine or work on accuracy?

A: Accuracy is 3rd level concept.

Q: *(L)* Well, you do understand that at this level we determine whether information is correct or good by whether it happens or comes true, particularly in terms of prognostications.

A: Yes.

Q: *(L)* And if a source misses on a prognostication, very often people lose faith in that source. Is that an unrealistic expectation?

A: Yes.

Q: *(L)* Is that because accuracy is an impossible task because of variability of reality?

A: If it were possible there would be no existence. The universe is nothing more than a learning laboratory.

Q: *(L)* OK, well, at this point I am wondering if there is any point in writing to Karla and sharing our information with her at all?

A: Of course. You are all learning. Share information to learn more faster.

---

[1] I did, and our correspondence continued for a bit as noted above.

33 **Q:** *(L)* Is there anything that can be said to her to help her in a positive way?

34 **A:** Have empathy. She was raised to put others before herself.

35 **Q:** *(L)* Well, OK, tell us about this, with the existing probabilities, will Terry and Jan be with us this coming Saturday?

36 **A:** Yes. But up to you. Ask and you shall receive.[2]

37 **Q:** *(L)* Jan was telling me that Terry's friends Shannon and Sara have bought into MF's thesis that I am the wicked witch of the west. Is this true?[3]

38 **A:** Yes.

39 **Q:** *(L)* Why is MF doing this?

40 **A:** Same as all other; this is a self serving, ego dominated world.

41 **Q:** *(L)* Is there any particular viciousness in him toward me, inspired for any particular reason?

42 **A:** Some, because of your sex references.

43 **Q:** *(L)* He is mad because I identified his motivations toward Scarlett as being sexually inspired? Was this true?

44 **A:** Yes. But truth hurts.

45 **Q:** *(L)* Can you tell us about this recent volcanic eruption? What was the cause?[4]

46 **A:** "Heating up" of Earth.

47 **Q:** *(L)* What is causing it to heat up?

48 **A:** Vibrational frequency changes.[5]

49 **Q:** *(L)* What is the source of these vibrational frequency changes?

50 **A:** Oncoming wave as we have told you before.

51 **Q:** *(L)* This oncoming wave, is this a wave which is so large or so vast that its effects are felt many years in advance of its absolute arrival point?

52 **A:** All waves in nature have a "contract" phase.

53 **Q:** *(L)* Does that mean like just before a wave comes up on shore it kind of sucks everything out?

54 **A:** Yes.

55 **Q:** *(L)* So we are in the sucking back phase [demonstrates with hand motion and sound effects].

56 **A:** Cute analogy.

57 **Q:** *(L)* Back in 1981 and 1982, my daughter A___[6] frequently saw something outside her window that she described as an alligator, and she would wake up screaming and we would get up and, on one occasion we saw what seemed to be a figure standing in a corner by the closet. The whole series of events ended up with my having a dream in which I confronted a dragon...[7]

58 **A:** Lizard.

---

[2] We did and they were.
[3] Good ole MF! UFO investigator extraordinaire, whacko, and sexual predator!
[4] Rabaul Volcano on the tip of the Gazelle Peninsula in East New Britain, Papua New Guinea. *The Wave* 1
[5] Interesting reference to 'global warming,' though certainly not in the context that Al Gore has propagated in his disinformation campaign to cover up Earth changes.
[6] All of my four daughter's names begin with the letter A. In this case, I was talking about my eldest. See *Amazing Grace* for details.
[7] *High Strangeness* 9

59 **Q:** *(L)* What were they doing at that time?

60 **A:** Scoping.

61 **Q:** *(L)* What did they discover from their scoping?

62 **A:** Potential abductees.

63 **Q:** *(L)* And did they abduct anyone at that time?

64 **A:** No.

65 **Q:** *(L)* Why didn't they?

66 **A:** You stopped it.

67 **Q:** *(L)* How did I stop it?

68 **A:** Knowledge is rooted in awareness.

69 **Q:** *(L)* So, my awareness is what stopped it?

70 **A:** Close.

71 **Q:** *(L)* When I had the dream about doing battle with the dragon, was that just a dream, an astral event, or an actual interaction with the Lizzies?

72 **A:** All three.

73 **Q:** *(L)* And what was their reaction to encountering my resistance to them?

74 **A:** Disappointment.

75 **Q:** *(L)* Have they tried to harass us since then?

76 **A:** Yes.

77 **Q:** *(L)* Have they succeeded on any of those occasions subsequent to that?

78 **A:** Yes.

79 **Q:** *(L)* In what way?

80 **A:** Alice.

81 **Q:** *(L)* Through my mother?

82 **A:** Yes.

83 **Q:** *(L)* Did they abduct her?

84 **A:** Garbled her emotions.[8]

85 **Q:** *(L)* Is that their best shot so far?

86 **A:** Yes.

87 **Q:** *(L)* Can it get worse?

88 **A:** It can always get worse.

89 **Q:** *(L)* So we just have to stay on our toes at all times?

90 **A:** Absolutely don't let others distract you. You have suffered many attempts at distraction away from truth. Now follow some proclamations: Pause. All there is is lessons. This is one infinite school. There is no other reason for anything to exist. Even inanimate matter learns it is all an "Illusion." Each individual possesses all of creation within their minds. Now, contemplate for a moment. Each soul is all powerful and can create or destroy all existence if know how. You and us and all others are interconnected by our mutual possession of all there is. You may create alternative universes if you wish and dwell within. You are all a duplicate of the universe within which you dwell. Your mind represents all that exists. It is "fun" to see how much you can access.[9]

91 **Q:** *(L)* It's fun for who to see how much we can access?

92 **A:** All. Challenges are fun. Where do you think the limit of your mind is?[10]

93 **Q:** *(L)* Where?

---

[8]It was a very traumatic time I went through when my mother became almost a complete stranger to me. Again, see *Amazing Grace* for details.

[9]Another statement describing something like a Universal Information Field.

[10]*The Wave* 12, 25

94 **A:** We asked you.

95 **Q:** *(L)* Well, I guess there is no limit.

96 **A:** If there is no limit, then what is the difference between your own mind and everything else?

97 **Q:** *(L)* Well, I guess there is no difference if all is ultimately one.

98 **A:** Right. And when two things each have absolutely no limits, they are precisely the same thing.

99 **Q:** *(L)* Is this all you are going to give for tonight?

100 **A:** Open. Can give more another time.

101 **Q:** *(L)* My husband wants to know why his ears have been ringing constantly.

102 **A:** Lizard move.

103 **Q:** *(L)* Why is this Lizard move causing his ears to ring?

104 **A:** They concentrate on those who are not protected or less protected by knowledge.

105 **Q:** *(L)* What can he do to stop this?

106 **A:** Open mind then learn.

107 **Q:** *(L)* And if he doesn't, what would be the result?

108 **A:** Further attack.

109 **Q:** *(L)* The other night when Terry and Jan were here and we were getting ready to sit down at the board, I had a sudden sharp pain in my left ear unlike anything I have ever had. It was three sharp jabs. What was that?

110 **A:** Electrical nerve surge.

111 **Q:** *(L)* What caused that?

112 **A:** DNA changing.

---

[11] *The Wave* 18

113 **Q:** *(L)* Well, [my daughter] A___ now has the ubiquitous pain in the shoulder. Is this because her DNA is changing?

114 **A:** Yes.

115 **Q:** *(L)* You said that each soul is all powerful and could create or destroy all existence... does this mean that an individual could create or destroy all of existence for all others?

116 **A:** Yes. But more complex than that will explain further another session.

117 **Q:** *(L)* If we were to ask specific questions, technically speaking, would you be able to tell us how to build a time machine or transdimensional transporter of some sort?

118 **A:** Yes. But where are you going to get all the hardware?

119 **Q:** *(L)* Well, I didn't say I was going to do it, I just wanted to know if you could tell us how.

120 **Q:** *(L)* Is there anything in a few words that you want to tell us before we end tonight?[11]

121 **A:** Network but be careful with whom.

122 **Q:** *(L)* Is anyone going to drop into our lives imminently who is going to help us with this?

123 **A:** Wait and see. Just beginning.

124 **Q:** *(L)* We thank you for all your help tonight. Are we going to receive spontaneous information regularly like we did tonight?

125 **A:** Occasionally when vibrations are right. Vibrations suggest invite Rodemerks. Energy is better with them.

126 **Q:** *(L)* When V___ is with us, would it be helpful for her to stand behind us and give Reiki while we work the board?

A: If you wish.

Q: *(L)* I get the feeling that means it doesn't really matter.

A: Open. Goodnight.

End of Session.

November 26, 1994

Terry and Jan were quite excited about their first interaction with the C's in the 19 November session, so they were back a week later for this one. It's long and goes in many directions and there is a definite shift in tone and information that can be detected with the addition of T&J. In general, it was beneficial energy but they did tend to get off on tangents sometimes. Nevertheless, some of the funniest moments in channeling history are due to Terry's comments. In this session, even Terry's digressions turn into insteresting discussions about the nature of 4th density. And finally, the session turns to the metaphoric nature of the communication and the problems with date-anchored predictions. All in all, a rich session.

Participants: 'Frank' and Laura, Terry and Jan

1 **Q**: Hello.

2 **A**: Thank you for altering the board.[1] We worked on your psyches to get you to do that.

3 **Q**: *(L)* Well, you didn't have to work on our psyches to get us to do it. It makes things faster for us too. We wanted to do it.

4 **A**: Everything is interactive when it comes to the "collective mind."

5 **Q**: *(T)* 'Endword' is for the end of every word not for the end of the sentence, so we can break the words up without having to do it... *(J)* I don't need it...

A: You will know the words as they come out.[2]

6

7 **Q**: *(L)* Now for the questions...

A: Who am I Laura? You are slipping.

8

9 **Q**: *(L)* Well, you told me last time that I didn't have to ask every time. OK, who do we have with us tonight?

A: Fun.

10

11 **Q**: *(L)* Your name is fun?

A: Silly.

12

13 **Q**: *(T)* We're being silly or we're just going to have a fun silly evening?

A: Laura needs to lighten up a bit.

14

---

[1] We had installed more punctuation marks. Our board now contains the following punctuation marks: quote, period, comma, colon, semicolon, exclamation mark, question mark, slash, equal sign, plus sign.

[2] We never used anything to indicate word separation because things just went too fast. It was impractical.

15 **Q:** *(L)* OK, can we have your name, please?

16 **A:** Murean.

17 **Q:** *(L)* [Attempt to pronounce] Glad to have you with us, Murean.

18 **A:** Accent on 2nd syllable.

19 **Q:** *(T)* Well, tonight we have Laura, Frank, and Terry on the board and Jan transcribing. Is this OK?

20 **A:** Of course, Terry.

21 **Q:** *(T)* Thank you.

22 **A:** You are welcome.

23 **Q:** *(T)* Something I noticed from last Saturday night: what you need is the energy from us in order to make the board work. It's not necessary that one or...

24 **A:** You add energy.

25 **Q:** *(T)* I personally add energy?

26 **A:** And Jan.

27 **Q:** *(L)* Just by being here? *(T)* Well, I don't want to feel that I am usurping V___'s position...

28 **A:** V___ is at earlier stage in learning process, so less energy.[3]

29 **Q:** *(L)* Well, V___ is part of the group and is learning along with the rest of us, and we are all at different stages in one way or another. She has a great gift of healing which is definitely needed in the group. *(T)* And LM[4] is a fisherman.

30 **A:** V___ is more emotional like a "Gemini" lover. She gives better Reiki because she has this emotional power.[5]

31 **Q:** *(T)* Well, I just don't want her to have hurt feelings or think that she is being replaced if I sit in.

32 **A:** Lighten up Terry.

33 **Q:** *(J)* I had a dream where I had vines growing out of my hair. I walked past a mirror and saw this and said, "I'm going to have to get rid of this stuff!" Is there some significance to this dream?

34 **A:** None.

35 **Q:** *(J)* What causes my sinus problems?

36 **A:** Emotional repression.[6]

37 **Q:** *(J)* Of what?

38 **A:** Feelings. Taught to be nondemonstrative in childhood.

39 **Q:** *(J)* There was a lot of repression of thought processes and creativity in my house as I was growing up. So what can I do to help my sinuses?

---

[3] This was another of the numerous subtle hints about V___ being disruptive. I was attributing this to Frank feeling ill-at-ease in her presence because she had challenged him on sexual issues a number of time. Frank was very anti-sex and V___ was very pro-sex and I had the impression that she would 'jump Frank's bones' if he would let her. I think he had that impression too, which was why he wasn't pleased when she attended the sessions.

[4] My husband at the time.

[5] I'm not entirely sure what the C's intended by "Gemini lover" except perhaps that Geminis are famed for romantic inconstancy, numerous affairs, serial and simultaneous.

[6] Something we have learned over the years is that many, if not most, physical conditions, are due to some kind of psychological or emotional blockage. See Gabor Mate's book *When The Body Says No* for insights.

40 **A**: Go out and smash a few flower pots. [Much laughter] Seriously. Harmless to others.[7]

41 **Q**: *(T)* Well there is a whole bunch of them out there. *(J)* Should I identify the things I am angry at and name the flower pots as I smash them?

42 **A**: If she wants to. We suggested flower pots because you have a surplus. [Laughter]

43 **Q**: *(T)* We do, big time! [Someone suggests shooting them]

44 **A**: Guns can cause harm unless extremely careful.

45 **Q**: *(J)* Why was Terry's mom so afraid of her cataract operation recently and why has she not yet healed and what can she do? *(T)* Too many questions. My mother just had a cataract operation and several other people in the family all had the same operation and all of them healed correctly and quickly. She is not healing correctly and she's scared to death that she is going to lose the sight in that eye. She was scared to death of this operation and she has had other operations which did not scare her.

46 **A**: Too many thought patterns.

47 **Q**: Why was she scared of this operation?

48 **A**: Her nature to be scared.

49 **Q**: *(J)* She claims that she has never been frightened of any other operation.

50 **A**: Incorrect.

51 **Q**: Is the eye going to heal?

52 **A**: If she changes her thoughts.

53 **Q**: *(L)* Have you given her Reiki in her eye? *(J)* No. *(T)* Well, go over there and do it this week some time.

54 **A**: Not recommended. She will resist strongly.

55 **Q**: *(L)* Is there anything Terry or Jan can do... *(J)* or what can she do...

56 **A**: Her lesson, not yours. Please limit inquiries of a personal nature.

57 **Q**: *(T)* It's a free will universe and they can't tell us. See, I read the book!

58 **A**: Good job, Terry. [Laughter]

59 **Q**: *(T)* I'm slow learning, but I do get the lessons eventually.

60 **A**: Not so slow.

61 **Q**: *(L)* Can we at least ask what kind of spirit animals Jan and Terry would have?

62 **A**: Jan, mouse. Terry, snake. [Laughter]

63 **Q**: *(T)* Does my snake totem refer to something about lizards or dragons?

64 **A**: No. You have been told that.

65 **Q**: *(T)* Well, I like dragons because I am into fantasy books. I'm not really crazy about lizards.

66 **A**: Dungeons and...

67 **Q**: *(T) Dungeons & Dragons*, one of my favorite games. Since I like Dungeons and Dragons, and kind of have this thing for that sort of thing...

68 **A**: We know.

69 **Q**: *(T)* We all have our hobbies. Why do I feel that there is a connection in my life to bladed weapons? What is the

---

[7]Finding a safe way to express anger is exactly what Gabor talks about in his book as the best solution to regaining balance in your life if you suffer from many physical problems.

root of my liking for the medieval games and so forth?

A: Swords. Was killed by pirate in 1713.

Q: *(T)* Why was I killed by a pirate in 1713? *(L)* Because you were there. *(T)* Wrong place at the wrong time!

A: Close enough.

Q: *(L)* What was his name in that lifetime?

A: George Caldwell. Lived in Plymouth, England. Occupation: Navy.

Q: *(L)* Who were the group of pirates that he encountered that took his life?

A: British cutthroats.

Q: *(T)* What was my rank?

A: Leftenant.

Q: *(T)* What was the name of the ship?

A: HMS Siderail.

Q: *(T)* What type of a ship was that?

A: Schooner.

Q: *(T)* So, it was not a military ship, then?

A: Yes.

Q: *(T)* Well, it was not a fighting ship. *(LM)* They never used schooners for fighting ships.[8]

A: Yes. Commandeered, LM. [Laughter]

Q: *(T)* The British Navy commandeered this schooner?

A: Yes.

Q: *(T)* Is this listed in British Admiralty records anywhere? Is any of this recorded?

A: No. Covered up.

Q: *(T)* Are there still records about the navy personnel?

A: Yes. Go to London. Contact New Scotland Yard for access.

Q: *(T)* Who captained the schooner?

A: Ian Miller of Plymouth.

Q: *(L)* Was Terry married?

A: No.

Q: *(T)* How old was I when I died?

A: 23.

Q: *(T)* Did I have fun up to that point?

A: Open.

Q: *(J)* Can you tell me about a specific game I played when I was in junior high school with other girls, specifically Margaret S?

A: Margaret's basement appears very dark. Candles or pinpoints of light. Words spoken in "ritual" fashion.

Q: *(F)* What did you do? *(J)* Yes. *(L)* You're kidding? *(J)* No. *(F)* What did you do? *(J)* [Laughs]

A: We are seeing scene you speak of in present "time". It is difficult to interpret as there seems to be an effort to "cloak" activities from others in a somewhat "sneaky" fashion. But, it appears to be an effort to influence events or cast "spells".

Q: *(L)* Were you? *(J)* Um hmm. *(L)* Did it work?

A: Open.

Q: *(J)* You cannot get any specifics on this regarding words?

A: We can't decipher.

---

[8] My ex had entered the room at this point and contributed this.

109 **Q:** *(J)* If I concentrated on it more?

110 **A:** Maybe.

111 **Q:** *(T)* Do you have something you want to share with us without us asking questions?

112 **A:** Clear vibrations. There is much interference at this time.

113 **Q:** *(T)* What is the source of that interference?

114 **A:** Many and varied.

115 **Q:** *(L)* Is it our tenseness or expectation about getting those words that created static?

116 **A:** Partly. But remember, the primary point of this communication is to bring information to all that is of universal importance as opposed to personal exercises and data. We want to clarify and expand upon previous statement. It is alright if you would prefer to use this forum for personal data and gain, because that is of free will. However, if you would like this connection to retain its strength and, in fact, increase, then it would be wise to limit personal inquiries because that is of the service to self realm and that realm is limiting and will eventually lead to contamination by forces that are oriented toward service to self, unlike this one.

117 **Q:** *(L)* I'm tired. Do you guys really need me here?

118 **A:** "The more the merrier."

119 **Q:** *(L)* Can I ask my question now?

120 **A:** Okay, Laura. Go for it.

121 **Q:** *(L)* The other night we were talking about the 'mark of Cain' and I lost part of the tape. I would like to go back over that a little bit more at this time. What was the true event behind the story of the 'mark of Cain'?

122 **A:** Advent of jealousy.[9]

123 **Q:** *(L)* What occurred to allow jealousy to enter into human interaction?

124 **A:** Lizard takeover.

125 **Q:** *(L)* Wasn't the Lizard takeover an event that occurred at the time of the Fall of Eden?

126 **A:** Yes.

127 **Q:** *(L)* Was this story of Cain and Abel part of that takeover?

128 **A:** Symbolism of story.

129 **Q:** *(L)* This was symbolic of the Lizzie takeover, the advent of jealousy, and the attitude of brother against brother, is that correct?

130 **A:** Partly. The mark of Cain means the "jealousy factor" of change facilitated by Lizard takeover of Earth's vibrational frequency. Knot on spine is physical residue of DNA restriction deliberately added by Lizards. See?

131 **Q:** *(L)* OK, Jan is going to move her hand up my back and you tell her when to stop at the 'knot.'

132 **A:** Okay.

133 **Q:** *(L)* You mean the occipital ridge?

134 **A:** Yes.[10]

135 **Q:** *(L)* What was the configuration of the spine and skull prior to this addition?[11]

136 **A:** Spine had no ridge there. Jealousy emanates from there, you can even feel it.

---

[9] *High Strangeness* 10; *The Wave* 3, 68
[10] See session 7 November 1994 for previous discussion and my notes.
[11] *High Strangeness* 10

137 **Q:** *(L)* Do any of these emotions that we have talked about that were generated by DNA breakdown, were any of these related to what Carl Sagan discusses when he talks about the 'Reptilian Brain'?

138 **A:** In a roundabout way.

139 **Q:** *(L)* OK, at the time this 'mark of Cain' came about, were there other humans on the planet that did not have this configuration?

140 **A:** It was added to all simultaneously.

141 **Q:** *(L)* How did they physically go about performing this act? What was the mechanism of this event, the nuts and bolts of it?

142 **A:** Are you ready? DNA core is as yet undiscovered enzyme relating to carbon. Light waves were used to cancel the first ten factors of DNA by burning them off. At that point, a number of physical changes took place including knot at top of spine. Each of these is equally reflected in the ethereal.

143 **Q:** *(L)* Is that all?

144 **A:** No. But, do you need more?

145 **Q:** *(L)* Well, the question I do have is, how many people were there on the planet and did they have to take each one and do this individually?[12]

146 **A:** Whoa.

147 **Q:** *(L)* How many people?

148 **A:** 6 billion.

149 **Q:** *(T)* That's 500 million more than there are now.

150 **A:** No, 200 million.

151 **Q:** *(L)* OK, there were this many people on the planet, how did they effect this change on all of them?

152 **A:** Light wave alteration.[13]

153 **Q:** *(L)* And light waves, actual light waves, affect DNA?

154 **A:** Yes.

155 **Q:** *(T)* What was the origin of the light waves?

156 **A:** Our center.

157 **Q:** *(L)* What is your center?

158 **A:** Our realm. STO.

159 **Q:** *(L)* So, how did the Lizzies use the light from the service to others realm...

---

[12] I was having a hard time understanding this because I knew almost nothing about cosmic rays and how even they can affect DNA, nor did I have any knowledge about how virii can also be used to mass-manipulate DNA by the simple release/arrival of a pathogen to which the population has no immunity.

[13] *The Wave* 3, 68

[14] Keeping in mind that 'Lizzie technology' can be something that appears to be quite natural in our realm. All of this may simply refer to the solar system traveling around the galaxy in tandem with it's sun. We simply don't know what different regions of space are like or what they contain.

Further, as to whether or not light can change DNA, it seems that it can according to recent research. First, in a study published in the *Journal of Physical Chemistry* by London Imperial College Department of Chemistry, the idea of micro gravitational forces forming matter out of wave patterns was observed. Dr. Sergey Leikin placed different types of DNA in a salt water solution, and differentiated the various strands by coloring them. Remarkably, the colored DNA were drawn to one

160 **A**: They used sophisticated technology to interrupt light frequency waves.[14]

161 **Q**: *(L)* Well, what I am getting out of this that you are saying from what you are not saying is that it was almost like,... well, was there a battle and you guys lost?

162 **A**: Yes.

163 **Q**: *(L)* Is this the same battle that the Pleiadians talk about?

164 **A**: Yes.

165 **Q**: *(T)* Not to go off on a tangent, but I have only come into this recently, you are the Cassiopaeans?

166 **A**: Yes.

167 **Q**: *(T)* Are you also the Pleiadians?

168 **A**: No.

169 **Q**: *(T)* Are you connected to the Pleiadians?

170 **A**: Yes and so are others.[15]

171 **Q**: *(T)* You are all the family of light?

172 **A**: Yes. Exactly. You have been "doing your homework".

173 **Q**: *(T)* I'm trying to. Now, another force in what we term as the past, defeated you and used the power of the light in order to alter us in different ways, is this correct?

174 **A**: Yes. Now understand this: It is all part of natural grand cycle.[16]

175 **Q**: *(L)* If this is all a part of a natural grand cycle, and correct me if I am wrong here, it almost seems as if you guys, the 'good guys,' and the other 'bad' guys, that you just really kind of go at it just for fun, is that true?[17]

176 **A**: No.

177 **Q**: *(L)* But you say it is a natural thing or part of a natural grand cycle. Is this natural grand cycle just part of the interaction between light and darkness and another moving very far distances to find the corresponding matches, and in time every DNA strand was paired up correctly. Although Dr. Leikin equated the phenomenon with possible electrical charges, other research revealed that gravity was the likely culprit.

In an astonishing experiment performed by Nobel Prize winner Dr. Luc Montagnier, DNA was randomly created out of nothing but sterilized water. The experiment used two separate sealed test tubes, one containing sterilized water and the other carrying both sterilized water and DNA. After electrifying both tubes and letting the tubes sit for eighteen hours, Dr. Montagnier was surprised to see that the tube that had originally contained nothing but water had produced tiny DNA strands. This was a shock for many reasons, mainly because water only contains hydrogen and oxygen and a DNA molecule is much more complex. How could something like this possibly happen? It seemed as though the DNA had "teleported" from one tube to the other, like they were connected by an unknown force. Another study shows that UV light actively changes DNA. See: http://news.discovery.com/human/health/how-the-sun-changes-your-skin-140702.htm So the idea that light can change DNA is not so far-fetched.

[15] *The Wave* 65
[16] *Secret History* 12; *The Wave* 3, 26, 68
[17] *High Strangeness* 10

which just simply must be?

178 **A**: Yes. We are at "front line" of universe's natural system of balance. That is where one rises to before reaching total union of "The One". 6th level.

179 **Q**: *(L)* Do you like being at 6th level?

180 **A**: Do you like being at 3rd level?

181 **Q**: *(L)* Frankly no, I don't. *(T)* If you answer the question by asking the question, and we know that we are striving to reach higher, does this mean there are more levels above 6th level?

182 **A**: Yes. One.

183 **Q**: *(L)* Is that union with the one?

184 **A**: Yes.

185 **Q**: *(T)* Now, the battle you had with the other side...

186 **A**: Are having.

187 **Q**: *(T)* This battle goes on... do you have the light power back?

188 **A**: Never lost it, you did.

189 **Q**: *(T)* OK, I guess that for us the Lizzies are the main force even though they have others on their side...

190 **A**: Yes.

191 **Q**: *(T)* They took our light, not yours?

192 **A**: Not against you. Currently in union with you.

193 **Q**: *(T)* So we are but one battle in the universe in an overall, ongoing struggle?[18]

194 **A**: Yes. Balance is natural. Remember, it's all just lessons in the grand cycle.

195 **Q**: *(L)* I am really curious... when you guys and the Lizzies 'go to it,' what do you do? I mean, you obviously don't shoot guns at each other and you don't have tanks...

196 **A**: Too complicated for you to possibly understand because you are not at 4th level yet.

197 **Q**: *(J)* When you are fighting, is it any way at all possible for us to detect the battle?

198 **A**: First: We don't "fight." Second, yes; it's nature as in meteorology and Earth changes.

199 **Q**: *(T)* Your form of confrontation takes the form of physical changes in the atmosphere and environment of the planet?

200 **A**: And in space.

201 **Q**: *(T)* But that is how we detect it? The more activity, the more conflict is going on?

202 **A**: Remember, we are the light. They are the dark. We are both high level thought forms reflected at all levels of reality.[19]

203 **Q**: *(T)* So, what we perceive, then, is what comes through to 3rd density, which is not what we would perceive if we were looking at it from 4th or 5th or 6th.

204 **A**: Yes.

205 **Q**: *(T)* We are talking 4th density to 3rd density. Is this what Hoagland is referring to when he talks about the tetrahedral form he has detected from the Martian structures he has been studying that he postulated...

206 **A**: Yes. This is a bridge to 4th density.

---

[18] *The Wave* 3

[19] This exchange is immensely important, I think.

207 **Q:** *(L)* Isn't it a little unfair for you guys, at 6th level, to take on the Lizzies at only 4th level?

208 **A:** The "Lizzies" are the 4th level representatives of the forces of the darkness not the 6th level, and you are 3rd level representatives.

209 **Q:** *(L)* Is there a 6th level representative of the forces of darkness?

210 **A:** Yes.

211 **Q:** *(L)* And what is this 6th level representative known as, or called, or look like or whatever?

212 **A:** Orion in your "neighborhood."

213 **Q:** *(L)* The Orions are 6th level STS beings?

214 **A:** Yes.

215 **Q:** *(L)* Are they like you, thought forms?

216 **A:** Yes.

217 **Q:** *(L)* Do they ever appear in physical matter?

218 **A:** Can.

219 **Q:** *(L)* And they are the driving force that controls the Lizzies?

220 **A:** Close.

221 **Q:** *(L)* Is there some intermediary between the 6th level Orions and the 4th level Lizzies, such as a 5th level force or being?

222 **A:** 5th level is contemplation zone for both "sides".

223 **Q:** *(L)* Does that mean that at the contemplation level that there is no activity? *(J)* Is it like a 'time out'?

224 **A:** Close. Balancer.

225 **Q:** *(L)* Is there a 3rd level representative of the forces of the light?

226 **A:** Yes.

227 **Q:** *(L)* Who or what are they?

228 **A:** Don't exist on your planet.

229 **Q:** *(L)* Do they have a planet of their own?

230 **A:** Have quadrillions of them.

231 **Q:** *(L)* Well, this is beginning to sound like we are in pretty bad shape here. This is like the Siberia of the universe as Gurdjieff said.

232 **A:** The Universe is infinitely huge.

233 **Q:** *(L)* If there are planets where there are 3D beings who are STS oriented, in other words, in a physical body, do they look something like us?

234 **A:** You are STS oriented. Did you really mean to say STO?

235 **Q:** *(T)* Is there a 3D race in this universe that is STO?

236 **A:** Yes. Already stated thus.

237 **Q:** *(L)* If there are planets with STO beings...

238 **A:** Some look like you.

239 **Q:** *(L)* What is life like on that sort of place? *(T)* They are not going to tell us that. That is something that we are going to have to develop to find out.

240 **A:** Exactly.

241 **Q:** *(J)* Is part of being STS being so appearance oriented as we are?

242 **A:** Not physical issue at 3rd level.

243 **Q:** *(T)* Who talks to me when I am having conversations with myself in my head?[20]

---

[20] *The Wave* 24

A: You.

Q: Am I talking to other beings?

A: Have.

Q: Do we all do this?

A: No.

Q: *(T)* Does Laura communicate like this?

A: Has.

Q: *(T)* Does Frank?

A: Ditto.

Q: *(T)* Should I continue communicating with whoever it is?

A: Up to you.

Q: *(T)* Are they connected to you?

A: No.

Q: *(T)* Do you know who I am talking about?

A: Yes.

Q: *(T)* Can you tell me who they are?[21]

A: Lizards.

Q: *(T)* Why are they talking to me?

A: Trying to convert you. Remember, Terry, your chronic depression represents a "battle" zone.

Q: *(T)* I no longer am depressed and they are talking to me more. *(J)* They are trying to get you back into it. *(T)* But they are not doing anything to convince me to be depressed.

A: Watch out!

Q: *(T)* Can I turn them off?

A: Yes.

Q: *(T)* Who is 'Sing'?

---
[21] *The Wave* 24

A: Leader of forces assigned to influence you.

Q: *(T)* Forces, as in many are assigned to me personally?

A: Yes.

Q: *(T)* How many are in this force?

A: Seven.

Q: *(T)* Do they do this because of the implants that are in me?

A: All part of process.

Q: *(T)* Do I have implants?

A: Yes.

Q: *(T)* These implants are what they use to control my emotions and amplify them so that they can feed off of them?

A: Not control, influence.

Q: *(T)* No, not to control; influence. But when, say, I get angry, then I'm angry for a short time but then I'm angry for a long time because they have used this technology to amplify and extend this; is this what they do?

A: Yes. Knowledge protects, ignorance endangers.

Q: *(T)* Can I feed back through their equipment what I choose?

A: Not necessary.

Q: *(T)* In other words, if I get angry and realize that I am being more angry than I should be, and I change that to something positive, and feed that back to them while they have their amplifiers wide open, will that affect them? Sour their milk, so to speak?

A: Now you are "fighting fire with fire."

Q: *(T)* Well, is that something that we are supposed to be doing?

A: Open. But what does phrase imply?

287 **Q**: *(L)* If you feed it back at them, in other words, what they are saying is, I think, when you feel yourself getting angry, the only way to stop the whole thing is to stop being angry and be happy or at peace. When you are happy and at peace there is not in you the desire to send anything back.

288 **A**: Bingo.

289 **Q**: *(J)* Redirect the energy into something positive. *(F)* You can't fight fire with fire. *(LM)* Well, actually you can in reality. *(T)* What I am getting at is, is it possible to do that, to change the emotional state to something more positive than what they are expecting and feed that back to them. Is that a possibility?

290 **A**: Why.

291 **Q**: *(T)* Just to give them a taste of their own for a change. *(J)* Do you want to antagonize them? You are still feeding them your energy. *(L)* The only change you could really have would be the opposite emotion which would be peace and if you are truly feeling peace...

292 **A**: 4th density STSers feed off negative energy.

293 **Q**: *(J)* So, give them nothing. *(T)* But what I am thinking about is the energy... I have a natural... They are feeding off negative energy. They put something in me, some technological thing, because they come into 3rd density to mess with us...

294 **A**: Yes.

295 **Q**: *(T)* ... that will amplify this for them. Make it even stronger.

296 **A**: Analogy follows: How effective is a light socket without a plug in it?

297 **Q**: *(T)* Well, how effective is a light socket without a socket in it... I'm trying to learn here so you guys give me some latitude.

298 **A**: What?

299 **Q**: *(T)* If you take a light socket and pull the socket... pull the plug on the light socket you no longer have light. *(L)* Well, the Lizzies are the light bulb and you are the power source so you just pull out their plug. *(J)* Unplug yourself. *(T)* Am I the socket?

300 **A**: How effective is a motor that is never turned on?

301 **Q**: *(J)* Do not be their source. If they feed off negative energy, starve them.

302 **A**: Implants are ineffective if not used.

303 **Q**: *(J)* The power source has to be on for the implant to work for them to get the juice, and the power is negative thoughts and emotions. *(T)* But I am still a 3rd density being. I have all the emotions of a 3rd density being, the whole gamut, and that is part of what makes me a 3rd density being. Therefore I can't turn one emotion off without upsetting the balance of the other emotions. Emotions are almost an analogy to the light and the dark.

304 **A**: No.

305 **Q**: *(T)* I have positive emotions and I have negative emotions; they both make up who I am.

306 **A**: If you choose, you may have only positive emotions.

307 **Q**: *(T)* Now, if I have only positive emotions, which is a nice thing to have and I'd like to have that, what does that do to the sensor equipment of the Lizzies?[22]

308 **A**: Cancels them.

---

[22] *The Wave* 24

309 **Q:** *(T)* So they are tuned to negative frequencies?

310 **A:** Yes.

311 **Q:** *(T)* Having positive feelings cuts off the implants. If I cut off the sensors by having positive feelings, what will the Lizards do?

312 **A:** Go elsewhere.

313 **Q:** *(L)* Am I correct in my thought that when you first start turning this off that they may increase their efforts for a period and then finally they realize that you are really in charge here and then they go away?

314 **A:** Exactly.

315 **Q:** *(L)* So, when you first get a clue and you start getting a grip on your emotions and dealing with everything that happens to you with acceptance and knowledge that all is a manifestation of your own creation and for your ultimate good, for a period of time they may try ten times harder to get you back as a food source, but then once they realize they can't, then they do finally let loose?

316 **A:** You and Frank are experiencing this right now.

317 **Q:** *(L)* This is true. *(F)* We have both been under massive attack. Just doing this work has been a struggle to keep at it with everything coming from every direction. *(L)* The hardest has been to stay in a frame of mind to do it. *(J)* Am I under attack?

318 **A:** Not yet.

319 **Q:** *(T)* Is what I have been under the past few months the first assault?

320 **A:** Yes.

321 **Q:** *(T)* Now they are trying to sweet talk me?

322 **A:** Only first assault.

323 **Q:** *(T)* So, the more positive I become, the more they are going to continue trying, and I am assuming that because you said I have seven beings of some kind assigned to me, that they find something interesting in me that they want to keep?

324 **A:** Close.

325 **Q:** *(T)* Should it make me happy that they think I am important enough to have seven beings assigned to me personally? Should I take that as a compliment?

326 **A:** No.

327 **Q:** *(J)* Is Terry's level of negativity what makes him attractive to them? His capability for strong negativity?

328 **A:** Vice versa.

329 **Q:** *(J)* Please explain. *(L)* Well, what did they say, is his negativity what makes him attractive? No. He has attracted them and that is what makes him negative? So what makes him attractive to them?

330 **A:** Not attractive, a threat.

331 **Q:** *(L)* Now, that is a point. I think there are a lot of people they start working on very early in life because they do like an aura reading or aura scan and determine and know that a person has potential for great light, so they start working on them when they are young and defenseless to try and take them out of the game, so to speak. *(F)* Not only great good, but also potential for knowledge. *(L)* Is this the case here?

332 **A:** Yes.

333 **Q:** *(L)* There you go. It isn't your potential for negativity, it is your potential for good.

(F) Right. If you look around you, you will see the mainstream of society, and they just seem to move through life and enjoy wallowing in materiality. These people don't seem to suffer as much.

(L) There seems to be two classes of people the Lizzies like to go after, extremely weak ones and those they haul off and eat or experiment on; and those who have potential strength and positivity.

(F) To give you an example is, the people they don't attack are those who they already have and they don't have to work on them. If you have the potential to rise above the service to self orientation, then you are a threat. And, if you look around at most of the people who are 'making it' in this world, those are the ones that are usually the most viciously service to self.

(T) Very true.

(J) That's the way it is.

(L) And how many times have you heard these 'New Age' teachers talk about "well, if your impression of people who have material possessions is that they are negative, then you are bringing this on yourself and you will just have to concentrate on prosperity more," that is, in a roundabout way promoting a very service to self philosophy. It's not that having things is bad, it's not that money is evil, it's the focus on it over and above helping others.

(T) I want to tell a little story. A guy I work for is a 'born-again Christian.' Only a-year-and-a-half born again. He's hobbying at it. He's looking for a lifestyle. He was pooh-poohing metaphysics and New Age philosophies in general, saying: "New Age! That's the devil's work!" He has no idea what it is, but he is shutting it down because someone told him to shut it down and he is doing it to be part of the lifestyle. I said: "Where do you get this stuff?" He said: "It's in the Bible." I said: "What do you mean it's in the Bible?" He said: "Well, it's in the books." So, I asked: "Well, where did the books come from? Some of them were written many hundreds of years ago and the New Testament books were written hundreds of years after Christ lived, that is, after the fact."

So, he said: "See, those who wrote the Bible didn't really write it, they got it from the Holy Spirit." So, I say, OK, I can buy that. The Holy Spirit wrote the Bible. I can follow this. Fine. I ask him: "How do they know this was the Holy Spirit?" And I'm only bringing up a question, I am not putting him down. So, he comes back and says: "Well, the books say the Holy Spirit came down and did this, and since it is in the book, it must be true." I said: "Wait a minute. The Holy Spirit came down and wrote these books through these people, gave them this information and helped them do this, and wrote in the book that it was the Holy Spirit that did this, therefore it makes it true because whoever brought this information said they brought this information. But, on a whole different level, the Holy Spirit brought this information to these people, and they didn't write the books, did they not 'channel' these books?" And he stopped there and it was like: "Well, I never thought of it that way."

And I said: "Well, you just said that all of this was of the devil, New Age, paranormal events, UFOs, the Rolling Stones..." So, he thought about it for a minute and then he said: "But it's OK. It was the 'right' channel!" And I say: "Wait a minute! Slow down here! Take this home and think about it for a few days. These books that you are putting your faith in, that you don't know where they came from, were channeled to people by means that you say are the devil's work if anybody else does it. And, the only reason you are accepting these works is because, *in* these works it says that it was the Holy Spirit that did it, but it was the Holy Spirit that told them to do this."

(F) And it was the Holy Spirit that told them that it was the Holy Spirit.

(T) Yeah, right! I told him: "Think about it. Just *think* about what you are saying." But he is just not seeing it.

(L) It's hypnosis.

(T) And, he's looking for a lifestyle. He talks about: "I heard this great group the other day, they're a Christian band." And a couple days later: "Hey, did you hear such and such, they're a Christian band." I said: "Gee, James, know any good Moslem bands?" I told him I liked Garrison Keilor and he said: "That's a Christian show." I said: "Where did you get that?" He said: "Well, my pastor said he was because he's from Minnesota!"

(F) Well, there are two points that this brings up. The first is that circular thinking and this whole idea is following what others tell you or what has been written without questioning it. You are not supposed to think. And then, the second thing, this source said once way back: "Don't take anything at face value, including this." Part of the light of knowledge is that you would always be open to new information.

(L) Well, that is the parable of the talents. I keep hammering on that one and one of these days I am going to write a little monograph on the parables of Jesus. The parable of the talents is prefaced by the phrase: "Now, knowledge of the kingdom is like unto a certain man who went on a journey..." and he called his three servants together and gave them each a certain number of talents. The talents represent knowledge. Two of the servants invested their talents. They were willing to take risks and give up what they had to get more. The third was afraid of losing the little he had and he buried his talent. So, the two increased their knowledge by repeatedly giving up and getting back more. The master came back and the two showed how they had made a killing on the market and the master was pleased. But the servant who had buried his talent said: "Master, I knew you were a hard man and you reaped where you did not sow and I was afraid..." The master cast him into outer darkness. And, remember, remember, remember, we are talking about knowledge. He took his little bit of knowledge and he closed himself off and hung onto that little bit for dear life...

(F) Yet another demonstration of service to self. He buried it so he could have it instead of sharing it. It is continually reflected over and over. Everybody out there has their one little talent and they are all burying it for dear life.

(T) OK. Where were we? Just by being positive will shut off the Lizzies' desire to mess with me?

A: Yes.

Q: *(T)* That's all there is to it? But the implants will still be there?

A: So what?

Q: *(T)* Do the implants do anything besides transmit the frequency?

338 **A**: No.

339 **Q**: *(T)* And, as long as I am negative it is transmitting and they can track me that way?

340 **A**: Close.

341 **Q**: *(T)* If I shut them off by being positive, they can't track me any longer?

342 **A**: Can track but not influence.

343 **Q**: *(T)* Why did they tell me that I gave them permission to do it when they abduct me?

344 **A**: "Bullshit!"

345 **Q**: *(T)* If I tell them it's bull will they leave me alone?

346 **A**: No.

347 **Q**: *(T)* If I shut them off will they continue to abduct me?

348 **A**: No.

349 **Q**: *(T)* I am not buying into the victim line. *(L)* There is another aspect here. Knowledge breeds awareness which gives you the ability to detect it when they try to influence you in very subtle ways so that you can begin to control your mind and resist early on and that is the key.

350 **A**: Close enough.

351 **Q**: *(L)* And you have to persist with positive thoughts and feelings sometimes in the face of incredible adversity. No one said it was going to be easy, but it is worth it. *(T)* Are my tarot cards telling me the truth?

352 **A**: Maybe. Enough on this subject, please.

353 **Q**: *(T)* One last question. How do I know you are telling me the truth?[23]

---

[23] *The Wave* 12

354 **A**: Open. For you to decide. Listen: Revelations follow. Now would be a good "time" for you folks to begin to reexamine some of the extremely popular "Earth changes" prophecies. Why, you ask. Because, remember, you are third density beings, so real prophecies are being presented to you in terms you will understand, i.e. physical realm, i.e. Earth changes. This "may" be symbolism. Would most students of the subject understand if prophecies were told directly in fourth density terms?

355 **Q**: *(L)* Is this comparable to my idea about dream symbolism. For example, the dream I had about the curling cloud which I saw in a distance and knew it was death dealing and I interpreted it to be a tornado, but it was, in fact, a dream of the Challenger disaster. I understood it to be a tornado, but in fact, what I saw was what I got, a death-dealing force in the sky, a vortex, in the distance. I guess my dream was a 4th density representation but I tried to interpret it in terms I was familiar with. Is this what you mean?

356 **A**: Close. But it is easy for most to get bogged down by interpreting prophecies in literal terms.

357 **Q**: *(L)* Is there more information you plan to deliver on this subject?

358 **A**: Okay.

359 **Q**: *(L)* Let me ask a quick one. Did the Gulf Breeze Six, as they are called, who were supposedly receiving information via the Ouija board, did they receive prophetic information of some sort?

360 **A**: Yes.

361 **Q**: And, from what source did they receive this information?

362 **A:** Mixed.

363 **Q:** *(L)* Was their information accurate?

364 **A:** Mixed.

365 **Q:** *(L)* Why were they, their board, their transcripts and so forth confiscated?[24]

366 **A:** Paranoia.

367 **Q:** *(L)* In terms of these Earth changes, Edgar Cayce is one of the most famous prognosticators of recent note. A large number of the prophecies he made seemingly were erroneous in terms of their fulfillment. For example, he prophesied that Atlantis would rise in 1969, but it did not, though certain structures were discovered off the coast of Bimini which are thought by many to be remnants of Atlantis. These did, apparently, emerge from the sand at that time.[25]

368 **A:** Example of one form of symbolism.

369 **Q:** *(L)* Well, in terms of this symbolism, could this be applied to the remarks you made about the two little boys who were missing in South Carolina?

370 **A:** Yes.

371 **Q:** *(L)* And the symbolism was that you were reading the event from 3rd density into 6th density terms and then transmitting it back into 3rd, and while the ideation was correct, the exact specifics, in 3rd density terms, were slightly askew. Is that what we are dealing with here?

372 **A:** 99.9 per cent would not understand that concept. Most are always looking for literal translations of data. Analogy is novice who attends art gallery, looks at abstract painting and says "I don't get it."

373 **Q:** *(L)* Well, let's not denigrate literal translations or at least attempts to get things into literal terms. I like realistic art work. I am a realist in my art preferences. I want trees to look like trees and people to have only two arms and legs. Therefore, I also like some literalness in my prognostications.

374 **A:** Some is okay, but, beware or else "California falls into the ocean" will always be interpreted as California falling into the ocean.

375 **Q:** [General uproar] *(F)* Wait a minute, what was the question?

(L) I just said I liked literalness in my prophecies.

(F) Oh, I know what they are saying. People believe that California is just going to go splat and that Phoenix is going to be on the seacoast, never mind that it's at 1800 feet elevation, it's just going to drop down to sea level, or the sea level is going to rise, but it's not going to affect Virginia Beach even though that's at sea level. I mean... somehow Phoenix is just going to drop down and none of the buildings are going to be damaged, even though its going to fall 1800 feet...

(T) Slowly. It's going to settle.

(F) Slowly? It would have to be so slowly it's unbelievable how slowly it would have to be.

(T) It's been settling for the last five million years, we've got a ways to go in the next year and a half!

(F) Right! That's my point.

---

[24] The rumor was that they were shut down by the military and their work confiscated and classified.

[25] *The Wave* 12

(T) In other words, when people like Scallion and Sun Bear and others say California is going to fall into the ocean, they are not saying that the whole state, right along the border, is going to fall into the ocean; they are using the term California to indicate that the ocean ledge along the fault line has a probability of breaking off and sinking on the water side, because it is a major fracture. We understand that that is not literal. Are you telling us that there is more involved here as far as the way we are hearing what these predictions say?

376 **A**: Yes.

377 **Q**: *(T)* Are we understanding what you are saying?

378 **A**: Some.

379 **Q**: *(T)* So, when we talk about California falling into the ocean, we are not talking about the whole state literally falling into the ocean?

380 **A**: In any case, even if it does, how long will it take to do this?

381 **Q**: *(LM)* It could take three minutes or three hundred years. *(T)* Yes. That is 'open' as you would say.

382 **A**: Yes. But most of your prophets think it is not open.

383 **Q**: *(J)* Yeah, because they think they have the only line on it. *(T)* OK. So they are thinking in the terms that one minute California will be there and a minute and a half later it will be all gone. Is this what you are saying?

384 **A**: Or similar.

385 **Q**: *(T)* So, when we are talking: "California will fall into the ocean," which is just the analogy we are using, we are talking about, as far as Earth changes, is the possibility that several seismic events along the fault line, which no one really knows the extent of...

386 **A**: Or it all may be symbolic of something else.

387 **Q**: *(L)* Such as? *(J)* All the fruitcakes in California are all going to go off the deep end together. *(L)* Symbolic of what?

388 **A**: Up to you to examine and learn.

389 **Q**: *(L)* Now, wait a minute here! That's like sending us out to translate a book in Latin without even giving us a Latin dictionary.

390 **A**: No it is not. We asked you to consider a reexamination.

391 **Q**: *(L)* You have told us through this source that there is a cluster of comets connected in some interactive way with our solar system, and that this cluster of comets comes into the plane of the ecliptic every 3600 years. Is this correct?[26]

392 **A**: Yes. But, this time it is riding realm border wave to 4th level, where all realities are different.

393 **Q**: *(L)* OK, so the cluster of comets is riding the realm border wave. Does this mean that when it comes into the solar system, that its effect on the solar system, or the planets within the solar system, may or may not be mitigated by the fact of this transition? Is this a mitigating factor?

394 **A**: Will be mitigated.

395 **Q**: *(T)* Is this what the Star Trek movie *Generations* is telling us?

396 **A**: Possible.

---

[26] *The Wave* 1

397 **Q:** *(T)* Are you or someone in the Federation influencing the writers of that program?

398 **A:** Open.

399 **Q:** *(L)* Does any of this mean that the Earth changes that have been predicted may not, in fact, occur in physical reality as we understand it?

400 **A:** You betcha.

401 **Q:** *(L)* Does this mean that all of this running around and hopping and jumping to go here and go there and do this and do that is...

402 **A:** That is strictly 3rd level thinking.

403 **Q:** *(L)* Now, if that is 3rd level thinking, and if a lot of these things are symbolic, I am assuming they are symbolic of movement or changes in energy.

404 **A:** Yes.

405 **Q:** *(L)* And, if these changes in energy occur does this mean that the population of the planet are, perhaps, in groups or special masses of groups, are they defined as the energies that are changing in these descriptions of events and happenings of great cataclysm? Is it like a cataclysm of the soul on an individual and or collective basis?

406 **A:** Close.

407 **Q:** *(L)* When the energy changes to 4th density, and you have already told us that people who are moving to 4th density when the transition occurs, that they will move into 4th density, go through some kind of rejuvenation process, grow new teeth, or whatever, what happens to those people who are not moving to 4th density, and who are totally unaware of it? Are they taken along on the wave by, in other words, piggy-backed by the ones who are aware and already changing in frequency, or are they going to be somewhere else doing something else?

408 **A:** Step by step.

409 **Q:** *(T)* In other words, we are looking at the fact that what's coming this time is a wave that's going to allow the human race to move to 4th density?

410 **A:** And the planet and your entire sector of space/time.

411 **Q:** *(T)* Is that what this whole plan is about, then, if I may be so bold as to include all of us here in this? We, of the beings of light who have come here into human form, to anchor the frequency, is this what we are anchoring it for, for this wave, so that when it comes enough of us will be ready, the frequency will be set, so that the change in the planet can take place as it has been planned?

412 **A:** Yes.

413 **Q:** *(L)* When this happens, will we piggy-back all those who are still unaware?

414 **A:** Open.

415 **Q:** *(T)* OK, when the people are talking about the Earth changes, when they talk in literal terms about the survivors, and those who are not going to survive, and the destruction and so forth and so on, in 3rd, 4th, 5th level reality we are not talking about the destruction of the planet on 3rd level physical terms, or the loss of 90 per cent of the population on the 3rd level because they died, but because they are going to move to 4th level?

416 **A:** Whoa! You are getting "warm."

417 **Q:** *(T)* OK. So, we are anchoring this. So, when they talk about 90 per cent of the population not surviving, it is not

that they are going to die, but that they are going to transform. We are going to go up a level. This is what the whole light thing is all about?

418 **A:** Or another possibility is that the physical cataclysms will occur only for those "left behind" on the remaining 3rd level density Earth.

419 **Q:** *(T)* OK, what you are saying, then, is that we are anchoring the frequency, so that when the wave comes, we move to 4th level density as many people as possible, in order to break the hold the 'Dark T-shirts' have got on this planet, those who remain behind will not have enough energy left for the 'Dark T-shirts' to bother with the planet any longer. There will be less of them so the planet will be able to refresh and they will be able to move on in their lessons without interference?

420 **A:** Close.

421 **Q:** *(L)* At this point of dimensional transition, is what we are doing, anchoring a frequency, are we creating a sort of 'super string' network that will literally create another Earth in 4th density, which will then exist in 4th density, and the old 3rd density Earth – almost like the splitting of a one-celled organism, only in this splitting one half of it moves into another dimension and is energized and quite literally created by the anchoring frequency, while the old one remains and experiences 3rd density reality?

422 **A:** Step by step.

423 **Q:** *(L)* Are we anchoring frequency to create a split?

424 **A:** One developing conduit.

425 **Q:** *(L)* We are developing a conduit?

426 **A:** Yes. One.

427 **Q:** *(J)* How many conduits do we need?

428 **A:** Open.

429 **Q:** *(T)* Is this conduit going to allow those who remain behind to be able to move to 4th density easier when they are ready?

430 **A:** No.

431 **Q:** *(T)* What is the conduit for?

432 **A:** You and those who will follow you.

433 **Q:** *(T)* Oh, this is for those of us who will move to 4th density. We will move through and they will follow us through the conduit. *(J)* Oh, others who are ready?

434 **A:** Your group here tonight.

435 **Q:** *(L)* Does this mean we will have followers or just us here now?

436 **A:** Open. Up to you.

437 **Q:** *(L)* This conduit. Is this a conduit through which an entire planet will transition?

438 **A:** You are one. There are others.

439 **Q:** *(L)* There are other planets...

440 **A:** No. Conduit.

441 **Q:** We are one conduit and there are conduits...

442 **A:** No. Developing at this point.

443 **Q:** *(J)* So, at this point we are developing a conduit?

444 **A:** Yes.

445 **Q:** *(T)* There are other groups on this planet developing their own conduits?

446 **A:** Yes.

447 **Q:** *(T)* These are conduits for us to move to 4th density in?

448 **A**: Knowledge is the key to developing a conduit.[27]

449 **Q**: *(T)* I am working on the assumption that all of us here are part of the family of light. Is this true?

450 **A**: Yes.

451 **Q**: *(T)* And we have been drawn together in order to develop this conduit from where we are?

452 **A**: Yes.

453 **Q**: *(T)* Are there others in this area?

454 **A**: Yes.

455 **Q**: *(T)* Are they supposed to join with us or are they working on their own?

456 **A**: Open.

457 **Q**: *(T)* OK, so it is up in the air as to whether we join with them, they join with us, or we all work independently.

458 **A**: It is up to how much publicity you manage to get.

459 **Q**: *(T)* Do we want publicity on this?

460 **A**: Open.

461 **Q**: *(L)* Would it help us?

462 **A**: Open.

463 **Q**: *(T)* We're developing a conduit to move us from 3rd density to 4th density. Once we have moved through the conduit does that mean we have completed what we came here to do, and that is anchor the frequency?

464 **A**: Partly.

465 **Q**: *(T)* Is the conduit kind of like an escape hatch for us?[28]

466 **A**: Close.

467 **Q**: *(L)* Let me get this straight. When we move through this conduit, are the other...

468 **A**: You will be on the 4th level Earth as opposed to 3rd level Earth.

469 **Q**: *(L)* What I am trying to get here, once again, old practical Laura, is trying to get a handle on practical terms here. Does this mean that a 4th density Earth and a 3rd density Earth will coexist side by side...

470 **A**: Not side by side, totally different realms.

471 **Q**: *(L)* Do these realms interpenetrate one another but in different dimensions...

472 **A**: Close.

473 **Q**: *(L)* So, in other words, a being from say, 6th density, could look at this planet we call the Earth and see it spinning through space and see several dimensions of Earth, and yet the point of space-time occupation is the same, in other words, simultaneous. *(J)* They can look down but we can't look up.

474 **A**: Yes.

475 **Q**: *(L)* So, in other words, while all of this cataclysmic activity is happening on the 3rd dimensional Earth, we will be just on our 4th dimensional Earth and this sort of thing won't be there, and we won't see the 3rd dimensional people and they won't see us because we will be in different densities which are not 'en rapport,' so to speak?

476 **A**: You understand concept, now you must decide if it is factual.

End of Session

---

[27] *The Wave* 1
[28] *The Wave* 1, 12

It's been twenty years since this explication of prophecy and Earth changes and reality splits was given and I have learned a lot more about it along the way; you could even say that I have had some experiences in 'reality shifting.' I've made a series of videos that are posted on YouTube which explain these things in terms of Information Theory and the Many Worlds Interpretation of Quantum Physics. You can access them from my website.[29] The bottom line is, what the C's said eventually made a lot of sense.

---

[29] http://cassiopaea.org/2013/10/17/a-course-in-knowledge-and-being-part-1/

November 27, 1994

This was a short, private session when my ex-husband was present for the first 10 minutes or so.

Participants: 'Frank', Laura and LM

1 **Q**: Hello.

2 **A**: Hello. Illo.

3 **Q**: *(L)* Your name is Illo? Who are you and where are you from?

4 **A**: Cassiopaea.

5 **Q**: *(L)* I have a few little questions I want to ask, and I know they are personal and I know how you feel about personal questions but there is a reason for the importance of these questions. The first is why is it every time I think about sitting at the board my left ear starts doing strange things?

6 **A**: DNA responding.

7 **Q**: *(LM)* Why or how would DNA make your ear hurt?

8 **A**: Changes.

9 **Q**: *(L)* How can DNA changing affect an ear or shoulder, for example?

10 **A**: Complex; read "Bringers of the Dawn".

11 **Q**: *(L)* My husband is really concerned about his truck. This may sound like a simple thing, but for us it isn't because we can't just go and spend money on fixing it only to find out that is the wrong thing and something else needs fixing. We need to know what is wrong with it so that we can fix it with the least amount of expenditure.

12 **A**: Catalytic converter.

13 **Q**: *(LM)* It doesn't have one. *(L)* He doesn't have one. What is wrong with the truck?

14 **A**: Space where converter should be.

15 **Q**: *(LM)* Whoever is telling you this is abysmally mechanically ignorant. No 1978 truck ever had a catalytic converter.

16 **A**: Check it. Your assertion. Fuel line clogged at bottom where "cc" should be.[1]

17 **Q**: *(L)* Is it possible to do hypnotic future progressions that give accurate information in a general sense?

18 **A**: Yes.

19 **Q**: *(L)* In the book *Mass Dreams of The Future*, are these statistically analyzed mass dreams in any way accurate?

20 **A**: In a sense.

21 **Q**: *(L)* Is it possible, since they showed several different scenarios... why am I feeling so strange at this moment?

22 **A**: Anemic/low blood sugar.

---

[1]This proved to be absolutely correct! A rubber cap was missing which led to the obstruction and LM was amazed.

Q: *(L)* So it is not an emotional reaction to my husband's hostility?[2]

A: Maybe.

Q: *(L)* Well, in that sense, I would like to know.

A: Know what?

Q: *(L)* Are you sure you are a Cassiopaean?

A: Yes.

Q: *(L)* Well, you don't seem to be really in tune or accurate about what is going on here tonight.[3]

A: In tune, but your energies are low; it "takes two to tango".

Q: *(L)* Now, last night you said you affected our psyches in order to have us make changes on the board. It occurred to me that you might have the ability to change the electromagnetics of the body, which would then affect the physical body. Is this correct?

A: Maybe.

Q: *(L)* So, could you perform an electromagnetic healing on me, that is, on the etheric or spirit body, which would then manifest in the physical body?

A: Do.

Q: *(L)* You do? Well, I would like to have more of it, more often. I would like you to speed up the process because I am fairly miserable in the physical sense. Is that possible?

A: Cycle will pass.

Q: *(L)* Well, I want to know why my arm hurts so bad and why my heart feels like an elephant is sitting on it?

A: Energy low.

Q: *(L)* Is the answer to that just simply to rest?

A: Yes. Absolutely. Last session was particularly draining. Don't overdo it, just pace it.

Q: *(L)* Well, let's go back to the truck. Do you think you can tap into anybody who is a mechanic and just give us...

A: Truck problem will be resolved by your tomorrow and will be easy to resolve.[4]

Q: *(L)* I talked to Tom M tonight and I wonder if he is going to be willing and able to compensate Frank for the electric bill.

A: Yes. But explain in detail. And point out his good fortune.

Q: *(L)* I want a new vehicle. Look into the future for me, please, and tell me which is there for me around the corner, is it a car or a nice, big van?

A: Either.

Q: *(L)* Is it very close in the future for me.

A: Maybe.[5]

Q: *(L)* Now, I want to know in terms of this activity, what percentage of our energy is utilized in this channeling process? Is it say, 60% Frank and 40% me or whatever?

A: Varies.

Q: *(L)* With Jan and Terry here, is that a more energetic session?

A: Yes.

---

[2]LM had left the room.
[3]I was assuming that the response about the truck was wrong.
[4]Absolutely accurate.
[5]It was. I found exactly what I wanted within my price range.

53 **Q:** *(L)* Does it help to have more people in the room?

54 **A:** If they are not hostile.

55 **Q:** *(L)* Does hostility cut back the energy?

56 **A:** Immensely and negative moods as well.

57 **Q:** *(L)* Is LM more hostile and negative than he believes he is or than he lets on?

58 **A:** Varies.

59 **Q:** *(L)* Are you going to be able to do something to my psyche that is going to make my body start dropping tons of weight with no necessity for me to focus on that issue at all?

60 **A:** Not necessary, once project gets going, your energy will greatly increase, thus weight loss follows.[6]

61 **Q:** *(L)* On many occasions I have had dreams about being on a train. What do these dreams mean to me?

62 **A:** Not significant.

63 **Q:** *(L)* What about the dreams of putting on makeup?

64 **A:** Hiding your self.

65 **Q:** *(L)* What level are the Pleiadians who channel through Barbara Marciniak?

66 **A:** 6th density.

67 **Q:** *(L)* OK, I would like to know where AG is and what she is doing currently.

68 **A:** North Carolina, nursing.

69 **Q:** *(L)* Is she still with Tom?

70 **A:** No.

71 **Q:** *(L)* Why?

72 **A:** Split.

73 **Q:** *(L)* Where is he?

74 **A:** Tarpon Springs.

75 **Q:** *(L)* Why is he there?

76 **A:** Engineering.

77 **Q:** *(L)* What about CS?

78 **A:** In Atlanta. Artist.

79 **Q:** *(L)* I talked to CP the other day, she seemed to be hostile. Is this a valid assessment?

80 **A:** Close.

81 **Q:** *(L)* Why does she feel this way?

82 **A:** Not on same wavelength.

83 **Q:** *(L)* Should I just forget her?

84 **A:** Up to you.[7]

End of Session

---

[6]This was true, but the project didn't 'really get going' until after I separated from my husband at the time and Ark entered the picture. That was still almost two years in the future.

[7]The funny thing is, I don't even remember who the people were that I was asking about. There sure was a lot of stuff occupying space in my brain then that wasn't worth my time or energy.

December 1, 1994

The ongoing uproar amongst the local UFO/metaphysical community had been brewing for months now and appeared to be coming to a head. As I described in *Soul Hackers* (this is *The Wave* Vol. 2, chapter 14: "Candy will ruin your teeth"), things had gotten a bit serious when my third daughter had contracted a serious illness from one of Scarlett's daughters.

When I originally wrote *The Wave*, I had to find a pseudonym for Scarlett that related to an illness or condition so that I could convey in some way how the clues were developing: 'Candy' seemed usable in relation to 'candidiasis.' But my daughter contracted scarlet fever, which is a bit more serious (and contagious) than candidiasis. Nowadays, with antibiotics, it can be managed, but in the old days, it used to be a major cause of death or permanent damage in children.

In any event, the whole dynamic with Scarlett, the 'super UFO investigator' Mike F, the local self-proclaimed super magician Andrew B, the Sitchin devotee John W (who was pure and self-righteous and would never have anything to do with any magical doings), was turning into a big drama. Scarlett had gotten a sum of money from me based on her plan to create a business but then, as soon as Mike F had entered the picture with all his claims and schmoozing, had dumped the idea and never bothered to think about repaying that money to me. Mike F and Andrew B, the big pooh-bahs of the Clearwater MUFON group, were determined to hush up anything that suggested that aliens were not here with our best interests at heart and that abductions weren't good for you and made you 'speshul.' John W was determined to evangelize the gospel according to Zecharia Sitchin and Scarlett was just in it for who could do the most for her in any number of ways. I also think she loved the drama.

Regarding Mike F and Andrew B, I do think it is possible that they were conscious agents of disinformation. They were certainly working overtime to make sure that my reputation was trashed with every lie they could come up with and using Scarlett, the poor victimized abductee, as capital in their negotiations.

At this point in time, I was getting crazy phone calls at all hours of the day and night: breathers, strange noises, threats, threatening and upsetting my children; you name it. I had never heard of a channeling project that brought on such a reaction from others!

Meanwhile, I had learned from one individual who was familiar with all the parties that they all had one thing in common: ritual magic. Some of them were members of a coven that was covertly run under the guise of the local metaphysical church; others claimed to be members of the Hermetic Order of the Golden Dawn.[1] I think that both groups were very upset that the C's had declared that rituals were STS inspired. They sure had a lot invested in that nonsense.

So, this session was held after a particularly nasty series of threatening phone calls and warnings from others that I should stop what I was doing if I knew what was good for me and my family.

Participants: 'Frank', Laura, J___- (Laura's son, age almost 12) and A_-_ (Laura's daughter, age 13)

1 **Q:** *(L)* Hello.

2 **A:** Hello. You like puppies.[2]

3 **Q:** *(L)* And who do we have tonight?

4 **A:** Romommea.

5 **Q:** *(L)* Who are you and where are you from?

6 **A:** Cassiopaea.

7 **Q:** *(L)* Should A___ participate?

8 **A:** Should sit quietly; she's at a "sensitive" age.

9 **Q:** *(L)* Does that mean it is better for her to not use the board?

10 **A:** Yes. Bad influences are near.

11 **Q:** *(L)* Bad influences are near? And what are these "bad" influences?

12 **A:** Discarnate "gargoyles".

13 **Q:** *(L)* What are they near for?

14 **A:** A___ is near the board.

15 **Q:** *(L)* Should she sit in the other chair?

---

[1] The Hermetic Order of the Golden Dawn (or, more commonly, the Golden Dawn) was an organization devoted to the study and practice of the occult, metaphysics, and paranormal activities during the late 19th and early 20th centuries. Known as a magical order, the Hermetic Order of the Golden Dawn was active in Great Britain and focused its practices on theurgy and spiritual development. Many present-day concepts of ritual and magic that are at the center of contemporary traditions, such as Wicca and Thelema, were inspired by the Golden Dawn, which became one of the largest single influences on 20th-century Western occultism.

[2] This was probably addressed to my daughter who was (and is) a serious dog/puppy lover.

A: Yes.

Q: *(L)* Is that better now?

A: Yes.

Q: *(L)* And, what would these gargoyles like to do?

A: Overtake communication.

Q: *(L)* Well, begone! Did that do it?

A: No.

Q: *(L)* Well, tell them to scram.

A: We are free will, we can advise.

Q: *(L)* Well, then advise them to leave, please.

A: Open. There is much interference.

Q: *(L)* What can we do to enhance communication at this end?

A: Communication is best when pure.

Q: *(L)* What is not pure tonight? Is it my attitude or activities?

A: No.

Q: *(L)* What is not pure?

A: Interference.

Q: *(L)* What is causing the interference?

A: We are not certain.

Q: *(L)* Is there anything we can do... should we have the children leave the room?

A: Maybe.

Q: *(L)* If they leave the room will you be better able to communicate?

A: Thought patterns show static.

Q: *(L)* My thought patterns show static?

A: Someone's.

Q: *(L)* Is it someone in this room?

A: Possibly, but not clear. It's someone apart from channel.

Q: *(L)* What are Mike F and Scarlett doing at this moment?

A: Unreadable.

Q: *(L)* Why is that?

A: Static energy field.

Q: *(L)* Is that possibly where the static is coming from?

A: Possible.

Q: *(L)* [Son leaves and goes to bed] OK, did that help?

A: Remember, children most vulnerable when attack underway. You are currently under psychic onslaught.

Q: *(L)* OK. [Daughter leaves and goes to bed] Is that better?

A: Better, but you are definitely being deliberately assaulted by some source right now.

Q: *(L)* Well, my ears are ringing to beat the band. What is this source?

A: Earth bound.

Q: *(L)* Is the originator of this negative energy Ms. Scarlett H who claims to have practiced witchcraft in her youth?

A: Maybe.

Q: *(L)* Is another of these attackers Mike F who also claims to have practiced witchcraft in his youth?

A: Yes.

Q: *(L)* And is another one Mr. Andrew B who claims to be Florida's greatest sorcerer, if not the world's?

A: Maybe.

Q: *(L)* Are they all in cahoots?

A: Maybe.

Q: *(L)* Can you give me any definite answers on this situation?

A: Static around all mentioned. Phone opened line of attack one attacker believes he has powers to damage you.

Q: *(L)* Is that attacker Mike F?

A: Maybe.

Q: *(L)* OK, the situation is that, from any point of view, Mike and Scarlett have really treated me badly and I tried to be real low key and understanding and forgiving about the whole thing. However, when I learned that they had stolen from me, I got very upset. So, did I take the right approach in having my attorney send the demand letter to Scarlett?

A: Yet to be seen.

Q: *(L)* Well, I decided that it was time for the buck to stop. These people have gone around doing what they are doing for as long as I am willing to tolerate not having my side heard. I never believed that people could be so vicious.

A: Will they share your beliefs?

Q: *(L)* Probably not, but I can only stay buried so long. And, it is definitely rattling some bushes.

A: Yes.

Q: *(L)* From your position of all-knowingness and all-seeingness, can you give me a little guidance on this?

A: No one is "all-knowing" and seeing.

Q: *(L)* OK, you can't see Andrew, Mike, or Scarlett, is that correct?

A: Static.

Q: *(L)* What is creating the static around them? Are they performing some Lizzie rituals?

A: Machinery of some kind is being used to create the static.

Q: *(L)* Are they doing this to protect themselves from some sort of imagined attack from me (because I am sure Scarlett has convinced them I am an evil witch)?

A: Assault upon Laura directly.

Q: *(L)* They are using some kind of machinery to attack me directly?

A: Yes.

Q: *(L)* What kind?

A: Lights, bells, smoke, siren, oscillator, EM waves.

Q: *(L)* Are they going to try to burn my house down?[3]

---

[3] The words "siren" and "smoke" triggered in me the fear of these nuts setting my house on fire. I suppose that the description could have been of some other type of activity such as some sort of ritual being conducted in St. Petersburg, where Andrew lived, and there could have been sirens in the background, which was common in the city. On the other hand, Andrew and Mike may have cooked up or constructed some kind of weird 'magic machine.' Of course, it's not beyond possibility that they actually had some sort of gadget such as the tech described by Nick Redfern in his book *Close Encounters of the Fatal Kind*. In a sub-chapter entitled "Murder by Microwave and Psychic Phenomena" he writes:

> In Chapter 7 of this book ... I referenced a March 1976 report titled "Biological Effects of Electromagnetic Radiation (Radiowaves and Microwaves) Eurasian Communist Countries," which was prepared for the Defense Intelligence Agency by Ronald L. Adams and Dr. R. A. Williams of the U.S. Army's Medical Intelligence and

86 **A**: Open.

87 **Q**: *(L)* I need to know, this is serious.

88 **A**: Cannot tell.

89 **Q**: *(L)* Well, what you have described sounds like a fire-truck.

90 **A**: Knowledge protects. We have helped you to gain knowledge.

91 **Q**: *(L)* So, I should just be alert and aware?

92 **A**: Good idea.

93 **Q**: *(L)* Did Andrew B call Mike F?

94 **A**: Probable.

95 **Q**: *(L)* Is Mike F the person who called earlier this evening?

96 **A**: Was some sort of device.

97 **Q**: *(L)* Who called after Frank was here and did not leave a message?

98 **A**: Same.

99 **Q**: *(L)* How come all of this stuff started happening today?

100 **A**: Energy flow and John W "bush rattling." From remote location.

101 **Q**: *(L)* How can Mike F attack me from a remote location?

102 **A**: He may try machinery.

103 **Q**: *(L)* What kind of machinery could cause my house to burn?

104 **A**: Not could cause, thinks could cause. Machines are frightening Scarlett.

105 **Q**: *(L)* What is the likelihood of Scarlett paying back what she owes me? It's a lot of money.

106 **A**: Depends on course of events.

107 **Q**: *(L)* And what are the possible courses?

108 **A**: 956,000 possibilities.

109 **Q**: *(L)* Is it better for the kids not to take the melatonin tonight in case Mike F tries to burn my house down?

110 **A**: Okay either.

111 **Q**: *(L)* Should I just not have said or done anything?

112 **A**: Cannot "should have" done anything.

113 **Q**: *(L)* I would also like to ask you guys to use your abilities to counteract some of this influence in the sense of at least shielding.

114 **A**: Knowledge is shield.

115 **Q**: *(L)* Why is A___ [daughter] depressed?

116 **A**: Biological changes.

117 **Q**: *(L)* Is it just a phase?

118 **A**: Close. Scarlett "crumbling".

119 **Q**: *(L)* Why is she crumbling?

120 **A**: Mixed feelings.

121 **Q**: *(L)* Did she do the things she did toward me deliberately?

122 **A**: Mike F heavy influence.

123 **Q**: *(L)* What does she think about Mike F Now?

124 **A**: Getting progressively "spooked".

125 **Q**: *(L)* By him?

126 **A**: Yes.

Information Agency. The document is made notable ... because it makes significant mention of how a heart attack can be induced vie the use of directed, microwave technology. ... let's not forget that this particular document deals with the use of microwaves from the perspective of utilizing them as weapons against targeted individuals.

Q: *(L)* Is she figuring out how crazy he is?

A: Subjective.

Q: *(L)* Are Shannon and Sara S[4] believers in the Gospel according to Mike F?

A: Naive.

Q: *(L)* Is this fiasco going to open their eyes?

A: Open.

Q: *(L)* Is there any other thing I need to know about this situation?

A: Just be aware.

Q: *(L)* Will I be able to sleep safely tonight?

A: Should, but pray.

Q: *(L)* And who should I pray to?

A: Same as always.

Q: *(L)* Is there such a being as St. Michael?

A: In a sense.

Q: *(L)* Which higher being is most able to help a person in a situation of danger?

A: Universe.

Q: *(L)* Pray to the Universe?

A: Refer to recent session.

Q: *(L)* And what was in the recent session that I need to refer to?

A: November 26.

Q: *(L)* What was in that session?

A: Universe.

Q: *(L)* About universes, alternate universes, etc?

A: Yes.

Q: *(L)* Anything else I need to know?

A: No.

Q: *(L)* Is it alright if we have Chuck attend?[5]

A: Good boy!

Q: *(L)* OK then, good night.

A: Good night.

End of Session

---

[4]Still other members of the Clearwater MUFON. Looking back on this whole situation, it really does appear that Andrew and Mike were agents provocateur sent in to break up that organization.

[5]A local private investigator/ex cop whom I had called on for help in investigating Scarlett's alleged abduction case. He had arranged for the dress she was wearing at the time, which was supposed to have Bigfoot hairs and strange fluids on it, to be examined in a police lab. However, the day he was going to pick up the bagged dress that Scarlett had left with me, she came and demanded it back because Mike F told her to get it, that I was just using her to achieve fame and glory with her great abduction case. Sheesh! (See *The Wave* chapter 19 for details.)

December 3, 1994

The crazy situation described at the beginning of the previous session had cooled a bit but was still running in the background. Since nothing serious had happened, I acquired a bit of confidence that 'mental blocking' and awareness were, in fact, quite effective. If you know somebody is trying to shoot nasty energies at you, you sort of send out blocking signals; and this is especially easy if you understand how pathetic they are and how silly they appear.

VG was present at this session and, as usual, tried to divert everything to her own personal questions, but, as you will see, the C's handled that on their own. There are predictions, a new Reiki symbol to use, and a long discussion about realms and the Wave. Most interesting overall, though I'll have a few remarks here and there.

Participants: 'Frank', Laura, VG

1 **Q:** Hello.

2 **A:** Hello.

3 **Q:** *(L)* Who do we have with us tonight?

4 **A:** Wasanna.

5 **Q:** *(L)* V___ had an incident at school where a small pile of powder appeared on her books after she had put her head down on them. What was this?

6 **A:** Materialized thoughts passed through frontal lobe.

7 **Q:** *(V)* Well, that is just amazing.

8 **A:** Amazement is fun.

9 **Q:** *(V)* I would like to know the source of the tension between my mother and myself.

10 **A:** Maternal influences. Psychological anxiety. Mother daughter rivalry for male attention. Enough personal dilly dallys. Long message to follow. Pause: Ukraine explosion; chemical or nuclear.[1] Hawaii crash; aviation, possi-

---

[1] If you want to look at this metaphorically, you could say that there has already been an important 'explosion' in Ukraine in terms of the recent political events (1st half of 2014). However, there is still the possibility of a nuclear explosion there what with the psychopaths running the U.S., the EU, and NATO. What I do find interesting is that this came first as though it were some sort of 'marker' event. When you take that in the context of the discussion of the 'realm border' and 'convergence point' following, it seems that we may, indeed, be on the verge of some dramatic changes.

bly involving military.² More California seismic activity after 1st of year: San Diego, San Bernardino, North Bakersfield, Barstow: all are fracture points. Hollister, Palo Alto, Imperial, Ukiah, Eureka, Point Mendocino, Monterrey, Offshore San Luis Obispo, Capistrano, Carmel: these are all stress points of fracture in sequence. "Time" is indefinite. Expect gradual destruction of California economy as people begin mass exodus.³ Also, Shasta erupts; Lassen activity. Ocean floor begins to subside.⁴ Leave channel open and pause: Queen Elizabeth serious illness; blood related.⁵ Princess Diana suicide attempt.⁶ Gas explosions this winter in NE United States, Texas and other. Supernova and unusual weather all over.⁷ Memphis feels tremors.⁸ Minneapolis banking scandal relates to mysterious Nordic covenant.⁹ Evangelical sexual tryst exposed.¹⁰ Gold is discovered in California after one of the

---

²Considering the many years in advance that this set of marker events was forecast, I'm wondering if the "Hawaii crash" might not refer to the missing Malaysian jetliner, Flight 370, that disappeared pretty much at the same time that Ukraine was going off?

³Based on the "after first of year" qualifier, and if this goes with the 'set of markers,' perhaps it is yet to come?

⁴This is particularly interesting considering what the Gulf Breeze Six included in their predictions, which I included with the 6 November 1994 session. You might want to check them for comparisons. Obviously, their dates are way off, but still, there is something!

⁵If these are marker events, and Ukraine is the big one, I guess we can wait and see on this one.

⁶Well, by now we know that Diana took a different path, or her end was deliberately planned and executed for some reason. The fact that Diana had attempted suicide a few times was not 'news,' since it was reported in 1992. See: http://articles.latimes.com/1992-06-08/news/mn-125_1_princess-diana-said and: http://www.dailymail.co.uk/news/article-299776/Diana-tapes-tell-Camilla-clash.html and http://abcnews.go.com/GMA/story?id=126905

⁷"Unusual weather all over" is sort of the watchword of our times. But when the C's said this, we had no idea how 'unusual' it could be. But then, they revealed further things in coming sessions about this. As to the supernova and gas explosions, again, if these are marker events headed up by the situation in Ukraine, I expect they are yet to come if they happen at all.

⁸I haven't heard of any earthquakes in Memphis, though Oklahoma has been being plagued due to fracking.

⁹There have been scads of banking scandals in the years since 9/11, so I don't know if this one is an 'off-side' hit or if it is yet to come. Maybe it should be taken with the group as 'marker events' and keep our eyes open for something more to come?

¹⁰Christian leaders getting caught with their pants down is rather common these days, so no cigar for this one unless it turns out to be so big and scandalous that we can't ignore it.

¹¹That would definitely be interesting!

quakes.[11] UFOs dramatic increase and Gulf Breeze gets swarmed, becomes massive "Mecca". Laura sees much more UFO activity. Huge wave of UFO activity. All manner and origins. Just you wait, it will give you chills and that feeling in the pit of your stomach. Many aliens will appear and we will be visible too. Think of it as a convention. All must awaken to this. It is happening right now. The whole populace will play individual roles according to their individual frequencies.[12] This is only the beginning. Just you wait "Henry Higgins," just you wait!

Q: *(L)* Are you a Rodgers and Hammerstein fan?[13] [14]

A: Yes.

Q: *(L)* How do you relate to the Pleiadians?[15]

A: Pleiadians are communicating with many others; we are bursting upon the scene with you, but we are essentially the same, just at slightly different focus points on the realm border.

Q: *(L)* Well, why is all this activity happening now?[16]

A: The grand cycle is about to close presenting a unique opportunity.

Q: *(L)* Does this mean that this is a unique opportunity to change the future?

A: Future, past and present.

Q: *(L)* Well, that sort of makes me think that if things are not changed somewhat at this point on the grand cycle that things could get really direfully screwed up, is that correct?

A: But they won't. You have not grasped concept.[17]

Q: *(L)* Yeah I have, I got you, I understand. It's just part of the cycle. It's all a cycle. I mean their being here is part of us being here...

A: You do??? [inscribed giant question mark on board][18]

Q: *(L)* Do what?

A: You said you understood concept. Really? Learn.

Q: *(L)* Well, since you guys can do that [referring to the big question mark], why

---

[12]Definitely read Pierre Lescaudron's book *Earth Changes and the Human-Cosmic Connection* to understand what is going on and what this can mean!

[13]While "Rodgers and Hammerstein" is what I said, and the creators of *My Fair Lady* were actually Lerner and Loew, the general intent of the question was "musical comedy" and the C's answer to my question stands even though I made the wrong connection.

[14]*The Wave* 1

[15]*The Wave* 71

[16]*The Wave* 22

[17]No, I hadn't. I was still thinking in terms of saving the world from any suffering; I had not come to the full realization that much of our civilization is going to be wiped away and the population of the planet along with it, one way or another, and that's just the way things are. It's an extinction cycle running its course.

[18]*The Wave* 17

[19]I was fascinated by the C's inscribing that question mark. In an instant, all kinds of possibilities occurred to me!

can't you teach us power symbols that will enhance our Reiki?[19]

A: You are not ready.

Q: *(L)* But if we work on the Reiki will you teach us more power symbols?

A: Okay, we'll give you one. [Draws symbol][20]

Q: *(L)* What is this symbol called?

A: Anuki. Pronounced: AH – NEW – KEY.

Q: *(V)* And, as it applies to Reiki, what does it do? What does it represent?

A: Retention of energy at location most in need.

Q: *(V)* So, if we work on somebody, do we use the symbol at the beginning or at the end?

A: All Reiki you have as yet learned involves passage of healing energy, this one involves prolonged retention for strengthened power, thus results.

Q: *(L)* Where are you getting this from?

A: Access is Universal.

Q: *(L)* Did Dr. Usui also receive this and then not remember it?

A: Usui did not reveal all to Takata.

Q: *(L)* Why?

A: He was told that the knowledge was priceless and must not be wasted by too much dissemination particularly to those who do not have the burning desire for truth. Those who did, as you do, would find some way of accessing knowledge.

Q: *(V)* Are we also advised not to divulge this information?

[20]See *The Wave* chapter 17 for symbol.
[21] *The Wave* 17

A: As always, be discreet.

Q: *(L)* Is this something we should pass to [two local Reiki practitioners of our acquaintance]?

A: Open.

Q: *(L)* Is it necessary to line the points up and the ascending line with geometric precision?

A: Yes.

Q: *(L)* And then, the circle elongated or more a perfect circle?

A: [Demonstration of drawing of circle part of symbol]

Q: *(V)* Has there ever been a crop circle that looks like this? It looks like one I saw.

A: Precisely. All are interrelated

Q: *(L)* Is it true that crop circles are a kind of grand Reiki being given to the planet?[21]

A: But also messages and lessons.

Q: *(L)* Well, could it also be said that Reiki symbols as applied to the body are etheric messages to the etheric body?

A: Yes.

Q: *(L)* Do they communicate information into our field, so to speak?

A: Everything that exists at all levels is just lessons.

Q: *(L)* Well, in the case of Reiki, what I specifically want to know is if, say an individual is psychically, spiritually, karmically, or otherwise wounded or discombobulated, does the application of

Reiki symbols give messages to the electromagnetic field to re-form or re-arrange the pattern in the perfect pattern intended?

A: Yes.

Q: *(L)* And can repeated application of this, can not only physical things, but also etheric things, be healed? That is, karma and so forth?

A: Yes.

Q: *(L)* So that our continual use of Reiki and application to ourselves and each other literally would cleanse us from our karmic burdens, memories, or scars of the soul?

A: Yes.

Q: *(V)* I am just concerned about the previously mentioned "convention"...[22]

A: Convention is because of realm border crossing.[23]

Q: *(L)* And why is there a convention attending this realm border crossing? I mean, is it just a "reely big shew!"?[24]

A: It is an opportunity.[25]

Q: *(V)* As in the windows are all opening at one time so that all these beings can get in at one time?

A: As in an opportunity to affect whole universe. Picture cosmic playing of "Pomp and Circumstance" AKA "Hope and Glory."[26]

Q: *(L)* How can a convention with slews of different kinds and races of people, converging on a single little pinpoint planet on the outer edges of an insignificant galaxy, at the farthest reaches of this enormous universe, affect the whole thing?

A: That is your perception.

Q: *(L)* Well, what is the correct perception? Is the planet Earth and the people thereon, and the things that are going on in this spot, the Earth specifically, more important than maybe we would ordinarily have thought?

A: The Earth is a Convergence point.

Q: *(L)* Has it always been a convergence point? Was it designed to be a convergence point? Or, is it just going to be a convergence point this once?

A: Too many questions at once.

Q: *(L)* Was it designed to be a convergence point from the beginning?

A: Natural function.

Q: *(L)* Has it been a convergence point all along? Is that why so many weird things happen here?

A: That is difficult to answer because you have no understanding of "time".

Q: *(V)* Has this type of convention thing happened on other planets with other groups of beings?

A: Has, is, and will.

---

[22] *The Wave* 71
[23] *The Wave* 1
[24] I'm dating myself: Ed Sullivan used to say this.
[25] *The Wave* 22
[26] Considering all we have learned about this 'realm border crossing' in the years since these early sessions, this makes a lot more sense. It's hard, in the beginning, to understand how the acceleration of horrific conditions on a planet can be beneficial. However, with an understanding of Information Theory and the possibilities that a cleansing can create conditions for a new beginning, it all begins to make sense.

81 **Q:** *(L)* So, in other words, there are other planets, I don't mean similar in structure or occupation, but other planets, that are convergence points? *(V)* Are they parallel universes?

82 **A:** Drifting.

83 **Q:** *(L)* If these convergence points are scattered around the universe, is the convergence of this realm border crossing going to occur simultaneously at all points in the universe that are convergence points?

84 **A:** No.

85 **Q:** *(L)* It only happens at say one, or selected, convergence points at any given point?

86 **A:** Close.

87 **Q:** *(L)* So, do realm borders have something to do with location?[27]

88 **A:** Realm borders ride waves.

89 **Q:** *(L)* And where do these waves come from?

90 **A:** They constantly cycle.

91 **Q:** *(L)* Does it have something to do with the movement of the planet Earth into it or does it move onto us?

92 **A:** Either or.

93 **Q:** *(F)* Does this convention or convergence have something to do with the fact that there are living beings on the Earth?

94 **A:** Yes. And because you are at critical juncture in development.

95 **Q:** *(L)* I would like to know in terms of prophecy if the prophecies you gave us in the first session are still valid and upcoming?

96 **A:** They are evolving.

97 **Q:** *(L)* Does that mean that they are evolving to the point that they are going to happen soon?

98 **A:** Fluid.

99 **Q:** *(L)* Does that mean that some of them may not happen?

100 **A:** Yes.[28]

101 **Q:** *(L)* And the prophecies that you gave tonight, are they subject to change also?

102 **A:** Maybe.

103 **Q:** *(L)* Are they more solid?

104 **A:** Open.

---

[27] *The Wave* 71

[28] This is probably the best explanation for how predictions can manifest I've seen: they 'evolve' or 'devolve', I guess, depending on changing variables. But what seems evident is that there is no avoiding the arrival of the 'cycling wave/realm border,' though the end results may be variable.

[29] Ken Carey, a contemporary New Age medium and channel, was a postal worker as a young man. Frustrated, he and his family moved to a farm where they lived without most modern conveniences such as electricity, plumbing, radio, television, newspapers, and magazines. Carey apprenticed himself to an Amish farmer. At one point in the later 1970s, lying in bed with a severe cold, he felt a presence and heard a low humming he described as an energy field. Then a voice spoke to him. During the winter of 1978–79 he channeled for 11 days. The entities that spoke through him sometimes appeared as angels (including the angel Raphael) or extraterrestrials. However, during the later sessions, an entity declared, "I am

105 **Q:** *(L)* I would like to know who is communicating with Ken Carey.[29] Who does he get this information from?

106 **A:** Many.

107 **Q:** *(L)* Are these individuals 'good guys' from our perspective?

108 **A:** Yes, some. Some is corrupted.

109 **Q:** *(L)* Is some of the information that comes through this channel corrupted?

110 **A:** Not as yet.[30]

111 **Q:** *(L)* Are the 6th density Orions, also known as Transient Passengers, are they the same TPs that have been referred to as the ones who genetically engineered us or put us here?[31]

112 **A:** Close. They are Wave riders.[32] [33]

113 **Q:** *(L)* Are those groups that ride the wave, is riding the wave part of the definition of Transient Passengers?

114 **A:** Yes.

115 **Q:** *(L)* Do they like to ride this wave?

116 **A:** Is it "fun" for you to live on Earth?

117 **Q:** *(L)* Well, I like living on Earth a great deal, but I don't like pain and suffering, and I don't like man's inhumanity to man and I don't like to see other people suffer.

118 **A:** Do you live on Earth for amusement?

119 **Q:** *(L)* I would like to live on Earth for amusement but I haven't had a whole heck of a lot of laughs since I have been here this time. I would like to have a life on the planet where things were pleasant...

120 **A:** You misunderstood.

121 **Q:** *(L)* I see what you are saying. That's where they live because that's where they live.

122 **A:** Yes.

123 **Q:** *(F)* In other words, did you choose to live on Earth because you bought a

---

Christ. I am coming this day through the atmosphere of your consciousness.... I am the bridegroom, spoken of old. I came to you first through the man named Jesus." The transcripts of these sessions were published as *The Starseed Transmissions* in 1982 and became an early channeled New Age classic. The entities who spoke through Carey emphasized the central New Age message. They had emerged in order to assist human evolution. It was time to lift the spell of matter and to bring forth a new planetary being. Humankind, Carey argued, is poised on the brink of a momentous transformation: The Earth is ripe for harvest. Two resources are available to assist humans in the transformative period: the advanced intelligences, such as those channeling through Carey; and the creative power of thought. See: http://www.answers.com/topic/ken-carey#ixzz36PvSaAQ5

[30]I guess there is a difference between being corrupted and being skewed because we have certainly seen evidence of skewing and the C's even said that persons who were hostile could dramatically affect the sessions.

[31]See sessions 7 October 1994 and 22 October 1994.

[32]Not surprising that the C's said "close" since I made a misstatement in my question. The C's had not said that there were 6th density Orions known as Transient Passengers, nor that Transient Passengers were the ones who genetically engineered humans. What they said was that the creators of the Cassiopaeans were "Your super ancient spiritual ancestors."

[33]*Secret History* 12; *The Wave* 26, 71

ticket? *(L)* I got it, Frank. I do want to ask about the *Course in Miracles* that is supposed to be channeled by Jesus Christ or the Holy Spirit. Is this true?

A: No.

Q: *(L)* What is the source that this is channeled from?

A: Variable sources.

Q: *(L)* Are they good guys?

A: Some.

Q: *(L)* So, even the *Course in Miracles* must be taken with a grain of salt?

A: Good idea.

Q: *(L)* I sent the answers to Karla, is this what she wanted?

A: Yes. She is diverted at the moment by others.[34]

Q: *(L)* Is it possible to do hypnotic future progressions and get accurate responses?

A: Yes.

Q: *(L)* In the book *Mass Dreams of the Future*, there are 4 scenarios described; are all of these scenarios accurate in terms of general experience?

A: Possible futures.[35]

Q: *(L)* So, when a person does a future progression, they are seeing a possible future and not necessarily...

A: Depends on quality of channel.

Q: *(L)* So, some people can be hypnotically progressed and get really accurate information?

A: Yes.

Q: *(L)* I would like to know, in the description of the Pentecost, it was said that the disciples gathered in a room and prayed for days and days and suddenly a wind came rushing in and flames danced over their heads and they all began speaking in tongues. I would like to know if this event or something similar occurred.

A: No.

Q: *(L)* In other words, the true baptism of the 'Holy Spirit' was when Jesus breathed on his disciples and transmitted something like the Reiki initiation?

A: Close.

Q: *(L)* Now, I had an experience a number of years ago when I was in church, when it seemed to me that I was speaking in tongues. Was that, in fact, what happened to me?

A: Suggestion.

Q: *(L)* It was suggested to me and therefore that is what occurred?

A: Yes.

Q: *(L)* Was any kind of psychic event occurring to me at that time?

A: Close.

Q: *(L)* Who or what energy is behind Jacques Vallee, the great scientist, investigator, and writer? Sometimes it seems like he is missing the point and sometimes it seems like he is the only one who knows what is going on.

A: He means well and his intentions are pure and good.

---

[34] I did receive a response from Karla shortly after this session as I described previously. We had a short exchange via snail mail until she went silent and some time later I learned that it was due to being diagnosed with cancer and undergoing surgery and other therapies.

[35] *The Wave* 22

153 **Q:** *(L)* What did Jesus look like? How tall was he?[36]

154 **A:** 5'9"

155 **Q:** *(L)* What color eyes did he have?

156 **A:** Blue.

157 **Q:** *(L)* What color hair did he have?

158 **A:** Strawberry blond.

159 **Q:** *(L)* What was his skin tone?

160 **A:** Fair.

161 **Q:** *(L)* What was his weight?

162 **A:** 160.

163 **Q:** *(L)* Was he muscular?

164 **A:** Average.

165 **Q:** *(L)* Was he what we would consider handsome?

166 **A:** Open.

167 **Q:** *(L)* Is there anybody I or Frank would know who bears a resemblance to him in facial features?

168 **A:** Maybe.

169 **Q:** *(L)* Could you name someone?

170 **A:** Scanning....

171 **Q:** *(L)* OK what was his occupation?

172 **A:** Carpenter.

173 **Q:** *(L)* Did he own his own home?

174 **A:** No.

175 **Q:** *(L)* Did John the Baptist really lose his head?

176 **A:** No.[37]

177 **Q:** *(L)* In talking about the new level of being after transition to 4th density, will this be something like what is described in the book *Celestine Prophecy*?

178 **A:** Close.

179 **Q:** *(L)* Is the carbon 14 dating process fairly accurate? If not, what is its major weakness?

180 **A:** To an extent.

181 **Q:** *(L)* What is its major weakness?

182 **A:** Same as yours.

183 **Q:** *(L)* Which is?

184 **A:** "Time" does not exist.

185 **Q:** *(L)* When was the last time a realm border crossed as far as the Earth is concerned?[38]

186 **A:** As you measure, on Earth, 309,000 years ago.

187 **Q:** *(L)* What does this wave consist of in terms of energy?

188 **A:** Feeling.

189 **Q:** *(L)* This wave is feeling? It is a wave of emotion?

190 **A:** Hyperkinetic sensate.

191 **Q:** *(L)* What does that mean?

192 **A:** All.

193 **Q:** *(L)* We don't understand

194 **A:** Too complex for this medium.

---

[36] Notice that the entire description from this exchange matches artistic representations and thus fit my assumptions that Jesus, as a historical character living in Palestine, actually existed. The C's were not lying; they were giving me what I asked for. In fact, lying or not lying is not really a very good point for assessment of a channeled source; rather whether the information can be determined as STS or STO.

[37] But Pompeius Magnus did. See Francesco Carotta's book *Jesus was Caesar*. Also see: http://www.carotta.de/subseite/texte/esumma.html

[38] *The Wave* 1, 22

195 **Q:** *(L)* OK. How many times has the wave come and involved the Earth as we know it?

196 **A:** Infinite number.

197 **Q:** *(L)* I would like to know if the Shroud of Turin was ever wrapped around Jesus.

198 **A:** No.

199 **Q:** *(L)* Was it wrapped around somebody who was crucified?

200 **A:** No.

201 **Q:** *(L)* How was it made?

202 **A:** Wrapped around Roman worker.

203 **Q:** *(L)* What caused the image on the shroud?

204 **A:** Body oils, hormones and other physiological chemicals.

205 **Q:** *(L)* Well, the kids have wanted me to ask this one for a long time and I keep forgetting. There was a woman out in California who was taken to the emergency room. Several attendants and a doctor collapsed while treating her and there was a big hoopla about contaminated blood.

206 **A:** Air conditioning system spread pesticides.[39]

207 **Q:** *(L)* Recently there was a supposed secret diary of Edgar Cayce reported in the tabloids. Was there such a diary?

208 **A:** No.

209 **Q:** *(L)* I received an article from Piers[40]

---

[39] Wrong, in my opinion, and probably due to strong prejudice toward this explanation. There is a much better explanation for what happened there on Wikipedia:

> Gloria Ramirez (January 11, 1963 – February 19, 1994) was a Riverside, California, woman dubbed "the toxic lady" by the media when several Riverside General Hospital workers became ill after exposure to her body and blood. Livermore Labs postulated that Ramirez had been using dimethyl sulfoxide *(DMSO)*, a solvent used as a powerful degreaser, as a home remedy for pain. Users of this substance report that it has a garlic-like taste, sold in gel form at hardware stores, it could also explain the greasy appearance of Ramirez's body. The Livermore scientists theorized that the DMSO in Ramirez's system might have built up, due to urinary blockage caused by her kidney failure. Oxygen administered by the paramedics would have combined with the DMSO to form dimethyl sulfone (DMSO2). DMSO2 is known to crystallize at room temperature, and crystals were observed in some of Ramirez's drawn blood. Electric shocks administered during emergency defibrillation could have then converted the DMSO2 into dimethyl sulfate (DMSO4), a powerful poisonous gas, exposure to which could have caused the reported symptoms of the emergency room staff.
> [http://en.wikipedia.org/wiki/Gloria_Ramirez]

This is why it is so, so important to research channeling. Answers given to questions with no emotional attachment are much more likely to be 'true.'

[40] Piers Anthony Dillingham Jacob: English American author in the science-fiction and fantasy genres, publishing under the name Piers Anthony. He is most famous for his long-running novel series set in the fictional realm of Xanth. We had a fairly lengthy correspondence off and on for years because of our mutual acquaintance, Keith Laumer. I was sending Piers updates now and again about the channeling experiment and he would send me articles or explanations for any apparent 'supernatural' phenomena.

about experiments by a fellow named Persinger who has been trying to duplicate the 'abduction' experience by subjecting people to EM fields in a sensory deprivation chamber. I would like comments on that, and second...

A: Nonsense, some have closed mind inspired by fear.[41]

Q: *(L)* My concern is that if he is doing this to people, and we have talked about electromagnetic energy blowing holes in the dimensional boundaries, my concern is that this experimentation could be detrimental to the persons being experimented on; is this a possibility?

A: Yes.

Q: *(L)* What could be the results of subjecting someone to these electromagnetic fields?

A: Cessation of body.

Q: *(L)* In other words, it could kill them?

A: Yes.

Q: *(L)* Could it also open doors between dimensions and allow other things to enter in?

A: Yes.

Q: *(L)* Could they be subjected to spirit or demonic possession by this method?

A: Yes.

Q: *(L)* Could they also be subjected to further programming by aliens through this method?

A: Yes.

Q: *(L)* Anything else you wish to say on this?

A: Always keep open mind.

---

[41] *High Strangeness* 8; *The Wave* 9, 20
[42] *The Wave* 35

Q: *(L)* Are there any psychological effects that could occur to a person as a result of this type of experimentation?

A: Maybe.

Q: *(L)* In the establishing of an ongoing connection between an abductee and the abductor, what methods or techniques are used? Is it a psychic bond?[42]

A: Close.

Q: *(L)* Is it formed technologically?

A: Partly.

Q: *(L)* There are so many stories of the 'gazing' process where the alien controls that abductee by staring into their eyes and the abductee feels full of love and harmony and thereby thinks that the experience is beneficial. This makes me wonder just exactly what is the purpose of this 'gazing'?

A: Hypnotic.

Q: *(L)* Does it also form a bond?

A: Yes.

Q: *(L)* What is the substance of this bond? Is there a psychic cord or connection and is it true that the same...

A: Channel wavering... [Planchette spinning around board]

Q: *(L)* Is that all you are going to say on that?

A: Please say good night.

Q: *(L)* Why?

A: Energy going.

Q: *(L)* Are you tired, Frank? *(F)* Not particularly. *(L)* Well they have never had their energy go before... and, especially since I am asking this particular question... is there some reason you do not want to answer this particular question?

A: Save...[43]

Q: *(L)* Goodnight

End of Session.

---

[43] I have the feeling that the asking of that question invited interference from those monitoring, whoever they might have been.

December 5, 1994

A little background on this session: remember the old boyfriend I wrote about in *Amazing Grace* and all the crazy stuff going on back then? Well, it happened that his mother lived on the same street where the house we bought in 1990 was also located; probably ten blocks away. As things happen, he learned we had bought the house. He called me shortly before this session and I filled him in on all the things I had been doing in the years since I had seen him last. He was not doing so well, however. His health was deteriorating rapidly and he blamed it on being exposed to toxic chemicals in Vietnam as well as the psychological damage he had experienced there. Then he told me something very peculiar: a raft of dead and dessicated frogs were appearing all over his house. Not just freshly dead, but mummified. Knowing how OCD[1] he was about cleanliness (the only person I ever knew who folded his dirty laundry to put it in the hamper!) and that he would surely have his house sealed against the incursion of critters, I was puzzled too. So, I suggested that we might ask at the session where the darn things were coming from.

Another odd thing about this session is the 'crankiness' of the C's in the beginning. The C's had made a number of remarks that suggested that I was their connection, though Frank was 'the channel' through which the information was transduced into language. Fair enough. What happened here was that V___ and I were sitting around waiting for Frank to show up (he liked to arrive as late as possible, which was quite annoying) so we decided to try to see if we could make contact with the C's without him. There was no instant contact and I'm not surprised in retrospect, because V___ was the last person it would have worked with. Anyway, Frank was quite annoyed that we had been doing this and his annoyance sure came through at the beginning and in a couple instances during this session! Nevertheless, as always, there

---

[1] Obsessive-compulsive disorder.

are some real gems in this one.

Participants: 'Frank', Laura, VG

Q: *(L)* Hello.

A: Hello.

Q: *(L)* Celestial dudes!

A: Look upon that as a sign.[2]

Q: *(L)* A sign of what?

A: Kindly remove ridge from board.

[Adjustments made]

A: Move board away from center of table.

Q: [Further adjustments made] *(L)* Is that better?

A: Okay.

Q: *(L)* Now, look upon what as a sign?

A: Channel.

Q: *(L)* Channel? How is that a sign channel? I don't get it?

A: Who? [Draws large question mark]

Q: *(L)* Who?

A: Is.

Q: *(L)* OK, you mean who is the channel?

A: Yes.

Q: *(L)* They are trying to tell us Frank is the channel. Who do we have with us tonight?[3]

A: Urua.

Q: *(L)* I have a number of questions prepared. Now, the beginning questions may seem a little bit personal, and we understand that you are STO. We are in need of a little service tonight. Is this alright?

A: Okay, but you are supposed to be moving toward STO.

Q: *(L)* Well, we are. The answering of some of these questions will stabilize certain aspects of our lives which will then enable us to devote ourselves more fully to helping others. Is that understandable?

A: Turn board, please.

Q: *(L)* Which way?

A: Not important, just turn slightly.

Q: *(L)* Will that do it?

A: Okay.

Q: *(L)* First question asked by neighbor down the street: what is the nature of the frog phenomenon?

A: Drugs.

Q: *(L)* How does this relate to drugs?

A: Left over influence.

Q: *(L)* Where are these frogs coming from?

A: Energy brings.

Q: *(L)* His energy manifests them? Or the drug energy manifests them?

A: Same.

Q: *(L)* Same? So, these are a manifestation of the frequency of drug use, is that a way of stating it?

A: Past drug use.

Q: *(L)* It is his own and not anyone else in the house?

---

[2] *The Wave* 35

[3] Clearly, this was Frank himself who felt threatened by the fact that anyone try the board without him, as became abundantly clear later.

39 **A**: Yes.

40 **Q**: *(L)* What do the frogs signify? What is the symbolism of the frogs?

41 **A**: Not signify, consequence.

42 **Q**: *(L)* Are these actual, physical frogs coming from somewhere?

43 **A**: Brought on.

44 **Q**: *(L)* I don't understand. Are we talking in circles here?

45 **A**: Your perception.[4]

46 **Q**: *(L)* Well, if you are a STO being, isn't our perception the one that matters? The one you are serving by clarification?

47 **A**: Serve by help to learn, learn by using mind. Direct answers don't help to learn.

48 **Q**: *(L)* OK, is there anything this individual can do to...

49 **A**: What would you do?

50 **Q**: *(L)* What would I do in his situation? Well, I would quit all drugs, I would begin meditating, and I would try in all ways to straighten myself out because a bunch of desiccated frogs suddenly appearing all over the place in my house would probably freak me out.

51 **A**: Yes, and? [Large question mark]

52 **Q**: *(L)* Obviously I am supposed to think of something else...

53 **A**: SRT.

54 **Q**: *(L)* What does that mean? Is that an abbreviation?

55 **A**: Yes. You have used the two words together extensively recently. Okay now, is part of book title.

56 **Q**: *(L)* Spirit Releasement Therapy?

[4] *The Wave* 3

57 **A**: Yes.

58 **Q**: *(L)* OK, so what this person needs is spirit releasement?

59 **A**: Bingo!

60 **Q**: *(L)* And so, what did we just learn from all of that?

61 **A**: How to use your mind.

62 **Q**: *(L)* OK, so he has some attachments. V___'s friend, BP, says she has channeled in the past. Who does she channel?

63 **A**: Lizards.

64 **Q**: *(V)* When she was channeling did she realize... well, obviously she didn't realize...

65 **A**: Most channel them.

66 **Q**: *(V)* So, then, it wouldn't be advisable to compare her channeled information with this information?

67 **A**: Up to you.

68 **Q**: *(L)* My mom wants to know about the physical condition of the lady she is taking care of whose name is MF. Is there anything she can do to improve the condition of this lady? Or, can you tell how long this lady will be in this plane?

69 **A**: Rub for circulation.

70 **Q**: *(L)* Is there any possibility of this lady getting better so that she can get about on her own to any extent?

71 **A**: Always possible.

72 **Q**: *(L)* What is the likelihood of her acceptance of getting better soon?

73 **A**: Open.

74 **Q**: *(L)* OK, is it seen in the immediate future that this lady has chosen to transition?

75 **A:** Open.

76 **Q:** *(L)* Mother also wanted me to ask if it would be advisable to invest funds in the marketing of my face cream.[5]

77 **A:** Please understand, we are not here to lead you by the hand, because, that would interfere with your free will, which is how you learn, which is how you progress.

78 **Q:** *(L)* Well, all things considered, I would still like to know if investing money in that project would be one of the better courses of action to take as far as developing a source of income.

79 **A:** What have we just told you?

80 **Q:** *(L)* Yeah, yeah. Is Paul Z going to accept the paperwork for the mortgage assignment as it is being drawn up?[6]

81 **A:** What are you going to do to help yourself?

82 **Q:** *(L)* Well, I am actually asking this as a test question to test your ability to predict, because it doesn't matter a whole lot if he accepts it the way it's being drawn up because if he wants to have it changed we can always change it. It's no big deal.

83 **A:** This is deteriorating into a personal forum.[7]

84 **Q:** *(L)* Well, somehow I don't feel that it is wrong to ask personal questions to test our source, because that is the only way we can determine what kind of information we are getting.

85 **A:** Ask test questions that potentially affect all. Paul Z is not particularly well known in Katmandu, for example.

86 **Q:** *(L)* I would like to ask about a book called *The "I AM" Discourses*. Could you tell us the source of this book?[8]

87 **A:** Good.

88 **Q:** *(L)* What density level is the source of this book?

89 **A:** Sixth level.

90 **Q:** *(L)* Can you tell us the name of the group behind this book?

91 **A:** All is one and the same.

92 **Q:** *(L)* As a service to another person can we get a health reading?

93 **A:** Is this of benefit to all?

94 **Q:** *(L)* Well, does this mean that we are going to be restricted forever to general questions that we can't verify?

95 **A:** Verification is not dependent upon personal nature. It is not STO if it limits.

96 **Q:** *(V)* So, asking about just one person is not service to all, it is just service to the one person?

97 **A:** And you.

---

[5] I have a channeled face cream formula.

[6] We were paying a mortgage on our house, held a mortgage on our old place, and were trading the latter for satisfaction of the former.

[7] Another discouragement from the C's to ask personal questions.

[8] *The "I AM" Discourses* are the original 'Ascended Master Teachings' religious movement founded in the early 1930s by Guy Ballard and his wife Edna in Chicago, Illinois. It is an offshoot of theosophy and a major precursor of several other New Age religions including the Church Universal and Triumphant. The movement had up to a million followers in 1938 and is still active today on a smaller scale. See: http://en.wikipedia.org/wiki/%22I_AM%22_Activity

98 **Q:** *(L)* Well, I am starting to wonder... I mean, if I didn't have to go back and start all over on prehistoric Earth, in the primordial soup, I would think this STO road is just a little bit rough.

99 **A:** No pain, no gain.

100 **Q:** *(L)* I don't want any more pain!

101 **A:** You are in the wrong place then.

102 **Q:** *(F)* I think this should be noteworthy, if Karla Turner claims that you can't trust anything that comes from this source because it will only tell you what it wants you to hear and so forth, this proves that this source does not just tell us what we want to hear. *(L)* Most assuredly. [Speaking sarcastically] *(F)* It sometimes tells us what we don't want to hear and sometimes it tells us whatever it feels like. Another thing that should be noteworthy is, every time you try to do something to verify something, it keeps answering that verification does not depend upon personal information. *(L)* Does this mean that I have to can my last three questions?[9]

103 **A:** Aren't things of universal significance more important?

104 **Q:** *(L)* Well, did you say before, when I was asking things that had to do with the various events of the past two years, that knowledge of them was protection? If that is the case, why can't I ask about these things now?

105 **A:** Yes, but we have repeatedly told all you need to know for your protection.[10]

106 **Q:** *(L)* In regards to my protection and V___'s and Frank's, and this is going to be the last on this series of questions, V___ and I both received cards from Ann B who, as you know, is hooked up with the metaphysical church group, I also received a card from Susan V, who is hooked up with Gene and Judy [also hooked up with the metaphysical church/coven]. Is there any underlying motivation from these individuals to send these cards and should we just disregard them?

107 **A:** Up to you.

108 **Q:** *(F)* Well, Laura, you can't ask for advice every step of the way on how to deal with everybody you know. *(L)* I know. *(V)* Have I been abducted in the last month?

109 **A:** No.

110 **Q:** *(V)* Do we need to interpret our

---

[9]Frank was practically crowing with glee that the C's were chastising me. However, I will point out here that the C's were quite often telling us what we wanted to hear because we had emotional investment in it. That's because they are STO and 'give what is asked.' Indeed, on other occasions, the C's told us things that were unpleasant that turned out to be true (or likely), which we didn't like, but that was when we had no pre-conceived notions combined with strong emotions attached to the questions. There were other cases where they would tell us the opposite of what we expected to hear, proving to be correct, but only if there was *no* emotional attachment to the idea. So, one has to be careful making blanket assumptions about the C's as Frank was doing here. As I said in the intro to this section, this "take that, I'm not going to answer your questions" emotional attitude was quite evident in Frank at this time. He was quite emotionally attached to being 'the channel' and anything that threatened that exalted position resulted in quite emotional displays.

[10]Not even close. Frank was just skewing the session.

dreams through this source?

111 **A**: Why not?

112 **Q**: *(L)* You mean you will discuss our dreams?

113 **A**: Up to you.

114 **Q**: *(L)* What a relief! A concession! OK, I had a dream last night, I dreamed about large mechanical flying 'V's' that had flapping wings like metal bat boxes. They scared me. Then, I was with my family and we were going to see my cousin who is deceased and she had just had a baby. The baby was walking and talking and quoting Shakespeare. My Aunt got very upset and said it was unseemly because the baby was illegitimate and she walked out in anger. The baby was only 10 days old. My aunt ran out the door and said it was evil.

115 **A**: Suggestion, get on computer net ASAP.[11]

116 **Q**: *(L)* In other words, I really need to take my computer down and get the A drive fixed, etc., and log onto the network?

117 **A**: Yes.

118 **Q**: *(V)* What does that have to do with the dream? *(L)* I think it relates back to when Terry and Jan were here and we were talking about dreams and the suggestion was given to hook up to the network and discuss and share dreams. Like a dream forum kind of thing. Is there any significance to the ten days in this dream?

119 **A**: When you network, your entire life will dramatically improve immediately! See, sometimes we do advise when appropriate.[12]

120 **Q**: *(L)* Alright. Point well taken. Would you please elaborate on the concept that alien abductions are 'the scourge of God' and are manifested so that consciousness may grow and differentiate itself by a refusal to accept negative experience within the delusive material world?

121 **A**: Nonsense!

122 **Q**: *(L)* Well, that was real elaborate! Would you comment on the Biblical command to not make graven images? Why was this command issued?

123 **A**: In order to prevent control by too many sources.

124 **Q**: *(L)* How would not making graven images prevent control by other or too many sources?

125 **A**: Deception.

126 **Q**: *(L)* Who issued this command to not make graven images?

127 **A**: Central.

128 **Q**: *(L)* What is "Central"?

129 **A**: Level 7.

130 **Q**: *(L)* What is the true symbolism of the Egyptian scarab and why was it invented?

131 **A**: Operation.

132 **Q**: *(L)* The symbolism was operation? What do you...

---

[11] *The Wave* 18, 35

[12] "Immediate," to the C's, is a relative term. However, it was almost immediately in human terms. When I finally got hooked up to the internet, it was only months before Ark and I 'met' and the rest is history. So, we see here, again, the C's sending coded information through Frank who, when no emotion was involved, functioned as a very efficient metaphor-to-language transducer or psychic 'reader.'

133 **A**: Was an operation.

134 **Q**: *(L)* How was a scarab an operation?

135 **A**: Think. Action.

136 **Q**: *(L)* The scarab is a dung beetle. It rolls dung into little balls. Am I onto something here?

137 **A**: Continue.

138 **Q**: *(L)* And supposedly the scarab symbolized eternal life because it represented the rolling of the sun... oh dear, wait a minute... the rolling of the sun across the sky is what the Egyptians understood... but what the dung beetle really does is simply rolls dung up into little balls... is this the operation you are talking about... the rolling of dung into little balls?

139 **A**: Close.

140 **Q**: *(L)* Well, that's all I know about the scarab so you are going to have to help me out here.

141 **A**: Life cycle.

142 **Q**: *(L)* OK, the life cycle. I would like to know what force was behind the rise and domination of Oliver Cromwell?[13]

143 **A**: Lizards.

144 **Q**: *(L)* OK, there is a woman named Jane Allyson who channels an entity known as Zeena. I would like to know who or what is Zeena?[14]

145 **A**: Just Jane.

146 **Q**: *(L)* So, she is just channeling herself? What is the significance of the number 444 as repeated by Cytron, a robot channeled by Jane Allyson, a super cyborg?

147 **A**: Zilch. [Much laughter]

148 **Q**: *(L)* I would like to know what is the karmic ramification of the killing of those two little boys in South Carolina by their mother? Everybody in the U.S. will be interested in this one, maybe not Katmandu, though.

149 **A**: Pain teaches.

150 **Q**: *(L)* And, in this case is the mother suffering the pain?

151 **A**: And all others involved including the whole nation. All is lessons.

152 **Q**: *(L)* Did these two little boys volunteer to come in for this purpose?

153 **A**: Yes. Were higher density beings on mission.[15]

154 **Q**: *(L)* Do 4th density STO's feed off of 3rd density energy?

155 **A**: No.

156 **Q**: *(L)* I would like to ask about the *Starseed Transmissions*. I would like to know about the Bird Tribes. What is this source?

---

[13] I had had a particularly vivid dream about a past life during the time of Cromwell, when I was an abused servant in the house of one of Cromwell's officers, whom I recognized as Keith Laumer. It seemed to me to explain the dynamic between us that had transpired in this life. See *Amazing Grace* for details.

[14] There were so many people channeling so many critters it was hard to keep up with it all.

[15] Well, I don't know about that; I do know that reading the story of the mother who committed this awful deed was very sad. She was very damaged herself and the whole thing was an ugly mess.

157 **A:** Ken Carey is only channeling his alternate self.[16]

158 **Q:** *(V)* Who are good channels, then, if every one we ask about is channeling themselves or false channels? Who can we look to as a clean channel?

159 **A:** We have already told you of one example.

160 **Q:** *(L)* Barbara Marciniak?

161 **A:** This session.

162 **Q:** *(L)* The *"I AM" Discourses*?

163 **A:** Review. Graven images.

164 **Q:** *(L)* Could you tell me what source of information was behind the...

165 **A:** Akashic records.

166 **Q:** *(V)* I wanted to ask about that and I had totally forgotten! Are the Akashic records the same thing as the source that you called "Central"?

167 **A:** No.

168 **Q:** *(L)* Are the Akashic records the same source that *The "I AM" Discourses* come from?

169 **A:** All is one at base but different "branches".

170 **Q:** *(L)* Was Nostradamus getting his information from the Akashic records?

171 **A:** Yes.

172 **Q:** *(L)* So, Nostradamus' quatrains, if interpreted correctly, would actually be valid.

173 **A:** Interpretation is the key.

174 **Q:** *(L)* If we were to hold a series of sessions about the quatrains of Nostradamus, would you be able to help us interpret them?

175 **A:** Yes.

176 **Q:** *(L)* Would that be a worthwhile project for us?

177 **A:** Up to you.

178 **Q:** *(L)* Are the 6th density STS individuals that you indicated are the Orions, these are the same beings, I understand, that genetically engineered or created mankind, is that correct?

179 **A:** No.

180 **Q:** *(L)* Are they the first to alter us after creation?

181 **A:** Close.

182 **Q:** *(L)* Are the 6th density Orions known as Transient Passengers?

183 **A:** Yes.

184 **Q:** *(L)* So there are Transient Passengers that are STO as well as STS?

185 **A:** TP is "wanderer".

186 **Q:** *(L)* And what is a wanderer?

187 **A:** TP.[17]

188 **Q:** *(L)* Well, the idea of the Wanderers, according to the *Ra Material*, is 4th or 5th density beings that have chosen to come back into 3rd density to help us. Would that be the same kind of Wanderer?

189 **A:** 5th or 6th density.

190 **Q:** *(L)* Is Frank a Wanderer?

---

[16] On 3 December, I'd asked this question in a different way and the response was that he was channeling "many" and some of his information was good, and some corrupted. So "only channeling his alternate self" gets no cigar.

[17] See 1994 sessions 7 October, 18 October, 22 October, 16 November, 3 December and notes. Here, again, I was making assumptions but I believe I was doing it deliberately to check consistency.

191 **A**: Open.

192 **Q**: *(L)* Am I or V___?

193 **A**: Open.

194 **Q**: *(V)* What if we felt like we were?

195 **A**: Check it out.

196 **Q**: *(L)* How?

197 **A**: How would you think?

198 **Q**: *(V)* Faith, I guess, and how I feel. What else do you have to go on?

199 **A**: Not answer, try again.

200 **Q**: *(L)* Would hypnosis be the solution?

201 **A**: Bingo!

202 **Q**: *(L)* OK. Now, I would like to know, for the sake of all the Theosophists around the world, what was the source of the information in the book *Isis Unveiled* by Helena Blavatsky?

203 **A**: Orions STS and STO. 6th density.

204 **Q**: *(L)* So, her information was from both sides? And it is up to the reader to figure out which is which?

205 **A**: Good idea.[18]

206 **Q**: *(L)* Is there any possibility that the information we get through this source is STS oriented?

207 **A**: Yes. Always possibility.

208 **Q**: *(L)* I would like to know what is the definition of, and would you describe for us, a dimensional curtain?[19]

209 **A**: Self-explanatory. Think.

210 **Q**: *(L)* When we are talking about dimensional curtains we are talking about divisions at the same level of density, is that correct?[20]

211 **A**: Maybe.

212 **Q**: *(L)* Can dimensional curtains be between dimensions at the same level of density?

213 **A**: Yes.

214 **Q**: *(L)* Are dimensional curtains also something that occurs between levels of density?

215 **A**: Yes.

216 **Q**: *(L)* So, a dimensional curtain is a point at which some sort of change takes place... what causes this change?

217 **A**: Nature.

218 **Q**: *(L)* In specific terms of the engineering of it, what defines this change?

219 **A**: Experience.

220 **Q**: *(L)* Is it in any way related to atomic or quantum physics or the movement of atoms?

221 **A**: Yes.

222 **Q**: *(L)* OK. An atom is in 3rd density. What distinguishes it from an atom in 4th density?

223 **A**: Reality.

224 **Q**: *(L)* What distinguishes one realm from another?

225 **A**: Assumptions.

226 **Q**: *(L)* OK, what you assume or expect is what you perceive about that atom depending upon which reality you are in, is that correct?

227 **A**: Close.

---

[18] Interesting answer since the "I AM" material from Godfre Ray King mentioned above relied to some extent on concepts developed or brought forward by Blavatsky.
[19] *The Wave* 1, 9
[20] *Secret History* 12; *The Wave* 26

228 **Q:** *(L)* What determines your assumptions?

229 **A:** Experience.

230 **Q:** *(L)* My experience of atoms is that they congregate in such a way as to form solid matter...

231 **A:** Every thing that exists is merely a lesson.

232 **Q:** *(L)* OK, so once we have learned certain lessons, as in experience of certain things, then our assumptions change?

233 **A:** Yes.

234 **Q:** *(L)* OK, is this wave that is coming our direction going to give us an experience that is going to change our assumptions?

235 **A:** Catch 22: One half is that you have to change your assumptions in order to experience the wave in a positive way.[21]

236 **Q:** *(L)* And what does this wave consist of in absolute terms?

237 **A:** Realm border.[22]

238 **Q:** *(L)* Is that realm border as in a cutoff point between one reality and another?

239 **A:** Yes.

240 **Q:** *(L)* Is that realm border as in dimensional curtain?

241 **A:** Yes.

242 **Q:** *(L)* So the planet Earth is going to pass through a dimensional curtain?

243 **A:** Or an Earth. All is merely a lesson, and nothing, repeat nothing, more.

244 **Q:** *(L)* Well, my experience with lessons has been that they are generally painful. Is this realm border crossing, or this merging experience, going to be what we, or I, in the 3rd density, would perceive as painful?

245 **A:** Wait and see.

246 **Q:** *(V)* Is the realm border 3rd density?

247 **A:** Have answered; stop and contemplate.

248 **Q:** *(L)* What exactly are crop circles and how are they formed? I know we have asked about crop circles before, but I would like to know the specific mechanism by which they are formed.

249 **A:** Not issue, but energy vortex.

250 **Q:** *(L)* Does this energy vortex arise from within the Earth itself?

251 **A:** No.

252 **Q:** *(L)* Where does this energy vortex issue from?

253 **A:** Here. Sixth density.

254 **Q:** *(L)* Do you want to give us more on the wave, or realm curtain?

255 **A:** No, not at this time. You have enough for now. Goodnight.

End of session.

---

[21]The exchange leading up to this response is actually quite fascinating because it connects several concepts together: observer-influenced reality, Many Worlds Interpretation of Quantum Theory, and Information Theory.

[22]*High Strangeness* 14

December 9, 1994

In the days between the last session and this one, I had been contacted by yet another woman who believed she had been abducted by aliens and wanted to schedule a hypnotic regression to explore the possibility. As should be well known by my readers, I saw each such case as a possible opportunity to find some explanation other than 'alien abduction.' I did think it was kind of strange that, after 20 years of doing hypnosis sessions for many, many people, and having never encountered a single case of alleged alien abduction, now, all of a sudden, cases were coming out of the woodwork and calling me! If awareness, assumptions, and experience determine your reality, as the C's suggested in the previous session, I was definitely entering a different realm!

As I wrote in the second chapter of *The Wave*, the client in question here was a woman, Diana M, about 45 years old, who was a science instructor at one of the local high schools. She had begun to experience some rather strange things in her life after becoming associated with a metaphysical church in Tampa, about 40 miles distant from my home at the time. (Recall from *The Wave* that Scarlett, AKA 'Candy,' had also suddenly become convinced that she had been abducted by aliens after joining the local metaphysical church/coven that had been giving me so much grief because of the C's communications.) I gave her the pseudonym 'Ruth' in *The Wave*.

As with Scarlett's case, and most cases of this kind, the initiating events are so lost in a confusing mess of contradictory details that it is difficult to sort out what exactly happened in what sequence. The person appears to be in such a state of post-traumatic stress disorder *(PTSD)* that it is difficult to get them to make any sense.

The transcript of the hypnosis session is published in *The Wave* so I won't include it here; I'll just mention that it included witnessing praying mantis–type aliens eating human children. (And believe me, I am strict about not asking leading questions!) By the time the session was over, I was almost as traumatized as the client, though I certainly did not reveal that to her. Needless to say, I wanted to see what the C's would say about this.

Participants: 'Frank' and Laura

1 **Q**: *(L)* Hello.

2 **A**: Hello.

3 **Q**: *(L)* And who do we have with us this evening?[1]

4 **A**: [Name lost]

5 **Q**: *(L)* And where are you from?

6 **A**: Cassiopaea.

7 **Q**: *(L)* Now, tell me the name of the beings Diana M experienced as praying mantises in her hypnosis session?

8 **A**: Her essence.

9 **Q**: *(L)* But, in that reality don't they have a name?

10 **A**: Too complex to answer adequately in this medium.

11 **Q**: *(L)* Well, you said that the [praying mantis] beings that V___ encountered were Minturians, aren't they the same?[2]

12 **A**: No.

13 **Q**: *(L)* Is there a difference between essence beings and incarnate beings?[3]

14 **A**: Yes.

15 **Q**: *(L)* So we have a distinct difference. OK, who were the ant/fly beings she described?

16 **A**: Her essence too.

17 **Q**: *(L)* And what were those snakey, slug-like beings that she saw?

18 **A**: Same.

19 **Q**: *(L)* Are you saying that all of this stuff is who she is? All of these horrible creatures and these..

20 **A**: In some of the alternate realities.

21 **Q**: *(L)* Do I have creatures like that that are my essence?

22 **A**: Yes.

23 **Q**: *(L)* My essence is something that horrible and dark and icky?

24 **A**: Subjective.

25 **Q**: *(L)* Well, weren't those horrible icky beings eating little children? Weren't those real human children?

26 **A**: How do you think you are viewed by deer, for example?

27 **Q**: *(L)* Well, I can immediately see that. I saw that already. I mean, cows and chickens would have to view us that way. I mean, it's pretty gross.

28 **A**: Roaches, too.

29 **Q**: *(L)* Is that why the night before Diana's session, I dreamed of ants that I could have stepped on and smashed, and for some reason I decided I did not want to take the life of even a single ant?

30 **A**: Yes.

31 **Q**: *(L)* Was that dream preparing me for what I was going to experience in that session?

32 **A**: Yes.

33 **Q**: *(L)* Well, what do we do about these essence parts of ourselves? I mean, I

---

[1] *The Wave* 33
[2] See sessions 16 October and 23 October 1994.
[3] *The Wave* 2

don't like it that there may be something of the predator in me. I would like to not have it, or get rid of it, or transform it, or whatever.

34 **A**: Wait and see.

35 **Q**: *(L)* Well, am I going to have to remember myself doing things like that in order to come to terms with it?

36 **A**: Yes.

37 **Q**: *(L)* Is that going to happen to me, that I am going to have memories like that surfacing?

38 **A**: Yes.

39 **Q**: *(L)* Well, I can't even cope with it in someone else, how am I going to deal with it in myself?[4]

40 **A**: You will.

41 **Q**: *(L)* Is this something we are all going to have to do?

42 **A**: All eligible.

43 **Q**: *(L)* And who is eligible?

44 **A**: 4th density candidates.

45 **Q**: *(L)* Is Frank going to have to remember these things, too?

46 **A**: Yes.

47 **Q**: *(L)* How does one know that one is a 4D candidate?

48 **A**: You gradually "awaken".

49 **Q**: *(L)* Are my children 4D candidates? And my husband? You have to tell me this. If I have to deal with things, let me do it a little at a time.

50 **A**: You are not in correct frame of mind.

51 **Q**: *(L)* Well, that sounds ominous.

52 **A**: Wait for answer.

53 **Q**: *(L)* Wait until when?

54 **A**: You are ready.

55 **Q**: *(L)* So, in other words, some people may have to leave behind children or mates, or siblings or parents, is that true?

56 **A**: If so, will be prepared.

57 **Q**: *(L)* Is there any way to tell if someone is a 4D candidate?

58 **A**: Inquire of them.

59 **Q**: *(L)* And, will they know?

60 **A**: Yes, at some level. In a sense. Those who are chosen feel it. You will know.

61 **Q**: *(L)* Well, I happen to think that my family is extremely special.

62 **A**: So do all.

63 **Q**: *(L)* I have taken a great deal of time and care with spiritual matters. Is that because it was my obsession or did they choose me because of this?

64 **A**: Open.

65 **Q**: *(L)* Did the Minturians, the praying mantis beings that V___ experienced in her regression, did those praying mantises eat people?

66 **A**: Too complex for your thought patterns of this session. You are upset.[5]

67 **Q**: *(L)* Well, is that what is wrong with me tonight? You aren't telling me much.

---

[4]To say that I was pretty horrified at this revelation about our reality is putting it mildly. This is one of the instances where the C's give what is asked for: the truth, and since I had no preconceived beliefs or emotional attachment to belief, the information was probably accurate even if distressing.

[5]No kidding!

68 **A:** Biological, and we are telling plenty, you are not "hearing" because biological factors have temporarily pushed you back more into 3D.

69 **Q:** *(L)* Would it be a good idea to do the Reiki exercises and stop the cycle?

70 **A:** Your cycle may stop soon anyway.

71 **Q:** *(L)* Well, is it true that that exercise, when it stops your cycle, it also stops the aging process?

72 **A:** Somewhat.

73 **Q:** *(L)* Would it be beneficial.

74 **A:** Maybe.

75 **Q:** *(L)* But, I thought you guys said I had another baby waiting to come in?

76 **A:** Does not necessarily mean will make it.

77 **Q:** *(L)* So, am I going through the change here?

78 **A:** Not yet.

79 **Q:** *(L)* When will it start?

80 **A:** Open.

81 **Q:** *(L)* Is Scarlett going to pay me the money she owes me?

82 **A:** Maybe.

83 **Q:** *(L)* What are the odds?

84 **A:** Depends on your efforts.

85 **Q:** *(L)* Does that mean that I have to now send her a certified letter through my attorney?

86 **A:** Up to you.

87 **Q:** *(L)* And, if I do this, will she pay?

88 **A:** Maybe.

89 **Q:** *(L)* Have the B___s made their final payment to Fleet?[6]

90 **A:** Not yet.

91 **Q:** *(L)* Will they pay on Monday?

92 **A:** Probably.

93 **Q:** *(L)* When will I get my SSI check?

94 **A:** Within 10 days?

95 **Q:** *(L)* When will I get my monthly check?

96 **A:** The same.

97 **Q:** *(L)* And how much will the back pay be?

98 **A:** 3000 approximately.[7]

99 **Q:** *(L)* And how much will we get from Paul with the deed to the house?

100 **A:** Open.

101 **Q:** *(L)* Back, a year or so ago, when we talked to Keith on the board, and you verified that it was Keith, Keith gave us a set of [lotto] numbers that came in within 8 days of the day he gave them to us. Now, if he, as an earthbound spirit, was capable of giving us a set of numbers that came in within 10 days, could you not do the same?

102 **A:** Maybe, when all is well.

103 **Q:** *(L)* In other words, when I am not in this crummy mood?

104 **A:** Okay.

105 **Q:** *(L)* Is there any qualification that needs to be established for us to get the lottery numbers? Is there some thing we have to do, or be, or think, or say?

106 **A:** Completely pure intent, i.e. open.

107 **Q:** *(L)* Completely open?

---

[6]Mortgage broker. As mentioned in previous session, we were trading a mortgage we held for the satisfaction on the house we lived in.

[7]Correct, but no cigar.

108 **A**: Nonanticipatory.

109 **Q**: *(L)* Our anticipation constricts the channel when we ask for that kind of information?

110 **A**: Yes.

111 **Q**: *(L)* We have to be completely uncaring whether we get it or not, so to speak?

112 **A**: Happy-go-lucky attitude helps. As you were before.

113 **Q**: *(L)* So, as long as we are worried, tense, anticipatory, and attached to the idea, we constrict the flow?[8]

114 **A**: Yes.

115 **Q**: *(L)* Now, you said in an earlier session that you were making financial arrangements for us. Well, I am not putting any weight or pressure on that, but, does that have anything to do with Martie T and referrals for hypnosis?

116 **A**: Maybe. Don't be anticipatory. Faith, dear.

117 **Q**: *(L)* Thank you and good night.

118 **A**: Good night.

End of Session

---

[8] It was hard to be anything other than worried and tense about finances with 5 kids and my health going down the tubes.

December 10, 1994

Terry and Jan drove up from St. Petersburg for this session. It begins with an interesting word that was, apparently, in Jan's head, because she had been in a location earlier that day where many poinsettias were being brought in as Christmas decorations. She was quite surprised and pleased.

Before the session, I had given Terry and Jan a recap of the hypnosis session with Diana M and her praying mantis essence-beings. Overall, this is a really interesting session and I think that is attributable to the presence of T&J and their positive energy. Looking back, I think that, at this point in time, Frank's negative energy was easily able to overpower me because I was still in a rather fragile state of health. This is the session where the C's introduced the concept "We are you in the future."

Participants: 'Frank', Laura, Terry and Jan

1 **Q:** *(L)* Hello.

2 **A:** Hello. Poinsettia.

3 **Q:** *(L)* What?

4 **A:** Just came to mind.

5 **Q:** *(L)* Is that in our minds?

6 **A:** No, ours.

7 **Q:** *(L)* Who do we have with us tonight?

8 **A:** Cassiopaea calling.

9 **Q:** *(L)* What is your name?

10 **A:** Rodann.

11 **Q:** *(L)* I want to ask again for the benefit of Terry and Jan, what or who were the beings seen by DM in her hypnotic regression the other night?[1]

12 **A:** Her essence.

13 **Q:** *(L)* Were these in any way physical beings on the Earth we occupy in space-time from where we are at this moment?[2]

14 **A:** No.

15 **Q:** *(L)* This happened in a so-called alternate reality?

16 **A:** Is still.

17 **Q:** *(L)* So, in some alternate reality, DM is a praying mantis being eating little

---

[1] This session is recounted in *The Wave* Series in some detail, including direct transcript.
[2] *The Wave* 2

children?

A: And so are you. And all others.

Q: *(L)* This is an essence of what?

A: Her being.

Q: *(L)* Are these aspects of our being coming to Earth as part of the realm border crossing?

A: Yes.

Q: *(L)* Are all of us going to have to face these aspects of ourselves as other beings?

A: Yes.

Q: *(L)* Are there other parts of us in all realms doing other things at this moment?[3]

A: Yes.

Q: *(L)* And how is this going to be affected by the realm border crossing?

A: Will merge.

Q: *(L)* Do we need to do extensive hypnosis to bring these aspects of ourselves up and deal with these things a little at a time?

A: Will happen involuntarily. Will be like a thermonuclear blast. Message follows: See pattern. Orion, Pleiades, Arcturas, Cassiopaea; check distances from Earth; progress locator for wave combined with Earth references of space time. For you to figure out. Cross reference channeled messages, printing dates and location. We are where we are.

Q: *(L)* What do you mean you are where you are?

A: Cross reference time and distance.

Q: *(L)* What book do we need to cross reference?

A: Any star chart and Marciniak, Arcturas Channel, Orion literature and Us. We speak from "crest" of wave, now, where are we?

Q: *(L)* Is this a riddle?

A: From, not of.

Q: *(L)* You speak from the crest of the wave? *(T)* Are you riding the wave?

A: Yes.

Q: *(L)* You said in another reading that you were 6 thousand miles...

A: Window of transmission.

Q: *(L)* We are certainly hoping that you are going to make all of this plain and clear...

A: It is.

Q: *(L)* Well, can you help us poor 2-strand DNA creatures to understand this?

A: How far away is Cassiopaea?[4]

Q: *(L)* Do we need specific distances?[5]

A: General is okay.

Q: *(L)* So, if we just find the general distances... and does each of these star clusters represent a general area of the wave?

A: Each represents locator in space time. You can judge speed and ETA by cross referencing distance with publishing dates and these messages from us.

Q: *(L)* I got it! You mean that *you* are the Arcturians, the Pleiadians, and now

---

[3] *The Wave* 6
[4] This is somewhat related to the concepts presented by Arkadiusz Jadczyk's article "Feeling the Future," included as a foreword to this volume.
[5] *The Wave* 2

you are the 'Cassiopaeans' because you "are where you are"! And you are riding the wave. Is this wave a straight line connecting all these constellations?

50 **A**: Circuitous or cyclical route.

51 **Q**: *(L)* So, is it like a spiral?

52 **A**: Yes.

53 **Q**: *(L)* So we really need to set up a map so we can draw it?

54 **A**: Yes.

55 **Q**: *(L)* When we speak from Orion we are 'Orions.' When from Pleiades, we are 'Pleiadian,' and so on.

56 **Q**: *(L)* So, all of these channeled books you have mentioned are coming from the same basic source, through different channels, that they are able to connect with because of their different positions in space-time and preparation level of the channels, is that correct?

57 **A**: Close. We have given you a Wave crest locator. We are from where we are and speak. Get it?

58 **Q**: *(L)* You are the wave crest?

59 **A**: We are Marciniak's Pleiadians. We are where we are.

60 **Q**: *(T)* So, you are not really Cassiopaeans from the constellation Cassiopeia?

61 **A**: We are Transient Passengers.

62 **Q**: *(T)* So, when the Wave reaches Earth and you are transmitting to somebody else out there you will represent yourselves as the 'Terrans'?

63 **Q**: When Wave reaches Earth, we merge with you.

64 **A**: *(L)* When you were at Orion, did you merge with the Orions?

[6] *The Wave 2*

65 **A**: Not on same frequency for realm border crossing.[6]

66 **Q**: *(L)* What effect did the wave have on the Orion sector?

67 **A**: None. Already at 4th density level.

68 **Q**: *(L)* Where did the wave originate?

69 **A**: Did not.

70 **Q**: *(L)* Has it always been cycling through the universe?

71 **A**: Close.

72 **Q**: *(T)* OK, you are riding on the crest of this wave in 6th density, is this true?

73 **A**: Yes. We are you in 6th density.

74 **Q**: *(T)* You are we, that is me Terry, Laura, Jan, and Frank?

75 **A**: Yes.

76 **Q**: *(L)* Are you alternate selves extending into higher densities?

77 **A**: At your current reference point in space time, we are you in the future.

78 **Q**: *(T)* We are your destiny?

79 **A**: And vice versa.

80 **Q**: *(L)* You are not, by any chance, one of those weird ant or preying mantis beings are you?

81 **A**: Yes and no.

82 **Q**: *(T)* You are just another part of ourselves? You, us, the Lizards, the ants, the Grays, the trees...

83 **A**: We are your whole self as you/we are in 6th density.

84 **Q**: *(T)* So, what we are working to become is you? You are us?

85 **A**: Yes.

86 **Q**: *(T)* So, when we move to 4th density and become whole with ourselves, we will know you also for a short time?

87 **A:** Not whole yet when at 4th density.

88 **Q:** *(T)* But in order to move to 4th density...

89 **A:** Closer.

90 **Q:** *(T)* We, us, in this room, are closer than others are?

91 **A:** No. Closer when at 4th density.

92 **Q:** *(L)* When Scarlett was under hypnosis she described seeing a fleet of space ships "riding a wave" and this unnerved her. She felt this wave was a fearful, invasion-type thing. Was this you and your wave she was perceiving?

93 **A:** Wave is transport mode.

94 **Q:** *(L)* Is that transport mode for many beings?[7]

95 **A:** Yes.

96 **Q:** *(L)* Are you coming to invade us?

97 **A:** No, merge.

98 **Q:** *(L)* Are others coming with the intention of invading us?

99 **A:** Yes.

100 **Q:** *(L)* And, when you merge with us, are you going to empower us to resist and defend ourselves?

101 **A:** Wave is "crowded."

102 **Q:** *(T)* So, everybody out in the whole universe who want a piece of the Earth action are on this wave?

103 **A:** At realm border crossing.

104 **Q:** *(L)* Let me ask a couple of quick questions to get them out of the way, unless you have something you really... I mean, you pretty much gave us what we need on that... this channeled material received here...

105 **A:** Oh yeah?

---

[7] *The Wave* 71

106 **Q:** *(L)* Well, I guess they are telling me that we did not get all we needed on that subject. But, we can come back to it.

107 **A:** You may ask questions if you wish.

108 **Q:** *(L)* Well, I don't want to cramp anybody's style here. *(T)* Oh, go ahead, they're crowded on the wave already anyway. OK, here is a transcript I received in the mail from a group called 'Cosmic Awareness'...

109 **A:** Dezinformatzia.

110 **Q:** *(T)* Well, I love a 6th density being with a sense of humor. *(L)* Has the base at Area 51 been moved to Kirtland as this stuff says?

111 **A:** No.

112 **Q:** *(T)* Is there a base at Area 51?

113 **A:** Yes. Kirtland has a new addition.

114 **Q:** *(L)* Is the base at area 51 where our military and aliens are working in conjunction?

115 **A:** They have recovered craft of Grays, but human and alien personnel are not working together there.

116 **Q:** *(T)* Are the craft actually captured?

117 **A:** Recovered from crash.

118 **Q:** *(T)* Have any alien beings given the government craft?

119 **A:** No.

120 **Q:** *(L)* Why not?

121 **A:** Would you give mice TV sets?

122 **Q:** *(L)* How do these insect beings, these other manifestations of ourselves, how do they view our treatment of insects on this planet?

123 **A:** Unconcerned.

124 **Q**: *(L)* Is that because the insects on our planet are not sentient beings?

125 **A**: Different.

126 **Q**: *(T)* How do the insect beings handle insects on their planet?

127 **A**: They are the insects on their planet.

128 **Q**: *(L)* Do they have pests on their planet like little miniature humans that run around and tear up their groceries? *(T)* Any energizer bunnies?

129 **A**: Mirth!

130 **Q**: *(L)* But really, do they have pests?

131 **A**: No.

132 **Q**: *(L)* Well, with serious intent, do they have pests on their planet like we do?

133 **A**: No. Microbic.

134 **Q**: *(L)* Well, do they exterminate them like we do?

135 **A**: No.

136 **Q**: *(L)* Can we understand our pests as something that has been inflicted on us by the Lizzies? I always did wonder why God created mosquitoes.

137 **A**: No.

138 **Q**: *(L)* When we go into 4th density are we going to be free of mosquitoes, roaches, slimy worms, slugs and so on?

139 **A**: No.

140 **Q**: *(L)* In conjunction with DNA changes, is there any similarity between the human race and the idea of transformation relating to populations such as grasshoppers into locusts?

141 **A**: Yes.

142 **Q**: *(L)* When grasshoppers turn into locusts, they swarm when their population gets too large.

143 **A**: All is part of natural cyclical process.

144 **Q**: *(L)* Was the DNA change that we are experiencing programmed into us so that after so many generations these changes would just sort of kick in?

145 **A**: Close.

146 **Q**: *(L)* So, we all selected certain bodies before we incarnated that would be prime for this programming?

147 **A**: Are you ready to be hermaphrodites?

148 **Q**: *(L)* Is that what we are going to be?

149 **A**: Wait and see.[8]

150 **Q**: *(T)* Since you are riding this wave, in order to communicate, since the wave is what you are using to focus this contact with, and you are, whoever you may be at whatever point the wave is, you gave Barbara Marciniak information under the name 'Pleiadians.' You are telling us this. Have you told the other people, such as Barbara Marciniak, that you are contacting other people?

151 **A**: No.

152 **Q**: *(L)* So, Barbara may not know that the contacts are the same only under a different name?

153 **A**: No.

154 **Q**: *(L)* Is it because she didn't ask?

155 **A**: Progressive information. Also, system is like mosaic.

156 **Q**: *(L)* Does this mean that different people get different pieces of the mosaic?

---

[8] In the 16 November 1994 session I asked "Was there ever a time when there was a physical human race that contained within a single body both sexes?" The answer was "No." But I guess that this may not apply to 4th density.

157 **A**: Yes.

158 **Q**: *(T)* But, you have told us that you have contacted others under other names?

159 **A**: Yes.

160 **Q**: *(T)* Have you told the others?

161 **A**: No.

162 **Q**: *(T)* Why have you not contacted the others and told them this?

163 **A**: Just answered. Progressive.

164 **Q**: *(T)* Are you still contacting Barbara?

165 **A**: Not at this point. She is in pause mode.

166 **Q**: *(T)* Does she know this?

167 **A**: Yes. Write to her and tell her to call "Cassiopaea". Next stop is Leo.

168 **Q**: *(T)* In some time in the future, the next sending point is Leo. Does that mean that at some point we will not be able to contact you?

169 **A**: We just told you who to call.

170 **Q**: *(T)* Well, what I am having trouble understanding is why we have to call to a certain space point. We are now in touch, does this channel not stay open?

171 **A**: Reference point.

172 **Q**: *(T)* So it doesn't matter as long as we meet regularly to talk with you?

173 **A**: Yes.

174 **Q**: *(T)* Barbara is also able to continue talking to you even though you are no longer the Pleiadians?

175 **A**: She may talk to someone else.

176 **Q**: *(T)* Are you saying that she is channeling some other source at this point?

177 **A**: Maybe.

178 **Q**: *(L)* J. Z. Knight supposedly channeled Ramtha. Who was Ramtha?

179 **A**: Originally valid source.

180 **Q**: *(L)* Did that change?

181 **A**: Greed.

182 **Q**: *(T)* So she faked it?

183 **A**: Yes.

184 **Q**: *(L)* I wanted to ask about something you mentioned last night; I haven't transcribed the tape, but you said something about being a 4th density candidate and I had not heard you use the term before. What is a 4th density candidate?

185 **A**: Self-explanatory.

186 **Q**: *(L)* How does one get to be a 4th density candidate?

187 **A**: Natural progression.

188 **Q**: *(L)* Is everyone on this planet a 4th density candidate?

189 **A**: No.

190 **Q**: *(L)* How many are there?

191 **A**: Open.

192 **Q**: *(L)* Could someone become a candidate overnight who is not now a candidate?

193 **A**: Yes.

194 **Q**: *(T)* How many strands of DNA do we have?

195 **A**: Terry, 4; Frank, 4; Jan, 3; Laura, 3.

196 **Q**: *(L)* Well, gee... does this have anything to do with sex?

197 **A**: No.

198 **Q**: *(L)* Are you telling us that Frank and Terry are smarter than Jan and me?

199 **A**: You are growing your 4th, 5th and 6th right now.

200 **Q**: *(T)* If our 3rd density were to examine our DNA right now would they see this?

201 **A**: They would call it Junk DNA.

202 **Q**: *(T)* Would it be noticeable as DNA that was not there before?

203 **A**: Maybe.

204 **Q**: *(F)* They would have to compare to a baseline.

205 **Q**: *(L)* Were Atlantis and Lemuria the most ancient of Earth's civilizations?

206 **A**: No.

207 **Q**: *(L)* What advanced civilizations were before Atlantis and Lemuria?

208 **A**: Many.

209 **Q**: *(L)* Was there an ancient advanced civilization located in the area we now call Antarctica?

210 **A**: Yes.

211 **Q**: *(L)* What was the name of this civilization?

212 **A**: Gor.

213 **Q**: *(L)* What kind of individuals lived in Gor?

214 **A**: 18 feet tall.[9]

215 **Q**: *(L)* Were they humanoid and did they look like us?

216 **A**: Close.

217 **Q**: *(L)* Were they male and female like us?

218 **A**: Yes.

219 **Q**: *(L)* And did they have space travel capabilities?

220 **A**: No interest.

221 **Q**: *(L)* Are there any remains of their civilization left?

222 **A**: Yes.

223 **Q**: *(L)* Did they only inhabit Antarctica?

224 **A**: No.

225 **Q**: *(L)* Did they inhabit the whole world?

226 **A**: Close.

227 **Q**: *(L)* Are there any remains in Florida?

228 **A**: No.

229 **Q**: *(L)* Where might the remains be found?

230 **A**: South America.

231 **Q**: *(L)* Where in South America?

232 **A**: Amazon. Ancient legend of Amazons.

233 **Q**: *(L)* Do our scientists know any of this?

234 **A**: Yes.

235 **Q**: *(L)* Are there remains of Atlantis and Lemuria?

236 **A**: Yes.

237 **Q**: *(L)* Do our scientists know of any of those?

238 **A**: Yes.

239 **Q**: *(L)* Are they withholding information on purpose?

240 **A**: Yes.

241 **Q**: *(L)* Have they any intention of telling about it?

242 **A**: No.

243 **Q**: *(L)* Do they have relics of these stored?

244 **A**: Yes.

---

[9] Reminds me of the ancient Greek myths of the Giants and Titans.

Q: *(L)* I would like to know if there is anything Tom G could do to enhance his recovery from cancer?

A: PMA. Positive Mental Attitude.

Q: *(L)* In our cultural experience we have a lot of very strange things that our young people participate in. Among these activities is the use of extremely loud stereo systems that quite literally vibrate the cells in their bodies until they turn to jelly. Could you tell me, please, the long term physiological effects of this kind of exposure of the human body to these loud booming noises?

A: Strange thought patterns.

Q: *(L)* What effects are these violently loud stereos having on people?

A: Varies.

Q: *(L)* Are these effects negative?

A: Open.

Q: *(L)* Are these effects less than conducive to optimum health?

A: Maybe.

Q: *(L)* What can these very loud booming sounds do to the body?

A: Make the body go "boom boom." [Much laughter]

Q: *(J)* Blue Cheer concert, 1969; group advertised as the loudest in existence, and they were. I sat ten feet from the speakers and couldn't hear for three hours afterward and had ringing in the ears for several days. That was the last concert I went to. *(L)* Is this part of a plot to destroy the minds and bodies of our young people?

A: Maybe.

Q: *(J)* Or are they just being stupid?

A: Good answer.

Q: *(L)* On two separate occasions you have mentioned Andarans.[10] I have never heard of them before. Who are they and why have you mentioned them? Where did they come from and what did they look like?

A: One question at a time.

Q: *(L)* Who are the Andarans?

A: Thought forms for STS.

Q: *(L)* What level of density are they?

A: 5th.

Q: *(L)* So, they are at the contemplative level?

A: Yes.

Q: *(L)* Where do they come from?

A: 5th level.

Q: *(L)* Can you tell us what is the Rainbow Bridge referred to in *Bringers of the Dawn*. Is this what you were talking about when you spoke of our group being a conduit?

A: Yes.

Q: *(L)* What happens psychically at the moment of orgasm?[11]

A: For whom?

Q: *(L)* For anybody. In just a general way. Does anything happen to a person psychically when they have sexual climax.

A: Open.

Q: *(L)* Is it different for each individual?

---

[10] I was confused. See 5 October 1994 for reference to Andarans and 7 October 1994 for reference to Antareans.
[11] *High Strangeness* 11; *The Wave* 24

278 **A:** Close.

279 **Q:** *(L)* Is it different for males from females?

280 **A:** Usually.

281 **Q:** *(L)* The reason I ask is because a man named Wayne Cook did some work with dowsing and he found out that the human body, after sexual climax, dowses the same pattern as a dead body. Why is this? *(T)* Draining of energy.

282 **A:** Yes.

283 **Q:** *(L)* OK, where does the energy drain to?

284 **A:** To the ether.

285 **Q:** *(L)* Does the energy go to one or the other partner?[12]

286 **A:** Maybe.

287 **Q:** *(L)* Is it possible, during this activity, for Lizzies or other beings to be hanging around and be drawing this energy?

288 **A:** Yes.

289 **Q:** *(L)* Is that, in a general sense, what often happens?

290 **A:** Yes.

291 **Q:** *(L)* Is this one of the reasons that sex has been promoted and promulgated in our society to such an extent...

292 **A:** Yes, yes, yes.

293 **Q:** *(T)* Was there anybody hanging around us last night? *(L)* Terry!

294 **A:** Sure, why not.

295 **Q:** *(T)* Cause we're that good? *(L)* Terry! Now, Otto Muck came to the conclusion that the final breaking up of Atlantis occurred on June 5, 8498 BC. Is this pretty close?[13]

296 **A:** Close.

297 **Q:** *(L)* What happened to the Mayans?

298 **A:** Taken by Lizard beings to cosmos in 4D. "Lizzieland."

299 **Q:** *(L)* What did they do with them there?

300 **A:** Many possibilities.

301 **Q:** *(L)* Do any of those possibilities include having them for dinner? Sorry about that, I couldn't help myself. *(J)* "Mayan Helper." And I helped!

302 **A:** Maybe.

303 **Q:** *(L)* How big was the main island of Atlantis?

304 **A:** 1,354,000 square miles.

305 **Q:** *(L)* There is a woman named Jane Allyson who channels a robot named Cytron. Is this a put-on or is she really channeling a super cyborg?[14]

306 **A:** Nonsense.

307 **Q:** *(T)* Emergency, emergency, Dr. Smith! *(L)* A few months ago I had A___ in trance to do spirit viewing for several people. In several frames of reference she saw a funny little grinning man with big, pointed ears, wearing black, boots, and holding a whip, darting about and hiding behind people. Who was this little guy?

308 **A:** He was a carnal thought form.

309 **Q:** *(L)* And who created this carnal thought form that was zipping around?

310 **A:** Host.

311 **Q:** *(L)* Who was the host?

---

[12] *High Strangeness* 11
[13] *The Secret of Atlantis* (1979), HarperCollins.
[14] I had asked about this previously on 5 December 1994.

312 **A:** The subject with whom it appeared. It indicated an individual with many carnal thoughts.[15]

313 **Q:** *(L)* I would like to know... my friend, Keith Laumer, who died last year, I am a little bit curious since he came and hung around me for a time after death, did we have a past life relationship and if so what were the dynamics?

314 **A:** Yes. You must learn this yourself. Are you learning yet? You keep asking 3rd level questions.

315 **Q:** *(T)* You talk about both STO and STS. Yet you tell us that we need to learn to be STO. Why is there a difference between what we have to do and what you are doing?[16]

316 **A:** STO is balance because you serve self through others.

317 **Q:** *(T)* You have said a couple of times that you are STS by being STO. Is this not true?

318 **A:** Yes. Already answered.

319 **Q:** *(T)* Kind of like: what goes around, comes around?

320 **A:** Yes.

321 **Q:** *(T)* Is STO a means to an end for STS?

322 **A:** No. STO is balance. STS is imbalance.

323 **Q:** *(T)* How can you be STS through STO if STS is imbalance?

324 **A:** STO flows outward and touches all including point of origin, STS flows inward and touches only origin point.

325 **Q:** *(T)* Well, they refer in the material that I am reading through, that they are STS through STO. *(L)* They serve self *by* serving others. *(T)* Is that what they mean? *(L)* Yeah. *(T)* Is that what we're supposed to do, serve ourselves by serving others? *(L)* Yeah! Because what goes around, comes around. If you serve others then you get things back. *(F)* Because when you serve yourself, all there is is an infinite number of individuals serving self. *(T)* There is no energy exchange, no synergy within the group; there is no exchange. *(F)* Everything moves inward. *(T)* There is no sharing, no growth, there is no nothing. *(F)* No interconnecting. *(T)* Right! There is no learning. *(L)* In terms of major STS, this may or may not be related, could you tell us the nature of a black hole?

326 **A:** Grand Scale STS.

327 **Q:** *(L)* Is it like a being that has achieved such a level of STS that it has literally imploded in on itself in some way?

328 **A:** Close analogy.

329 **Q:** *(T)* Possibly an entire civilization of STS?

330 **A:** No.

331 **Q:** *(L)* Well, maybe a civilization can't do it because that implies working together. It must need to be an individual being.

332 **A:** Black holes are a natural force reflection of free will consciousness pattern of STS. Notice that black holes are located at center of spiral energy forces, all else radiates outward.

333 **Q:** *(L)* Now, you say "spiral" energy forces, and you also have said that this wave is a spiral. Is the central point of this wave that is spiraling, a black hole?

---

[15] Another example of the metaphoric nature of information.
[16] *The Wave* 8

334 **A**: No.

335 **Q**: *(L)* Is it a radiating wave?

336 **A**: All in creation is just that: a radiating wave.

337 **Q**: *(L)* Where does the energy go that gets sucked into a black hole?

338 **A**: Inward to total nonexistence.

339 **Q**: *(L)* Well, if a black hole continues to suck stuff in, is it possible that it would eventually suck in the entire creation?

340 **A**: No.

341 **Q**: *(L)* Why is that?

342 **A**: Universe is all encompassing. Black holes are final destination of all STS energy.

343 **Q**: *(F)* So, does this mean that we, or anyone else who is classified as STS, remains on said path, that we will eventually end up in a black hole?

344 **A**: Close.

345 **Q**: *(L)* Well, that is pleasant. And what happens to energy that is "total non-existence"?

346 **A**: Total non-existence balances total existence. Guess what is total existence?

347 **Q**: *(L)* Well, is it kind of like a balancing force?

348 **A**: "God."

349 **Q**: *(T)* Are we talking about the creator god as in the Pleiadians?

350 **A**: Not Pleiadians. Prime Creator.

351 **Q**: *(T)* What is the difference between the Prime Creator and 'God'?

352 **A**: None. As long as you exist, you are of the Prime Creator.

353 **Q**: *(L)* Now, this stuff that goes into black holes, that goes into non-existence, is that, then, not part of the Prime Creator?

A: Correct.

355 **Q**: *(L)* How can Prime Creator lose any part of him or itself?

356 **A**: Prime Creator does not "lose" anything.

357 **Q**: *(L)* Well, then, how would you describe this energy that was in existence and then is no longer in existence because it has become or gone into a black hole?

358 **A**: Reflection is regenerated at level 1.

359 **Q**: *(L)* So, this energy goes into a black hole and... does it come out on the other side?

360 **A**: No.

361 **Q**: *(L)* Does it become like a primal atom?

362 **A**: No.

363 **Q**: *(T)* Does it go back into the cycle?

364 **A**: No. Reflection regenerates as primal atoms.

365 **Q**: *(L)* So, this energy that is sucked into the black holes... what... *(T)* When we put out energy as positive or negative energy, and there are beings on other levels that feed on this energy, is this true?

366 **A**: Yes.

367 **Q**: *(T)* OK, and you said that the Lizzies feed on the negative energy?

368 **A**: Yes.

369 **Q**: *(T)* Who feeds on the positive energy?

370 **A**: You do.

371 **Q:** *(T)* How do we feed on the positive energy?

372 **A:** Progression toward union with the one, i.e. level 7.

373 **Q:** *(L)* In other words, you fuel your own generator instead of fueling someone else's. *(T)* You are at level 6, what do you feed on?

374 **A:** You have the wrong concept. We give to others and receive from others of the STO. We feed each other.

375 **Q:** *(L)* So, by feeding each other you move forward and grow but those of the STS path do not feed each other so must feed off of others. *(T)* Now, you are talking to us now. This is considered STO?

376 **A:** Yes.

377 **Q:** *(T)* We are providing energy for the channel also, does that provide you with energy?

378 **A:** No.

379 **Q:** *(F)* You are not keeping up with the program, Terry. *(L)* What do you want from us?

380 **A:** We don't want when pure STO. We came because YOU wanted. But that is STS until you share with others.

381 **Q:** *(L)* So, it is necessary that we share this information?

382 **A:** Up to you, it is a free will choice.

383 **Q:** *(L)* Is there some risk to ourselves by sharing this information?

384 **A:** At some level, but there is "risk" to all things.

385 **Q:** *(T)* I have a question: where do you get all your cute little cliches and sayings?

386 **A:** We access the human condition.

387 **Q:** *(L)* In one of my *Fate* magazines over there I read a story about a fellow who discovered an enormous structure in a cave when he was wounded and hiding there during the war. It was in Europe somewhere. I am visualizing the image. What was this thing this man found in this cave?

388 **A:** Magnesium wall made by Lizard beings. Constructed 309,448 years ago. It was part of a base. It was buried during cataclysms.[17]

389 **Q:** *(L)* What is buried on Oak Island?

390 **A:** Regenerator.

391 **Q:** *(L)* What is a regenerator?

392 **A:** Remolecularizer.

393 **Q:** *(L)* Who put it there?

394 **A:** Lizard beings.[18]

395 **Q:** *(L)* When did they put it there?

---

[17] *The Wave* 29. "Hidden deep within a Czech mountain is an ancient shaft and tower seemingly built by advanced technology but older than the bones of extinct beasts..." The author, Antonin T. Horak, wrote down the cave exploration adventure of a member of the Czech resistance, which occurred in October of 1944, during WWII. Mr. Horak stated that the account was confirmed by friends of his in Czechoslovakia in 1965. The story was first printed in the March 1965 issue of *National Speleological Society* in an attempt to interest other speleologists in mounting an expedition. The captain of the Slovak Resistance who told the story for the speleology magazine was apparently hidden in this cave, along with a companion who was wounded, by a farmer near the villages of Plavince and Lubocna at 49.2 N 20.7 degrees E. The farmer's name was Slavek.

[18] *Secret History* 11; *The Wave* 32

396 **A**: 10,000 years ago, approximately.

397 **Q**: *(L)* Do they use it from time to time?

398 **A**: No.

399 **Q**: *(L)* Does it still work?

400 **A**: It could.

401 **Q**: *(T)* What is the purpose of a remolecularizer? *(L)* Yeah, what do you use it for? Entertain your friends at parties?

402 **A**: Regenerate matter.

403 **Q**: *(L)* Such as physical bodies?

404 **A**: Yes.

405 **Q**: *(L)* So, you just go and stand next to it or inside it or whatever and it regenerates you?

406 **A**: Any matter.

407 **Q**: *(L)* Well, that would be a really handy thing to have in the barn. Is there any way to get it out of there?

408 **A**: Maybe. Are you planning an expedition?

409 **Q**: *(L)* No, we're just being nosy. How deep is it buried?

410 **A**: Deep.

411 **Q**: *(T)* Well, we can send it in to a treasure hunter's magazine and give somebody an idea of how far they have to go. *(L)* Yeah, tell them what it is and they will go whole hog for it! *(T)* Yeah. It's a regenerator. "What?" Well, it's a remolecularizer. What's wrong with you? Where have you been? You never wanted to be regenerated? You, too, can be a Time Lord! *(L)* Amaze your friends, confound your enemies, you can hypnotize any woman from a distance by the power of your... *regenerator!* *(T)* Wow! Look at the size of his regenerator! [Much laughter] Thank you.

412 **A**: Good Night.

End of session.

December 17, 1994

Diana M is the woman discussed in the previous two sessions who, under hypnosis, described being abducted by praying mantis beings who ate children. As described in *The Wave*, Chapter Two, she was a science teacher at a local high school, divorced from a history professor at the University of South Florida, and had a rather wild teen-aged daughter whom she obsessed over. We had earlier attended a reception at a New Agey bookstore where an alleged expert on Mayan cosmology and/or esoteric teachings was holding court. Liquor had been served and we had all had a couple of drinks, which was unusual in the extreme for me. During the reception we told DM about the C's and she was very anxious to consult them, so we all left the party and went back to the house to see what would come out.

I should also mention the fact that the UFO/alien abduction–crowd celebrity of the moment, Eddie Page, had been at the party also. He is mentioned in session 4 November 1994. I first heard about him from Scarlett some months back and she and Mike F were apparently part of the Eddie Page fan club.

Eddie's story was that he was a Pleiadian-human hybrid and he had been killed in battle in Vietnam, but his Pleiadian 'father' had sent a team to rescue him. They took him onboard a spaceship and gave him a new heart and new blood. The result was that he had two hearts and black blood. My companions of the evening were absolutely aghast when I announced that I wanted to ask Eddie to give me a blood sample right there! He was *such* an obvious fraud![1] *But*, Diana M, Scarlett, and a host of other gullible people believed every word that came out of his mouth no matter how outrageous it was. Darndest thing I'd ever seen – except in a fundie church. But I digress. You'll see that the topic of Eddie Page takes up a lot of this session and the C's were

---

[1] You are invited to entertain yourself with a video of Eddie Page 'under hypnosis' here: http://ufovideoreview.com/UFO-Aliens/category/abduction-story/eddie-page-ufo-abduction-hypnosis-regression-analysis

quite patient with DM in trying to disabuse her of her illusions. This is an excellent example of how they operate with someone who has very strong beliefs and emotional attachment to those beliefs. I included more details about Eddie and his fabulous fraud and how it unraveled in *The Wave*.

Participants: 'Frank', Laura, VG, Diana M

1 **Q**: *(L)* Hello.

2 **A**: Hello.

3 **Q**: *(L)* Celestial dudes!

4 **A**: That was cute!

5 **Q**: *(L)* Who do we have with us tonight?

6 **A**: Porsonea.

7 **Q**: *(L)* I guess you were with us at the party tonight? [Talk about the speaker who was guest of honor at party] What was his talk about?

8 **A**: Mayan, Laura.

9 **Q**: *(L)* Was our alcohol consumption bad for us?

10 **A**: Only if in excess.

11 **Q**: *(L)* Did I have too much?

12 **A**: Some.

13 **Q**: *(L)* We would like to ask what is the source of the warts Diana and Eddie Page's[2] wife have in various places on their bodies?

14 **A**: Genes oriented.

15 **Q**: *(L)* Does this mean warts are genetic?

16 **A**: Oriented.

17 **Q**: *(L)* Is it the same for both of them?

18 **A**: Not exactly.

19 **Q**: *(L)* How can warts be connected to genetics?

20 **A**: Progression to 4th density.

21 **Q**: *(L)* Why does it have to be so hard?

22 **A**: Many things are. Backaches, for example.

23 **Q**: *(L)* Backaches are one thing, but warts are very unpleasant.

24 **A**: Unpleasant is subjective.

25 **Q**: *(L)* How does Diana get rid of her warts?

26 **A**: Not the point.

27 **Q**: *(L)* What is the point.[3]

28 **A**: Natural progression. Warts are not the issue. All have symptoms, but not all are the same.[4]

29 **Q**: *(DM)* What can I do to get rid of the warts? They make me feel awful.

30 **A**: Adjust your feelings.

31 **Q**: *(DM)* Am I getting these warts because I am transitioning to 4th density?

---

[2] Eddie Page: alleged abductee doing the UFO speakers' circuit. I thought he was a fraud, but DM was very taken by his nonsense. His wife was literally covered, all over the exposed parts of her body, with hundreds of warts. D's warts were a more minor thing, with only a dozen or so.

[3] *High Strangeness* "Appendix"; *The Wave* 21

[4] I was sure glad that none of my symptoms were warts! One also wonders if there is something symbolic in warts?

A: All are headed to 4th density. So, what does it matter, remember, transformation is always accompanied by some difficulty.

Q: *(L)* Is there anything that can be done physically to help Diana with her warts?

A: Can be accomplished, try adjustment of mind and diet. You are missing potassium. You must also adjust your mind.

Q: *(L)* Adjust her mind in what way?

A: Anti stress measures.

Q: *(L)* Is this the same thing Mrs. Page needs to do?

A: Help, but not cure.

Q: *(L)* What will work for her?

A: Compresses.

Q: *(L)* What kind of compresses?

A: Mud nourished with minerals. Check with horticulturist.

Q: *(L)* How do we find a horticulturist? Network?[5]

A: Always "network". Networking is 4th density STO concept seeping into 3rd density with upcoming realm border crossing.

Q: *(DM)* Networking is the way to get things done from 3rd level into 4th level?

A: Coming from 4th level into 3rd because of influence of wave.

Q: *(DM)* So, each of us has a skill that we develop and help each other. *(L)* We are all part of a body.

A: This is the way lives in STO! Diana on board, V___ write. V___ not to feel bad, will return. Please be patient. Hello, Diana.

Q: *(L)* Who has Eddie Page been abducted by that he says look like us?

A: 4th density Orion STS.

Q: *(V)* Well, he is under the impression that it is the Pleiadians. Why does he...

A: All can create false impression.

Q: *(V)* Well, he is planning in 6 months to leave his family and the planet and heading off toward the Pleiades.[6]

A: Free will.

Q: *(V)* So, his free will is going to propel him into the Pleiades?

A: Your free will propels you always.

Q: *(DM)* The Pleiadian he talks of is his father, is this correct?

A: No.

Q: *(DM)* Are you saying that he is not a hybrid? Is this correct?

A: If he chooses to be hybrid, then that is his choice.

---

[5] *The Wave* 18

[6] This was part of his story. What actually happened was that he went to a UFO conference and hooked up with another looney who claimed that she was also a Pleiadian-human hybrid, that she and Eddie were siblings, and that in Pleiadia (or wherever) it was the custom to mate with your sibling! So, Eddie moved the floozie into his house with his wife and moved his wife out onto the sofa. I think she put up with this for a while before some more rational members of the UFO community talked sense into her and she kicked Eddie and the floozie out. Eddie soon abandoned the floozie and got a job working in the pits at a racetrack in North Carolina, I think it was.

61 **Q:** *(L)* Are you saying... *(DM)* How can be being a hybrid be a choice?

62 **A:** How can anything?

63 **Q:** *(L)* You mean it is a subjective choice to perceive that way? *(DM)* Is his father a Pleiadian?

64 **A:** No.

65 **Q:** *(L)* Why does he think is father is? *(DM)* Is he giving false information?

66 **A:** He believes what he is saying.

67 **Q:** *(DM)* So, what he is saying, he believes to be the truth?

68 **A:** Yes.

69 **Q:** *(L)* But, is it the truth?

70 **A:** It is, but on what level? That is the question.

71 **Q:** *(L)* On what level? *(DM)* Is this 5th density?

72 **A:** Okay, time to learn... [Groans of dismay] The past and the future are all in the present!

73 **Q:** *(DM)* So, we are talking about different levels all at the same time...

74 **A:** But you know that by now, Diana.

75 **Q:** *(L)* OK, at some level... *(DM)* Are all of his levels together, now?

76 **A:** Integrating.

77 **Q:** *(DM)* So, he is integrating into one, is this correct?

78 **A:** Close enough.

79 **Q:** *(DM)* Does this mean that, as soon as he has integrated, that he will leave this planet?

80 **A:** If he chooses.

81 **Q:** *(DM)* And he will choose, is this correct?[7]

82 **A:** Open.

83 **Q:** *(L)* Well, what worries me is that they are saying the STS guys have ahold of him and that's not good. *(DM)* Is Eddie STS?

84 **A:** You all are still. You all are moving toward graduation to STO.

85 **Q:** *(F)* We all are still STS?

86 **A:** Yes.

87 **Q:** *(L)* Well, I still don't understand about Eddie... *(DM)* Would you please explain to me what service to others entails?

88 **A:** Complete lack of concern for self.

89 **Q:** *(L)* Well, that's a real tough one. *(DM)* It would be like being Mahatma Gandhi, is this correct?

90 **A:** Closer.

91 **Q:** *(DM)* Then there is no one that I know of that is going to make this?

92 **A:** Do you know anyone who is in 4th density?

93 **Q:** *(L)* Of course not. *(DM)* I'm not sure. *(V)* So, when we transition from 3rd density to 4th density we lose that need for service to self?

94 **A:** If you transition, you are ready to do so if you choose.

95 **Q:** *(DM)* So, it's like an instant thing? As soon as you are ready, you are gone!

96 **A:** No. Realm border crossing.

---

[7]It's really amazing to observe how this woman's emotional attachment to the Eddie Page story made it almost impossible for her to understand what the C's were saying. Their patience with her was also amazing. But I was getting tired of this dancing around.

97 Q: *(L)* At the time of the realm border crossing those who are of the correct vibrational frequency to transition will do so, as it says in the Bible, in the twinkling of an eye. Almost instantaneously. We are getting ready... you have to be at least a certain level... it all has to do with the coming of this wave...

98 A: We ride the wave.

99 Q: *(L)* Who does Eddie Page channel?

100 A: Many.

101 Q: *(L)* Many who are what? *(DM)* Does he channel his father?

102 A: Not in the sense you mean. All are "father" in some sense.

103 Q: *(DM)* So, when he talks to his father he is talking to many because many are the father? So then, are we speaking of his father as being a collection of DNA composite?

104 A: No. Collection of consciousness.

105 Q: *(DM)* The universal consciousness?

106 A: Close.

107 Q: *(V)* A male consciousness?

108 A: No.

109 Q: *(L)* OK, you say it is not his father in the sense of being a genetic line, is that correct?

110 A: Okay.

111 Q: *(L)* Is Eddie Page genetically mutated or altered in some way?[8]

112 A: No. Not in this space time.

113 Q: *(L)* So, in other words, what he may be tapping into is similar to what Diana was tapping into in her hypnosis as carnivorous praying mantis beings, another aspect of himself, and he is misinterpreting this aspect of himself as being who and what he is now?

114 A: Not misinterpreting.

115 Q: *(L)* Does he fully understand what is going on?

116 A: No. Neither do you.

117 Q: *(DM)* Will I be meeting some Pleiadians Tuesday night at 10 o'clock? Will they be coming to my house?[9]

118 A: In a sense. Review concept.

119 Q: *(L)* In case you haven't figured it out, this whole operation is a learning process. The Cassiopaeans make us go through all kinds of hoops to get stuff.

120 A: If you review you learn. Knowledge protects.

121 Q: *(DM)* But, am I going to be visited by Pleiadians?

122 A: Bring Diana "up to speed."

123 Q: *(DM)* OK, then what I can expect is a psychic connection with you if you are connected to the Pleiadians?

124 A: We only rarely appear as human.

125 Q: *(DM)* I am going to have humans come to me Tuesday night and they are going to be Pleiadians?

126 A: No.

127 Q: *(DM)* What is going to be at my house Tuesday night at 10 o'clock?

128 A: Nice people.

129 Q: *(DM)* But are they Pleiadians?

130 A: Review.

---

[8]He claimed to have two hearts and black blood; however, he never provided any proof of this and when I asked for it, I was considered a heretic.

[9]Eddie Page told her that the Pleiadians were going to visit her. She gave him a large donation after that!

131 **Q**: *(DM)* Will I understand what is going to happen Tuesday when it happens?

132 **A**: Keep mind open.

133 **Q**: *(V)* What is it that is supposed to happen Tuesday night at your house? *(DM)* Eddie Page told me the Pleiadians were going to visit me.

134 **A**: Wait and see.

135 **Q**: *(DM)* OK, that's cool. *(F)* Well, it said to keep your mind open and wait and see. *(DM)* But they are not saying no!

136 **A**: Mind is not currently open.

137 **Q**: *(DM)* Why?

138 **A**: Expectations are influenced by various sources.

139 **Q**: *(DM)* Then, Eddie is one of these sources, is that correct?

140 **A**: Yes.

141 **Q**: *(L)* Should she be surprised if nothing happens at all?

142 **A**: Up to Diana.

143 **Q**: *(DM)* I don't think I am going to be surprised. But why isn't my mind open? *(L)* Maybe because you decided to believe what Eddie told you, is that it?

144 **A**: Open.

145 **Q**: *(DM)* Well, somebody's going to come to my house Tuesday! *(L)* Well, I am really confused about Eddie. You say he is being abducted by Orion STS guys. What level of beings are doing this abducting?

146 **A**: Has been.

147 **Q**: *(L)* Has he been abducted by other groups?

148 **A**: Yes.

149 **Q**: *(L)* What other groups?

150 **A**: Grays.

151 **Q**: *(V)* Well, he thinks the Grays are just hunky-dory friendly fellows. *(DM)* Are the Grays STO?

152 **A**: No. Cybergenetic.

153 **Q**: *(L)* Who has told Eddie that the Grays are good? Why is he convinced of this?

154 **A**: Many.

155 **Q**: *(DM)* Am I channeling this?

156 **A**: Starting to.

157 **Q**: *(DM)* Have I been channeling the questions too?

158 **A**: Sara is okay. [DM's daughter]

159 **Q**: *(DM)* I have been wanting to ask questions about Sara.

160 **A**: On your mind. Ease up.

161 **Q**: *(DM)* Am I being too controlling?

162 **A**: Yes and too concerned.

163 **Q**: *(DM)* Is her boyfriend into drugs?

164 **A**: Has been.

165 **Q**: *(DM)* Is she into drugs?

166 **A**: Not at the moment.

167 **Q**: *(L)* Is it true that this is Sara's choice and Sara's lessons?

168 **A**: As with all.

169 **Q**: *(DM)* Is her father influencing her actions?

170 **A**: No.

171 **Q**: *(DM)* Does he have any intentions of doing that?

172 **A**: Intentions are transitory.

173 **Q**: *(DM)* Are there any actions I can take that will be beneficial for Sara?

174 **A**: Open. Free will.

175 **Q:** *(DM)* Am I going to have a problem with her father before October?

176 **A:** Okay now. Worry no more.

177 **Q:** *(L)* Can we ask about John Reed?

178 **A:** Why so much interest in individual students?

179 **Q:** *(L)* He is a student?

180 **A:** All are. Us too.

181 **Q:** *(DM)* Everyone has a creator.

182 **A:** We are not creator any more than you are. We are all creator!

183 **Q:** *(L)* Diana was telling me on the ride over about Eddie Page telling her about an event that happened to her when she was a child. She perceived this as a demonstration of psychic ability and therefore goodness. Can you tell me how, if he is being influenced by the STS guys, how he can have this psychic ability?

184 **A:** All have ability, it just depends on how it is used.

185 **Q:** *(L)* Was Eddie Page killed in battle?[10]

186 **A:** Yes.

187 **Q:** *(L)* Was he revived by aliens?

188 **A:** Yes.

189 **Q:** *(L)* Who revived him?

190 **A:** Orion STS.

191 **Q:** *(L)* What was their purpose in reviving him and restoring him to life?

192 **A:** Purpose already determined.

193 **Q:** *(L)* And that is...

194 **A:** Many faceted.

195 **Q:** *(L)* What is the primary purpose?

196 **A:** Complex.

197 **Q:** *(L)* We know it is complex, give us one...

198 **A:** Very important for all to review, what happens at realm border crossing?

199 **Q:** *(L)* We transition to 4th density, is that correct?

200 **A:** Partly.

201 **Q:** *(L)* We either choose to transition as STS or STO, is that correct?

202 **A:** Partly.

203 **Q:** *(L)* And we do this based upon knowledge, is that correct?

204 **A:** Partly.

205 **Q:** *(L)* And Eddie Page has been given a certain...

206 **A:** What do STS 4th density intend to do?

207 **Q:** *(L)* The 4th level STS beings intend to set things up so that they can rule us and feed off of us in 4th density. They want to bring everybody over to their way of thinking and their domination so that we will give them our energy and give up our free will... *(DM)* So, we are being set up. *(F)* Well, that is part of it. Don't you remember the battle that is supposed to ensue that has already begun at some level, and this will determine, in part, whether we will be STS or STO, which also is known at some level... *(L)* Has Eddie Page been subverted and programed to lead people astray?

208 **A:** No.

209 **Q:** *(L)* Well, then I don't understand.

210 **A:** You are reading into situation.

211 **Q:** *(DM)* What is it that she is reading into the situation that isn't there?

---

[10] In Vietnam – his claim to fame; that he died and was saved by aliens.

212 **A**: Page is experiencer, you are witnesses, that is all!

213 **Q**: *(L)* What is he experiencing?

214 **A**: We have told you already.

215 **Q**: *(L)* What he is experiencing is... *(DM)* We are watching him put himself all together. *(L)* Is this what we are witnessing, him integrating?

216 **A**: Yes.

217 **Q**: *(L)* He is integrating, we are witnessing. He is integrating.... *(DM)* He is putting himself together at all the different levels... there isn't anything more. *(L)* Is this true?

218 **A**: Yes.

219 **Q**: *(L)* Well, in another session we were told that a lot of what Eddie Page is saying is disinformation designed to take people in, is that true?

220 **A**: Yes.

221 **Q**: *(L)* And what is the source of that disinformation?

222 **A**: Orion STS.

223 **Q**: *(L)* Are they trying to, to put this in plain terms, are they trying to 'take his soul'?

224 **A**: No.

225 **Q**: *(L)* Are they trying to win the battle in terms of dominating him in 4th density?

226 **A**: And you and all others.

227 **Q**: *(L)* Well that is pleasant...

228 **A**: We have told you this before, knowledge protects, ignorance endangers.

229 **Q**: *(L)* How does one...

230 **A**: All knowledge is good.

231 **Q**: *(L)* How can one, such as Eddie, defend himself against beings of such superior capabilities of mind control, that they can literally put thoughts in his head; I mean, what chance is there for anybody?

232 **A**: He has participated in process.

233 **Q**: *(L)* So, at some level he has chosen the STS pathway, is that what you are saying here?

234 **A**: Yes.

235 **Q**: *(L)* And part of this STS pathway is just going off and leaving his family, is that it?

236 **A**: Close. But please don't read into situation. Open your mind.

237 **Q**: *(DM)* Is this just something that we are going to have to see in the future?

238 **A**: Okay. Get to know Page.

239 **Q**: *(DM)* In what respect?

240 **A**: Open your minds. He is experiencing, you are witnessing. Just watch and see. Look, listen and learn.

241 **Q**: *(L)* OK, thank you and good night.

242 **A**: Good night.

End of Session

December 23, 1994

Diana M is back again at this session. Frank was really taken with her. At the time, I really didn't understand why Frank was so anxious to have her sit in on the sessions, but he was. Perhaps part of it was because she was a high school science teacher and he liked to show off his knowledge of science by engaging her in discussions. But mainly, I think, there was some sort of feeling of affinity because of the claimed alien abductions that both had experienced (or claimed to) and their 'victim' status.

Anyway, you will notice something very odd in this session: it is almost entirely personal and devoted to Diana's personal problems despite the number of times the C's had declared that personal issues were of little importance and, when Frank was in a cranky mood, they would refuse to answer any such questions for me at all. That, in my opinion, is indicative of Frank's wish to impress Diana and acquire her as a devotee. Nevertheless, once again, in spite of such issues, the session did produce some good material of general value to all though it was 'off-side,' so to say.

Participants: 'Frank', Laura, Diana M

1 **Q**: Hello.
2 **A**: No ritual.
3 **Q**: *(D)* Explain, please?
4 **A**: No ritual.
5 **Q**: *(F)* Did somebody do a ritual? *(L)* No. Did you do one in your mind, Diana? *(D)* I just rubbed my hands together. *(L)* No, I don't think that is what they are talking about. It's because we were talking about rituals and why we don't do them. OK, why did you tell us "no ritual"?
6 **A**: Diana. Caution.
7 **Q**: *(L)* Tell Diana, please, why we don't do rituals.
8 **A**: Rituals constrict. Who are we?
9 **Q**: *(L)* What is your name, please?
10 **A**: Oplea.
11 **Q**: *(L)* Are you a discarnate?
12 **A**: No, Cassiopaean.
13 **Q**: *(L)* Let me ask you about your spelling of the word 'Cassiopaea.' It is the archaic spelling of Cassiopeia, but not the one currently used. However, the last part of the word, as you spell it,

is the word *paean*, which is a 'warning' sound or an announcement or message. 'Something that calls people to attention.' Is there any chosen symbology in your use of this spelling?

A: No, but nice analogy.

Q: *(D)* I want to thank you very much for the advice you gave me. It was something that was very much on my mind and your advice probably saved my daughter from running away.

A: You are welcome.

Q: *(D)* I want to impose on you, and I hope you don't mind. Sara's father has influence on her; is he someone I need to warn her about? [Asking about her daughter]

A: Worry not.

Q: *(L)* Does that mean that the less Diana says, the sooner Sara will figure things out for herself?

A: Open.

Q: *(D)* Will be Sara be OK by herself if I leave the state?

A: You're not leaving.

Q: *(L)* Well, that is a pretty definite statement. Is she going to get... *(D)* Do you have a use for me here?

A: Your use is your pathway of learning.

Q: *(D)* My pathway... I am not understanding... *(L)* In other words, they may not specifically have a use for you in the sense of being used, but your pathway of learning is what you are here doing. *(D)* I am supposed to be learning and I'm supposed to stay here until I learn?

A: Yes. Everyone is always learning.

Q: *(L)* Why do you say she is not leaving? That is a pretty definite statement and you guys don't usually make real definite statements like that.

A: Because she is not.

Q: *(D)* Am I to be working with Eddie Page?[1]

A: Wait and see.

Q: *(D)* I have felt that I was going to sell my house and would be doing something significant and that would be in North Carolina... *(L)* Well, maybe you will end up in North Carolina. I wanted to go to Montana and I ended up on Montana Avenue. I guess that is as close as I am going to get.

A: Pressing does not work.

Q: *(D)* Well, I was trying to press things. *(L)* I was a presser too, and still do from time to time, but it never works... I'm learning to let things happen.

A: House sells, but move isn't far. How do you like New Port Richey?[2]

Q: *(D)* Well, I don't know there is a position open or opening and I do know the people over here and...

A: Bingo!

Q: *(L)* Well, why don't you tell Frank and me stuff like that? Am I going to sell my house? I want to move too!

A: We tell that which needs to be told.

Q: *(L)* Well, Diana gets told stuff and I don't. That's not fair...[3]

A: Yes you do!

Q: *(L)* Would it be a good idea for Diana to get the Reiki initiation?

---

[1] See previous session for details on Eddie Page.
[2] That is definitely Frank wanting a devotee there, I think.
[3] I was just pointing out the obvious and trying to see what the C's would say.

42 **A**: Up to Diana. You are pressing again.

43 **Q**: *(D)* Well, I understand that Laura wants me to and she has given me the reasons. What I do is listen and assemble the information... probably I will.

44 **A**: You know. You are soft spoken.

45 **Q**: *(D)* I discovered that if I put vitamin E oil on my warts it stopped them from itching...

46 **A**: Potassium.

47 **Q**: *(D)* Yes, I am eating bananas! I put some antibiotic oil on them also, and then I could scratch off part of it and it stopped itching so much. I am sure the potassium did help. I have been eating bananas. *(L)* Well, we were talking earlier about all the synchronous events that happened during the year prior to the beginning of this contact, and I would like to know if those events were, in part, engineered by you guys.

48 **A**: Open.

49 **Q**: *(L)* What was it that caused the repeated swelling of my eyes and other soft tissue of the body?

50 **A**: Learning comes with discovery.[4]

51 **Q**: *(D)* You were discovering. You were being led. *(L)* Oh, see what they are saying. *(D)* Just like I am being led to live here and work with you. *(L)* Is Diana part of the conduit?

52 **A**: You will see. Forum first.

53 **Q**: *(D)* That means yes. *(L)* In the forming of this conduit, is the conduit not only something that brings energy into us, but also through which we can travel into other dimensions as well? Does it go both ways?

54 **A**: Learn by discovery!

---

[4]Notice how I am being dissed repeatedly!

55 **Q**: *(L)* In other words, do it! We got the program loaded for the computer net, which you told us once we got online our lives would change suddenly and dramatically. *(D)* Are we not quite ready for this?

56 **A**: Discover.

57 **Q**: *(L)* You told us that if we created the maze in the yard and walked it, that it would change our vibrations to the point that we would be able to see you. If we did that as a group, what would be the result?

58 **A**: Same.

59 **Q**: *(L)* Would a group moving in that energy format create a greater energy than, say, a single individual?

60 **A**: Yes.

61 **Q**: *(D)* So, what if we had a lot of people do that? *(L)* They told us that this was similar to what they did at Stonehenge, that walking a pattern like a maze design would concentrate energy. A spiral.

62 **A**: [Planchette demonstrates by moving in a gradually expanding spiral which then gradually got smaller]

63 **Q**: *(L)* Are you demonstrating the pattern that should be used?

64 **A**: Cycle.

65 **Q**: *(L)* Would this do a lot to empower us as well as hasten the bundling of the DNA?

66 **A**: Wait and see.

67 **Q**: *(L)* In other words, you just want us to do things, to get moving on these projects, get these transcripts organized, get the maze built, do our spinning...

68 **A**: We want you to do what you will do.

69 **Q**: *(L)* Well... *(D)* Thanks a lot... *(L)* I guess that is what it comes down to: get free, get happy...

70 **A**: Above all learn.

71 **Q**: *(D)* Is there something we can do to help other people?[5]

72 **A**: Access instincts, network.

73 **Q**: *(D)* Are you talking about the computer network?

74 **A**: In general.

75 **Q**: *(D)* Now, wait a minute. They may mean networking people and their uses. *(L)* Does network in general mean, as Diana says, contacting people, spread the word, bring others in, along that line?

76 **A**: Why Sara so many viruses?[6]

77 **Q**: *(L)* What do you mean? Who has so many viruses?

78 **A**: Sara.

79 **Q**: *(L)* Well, does Sara have a lot of viruses? Why does Sara have so many viruses?

80 **A**: We asked you.

81 **Q**: *(D)* Well, she's having her tonsils out Tuesday. I don't know why.

82 **A**: Have you not noticed?

83 **Q**: *(D)* Well, I hadn't put things together. *(F)* Is it true? *(D)* Yes, she does. She has, different kinds of viruses... *(L)* Well, are you going to give us a clue on this one?

84 **A**: Emotions reflect in physical body.

85 **Q**: *(L)* What is the nature of her emotional upset?

86 **Q**: *(D)* It's her father. Is it her father?

87 **A**: No.

88 **Q**: *(L)* What is it? *(D)* Has she been abducted?

89 **A**: That is not the point.

90 **Q**: *(L)* What is the nature of her emotional viruses?

91 **A**: Complicated but, mother-daughter soul connection is unusually strong in this case!

92 **Q**: *(L)* How many lifetimes have Diana and Sara had together?

93 **A**: 59.

94 **Q**: *(L)* Well, that's high. *(D)* Let me tell you something, the last time I killed her...

95 **A**: Twins.

96 **Q**: *(L)* Which one of...

97 **A**: Last was tragic.

98 **Q**: *(D)* I killed Sara... *(L)* Could you tell us the dynamics of that last lifetime that are so strong...

99 **A**: Diana reveal.

100 **Q**: *(L)* Should Diana do this through hypnotherapy?

101 **A**: Okay but has done work already.

102 **Q**: *(L)* What could Diana have done for or to or with Sara in the lifetime that is most heavily affecting this lifetime, to have resolved the issue then?

---

[5] *The Wave* 18

[6] Really bizarre that the C's were almost insisting on giving a 'personal session' to this woman, while questions of general interest were being shunted aside. I think Frank was so emotionally desperate for a personal devotee that it was the overriding tenor of this session.

103 **A**: Not important, this one is!

104 **Q**: *(L)* What does she need to do now?

105 **A**: On right path since Tuesday.

106 **Q**: *(L)* What did you do Tuesday? *(D)* Tuesday... *(L)* What happened Tuesday that was so significant?

107 **A**: Discover.

108 **Q**: *(L)* Does it have something to do with the roller blades Diana bought Sara Tuesday?

109 **A**: Now you are learning, so we will help. Now you see?! She needs the childhood she never had.

110 **Q**: *(L)* Why did she never have a childhood? *(D)* Because she was sexually abused by her father she always felt that she had to be the grown-up; she had to be between her father and myself; she had to pull everything together. She always felt that responsibility and she... oh! I see! Thank you! I took her shopping. We went to the mall. She saw things that she didn't get when she was a kid and I explained to her that now she wasn't a kid and she couldn't really enjoy those things but she could enjoy the things that would be more her age level. She got down and saw little doodads that she always wanted. *(L)* Well, get them for her. Can you? *(D)* Yes! *(L)* Is that the answer? Give her the childhood things?

111 **A**: Continue...

112 **Q**: *(D)* I'll go down and buy her those things tomorrow.

113 **A**: Okay. Childhood is stepping stone to spiritual growth in each lifetime.

114 **Q**: *(D)* I want to thank you!

115 **A**: We are helping you with this because you simply must resolve this issue before you can properly progress to important work, see?[7]

116 **Q**: *(D)* I have to solve this... *(L)* They just told you that you had important work to do which is pretty close to a prophecy... am I correct on that, that she has important work to do and that you have plans for her?

117 **A**: Yes. Diana has been "discombobulated".

118 **Q**: *(L)* You have been discombobulated? *(D)* I can handle that. *(L)* Is there anything else you can add to help solve this issue that maybe we haven't asked? *(D)* I think I just need to enjoy my daughter rather than trying to control her...

119 **A**: Now you are on the right path.

120 **Q**: *(D)* I haven't been talking against her father and I have been telling her, encouraging her... I have been forgiving him... and I told MT today that I found out from Sara that her father is the one who took her to get the abortion, and he paid for it, and I said something about mixed feelings, not everything is bad. There's something good in everything, and I referred her to different parts of different books... page 29 in the *Ra Material*, and not showing the anger... and that is what I have been doing: showing anger, getting that emotion out and feeding the Lizzies... and getting wrinkles and gray hair and growing warts... and warts?

121 **A**: Yes.

122 **Q**: *(D)* They said to get rid of stress situations. *(L)* I would almost say that what you just learned was that a lot

---

[7] Almost feels like manipulation of a very gullible person to me.

of your stress is self-generated... *(D)* Exactly... my hat is off to you guys, I thank you...

123 **A**: Now Diana, do you still want to move to North Carolina?[8]

124 **Q**: *(D)* No. That's cool! Thank you very much. I don't need to flee! I can stay. *(L)* I guess that is what you needed to be here tonight for. *(D)* And I thought that I was going to help mankind and I got helped...

125 **A**: This is only the beginning of this work!

126 **Q**: *(D)* How can I thank them?

127 **A**: Not necessary because we are working together.

128 **Q**: *(D)* I also started telling Sara about spirituality and God and things like that, and I told her that what you first have to understand is there is no such thing as sin... *(L)* It's all lessons... *(D)* There is no such thing as sin and then I named all the negative emotions and said that what we need to do is have a lot less of that and more of love, caring, sharing and that kind of thing... and she really listened! So, I have started teaching her. And, I want her to have something to... Oh!, here's a good question: Could you help me out and guide me into what book would be good for Sara to read?

129 **A**: No, this is up to Sara. It is all just lessons for each individual. That is all there is, nothing else.

130 **Q**: *(L)* I guess it is like dancing, you follow the signals and the music to know what step to do next. Take your cues from Sara.

131 **A**: There is nothing, repeat nothing, but lessons.

132 **Q**: *(L)* I guess it is a big laboratory and we are the guinea pigs...

133 **A**: No, everything that exists in all of creation is a lesson, there is no laboratory.

134 **Q**: *(L)* Sorry guys. *(F)* So, absolutely everything is a lesson. *(L)* Let me ask this: On Tuesday when Diana was reading and fell asleep, did she get a visit or a contact from any source?

135 **A**: Hypnotize her to access this information.

136 **Q**: *(D)* Was there something pertinent that happened that night?

137 **A**: Discover.

138 **Q**: *(D)* OK, so we should discover through the hypnosis. *(L)* Did the Pleiadians come?

139 **A**: Laura, you are such a card![9]

140 **Q**: *(L)* Well, I thought I would try to sneak that one by them. Let me ask: On the night the big black boomerang came over my house, was I or one of my children abducted?

141 **A**: Why do you think you learned hypnosis, to put it on the shelf for a conversation piece, maybe?

142 **Q**: *(L)* Are you saying that I need hypnosis myself?

143 **A**: Others. Children will have answers.

---

[8]The smarminess of this session is unbelievable!

[9]Yeah, I admit I was being a little nasty here. Diana had been told by Eddie Page that the Pleiadians would be visiting her. This was discussed at the last session. Obviously, no Pleiadians were really coming, nor did they come, so I was just getting in a dig here.

144 **Q:** *(L)* Oh, good, that's clever! I never thought about that. OK, that's how I'll find out. It's too simple. I'm beginning to feel brain-dead. Why have my eyes been bothering me so much for the last year?

145 **A:** Eyes do that on 3rd density.

146 **Q:** *(D)* I have been having similar problems. *(F)* I have been getting nearsighted in the last year. *(L)* Anybody got any questions? *(D)* Not me, I just had a huge, huge problem solved in just a few words... what else could I want to know? But, there is something... David N, how does he fit in my life?

147 **A:** Open.

148 **Q:** *(D)* Is he a good guy? *(L)* They are not going to tell you that.

149 **A:** Subjective.

150 **Q:** *(L)* I guess it depends on your point of view. I'm sure Hitler thought he was a good man. That is subjective. Good and evil are subjective. *(D)* Would he and I be compatible?

151 **A:** Discover on your own. Free will.

152 **Q:** *(L)* Well, there is a way you might be able to find out something. Since all minds are one mind, the Cassiopaeans don't mind telling you what another person thinks or how they think. What does David N think of Diana?

153 **A:** Jumbled thought patterns.

154 **Q:** *(L)* Is this David N that Diana has met, is he the same David N that Sally B was acquainted with in St. Petersburg?

155 **A:** How many are there with that name?

156 **Q:** *(L)* Well, there are probably more than one, but I don't think all of them in this area would be involved in the metaphysical community. That would narrow it down. Was Sally B accurately reading the situation when she said that the David N she knew was a little hung up on sex?[10]

157 **A:** Many are.

158 **Q:** *(L)* OK, what are David N's intentions toward Diana?

159 **A:** Open.

160 **Q:** *(D)* Would he like to get me in bed?

161 **A:** We might ask the same question of you.

162 **Q:** *(L)* What are your intentions? *(D)* I don't have any intentions until I find out whether or not he has good intentions. I am not going to jump in the hay with anybody unless I find out that they really care for me. So, that is why I am asking.

163 **A:** Okay.

164 **Q:** *(L)* I don't think they are going to help you out on this one. The closest we are going to get is that he has jumbled thoughts and he is probably the same guy Sally knew.

165 **A:** The "bedroom" is not our specialty.

166 **Q:** *(D)* Not mine either, fortunately or unfortunately. *(L)* Well, let's ask about JR. Has he read the transcripts all or in part, and, if so, what is his reaction?

167 **A:** Dreamy person.

168 **Q:** *(L)* What do you mean by dreamy? He dreams a lot?

169 **A:** Self explanatory.

---

[10] Sally (my Reiki master) had a *lot* more to say about this guy, David N, than that! He was, apparently, a real predator/gigolo. So, once again, Diana M was showing how gullible she was.

170 **Q:** So, "dreamy person" is his reaction to the transcripts?

171 **A:** Dreamy person is he.

172 **Q:** *(L)* Does this mean that he lives in the world of dreams and not reality? *(D)* Or, is he someone who initiates his thoughts in the dream state?

173 **A:** We are merely relating our observations.

174 **Q:** *(L)* Has he read the transcripts?

175 **A:** Some.

176 **Q:** *(L)* What did he think in reaction to them?

177 **A:** Went into dream state.

178 **Q:** *(D)* Oh, he was reading it and it hit something? *(L)* Is that it, what Diana is saying?

179 **A:** Maybe.

180 **Q:** *(D)* Well, it hit something and he went off into a dream. So, it hit some of his reality. *(D)* I want to ask some questions about Martie: will she and Eddie Page reestablish communication? *(L)* I didn't know they were on the outs. But, I don't know either of them well enough to ask questions. *(D)* Well, apparently the story is that Martie told someone else that Eddie was having affairs with other women and it got back to Eddie's wife.[11]

181 **A:** People have shortcomings.

182 **Q:** *(D)* Will they get back together?

183 **A:** Open.

184 **Q:** *(L)* Did Martie relay a falsehood about Eddie? *(D)* Eddie said she did, anyway.

185 **A:** Subjective.

186 **Q:** *(D)* She said that Eddie had mistresses.

187 **A:** That is not important.

188 **Q:** *(D)* Well, that is OK. *(L)* On the day that we saw Eddie, I guess it was last Saturday, he told us that he had been abducted three days before. Was this a physical abduction or was it a virtual-reality abduction?

189 **A:** It was the latter.

190 **Q:** *(L)* Of the many abductions he claims to have experienced, how many are of the VR type?

191 **A:** Half or thereabouts.

192 **Q:** *(L)* In a virtual-reality abduction, does any part of the person actually leave and go into another dimension?

193 **A:** Soul replication.

194 **Q:** *(L)* So, a replica of their soul, like a shadow of the soul, so to speak, like maybe a holographic part of the soul gets moved into another dimension and experiences events; is that what you mean?

195 **A:** That is close.

196 **Q:** *(L)* So, when a person experiences a virtual-reality abduction it's virtually real in the sense that it happens to them on some level, or to some part of them?

197 **A:** It is real.

198 **Q:** *(L)* But, their physical body is not being abducted and going anywhere?

199 **A:** The original does not.

200 **Q:** *(L)* Well, that's intriguing. *(D)* Is that like... *(L)* It's soul replication...

201 **A:** Think of photo copier, similar concept.

---

[11] And people wonder why I distanced myself from the whole metaphysical/New Age/UFO crowd? Sheesh!

202 **Q:** *(L)* A photocopy? So, half of Eddie's abductions are virtual-reality abductions...

203 **A:** Yes.

204 **Q:** And the other half are actual physical abductions?

205 **A:** Yes.

206 **Q:** *(L)* Who is he being abducted by? I know we asked this before, but I want to clarify something...

207 **A:** Orion STSers.

208 **Q:** *(L)* And what level of density are these abductors who abduct him?

209 **A:** 4th level.

210 **Q:** So, the 4th level Orion STS group abduct Eddie Page. What do they look like?

211 **A:** They rearrange appearance.

212 **Q:** *(L)* Well, to look like what? He perceives...

213 **A:** Whatever is anticipated by the abductee.

214 **Q:** *(L)* Well, he told me they were beautiful. *(D)* His father is one of them, he says. Beautiful people, the way I see it, means from the heart... not like physical beauty... *(L)* Does he perceive them as physically beautiful?

215 **A:** That is subjective.

216 **Q:** *(L)* And, since you say that they rearrange their appearance, in their natural state, before they are rearranged, what do they look like?

217 **A:** Natural state is variable.

218 **Q:** *(D)* Are they robots?

219 **A:** Some.

220 **Q:** *(L)* What do the robots look like?

221 **A:** Grays.

222 **Q:** *(L)* OK, what do the other ones look like? *(D)* Are they 12-foot-tall robots...? *(L)* I get the feeling they don't want to answer this question...

223 **A:** 3rd density thinking.

224 **Q:** *(L)* I'm sorry. I guess you just want us to learn by this exercise, is that it?

225 **A:** Review material.

226 **Q:** *(L)* What do the 4th density STS Orions look like? I know what the answer is... are they Lizzies?

227 **A:** Some.

228 **Q:** *(L)* So, Eddie Page is getting hauled out by the Lizzies and the Grays and they make themselves look and seem nice to him, is that it?

229 **A:** Laura, 3 and 4 don't jibe.

230 **Q:** *(L)* Are there 3rd level Lizzies?

231 **A:** All these are 4th who sometimes travel to 3rd rules are totally different in 4th density have you not grasped this yet?[12]

Tape runs out. We decided to stop at this point as we were tired.

End of Session

---

[12]Yeah, I had grasped a lot, mainly that this session was all about Frank and his desire to be a channeling star with devoted followers of the gullible kind.

December 28, 1994

As noted, I had not been happy with the tone of the previous session, so I was in a bit of a challenging mood myself at this one. While I don't recall the specifics, I'm sure there was some discussion during the week about Diana M and her gullibility to the Eddie Page scam and how likely it was that she had been a skewing presence. While I had said I didn't want her at any future session, I was trying to stay open about the possibility that she would learn a serious lesson in her 'Pleiadian interactions.'

As you will see towards the end, I had been in a rather unusual auto-accident on Christmas Eve, just four days before this session. The rotator muscles in my left arm were torn, I had a concussion, a cracked vertebra in my neck, etc. I didn't realize it at the time of this session that these injuries were going to progressively worsen and cause me problems for the next few years. I think I was still in shock from the accident, but determined to 'carry on' as usual even though I was wearing a neck/head brace and could barely use my arm.

Just before the session here, VG and I had been discussing the problems with modern psychology as it is currently taught. There was a little bit of emotional attachment to our various ideas here, but not much, and there was some balance from the various sides, so the information that came through on this topic appears to be rather good.

Participants: 'Frank', Laura, VG

1 **Q**: Hello.

2 **A**: Hello. Wonderland.

3 **Q**: *(L)* What does "Wonderland" have to do with anything?

4 **A**: It just popped to mind.

5 **Q**: *(L)* Since this happens from time to time, an odd word or phrase pops to mind as the connection is made, is this because that particular thought is occupying the point in space-time where the connection is made?

6 **A**: Laura, such an active imagination[1]

---

[1] Rather condescending if you ask me, which was exactly how Frank was acting towards me at the time.

you have, my dear!¹

7 **Q:** *(V)* I think they just mean they see all the Christmas cheer and so forth... *(L)* Well, why do these little phrases just 'pop' in...? It's curious.

8 **A:** Why not?

9 **Q:** *(L)* Who do we have with us tonight?

10 **A:** Rollaea?

11 **Q:** *(L)* Haven't you been with us before?

12 **A:** No. And yes.

13 **Q:** *(L)* Well, we have two or three things on the agenda tonight. The first thing I would like to ask for Suzanne Konicov...

14 **A:** Where are we from?

15 **Q:** *(L)* I'm sorry, where are you from?

16 **A:** Cassiopaea. If you don't ask, how do you know who we are?²

17 **Q:** *(L)* Well, good point. If you were the Lizzies and I asked, wouldn't you answer that you were the Cassiopaeans to deceive me?³

18 **A:** They would not.

19 **Q:** *(L)* Well, aren't they telling Eddie Page that they are the Pleiadians?

20 **A:** Not Lizzies.

21 **Q:** *(L)* OK, who is telling Eddie Page that they are the Pleiadians?

22 **A:** Orion STS.

23 **Q:** *(L)* Well, if you were Orion STS and we asked who you were, wouldn't you say you were the Cassiopaeans?

24 **A:** No. Pleiadians. That is "trendy" thus deceptive.⁴

25 **Q:** *(L)* Back to my question. Now, at one point in the transcript of past sessions you said that you could not help the Jews or the Native Americans who called upon you, and yet, you say that when we call on you that you can help us. What is the difference?

26 **A:** Did not say that, review transcript now!

27 **Q:** *(L)* Well, what I remember is that I asked if our race was going to be wiped out by the Lizzies and the answer was "Maybe." And then... well, I'll get it out now... OK, it says here: "We don't want to be abducted, can't we stop it?" And you answered: "Not likely, they have more power than you." Then I asked: "Why can't you help us?" and you answered: "Would interfere in natural progression of your race and theirs. The Jews called upon us to save them and we could not. And the natives of your land called upon us and we could not save them from your race. We could not stop that either. It is natural progression, see?" And then I asked: "Are we going to be wiped out by aliens as part of this natural progression?" Answer: "Maybe..." OK, so, in a sense, the question related specifically to stopping abductions and you said no, you could not stop that and you said that you could not save the Jews or the Native Americans because it would interfere in natural progression... yet you said you could help us individually if we called upon you for help... What is the difference?

28 **A:** We cannot interfere to help, knowl-

---

²Yet previously they had said there was no longer any need to ask the identifying series of questions.

³Here you see my suspicion spelled out.

⁴Not an adequate answer in my opinion.

edge protects, ignorance endangers. You can help yourselves to gain knowledge, we can be the "conduit."

29 **Q**: *(V)* So, that is a misinterpretation on all our parts of what this help might or might not be? *(L)* We have a couple of other things that we have been discussing here this evening that I am sure that we all want to know about. The first thing is: Could we have a little reading for our friend Sandra D, who has been in the hospital? What is the root of the problem and how can we help her or how can she help herself to get better?

30 **A**: Sandra has chosen her karmic path. Her problem is manifesting in several locations: heart, weight affects all other organs in the body.

31 **Q**: *(L)* Does Sandra have attachments causing physical problems?

32 **A**: Not the issue. Physical reflection.

33 **Q**: *(L)* If she changes her diet will her health improve?

34 **A**: She will improve only if she chooses to. We cannot interfere, but she could always choose to explore her subconscious, but we must warn this will be a "tall order."

35 **Q**: *(L)* Now, before Frank arrived, V__-__ and I were having a discussion about physics and psychology and it is my understanding from experience and study that emotions, as human beings term them, are related to physiology, to chemicals, and can be controlled by thoughts. And, that if we choose to change our emotions, we have only to change our thinking. Is this correct?

36 **A**: Partly.

[5] *The Wave* 64

37 **Q**: *(V)* What you are saying is true, and that is all fine and dandy, but how many of the population can do that? Would even believe that they could do that? *(L)* Not very many. Less than ten percent. *(V)* Well, then, how does the definition...

38 **A**: That is not the issue?[5]

39 **Q**: *(L)* Well then, what is the issue?

40 **A**: Karma.

41 **Q**: *(L)* Are emotions that are carried over karmically, do they affect the physical body that they come into in a chemical way...

42 **A**: Can.

43 **Q**: *(V)* So Laura's hypothesis that all emotions stem from chemicals is not necessarily true as an exclusive statement?

44 **A**: Okay.

45 **Q**: *(L)* Does the soul have emotions of its own as we human beings term emotions?

46 **A**: Close.

47 **Q**: *(L)* What emotions does the soul experience?

48 **A**: Complex.

49 **Q**: *(L)* Can the soul, at an absolute level, experience hatred, for example?

50 **A**: Not same state.

51 **Q**: *(L)* Well, when one is dealing with psychology, what would be the best approach... what is the true aspect of the self or the being that one should inquire into in order to heal?

52 **A**: Subconscious mind.

53 **Q:** *(V)* Is the statement that psychology studies emotions, is that a fair statement?

54 **A:** No. Subconscious is same in body or out.

55 **Q:** *(V)* The subconscious is part of the soul?

56 **A:** One and same.[6]

57 **Q:** *(V)* Is the higher self the same as the soul and the subconscious?

58 **A:** Yes.

59 **Q:** *(V)* Please define true psychology for me.

60 **A:** Half.

61 **Q:** *(L)* What do you mean by half? What is the half?

62 **A:** Half spirituality.

63 **Q:** *(V)* Do you think that the spiritual part put together with the subconscious part is a good way to approach psychology as I have been planning?[7]

64 **A:** Be careful of "influences," you are easily influenced.

65 **Q:** *(V)* Is this directed at me and my idea of spiritual psychology?

66 **A:** Yes. And no.

67 **Q:** *(V)* What influences?

68 **A:** Any.

69 **Q:** *(V)* That is kind of open, isn't it? *(L)* Well, you never answered the question about 'true' psychology. You only said "Half." What is true psychology? Is it the investigation of the subconscious mind?

70 **A:** True psychology only half.

71 **Q:** *(L)* And what is true psychology, a definition? Was it as I said, an investigation of the subconscious mind?

72 **A:** Physiologically directed study of mind.

73 **Q:** *(L)* The effects on the mind of the physiology, the hormones, blood sugar levels and so forth, input and output of the various organs and how that can affect the thought processes, is that correct?

74 **A:** Close.[8]

75 **Q:** *(L)* And that is half of it. What else?

76 **A:** Spirit is missing half.

---

[6]This is actually quite interesting in view of the work done by Gabor Mate (*When the Body Says No*), Timothy Wilson (*Strangers to Ourselves*), Daniel Kahneman (*Thinking: Fast and Slow*), Martha Stout (*The Myth of Sanity*), others, and, of course, Gurdjieff whose ideas have been vindicated and augmented by modern cognitive psychology. But cognitive psychology was still in its infancy when this session was held. Ulric Neisser is credited with formally having coined the term 'cognitive psychology' in his book *Cognitive Psychology*, published in 1967. Modern perspectives on cognitive psychology generally address cognition as a dual process theory, introduced by Jonathan Haidt in 2006, and expounded upon by Daniel Kahneman in 2011. Of course, even modern cognitive psychology does not address the issues we were trying to get at here.

[7]VG was studying psychology at university.

[8]Which is where our research has led us over the years: the importance of studying the 'machine,' as Gurdjieff referred to it, though our approach even takes diet into consideration.

Q: *(L)* And what would the person who is working on the spiritual half of it focus their energies on? Would it be techniques of meditation, understanding the nature of the universe, would it have to do with physics, what area?

A: Apples and oranges.

Q: *(L)* All of those things are apples and oranges compared to the spiritual application of psychology that you intend?

A: No. Spirit has nothing to do with psychology as you know it.

Q: *(L)* But, in this theoretical psychology that you are telling us about, how would you fit the spiritual aspect into it?

A: Totally restructure theory.

Q: *(L)* OK, and how would you present this totally restructured theory?

A: Much too complex.

Q: *(L)* In the discussion of psychology that we have had here, obviously you think that there is something about the way you have discussed it that V___ has missed or would miss because of influences from other sources, is that correct?

A: Yes.

Q: *(L)* In terms of these sources that influence her, by what means of her system, her organic or spiritual system, do these influences tap into her being?

A: Visual and auditory.

Q: *(L)* OK, so she sees things and hears things that influence her, is that correct?

A: Yes.

Q: *(L)* And where does she usually see or hear these things?

A: Scholastic.

Q: *(L)* So, these are scholastic things that you are talking about. She hears and sees things at school that influence her, that you say these influences are not going to be helpful in what she is ultimately trying to achieve, is that correct?

A: Bingo!

Q: *(L)* These things that she sees and hears, are they people and words that the people speak, or are they images such as film images, or just general...

A: All of the above.[9]

Q: *(V)* OK, now listen guys: if I don't go to school to get an education, and, in other words, to get the degree and get the credibility, then how am I going to be able to do any work? *(L)* Did you ever think that the people you would want to work with wouldn't come to anybody with a traditional degree?

A: Laura, let us answer.

Q: *(L)* I'm sorry. I'll butt out.

A: Why do you think you need a degree?

Q: *(V)* Well, the professional world here on planet Earth is built around degrees. I'm sure you are aware of that.

A: Incorrect!

Q: *(L)* People with degrees are in breadlines... I'm sorry... I'll shut up. *(V)* Well, my goodness... so then I...

A: Disinformation cleverly and carefully orchestrated.

Q: *(L)* For what purpose?

A: To mislead.

---

[9] *High Strangeness* "Appendix"

107 **Q:** *(V)* To mislead in what way? What am I being led away from?

108 **A:** Not just you.

109 **Q:** *(V)* All psych students are misled?

110 **A:** All humans.

111 **Q:** *(L)* Are you saying that the public school system, including the college system, is deliberately designed and implemented to fill one's brain with false knowledge, to perpetuate Lizzie rule?

112 **A:** Close but this manifests at lower levels too.

113 **Q:** *(V)* Well, let me ask this question... is this the only species in the universe that studies this concept of psychology? Are there psychologists in Orion, are there psychologists in Cassiopaea?

114 **A:** Narrow concept.

115 **Q:** *(L)* What do you mean it's a narrow concept? *(V)* I mean, I mean... *(L)* Do you understand what they mean? *(V)* No, but what I mean is are we the only thinking, intelligent types of people that... *(L)* I don't think that's what they meant to imply. *(V)* Well, it's not coming out right. You know, I sit here and I try and put things into words and it's so hard...

116 **A:** Expand your mind.

117 **Q:** *(V)* I'm trying to. *(L)* By what means?

118 **A:** Less prejudice.

119 **Q:** *(L)* Bet you never thought you would be called prejudiced, did you? *(V)* Prejudice about what? I don't think they are talking about blacks and whites... *(L)* I know, but there are other kinds...

120 **A:** The universe is an infinite illusion.

[10] VG really was getting upset here.

121 **Q:** *(V)* Jesus Christ! You guys...[10]

122 **A:** We are not Jesus Christ.

123 **Q:** *(V)* That was just an exclamation... *(L)* They know that. I think they are being funny. *(V)* Ha, ha. Well, then, I guess... OK, when you say the universe is an infinite illusion, then why not close the eyes, lights out and the illusion is over?

124 **A:** Stop focusing so narrowly and rigidly.

125 **Q:** *(V)* Now, I don't think that's fair because I sit around all the time not focusing on narrow... *(L)* I know nothing! They already told me to shut up! Alright, you guys, you better help V__ out here because she is losing it... *(V)* Well I'm, I'm...

126 **A:** Blast your mind open.

127 **Q:** *(V)* Alright. You guys have said you are with us at all times, then you must know that I constantly am thinking about the possibilities... not even to think about possibilities, just accept that there is endless, boundless possibilities and move forward every day from that point of view?

128 **A:** That's a good start.

129 **Q:** *(V)* Well, if I have as open a mind as I do, I mean, I think I have a pretty open mind, what do you guys consider an open mind? Does anybody sitting here have the ultimate open mind? *(L)* Don't include me in this... I don't want them starting on me! *(V)* No, I mean how... as 3rd dimensional beings, how open can our minds be? Can you not tell that I am trying?

130 **A:** You are moving to 4th level, but all are not at same level of progression.

131 **Q:** *(L)* Are you saying here that V___ is much farther along than many people?

132 **A:** No.

133 **Q:** *(L)* Well, are you saying that she's got a good start? *(V)* Am I doing... let's put it this way, if I am moving on in my progression, what are the most critical things that I am doing in my moving and my progressing to move faster, that's making it happen? What are the key things that I do...

134 **A:** Association with individuals who speed your progress.

135 **Q:** *(V)* And naturally, that's Laura and Frank, correct?[11]

136 **A:** Maybe. That is up to you.

137 **Q:** *(V)* OK, association with individuals who speed my progress, that's one of the things that I do right, that's what you said, right?

138 **A:** Okay.

139 **Q:** *(V)* Is that the only key thing that I do?

140 **A:** Learning involves discovery.

141 **Q:** *(V)* Alright... So then, am I wasting my precious time going to school to get a degree in psychology?

142 **A:** Open.

143 **Q:** *(L)* I just think if going to school makes you happy, do it, but don't take it too seriously. *(V)* Are you saying that I can be so influenced that I...

144 **A:** Influence comes not from experience but belief.

145 **Q:** *(V)* Well, if you guys hadn't just instilled within me that what I am doing, my education, is also being highly influenced, then would I ever have had the belief that you are talking about? Are you part of the influence? *(L)* What are you saying here? *(V)* Influence comes not from experience but belief... I didn't have a belief before this that I could... *(L)* OK, in other words you have warned her about influences therefore, it is now OK for her to continue on her daily path as it is currently set up because she has been warned and is aware, is that correct?

146 **A:** Close.

147 **Q:** *(V)* My understanding is that the whole psychology thing, you know because Frank pooh poohs it all the time, and its that even though the teachings of Freud and all the others, Erikson, Horney and so forth, may not apply to the whole universe, they do apply to the species as a society...

148 **A:** Application is subjective.

149 **Q:** *(L)* So V___ is OK to continue along her current path, and there are a lot of benefits she is receiving from going to school including networking, as it exists for her... *(V)* Yes, I do a lot of seed planting while I am at school...

150 **A:** Okay, but be careful of influences.

151 **Q:** *(L)* Well, I guess that is it. You have the knowledge now and you're loaded for bear.

152 **A:** Now, you could gain much more knowledge by independent study and meditation.

153 **Q:** *(V)* Well, the knowledge that I want to gain in psychology and in school, and

---

[11] VG had also noted a certain self-promotion about Frank as 'the channel to end all channels,' which he went on about on numerous occasions, so she was on guard here, I think.

all of this is in order to help other people grow. *(L)* I think that what they are telling you is that the knowledge that you want you are not going to get there. That is the whole issue.

154 **A**: Why do you feel you need a degree?

155 **Q**: *(V)* Like I said, for credibility. It's also a legal aspect of practicing. You just don't practice...

156 **A**: Nonsense![12]

157 **Q**: *(V)* But you are not going to tell me how I can do this otherwise, are you?

158 **A**: We just did, but because you are not yet open, you did not recognize this.

159 **Q**: *(V)* So, independent study and meditation is the true way that I could find how to help other people?

160 **A**: Yes.

161 **Q**: *(V)* So, in other words, if it is going to happen, it is going to happen. No need to force the issue, huh? OK, once this is published and people start being aware of what we do, what will they be looking for?

162 **A**: Everything.

163 **Q**: *(L)* You did say that once we got on the network, things would happen suddenly and dramatically. Now, as you must know, I did have an automobile accident the [very] day after I got hooked up to the network (Christmas Eve)! I am put back together now with screws and tape! I'm surprised they didn't keep me in the hospital longer. Now, oddly, as I was driving, just a few minutes prior to the accident, I was thinking very strongly of the fact that you Cassiopaeans were with me and I was saying to you in my mind that I wished you would also go and help my friend, Sandra, who was in the hospital. I was planning on rushing through my Christmas Eve and going to the hospital to give her Reiki. And then, Kowabonga! I got the smasho-smacko in the rear. Why did this happen? What did I do wrong? Is this what you meant by "sudden and dramatic"?

164 **A**: All happens for a reason.[13]

165 **Q**: *(L)* Was there something I was supposed to learn from this smash-up?

166 **A**: If so, learn by meditating.

167 **Q**: *(L)* Is there something about our state of being that we can be sitting there thinking loving thoughts about others and then we get smashed?

168 **A**: Meditate.

169 **Q**: *(V)* Is her accident directly connected with getting online? *(L)* Well, they didn't kill me, though they tried! *(V)* Back to my question...

170 **A**: Not necessary to answer.

171 **Q**: *(L)* Is that because I know the answer?

172 **A**: Okay.

---

[12] In my opinion, this approach toward the topic is not reasonable or realistic and not what I, personally, advocate or teach as a result of long research, including channeling and analyzing these sessions. It also doesn't reflect the later developments in the Cassiopaean communications after Frank was gone and a clearer channel was established.

[13] *The Wave* 18. Indeed, the therapy I was able to get as a result of the accident (paid for by the insurance) led to my separation from my then husband a little over a year later, following which I met Ark and, as they say, the rest is history.

173 **Q:** *(L)* And my answer is that there is a definite connection between the accident and getting hooked up, is that correct?

174 **A:** You explore well.

175 **Q:** *(L)* I think... now, my whole spinal column snapped like a whip on impact and I did have a concussion [and fractured vertebra]... and my shoulder is in *really* bad shape... It's going to take a long time to recover.

176 **A:** You must be a "Whippersnapper."[14]

177 **Q:** *(L)* Are there going to be some really positive results from the computer net? I mean, this is a rather painful beginning.

178 **A:** What have we told you?[15]

179 **Q:** *(V)* Well, let's turn it on now.

180 **A:** Good idea.

181 **Q:** *(L)* Good night.

End of Session

---

[14] Definition: "a young and inexperienced person considered to be presumptuous or overconfident." Yeah, I really was over-confident and still in the illusion that if you just think nice and loving thoughts all the time, surround yourself with light and warm fuzzies, nothing bad will ever happen.

[15] Yeah, yeah: "no pain, no gain." As I said in note above, the therapy I was able to get led to massive changes in my life. In a funny way, it relates to the topic of this session: psychology. During the course of over a year of therapy, I was able to address many past-life and what can be called 'psychic' issues. I came to realize that this accident was a reflection of past-life issues and worked on clearing those out. Perhaps I'll write about this process specifically one day because it truly was amazing that something that appears to be so negative at the outset could bring so many benefits at the end.

December 31, 1994

At this point in time, we were well and truly shunned by the metaphysical/spiritualist community because we (shudder) were concerned with UFOs and aliens, acknowledging that they could have played a big part in paranormal phenomena down through the centuries. That wasn't 'spiritual' to that crowd. On the other side, the UFO/alien research community looked on what we were doing – using what was perceived as paranormal means of getting some answers about aliens and UFOs – as not scientific. The UFO/alien contactee community wasn't happy because the C's did not describe their vaunted abductors as the saviors of humanity; in fact, the C's had given some shocking and unsettling responses to questions about 'what was really going on' behind the phenomenon.

Nevertheless, there were representatives from each of these crowds at the New Year's Eve party session below. That was due to the lobbying of Terry and Jan, who really wanted some of their wide circle of acquaintances in those milieus to 'check it out!' Additionally, Frank had invited a friend of his and the friend's friend. I've got as many of the names included as I can remember with notes as to who is who.

Frank was in his element at this session, the star, the center of attraction, holding court as The Channel, bringing in dead dudes and more. I was perfectly happy to let him enjoy himself, but the session itself reflects a bit of all these conflicting energies. Still, there is some very good material here in spite of the C's having to cater to so many beliefs and emotional investments. Also, the session went on a long time and we took a break for midnight. The second half is included even though it actually occurred in 1995!

Participants: 'Frank', Laura, Terry, Jan, Diana M,[1] VG, Gene and Jean Brown,[2] Mark E and his wife Luanne, Billy (Luanne's brother), Glenn and several others

New Year's Eve Party in progress as we sit at the board. A message is spelled out quickly before we even get started properly.

We began with four at the board: 'Frank', myself, VG and Terry; we made several changes as the night went on.

1 **Q:** Hello.

2 **A:** Hello. Did you get last message?

3 **Q:** Yes, the last message was: We are happy to see more people here.

4 **A:** Yes. Say hello to Mark and Billy, Luanne, Glenn and others. You have visitors in ethereal plane because of holiday get together and we brought 4 here because it is time for exposure. Terry keep up, this is the night for important stuff.

5 **Q:** *(L)* OK, who needs to be on the board? You asked for Terry, can I trade with Diana?

6 **A:** Okay now. Diana. [I gave up my place at the board to Diana]

7 **Q:** *(DM)* Hi.

8 **A:** Ease up on pressure. Very important: this time measurement year represents big changes.

9 **Q:** *(L)* Changes of what sort?

10 **A:** Spiritual linked to physical on planet.

11 **Q:** *(L)* I guess you are going to tell us?

12 **A:** Terry on board. Keep fingers on. [The pointer was literally flying around the board and, at this point, actually sailed off the table]

13 **Q:** *(T)* It's hard, you're moving so fast tonight. Energy's up.

14 **A:** Power is explosive. [Many spins around board]

15 **Q:** *(T)* Well, happy New Year to y'all, too!

16 **A:** We want you all to succeed this year.

17 **Q:** *(DM)* In what?

18 **A:** To send messages.

19 **Q:** *(DM)* Thank you.

20 **A:** Diana easy on pressure.

21 **Q:** *(T)* You guys are moving so fast tonight we have to hang on. *(DM)* I'm just trying to keep up.

22 **A:** You're correct.

23 **Q:** *(V)* Are you guys ready for a couple of questions?

24 **A:** Okay.

25 **Q:** *(V)* This right here I picked up at the Tampa metaphysical bookstore. [Holds up rock] It is supposed to be a piece of meteorite. What can you tell me about this? I was told that it's used for transformation.

26 **A:** Bogus. [Laughter]

27 **Q:** *(DM)* It's funny, the word came into my mind!

28 **A:** We are going through you and Frank tonight. Easy, Diana. Diana sell house this month.[3]

29 **Q:** *(DM)* Yes! Can you give me a day?

---

[1] Representing the UFO/alien contactee, Eddie Page–type crowd.
[2] State Section Directors of MUFON. See: http://www.i-b-r.org/UFO-Ladingtest.pdf
[3] This is more of Frank looking to Diana to become his devotee and possible financial patron. I think she did, actually, sell the house though.

30 **A:** 19th. Drop price 2,000 dollars.

31 **Q:** *(DM)* I can live with that.

32 **A:** You got it.

33 **Q:** *(DM)* Should I drop it or dicker it?

34 **A:** Drop it now.

35 **Q:** *(V)* Let's ask about this letter. I received a letter in the mail today that is really perplexing us all. Can you tell me what this letter is about?[4]

36 **A:** Third party got ahold of privileged info.

37 **Q:** *(T)* Who is the third party?

38 **A:** Amos Sanders.[5]

39 **Q:** *(V)* Is it my privileged information?

40 **A:** No. Consortium.

41 **Q:** *(L)* What is the intent of this letter?

42 **A:** 3rd party got your bio off files.

43 **Q:** *(V)* What files?

44 **A:** Computer grid.

45 **Q:** *(T)* What computer grid?

46 **A:** FBI.

47 **Q:** *(T)* Has this letter been set up by the FBI?

48 **A:** No. Amos Sanders broke into system.

49 **Q:** *(V)* How am I mixed up in this? *(T)* Who is Amos? *(DM)* Maybe it's an acronym.

50 **A:** New license.

51 **Q:** *(V)* I just got a new license in November. *(T)* A driver's license? *(V)* Yes. *(T)* Is this the DMV computer system?

52 **A:** FBI.

53 **Q:** *(T)* Why is V___ in the FBI computer system?

54 **A:** You all are on file.

55 **Q:** *(L)* Is that "you all" as in everybody in the country or just us specifically?

56 **A:** You and others.

57 **Q:** *(V)* Well, what course do I need to contact... the police... what course of action do I need to take with this? This is fraud...

58 **A:** Ignore it.

59 **Q:** *(T)* Is this letter a set-up?

60 **A:** No Amos is "nuts." Crazy "genius." Breaks into files.

61 **Q:** *(T)* The guy mentioned in the letter is 'Wilbur.'

62 **A:** False name.

63 **Q:** *(V)* So this is in no way... this is not a threat to me financially or in the future legally wise... somebody...

64 **A:** But you are on FBI file.

65 **Q:** *(T)* Why is she on the FBI file? *(V)* Because I know too much?

66 **A:** Piano.

67 **Q:** *(T&L)* Piano? *(V)* I have a piano debt. Why would that be on the FBI file? *(J)* What? *(V)* Is there a warrant out for my arrest? [Laughter] *(T)* Why

---

[4] VG had received a letter of inquiry that was basically asking "Are you this person?" and included her driver's license number, her Social Security number, and other private details. It didn't state the nature of the business that triggered the inquiry and I had never seen anything exactly like it before.

[5] Who knows? But I doubt the name is correct unless it was another of the crowd of dead dudes around!

do they have her on file for a debt for a piano?

A: Tracer. They know all and keep track of everyone and every thing.[6]

Q: *(T)* Is there more to this than just general tracing of debt and license accessed by a nut?

A: Not yet.

Q: *(T)* Well why, besides the debt, would they be interested in watching her?

A: Your activities.

Q: *(L)* In specific?

A: Metaphysical.

Q: *(T)* The FBI is watching people who are involved in metaphysics?

A: And UFOs.

Q: *(T)* Well, they always watch us UFO people... *(DM)* Are they watching people like Eddie Page?

A: Eddie Page file "one."

Q: *(T)* What is a file "one"?

A: Top priority.[7]

Q: *(V)* Well, let's hope my file is a '200.' What priority is my file?

A: Four.

Q: *(T)* What is a level "four" file?

A: 4th most important.

Q: *(V)* Well, what about Frank? *(T)* Is Eddie Page telling the truth?

A: Some.

Q: *(DM)* What is he not telling the truth about?

A: Too many things.

Q: *(T)* So, his story is mostly false?

A: He believes.[8]

Q: *(V)* Are these FBI files that have to do with metaphysical and UFO business and what have you, are they more than just the government? Are they connected to...

A: Are you listening?

Q: *(V)* Am I listening? Of course I'm listening.

A: FBI tracks everyone.[9]

Q: *(V)* OK, so just don't worry about it. *(T)* I can just imagine what my

---

[6] This whole exchange was quite bizarre to us at the time, but with all the revelations about the NSA in the past year (2013–14) it is not impossible that this kind of information was already being compiled back then. We certainly know that the FBI kept extensive files on activists of all kinds back in the 1970s. As for the computer hacking part: I guess it is possible. It is certainly something that we hadn't heard very much about as a concept back then.

[7] Probably because Eddie Page was set up to be a spreader of disinformation and was being handled. This issue will actually come up again, so keep the name in mind along with the name of Eddie's 'handler,' Jiles Hamilton.

[8] I think this conflicts with previously given information where it was suggested that Eddie was aware that he was a fraud. On the other hand, years of research and evidence of mind control experiments such as MKULTRA being real suggest that it is possible that Eddie was a subject of such experimentation.

[9] I guess that got taken over by the NSA or the NSA started their own program and elbowed the FBI out.

file looks like! *(L)* The computer systems are so advanced it is no trouble for them to even know what color toilet paper you buy. [Laughter] I mean, the checker at the store tells what color toilet paper you buy on your receipt... "Scottissue:blue"...

96 **A**: V___ prefers green.

97 **Q**: *(L)* Do you prefer green? *(V)* Yes, but I have white. *(V)* Are you telling me I'm supposed to use green toilet paper? *(T)* They are perfecting 3rd level humor at 4th level. [Laughter]

98 **A**: Joke.

99 **Q**: *(T)* You're getting good at it too! *(DM)* I'd like to know what they look like. *(L)* Did you read the transcripts? We already asked that. *(DM)* No, I haven't gotten to it yet.

100 **A**: We are light beings, we are you in the future.

101 **Q**: *(L)* Susanne K talked to me about Al Bielek. Previously you had said that Al was an agent of the government disseminating disinformation for one thing, number two: that he knew that he was an agent of the government; there's a little confusion about his participation in the Philadelphia Project; I found a reference to him in an Ivan Sanderson book published some time ago. Susanne says that this poor guy just lives from hand to mouth, and she finds it hard to believe that he is an agent of the government since he lives such a poverty-stricken existence. Could you comment, please, on Al Bielek and his activities? *(T)* Is Al an agent for the government?

102 **A**: Al Bielek is many faceted. Poverty is subjective.

103 **Q**: *(L)* Is he an agent for the government? *(T)* They say he is many faceted.

104 **A**: Yes. But he is involved in activities.

105 **Q**: *(T)* In one session you talked about Al Bielek you indicated he was, um, not actually involved in the Philadelphia Experiment, that he was a technician on shore, and that he is now feeding out information that is provided to him, or that he had knowledge above and beyond his involvement with the experiment...

106 **A**: Close.

107 **Q**: *(T)* OK, if he is working partly with the government and then partly for his own purposes, what is it that he expects to get out of this?

108 **A**: Exposure.

109 **Q**: *(T)* What does he want from the exposure?

110 **A**: He wants people to know.

111 **Q**: *(L)* Is it possible that he is giving out some true information along with disinformation, so that the information itself can be gotten out? Could it be that his intentions might be...

112 **A**: Confused thought pattern.

113 **Q**: *(L)* Is that my thoughts or Al's thoughts?

114 **A**: Bingo! Laura's.

115 **Q**: *(T)* Does Al know that he is giving out false information... does he know that the information the government is giving him is false?

116 **A**: He is so involved you would not believe.

117 **Q**: *(T)* He is involved with the government cover-up?

118 **A**: With all of it. He knows that what he is saying is false but he has no choice because he is entangled in the web. They are using him.

119 **Q:** *(L)* What about this letter Susanne sent from some source that states that Jesus was a mythical character?

120 **A:** No, Jesus was not mythical.[10]

121 **Q:** *(T)* What about this information from this Acharya?

122 **A:** Babble.

123 **Q:** *(L)* What is the point of this stuff? It is very well done. Why are they trying to prove that Jesus never existed?

124 **A:** Nonsense. It is disinformation. Desinformatzia. Russki.

125 **Q:** *(T)* This is from Russia?

126 **A:** No, we were having some fun with words.

127 **Q:** Mirth! Mirth! *(T)* Are any of the people they are copying this to believing this stuff?

128 **A:** Some.

129 **Q:** *(T)* Is *UFO Library* going to print this?

130 **A:** Who knows.

131 **Q:** *(T)* Well, I wouldn't be surprised if it is in there next month.

132 **A:** There is a lot of garbage in there each month.

133 **Q:** *(L)* Well, this is on a different subject, but, has Mark ever been abducted by aliens?

134 **A:** Yes, starting at age three. Do you remember "ghost at corner window" at 3 yrs old?

135 **Q:** *(M)* I remember something very vaguely. I think I told Frank the story. Something happened and I think I woke up screaming. I saw something. When was the last time?

136 **A:** At age 22.

137 **Q:** *(V)* How many times has Mark been abducted?

138 **A:** 23 times.

139 **Q:** *(M)* Will I be abducted again?

140 **A:** Yes.

141 **Q:** *(M)* When?

142 **A:** It depends on belief center.

143 **Q:** *(L)* I think it might depend on how much knowledge you acquire as to whether you will be abducted again or under what circumstances.

144 **A:** Grandfather let you in on secrets of life.

145 **Q:** *(M)* Yes, yes. He taught me a lot and I think that's what they mean.

146 **A:** He was a "Priority One Soul."

147 **Q:** *(L)* What is a "Priority One Soul"?

148 **A:** One who sacrifices life's pleasures to teach others. He was your teacher. You are lucky, Mark. He kept you from "trouble."

149 **Q:** *(L)* Who abducted M___?

150 **A:** Grays.

151 **Q:** *(L)* What was the purpose of Mark's abduction?[11]

152 **A:** To study his mind. He has a very strong mind and resolve.

153 **Q:** *(L)* Did they put an implant in him?

154 **A:** Yes.

155 **Q:** *(L)* And what do they do with that implant?

156 **A:** Is monitor. Frequent ringing in ear signifies monitoring activity.

---

[10] That's certainly true. Jesus was Julius Caesar. But I wasn't ready for that then.
[11] *High Strangeness* 8

157 **Q**: *(F)* Do you have frequent ringing in your ear? *(M)* Yes. *(L)* One ear more than another? *(M)* Yes. It is kind of a tone. *(T)* Last session when I was here you were giving us information on how to calculate when the wave is going to reach Earth. I was able to plot two of the four for distance, but two were constellations. I cannot plot those distances.

158 **A**: Check third most distant star in Cassiopaea and middle "belt" star in Orion, closest star in Leo. Welcome Mark to the board. [Diana gives up her place at the board to Mark]

159 **Q**: *(M)* Well, just tell me what to do.

160 **A**: Hi, Mark. We are glad to have you here with us tonight. We have been trying to reach you for 18 years as you measure time.

161 **Q**: *(M)* Why?

162 **A**: You are destined just like the others and you know it inside. We have gone to great lengths to reach you. That is why you were brought together with Frank. Do you not remember feeling different back then?[12]

163 **Q**: *(M)* What does that mean? *(V)* Well, when you met Frank did you feel different? *(M)* Yes, I guess so. *(L)* Anybody who meets Frank feels different! *(M)* Amen! Thank you! *(J)* I would like to point out that we have all male energy on the board. That is different!

164 **A**: You and Terry knew each other in last life, remember?

165 **Q**: *(M)* Well, no, I don't. *(V)* You would probably remember if you would start meditating. *(L)* You could have past life regressions. *(T)* He wasn't that guy that got me with the sword when I was in the British Navy, was he? Those cutthroats?

166 **A**: No, but on same ship! This is why you returned to England!

167 **Q**: *(V)* Why you returned to England. Were they brothers?

168 **A**: No.

169 **Q**: *(L)* Mark was born in England.

170 **A**: That you returned to sea. You love the water.

171 **Q**: *(M)* I'm confused. *(T)* So, Mark and I knew each other in our last life? When was this?

172 **A**: 1700's.

173 **Q**: *(T)* We didn't have any other lives between 1700s and now?

174 **A**: Not for Mark. He was a sea captain with the same last name. You, Mark, are your great, great, great grandfather Simon E____.[13]

[Break for New Year's]

January 1, 1995: Continuation of 31 December 1994 session after break for New Year celebration.

175 **Q**: *(L)* Who do we have with us tonight?

176 **A**: Cassiopaea calling. Sorrona.

177 **Q**: *(L)* And who are our guests?

178 **A**: You must network tonight as there are those who are awaiting your message as promised.

179 **Q**: *(L)* Do you mean do the board and transfer it to the network?

180 **A**: Open.

---

[12]I never trusted this sort of 'you are speshul' material. On several other occasions, the C's actually said that nobody is special unless they choose to act in special ways.

[13]That really was a fascinating remark if true but no way to prove.

181 **Q:** *(V)* Have you promised somebody else that you work through that we will... *(L)* No, we promised on the network...

182 **A:** You did.

183 **Q:** *(L)* Frank and I promised that we would channel online. Yes, we logged on and made the announcement and the next day I had the wreck.[14] I had been promised that my life would change suddenly and dramatically.

184 **A:** It is.

185 **Q:** *(L)* My life is changed?

186 **A:** Yes. In process.

187 **Q:** *(L)* We want to know who the ethereal visitors are tonight... *(T)* And have they left since all the noise started?

188 **A:** Mary, Laura, John, Ruth, Terence, Todd, Vance, There's a Ronald.

189 **Q:** *(L)* Is the Laura someone who is related to me?

190 **A:** Grandma.[15]

191 **Q:** *(L)* Does anybody else recognize any of those names? *(V)* I recognize John, my uncle. Are each one of these names like a guide for each one of us?

192 **A:** No. Visitors. Attracted by energy center.

193 **Q:** *(V)* Have I had contact with John before?

194 **A:** Yes. Uncle.

195 **Q:** *(T)* Am I related to any... *(V)* My uncle that's just passed on?

196 **A:** Yes.

197 **Q:** *(L)* Is Terry related to any of these people?

198 **A:** Yes.

199 **Q:** *(L)* Who?

200 **A:** Vance.

201 **Q:** *(T)* Who is Vance? *(V)* Do they have messages for us? *(L)* Who is Vance?

202 **A:** Great Uncle.

203 **Q:** *(L)* Do any of these people have messages for any of us?

204 **A:** No.

205 **Q:** *(V)* About 5 or 6 weeks ago I was surrounded by a smell of...

206 **A:** Yes.

207 **Q:** *(V)* It was my uncle Wayne?

208 **A:** Yes.

209 **Q:** *(V)* His name was John Wayne... *(L)* Has Diana ever been abducted?[16]

210 **A:** Yes.

211 **Q:** *(L)* When was she first abducted?

212 **A:** Age 2.

213 **Q:** *(L)* How many times?

214 **A:** 59.

215 **Q:** *(V and L)* You got the record! *(T)* How many were physical?

216 **A:** Not correct thinking pattern.

217 **Q:** *(L)* In a sense they are all physical? How many of these abductions were virtual-reality abductions?

218 **A:** Everything is that.

---

[14] Automobile accident.

[15] My great-grandmother's name was Laura; I was named for her.

[16] Even though I knew that Diana claimed to have been abducted and I had done the hypnotic regression with her as described in previous session, I often would toss out quick questions like this for 'checking.'

219 **Q**: *(L)* Well, how many of these level 1 abductions?

220 **A**: 9.

221 **Q**: *(T)* How many were alpha-state abductions?

222 **A**: Two weeks ago felt "tingle."

223 **Q**: *(V)* Well, two weeks ago was the night of the party at the bookstore in Tampa. *(L)* OK, has Luanne ever been abducted?

224 **A**: Yes.

225 **Q**: *(L)* How many times?

226 **A**: 17.

227 **Q**: *(LE)* No way! *(L)* When was the first time?

228 **A**: When lived in red house.

229 **Q**: *(L)* Did you ever live in a red house? *(B)* Yeah, we lived in a brick house. *(L)* How old were you? *(LE)* When I was five.

230 **A**: 4

231 **Q**: *(LE)* Correct. We moved there when I was four right before I was five. *(L)* Does she have an implant?

232 **A**: No.

233 **Q**: *(L)* Does Diana have an implant?

234 **A**: She has 4.

235 **Q**: *(D)* Has 4 implants?

236 **A**: Yes.

237 **Q**: *(L)* Where are they?

238 **A**: In brain.

239 **Q**: *(L)* In her brain? Ar-r-r-gh! *(LE)* I had lots of allergies. *(D)* What is their purpose?

240 **A**: Monitor.

241 **Q**: *(L)* That's what they all are, monitors. *(D)* But, why?

242 **A**: You are aware.

243 **Q**: *(L)* They want to monitor you because you are aware. *(T)* They don't have cable... *(L)* Is Susan going to be here shortly?[17]

244 **A**: Open.

245 **Q**: *(L)* We want to know, what kind of energy is behind Budd Hopkins?

246 **A**: Divergent.

247 **Q**: *(L)* Is he on the right track in his research?

248 **A**: Halfway.

---

[17]Recall that in session 5 December 1994 I had mentioned receiving a Christmas card from Susan and commented that she was friends with Gene and Judy, who were associated with the metaphysical/spiritualist church crowd that considered my channeling experiment to be an attack on their beliefs. I had called Susan after receiving the card and probed a bit for info. She had said that her only connection with Judy was that, as a massage therapist, she had given them a few massages in the past but there was not much of a relationship. She had called earlier in the evening to wish us a Happy New Year, so I felt sort of obligated to invite her to the New Year's party.

[18]From: http://www.ufocasebook.com/Manhattan.html:

> An extremely compelling and controversial case of alien abduction is that of Linda Napolitano (originally aliased as Cortile), which was researched by the well-known and respected Budd Hopkins. Napolitano claimed that she was abducted by the so-called "greys," who floated her from a closed bedroom window into a hovering

249 **Q:** *(T)* Is the Linda Cortile case[18] a set-up to discredit him?

250 **A:** No.

251 **Q:** *(T)* Everything that she says happened really happened to her?

252 **A:** In 4th density.[19]

253 **Q:** *(T)* Well, all the abduction stuff was in 4D, but being pulled out of the apartment from the 17th floor or wherever it was, and being sucked up in the beam of the light, that actually happened to her?

254 **A:** In 4th density.

255 **Q:** *(T)* How did people in 3rd density see it?

256 **A:** Only those who were tuned in saw it.

257 **Q:** *(L)* Were there people there who did not see it?

258 **A:** Yes.

259 **Q:** *(T)* What or who were some of the people who didn't see it?

260 **A:** Not important.

261 **Q:** *(L)* Now, Whitley Strieber. *(T)* Can implants be removed?

262 **A:** No.

UFO. The craft was waiting for her above a Manhattan apartment building at about 3:00 A.M. November 30, 1989. More than a year after Cortile's experience, Hopkins received mail correspondence from two witnesses (known as Richard and Dan), who claimed to have actually seen the abduction. Agreeing perfectly with Linda's account of the abduction, the two men were bodyguards of a senior United Nations statesman who was visiting Manhattan. This diplomat would eventually be identified as Javier Perez de Cuellar, who, according to his two bodyguards, was visibly shaken while viewing the surreal scene. These three men encountered an unbelievable sight...the plight of a woman being floated through the air, and not only that...but three entities were also being floated, accompanying her on a short trip to a massive hovering flying craft. Hopkins' investigation would gain additional momentum when more witnesses to the event would come forward with their stories.

The bodyguards would go on to become irrational and psychotic, and one of them began to think of Linda as having some unusual, extraordinary power or influence on others. The actions of the two bodyguards, whom would later be revealed as CIA agents, presented a strange enigma to Hopkins. On April 29, 1991, they kidnapped Linda, bundled her into their car in broad daylight and quizzed her for three hours. Dan became increasingly upset with Linda as she repeated stated that she had no idea why it (the abduction) had happened. Linda would be kidnapped a second time by the men who tried to pry information from her, thinking she had a part in the alien abduction herself, which brought them into the case involuntarily.

Although Cuellar corresponded with Hopkins and verified the abduction, he explained to Hopkins that he could not go public for obvious reasons. Cuellar went even as far as to meet privately with Hopkins to discuss details of his observations that night, but demanded that he remain anonymous.

The Linda Napolitano affair is without question one of the best documented alien abduction cases in UFO history. Most of these cases are related to authorities and investigators by a single person. It is extremely unusual to have multiple witnesses, especially those totally unknown to the experiencer, to validate the facts of an alien abduction. Hopkins did an exceptional job of holding together the case, despite some unusual twists and turns.

[19] *High Strangeness* 8; *Secret History* 12; *The Wave* 26

263 **Q:** *(L)* What is the energy fueling Whitley Strieber and his work?

264 **A:** Grays.

265 **Q:** *(L)* He is an agent of the Grays?

266 **A:** No. Instrument of the Grays.

267 **Q:** *(T)* So, all his writing is compromised by the Grays?

268 **A:** Influenced by them.

269 **Q:** *(T)* Well, he says that, too. *(L)* Well, he now thinks he has learned how to be a companion of God through these experiences.

270 **A:** Wolfen reflects Lizzie reality.

271 **Q:** *(L)* Who's read the book, what's it about? *(T)* I saw the movie but I never read the book. I can't stand his Gothic style of writing. *(L)* I can't stand to read his stuff either. *(T)* I only got halfway through *Communion* and gave it up. *(L)* Well, let me ask, while we are on the subject of writing, is Anne Rice channeling her concepts in her vampire books?

272 **A:** She also is influenced by the Grays.[20]

273 **Q:** *(T)* What about Stephen King?

274 **A:** Carnal influences.

275 **Q:** *(T)* He's writing from his cojones, eh? [Laughter]

276 **A:** Okay, Terry.

277 **Q:** *(L)* Are there any further comments or do you want us to go online now?

278 **A:** Yes.

[Break – lively discussion. Someone mentions to V___ that she projects a lot of sex energy from her lower chakras in her behavior; she is offended]

279 **A:** V___, do not be offended, we are all learning.

280 **Q:** *(V)* Well, thank you so much for the honesty from everybody in the room, I really appreciate it. *(LM)* I wasn't being honest, don't blame me. *(V)* [Gene whispers to V___ and she asks the question] What chakra level is Gene operating at?

281 **A:** Chakras are like escalators, you choose your step and rise accordingly.

282 **Q:** *(G)* Well, I was hoping they would give me a number. I don't know much about chakras.

283 **A:** Learn.

284 **Q:** *(T)* The whole thing is that we are supposed to learn for ourselves. They will point us in the right direction, but then we are supposed to go out and do it. If you don't learn it on your own, you don't really learn. You have to go out and fall off the log a couple times to learn to walk the log. *(V)* Eric just told me about something that happened. Can you give me some insight?[21]

285 **A:** Imagination.

286 **Q:** *(V)* Are the boys fine? Are the boys OK?

287 **A:** Boys will be boys.

288 **Q:** *(V)* They thought they saw a witch. *(T)* Who was she? It was the neighbor lady again. *(L)* Where was she and what was she doing? *(V)* What do you mean over a car that just started? Their imaginations are just going.

289 **A:** How do peyote users see Santa Claus? [Laughter]

290 **Q:** *(V)* Are the boys doing drugs tonight?

---

[20] I didn't like that answer because Anne is one of my favorite authors.
[21] V___ had called home to check on her son, Eric.

291 **A**: Nope. [Undecipherable comment from Gene amidst laughter] When did you last see this in Rochester, Gene?

292 **Q**: *(G)* Never! [Much laughter]

293 **A**: Bingo!

294 **Q**: *(V)* That kind of smacks of Frank's "When did you ever see this in Half-Moon Bay, V___?" *(L)* Where do you think Frank is getting it from? *(V)* Aren't we all being enlightened? *(T)* Is this...²²

295 **A**: Frank is channel. Others are grooving rapidly.

296 **Q**: *(T)* Others of us?

297 **A**: Yes. Forming conduit.

298 **Q**: *(V)* You were real happy to see all of us here together this evening...

299 **A**: Yes.

300 **Q**: *(V)* Can we look forward to a greater group and a greater gathering as the year progresses?

301 **A**: Yes.

302 **Q**: *(T)* Will it reach a point where there are too many people?

303 **A**: No.

304 **Q**: *(V)* Is this like a community gathering? A society?

305 **A**: A conduit.

306 **Q**: *(T)* If I am not supposed to be at Home Shopping [employer], where am I supposed to be?

307 **A**: Discover.

308 **Q**: *(T)* Am I supposed to be doing another kind of a job or is there something entirely different that I am supposed to be doing?

309 **A**: Discover.

310 **Q**: *(L)* Is he going to come to this awareness after he does some hypnotic work and processes?

311 **A**: Open.

312 **Q**: *(V)* With meditation and metaphysical exercise, I can lift my chakras higher, is this correct?

313 **A**: Yes.

314 **Q**: *(V)* Dedication?

315 **A**: Yes.

316 **Q**: *(V)* Is it all in what I perceive my purpose to be?

317 **A**: Yes.

318 **Q**: *(L)* [Indicating little plastic dinosaur] Do you like our little mascot here on the table?

319 **A**: Okay.

320 **Q**: *(V)* Do you have any messages for us before we say goodnight?

321 **A**: No. Goodnight.

322 **Q**: *(L)* Thank you very much.

End of Session

---

²² *The Wave* 37

Appendix: Images

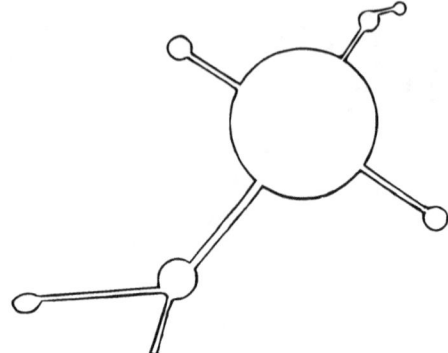

Figure 1: Crop Circle attributed to Dennis Healy, date unknown; Drawing by J. Rodemerk 1997

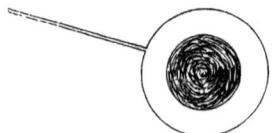

Figure 2: Crop Circle found near Pepperbox Hill Whiteparish, Wiltshire in 1987; Drawing by J. Rodemerk 1997

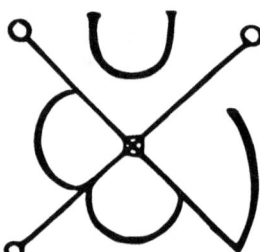

Figure 3: "Seal of Mars", Figure 26 in H. Stanley Redgrove, B.Sc., "Magic and Mysticism: Studies in Bygone Beliefs", New Jersey, Citadel Press 1972, p. 72

Figure 4: Crop Circle found in Ickleton, near Cambridge, in 1991; Drawing by J. Rodemerk 1997

Figure 5: Crop Circle found near Barbury Castle, in 1991; Drawing by J. Rodemerk 1997

Figure 6: Crop Circle found in Foxfield near Hungerford in 1991, Drawing by J. Rodemerk 1997

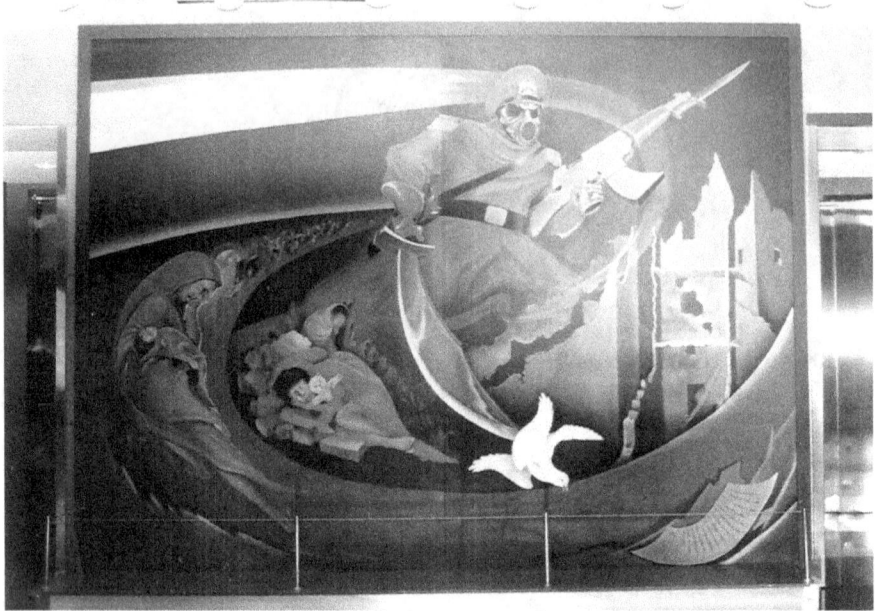

Figure 7: Denver Airport Mural 1: An oppressing force causing death and misery?

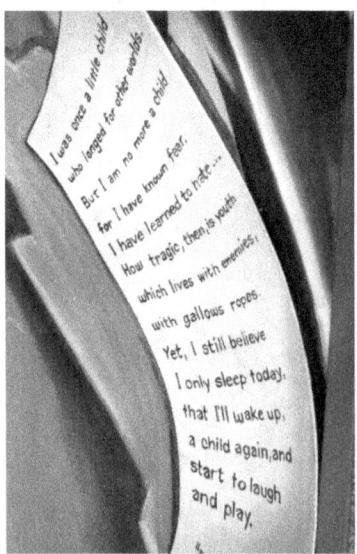

Figure 8: Detail of Denver Airport Mural 1: Letter

Figure 9: Denver Airport Mural 2: Destruction and Death?

Figure 10: Denver Airport Mural 3: Fighters with Falling Rocks in the sky?

Figure 11: Denver Airport Mural 4: Mass Exodus?

Figure 12: Denver Airport Mural 5: Victory over Evil?

Figure 13: Detail of Denver Airport Mural 5: "War, Violence, Hate"

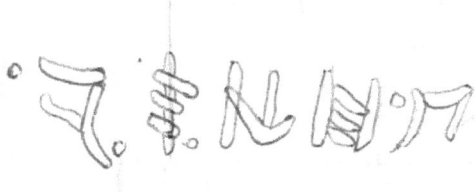

Figure 14: Symbols drawn by A__

Chapters of "The Wave"

"The Wave" originally was a series of articles written by Laura Knight-Jadczyk for the Internet only. These articles have been expanded and published as a series of volumes (1–8), in paper and in electronic formats. Over the years, a number of editions have been produced for each of these volumes. Some of these editions do not have chapter numbering, and for some, the chapter numbering has been re-started from one. However, the chapter titles are identical in all editions. For this reason, the following table summarizes all chapters of *The Wave* Series and gives chapter number, chapter title, and shows into which volume a particular chapter number has been included (VP = volume number in print, VE = volume number in electronic format), and where a chapter can be found on the Cassiopaea website. Please refer to the bibliography, section "Esotericism", for additional details about the volumes of *The Wave*.

Nr.	Chapter Title	VP	VE	http://cassiopaea.org/
1	"Riding The Wave"	1	1	/the-wave-chapter-1
2	"Multi-Dimensional Soul Essences"	1	1	/the-wave-chapter-2
3	"Dorothy and The Frog Prince"	1	1	/the-wave-chapter-3
4	"The C's go for a 'Test Drive'"	1	1	/the-wave-chapter-4
5	"Perpendicular Realities"	1	1	/the-wave-chapter-5
6	"Animal Psychology"	1	1	/the-wave-chapter-6
7	"Laura Falls Into the Pit"	1	1	/the-wave-chapter-7
8	"Everywhere You Look..."	1	2	/the-wave-chapter-8
9	"The Beast of Gévaudan"	1	2	/the-wave-chapter-9
10	"The Truth Is Out There"	2	2	/the-wave-chapter-10
11	"Roses Grow Best In Manure"	2	2	/the-wave-chapter-11
12	"All There Is Is Lessons"	2	2	/the-wave-chapter-12
13	"Some Further Remarks"	2	2	/the-wave-chapter-13
14	"Candy Will Ruin Your Teeth"	2	2	/the-wave-chapter-14
15	"He Hideth My Soul..."	2	2	/the-wave-chapter-15
16	"Laura Finds Reiki"	2	2	/the-wave-chapter-16
17	"Wandering In 3rd Density"	2	2	/the-wave-chapter-17
18	"A Trip to 'Alligator Alley'"	2	2	/the-wave-chapter-18
19	"Dr. Greenbaum"	2	2	/the-wave-chapter-19

20	"Black Lightning Strikes"	3	3	/the-wave-chapter-20
21	"Roswell Revisited"	3	3	/the-wave-chapter-21
22	"The Nexus Seven"	3	3	/the-wave-chapter-22
23	"Lucifer and the Pot of Gold"	3	3	/the-wave-chapter-23
24	"The Bacchantes Meet Apollo"	3	3	/the-wave-chapter-24
25	"A Walk in Nature"	3	3	/the-wave-chapter-25
26	"The Tree of Life"	3	3	/the-wave-chapter-26
27	"Stripped to the Bone"	3	3	/the-wave-chapter-27
28	"Technicians of Ecstasy"	4	4	/the-wave-chapter-28
29	"The 3-5 Code"	4	4	/the-wave-chapter-29
30	"Grape Wine In a Mason Jar"	4	4	/the-wave-chapter-30
31	"The Priory of Sion"	4	4	/the-wave-chapter-31
32	"Torah, Kaballah..."	4	4	/the-wave-chapter-32
33	"Introduction"	5	5	/the-wave-chapter-33
34	"The Channel"	5	5	/the-wave-chapter-34
35	"A Strange Interlude"	5	5	/the-wave-chapter-35
36	"A Vile Superstition"	5	5	/the-wave-chapter-36
37	"Critical Channeling"	5	5	/the-wave-chapter-37
38	"The Feminine Vampire"	5	5	/the-wave-chapter 38
39	"The Court of Seven"	5	5	/the-wave-chapter-39
40	"Secret Agents from Alpha 1"	5	5	/the-wave-chapter-40
41	"The Realm of Archetypes"	5	5	/the-wave-chapter-41
42	"The Tradition"	5	5	/the-wave-chapter-42
43	"The Head of Bran"	5	5	/the-wave-chapter-43
44	"The Crane Dance"	5	5	/the-wave-chapter-44
45	"The Gulf Breeze"	5	5	/the-wave-chapter-45
46	"The Theological Reality"	5	5	/the-wave-chapter-46
47	"Semiotics and the Content Plane"	5	5	/the-wave-chapter-47
48	"The Juvenile Dictionary"	6	6	/the-wave-chapter-48
49	"Frequency Resonance Vibration"	6	6	/the-wave-chapter-49
50	"Shifts in the Matrix"	6	6	/the-wave-chapter-50
51	"The Psychomantium"	6	6	/the-wave-chapter-51
52	"The Cryptogeographic Being"	6	6	/the-wave-chapter-52
53	"Strange Birds"	6	6	/the-wave-chapter-53
54	"Glimpses of Other Realities"	6	6	/the-wave-chapter-54
55	"Albert Einstein, Free Energy..."	6	6	/the-wave-chapter-55
56	"Intolerance, Cruelty..."	6	6	/the-wave-chapter-56
57	"It's Just Economics"	7	7	/the-wave-chapter-57
58	"Alien Reaction Machines"	7	7	/the-wave-chapter-58
59	"An Encounter with the Unicorn"	7	7	/the-wave-chapter-59
60	"The Unicorn's Closet"	7	7	/the-wave-chapter-60
61	"Ira's Inner Cesspool"	7	7	/the-wave-chapter-61
62	"Secret Games at Princeton"	7	7	/the-wave-chapter-62
63	"Murdering the Feminine"	7	7	/the-wave-chapter-63
64	"Crossing the Threshold"	8	8	/the-wave-chapter-64

65	"The Way of the Fool"	8	8	/the-wave-chapter-65
66	"The Zelator"	8	8	/the-wave-chapter-66
67	"Food for the Moon"	8	8	/the-wave-chapter-67
68	"As Above, So Below"	8	8	/the-wave-chapter-68
69	"The Whirlpool of Charybdis..."	8	8	/the-wave-chapter-69
70	"You Take the High Road..."	8	8	/the-wave-chapter-70
71	"If I Speak in the Tongues..."	8	8	/the-wave-chapter-71
72	"Nonlinear Dynamics of Love..."	8	8	/the-wave-chapter-72

Recommended Reading

This is a subset of the "Recommended Reading" list at
http://cassiopaea.org/forum/index.php/topic,33 092.0.html

9/11

- Griffin, David Ray – *The 9/11 Commission Report: Omissions And Distortions*, Olive Branch Pr 2004
- Griffin and Falk – *The New Pearl Harbor: Disturbing Questions About the Bush Administration and 9/11*, Interlink Pub Group 2004
- Quinn and Knight-Jadczyk – *9/11 The Ultimate Truth*, Red Pill Pr 2006
- Wood, Judy – *Where Did the Towers Go? Evidence of Directed Free-energy Technology on 9/11*, The New Investigation 2010

Ancient Civilizations

- David-Neel, Alexandra – *Magic and Mystery in Tibet*, Dover 1971
- Dunn, Christopher – *The Giza Power Plant: Technologies of Ancient Egypt*, Bear & Company 1998
- Firestone, West, Warwick-Smith – *The Cycle of Cosmic Catastrophes: How a Stone-Age Comet Changed the Course of World Culture*, Bear & Company 2006
- Fox, Hugh – *Gods of the Cataclysm: A revolutionary investigation of man and his gods before and after the Great Cataclysm*, Aardwolfe Books 2011
- von Hassler, Gerd – *Lost Survivors of the Deluge*, Signet 1978
- Muck, Otto – *The Secret of Atlantis*, HarperCollins 1979

Astronomy

- Clube and Napier – *The Cosmic Serpent*, Universe Pub 1982
- Clube and Napier – *The Cosmic Winter*, Blackwell Pub 1990
- Knight-Jadczyk, Laura – *The Apocalypse: Comets, Asteroids and Cyclical Catastrophes*, Red Pill Pr 2012
- Velikovsky, Immanuel – *Worlds in Collision*, Paradigma Ltd 2009

Bible History

- Davies, Philip R. – *The Origins of Biblical Israel (Library Hebrew Bible/Old Testament Studies)*, T&T Clark 2009
- Finkelstein and Silberman – *David and Solomon: In Search of the Bible's Sacred Kings and the Roots of the Western Tradition*, Free Pr 2007
- Garbini, Giovanni – *History and Ideology in Ancient Israel*, Crossroad Pub Co 1988
- Mack, Burton – *The Lost Gospel: The Book of Q and Christian Origins*, HarperOne 1994
- Mack, Burton – *A Myth of Innocence: Mark and Christian Origins*, Augsburg Fortress Pub 1998
- Silberman, Neil Asher – *The Bible Unearthed: Archaeology's New Vision of Ancient Israel and the Origin of Its Sacred Texts*, Touchstone 2002
- Thompson, Thomas L. – *The Mythic Past: Biblical Archaeology And The Myth Of Israel*, Basic Books 2000
- Thompson, Thomas L. – *The Messiah Myth: The Near Eastern Roots of Jesus and David*, Basic Books 2005

Cassiopaea Experiment

- Koehli, Harrison – "The Cs Hit List 01: Prophecy, Prediction, and Portents of Things to Come", *Signs Of The Times*, sott.net/article/236777
- Koehli, Harrison – "The Cs Hit List 02: Space and Weather Science Gone Wild", *Signs Of The Times*, sott.net/article/237356
- Koehli, Harrison – "The Cs Hit List 03: History Is Bunk", *Signs Of The Times*, sott.net/article/238372
- Koehli, Harrison – "The Cs Hit List 04: Nature, Nurture, and My Monkey Genes", *Signs Of The Times*, sott.net/article/239307
- Koehli, Harrison – "The Cs Hit List 05: Dr. Greenbaum and the Manchurian Candidates", *Signs Of The Times*, sott.net/article/240587
- Koehli, Harrison – "The Cs Hit List 06: Let's Do the Planetary Twist to the Tune of the Brothers Heliopolis", *Signs Of The Times*, sott.net/article/242280
- Koehli, Harrison – "The Cs Hit List 07: Sun Star Companion, Singing Stones and Smoking Visions", *Signs Of The Times*, sott.net/article/244819
- Koehli, Harrison – "The Cs Hit List 08: Of Oracles and Conspiracies: TWA 800, 9/11, H1N1, and VISA", *Signs Of The Times*, sott.net/article/247080
- Koehli, Harrison – "The Cs Hit List 09: DNA, Rational Design and the Origins of Life", *Signs Of The Times*, sott.net/article/250256

Esotericism

- Campbell, Joseph – *The Hero with a Thousand Faces*, Princeton University Pr 1972
- Chittick, William – *The Sufi Path of Knowledge: Ibn al-'Arabi's Metaphysics of Imagination*, State University of New York Pr 1989
- Hall, Manly – *The Secret Teachings of all Ages*, Wilder Publications 2009
- Knight-Jadczyk, Laura – *Amazing Grace*, Red Pill Pr 2012
- Knight-Jadczyk, Laura – *Riding the Wave: The Truth and Lies about 2012 and Global Transformation* (The Wave Series Vol. 1), Red Pill Pr 2010
- Knight-Jadczyk, Laura – *Soul Hackers: The Hidden Hands Behind the New Age Movement* (The Wave Series Vol. 2), Red Pill Pr 2010
- Knight-Jadczyk, Laura – *Stripped to the Bone: The Path to Freedom in the Prison of Life* (The Wave Series Vol. 3), Red Pill Pr 2010
- Knight-Jadczyk, Laura – *Through a Glass Darkly: Hidden Masters, Secret Agendas and a Tradition Unveiled* (The Wave Series Vol. 4), Red Pill Pr 2011
- Knight-Jadczyk, Laura – *Petty Tyrants & Facing the Unknown: Navigating the Traps and Diversions of Life in the Matrix* (The Wave Series Vol. 5/6), Red Pill Pr 2011
- Knight-Jadczyk, Laura – *Almost Human: A Stunning Look at the Metaphysics of Evil* (The Wave Series Vol. 7), Red Pill Pr 2009
- Knight-Jadczyk, Laura – *Debugging the Universe: The Hero's Journey* (The Wave Series Vol. 8), Red Pill Pr 2012
- Ouspensky, P. D. – *In Search of the Miraculous: Fragments of an Unknown Teaching*, Harvest/HBJ 1977

Information Theory, Metaphysics and Evolution

- Davies and Gregersen – *Information and the Nature of Reality: From Physics to Metaphysics*, Cambridge University Pr 2010
- Hardy, Alister – *The Living Stream: Evolution and Man*, Harper & Row 1965
- Milton, Richard – *Shattering the Myths of Darwinism*, Inner Traditions 1997
- Morgan, Elaine – *The Scars of Evolution: What Our Bodies Tell Us About Human Origins*, Oxford 1990
- Nagel, Thomas – *Mind and Cosmos: Why the Materialist Neo-Darwinian Conception of Nature Is Almost Certainly False*, Oxford University Pr 2012
- Pierce, John R. – *An Introduction to Information Theory: Symbols, Signals and Noise*
- Shiller, Bryant M. – *Origin of Life: The 5th Option*, Trafford Pub 2006

Health

- Keith, Lierre – *The Vegetarian Myth: Food, Justice and Sustainability*, PM Press 2009
- Mate, Gabor – *When the Body Says No: Exploring the Stress-Disease Connection*, Wiley 2011

History

- Baigent and Leigh and Lincoln – *Holy Blood, Holy Grail: The Secret History of Christ & The Shocking Legacy of the Grail*, Dell Trade Paperbacks 2004
- Baillie, Mike – *Exodus to Arthur: Catastrophic Encounters With Comets*, B T Batsford Ltd 1999
- Baillie, Mike – *New Light on the Black Death*, Tempus 2006
- Carotta, Francesco – *Jesus Was Caesar: On the Julian Origin of Christianity: An Investigative Report*, Aspekt 2005
- Garnier, John – *The Worship of the Dead, or the Origin and Nature of Pagan Idolatry and Its Bearing Upon the Early History of Egypt and Babylonia*, Chapman & Hall 1904
- Knight-Jadczyk, Laura – *The Secret History of the World: And how to get out alive* (Secret History Series Vol. 1), Red Pill Pr 2005
- Knight-Jadczyk, Laura – *Comets and the Horns of Moses* ("Secret History" Series Vol. 2), Red Pill Pr 2013
- Langer, Walter C. – *The Mind of Adolf Hitler: The Secret Wartime Report*, Basic Books 1972
- Lescaudron and Knight-Jadczyk – *Earth Changes and the Human Cosmic Connection* (Secret History Series Vol. 3), Red Pill Pr 2014
- Malkowski, Edward F. – *Ancient Egypt 39,000 BCE: The History, Technology, and Philosophy of Civilization X*, Bear & Company 2010
- Momigliano, Arnaldo – *On Pagans, Jews, and Christians*, Wesleyan 1987
- Shreeve, James – *The Neandertal Enigma: Solving the Mystery of Modern Human Origins*, Avon 1996
- Sitchin, Zecharia – *The 12th Planet*, Harper 2007
- Thompson and Cremo – *The Hidden History of the Human Race (The Condensed Edition of Forbidden Archeology)*, Bhaktivedanta Book Pub 1999
- Wilkens, Iman – *Where Troy Once Stood: The Mystery of Homer's Iliad & Odyssey Revealed*, St Martins Pr 1991

Hyperdimensions

- Abbott, Edwin A. – *Flatland: A Romance of Many Dimensions*, Signet 1984
- Kaku, Michio – *Hyperspace: A Scientific Odyssey Through Parallel Universes, Time Warps, and the 10th Dimension*, Anchor 1995
- Ouspensky, P.D. – *Tertium Organum: A Key to the Enigmas of the World*, Vintage 1981
- Rucker, Rudy – *The Fourth Dimension: A Guided Tour of the Higher Universes*, Houghton Mifflin 1984

Politics and Pathocracy

- Allen, Gary – *None Dare Call It Conspiracy*, Gsg & Assoc 1971
- Douglass, James W. – *JFK and the Unspeakable: Why He Died and Why It Matters*, Touchstone 2010
- Klein, Naomi – *The Shock Doctrine: The Rise of Disaster Capitalism*, Picador 2008
- Knight-Jadczyk, Laura – *JFK: The Assassination of America*, Red Pill Pr 2013
- Prouty, L. Fletcher – *JFK: The CIA, Vietnam, and the Plot to Assassinate John F. Kennedy*, Skyhorse Pub 2011
- Prouty, L. Fletcher – *The Secret Team: The CIA and Its Allies in Control of the United States and the World*, Skyhorse Pub 2011

Psychology

- DiSalvo, David – *What Makes Your Brain Happy and Why You Should Do the Opposite*, Prometheus 2011
- Donaldson-Pressman, Stephanie – *The Narcissistic Family: Diagnosis and Treatment*, Jossey-Bass 1997
- Golomb, Elan – *Trapped in the Mirror: Adult Children of Narcissists in their Struggle for Self*, William Morrow & Co 1995
- Hort, Barbara E – *Unholy Hungers: Encountering the Psychic Vampire in Ourselves & Others*, Shambhala 1996
- Kahneman, Daniel – *Thinking, Fast and Slow*, Farrar, Straus and Giroux 2013
- McRaney, David – *You Are Not So Smart: Why You Have Too Many Friends on Facebook, Why Your Memory Is Mostly Fiction, and 46 Other Ways You're Deluding Yourself*, Gotham 2012
- Simon, George K. – *Character Disturbance: the phenomenon of our age*, Parkhurst Brothers 2011

- Stout, Martha – *The Myth of Sanity: Divided Consciousness and the Promise of Awareness*, Penguin 2002
- Wilson, Timothy D. – *Redirect: The Surprising New Science of Psychological Change*, Little, Brown and Company 2011
- Wilson, Timothy D. – *Strangers to Ourselves: Discovering the Adaptive Unconscious*, Belknap Pr 2004

Psychopathy

- Babiak and Hare – *Snakes in Suits: When Psychopaths Go to Work*, HarperBusiness 2007
- Brown, Sandra – *Women Who Love Psychopaths: Inside the Relationships of inevitable Harm With Psychopaths, Sociopaths & Narcissists*, Mask Pub 2010
- Cleckley, Hervey – *The Mask of Sanity: An Attempt to Clarify Some Issues about the So-Called Psychopathic Personality*, Literary Licensing 2011
- Hare, Robert D. – *Without Conscience: The Disturbing World of the Psychopaths Among Us*, Guilford Pr 1999
- Lobaczewski, Andrzej – *Political Ponerology: A Science on the Nature of Evil Adjusted for Political Purposes*, Red Pill Pr 2007
- Stout, Martha – *The Sociopath Next Door*, Harmony 2006

Religion

- Hoyle, Fred – *Origin of the Universe and the Origin of Religion (Anshen Transdisciplinary Lectureships in Art, Science, and the Philosophy of Culture, Monograph)*, Moyer Bell 1997

Spiritualism

- Ashe, Geoffrey – *The Ancient Wisdom: A Quest for the Source of Mystic Knowledge*, Macmillan 1997
- Baldwin, William – *Spirit Releasement Therapy: A Technique Manual*, Headline Books 1995
- Barrett and Hyslop – *Evidence Of Survival After Death*, Kessinger Publishing 2010
- Blum, Deborah – *Ghost Hunters: William James and the Search for Scientific Proof of Life After Death*, Penguin Books 2007
- Davis, Vance A. – *Unbroken Promises: A True Story of Courage and Belief*, White Mesa Pub 1995
- Doyle, Arthur Conan – *The History of Spiritualism*, Fredonia Books 2003

- Carrington and Fodor – *Haunted People: The Story Of The Poltergeist Down The Centuries*, Kessinger Publishing 2006
- Ebon, Martin – *Prophecy in our Time*, New American Library 1968
- Elkins, Rueckert, McCarty – *The Ra Material*, L/L Research 1984
- Fiore, Edith – *The Unquiet Dead: A Psychologist Treats Spirit Possession*, Ballantine 1995
- Fodor, Nandor – *The haunted mind: A psychoanalyst looks at the supernatural*, Garrett Pub 1959
- Garret, Eileen – *Many Voices: The Autobiography of a Medium*, Putnam Pub
- Kardec, Allan – *The Spirits Book*, White Crow Books 2010
- Lethbridge, T. C. – *The Power of the Pendulum*, Penguin Books 1991
- Marciniak, Barbara – *Bringers of the Dawn*, Bear & Company 1992
- Martin, Malachi – *Hostage to the Devil: The Possession and Exorcism of Five Contemporary Americans*, HarperOne 1999
- Roll and Storey – *Unleashed: Of Poltergeists and Murder: The Curious Story of Tina Resch*, Pocket Books 2007
- Stevenson, Ian – *Twenty Cases Suggestive of Reincarnation*, University of Virginia Pr 1980
- Vickers, Brian – *Occult Scientific Mentalities*, Cambridge University Pr 1986
- Whitten and Fisher – *Life between Life*, Grand Central Pub 1988
- Wickland, Carl – *Thirty Years Among the Dead*, White Crow Books 2011
- Wilson, Colin – *The Siren Call of Hungry Ghosts: A Riveting Investigation Into Channeling and Spirit Guides*, Paraview Press 2001

UFOs/Aliens

- Bramley, William – *The Gods of Eden*, Avon 1993
- Corso, Philip – *The Day After Roswell*, Pocket Books 1998
- Dolan, Richard – *UFOs and the National Security State: Chronology of a Cover-Up, 1941–1973*, Keyhole Pub 2009
- Dolan, Richard – *UFOs and the National Security State: The Cover-Up Exposed, 1973–1991*, Keyhole Pub 2010
- Fort, Charles – *The Complete Books of Charles Fort*, Dover 1974
- Fowler, Raymond E. – *The Andreasson Affair: The Documented Investigation of a Woman's Abduction Aboard a UFO*, Wild Flower Pr 1994
- Fuller, John G. – *The Interrupted Journey*, Dial Pr 1967
- Jessup, Morris – *The Case for the UFO*, New Saucerian Books 2014

- Knight-Jadczyk, Laura – *High Strangeness: Hyperdimensions and the Process of Alien Abduction*, Red Pill Pr 2008
- Moulton Howe, Linda – *Glimpses of Other Realities Vol. 1: Facts and Eyewitnesses*, LMH Prod 1993
- Moulton Howe, Linda – *Glimpses of Other Realities Vol. 2: High Strangeness*, LMH Prod 1998
- Keel, John – *Operation Trojan Horse*, Anomalist Books 2013
- Keel, John – *The Mothman Prophecies*, Tor 2002
- Keel, John – *The Eighth Tower*, Anomalist Books 2013
- Picknett and Prince – *The Stargate Conspiracy: The Truth about Extraterrestrial life and the Mysteries of Ancient Egypt*, Berkley 2001
- Redfern, Nick – *Close Encounters of the Fatal Kind: Suspicious Deaths, Mysterious Murders, and Bizarre Disappearances in UFO History*, New Page Books 2014
- Sanderson, Ivan T. – *Invisible Residents: The Reality of Underwater UFOs*, Adventures Unlimited Pr 2005
- Strieber, Whitley – *Majestic*, Tor 2011
- Turner, Karl – *Into the Fringe: A True Story of Alien Abduction*, WordMean 2014
- Turner, Karl – *Taken: Inside the Alien-Human Agenda*, WordMean 2013
- Vallee, Jacques – *Passport to Magonia: On UFOs, Folklore, and Parallel Worlds*, Contemporary Books 1993
- Vallee, Jacques – *Dimensions: A Casebook of Alien Contact*, Anomalist Books 2008

Books and DVDs from Red Pill Press

Visit redpillpress.com for more information!

The Secret History of the World, Vol. 1

... and how to get out alive

Laura Knight-Jadczyk

If you heard the Truth, would you believe it? Ancient civilisations. Hyperdimensional realities. DNA changes. Bible conspiracies. What are the realities? What is disinformation?

The Secret History of The World and How To Get Out Alive is the definitive book of the real answers where Truth is more fantastic than fiction. Laura Knight-Jadczyk, wife of internationally known theoretical physicist, Arkadiusz Jadczyk, an expert in hyperdimensional physics, draws on science and mysticism to pierce the veil of reality. Due to the many threats on her life from agents and agencies known and unknown, Laura left the United States to live in France, where she is working closely with Patrick Rivière, student of Eugene Canseliet, the only disciple of the legendary alchemist Fulcanelli.

With sparkling humour and wisdom, she picks up where Fulcanelli left off, sharing over thirty years of research to reveal, for the first time, The Great Work and the esoteric Science of the Ancients in terms accessible to scholar and layperson alike.

Conspiracies have existed since the time of Cain and Abel. Facts of history have been altered to support the illusion. The question today is whether a sufficient number of people will see through the deceptions, thus creating a counter-force for positive change - the gold of humanity - during the upcoming times of Macro-Cosmic Quantum Shift. Laura argues convincingly, based on the revelations of the deepest of esoteric secrets, that the present is a time of potential transition, an extraordinary opportunity for individual and collective renewal: a quantum shift of awareness and perception which could see the birth of true creativity in the fields of science, art and spirituality. *The Secret History of the World* allows us to redefine our interpretation of the universe, history, and culture and to thereby navigate a path through this darkness. In this way, Laura Knight-Jadczyk shows us how we may extend the possibilities for all our different futures in literal terms.

With over 850 pages of fascinating reading, *The Secret History of The World and How to Get Out Alive* is rapidly being acknowledged as a classic with profound implications for the destiny of the human race. With painstakingly researched facts and figures, the author overturns long-held conventional ideas on religion, philosophy, Grail legends, science, and alchemy, presenting a cohesive narrative pointing to the existence of an ancient techno-spirituality of the Golden Age which included a mastery of space and time: the Holy Grail, the Philosopher's Stone, the True Process of Ascension. Laura provides the evidence for the advanced level of scientific and metaphysical wisdom possessed by the greatest of lost ancient civilizations - a culture so advanced that none of the trappings of civilization as we know it were needed, explaining why there is no 'evidence' of civilization as we know it left to testify to its existence. The author's consummate synthesis reveals the Message in a Bottle reserved for humanity, including the Cosmology and Mysticism of mankind Before the Fall when, as the ancient texts tell us, man walked and talked with the gods. Laura shows us that the upcoming shift is that point in the vast cosmological cycle when mankind - or at least a portion of mankind - has the opportunity to regain his standing as The Child of the King in the Golden Age.

If ever there was a book that can answer the questions of those who are seeking Truth in the spiritual wilderness of this world, then surely *The Secret History of the World and How to Get Out Alive* is it.

Comets and the Horns of Moses

The Secret History of the World, Vol. 2
Laura Knight-Jadczyk

The Laura Knight-Jadczyk's series, The Secret History of the World, is one of the most ambitious projects ever undertaken to provide a cogent, comprehensive account of humanity's true history and place in the cosmos. Following the great unifying vision of the Stoic Posidonius, Laura weaves together the study of history, mythology, religion, psychology and physics, revealing a view of the world that is both rational and breathtaking in its all-encompassing scope. This second volume, Comets and the Horns of Moses, (written in concert with several following volumes soon to be released) picks up the dangling threads of volume one with an analysis of the Biblical character of Moses – his possible true history and nature – and the cyclical nature of cosmic catastrophes in Earth's history.

Laura skillfully tracks the science of comets, revealing evidence for the fundamentally electrical and electromagnetic nature of these celestial bodies and how they have repeatedly wreaked havoc and destruction on our planet over the course of human history. Even more startling however, is the evidence that comets and cometary fragments have played a central role in the formation of human myth and legend and the very concept of a 'god'. As she expertly navigates her way through the labyrinth of history, Laura uncovers the secret knowledge of comets that has been hidden in the great myths, ancient astronomy (and astrology) and the works of the Greek philosophers. Concluding with a look at the political and psychological implications of cyclical cometary catastrophes and what they portend for humanity today, Comets and the Horns of Moses is a marvel of original thought and keen detective work that will rock the foundations of your understanding of the world you live in, and no doubt ruffle the feathers of the many academics who still cling to an outdated and blinkered view of history.

Earth Changes and the Human-Cosmic Connection

The Secret History of the World, Vol. 3
Pierre Lescaudron and Laura Knight-Jadczyk

Jet Stream meanderings, Gulf Stream slow-downs, hurricanes, earthquakes, volcanic eruptions, meteor fireballs, tornadoes, deluges, sinkholes, and noctilucent clouds have been on the rise since the turn of the century. Have proponents of man-made global warming been proven correct, or is something else, something much bigger, happening on our planet?

While mainstream science depicts these Earth changes as unrelated, Pierre Lescaudron applies findings from the Electric Universe paradigm and plasma physics to suggest that they might in fact be intimately related, and stem from a single common cause: the close approach of our Sun's 'twin' and an accompanying cometary swarm.

Citing historical records, the author reveals a strong correlation between periods of authoritarian oppression with catastrophic and cosmically-induced natural disasters. Referencing metaphysical research and information theory, *Earth Changes and the Human-Cosmic Connection* is a ground-breaking attempt to re-connect modern science with the ancient understanding that the human mind and states of collective human experience can influence cosmic and earthly phenomena.

Covering a broad range of scientific fields, and including over 250 figures and 1,000 sources, *Earth Changes and the Human-Cosmic Connection* is presented in an accessible format for anyone seeking to understand the signs of our times.

The Wave 1 – "Riding the Wave"

... The Truth and Lies about 2012 and Global Transformation
Laura Knight-Jadczyk

As 2012 fast approaches, opinions about what to expect on this much-anticipated date are sharply polarized. Will humanity experience a global, spiritual transformation? Cataclysmic Earth Changes? Or both? Or nothing? If Earth and its inhabitants are scheduled for some life-changing or life-ending event, we should ask ourselves what we know and how we know it, and how to prepare for our future.

Drawing on decades of research into history, religion, and the esoteric, Laura Knight-Jadczyk introduces the concept of "the Wave" to describe the possible phenomena behind all the hype surrounding global transformation. *Riding the Wave* not only collects the most probable scenarios we may face in the near future – it provides the context to make it all intelligible.

With roots in the science of hyperdimensions made popular by physicist Michio Kaku and the Fortean theories of the late John Keel, *Riding the Wave* suggests that many of the noticeable changes to our world in the last century are symptoms of the approaching Wave. From climate change, extreme population growth and technological development, as well as novel social and political movements, to the advent of UFO sightings, crop circles, and a variety of otherworldly experiences, something is up on the Big Blue Marble, and it all seems to be leading to a sea change in the way we see and interact with the world. The only question is, will it be for the better or the worse?

An intimate blend of science and mysticism, this volume of Laura Knight-Jadczyk's Wave Series initiates the process of unveiling the truth about life on Earth, and the man behind the curtain...

The Wave 2 – "Soul Hackers"

... The Hidden Hands Behind the New Age Movement
Laura Knight-Jadczyk

Why are we here? Why do we suffer? If this is an infinite school, what are we here to learn? And why do our efforts at "fixing" our lives often do exactly the opposite? As mystic and researcher Laura Knight-Jadczyk writes in this volume of her expansive Wave Series: "when you ask a question – if the question is a burning one – your life becomes the answer. All of your experiences and interactions and so forth shape themselves around the core of the answer that you are seeking in your soul. In [my] case, the question was: 'How to be One with God,' and the answer was, 'Love is the answer, but you have to have knowledge to know what Love really is.'"

Soul Hackers is a deeply personal and insightful account of this very process – of burning questions and transformative answers. Through the story of her own struggle with mainstream and alternative religion and the solutions they claim to offer, Knight-Jadczyk lays bare the problems inherent in the New Age movement as a whole – from Reiki, Wicca, and the phenomenon of channeling, to the very real problems of spirit attachments, mind control, and otherworldly predators posing as benevolent beings. She asks what it really means to "create your own reality." Is it merely self-hypnosis, or is something more hidden in this New Age truism?

The answers lie in the very nature of the Wave – the cosmic force and fabric of personal and collective evolution. For anyone wishing to understand the deeper meaning and reality of the human experience, and what our very near future may very well have in store for us, *Soul Hackers* provides a map to our symbolic reality and the knowledge necessary to weather the approaching storm.

The Wave 3 – "Stripped to the Bone"

... The Path to Freedom in the Prison of Life
Laura Knight-Jadczyk

Media propaganda. Official cover-ups. Dishonest science. "Non-lethal" weaponry. Mind control technology. Racial stereotypes. Social engineering. Religious programming. The cold pursuit of profit. And the unrelenting pull of materialism... In a world where "freedom" is exported at the barrel of a gun, true freedom seems more like a distant fairytale, blocked for us in more ways than we can imagine.

In *Stripped to the Bone*, author Laura Knight-Jadczyk lays bare the forces seeking to keep humanity in a prison of its own creation. She lucidly describes evil's place in the cosmos, from the dark world of political conspiracy and government mind control to the reality behind the UFO phenomenon. But in response to the grim state of affairs on the Big Blue Marble, she also asks: Is there a solution? What can we learn from those who came before us? *Stripped to the Bone* suggests that this knowledge was not only known and widely practiced in humanity's prehistory, but that it can be rediscovered.

Through her extensive reading on all things esoteric, Knight-Jadczyk maintains that by knowing our limitations, we may overcome them. In this volume of her acclaimed Wave Series, she tears down our illusions about freedom and the idea that it can be won in any war. Rather, the path to freedom is an inner battle against the many limitations placed on our ability to choose by official culture, our own beliefs, and the forces behind the reality of our everyday experience.

By showing us our own limitations she also succeeds in presenting anew the real possibilities and true potential of a free humanity.

The Wave 4 – "Through A Glass Darkly"

... Hidden Masters, Secret Agendas and a Tradition Unveiled
Laura Knight-Jadczyk

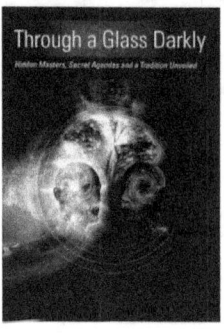

Behind the surface of everyday life lie secrets that have been kept from the eyes of the humanity. In every field of knowledge, we seem to take a wrong turn, coming to conclusions that are diametrically opposed to the truth of the matter. It seems that true science, history, the purpose and aim of human life, our past and potential futures are all off limits to public consumption. How can this be the case, and can these truths come to be known?

In *Through a Glass Darkly*, Laura Knight-Jadczyk continues to make it clear that nothing is what it appears to be. From the stories stitched together to make up our own personal identities to the myths of history on which nations are founded, we live in a sea of lies and half-truths. Just as we lie to ourselves and each other about who we really are, often putting ourselves in the best light possible, there are those who manufacture, manipulate, and shape current and past events to suit their own vested interests. And the current events of today will become the history of tomorrow, erroneously shaping our notions of who we are as a people, just as those of the past have done before.

But behind this sorry state of affairs, the truth awaits discovery. In this fourth volume of her series *The Wave or Adventures with Cassiopaea*, Knight-Jadczyk follows the trail of the hidden masters of our planet, exposing the agenda behind the alleged secret society, the "Priory of Sion", and that mystery's connections with alchemy, Oak Island, and the Kabbalists of old. In the process she reveals aspects of the tradition kept under wraps by these very groups. By exposing the agendas and conspiracies of the elite, we can come to know the truth about ourselves, and why it is has been kept hidden.

The Wave 5 & 6 – "Petty Tyrants & Facing the Unknown"

... Navigating the Traps and Diversions of Life in the Matrix

Laura Knight-Jadczyk

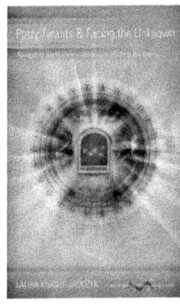

From the myths of romance to the tales of the hero's journey, the quest for knowledge and being has always been portrayed in terms of struggle. Far from home, the hero faces obstacles and tests of his or her courage, will, and cunning. But how do the labyrinths and monsters of these 'messages in a bottle' from our remote ancestors relate to our lives in the 21st century? In an age of mass media, the worldwide web, and multinational corporations, how do these archetypal dramas play themselves out?

In these two volumes of her revolutionary series, *The Wave or Adventures with Cassiopaea,* Laura Knight-Jadczyk continues her project of laying bare the nature of our reality. Through her own experiences and interactions over the course of the Cassiopaean Experiment, many of which just go to show that truth is stranger than fiction, Laura describes the real-life dynamics only hinted at in myth. Most importantly, she gives the tools and clues necessary to actually read the symbols of reality: the theological substrate in which our ordinary psychological motivations are embedded.

With these stunning revelations, Shakespeare's famous words take on a whole new meaning: "All the world's a stage, and all men and women merely players."

First published on her groundbreaking website cassiopaea.org, *Petty Tyrants & Facing the Unknown* have now been fully revised and packaged together in one attractive volume. For anyone interested in the world of esoteric knowledge, studies in the paranormal and everything 'alternative', or even just curious about life in general and its possible significance and meaning, these volumes are a must-read.

The Wave 7 – "Almost Human"

... A Stunning Look at the Metaphysics of Evil

Laura Knight-Jadczyk

In this volume of her prescient Wave series, Laura Knight-Jadczyk brings order to the chaotic and labyrinthine world of murder, conspiracy, and the paranormal. In a unique and probing synthesis of science and mysticism she presents a detailed series of case studies and application of her hypothesis of hyperdimensional influence.

From interpersonal relationships and their expression of archetypal dramas to the vectoring of human behaviour to achieve hyperdimensional purposes, *Almost Human* reveals the mechanics of evil, how it creeps into our lives, and what we need to be aware of in order to avoid it.

The case studies of John Nash, the schizoidal creator of Game Theory, and Ira Einhorn, the New Age psychopath who murdered his girlfriend, are the window through which Knight-Jadczyk unravels the intricate web of deception, aims, and counter-aims of the Powers That Be.

Almost Human is essential reading for anyone wondering why our world is becoming increasingly controlled and our freedoms more restricted.

The Wave 8 – "Debugging the Universe"

... The Hero's Journey

Laura Knight-Jadczyk

The Path of the Fool, the Hero's Journey, the Great Work – by whatever name it takes, the path of self-development and growth of knowledge is one fraught with difficult lessons and intense struggle. But what exactly is the nature of those lessons, and what insights can the latest advances in modern science provide for us along the way?

Debugging the Universe takes us into the heart of what it means to be human, from the molecules of our DNA to our life purpose and true place in the universe, and everything that separates us from embodying that higher potential. Explored within are real-life applications of the Hero's archetype, the relevance of neuroscience and the 'molecules of emotion', the hidden meaning behind the enigmatic symbols of esoterica, and what it means to live inside a complex system: the universal breath of chaos and order.

This volume concludes the publication in print of Laura Knight-Jadczyk's unparalleled and controversial magnum opus: *The Wave or Adventures with Cassiopaea*. Originally published online at www.cassiopaea.org, The Wave is a fully modern exposition of the knowledge of the ancients, with subjects ranging from metaphysics, science, cosmology, and psychology to the paranormal, UFOs, hyperdimensions and macrocosmic transformation.

"High Strangeness"

... Hyperdimensions and the Process of Alien Abduction
Laura Knight-Jadczyk

High Strangeness: Hyperdimensions and the Process of Alien Abduction is an enlightening attempt to weave together the contradictory threads of religion, science, history, alien abduction, and the true nature of political conspiracies. With thorough research and a drive for the truth, Laura Knight-Jadczyk strips away the facades of official culture and opens doors to understanding our reality.

The Second Edition includes additional material that explains the hyperdimensional mechanisms by which our reality is controlled and shaped by 'alien' powers. The self-serving actions of unwitting puppets – psychopaths and other pathological types – who may have no knowledge that they are being used, become the portals through which an agenda that is hostile to humanity as a whole, is pushed forward.

High Strangeness takes the study of ponerology into a whole new dimension!

"9/11 – The Ultimate Truth"

Joe Quinn and Laura Knight-Jadczyk

In the years since the 9/11 attacks, dozens of books have sought to explore the truth behind the official version of events that day - yet to date, none of these publications has provided a satisfactory answer as to **why** the attacks occurred and who was ultimately responsible for carrying them out.

Taking a broad, millennia-long perspective, Laura Knight-Jadczyk's *9/11: The Ultimate Truth* uncovers the true nature of the ruling elite on our planet and presents new and ground-breaking insights into just how the 9/11 attacks played out.

9/11: The Ultimate Truth makes a strong case for the idea that September 11, 2001 marked the moment when our planet entered the final phase of a diabolical plan that has been many, many years in the making. It is a plan developed and nurtured by successive generations of ruthless individuals who relentlessly exploit the negative aspects of basic human nature to entrap humanity as a whole in endless wars and suffering in order to keep us confused and distracted to the reality of the man behind the curtain.

Drawing on historical and genealogical sources, Knight-Jadczyk eloquently links the 9/11 event to the modern-day Israeli-Palestinian conflict. She also cites the clear evidence that our planet undergoes periodic natural cataclysms, a cycle that has arguably brought humanity to the brink of destruction in the present day.

For its no nonsense style in cutting to the core of the issue and its sheer audacity in refusing to be swayed or distracted by the morass of disinformation that has been employed by the powers that be to cover their tracks, *9/11: The Ultimate Truth* can rightly claim to be **the** definitive book on 9/11 - and what that fateful day's true implications are for the future of mankind.

The new Second Edition of *9/11: The Ultimate Truth* has been updated with new material detailing the real reasons for the collapse of the World Trade Center towers, the central role played by agents of the state of Israel in the attacks, and how the arrogant Bush government is now forced to dance to the Zionists' tune.

JFK: The Assassination of America

Laura Knight-Jadczyk

Anyone who has taken the time to study the facts about that fateful day in Dallas, TX, November 22, 1963, will already know that John F. Kennedy was deliberately murdered by a cabal of psychopathic warmongers who were opposed to his plans for a more peaceful world. This ebook written by Laura Knight-Jadczyk brings into focus how the convergence of greed and the power-mad forces of big oil, organized crime, and the military-industrial complex brought about the destruction of JFK. Drawing on an early analysis of Kennedy's assassination, *Farewell America*, which was produced by a French intelligence group, Mrs. Knight-Jadczyk brings a deeper understanding of this tragic event by placing it in the light of the psychopathic motivations of these criminal elements. *JFK: The Assassination of America* shows a world that could have been, and a great man silenced by forces who will stop at nothing to keep that world from becoming a reality.

Amazing Grace

Laura Knight-Jadczyk

Laura Knight-Jadczyk has lived intimately – and mysteriously – with the world of spirit. In *Amazing Grace*, Laura takes us back to her beginnings in a Gulf Coast Florida childhood, mapping the first decades of her extraordinary search for an objective reality of spirit, of the play of forces that exist as a subtext to the lives of all human beings – a journey toward knowledge and understanding.

From her first experiences with a terrifying Face at the Window in childhood, to her work as an exorcist, chronicled by Pulitzer Prize–winning journalist Thomas French in the *St. Petersburg Times*, Laura relates the many experiences in her search for the existence of truth about our reality, which forced her to recognize the validity of perceptions beyond those of materialism.

This is also the story of how the Cassiopaeans came to be a part of her life. Their channeled messages, which include important concepts of physics and the underlying nature of reality, have drawn the attention of intellectually advanced yet spiritually hungry people from all over the world. This is not just the story of one woman's experience with personal quantum jumps from one reality to another, but is also the greater story of the potential that exists in every seeker. We have the potential to discover the genuine existence of spirit and the play of the archetypal forces of the world, and to connect with them in a dynamic way. Amazing Grace, or Quantum Future, can be a reality in our lives.

The Apocalypse: Comets, Asteroids and Cyclical Catastrophes

Laura Knight-Jadczyk

For untold millennia, comets and asteroids have struck fear into the hearts of humankind. Their stark radiance was observed everywhere with a sense of impending doom, interpreted as signs of the gods' judgment, omens of plague, mass destruction and the end of time. Astronomers recorded their appearance the world over, building large scale observatories to track their movements and predict their ominous arrival. What was it about these majestic wonders of the heavens that inspired such dread? Was it simply a product of mere superstition and social hysteria?

The latest scientific analysis and historical analysis strongly suggest otherwise. Our ancestors knew something we have since forgotten, their secrets deeply embedded in the archaeological record and the myths passed on throughout generations. And we have only begun to unravel their mysteries ...

Spurred on by the discovery of a little known letter of warning to the European Office of Aerospace Research and Development by astrophysicist Victor Clube, author Laura Knight-Jadczyk began an in-depth research project to get to the bottom of the very real threat to humanity posed by these celestial visitors. In *The Apocalypse: Comets, Asteroids, and Cyclical Catastrophes*, Knight-Jadczyk shares what she found: historical evidence for mass destructions, comet-borne plagues, and repeated cover ups littering our past, as well as clues that a similar fate may be fast approaching.

The Noah Syndrome

Laura Knight-Jadczyk

"As it was in the days of Noah ..."

Technological progress married with moral decay. A people enraptured by the trivial and superficial, entrenched in a culture of materialism and endless warfare. A civilization whose time has come. If a phrase defines the condition of our era, it is this: The Noah Syndrome.

After twenty-six years, Laura Knight-Jadczyk's unpublished book is now in print for the first time. And it's more relevant than ever. Drawing on prophecies ancient and new - from biblical narratives to modern-day visionaries - yet grounded in cutting-edge scientific discoveries about earth's cataclysmic history, this book presents a remarkable vision of humanity's dramatic past and extremely hazardous future.

The Noah Syndrome also introduces the concept of quantum cosmic metamorphosis - the spiritual ark that may carry us through the coming catastrophe. If our past is the key to our future, as Laura suggests, heeding the counsel in these pages could mean the difference between transformation and destruction.

Evidence of Revision

Quantum Future Group

Evidence of Revision is a six part documentary containing historical, original news footage revealing that the most seminal events in recent American history have been deeply and purposefully misrepresented to the public. Footage and interviews provide an in-depth exploration of events ranging from the Kennedy assassinations to the Jonestown massacre, and all that lies between.

The footprints left in this archival footage reveal the coordinated, clandestine sculpting of the America we know today. Evidence of Revision proves once and for all that history has been revised even as it was written!

Part 1: The Assassinations of Kennedy and Oswald
Part 2: The why of it all referenced to Vietnam and LBG
Part 3: LBJ, Hoover and others: what so few know even today
Part 4: The RFK assassination as never seen before
Part 5: RFK assassination, MKULTRA and the Jonestown massacre
Part 6: The assassination of Martin Luther King

6 parts – 3 DVD set – Region-Free DVDs – Watch on any DVD player or computer anywhere in the world.

Newly subtitled in English, Spanish, French and Polish – the documentary is filmed in English, the subtitles are for clarity due to archival footage on which the audio is, at times, unclear. Duration: 10 hours 25 minutes.

Éiriú Eolas, An Amazing Stress Control, Healing and Rejuvenation Program

Laura Knight-Jadczyk

Are you stressed? Do you suffer from chronic fatigue, conditions that your doctor cannot diagnose or that he thinks are "all in your head"? Are you in physical pain more often than not? Is your system toxified from living in today's polluted environment? Do you wish you could face life's challenges with greater calm and peace of mind? Would you like to actually feel healthy, happy and pain-free every day?

Introducing Éiriú Eolas (pronounced "AIR-oo OH-lahss"), the amazing scientific stress-control, healing, detoxing and rejuvenation program which is THE KEY that will help you to change your life in a REAL and immediately noticeable way:

Proven benefits of the Éiriú Eolas Program include: instantly control stress in high energy situations, detox your body resulting in pain relief, relax and gently work through past emotional and psychological trauma and regenerate and rejuvenate your body/mind.

Éiriú Eolas will enable you to rapidly and gently access and release layers of mental, emotional and physical toxicity that stand between you and a healthy, younger feeling and younger looking body!

Subtitles available in: English, Danish, German, Spanish, Greek, French, Croatian, Italian, Dutch, Polish, Russian, Serbian, Turkish and Vietnamese!

Red Pill Press
info@redpillpress.com
www.redpillpress.com

Index

666, 58, 98, 101, 105, 221

abduction, 19–21, 24, 25, 31–33, 46, 53, 54, 58, 67, 88–90, 98, 104, 115, 116, 121, 125, 131, 132, 149, 150, 156, 158, 161, 164, 178, 179, 183, 188, 190, 196–198, 204, 205, 207, 219, 235, 244, 245, 247, 251–253, 255, 265, 283, 295, 296, 300, 311, 317, 318, 323, 343–345, 348, 351, 354, 356, 358, 359, 362, 371, 376, 378–380, 401, 402, 414
abortion, 162, 355
Abraham, 54, 69
Adam, 69, 70, 94, 112, 113, 254, 298
Adamski, George, 254
Akashic records, 320
Alabama, 16
alien, 15, 16, 18, 20, 23–27, 31–33, 35, 36, 39, 46, 50, 53, 54, 58, 67, 86–88, 90, 102, 104, 106, 115, 120, 121, 125, 131, 134, 139, 149, 154, 155, 161, 162, 178, 181, 188, 190, 198–200, 202–205, 207, 219, 221, 229, 235, 239, 243, 247, 250, 253, 254, 256, 259, 261, 262, 295, 303, 311, 318, 323, 332, 343, 349, 351, 362, 371, 372, 376, 379, 380, 392, 402, 414
alternate reality, vi, 324, 329
alternative universe, 265
Alzheimer, 216
America, 27, 34, 77–80, 84, 111, 123, 127, 135, 149, 173, 174, 178, 207, 228, 251, 254, 255, 310, 335, 362, 399, 401, 416, 420
Andarans, 62, 336
Andreasson, Betty, 33, 252, 253, 255, 401
Andrus, Walt, 217
Angkor Wat, 135
animal, 34–36, 55, 133, 165, 166, 197, 214, 271, 391
Ankh, 146, 182
Annunaki, 25, 32, 52, 58, 76
Antarctica, 335
Antichrist, 249
anticipation, 63, 86, 122, 327, 359, 407
Appolyon, 217
archeology, vii, 398
Area 51, 18, 161, 332
Arizona, 17
ark, 67, 100, 140, 168, 169, 186, 187, 293, 318, 368, 419
Aryans, 62, 76, 83, 87, 95, 110, 111, 127, 150, 179, 181, 188
Asia, 40, 79, 124, 127
asteroid, 27, 57, 74, 76, 77, 142, 395, 418
Atlantis, 9, 20, 54, 67, 71, 79–81, 87, 121–123, 127, 134, 174, 178, 180, 181, 239, 240, 243, 257–259, 284, 335, 337, 395
atmosphere, 55, 78, 139, 140, 142, 153, 181, 216, 240, 276, 307
atom, 35, 83, 107, 112, 130, 142, 154, 155, 173, 180, 211, 237, 238, 252, 259, 321, 322, 339
attachments, 3, 39, 101, 155, 156, 162, 260, 310, 315, 317, 325, 344, 346, 361, 363, 408
attack, xxviii–xxx, 13, 24, 115, 151,

163, 167, 175, 179, 183, 216,
241, 255, 266, 280, 281,
297–299, 379, 415
attention, vi, xxxii, 7, 17, 42, 48, 90,
102, 106, 109, 135, 139, 159,
188, 209, 247–249, 301, 352,
417
awareness, xvii, xviii, 4, 6–8, 11, 19,
26, 35, 43, 48, 113–115, 121,
130, 134, 136–138, 143, 151,
197, 201, 214, 219, 235, 248,
249, 251, 256, 263, 265, 283,
286, 299–301, 323, 332, 365,
367, 368, 374, 379, 382, 400,
403, 412

Baalbek, 122, 123
Babaji, 225
Babel, 67, 68, 141, 178, 239
Babylon, 51, 52, 68, 105, 125, 126,
154, 178, 398
Baldwin, William, 3, 50, 162, 169, 400
ball lightning, 217
Bar Mitzvah, 44
Basques, 79
battle, 23, 24, 66, 74, 141, 153, 171,
172, 194, 234, 265, 275, 276,
278, 343, 349, 350, 409
beast, 54, 101–106, 122, 177, 181, 201,
217, 229, 340, 391
Beelzebub, 217
belief, i, vii, xi, xv, xix, xxi, xxx, 5, 39,
44, 55, 63, 86, 94, 117, 164,
165, 298, 325, 344, 367, 371,
376, 379, 409
Bell Witch case, 215
Berlitz, Charles, 161
Bermuda Triangle, 243, 258
bible, 25, 26, 41, 44, 45, 51, 63, 70, 94,
100, 125, 208, 217, 218, 281,
347, 396, 403, 419
Bielek, Al, 78, 79, 250, 375
big bang, iv, 113, 238
Bigfoot, 32, 83, 84, 253, 300
Blavatsky, Helen, 321

blizzard, 23
blood, 41, 64, 74, 111, 119, 132, 291,
302, 310, 343, 347, 364
Boleyn, Ann, 216
book, i–iii, vii, viii, xi, xiii, xxv, 1, 2,
9, 13, 15, 16, 26, 27, 33, 34,
36, 40, 43, 49, 50, 68, 69,
75–77, 79, 84, 87, 90, 91,
93–95, 98, 99, 103, 113, 123,
126, 128, 136, 150, 152–155,
157, 161, 164, 166, 169, 171,
172, 174, 180, 181, 187, 189,
193, 195, 199, 203, 205, 207,
209, 218, 224, 225, 234, 238,
252, 253, 261, 270, 271, 281,
282, 285, 291, 298, 301, 303,
308, 309, 315, 316, 321, 330,
331, 343, 355, 356, 364, 372,
375, 379, 381, 395, 396,
398–404, 415, 416, 419
Boylan, Richard, 161
brain, xxii, 8, 67, 79, 88, 89, 91, 132,
178, 190, 198, 211, 212, 257,
274, 293, 357, 366, 379, 399
 frontal, 301
brainwashing, 67, 79
Branch Davidians, 64, 65
brotherhood, 95, 98, 99, 102, 113, 121,
190, 211, 217, 229, 249
Buddha, 51

Cain, 211, 273, 274, 403
California, 9, 10, 17, 23, 88, 130, 284,
285, 302, 310
Cana, 44, 84, 88, 256
cancer, xxx, 91, 162, 166, 262, 308,
336
carbon 14 dating, 309
Carey, Ken, 306, 307, 320
Cassiopaea, i–iii, v, vi, viii, x, xi, xiii,
xvi, xx–xxii, xxiv, 1, 16, 23,
25, 26, 29, 34, 35, 42, 44, 45,
49, 52, 53, 57, 61, 64, 66, 71,
73, 75, 80, 83, 94, 109, 119,
130, 145, 146, 153, 159, 166,

175, 185, 193, 202, 211, 221,
224, 227–230, 232, 233, 243,
263, 275, 291, 292, 296, 307,
324, 329–331, 334, 347, 351,
357, 362, 366, 368, 377, 391,
410, 411, 413, 417
Cassiopeia, 23, 331, 351
cataclysm, xviii, 55, 56, 64, 66, 70, 77,
79, 87, 100, 123, 140, 149,
165, 174, 175, 181, 190, 203,
240, 286–288, 340, 395, 407,
415, 419
Catholicism, 218
Caucasus, 111
Cayce, Edgar, 9, 15, 16, 130, 222, 284,
310
Celts, 77, 83, 110, 111, 127, 154, 181,
228
chakra, 196, 197, 381, 382
channeling, iii, xv, xvi, xix–xxiv, 1–7,
9, 15, 16, 24, 26, 27, 36, 37,
44, 45, 47, 66, 74, 85, 88, 89,
94, 96, 100, 110, 117,
127–130, 132, 135, 137, 145,
146, 149, 150, 156, 166, 168,
169, 194, 199, 202, 203, 205,
209, 213, 215, 221, 241, 245,
246, 252, 253, 261–263, 269,
281, 282, 292, 293, 296, 297,
302, 306–311, 313–317, 319,
320, 327, 330–332, 334, 337,
340, 347, 348, 359, 367, 368,
371, 378, 379, 381, 382, 392,
401, 408, 417
  conduit, 209, 287, 288, 336, 353,
363, 382
Chicago, 65, 206, 316
children, 19, 20, 25, 32, 36, 42, 43, 52,
63, 64, 98, 127, 159, 160,
168, 188, 198, 218, 222, 223,
295–297, 323–325, 330, 343,
356, 399
cholera, 23
Christ, 27, 39, 40, 42, 44, 64, 66, 81,
84, 86, 94, 105–107, 137,
138, 165, 180, 195, 204, 208,
251, 281, 282, 302, 307, 308,
329, 361, 362, 366, 368, 379,
395, 396, 398
church, 119, 120, 167, 187, 218, 296,
308, 317, 323, 343, 379
CIA, 79, 103, 251, 380, 399
civilization, xvii, xviii, 6, 40, 41, 43,
51, 52, 62, 80, 123, 138, 174,
181, 202, 234, 235, 239, 303,
335, 338, 404, 419
Clarke, Arthur, 125, 132
climate, vii, viii, 55, 71, 179, 189, 407
cluster, 56–58, 66, 67, 70, 74–77, 86,
106, 123, 130, 174, 175, 182,
185, 257, 285, 330
Coatzlmundi, 123
comet, i, viii, 1, 5, 19, 24, 26, 27, 35,
39, 49, 51, 52, 55–58, 66–70,
74–77, 79, 86, 89, 90, 106,
107, 123, 130, 153, 154, 157,
165, 174, 175, 177, 179, 181,
182, 189, 190, 257, 258, 285,
395, 398, 405, 406, 418
computer, xvii–xx, 3, 4, 13, 24, 27, 75,
78, 103, 166, 178, 200, 201,
244, 246–248, 250, 257, 318,
353, 354, 369, 373–375, 420
confusing of languages, 67
consciousness, v, xiii, xxiii, 1, 3–5, 7,
8, 11, 13, 21, 32, 46, 48, 49,
63, 85, 98, 109, 110, 114,
127, 130, 133, 156, 163, 195,
198, 222, 233, 236, 244, 245,
251, 253, 258, 295, 307, 318,
338, 347, 363, 364, 400
consortium, 18, 20, 25, 249, 373
conspiracy, viii, 12, 24, 54, 62, 399,
402, 409, 412
convergence point, 301, 305, 306
Cooper, William, 161
Course in Miracles, 308
creator, 40, 41, 45, 70, 71, 73, 75, 113,
114, 141, 148, 164, 165, 207,
303, 307, 339, 349, 412

Cromwell, Oliver, 319
crop circle, 171–173, 216, 241, 304,
    322, 407
cybergenetic, 53, 348

D'Ahnkiar, 236
Dahmer, Jeffrey, 150, 214
Dallas, 17, 416
death, xi, 2, 34, 40, 42, 48, 55, 57, 84,
    90, 91, 95, 96, 99, 102, 104,
    125, 131, 151, 154, 165, 181,
    203, 206, 213, 214, 218, 219,
    222, 237, 238, 251, 271, 283,
    295, 338, 398, 400, 402
  die, 12, 16, 23, 48, 99, 128, 140,
    147, 151, 182, 190, 215, 219,
    225, 238, 260, 343–350, 352,
    356, 358, 359, 361, 362, 372,
    374
  dying, 49, 54, 56, 58, 74, 75, 121,
    132, 133, 215, 237, 276, 364,
    413
debit, 98, 99, 165
deception, 4, 69, 70, 104, 136, 217,
    234, 239, 318, 362, 403, 412
defense, 20, 136, 177, 208, 280, 298
deities, 123, 134
deluge, 40, 41, 154, 240, 395, 406
delusion, iv, v, 119, 190, 244
density, v, xiii, xxi, 1, 9, 35, 44, 48, 65,
    66, 71, 80, 83, 96, 97, 106,
    107, 132–135, 138–140, 142,
    149, 150, 153, 157, 175, 176,
    182, 183, 196, 197, 212, 217,
    219, 235–239, 245, 247, 249,
    252, 253, 262, 269, 276, 279,
    283, 284, 286–288, 293, 307,
    309, 316, 319–322, 325,
    331–336, 344–346, 349, 350,
    357, 359, 380
  1st, 238, 339
  3rd, 9, 97, 99, 100, 128, 133, 134,
    140, 183, 217, 219, 235–238,
    253, 263, 276, 277, 279, 284,
    286–288, 319–322, 335, 338,
    345, 346, 357, 359, 375, 380
  4th, 96, 97, 106, 107, 132–134,
    149, 150, 153, 157, 176, 182,
    183, 196, 197, 199, 215,
    235–239, 245, 269, 276, 277,
    279, 283, 285–288, 309, 319,
    321, 325, 331–334, 344–346,
    349, 350, 359, 366, 375, 380
  5th, 247, 277, 286, 336
  6th, xiii, 9, 35, 71, 80, 134, 135,
    138, 276, 277, 284, 288, 293,
    307, 316, 320–322, 331, 332,
    340
  7th, 238, 318, 340
Denver, 17, 23, 135
depression, 99, 224, 225, 231, 245, 246,
    278, 299
destiny, 52, 63, 114, 116, 117, 171, 331,
    377, 404
devil, iv, xx, 4, 208, 231, 251, 281, 282,
    401
dimension, v, xiii, xxi, 1, 12, 34, 35,
    44, 48, 52, 96, 97, 131, 133,
    155, 173, 175, 176, 197, 198,
    208, 213, 216, 237, 249, 252,
    255, 258, 259, 266, 287, 288,
    311, 321, 322, 353, 358, 366,
    391, 399, 402, 403, 407,
    412–414
dinosaurs, 54, 55, 57, 73–75, 149, 239,
    382
discarnate, 1, 15, 23, 109, 153, 159,
    185, 193, 211, 243, 262, 296,
    351
disinformation, xi, xix, xx, xxii, xxiii,
    34, 62, 79, 99–101, 103, 106,
    161, 243, 248, 249, 251, 253,
    257, 264, 295, 350, 365,
    374–376, 403, 415
Druids, 150

earth changes, 9, 10, 24, 62, 64, 93,
    157, 227, 228, 243, 251, 256,
    257, 259, 264, 276, 283–286,
    289, 406

Earthquake, 125
earthquake, 62, 129, 203, 205, 206, 213, 259, 302, 406
Easter Island, 173, 174
Ecstasy, 392
ecstasy, 99, 231
Eden, 70, 71, 73, 146, 148, 173, 176, 273, 401
education, 9, 187, 365, 367
Egypt, 15, 26, 40, 41, 44, 51, 67, 80, 90, 91, 95, 101, 106, 125, 127, 141, 154, 158, 179, 180, 189, 239, 318, 319, 395, 398, 402
electricity, viii, 7, 36, 56, 97, 120, 183, 212, 213, 238, 260, 266, 275, 292, 306, 310, 405, 406
electromagnetism, 24, 27, 55, 56, 61, 67, 101, 107, 130, 132, 142, 145, 212, 213, 217, 252, 292, 298, 305, 311, 405
emotion, 3, 20, 33, 39, 44, 46, 47, 85, 106, 116, 156, 159, 160, 163, 193, 195, 196, 243, 265, 270, 274, 278–280, 292, 309, 310, 317, 318, 325, 344, 346, 354–356, 361, 363, 364, 371, 413, 421
    negative, 279, 356
    positive, 279
EMP, 26
energy, xviii, xix, 8, 9, 12, 29, 34, 36, 45, 53, 56, 58, 61, 62, 69, 71, 73, 75, 76, 85, 89–91, 99, 109, 112, 119, 125, 128, 129, 131–134, 142, 151, 153, 155, 161, 163, 167–169, 172, 174, 175, 180, 183, 186, 189, 193–197, 212, 216, 225, 233, 234, 237–239, 243, 244, 251–255, 259, 269, 270, 279, 286, 287, 292, 293, 297, 304, 306, 308, 309, 311, 314, 319, 322, 329, 337–340, 349, 353, 377–379, 381, 395, 421

    negative, 133, 134, 225, 279, 297, 329, 339
Enki, 52
Enlil, 40, 52
essence, xxviii, 13, 175, 324, 329, 330
Essene, 63, 95, 217
Ethiopia, 23, 94
Eve, 69, 70, 112, 113, 368, 371, 372
evolution, 1, 76, 123, 131, 154, 165, 195, 204, 208, 251, 261, 307, 395, 397, 408, 411
exodus, 26, 51, 66, 77, 106, 123, 189, 302, 398
exorcism, 2, 45, 121, 201, 218, 401, 417
experience, iv–vi, viii, xiv, xv, xxi, xxix, 1, 3, 5, 8, 12, 18, 27, 41, 46, 49, 74, 79, 86, 87, 96–98, 117, 126, 131, 134, 136–141, 147, 148, 153, 156, 161, 162, 201, 208, 216, 233, 245, 247, 250, 251, 253, 255, 256, 258, 287, 289, 308, 311, 313, 318, 321–325, 336, 350, 351, 358, 363, 367, 369, 380, 381, 406–409, 411, 417
extraterrestrial, xvi, 52, 188, 197, 259, 306, 402
Ezekiel, 113

fairies, 200
faith, iii, xix, 73, 100, 120, 136–138, 140, 165, 168, 169, 241, 254, 260, 263, 282, 321, 327
Fall of Man, 42, 70, 73, 105, 148, 149, 173, 176, 262, 273, 391, 404
FBI, 218, 373, 374
fear, vi, 40, 58, 66, 69, 102, 106, 117, 120, 132, 136, 177, 195, 208, 234, 256, 298, 311, 332, 418
federation, 16, 33, 35, 98, 125, 177, 202, 286
fiction, vii, 15, 80, 81, 124, 310, 399, 403, 411
finances, x, 18, 85, 98, 102, 117, 152, 194, 216, 224, 255, 257, 281,

291, 295, 299, 316, 326, 327, 372, 373
flood, 19, 51, 52, 54, 55, 67, 77, 87, 94, 100, 123, 139, 140, 180, 240
Florida, 1, 16, 17, 36, 88, 91, 117, 201, 207, 297, 335, 343, 417
Fodor, Nandor, 216, 401
food, 96, 99, 134, 280
Fort, Charles, 52, 201, 204, 396, 401, 407
forum, i, viii, ix, xxiv, 168, 173, 273, 316, 318, 395
Fowler, Raymond, 33, 53, 233, 234, 252, 401
free will, iii, iv, 5, 32, 33, 36, 66, 98, 99, 139, 149, 204, 217, 271, 273, 297, 316, 338, 340, 345, 348, 349, 357
Friedman, Stanton, 161

galaxy, 23, 57, 76, 112, 140, 185, 186, 274, 305
gamma ray, 216
Gandhi, Mahatma, 346
genetics, vii, xxxiii, 19, 25, 27, 52, 53, 74, 90, 111, 121, 122, 127, 139, 141–143, 147, 148, 150, 156, 174, 175, 212, 216, 239, 307, 320, 344, 347
    changes, 90, 239, 245, 333, 403
    DNA, 69, 89–91, 111, 127, 147, 152, 160, 175, 212, 239, 245, 266, 273–275, 291, 330, 333–335, 347, 353, 396, 403, 413
giant, 25–27, 32, 33, 41, 55, 74, 112, 122–124, 127, 149, 154, 155, 175, 225, 303, 335
Gilgamesh, 40, 41, 51
Gnosticism, 155
God, iv, xix, xxii, xxiii, 34, 40, 41, 51, 52, 68–70, 74, 81, 85, 102–105, 124, 153, 154, 179, 207, 231, 239, 333, 339, 356, 381

goddess, 74, 223, 239
gold, 25, 65, 84, 106, 117, 215, 222, 241, 296, 302, 392, 403, 404
Goliath, 146, 147
government, ix, x, 17, 18, 23, 24, 64, 75, 79, 86–88, 104, 130, 143, 166, 175, 177, 200, 203, 204, 206, 207, 243, 245, 246, 250–252, 255, 256, 258, 260, 332, 374, 375, 409, 415
grand cycle, 176, 232, 236, 275, 276, 303
gravity, 57, 61, 67, 76, 77, 101, 123, 130, 139, 142, 147, 274, 275
gravity wave, 61, 67, 101
grays, 33, 34, 53, 74, 79, 85, 87, 88, 90, 98, 120, 121, 127, 130, 132, 133, 146, 149, 150, 154, 155, 158, 161, 176, 178, 179, 183, 196, 244, 245, 253–256, 331, 332, 348, 355, 359, 376, 381
Gurdjieff, G. I., 149, 195, 197, 230, 277, 364
Gypsies, 121

Halloween, 154
hallucination, 215
hauntings, 91, 213, 215, 216, 401
Haywood, Ann, 253
healing, 47, 71, 120, 163, 233, 260, 270, 271, 292, 304, 421
Hebrew, 67, 68, 81, 94, 178, 396
hermaphroditism, 240, 333
hierarchy, 178, 235
Hitler, Adolf, 50, 87, 182, 357, 398
Hoagland, Richard, 257, 276
Holy Grail, 64, 398, 404
Hopkins, Budd, 115, 379, 380
Horus, 90, 153
hybrid, xxiii, 124, 343, 345, 346
hypnosis, 2, 3, 20, 46, 58, 63, 115, 121, 126, 129, 155, 166, 202, 205, 218, 222, 247, 249, 253, 260, 282, 291, 308, 311, 321, 323, 324, 327, 329, 330, 332, 341,

343, 347, 354, 356, 378, 382, 408

ignorance, 19, 230, 249, 278, 350, 363
   endangers, 19, 249, 278, 350, 363
Illuminati, 157, 177, 217, 224, 228, 229, 231, 232, 249
illusion, 148, 183, 239, 344, 366, 369, 403, 409
immortality, 52
implant, xxiv, 21, 24, 32, 67, 69, 88, 121, 156, 179, 204, 235, 262, 278–280, 282, 376, 379, 380
incarnation, 35, 50, 65, 66, 190, 203, 218, 219, 238, 324, 333, 401
India, 25, 33, 41, 44, 50, 79, 84, 85, 95, 111, 112, 123–125, 127
intermarriage, 111, 124
intuition, 163
Iran, 43, 203
iridium, 182
Isis, 89, 90, 321

Jack the Ripper, 49
Japan, 17, 50, 62, 258, 259
jealousy, 116, 120, 172, 211, 273
Jehova, 126
Jehovah, 81, 125
Jericho, 125, 178
Jesus, 27, 34, 35, 39, 40, 42–45, 47–51, 62–66, 76, 77, 84–86, 100, 137–139, 142, 164, 165, 282, 307–310, 366, 376, 396, 398
Jews, 26, 33, 51, 80, 81, 94, 95, 110, 142, 190, 212, 362, 398
Joan of Arc, 99, 153
John the Baptist, 65, 66, 309
Joseph, 42, 63, 96, 125, 126, 397
Joshua, 65
Jupiter, i, 5, 24, 26, 41, 51, 57, 58, 74–76, 80, 86, 122, 142, 154

Kaballah, 69, 151, 392
Kantek, 57, 110, 142, 240

karma, 20, 101, 110, 116, 127, 137, 162, 200, 213, 216, 235, 244, 304, 305, 319, 363
King, Stephen, 381
Kirtanah, 85
Knossos, 181
knowledge, iii, xi, xvi, xviii, xxxi, 1, 4, 6, 19–21, 32, 44, 52, 66, 69, 70, 73, 77, 89, 90, 93, 95, 96, 99, 105, 112, 113, 120, 126, 130, 136–140, 142, 167, 168, 177, 178, 182, 215, 224, 227, 234, 249, 251, 252, 265, 266, 274, 278, 280, 282, 283, 288, 289, 299, 304, 317, 347, 349–351, 363, 366–368, 375, 376, 397, 400, 404, 405, 408–411, 413, 414, 417
   protects, 20, 21, 182, 249, 251, 278, 299, 347, 350, 363

Laumer, Keith, 15, 225, 310, 319, 338
Lazar, Bob, 18, 48, 53, 161
lead, vii, x, xi, xiv, xviii, 2, 3, 50, 52, 65, 95, 99, 101, 103, 105, 154, 158, 162, 175, 187, 202, 203, 205, 207, 215, 273, 302, 316, 322, 323, 349, 365, 366, 407
learning, ii, viii, xiv, xxii, xxviii, 1, 5–8, 10, 17, 39, 41, 42, 53, 71, 73, 84, 86, 90, 97–99, 101, 105, 120–122, 126, 131, 133, 136–138, 146, 148, 149, 160, 162, 167, 168, 178, 181, 187, 196, 199, 209, 213, 214, 224, 229, 234, 254, 263, 265, 266, 270, 271, 279, 285, 289, 296, 298, 304, 305, 308, 313, 315, 316, 322, 338, 346, 347, 350, 352, 354–356, 359, 361, 368, 381, 408, 409
legend, 26, 43, 74, 85, 112, 121, 123, 146, 148, 154, 157, 181, 189, 190, 335, 403–405

Leithbridge, Thomas Charles, 216, 401
Lemuria, 173, 174, 335
lessons, xiv, 98, 116, 120, 213, 236, 265, 271, 276, 287, 304, 319, 322, 348, 356, 361, 391, 413
Leviathan, 217
Libra, 16, 24, 376, 396, 401
life force, 132, 196, 197, 222
lifetime, viii, 1, 43, 117, 219, 247, 272, 354, 355
light, vi, viii, xi, xiv, xxxii, 2, 7–9, 14, 29, 31, 41, 48, 53, 55, 56, 68, 74–76, 83, 85, 97, 98, 100, 109, 116, 123, 136, 145, 155, 157, 158, 161, 171, 181–183, 185, 189, 198, 201–203, 213, 217, 225, 231, 232, 238, 255, 269, 270, 272, 274–277, 279, 280, 282, 284, 286–288, 298, 302, 303, 314, 366, 369, 375, 380, 382, 392, 398, 410, 414, 416
Lincoln, Abraham, 54, 64, 398
lizard beings, 53, 67–69, 71, 73, 74, 76, 78–81, 83, 84, 86, 87, 90, 95, 96, 98, 99, 101, 102, 106, 107, 112–114, 119–121, 123, 125–127, 132–135, 140, 141, 146, 149, 150, 153–157, 161, 165–168, 176, 177, 179, 182, 183, 188, 190, 196, 198–200, 212, 217, 229–232, 234, 235, 239, 245, 246, 249, 251, 252, 254, 255, 259, 260, 264–266, 273, 274, 276–282, 298, 315, 319, 331, 333, 337, 339, 340, 355, 359, 362, 366, 381
Loch Ness, 149
London, xxxiv, 23, 154, 216, 272, 274
long wave cycle, 131
Lourdes, 233
LSD, 215
Lucifer, 148, 190, 392
Luke, 50, 100, 218

magi, iv, x, xix, 6, 13, 14, 40, 41, 43, 52, 65, 69, 90, 115, 132, 135, 142, 161, 178, 179, 202, 215, 222, 233, 249, 254, 295, 296, 298, 361, 374, 381, 395, 397, 409
Majestic 12, 33, 79, 247, 402
Maldek, 181
Malta, 223
manipulation, xviii, xxii, 74, 103, 140, 141, 155, 157, 197, 212, 230, 235, 274, 355, 410
Marciniak, Barbara, 195, 200, 293, 320, 330, 331, 333, 401
Marduk, 86, 157
Mars, 54, 57, 58, 66, 67, 74–76, 78, 83, 86, 139, 142, 155, 157, 172, 240, 257–260
Martek, 54, 67, 110, 123, 139, 140, 240
Mary, 15, 27, 42, 62, 63, 65, 66, 202, 233, 234, 378
masons, 93, 157, 227–229, 232
Matthew, 50, 100, 218
Mayans, 41, 80, 176, 178, 337, 343, 344
media, ix, xix, xx, xxx, 15, 16, 62, 75, 97, 103, 107, 185, 187, 211, 235, 250, 277, 310, 315, 318, 324, 411, 421
meditation, 19, 126, 130, 138, 196, 215, 218, 219, 259, 365, 367, 368, 382
Melchizedek, 65, 69, 126
memory, xviii, 20, 21, 41, 74, 78, 79, 98, 117, 126, 132, 141, 158, 197, 198, 204, 227, 244, 305, 325, 399
Merlin, 215
mermaids, 154
Mescalitos, 214
Mesopotamia, 40, 41, 52, 68
metabolism, 97, 132, 134
meteor, viii, 24, 55, 181, 276, 372, 406
Mexico, 23, 41, 88, 251
Miami, 17

military, 33, 79, 200–204, 206, 207, 256, 261, 272, 284, 302, 332, 416
Minoan civilization, 181
Minturians, 98, 149, 324, 325
miracle, xxviii, 45, 47–49, 104, 138, 163, 308
Missouri, 17
Mohenjo Daro, 123, 135, 150
monitoring, xvi, 32, 156, 179, 248, 312, 376, 379
Montana, 17, 23, 352
Moon, 86, 157, 382, 393
Moore, William, 161
Mormons, 96
mosaic, 333
Moses, 51, 65, 69, 77, 81, 95, 153, 157, 175, 189, 398, 405
Muck, Otto, 337, 395
MUFON, 1, 8, 197, 217, 222, 223, 246, 248, 250, 252, 295, 300, 372
murder, 2, 42, 64, 65, 84, 90, 91, 151, 159, 211, 213, 412, 416
music, 85, 93, 105, 189, 228, 235, 303, 356
mutation, 69, 111, 147, 195
Mycenaeans, 181
mysticism, xi, 54, 233, 400, 403, 404, 407, 408, 412
mythology, 26, 45, 49, 51, 52, 69, 74, 85, 86, 89, 90, 157, 204, 240, 258, 335, 364, 376, 396–398, 400, 405, 410, 411, 418

Nazca, 135
Neanderthal, 71, 127, 147, 182, 211, 212, 257, 259
negativity, 136, 142, 280
Nephilim, 122, 123, 140, 146, 147, 171, 173–177, 182, 183, 190, 225, 239
Neptune, 58, 217
network, 27, 246–248, 250, 266, 287, 318, 345, 354, 367, 368, 377, 378

New Age, xx, 3, 5, 15, 115, 165, 167, 202, 243, 281, 306, 307, 316, 343, 358, 397, 408, 412
New Testament, 94, 202, 218, 281
New World Order, 17, 36, 102, 208, 249
Nibiru, 57, 217, 225
Noah, 51, 54, 55, 67, 68, 77, 87, 94, 100, 123, 139, 140, 240, 419
Nordic types, 188, 254, 302
Nostradamus, 320
Nubians, 124
nuclear, 26, 55, 68, 95, 122, 259, 301, 330

Oak Island, 340, 410
Oakes, Harry, 84
obelisk, 68
objective, xxix, 235, 417
obsession, 137, 139, 142, 253, 325
Oklahoma, xxx, 24, 302
omnipresence, 25, 109, 160
orbit, 26, 51, 56, 57, 66, 67, 75, 76, 97, 112, 122, 123, 130, 185, 204, 255
Orient, 7, 50, 110–112, 174, 231, 273, 277, 281, 321, 344
Orion, 16, 25, 31–33, 35, 53, 98, 127, 140, 146–148, 174, 277, 307, 320, 321, 330, 331, 345, 348–350, 359, 362, 366, 377
Orlando, 17
Ormethion, 112, 113, 125
Osaka, 62
Osiris, 69, 89, 90, 93
overseers, 93, 227

pain, ix, 9, 19, 32, 34, 100, 133, 136, 164, 179, 219, 238, 245, 266, 284, 307, 310, 317, 319, 322, 369, 404, 421
Palestine, 44, 76, 85, 86, 309, 415
paranoia, 116, 155, 156, 217, 228, 284
paranormal, iii, viii, ix, xxviii, 3–5, 7, 26, 153, 204, 209, 228, 281, 296, 371, 411–413

parasite, 181
Paris, 23
past life, 98, 218, 219, 319, 338, 377
Pentecost, 308
Persia, 43, 95
Philadelphia Experiment, 78, 79, 243, 250, 251, 258, 375
philosopher's stone, 215
philosophy, 1, 4, 16, 109, 154, 180, 281, 398, 400, 404
phoenix, 10, 78, 112, 255, 284
planet, xx, 5, 6, 16, 18–20, 25–27, 29, 33–35, 43, 44, 51, 53–58, 62, 64, 65, 67, 68, 71, 74–78, 80, 83, 85–87, 97, 106, 107, 110–112, 121, 123, 126, 128, 130, 134, 135, 139, 140, 142, 146–149, 154, 155, 157, 168, 169, 172, 174–177, 179, 182, 183, 188–190, 195, 198, 201, 202, 213–215, 224, 225, 228, 229, 231, 235–237, 240, 257, 263, 274, 276, 277, 285–288, 303–307, 322, 332–334, 345, 346, 365, 372, 396, 398, 405, 406, 410, 415
Pleiades, 16, 53, 71, 98, 128, 149, 195, 275, 293, 303, 330, 331, 333, 334, 339, 343, 345–348, 356, 361, 362
poltergeist, 2, 222, 243, 253, 401
population, vii, 18, 41, 43, 68, 74, 90, 101, 107, 111, 112, 140, 141, 175, 177, 185, 195, 212, 274, 286, 303, 333, 363, 407
prayer, 43, 48, 168, 233
pregnancy, 162
projection, 48, 81, 96, 121, 126, 133, 154, 200, 211, 252, 254, 255
promised land, 189
propaganda, vii, x, 34, 101, 218, 409
prophecy, iii, iv, xix, 3, 4, 9–11, 13, 16, 17, 36, 43, 47, 65, 71, 80, 85, 93, 94, 101, 157, 189, 202, 203, 205, 207, 215, 228, 283–285, 289, 306, 309, 355, 396, 401, 402, 419
Prophet, Elizabeth Clare, 215
protection, 19, 21, 135–137, 167, 234, 317
pyramid, 44, 71, 123, 126, 134, 141, 180, 189, 259

quantum physics, xxiii, xxv, 321
Quorum, 93, 94, 157, 227–229, 231, 232

Ra Material, 13, 15, 16, 29, 40, 44, 129, 150, 202, 320, 355, 401
race, i, xvi, xxxiii, 1–3, 10–12, 15, 18, 19, 21, 23, 25, 31, 33, 34, 42–44, 52, 58, 68, 70, 73, 74, 76, 86, 90, 105, 110, 111, 116, 119–121, 125–127, 129, 133, 134, 137, 140, 141, 148, 157, 164, 172, 185, 202, 206, 222, 224, 229, 231, 234–236, 240, 247, 251, 255, 260, 264, 265, 277, 286, 305, 313, 319, 333, 345, 361, 362, 374, 397, 398, 404, 417
Radon, 17
reality, iii–vi, viii–x, xxi, 1, 6, 8, 11, 13, 16, 20, 24, 35, 39, 44, 48, 54, 70, 71, 86, 87, 90, 99, 113, 121, 134, 141, 142, 147, 148, 153, 155, 175, 182, 198, 200, 208, 209, 213, 232, 236, 245, 247, 248, 250, 252, 255, 262, 263, 276, 279, 286, 287, 289, 321–325, 358, 359, 378, 381, 392, 397, 402, 403, 408, 409, 411, 414–417
realm, 1, 9, 11, 13, 25, 43, 44, 49, 52, 62, 65, 83, 112–114, 128, 131, 134, 138, 149, 153, 175–177, 208, 209, 212, 235–237, 252, 273, 274, 283, 285, 288, 301, 303, 305, 306, 309, 310, 321–323, 330–332, 345–347, 349, 392

realm border, 112, 113, 175, 176, 236, 285, 301, 303, 305, 306, 309, 322, 330–332, 345–347, 349
realm crossing, 114, 236, 237
Reiki, 29, 45, 46, 119, 163, 188, 222, 223, 231, 245, 254, 255, 266, 270, 271, 301, 304, 305, 308, 326, 352, 357, 368, 391, 408
    Takata, Hawayo, 304
    Usui, Mikao Dr., 45, 231, 304
relationship, 24, 50, 65, 66, 94, 116, 122, 130, 159, 180, 189, 217, 219, 227, 228, 338, 379, 400, 412
religion, iv, viii, xix, 4, 39, 49, 50, 63, 64, 66, 85, 86, 94, 95, 104, 116, 145, 153, 154, 168, 181, 204, 207, 208, 251, 316, 400, 404, 405, 407–409, 414
Revelation, xi, 16, 80, 93, 98, 106, 128, 201, 207, 217, 225, 283
Rice, Anne, 381
ritual, 21, 44, 61, 95, 126, 135, 136, 167, 168, 181, 243, 296, 298, 351
Roberts, Jane, 213
robot, 132, 143, 319, 337, 359
Rome, 41–43, 63

Sagan, Carl, 274
salt, 69, 167, 274, 308
Sanksrit, 95, 101, 181, 254
Saturn, 58, 86, 89
scandal, xxxiii, 17, 19, 23, 135, 182, 201, 302
schizophrenia, 155, 156
Seattle, 17, 205
serpent, 26, 52, 71, 95, 112, 149, 153, 154, 395
Seth, 126, 213
sex, 27, 40, 86, 89, 115, 124, 150, 165, 188, 195–197, 216, 253, 264, 270, 302, 334, 336, 337, 355, 357, 381
shamanism, 3, 40, 165–168

Shandera, Jaimie, 161
Sheba, Queen of, 124
ship, 1–3, 24, 26, 42, 43, 47, 48, 50, 58, 65, 66, 68, 85, 94, 102–105, 116, 122, 123, 125, 127, 130, 134, 135, 154, 159, 175, 180, 186, 188, 189, 198, 202, 207, 217, 219, 223, 227, 228, 239, 250, 253, 272, 332, 338, 343, 377, 379, 398, 400, 412
short wave cycle, 131, 132
Shroud of Turin, 310
Sirius, 86
Sitchin, Zecharia, 25, 52, 56, 68, 80, 86, 116, 126, 134, 222, 241, 295, 398
sleep, x, 7, 47, 48, 50, 85, 100, 176, 230, 240, 244, 300, 356
Smith, Joseph, 96
smoking, 32, 166, 223, 249
snake, 41, 73, 95, 113, 214, 271, 324, 400
Socrates, 65
Sodom and Gomorrah, 26, 68, 69
solar system, 25, 26, 54, 56–58, 67, 74, 77, 112, 123, 126, 134, 240, 257, 274, 285
Solomon, 122, 125, 396
soul, xxiii, 18, 20, 21, 33, 34, 48–50, 53, 58, 65, 66, 74, 86, 96, 111, 115, 119, 120, 126, 131–134, 137–143, 146–148, 164, 165, 175, 178, 183, 190, 198, 214, 219, 236–238, 245, 247, 265, 266, 286, 295, 305, 350, 354, 358, 363, 364, 376, 391, 397, 408
sound, x, 5, 9, 74, 105, 122, 126, 130, 150, 151, 163, 164, 213, 255, 264, 277, 291, 299, 325, 336, 352
spaceship, 18, 43, 61, 79, 142, 189, 202, 343
speaking in tongues, 308
Sphinx, 71, 141, 239

Spirit Releasement Therapy, 2, 3, 5,
    50, 101, 260, 315, 400
  earthbound spirits, 100, 221, 326
St. Germaine, 215
St. Issa, 84
Starseed Transmissions, 307, 319
Steiner, Rudolf, 165
STO, 12, 13, 16, 81, 133, 165, 231,
    232, 274, 277, 309, 314–317,
    319–321, 338, 340, 345, 346,
    348, 349
Stonehenge, 150, 151, 217, 222, 353
Strieber, Whitley, 33, 79, 380, 381,
    402
struggle, 6, 172, 276, 280, 408, 411,
    413
STS, 12, 13, 16, 33, 34, 133, 142, 231,
    232, 273, 277, 279, 281, 282,
    296, 309, 320, 321, 336,
    338–340, 345, 346, 348–350,
    359, 362
study, i, vii–ix, xi, xiii, xxx, 1, 11, 15,
    21, 44, 46, 55, 74, 77, 80,
    174, 177, 178, 180, 189, 198,
    212, 223, 224, 237, 274–276,
    296, 363, 364, 367, 368, 376,
    405, 414, 416
subconscious, 3, 4, 7, 11, 21, 32, 85,
    98, 109, 156, 253, 363, 364
subjective, 20, 48, 63, 98, 109, 116,
    166, 183, 223, 230, 237, 260,
    300, 324, 344, 346, 357–359,
    367, 375
subliminal, 65, 166, 235
suffering, 20, 32, 34, 87, 91, 100, 123,
    133, 188, 193, 224, 231, 245,
    265, 271, 281, 303, 307, 319,
    408, 415, 421
Sufi, 223, 224, 397
suicide, 49, 64, 151, 213, 219, 302
Sumeria, 25, 51, 52, 57, 68, 74, 80, 86,
    122, 157, 225
sun, xiv, xxxii, 10, 11, 16, 24–26, 40,
    41, 43, 55–59, 75, 76, 85, 86,
    97, 128, 173, 178, 185, 195,
    257, 274, 275, 285, 307, 319,
    396, 406
superstition, 90, 165, 211, 239, 392,
    418
Swastika, 112
Switzerland, 64
sword, 40, 70, 103, 104, 272, 377
symbolism, vi, 9–11, 13, 23, 29, 45, 52,
    54, 66, 68–70, 74, 89–91,
    100, 105, 111, 112, 126, 135,
    140, 146, 167, 172, 175, 208,
    222, 229, 231, 234, 239, 254,
    257, 273, 283–286, 301, 304,
    305, 315, 318, 319, 344, 352,
    397, 408, 411, 413

Tahiti, 23
technology, xvi, xx, xxiii, 27, 79, 87,
    133, 155, 188, 248, 252, 257,
    259–261, 274, 275, 278, 299,
    340, 409
telekinesis, 47
telepathy, 2, 4, 11–13, 63, 65, 197, 202,
    204, 214
temple, 64, 68, 71, 95, 106, 122, 126,
    223
Texas, 16, 17, 302
The P'taah Tapes, 150
Thera, 3, 50, 123, 181, 315, 400
thought center, 112, 113
thought form, xiii, 141, 168, 276, 277,
    336, 337
Tiamat, 86, 157
Tibet, 90, 124, 225, 395
time, i, iii–v, vii, xiii, xiv, xvi, xvii,
    xix, xxi, xxv, xxviii,
    xxx–xxxii, 1, 7, 8, 11, 19, 24,
    26, 27, 35, 36, 39, 42–45,
    48–52, 54, 55, 57, 58, 61–65,
    67, 73, 75–81, 85–89, 91,
    93–97, 100, 107, 109, 110,
    112, 113, 116, 123, 128, 131,
    133–135, 137, 138, 140–143,
    145, 148, 153, 154, 158, 162,
    163, 165, 167, 171, 173–179,

181, 183, 186, 188, 189, 193,
194, 196, 198, 201, 204, 209,
219, 223–225, 227, 229, 231,
234, 236–240, 243, 250–253,
263, 265, 266, 269, 273–275,
277, 278, 280, 285, 286, 288,
291, 293, 295, 298, 302, 305,
307–310, 317, 319, 323, 325,
329–331, 333, 334, 338, 341,
346, 347, 352, 354, 361, 366,
367, 369, 371, 372, 375, 380,
398, 399, 403, 416, 419
Tokyo, 62
trance, 3–5, 27, 129, 135, 137, 138,
146, 202, 221, 222, 337
transdimensional, 155, 237, 249, 252,
258, 266
Transient Passenger, 75, 113, 141, 237,
307, 320, 331
Trismegistus, Hermes, 95, 157
trust, 18, 102, 129, 137, 163, 205, 252,
260, 317, 377
truth, iv, ix, x, xiv, xviii–xx, xxii, 4,
12, 13, 19, 34, 45, 47, 49, 70,
74, 80, 88, 94, 95, 120, 149,
151, 161, 207, 208, 218, 219,
223, 230, 251, 262, 264, 265,
283, 304, 325, 346, 374, 391,
395, 397, 402–404, 407, 410,
411, 414, 415, 417
turmoil, 99, 100, 196
Turner, Karla, 87, 90, 91, 155, 199,
253, 261, 263, 317, 402

UFO, 1, 8, 15, 26, 29, 32, 53, 87, 115,
132, 151, 160, 161, 187, 197,
200–202, 204, 205, 212, 213,
216, 217, 222–224, 228, 241,
243, 246, 248, 250, 252, 255,
256, 264, 281, 295, 300, 303,
343–345, 356, 358, 371, 372,
374, 376, 380, 401, 402, 407,
409, 413
unicorn, 181
United States, 23, 64, 78, 79, 88, 102,
183, 200, 201, 203, 204, 206,
219, 233, 245, 252, 302, 399,
403
universe, iii, iv, viii, xiii–xv, xvii, xviii,
xxii, xxxiv, 10–12, 33, 34,
78, 112–114, 117, 125, 131,
148, 154, 185, 209, 217, 231,
238, 263, 265, 271, 276, 277,
300, 305, 306, 331, 332, 339,
365–367, 395, 397, 399, 400,
404, 406, 413
Utnapishtim, 51, 67

Vallee, Jacques, 16, 128, 209, 308, 402
variability of physicality, 97
Vedas, 111
vegetarian, 36, 149, 398
Velikovsky, 26, 56, 67, 106, 395
Venus, 19, 26, 51, 56, 58, 66, 67, 77,
78, 86, 122, 123, 240, 258
violence, 89, 175
Virgin Mary, 202, 233, 234
virus, xix, 74, 126, 354
VISA, 98, 101, 104–106, 221, 396

Waco, 64
Wanderer, 320
Ware, Don, 161
water, 1, 10, 33, 41, 47, 52, 54, 67, 88,
91, 105, 119, 139, 140, 149,
159, 177, 185, 197, 233, 240,
249, 259, 274, 275, 285, 295,
300, 377, 402
Wave, i, ii, v, xxxii, 1, 5, 6, 9, 15, 16,
18, 20, 21, 23, 24, 27, 31, 33,
35, 36, 39, 40, 43, 45–48, 50,
53–58, 61–64, 67–71, 73–76,
79, 85, 87–90, 93–98, 101,
105, 110, 112, 113, 115, 121,
122, 127–132, 134, 135, 139,
141, 142, 145–148, 150, 154,
155, 157, 162, 163, 167, 168,
171, 173–175, 177, 181, 182,
187, 193, 195, 200, 205, 212,
214–216, 218, 221–225, 232,

233, 235–237, 244, 246, 248,
249, 252, 254–256, 264–266,
273–279, 283–288, 293, 295,
298–301, 303–311, 314, 315,
318, 321–324, 329–333, 336,
338–340, 343–345, 347, 354,
363, 368, 377, 380, 382,
391–393, 397, 407–413

we are you in the future, xiii, 1, 128, 331, 375
weapon, 26, 65, 181, 190, 252, 271, 299, 409
Wizard of Oz, 177
worship, 68, 85, 102–105, 123, 125, 127, 134, 135, 154, 217, 239, 398

www.ingramcontent.com/pod-product-compliance
Lightning Source LLC
Chambersburg PA
CBHW060513230426
43665CB00013B/1496